FUNCTIONAL PROGRAMMING

INTERNATIONAL COMPUTER SCIENCE SERIES

OTHER TITLES IN THE SERIES

Programming in Ada (2nd Edn.) *J G P Barnes*

An Introduction to Numerical Methods with Pascal *L V Atkinson and P J Harley*

Introduction to Expert Systems *P Jackson*

Modula-2: Discipline & Design *A H J Sale*

PROLOG *F Giannesini, H Kanoui, R Pasero and M van Caneghem*

Programming Language Translation: A Practical Approach *P D Terry*

Data Abstraction in Programming Languages *J M Bishop*

System Simulation: Programming Styles and Languages *W Kreutzer*

The Craft of Software Engineering *A Macro and J Buxton*

PROLOG Programming for Artificial Intelligence *I Bratko*

An Introduction to Programming with Modula-2 *P D Terry*

Parallel Programming *R H Perrott*

The Specification of Computer Programs *W M Turski and T S E Maibaum*

Software Development with Ada *I Sommerville and R Morrison*

Logic Programming and Knowledge Engineering *T Amble*

Performance Measurement of Computer Systems *P McKerrow*

Syntax Analysis and Software Tools *K J Gough*

Concurrent Programming *N Gehani and A D McGettrick (Eds)*

Practical Compiling with Pascal-S *M J Rees and D J Robson*

Ada from the Beginning *J Skansholm*

FUNCTIONAL PROGRAMMING

Anthony J. Field
Peter G. Harrison

Imperial College of Science and Technology
University of London

ADDISON-WESLEY
PUBLISHING
COMPANY

Wokingham, England · Reading, Massachusetts · Menlo Park, California
New York · Don Mills, Ontario · Amsterdam · Bonn
Sydney · Singapore · Tokyo · Madrid · San Juan

The programs presented in this book have been included for their instructional value. They have been tested with care but are not guaranteed for any particular purpose. The publisher does not offer any warranties or representations, nor does it accept any liabilities with respect to the programs.

Cover designed by Crayon Design of Henley-on-Thames
and printed by The Riverside Printing Co. (Reading) Ltd.
Typeset by Times Graphics, Singapore
Printed in Great Britain by The Bath Press, Avon.

First printed 1988. Reprinted 1989

British Library Cataloguing in Publication Data
Field, Anthony J., *1960–*
Functional programming.—(International computer science series).
1. Computer systems. Functional programming
I. Title II. Harrison, Peter G., *1951–*
III. Series
005.1

ISBN 0-201-19249-7

Library of Congress Cataloging in Publication Data
Field, Anthony J., 1960–
Functional programming.

(International computer science series)
Bibliography: p.
Includes index.
1. Functional programming (Computer science)
I. Harrison, Peter G., 1951– . II. Title.
III. Series.
QA76.6.F477 1988 005.1'1 88-1265
ISBN 0-201-19249-7

To Sarah

Preface

Over the last ten years or so there has been a growing interest in functional programming within both academic and commercial institutions. There are perhaps three major aspects of functional languages which make them appealing: firstly, functional programs are invariably much shorter, more abstract and easier to understand than their imperative language counterparts; secondly, functional programs are amenable to formal analysis and manipulation, and thirdly they are naturally amenable to implementation on a parallel machine. Each of these properties is attributable to the inherently mathematical nature of functional languages: the building blocks of a functional program are 'true' functions, i.e. mathematical functions, each of which describes the transformation of input values to output values with no concern for the environment in which the function is used. From the programming angle this is attractive in that functional programs look like the kind of hierarchical specifications so often used in software engineering. At the same time the formal manipulation of functional programs is relatively straightforward because we can appeal to the apparatus of conventional mathematics both to establish properties about them and to transform them into more efficient forms.

This book is concerned with three important aspects of functional programming technology: functional programming and functional languages in general, the implementation of functional languages and the formal manipulation of functional programs for optimization. The book is divided into three parts entitled 'Programming with Functions', 'Implementation' and 'Optimization', which reflect each of these areas.

The book is aimed at undergraduate and postgraduate students of computer science, and at professionals who wish to learn about the current state of the art in functional programming and the related technology. In writing this book we have tried to make it as self-contained as possible although some experience of conventional programming is obviously desirable. Those readers who already know something about functional languages but who would like to know more about implementation and/or optimization may wish to skip the first part of the book and move directly on to Parts II and III.

Acknowledgements

We are greatly indebted to the members of the Functional Programming Section at Imperial College for their numerous suggestions and comments regarding the material in this book. We would like to thank in particular Helen Pull and Lyndon While who devoted many hours of their time to reading the earlier drafts and who provided many detailed and perceptive comments which proved invaluable.

Imperial College
August 1987

Tony Field
Pete Harrison

Contents

Part I
PROGRAMMING WITH FUNCTIONS

Introduction

The operation of a conventional computer is based on the sequential execution of instructions retrieved in turn from a single, although possibly hierarchical, storage medium. This 'model of computation' is longstanding and almost universal, and has had a profound influence on the nature of programming languages, to the extent that even today we are still tied to the view of programs as high-level encodings of conventional instruction sequences. Although the various language developments in recent years have seen to it that many of the low-level details of the machine's architecture are hidden away, enabling the programmer to concentrate on the problem at ever higher levels of abstraction, the fact remains that conventional languages still present a style of programming based on providing recipes to the computer explaining *how* a given problem is to be solved. Consequently, the programmer must always bear in mind *how* the program is ultimately evaluated for only then can the correct sequence of operations be produced to solve the problem at hand. The philosophy behind the programming process is therefore one of 'I'll tell you how'; in other words it is based on the description of solutions to problems rather than on descriptions of the problems themselves. Such languages are often called **imperative** languages to reflect the fact that each statement in a program is a prescription of what to do next in solving the problem.

Despite the current status of progamming languages, however, the continuing trend has always been toward providing more and more abstract ways of solving problems, trading off programming simplicity with program execution speed, each of the major developments taking the language yet further from the model of sequential instruction execution. It seems, therefore, that a natural and almost inevitable development in language technology is one which divorces the programming process from the underlying computational model altogether. Only then can we depart from the view of a program as a recipe for computing an answer and instead develop the view of a program as a clear and concise statement of what the answer should be, ignoring to a large extent the way in which the answer is computed. The philosophy behind the programming process is then one of 'I'll tell you what, you work out how'; in other words it is based more on the abstract specification of problems rather than a description of their method of solution.

There have been a number of languages in recent years which have succeeded in breaking out of the mould of conventional imperative programming, one such class of language being the **applicative** or **functional** languages which are the subject of this book. Functional programs are built from 'pure' functions, i.e. mathematical functions, which in sharp contrast to the functions found in many imperative programs are side-effect free, meaning that their evaluation cannot alter the environment of the computation. In other words there is no assignable program state. Because of this we can no longer program 'by effect' so that the value to be computed by a program and the program itself are reduced to one and the same thing. Program execution then becomes a process of altering the form of the required final value in precisely the way that we can alter the form of '8 + 1' to '9' in the knowledge that they both denote the same value.

The first part of this book is dedicated to providing an informal and intuitive introduction to functional languages and functional programming concepts. The primary objective is to show that programming with functions is not only possible but also perfectly natural and leads to programs which are almost invariably much shorter than the imperative counterparts, easier to write and easier to understand. We shall pitch our discussions at the level of a conversion course for those readers who have no prior knowledge of functional languages but who have a basic understanding of conventional programming techniques; for example, we shall often refer to sections of Pascal programs in order to illustrate the important differences between the imperative and functional styles. For consistency we shall use a common source code throughout this book, namely that of a functional language called **Hope**, so that much of the material in this part is aimed at describing the Hope language and the general techniques of Hope programming. However, we should not wish to present Hope as the only functional language or even as the best functional language, since such assessments often rely very much on personal taste. Therefore, to provide a general feel for the alternative approaches to functional language design, we shall also look at the approaches taken in other functional languages. The objective here is to describe a representative cross-section of functional languages rather than present a full survey of the field.

Those readers who are already familiar with functional programming may wish to skip much of this part of the book and instead refer to Appendix A of the book for a summary of the Hope language features.

Chapter 1
Introducing functions

This chapter is intended to provide a very straightforward introduction to the idea of mathematical functions and how to use such functions to build programs using function composition. We shall see how a function can be viewed as a black box for solving a problem and how these boxes can be plugged together to make bigger and more powerful functions which can themselves then be viewed as black boxes for building even bigger functions. We shall then examine the property of referential transparency and will look at the problems associated with languages which do not have this property. As we shall see, using a conventional language like Pascal we can obtain some most curious behaviour from a program simply because the language allows side-effects which can alter the state of the computation.

1.1 Pure functions

In mathematics a function is something which provides a mapping from objects drawn from a set of values called the **domain** into objects in some 'target' set called the **codomain** or **range**.

A simple example of a function is one which maps any given integer into one of plus, minus or zero depending on whether the integer is positive, negative or zero respectively. We shall call this function 'sign' to reflect the mapping it performs. The domain of the sign function is therefore the set of integers and the range of the function is the set of values { plus, minus, zero }. We can characterize sign by showing explicitly the elements of the domain and the range and the individual mappings which it specifies (Figure 1.1).

Notice that sign maps each element of the domain into a single element of the range. This is important because it means that there is no ambiguity as to which range element a given domain element is mapped to. For this reason all functions are said to be **well defined** or **deterministic**.

Another way of representing the mappings between the domain and range elements is to use a set of equations, one for each element of the domain,

```
⋮
sign( −3 ) = minus
sign( −2 ) = minus
sign( −1 ) = minus
sign( 0 )  = zero
sign( 1 )  = plus
sign( 2 )  = plus
sign( 3 )  = plus
⋮
```

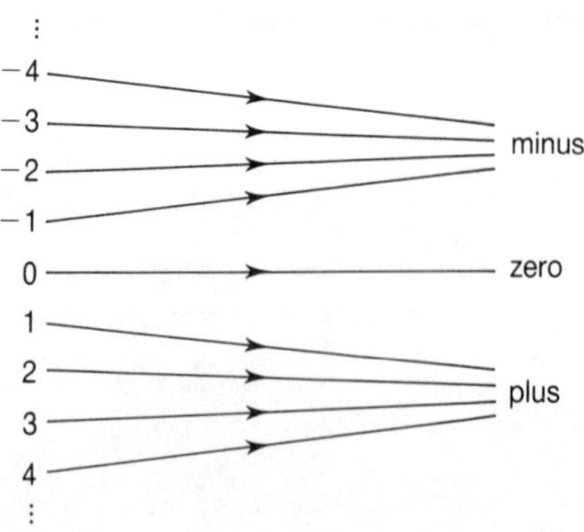

Figure 1.1 sign expressed as a mapping diagram.

For the sign function this notation is rather clumsy because we require an infinite number of equations to characterize it fully. The use of equations is not always a bad thing, however, as we shall see later on.

A third way of describing the mappings performed by sign is to specify a single rule:

$$\text{sign}(x) = \begin{cases} \text{minus} & \text{if } x < 0 \\ \text{zero} & \text{if } x = 0 \\ \text{plus} & \text{if } x > 0 \end{cases}$$

x here is called the **formal parameter** of sign and represents any given element of the domain of the function. The body of the rule (i.e. the right-hand side of the rule) simply specifies which element of the range the parameter x is mapped to. In this respect the rule for sign represents an infinite number of individual equations, one for each value in the domain. Because the function caters for *all* possible domain elements it is said to be a **total** function. If the rule were to omit one or more of the possible domain elements then it would be a **partial** function. For example

$$\text{sign2}(x) = \begin{cases} \text{minus} & \text{if } x < 0 \\ \text{plus} & \text{if } x > 0 \end{cases}$$

is a partial function over the domain of integers because there is no rule to cover the case where x is 0. We say that sign2 is **undefined** when $x = 0$.

We can view a function like sign as a black box with an input representing the parameter of the function and an output representing the result computed by the function. For sign, the output of the box will be one of minus, zero or plus depending on the value of the integer submitted on the input. The choice of which output value to produce is determined by the rule for sign which is embodied within the black box. For example, if we place the integer 6 on the input to the sign box we get the value plus delivered:

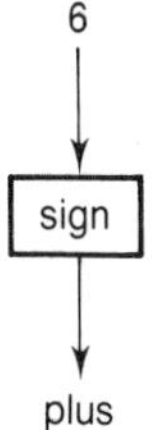

6 here is called the **actual parameter** of the function i.e. the value which is actually supplied to the function. The process of supplying an actual

parameter to the function is called function **application** and we say that sign is **applied** to 6, meaning that the rule for sign is invoked using 6 as the actual parameter. We shall often refer to the formal or actual parameter of a function as the **argument** of the function depending on the context. We can express the above application of sign using a mathematical notation:

```
sign( 6 )
```

We say that this expression **evaluates** to plus which we write

```
sign( 6 ) → plus
```

meaning that the black box delivers the value plus at its output when the value 6 is placed on its input. However, we can also read → as equals since the expression sign(6) is simply an alternative notation for the value plus. Here are some more examples:

```
sign( −4 ) → minus
sign( 0 ) → zero
```

The idea of a function being a canned-up rule for transforming inputs into outputs is one which is fundamental to functional programming. The black boxes provide the building blocks for a functional program and by joining these boxes together we can specify ever-more sophisticated operations. This process of 'joining the boxes' is called function **composition**.

To illustrate the process of function composition here is a function max which computes the maximum of a pair of numbers m and n:

```
max( m, n ) = m     if m > n
              n     otherwise
```

The domain of max is therefore the set of pairs of numbers and the range is the set of numbers. We can view max as a black box and use it to compute the maximum of two numbers. For example

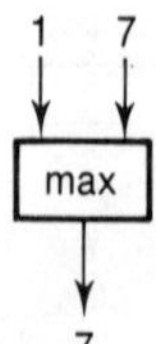

which we write

```
max( 1, 7 ) → 7
```

Also, we can use max as a building block for a more complicated function. Suppose we require a function which computes the maximum of three numbers instead of just two. We could define this new function (call it max3) in the following way:

$$\text{max3}(a, b, c) = \begin{cases} a & \text{if } a \geq b \text{ and } a > c \quad \text{or} \quad a \geq c \text{ and } a > b \\ b & \text{if } b \geq a \text{ and } b > c \quad \text{or} \quad b \geq c \text{ and } b > a \\ c & \text{if } c \geq a \text{ and } c > b \quad \text{or} \quad c \geq b \text{ and } c > a \\ a & \text{otherwise} \end{cases}$$

(The 'otherwise' case is required if $a = b = c$.)

This is rather a messy definition. A far more elegant way to develop the max3 function is to use the max function already defined:

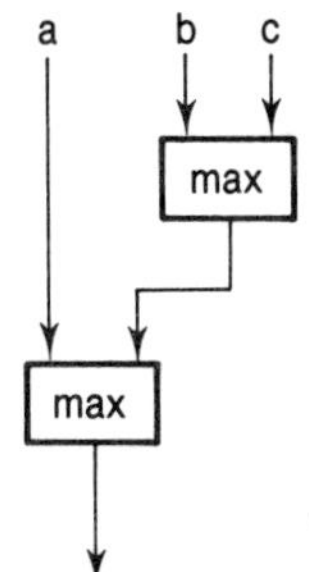

We write this in the following way:

```
max3( a, b, c ) = max( a, max( b, c ) )
```

Because max3 provides a deterministic mapping from triples of numbers to numbers we can treat it as a black box in its own right:

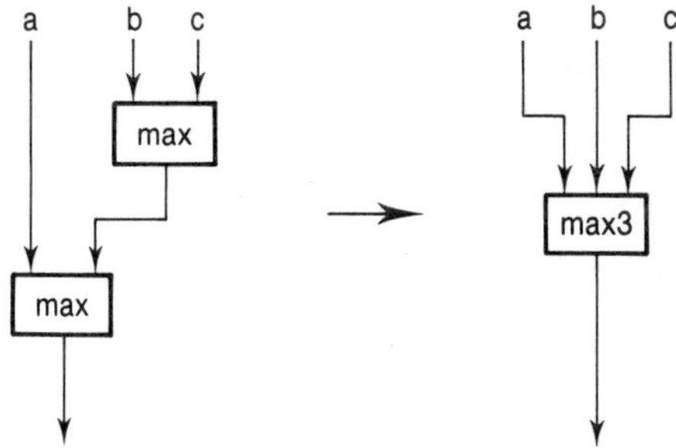

We can now forget about the internal workings of this new box and use it as a computational unit or a building block for other functions as we require. We can compute with it, for example

```
max3( 1, 4, 2 )
```

which yields the answer 4 and we can use it to build other functions such as the following which computes the sign of the maximum of four numbers a, b, c and d using the sign and max functions we have already defined:

```
SM4( a, b, c, d ) = sign( max(a, max3( b, c, d ) ) )
```

This can be represented as a black box as follows:

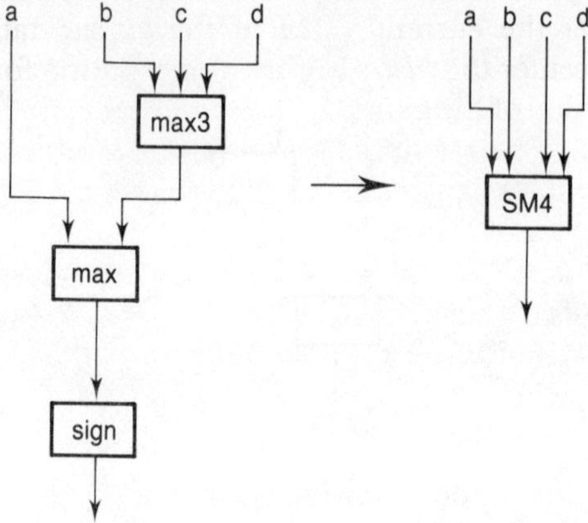

So, given a set of predefined black box functions, called **built-in** functions or **primitives**, for doing simple operations like basic arithmetic we can build new functions, i.e. new black boxes, to do more sophisticated things in terms of these primitives. We can then use these new functions as building blocks for even more sophisticated functions, and so on. As in conventional programming practice we can define new functions both to break up and so simplify the definition of a more complicated function or to describe a commonly used operation and so save writing out the same expression again and again.

1.2 Referential transparency

The fundamental property of mathematical functions which enables us to plug together black boxes in this way is the property of **referential transparency**. There are a number of intuitive readings of the term but essentially it means that each expression denotes a single value which cannot be changed by evaluating the expression or by allowing different parts of a program to share the expression. Evaluation of the expression simply changes the form of the expression but never its value. All references to the value are therefore equivalent to the value itself and the fact that the expression may be referred to from other parts of the program is of no concern. Referential transparency is therefore the distinguishing factor between mathematical functions and the functions we might write in imperative programming languages like Pascal, for within these languages we allow the functions to refer to *global* data and we allow destructive assignment to that data which can change its value from one invocation of the function to the next. Such dynamic changes in the value of data are often referred to as **side-effects**, and because of them the value produced by a function can change even though its arguments may be the same each time it is called. This makes the function very hard to use because in order to determine what value the function will generate we must consider the current value of the global data. This in turn requires us to consider the *history* of the computation for it is this which determines the value of the global data at any time. Imperative languages are therefore said to be **referentially opaque**. To illustrate the referential opacity of imperative languages let us look at an example program written in the syntax of Pascal:

```
program example ( output ) ;
var flag : boolean ;

function f ( n : integer ) : integer ;
begin
  if flag then f := n
         else f := 2 * n ;
  flag := not flag
end ;

begin
  flag := true ;
  writeln( f( 1 ) + f( 2 ) ) ;
  writeln( f( 2 ) + f( 1 ) )
end.
```

If we now execute this program we get the two numbers 5 and 4 printed at the terminal. This is rather curious, however, for mathematics tells us that the commutativity of addition enables us to substitute x + y with y + x for any x and y, and yet in this program we find that the Pascal expression f(1) + f(2) yields an answer which is different to f(2) + f(1)!

The problem, of course, is that the function f defined above is very different from the mathematical functions we have seen up until now. Our view of a mathematical function is one of a black box which computes output values solely in terms of input values. The function defined in the program above is a classical example of a function which is dependent on global data as well as its own parameters. This is not a problem in its own right for we might argue that the definition of a primitive function like + is something which is global to a program. The problem here is that the value of the global data (i.e. flag) in the Pascal program is allowed to be changed and it is this which destroys the referential transparency of the language. The value of the primitive function + does not change, that is it always denotes the function which adds things together. The heart of the problem in the Pascal program is therefore the **destructive assignment** statement:

```
flag := not flag
```

which changes the value of flag. If flag were true before execution of the statement then it will be false afterwards and vice versa. A statement like this is not allowed in mathematics; mathematical reasoning is based on the idea of equality and the replacement of one expression by another expression which means the same thing, i.e. which denotes the same value. For example we can replace the expression

$$4 + 8$$

by the expression

$$12$$

because both expressions are denotations of the same value, i.e. the number 12. It is a characteristic of functional programs that there are no destructive assignment statements. Instead of viewing a variable as a placeholder for a value which can be periodically updated by assigning different values to that variable, the variables in a functional program are like mathematical variables: if they exist then they have a value and the value cannot change. Instead of a program being a sequence of imperatives which describe *how* the computer must solve a problem in terms of state changes (updates to assignable variables), a functional program describes *what* is to be computed, that is the program is just an expression, defined in terms of the predefined and user-defined functions, the value of which consitutes the result of the program. There is no notion of program state and there is no notion of program history.

SUMMARY

- Pure (mathematical) functions can be used to build programs.
- New functions can be built by composing old functions together.
- Languages based on programming with functions are referentially transparent.

Chapter 2
An introduction to functional programming through Hope

The previous chapter should have provided a basic introduction to the idea of programming with functions. In the next three chapters we shall describe the basic techniques of functional programming using the Hope language as our notation; for consistency Hope will be used throughout the book as a 'common' source code. It should be noted that the version of Hope used in this book is a modest extension of the original Hope language which is described in Burstall *et al.* (1980).

In this chapter we shall cover some of the more elementary features of Hope starting with simple function declaration and definition and culminating in user-defined data types. A description of the more advanced features of Hope is deferred until Chapters 3 and 4. We shall not attempt to cover all of the features of the language, but sufficient at least to provide a thorough grounding in the techniques of functional programming and to enable the example programs given in Parts II and III of the book to be understood. A full description of the language can be found in Perry (1987) and we give a language summary in Appendix A.

2.1 Introducing a function

We have seen in Chapter 1 how a mathematical function can be defined in terms of a rule which specifies what the function must do with its argument or arguments in order to generate the required result. In Hope we describe a function in two steps. The first step involves writing down the *type* of the function, which states explicitly the domain and range of the function. The second step involves describing what the function does.

Let us consider a very simple function for squaring integers. The first thing we do is to name this function square and declare its type like this:

```
dec square : num → num ;
```

dec is a reserved word (all reserved words will be written in bold) which indicates the start of a type declaration. This is followed by the name of the function being typed i.e. square and a *type expression* which describes the type of that function. A colon (:) separates the function name and the type expression and the whole declaration is terminated with a semicolon (;). The above declaration may be read: 'square is a function from num to num'. num here is a *base type* (i.e. a predefined type) which represents the set of integers; we shall encounter the other base types of Hope later on.

The type declarations of all functions have a similar format, i.e.

```
dec name : A → B ;
```

A specifies the type of the argument(s) of the function (the domain) and B specifies the type of the result returned by the function (the range).

Hope is an example of a *strongly-typed* language, meaning that each function is defined to operate on objects of a specified type so that an application of the function to an object of inappropriate type is flagged as an error. Now, although the type of each function must be declared explicitly in Hope this is not a general requirement for strong typing. In Chapter 5 we shall see an example of a language in which the type of each function is inferred automatically, i.e. without the need for explicit programmer declarations. The Hope philosophy is that typing is a part of the intellectual process of programming and so should be enforced; the alternative philosophy is one of minimization, i.e. the less writing required the better.

The principal advantage of strong typing is that many programming errors can be eliminated *before* the program is submitted for execution. A surprising number of programming errors are due to functions being applied to the wrong type of argument. If the language is strongly typed then a type checker can report a meaningful error message to the programmer as soon as any type inconsistency in the program is detected. This is far more helpful than waiting for the program to fail at run-time and then wading through error dumps trying to locate the source of the problem. We shall come back to the issue of type checking in the later chapters of the book where we shall see that strong typing of the source program also has significant advantages for the efficiency of the implementation. The type checking algorithm itself is described in Chapter 7.

Referring back to our example, the definition of the function square describes what square does to its argument and has the following format:

```
--- square( x ) <= x * x ;
```

which is very similar to the mathematical notation used above. All function definitions are highlighted by preceding them with the string --- and consist of a left-hand side and a right-hand side separated by the arrow <=. The left-hand side indicates the name of the function being defined and lists the names of the formal parameter(s) of the function; the right-hand side (often called the function *body*) states what to do with those parameters once they have been passed. Again the whole definition is terminated by a semicolon. In this example the body consists of the expression x * x, the square of x. The * in this expression is an example of a **primitive** function. The fact that the function symbol * appears between its arguments is simply for notational convenience and we say that * is an **infix** function or infix operator. We could define * to be a **prefix** function so that we would write instead * (x, x) but the infix notation is more familiar from elementary mathematics. The complete set of primitive functions (operators) supported by Hope is given as part of the Hope language summary in Appendix A.

Having now defined square we can use it to compute squares by applying square to an integer argument as in

```
square( 3 )
```

The evaluation of this expression proceeds as follows:

```
square( 3 )
→ 3 * 3     from the definition of square
→ 9         from the predefined semantics of *
```

(The arrow → really means 'is equal to' although it should be apparent that it also implies simplification: the expression to the right of the arrow is the result of simplifying the expression to the left of the arrow.) Because square is a 'pure' function (as are all functions in Hope) we can be sure that the expression square(3) always evaluates to 9.

Let us now look at a slightly more complicated example. In Chapter 1 we defined the max function:

```
max( m, n ) = m   if m > n
            = n   otherwise
```

The domain of this function is the set of number pairs and the range is the set of numbers. This is reflected in the type declaration of the equivalent Hope function:

```
dec max : num # num → num ;
```

The type expression to the left of the → in this declaration specifies that max takes a pair of numbers as arguments rather than just a single argument as in the square function. It is read: 'num cross num'. The hash symbol (#) denotes the **Cartesian product** of types – in this case pairs of numbers.

The rule for max looks like this:

```
--- max( m, n ) <= if m > n then m else n ;
```

The function > (i.e. 'greater') is another example of a Hope primitive function. The **if** . . . **then** . . . **else** . . . is the *conditional* construct of Hope and has the obvious meaning.

We can now use max to define other functions, for example the max3 function of Chapter 1:

```
dec max3 : num # num # num → num ;
--- max3( a, b, c ) <= max( a, max( b, c ) ) ;
```

Notice that the type declaration specifies that max3 takes a triple of arguments instead of a pair.

The idea of an expression 'denoting a value' is important for it reflects the property of referential transparency alluded to earlier. We say that square(3) *denotes* the value 9 to mean that the expression square(3) can be unconditionally replaced by the value 9 wherever we see it. Thus, although the form of an expression may change, the value it represents does not.

2.2 Tuples

The word 'tuple' conjures up the idea of a collection of related values or objects. In fact we have already seen several examples of tuples, although they may not have been immediately obvious. In the expression:

```
max( 1, 2 )
```

we treated max as if it were a function of *two* arguments. Strictly, however, in Hope we must view the arguments as a single tuple of values rather than a collection of separate values. The type expression of max

```
dec max : num # num → num ;
```

should read: 'max takes a two-tuple of numbers (underlined) and returns a single number'. There is no notion of a tuple consisting of a single value. Indeed, if a function takes a single non-tuple argument then the parentheses around the argument in both the definition and application of the function can be optionally omitted. This means that both

square 12   and   square(12)

are valid applications of the square function defined earlier. Throughout this book we shall consistently adopt the latter notation in order that all function arguments have a similar format. In the case of single-argument functions the parentheses can be viewed simply as delimiters rather than as special syntax for constructing tuples.

This distinction between argument lists and tuples is not usually significant, indeed we shall usually talk of a function having 'more than one argument' meaning that it takes a tuple of arguments, but it does allow us to play one useful trick as will become apparent in the following discussion.

So far, we have concerned ourselves with functions which take one or more arguments and produce just a single result. However, we can define similarly a function which for any argument (or arguments) produces a result with more than one component, i.e. a tuple. An example of such a function is the function IntDiv which for a given argument pair computes the *quotient* and *remainder* of the integer division of those two numbers. For example,

```
IntDiv( 7, 3 )
```

will generate the pair (i.e. the two-tuple)

```
( 2, 1 )
```

The declaration and definition of IntDiv in Hope are as follows:

```
dec IntDiv : num # num → num # num ;
--- IntDiv( m, n ) <= ( m div n, m mod n ) ;
```

where div and mod are Hope infix primitives. Notice that the type of the argument of IntDiv is the same as the type of the result of IntDiv, namely num # num; if we apply IntDiv to two arguments (a tuple) we get two results (but packaged up in the form of a single tuple).

Now, because the result generated by each application of IntDiv is of the same type as the argument required by the max function for example, we can compose these two functions together. For example

```
max( IntDiv( 11, 4 ) )
```

yields 3 because IntDiv(11, 4) returns (2, 3) and max(2, 3) is 3.

In addition to the base type num which denotes the set of integers, Hope also supports the base types truval, real and char. The type truval (short for *tru*th *val*ue) represents the Booleans and has the values true and false as elements. real denotes the set of real numbers and char the set of characters. To illustrate how these base types may be used in practice we shall now develop a simple function called analyse which performs a simple analysis of real numbers. Given a real number, r, analyse will return a tuple with three components:

(1) A character '−' or '+' according to whether the number is less than 0.0 or not respectively.

(2) A truth value which indicates whether the number lies between −1.0 and +1.0 inclusive.

(3) The integer 'nearest' the given number.

The description of the problem immediately suggests the type of the function required:

```
dec analyse : real → char # truval # num ;
```

The body of analyse consists of a tuple of three expressions, one for each component of the result:

```
--- analyse ( r ) <= ( if r < 0 then '−' else '+',
                       ( r >= −1.0 ) and ( r =< 1.0 ),
                       round( r ) ) ;
```

The first component is a conditional expression returning one of the characters '−' or '+' depending on the value of r, the second component is a Boolean expression and the third component is a simple application of the primitive function round which rounds a real number up to the nearest integer, as we require. So, for example, the expression

```
analyse( −1.04 )
```

will evaluate to ('−', false, −1) since −1.04 is negative (hence the '−') does not lie between −1.0 and 1.0 (hence the false) and when rounded up yields −1.

Notice that in this definition we have used the primitive function > with two real numbers as its arguments, whereas in the definition of max given above we used the same function to operate on integers. This may appear slightly curious because we have implied that all functions (primitive functions included) are strongly typed, meaning that they can only be applied to objects of a certain type as dictated by their respective type declarations. It would be rather awkward, however, to have to use different symbols to denote the greater-than function according to whether its arguments are reals or integers, and also when one argument is a real and the other is an integer. Hope solves this problem by using **overloading** which enables a single function symbol to have a number of meanings depending on the context in which the symbol occurs. We can imagine there being four different versions of the > function,

```
dec > : num # num → truval ;
dec > : num # real → truval ;
dec > : real # num → truval ;
dec > : real # real → truval ;
```

with their associated (predefined) definitions. Although we used the same symbol > in both the analyse and max functions, the primitive function invoked in each case is actually different. The same rule applies to the other comparison functions and the arithmetic functions like + and − which may also operate on both reals and nums.

The other point to note in the example is that the elements of a tuple can be of mixed types; the components of the result tuple can consist of any triple of values so long as the first is a character, the second a truval and the third an integer. The tuples

```
( true, 'a', 'b' )     and     ('a', true, 'b' )
```

are therefore not of the same type even though they both contain two characters and a truval.

2.3 Recursive functions

Suppose we are required to write a function to compute the sum of the first n non-negative integers. We could proceed to write a very large function definition along the following lines:

```
dec sum : num → num ;
--- sum( n ) <= if n = 0 then 0 else
                if n = 1 then 1 else
                if n = 2 then 3 else etc.
```

The problem with this, of course, is that the function has infinitely many cases to consider (or rather a finite number dictated by the arithmetic limitations of the implementation). Now, in a conventional programming language we might solve the problem using a loop of some form. For example, in Pascal we might define the following function to do the job:

```
function sum( n : integer ) : integer ;
var
  loopcounter, acc : integer ;
begin
  acc := 0 ;
  for loopcounter := 1 to n do
    acc := acc + loopcounter ;
  sum := acc
end ;
```

This uses a **for** loop to update repeatedly the value of an accumulator acc which at the end of the looping process contains the required result. Now, in a functional language there are no looping constructs and there is certainly no destructive assignment facility which could update the value of a counter. In such languages the problem is solved using a **recursive** function. A recursive function is simply a function which calls itself. Of course, the recursive call must be to solve a simpler problem than the original one being solved, otherwise the recursion would proceed indefinitely. Part of the problem associated with writing a recursive function is therefore to split the problem at hand into one or more simpler problems but of a similar nature to the original. The function can then call itself to solve the simpler problem(s) and the complete solution can be constructed from the result(s) which are returned. In order to solve the summation problem using recursion let us look at the structure of the expression which sums the first n integers:

$$\text{sum}(\ n\ ) \equiv 1 + 2 + 3 + 4 + \ldots + (\ n - 1\ ) + n$$

An inspection of this exposes a relationship between the sum of the first n integers and the sum of the first $n - 1$ integers. If we remove the $+ n$ from the end of the above expression we are left with an expression precisely equivalent to sum(n − 1); this is often referred to as a **recurrence relationship**. This suggests that given the integer n we can use the sum function we are defining to sum the first $n - 1$ integers and then form the complete solution by adding n to the result returned. To complete the definition we have only to define a 'base case' which specifies where the recursive process should end. For the sum function the base case occurs when the argument is 0 and for this case we would expect the function to return 0 (the sum of the first zero integers is 0). Putting things together we end up with the following definition:

```
--- sum( n ) <= if n = 0 then 0 else sum( n - 1 ) + n ;
```

Although the definition of sum did not require us to think about how recursion works, we can see the effect of the recursion when we look at a sample evaluation:

```
sum( 4 )
→ sum( 3 ) + 4
→ ( sum( 2 ) + 3 ) + 4
→ ( ( sum( 1 ) + 2 ) + 3 ) + 4
→ ( ( (sum( 0 ) + 1 ) + 2 ) + 3 ) + 4
→ ( ( ( ( 0 + 1 ) + 2 ) + 3 ) + 4 )
→ 10
```

By comparing the Hope version of sum with the Pascal version given above we see the most important difference between an imperative solution and a functional solution to a problem: the Pascal solution is *ad hoc*; in order to understand why it is correct we have to understand what the machine will do when it executes each statement in the program. In the functional solution, on the other hand, we do not have to think about how the program will be evaluated by a computer; there is no notion of an updatable program state or of sequential instruction execution. The functional solution is in fact a statement of the problem itself rather than a recipe for its solution and it is in this sense that we talk of a functional program as being a specification of *what* to do instead of a sequence of instructions which describe *how* to do it.

We shall see many more examples of recursive functions in the later sections of this chapter and in other chapters of the book. Although recursion leads to very abstract and concise solutions to numerical problems, its real power becomes apparent when we consider functions which operate on user-defined data types. This topic will be covered in Section 2.6 below.

2.4 Declaring infix operators

The functions we have defined so far are written in **prefix** notation, that is with the function symbol preceding its argument or arguments. However, in elementary mathematics we are more familiar with expressions like

```
1 + 3
```

In this expression the function symbol appears between its operands and so is called an **infix** function or **infix** operator.

In writing programs, too, it is sometimes convenient to define our own infix functions and this can be done in Hope by using the reserved word **infix**. This introduces the name of a new operator and its associated priority. The priority of the operator is an integer between 1 and 10 which specifies the precedence of the operator relative to the other operators in the program. As a simple example of operator precedence, when we write

```
1 + 3 * 2
```

we usually assume that * has a higher priority than + so that the expression is actually read as 1 + (3 * 2) rather than (1 + 3) * 2. In Hope the priority of the operators + and * are respectively 5 and 6. (The priorities of all the infix primitives are given in Appendix A.) The higher priority of * means that the above expression will be bracketed as we expect.

To introduce a new operator OP with priority P we write

```
infix OP : P ;
```

The syntax of the type declaration of the operator is the same as that of a normal function except that it always has two arguments:

```
dec OP : Type1 # Type2 → Type3 ;
```

Where Type1, Type2 and Type3 are all type expressions. Similarly, when we define OP the left-hand side of the definition is itself written in infix format:

$$--- P_1 \text{ OP } P_2 \Leftarrow \ldots ;$$

where P_1 and P_2 are the formal parameters of OP.

To illustrate this mechanism, here is the declaration and definition of the infix operator ↑ which performs 'powering'. That is, given two integer arguments x and y it will compute x^y. In mathematics powering has higher priority than the other arithmetic operators so that the expression $a * b^c$ is read $a * (b^c)$ rather than $(a * b)^c$. To reflect this, we shall assign the priority 7 to the operator, one higher than the priority of *.

```
infix ↑ : 7 ;
dec ↑ : num # num → num ;
```

The definition of ↑ is recursive and based on the fact that

$$a^b = a * a^{b-1}$$

and with the 'base case' that $a^0 = 1$. Here it is in Hope:

```
--- x ↑ y <= if y = 0 then 1 else x * x ↑ (y − 1) ;
```

So, for example

3 + 7 ↑ 2 − 6 evaluates to 46

and

3 * 5 ↑ 2 evaluates to 75

2.5 Qualified expressions

Take a look at the following function:

```
dec f : num → num ;
--- f( x ) <= g( square( max ( x, 4 ) ) ) +
              ( if x =< 1 then 1 else g( square( max( x, 4 ) ) ) ) ;
```

In this definition the subexpression g(square(max(x, 4))) appears twice in the definition of f. Furthermore, if the argument to f (i.e. x) is greater than 1 then the body of f will be equivalent to

```
g( square( max( x, 4 ) ) ) + g( square( max( x, 4 ) ) )
```

which will cause the subexpression g(square(max(x, 4))) to be evaluated twice. This is rather wasteful since we know that the result generated by both calls will be the same – a consequence of referential transparency.

We can avoid this repetition in two ways. Firstly, we can define an extra function, f1 say, which takes the repeated subexpression as a parameter:

```
--- f( x )     <= f1( g( square( max( x, 4 ) ) ), x ) ;
--- f1( a, b ) <= a + ( if b =< 1 then 1 else a) ;
```

This relies on the fact that the arguments to a function are evaluated at most once (this will be made clearer in Chapter 6).

The second way of avoiding repeated evaluation is to use a so-called **qualified expression**. Qualified expressions enable us to attach a name to an expression and then use that name in the same way that we use a formal parameter. In some respects we can view the mechanism as one of 'extending the existing set of formal parameters'. In Hope there are two equivalent kinds of qualified expression: the **let** construct looks like this:

let ⟨name⟩ == ⟨expression⟩$_1$ **in** ⟨expression⟩$_2$

and the **where** construct is similar

⟨expression⟩$_2$ **where** ⟨name⟩ == ⟨expression⟩$_1$

⟨expression⟩$_1$ is sometimes referred to as the **qualifying expression** or **qualifier** and ⟨expression⟩$_2$ as the **resultant**. Both of these expressions have the effect of naming the qualifier expression so that it can be referred to by name in the resultant expression. The function f above can now be written

```
--- f( x ) <= let a == g( square( max( x, 4 ) ) )
               in a + ( if x =< 1 then 1 else a ) ;
```

or alternatively,

```
--- f( x ) <= a + ( if x =< 1 then 1 else a )
               where a == g( square( max( x, 4 ) ) ) ;
```

It is important to understand that the == merely associates a name with an expression; it should not be confused with <= and certainly not with the destructive assignment operator (:=) of imperative languages. The following example illustrates the point:

```
let x == E1 in
  if ( let x == E2 in E3 )
  then x
  else 1 + x
```

The outermost **let** expression attaches the name x to the expression E1. Once this has been done the value denoted by x is the value denoted by E1. The inner **let** expression in the predicate of the conditional does not change the meaning of the outer x. This **let** introduces a new name for the expression E2 which is coincidentally the same as that in the outer **let**. Consequently the references to x in the two branches of the conditional both refer to E1 rather than E2, but the inner **let** overrides the binding made by the outer **let** so that all references to x from within E3 actually refer to E2 rather than E1. The scope of a new name is therefore restricted to the expression following the **in** in a **let** expression and the expression preceding the **where** in a **where** expression.

Qualified expressions are usually used when a sub-expression is referred to more than once from within an expression but can also be used to improve the readability of a function definition. A third application, however, relates to the decomposition of tuples. As an example, consider the IntDiv function given above. Each call to IntDiv returns a pair of numbers, i.e. the quotient and remainder of the division of the two arguments. One way to extract just one of the two components of the result tuple is to devise auxiliary functions to do the decomposition, e.g.

```
dec quot : num # num → num ;
--- quot( q, r ) <= q ;
dec rem : num # num → num ;
--- rem( q, r ) <= r ;
```

For example,

```
let pair == IntDiv( x, y ) in quot( pair ) * y + rem( pair )
```

However, we can also use a qualified expression to decompose the tuple generated by IntDiv in the following way:

```
let ( q, r ) == IntDiv( x, y ) in q * y + r
```

This has the effect of simultaneously naming the first element of the resulting tuple q and the second element r. This is a simple example of what is called **pattern matching** in Hope. In the above expression we are matching the pair (q, r) with the result generated by the call to IntDiv, i.e. (2, 3) in this case. As a result of the matching process q is attributed the value 2 and r the value 3. We shall sometimes talk of **binding** and say that q is bound to 2 and r to 3. We shall see more of this in the next section.

2.6 User-defined data types

So far, all of our example functions have been defined to operate on base-type objects like nums, reals and chars. In most applications, however, the program is required to operate on a much richer set of data types, some of which are defined by the programmer. These are called **user-defined** data types.

Most languages offer, in addition to the base types of the language, a number of tools for building more general data structures. Pascal, for example, allows us to define records and pointers; we can use records to build the components of a structure and we can use pointers to refer to those records. In this way we can define lists in Pascal by using a record to represent each list 'cell', a pointer to refer to each cell and the special value NIL to represent the null pointer. The type definition of a list then looks like this:

```
type
  list = ^cell ;
  cell = record
           head : integer ;
           tail : list
         end ;
```

Here, we are encouraged to think about the representation of lists as 'cells and arrows'. For example, the list containing the elements 1, 2, and 3 will be represented by

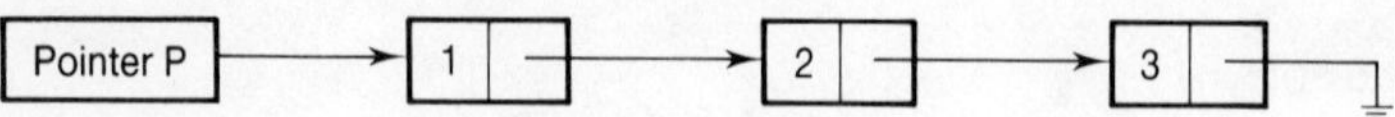

We build a list by creating new records and filling them in with appropriate values. The following section of program, for example, builds the list containing the single element 3:

```
NEW( L ) ;
with L^ do
begin
  head := 3 ;
  tail := NIL
end ;
```

In effect what we are doing here is manipulating memory, albeit at a rather high level, by explicitly claiming boxes and by explicitly filling them in with the values required to build the structure.

When we define lists in Hope we do so by introducing an entirely new type with its own building blocks rather than by using a predefined set of data-structuring primitives such as records and pointers. The advantage of this is that we have only to think about *what* the data structure looks like rather than *how* it can be represented in terms of predefined building blocks.

Suppose, then, that we wish to describe a list of numbers so that we can build such lists and pass them around between functions. We don't think about the storage representation of lists or of cells and arrows as is prescribed in Pascal; instead we concentrate on the recursive structure of a list:

> A list of numbers is a data structure which is either empty or else non-empty in which case it consists of a number (the head of the list) and another list of numbers (the tail of the list).

The syntax of the corresponding Hope data definition exactly reflects this description:

```
data NumList == nil ++ cons( num # NumList ) ;
```

nil and cons in this definition are called **data constructors**, because they serve only to construct, i.e. bind together, data. They are implicitly defined when they appear in the **data** statement. Constructors with no arguments (e.g. nil above) are sometimes called **data constants** and constructors in general are often referred to as **constructor functions**.

Using these constructors we can write down an expression which denotes the single-element list containing 3:

```
cons( 3, nil )
```

We notionally 'apply' the constructor just as though it were a normal function, hence the term 'constructor function'. Unlike other functions, however, constructor functions have no rules. The expression cons(3, nil) is therefore a *value* in that it cannot be further simplified by using any function rule. As a more complicated example, here is the list comprising the numbers 1, 2 and 3 expressed using the constructors nil and cons:

```
cons( 1, cons( 2, cons( 3, nil ) ) )
```

As a matter of terminology, we shall often refer to expressions formed by the application of a constructor as **constructed data** or as **compound data** terms.

Using the constructors nil and cons we can build arbitrarily large lists of numbers. Sometimes, however, we want to build lists of other things like characters, reals, or even lists. To represent a list of characters, for example, we could define a new data type CharList:

```
data CharList == NilCharList ++ ConsChars( char # CharList ) ;
```

We are not allowed to use the same constructor name as appears in some other data type, so we cannot use nil or cons here.

Observe, however, that the definition of CharList has an identical format to that of NumList defined earlier. This is because the overall 'shape' of a list of characters is the same as that of a list of numbers. In Hope we can avoid having to define new lists for each component object type by defining a **generic** or **polymorphic** (many-formed) data type. This encapsulates the idea that lists of 'anything' have identical overall structure. Polymorphism enables us to *parameterize* a list definition by the type of the objects contained in the list. Here is a polymorphic definition of lists which can be used to define lists of any type of object:

```
typevar any ;
data list( any ) == nil ++ cons( any # list( any ) ) ;
```

any is called a **type variable**, meaning that it is an identifier which denotes some type. New type variables are declared using the reserved word **typevar** as shown.

Using this single definition we can now use nil and cons to build lists of any type; for example

cons(1, cons(2, nil))	is a list of numbers
cons('a', cons('b', cons('c', nil)))	is a list of characters
cons(nil, cons(cons(1, nil), nil))	is a list of lists
nil	is a list of unspecified object types

Note that all elements of a given list must be of the same type. The list

```
cons( 1, cons( 'a', nil ) )
```

is therefore invalid because the components are a mixture of numbers and characters. For convenience, the type variables alpha and beta are predefined in Hope and may be used anywhere without prior definition.

Because lists are so commonly used these are also predefined. The empty list constructor is nil as above, and the non-empty list constructor is the infix constructor :: (pronounced cons) with priority 7. The definition of these predefined lists would look like this if written out in full:

```
infix :: : 7 ;
data list( alpha ) == nil ++ alpha :: list( alpha ) ;
```

The following expressions denote the same lists as those given earlier but using the predefined list constructors:

```
1 :: ( 2 :: nil )
'a' :: ( 'b' :: ( 'c' :: nil ) ) )
nil :: ( ( 1 :: nil ) :: nil )
nil
```

Hope allows a number of 'shorthand' notations to be used for list expressions. The list

$$e_1 :: (e_2 :: (e_3 :: (\ldots :: (e_n :: nil) \ldots)))$$

can be written

$[\ e_1, e_2, e_3, \ldots, e_n\ ]$

Furthermore, if the e_i are all characters, then we can juxtapose the component characters and enclose them in double quotes. For example, the list

```
'H' :: ( 'o' :: ( 'p' :: ( 'e' :: nil ) ) )
```

can be written using the previous shorthand

```
[ 'H', 'o', 'p', 'e' ]
```

or alternatively as the quoted string

```
"Hope"
```

Another mechanism provided by Hope is that of naming existing types and combinations (tuples) of these types. For example, we may wish to write a set of functions for processing grid coordinates where each coordinate is an (x, y) pair. Rather than write the type of the coordinate pair explicitly as

```
real # real
```

each time we require it we can name the type real # real using a **type** declaration:

```
type Coordinate == real # real ;
```

and use the type identifier Coordinate in place of real # real wherever we require it, for example

```
Coordinate → Coordinate
```

denotes exactly the same type as

```
real # real → real # real
```

Notice that a **type** declaration does not introduce a new type (like the **data** statement), it simply attaches a name to a type expression.

2.6.1 Defining functions over data types

Having defined a set of data types, we can write down functions which operate on those data types. To demonstrate how we go about writing such functions, we shall look at four example programs: the first three are straightforward list-processing examples; the third is based on a more complex user-defined data type, namely a tree.

EXAMPLE 1: JOINING TWO LISTS

In this first example we are going to write a function Join which given any two lists as arguments will join them together. For example,

```
Join( "ET", " phone home" )
```

will be required to produce the result

```
"ET phone home"
```

As with all the examples so far, we begin by writing down the type declaration of Join. An important characteristic of Join is that it can be used to join lists of an arbitrary type. For this reason Join is said to be a **polymorphic function**. This means that the declaration is expressed in terms of a type variable – we shall use the predefined type variable alpha:

```
dec Join : list( alpha ) # list( alpha ) → list( alpha ) ;
```

The two argument lists must contain objects of the same type for otherwise the resulting lists would contain mixed object types which is not allowed; this restriction is conveyed by the use of the same type variable alpha throughout the type expression.

The definition of a function which operates on a data type follows a very straightforward pattern: instead of using a single rule to specify the function we use a number of rules (sometimes called **rewrite rules** or **equations**), one for each possible 'form' that the argument can take, i.e. one for each constructor in the corresponding data definition. In the Join example, the arguments are lists and so there will be two cases to consider: one for the empty list (the nil constructor case) and one for the non-empty list (the :: constructor case).

We need not decompose the second argument of Join for we wish only to add the first argument to the front of it. Hence we have only to consider the form of the first argument when defining the function. The first question we ask is: 'what happens if we try to join an empty list to some list L?' Clearly the result is L unmodified, which we write as follows:

```
--- Join( nil, L ) <= L ;
```

Next we consider the non-nil case, that is when the first list is of the form x :: y for some x and y. To join this list onto a list L we simply join y to L and then add x to the front of the resulting list. We express this rule as follows:

```
--- Join( x :: y, L ) <= x :: Join( y, L ) ;
```

This definition is now complete since we have considered all possible forms which the first list can take.

nil and x :: y in the left-hand sides of these definitions are called **patterns**. A pattern serves two purposes: firstly it specifies the form that an argument must take before the corresponding rule can be applied; secondly it has the effect of decomposing the argument and naming its components (except, of course, when the pattern is a simple data constant). For example the pattern x :: y specifies that the corresponding list must be non-empty (i.e. built from ::) and has the effect of naming the head of the list x and the tail y if it is. x and y can then be used in the body of the rule to refer to the head and tail of the argument as required. Here is the example application of Join given above along with its definition:

Join("ET", " phone home")	
≡ Join('E' :: ('T' :: nil), " phone home")	Undoing some of the shorthand
→ 'E' :: Join('T' :: nil, " phone home")	'E'::('T':: nil) matches the second rule for Join with x = 'E', y = 'T' :: nil
→ 'E' :: ('T' :: Join(nil, " phone home"))	'T' :: nil matches the second rule for Join with x = 'T', y = nil
→ 'E' :: ('T' :: " phone home")	The first rule for Join applies
→ 'E' :: "T phone home"	Simple application of ::
→ "ET phone home"	Simple application of ::

Because Join is polymorphic we can also use it to join lists of other types, for example:

```
Join( [ true, true, false, true ], [ false, false ] )
```

will generate the list of truvals:

```
[ true, true, false, true, false, false ]
```

It is important to appreciate that when we join two lists in this way we do not change either argument list. Join actually generates an entirely new list from two old ones in exactly the same way that the expression x :: L generates a new list with x at the head and L at the tail without changing either x or L. Once again this relates back to the issue of referential transparency.

Clearly, in order that pattern matching can be performed there must be no ambiguity as to which rule to apply for any given argument or set of arguments. The easy way to avoid this ambiguity is to forbid overlapping left-hand sides such as the following:

```
f( nil ) <= . . .
f( x ) <= . . .
```

(if the argument of f is nil then both rules will match). However, Hope allows overlapping patterns provided that they are collectively *unambiguous*. The above definition is permitted because nil (which is a constructor) is more specific than x (which is a simple variable). With the exception of some trivial functions given in Part III all of the examples in this book will be written using non-overlapping patterns so that definitions like the one above will not arise. However, we shall return to the issue of overlapping patterns in Chapter 8 where we consider the translation of source programs into an intermediate form, a significant part of which involves the treatment of pattern matching.

The Join function given above is a particularly useful and commonly used function and so is predefined in Hope; it is called append and is defined as an infix operator ⟨⟩ with priority 5. Thus, we can write

```
"ET" <> " phone home"
```

which has the same effect as writing

```
Join( "ET", " phone home" )
```

EXAMPLE 2: REVERSING A LIST

We shall now develop a simple function Rev, expressed in terms of append, which reverses a list of arbitrarily-typed objects. The main objective of the exercise is to explain the technique of **accumulating parameters** in which auxiliary parameters are added to a function to accumulate the result, as the name suggests. The technique described is a simple one, yet it can have significant effects on the execution time of a functional program.

To illustrate what Rev is required to do, the expression

$$\text{Rev}\,(\,[\,e_1, e_2, \ldots, e_{n-1}, e_n\,]\,)$$

is expected to yield

$$[\,e_n, e_{n-1}, \ldots, e_2, e_1\,]$$

Notice that the types of the argument and result of the function are the same, hence the declaration:

```
dec Rev : list( alpha ) → list( alpha ) ;
```

Because the argument to the function is a list, there will be two rules to consider: firstly, if the list is empty then the result will be nil because reversing the empty list returns just the empty list; secondly, if the list is of the form x :: l then we can reverse it by reversing l and adding the list [x] to the end of the resulting list. Hence,

```
--- Rev( nil )   <= nil ;
--- Rev( x :: l ) <= Rev( l ) <> [ x ] ;
```

Note that [x] forms a singleton list containing just x; this is required before <> can be applied.

Although this definition is correct, we may wish to make it more efficient by eliminating the calls to <>. An examination of the Rev function will reveal that the total number of calls made to :: (including those resulting from calls to <>) is quadratic in the length of the list being reversed. We can reduce the number of calls to :: to linear dimensions if we use an accumulating parameter. This is an extra parameter (which is initially nil) which accumulates the required reversed list at each function call. Because we require a function with an extra parameter we shall define an auxiliary function Rev2 which will be called from Rev with the input list and the initial accumulating parameter value, i.e. nil:

```
dec Rev : list( alpha ) → list( alpha ) ;
dec Rev2 : list( alpha ) # list( alpha ) → list( alpha ) ;
--- Rev( L )          <= Rev2( L, nil ) ;
--- Rev2( nil, A )    <= A ;
--- Rev2( x :: l, A ) <= Rev2( l, x :: A ) ;
```

For example,

```
Rev( [ 1, 2, 3 ] )
→ Rev2( [1, 2, 3], nil )
→ Rev2( [2, 3], [1] )
→ Rev2( [3], [2, 1] )
→ Rev2( nil, [3, 2, 1] )
→ [3, 2, 1]
```

We see that the accumulated list is built up 'back-to-front' so that adding a new element to the result list consists of a single :: operation rather than a call to ⟨⟩. Because of this the number of calls made to :: is now linear with respect to the length of the argument list. The function Rev2 in this example is called a **tail-recursive** function because the result of the function in the non-base case is determined solely by the result of calling the function itself (with a 'simpler' argument). The following examples are therefore tail-recursive (the tail-recursive calls are underlined):

```
--- f( x ) <= if x = 0 then 0 else f( x − 1 ) ;
--- g( x ) <= let a == x − 2
                  in if P( a ) then a else g( a ) ;
```

We shall see in Chapter 18 how accumulating parameters may be applied to perform 'recursion removal', a transformation which automatically converts certain functions into tail recursive form or equivalently into imperative language loops which execute more efficiently on a conventional computer.

EXAMPLE 3: TOKENIZING A SENTENCE

In this example we shall develop a function for splitting up a sentence into its component words. We shall assume that the words are separated by one or more spaces (i.e. ' ' characters) although in practice there may be other delimiters such as end-of-line characters (crlf in Hope) and punctuation characters such as

‘ , ’, ‘ ; ’ etc. For example,

```
SplitUp( "The following words" )
```

will be required to produce the list of words:

```
[ "The", "following", "words" ]
```

As always, we shall first write down the type of the function being defined. To help us to read the program we shall also use the **type** statement to define words and sentences – these are both lists of characters, hence:

```
type word == list( char ) ;
type sentence == list( char ) ;
dec SplitUp : sentence → list( word ) ;
```

We can perform the splitting up of a sentence by repeatedly extracting the first word from the sentence and adding it to the result of splitting up the remainder of the sentence, terminating when the sentence is empty. This suggests that it would be helpful to define an auxiliary function which given the input sentence returns the first word of the input sentence and the input sentence with the first word removed. We shall call this function NextWord with the declaration:

```
dec NextWord : sentence → word # sentence ;
```

To define this function we have to consider the possible forms of the input sentence. The 'base' case is when the sentence is empty, in which case both the word and remaining sentence returned must be empty:

```
NextWord( nil ) <= ( nil, nil ) ;
```

If the input is non-empty then it will either have a terminator at its head (i.e. a space character) or some other character. If the head of the sentence is a space then we have reached the end of the next word and so must return nil and the remainder of the sentence:

```
--- NextWord( Next :: Rest ) <=
        if Next = ' '
        then ( nil, Rest )
        else . . . ;
```

If the head of the sentence is some other character then we can use NextWord to detach the remainder of the next word from the rest of the sentence and then add Next to the front of the next word returned. The complete definition therefore becomes:

```
--- NextWord( Next :: Rest ) <=
        if Next = ' '
        then ( nil, Rest )
        else let ( RestOfWord, RestOfSentence ) ==
                    NextWord( Rest )
                 in ( Next :: RestOfWord, RestOfSentence ) ;
```

For example (we use the abbreviations R for RestOfWord and S for RestOfSentence):

```
NextWord( "The trouble with Tribbles" )
→ let ( R, S ) == NextWord( "he trouble with Tribbles" )
   in ( 'T' :: R, S )
→ ( 'T' :: "he", "trouble with Tribbles" )
≡ ( "The", "trouble with Tribbles" )
```

In a similar way we can now use NextWord to define SplitUp:

```
--- SplitUp( nil ) <= nil ;
--- SplitUp( Next :: Rest ) <=
        if Next = ' '
        then SplitUp( Rest )
        else FirstWord :: SplitUp( RestOfSentence )
             where ( FirstWord, RestOfSentence ) ==
                       NextWord( Next :: Rest ) ;
```

By way of variety we have used **where** instead of **let** to decompose the returned tuple. The test for ' ' simply handles the original sentence.

Notice that in the definition of SplitUp if the next character in the sentence is not a space then the argument of NextWord is exactly the same expression as the argument to SplitUp itself. This is rather wasteful of effort (and writing) since the pattern matching decomposes the input and the body puts it back together again. Fortunately, Hope allows us to name a whole argument pattern so that we can avoid this:

```
--- SplitUp( TheInput & Next :: Rest ) <=
        ...
             where ( FirstWord, RestOfSentence ) ==
                       NextWord( TheInput ) ;
```

This says: 'The argument is called TheInput and it must be a non-nil list with a head called Next and a tail called Rest '.

In contrast to this idea of naming argument patterns, sometimes we are interested in not having to name arguments, for example if we are interested only in the form of the argument rather than its components. A good example of this is the function IsEmpty which returns true if a given argument is nil and false otherwise:

```
dec IsEmpty : list( alpha ) → truval ;
--- IsEmpty( nil )   <= true ;
--- IsEmpty( x :: l ) <= false ;
```

In the second equation we are not required to use x or l in the body of the function. To save us having to invent names for the head and tail of the list we can use a special symbol _ (underscore) to mean 'don't care':

```
--- IsEmpty( nil ) <= true ;
--- IsEmpty( _ :: _ ) <= false ;
```

Both & and _ can be nested within a pattern for naming (or not naming) the subcomponents of an argument. For example, all of the following are valid patterns:

```
x :: ( y & _ :: _ )
a & ( x :: l ) :: _
_ :: ( ( x & ( a :: b ) ) :: _ )
```

As another aside, note that we can also use any base-value constants in a pattern and that arbitrary patterns may be used in qualified expressions. For example, the following are also valid patterns:

```
'a'
"Pattern"
[ true, false, x, y ]
```

and the following are valid **let/where** expressions:

```
let ( Next :: Rest ) == SplitUp( "Big Ben" ) in Rest
3 :: P where [ u, P & ( y :: z ), [ v ] ] == f( x )
LabelName where ( 'L' :: ( '_' :: LabelName ) ) == Label
```

EXAMPLE 4: Treesort

Treesort is a program which sorts a list of numbers into ascending order by building the initial list of numbers into an ordered binary tree and then flattening that tree back into a (sorted) list. Here are some examples of binary trees:

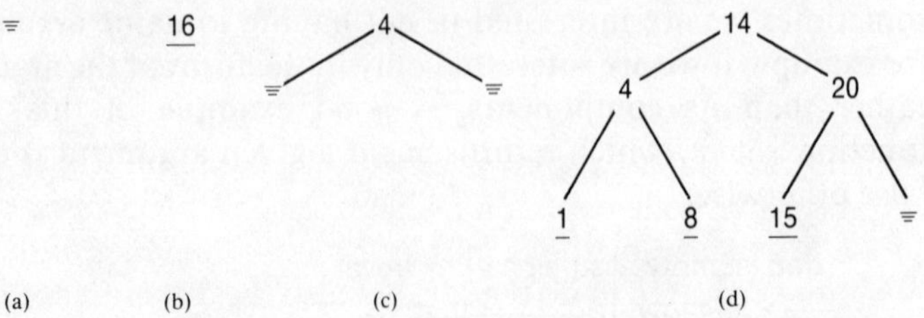

(a) is an **empty** tree; (b) is a tree with a single element called a **leaf** (shown underlined) which is a num; (c) and (d) are examples of multi-layer trees built from internal **nodes**, leaf nodes and empty trees. Each internal node contains a number and two subtrees. An *ordered* binary tree is a tree in which for every internal node the elements of the left subtree are all less than or equal to the value at the node and the elements of the right subtree are all greater than the value at the node. All of the examples show ordered binary trees. Flattening a tree notionally consists of squashing the tree in the direction of the leaf nodes so that the elements of the tree appear as a linear list. As an example of this, if we were to flatten tree (d) we would obtain the list [1, 4, 8, 14, 15, 20].

In order to write a Hope program to implement Treesort let us look at the overall structure of the problem. Treesort takes an unordered list of numbers and generates an ordered list of numbers, for example:

[5, 2, 1, 9] ——Treesort——→ [1, 2, 5, 9]

In doing so, however, it first builds an intermediate ordered binary tree and then flattens it:

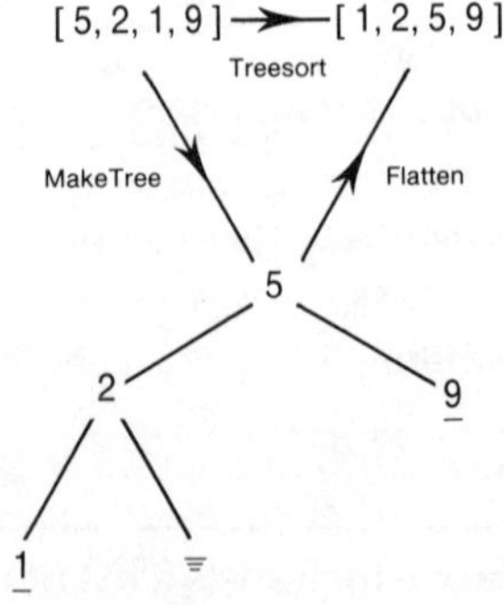

This description tells us everything we need to know about the structure of the Treesort program. Firstly from the definition of trees we can write down a Hope data definition:

```
data tree == empty ++ leaf( num ) ++ node( tree # num # tree ) ;
```

which says that a tree is either empty or a leaf containing a number, or a node containing a number and two subtrees.

The diagram above tells us not only the types of the main functions required to do the sort but also the definition of Treesort itself:

```
dec Treesort : list( num ) → list( num ) ;
dec MakeTree : list( num ) → tree ;
dec Flatten : tree → list( num ) ;
--- Treesort( UnsortedList ) <=
      Flatten( MakeTree( UnsortedList ) ) ;
```

All we have to do now is define the functions MakeTree and Flatten. Let us begin with MakeTree.

The argument of MakeTree is a list of numbers, so the definition of MakeTree will involve two cases: one for the empty (nil) list and one for non-empty lists. The 'base' case is straightforward:

```
--- MakeTree( nil ) <= empty ;
```

If the input list is non-empty with a head n and a tail rest then we can make the required tree by making a tree from the rest of the input and then doing an ordered insertion of n into the resulting tree. It will therefore be helpful to define an auxiliary function Insert which inserts a number into a tree in the right place, i.e. so as to preserve the orderedness of the tree. The operation which Insert is required to perform suggests its type declaration:

```
dec Insert : num # tree → tree ;
```

We can now complete the definition of MakeTree:

```
--- MakeTree( n :: rest ) <= Insert( n, MakeTree( rest ) ) ;
```

In order to define Insert we note that it is a function defined over trees, which suggests that there will be three rules, one for each possible tree constructor. Inserting a number into an empty tree

We introduce the concept in terms of simple induction on the integers which will probably be familiar to most readers. This principle states that we can establish some property $P(n)$, called the *inductive hypothesis*, for all non-negative integers n if we can prove $P(0)$ and that assuming $P(k)$, we can prove $P(k+1)$ for all integers $k \geqslant 0$. This is called the *principle of mathematical induction.* A simple example might be to prove that the sum, $S(n)$, of the first n numbers is $n(n+1)/2$. Here we would have for $P(n)$ the proposition '$S(n) = n(n+1)/2$'. Now, the base case occurs when n is 0 and it is easy to see that here $S(0) = 0$ so that $P(0)$ is true. Now assuming $P(k)$, i.e. assuming that '$S(k) = k(k+1)/2$' is true we have $S(k+1) = (k+1) + S(k) = (k+1) + k(k+1)/2 = (k+1)(k+2)/2$ so that $P(k+1)$ is true. Hence by mathematical induction $P(n)$ is true for all n.

An equally valid induction principle states that $P(n)$ holds for all non-negative integers n if $P(0)$ is true and that for all integers $k > 0$, assuming $P(j)$ for all $j < k$, we can prove $P(k)$. This is called *complete induction.* Induction works on the set of non-negative integers, $\mathcal{N}$, because $\mathcal{N}$ may be defined by the following axioms:

(1) 0 is in $\mathcal{N}$ (a 'base' value)
(2) if $n \in \mathcal{N}$ then $succ(n) \in \mathcal{N}$
(3) there are no other elements in $\mathcal{N}$

Notice that without (3) induction would not be valid since there would be some elements, n, of $\mathcal{N}$ for which $P(n)$ would not be considered at all.

Induction is not, therefore, confined only to the integers: any inductively defined set with a well defined ordering on its elements is amenable to the same technique which, generalized in this way, is called *well founded induction.* Now, in defining a recursive data type, for example a Hope list, we are defining just such a set, D say. The three axioms above are satisfied in generalized form for D (m, n and $J(i)$ are fixed finite integers, $1 \leq i \leq n$):

(1) the non-recursive 'base' expressions $b_1, \ldots, b_m$ are of type D, each being the application of a constructor (for example, empty and leaf in the tree data type above);
(2) if the syntactic expressions d_j are of type D_j, then the expression $c_i(d_1, \ldots, d_{J(i)})$ is of type D where c_i is a constructor of D of type $(D_1 \times \ldots \times D_{J(i)} \rightarrow D)$, $1 \leq j \leq J(i)$ (for example the node constructor above which has the type tree × num × tree → tree);
(3) there are no other elements in D.

Well founded induction applied to propositions over D then states that '$P(d)$ holds for all d of type D if $P(b_k)$ is true for $1 \leq k \leq m$ and that, for $1 \leq i \leq n$, assuming $P(d_j)$ for $1 \leq j \leq J(i)$ with $D_j = D$, we can prove $P(c_i(d_1, \ldots d_{J(i)}))$'. This principle is called structural induction. The base types $b_1, \ldots, b_m$ will often be constructors with no arguments, such as nil in the case of lists, but in general they may be constructors applied to types other than D – if so the base case step in any inductive proof will be more complex.

We can use structural induction to prove many properties about recursively defined functions and, although proof techniques are not a central theme to the book, we shall use structural induction in some of the later chapters. In fact inductive proofs go hand-in-hand with recursive functions: whenever we use recursion to write a program we may use induction to establish properties about it.

To give the reader a flavour of the type of proof which can be constructed using the technique let us now prove that the function Join:

```
--- Join( nil, L ) <= L ;
--- Join( x :: y, L ) <= x :: Join( y, L ) ;
```

which we developed earlier is associative, i.e. that

```
Join( Join( x, y ), z ) = Join( x, Join( y, z ) )
```

for all lists x, y, z. We prove this by structural induction on x which begins by looking at the base case.

When x = nil, Join(Join(nil, y), z) = Join(y, z) = Join(x, Join(y, z)) so the proposition holds for all lists y, z.

Now assume that Join(Join(u, y), z) = Join(u, Join(y, z)) for all lists u, y, z. Then, for arbitrary list item a,

```
Join( Join( a :: u, y ), z) = Join( a :: Join( u, y ), z )   by definition of Join
                            = a :: Join( Join( u, y ), z )   for the same reason
                            = a :: Join( u, Join( y, z ) )   by the inductive
                                                               hypothesis
                            = Join( a :: u, Join( y, z ) )   by definition of Join
```

Hence, by structural induction we have proved that Join is associative.

SUMMARY

- Hope is an example of a purely functional language.
- Hope is a strongly typed language.
- There are a number of predefined base types and primitive functions from which we can build other types and functions.
- Computations based on repetition are expressed functionally using recursion.
- Recursion provides a powerful and abstract way of solving problems.

- Expressions can be named to aid readability of a program, to save writing and to avoid repeated computation.
- New data types can be introduced and are defined in terms of constructor functions.
- Data types and functions can be polymorphic.
- Defining recursive functions over data types is simple, systematic and powerful.
- Pattern matching simplifies function definition and enables data structures to be decomposed into their constituent parts.
- Structural induction can be used to prove properties about functions over recursive data types.

EXERCISES

2.1 (a) Define a function convert of type num → num which converts a base 10 number into a base 2 number. For example, given the number 27, convert must produce the number 11011.

(b) Define a function sum of type num # num → num which performs addition on equal length base 2 numbers represented in the above way.

2.2 Consider the following function which sums the elements of a given list of numbers:

```
dec sum : list( num ) → num ;
--- sum( nil )   <= 0 ;
--- sum( x :: l ) <= x + sum( l ) ;
```

Define an equivalent function which uses an accumulating parameter to compute the sum. Does this reduce the algorithmic complexity of the function?

2.3 A *bag* is like a set except that a given element can occur more than once. A bag can be represented by a list of pairs where each pair consists of the element together with the number of times that element occurs in the bag. Write down a polymorphic type definition for bags together with the functions add for adding an element to a given bag; remove which returns an arbitrary element of the bag together with the bag with that element removed; isempty which returns true if a given bag is empty. Define a union function on bags in terms of the function add.

2.4 Write down the declaration and definition of a function search which scans a piece of text searching for (the first occurrence of) a given string, returning 0 if the string did not occur in the text and n if the string occurred starting at the nth character position in the text. The text is assumed to be held as a list of characters. For example, given the text "Hence home you idle creatures" and the search string "eat" the function should return 23.

2.5 *Insertion sort* is a sorting algorithm which accumulates a sorted list from its input list by repeatedly inserting the elements of the input list into the partial sorted list in their correct positions. For example given the input list [4, 1, 5, 3] the algorithm proceeds as follows:

input list	(partial) sorted list
[4, 1, 5, 3]	[ ]
[1, 5, 3]	[4]
[5, 3]	[1, 4]
[3],	[1, 4, 5]
[ ]	[1, 3, 4, 5]

result = [1, 3, 4, 5].

Implement insertion sort as a Hope function.

2.6 A **directed graph** is a network of nodes connected by one-way arcs. Suggest a representation for directed graphs in Hope. Define a function pathlength which given a graph and two nodes returns the minimum number of arcs it is necessary to traverse in order to go from the first node to the second. The function should return 0 if no path exists between the two nodes.

2.7 Suppose that the built-in type truval were not available in Hope. How might truvals be represented as a user-defined data type? For your chosen representation write down the declarations and definitions of the infix logical functions and, or and not.

2.8 (a) A university staff database is required in which the details of each member of the staff is recorded for administrative and organizational purposes. There are two types of staff member: teaching staff and support staff. For both staff types the name, sex, date of birth, date of enrolment at the university and address of the staff member are required to be stored. Each teaching staff member is affiliated with one of three departmental sections: systems, software or theory.

Their database records include in addition to the above information their associated section and a list of courses they currently teach (each represented by a unique course number). Each support staff member is classified as either secretarial, computer support or maintenance. Their database records include their associated classification in addition to the information above. Suggest a possible representation of this database in Hope and write down the **type** and **data** definitions required.

(b) Define Hope functions to do each of the following:

(i) count the total number of teaching and support staff in the database;

(ii) return the name of the teacher who teaches a given course;

(iii) compute the ratio of computer support staff to maintenance staff.

2.9 Prove by structural induction that addition defined on the natural numbers by:

```
data nat == zero ++ succ ( nat ) ;
dec add : nat # nat → nat ;
--- add ( n, zero ) <= n ;
--- add ( n, succ ( m ) ) <= succ ( add ( n, m ) ) ;
```

is associative and commutative. (*Hint:* For commutativity, show that add (n, succ (m)) = add (succ (n), m) for all n, m of type nat.)

Chapter 3
Higher-order functions

The features of Hope we have described so far enable us to define arbitrary data structures and arbitrary functions for processing those structures. We have seen how Hope provides a simple and abstract method of describing data as well as a mechanical way of structuring the functions which operate on that data. These features therefore lead to a style of programming based on the definition of functions by cases – one case covering each possible pattern of argument data.

In this chapter we shall look at another powerful feature of functional languages, namely that of higher-order functions. In the examples we have seen so far each function is viewed as a static piece of code for transforming input values to output values; we have, in effect, described the **first-order** subset of Hope. The basic idea behind higher-order functions is that functions themselves should have the same first-class status as any other data object so that they can themselves be passed as inputs to and returned as outputs from other functions. In this chapter we shall see how this capability can be used to express common patterns of recursion and so enable otherwise recursive functions to be re-expressed using a non-recursive application of a higher-order function. This technique leads to very concise and abstract programs which are often remarkably short for the complexity of computation which they perform. We shall examine the style of programming which is encouraged by higher-order functions and will look at a number of examples illustrating how they can be used in practice.

3.1 Patterns of recursion

Take a look at the following Hope functions:

```
dec IncList : list( num ) → list( num ) ;
--- IncList( nil ) <= nil ;
--- IncList( x :: l ) <= ( x + 1 ) :: IncList( l ) ;

dec MakeStrings : list( char ) → list( list( char ) ) ;
--- MakeStrings( nil ) <= nil ;
--- MakeStrings( c :: l ) <= [ c ] :: MakeStrings( l ) ;
```

Although these functions are different in that they perform different operations on lists of different types, they are similar in that they both perform a single operation on every element of a list. The first function increments every element of a list of numbers; the second maps every element of a list of characters into a singleton list. We say that the 'pattern of recursion' is the same in both cases.

In a functional language we can express this pattern of recursion using higher-order functions. A higher-order function is a function which takes a function as an argument or which generates a function as its result. More precisely, a first-order function is one with type A → B where there are no arrows in the type expressions A and B so that by a complementary argument a higher-order function is any function which is not first-order.

In the two examples given above a function is being applied to every element of a given list. In IncList that function has the defining equation

```
--- Inc( n ) <= n + 1 ;
```

while for MakeStrings the function's equation is

```
--- Listify( c ) <= [ c ] ;
```

(with the appropriate type declarations). We can capture the overall structure of functions such as MakeStrings and Inclist by defining a higher-order function which takes a function like Listify or Inc as an argument and applies it to each element of a given list which is supplied as a second argument. This is a commonly used higher-order function and is often called map to reflect the fact that a function is being mapped over every element of a list. Because we do not know in advance the type of the function being applied or the type of the list elements being processed, map must be declared as a polymorphic function. The complete definition looks like this:

```
dec map : ( alpha → beta ) # list( alpha ) → list( beta ) ;
--- map( f, nil ) <= nil ;
--- map( f, x :: l ) <= f( x ) :: map( f, l ) ;
```

We can now express IncList and MakeStrings using map and the auxiliary functions Inc and Listify which were defined above:

```
IncList( L )       ≅ map( Inc, L )
MakeStrings( L ) ≅ map( Listify, L )
```

This is fine provided we have predefined the functions Inc and Listify to map over the list. Explicitly defining such functions can be rather onerous, however, particularly if the function being mapped is simple like the two functions here and not used elsewhere in the program, for we have to both declare these functions and specify their rule(s). Fortunately, Hope allows us to write down directly a function-valued expression, called a **lambda expression**, which enables us to express Inc and Listify directly. Inc, for example, is written:

```
lambda x => x + 1
```

(The significance of the reserved word **lambda** will become apparent in Chapter 6.) This may be understood by reading **lambda** as 'the function of ...', and the => as '... which returns ...'. Thus in general the function f defined by the equation

```
--- f( x ) <= E ;
```

where f does not occur in E, can be expressed equivalently as a lambda expression:

```
lambda x => E
```

We can now express an application of the IncList function using map and a lambda expression:

```
IncList( L ) ≅ map( lambda x => x + 1, L )
```

and, in a similar way, the MakeStrings function:

```
MakeStrings( L ) ≅ map( lambda c => [ c ], L )
```

The body of a lambda expression can be any expression but note that a lambda expression of this form cannot be recursive for there is no associated function name to refer to! We can get round this problem, however, using a **let** or **where** statement outside the lambda. **let** and **where** introduce names which can be used within the expression defining that name if required. So, the function f defined by

```
f A <= ... f ... ;
```

where A is an arbitrary pattern can be defined *in situ* by using a **let** or a **where**:

```
let f == lambda A => ... f ... in E_f
```

or

```
E_f where f == lambda A => ... f ...
```

E_f here denotes some expression involving f. For example,

```
let f == lambda x => if x = 0 then 0 else x + f( x - 1 )
in f( 3 )
```

which computes the sum of the first three integers, i.e. 3 + 2 + 1 + 0 = 6. A **let** or **where** expression which introduces a recursive function is often referred to as a **recursive let** or a **recursive where** expression. In some languages recursive let expressions are distinguished from non-recursive ones by use of a separate keyword such as **letrec** or **whererec**. We shall see an example of such a language in Chapter 5.

In Hope, a lambda expression may also contain embedded rules (i.e. embedded patterns), each separated by a |. For example, the function IsEmpty defined by

```
--- IsEmpty( nil ) <= true ;
--- IsEmpty( _ :: _ ) <= false ;
```

can be written as a lambda expression:

```
lambda nil => true | _ :: _ => false
```

As another example, the expression

```
map( lambda nil => "?" | h :: _ => "Head is" <> [ h ],
    [ "Monsters", nil, nil, "from", nil, "the", "Id" ] )
```

evaluates to the list of strings:

```
[ "Head is M", "?", "?", "Head is f", "?", "Head is t", "Head is I" ]
```

and the expression

```
map( lambda c :: _ => c,
   SplitUp( "Time and relative dimension in space" ) )
```

(where SplitUp is as defined in the previous chapter) generates the string "Tardis".

The map function defined above has the effect of recreating the original list with each element transformed according to the function being mapped. Sometimes, however, we are interested in 'reducing' a list to some other value, for example a number representing the length of the list or the maximum value in the list. This type of recursive function can also be captured using a higher-order function:

```
dec reduce : ( alpha # beta -> beta ) # beta # list( alpha ) -> beta ;
--- reduce( f, b, nil ) <= b ;
--- reduce( f, b, x :: l ) <= f( x, reduce( f, b, l ) ) ;
```

To see how this works, observe that the expression

reduce(f, b, [e_1, e_2, . . . , e_n])

is equivalent to the expression

f(e_1, f(e_2, . . . f(e_n, b) . . .))

where b here is the 'base' value i.e. the value returned by reducing an empty list. Many list processing operations have this computational structure and can be expressed using reduce by supplying the appropriate function f and base case b. As a simple example, the following expression sums the elements of a list of numbers, L:

```
reduce( +, 0, L )
```

(Note that + is an infix function, whereas we defined reduce to accept only prefix functions. However, infix functions are automatically converted to an equivalent prefix form whenever they are passed as parameters.)

To illustrate how this works here is the evaluation sequence for L = [1, 2, 3] (note that the prefix version of + is written ⟨+⟩):

```
reduce( +, 0, [ 1, 3, 5 ] )
≡ reduce( +, 0, 1 :: ( 3 :: ( 5 :: nil ) ) )
→ ⟨+⟩( 1, reduce( +, 0, 3 :: ( 5 :: nil ) ) )
→ ⟨+⟩( 1, ⟨+⟩( 3, reduce( +, 0, 5 :: nil ) ) )
→ ⟨+⟩( 1, ⟨+⟩( 3, ⟨+⟩( 5, reduce( +, 0, nil ) ) ) )
→ ⟨+⟩( 1, ⟨+⟩( 3, ⟨+⟩( 5, 0 ) ) )
→ 9
```

In a similar way the expression

```
reduce( *, 1, L )
```

computes the product of a list of numbers, L (note that the base case is now 1 – the identity element for *). Here are some further examples which demonstrate the power and flexibility of reduce:

(1) Compute the maximum of a list of non-negative numbers, L, using the max function from the previous chapter:

```
reduce( max, 0, L )
```

(2) Find the number of people called "Spock" in a list of names, L:

```
reduce( lambda ( name, sum ) =>
          sum + ( if name = "Spock" then 1 else 0 ), 0, L )
```

(3) List search: returns true if el is in L; false otherwise

```
reduce( lambda ( next, isthere ) =>
          if next = el then true else isthere, false, L )
```

(4) The MakeTree function from the Treesort example given in the previous chapter. This makes a tree from a list of numbers, L:

```
reduce( Insert, empty, L )
```

(5) The identity function on lists:

```
reduce( ::, nil, L )
```

Note that in the last example the constructor function :: was passed as an argument to reduce. This is quite acceptable since, as we have already seen, a constructor behaves just like any other function except that it has no rules.

3.2 Binding

It is important to understand that the values of the variables in a lambda expression are determined when the expression is *defined* rather than when it is *used*. For example, if we write

```
let x == 1 in ( let f == lambda y => x + y in ( let x == 2 in f( x ) ) )
```

the x in x + y refers to the value 1, i.e. the value of x at the point of definition of f. This is called **static binding**. Some languages (for example some dialects of LISP) employ **dynamic binding** in which the values of the variables in a lambda expression are determined when the expression is eventually applied. If Hope were to use dynamic binding then the value of x used for the evaluation of x + y above would be 2 since x has the value 2 when f is applied. The original value of x is effectively forgotten.

Dynamic binding is generally considered to be confusing because the meaning of a function can change according to the context in which it is used. This means that it is possible for the same function call to produce different answers, which is contrary to the idea of referential transparency. All modern functional languages use static binding to avoid this problem. We shall return to the issue of binding in Chapter 9 where we shall see how static binding is supported in an interpreter for functional languages.

3.3 Other patterns of recursion

The higher-order functions we have seen so far aim to capture the recursive structure common to many list-processing functions. However, it is possible to define arbitrarily complex user-defined data types for which functions like map and reduce are inappropriate as 'recursion abstraction' functions. However, there is no reason why we cannot associate different higher-order functions with these types in order to capture the structure of many recursive functions defined over them. As a simple example, let us consider how certain recursive tree-processing functions can be described using the equivalents of map and reduce defined for lists. The same approach can be equally well applied to other user-defined types.

For generality we shall assume a polymorphic definition of trees in which the objects contained in the tree can be of arbitrary type alpha. Also for simplicity we shall consider only trees built from empty trees and internal nodes (i.e. omitting the leaf constructor used in the Treesort program in the previous chapter). The data definition therefore looks like this:

```
data tree( alpha ) == empty ++ node ( tree( alpha ) # alpha # tree( alpha ) ) ;
```

We can develop a generalized function which applies a given function to each element (of type alpha) in a tree by means of a higher-order function MapTree which is an obvious extension to the map function defined for lists:

```
dec MapTree : ( alpha → beta ) # tree( alpha ) → tree( beta ) ;
--- MapTree( f, empty ) <= empty ;
--- MapTree( f, node ( left, value, right ) ) <=
        node( MapTree( f, left ), f( value ), MapTree( f, right ) ) ;
```

For example, we can increment each element in a tree of numbers T by writing the expression

```
MapTree( lambda x => x + 1, T )
```

The equivalent of the reduce function for lists is more interesting because there are now several ways in which a tree can be traversed. For example, we can reduce both subtrees independently and then apply the reducing function to the results:

```
dec TreeReduce : ( alpha # beta # beta → beta ) # beta # tree( alpha )
                  → beta ;
--- TreeReduce( f, b, empty ) <= b ;
--- TreeReduce( f, b, node( left, value, right ) ) <=
        f( value, TreeReduce( f, b, left ), TreeReduce( f, b, right ) ) ;
```

so that, for example,

```
TreeReduce( lambda ( v, r1, r2 ) => r1 <> ( v :: r2 ), nil, T )
```

has the effect of flattening the tree T in the manner described in Chapter 2, and

```
TreeReduce( lambda ( v, r1, r2 ) => max( v, max( r1, r2 ) ), 0, T ) ;
```

computes the largest number in a tree of non-negative integers. However, we can also define a form of reduce which reduces the left subtree using the result of reducing the right subtree as the 'base' case:

```
dec TreeReduce2 : ( alpha # beta → beta ) # beta # tree( alpha ) → beta ;
--- TreeReduce2( f, b, empty ) <= b ;
--- TreeReduce2( f, b, node( left, value, right ) ) <=
        f( value, TreeReduce2( f, TreeReduce2( f, b, right ), left ) ) ;
```

Notice that the function parameter f is now required to be a two-argument function. Using this form of reduce we can rewrite the above expression to compute the maximum number in a tree T as follows:

```
TreeReduce2( max, 0, T )
```

As a variation on this we could have put the call to f in a different place:

```
dec TreeReduce3 : ( alpha # beta -> beta ) # beta # tree( alpha ) -> beta ;
--- TreeReduce3( f, b, empty ) <= b ;
--- TreeReduce3( f, b, node( left, value, right ) ) <=
        TreeReduce3( f, f( value, TreeReduce3( f, b, right ) ), left ) ;
```

Using this definition we can perform tree flattening without requiring the use of append:

```
TreeReduce3( ::, nil, T )
```

The astute reader may notice that this expression effectively flattens the tree using the 'base' value as an accumulating parameter. In the same way that the use of an accumulating parameter reduced the quadratic complexity of the Reverse function given in Chapter 2 to linear dimensions, here too it reduces the number of calls to :: from $O(n^2)$ to $O(n)$ where n is the number of elements in the tree. There are clearly other variations on the reduce function which reflect the various ways in which a binary tree can be traversed.

In general, then, by defining a small suite of higher-order functions to 'iterate' over each data type we can avoid writing down many explicit recursive functions on that type, using instead the higher-order functions appropriately parameterized. In a sense the technique can be compared with that of polymorphism: a polymorphic data type enables structures with the same overall shape to be described by a single definition; higher-order functions enable recursive functions with the same overall structure to be described by a single function.

3.4 An example application

In order to illustrate how higher-order functions may be used in practice we shall now consider a simple problem from text processing and will demonstrate how higher-order functions can be used to solve the problem in a very concise and abstract way. The problem we shall consider is one of producing a word count list from a file of text. The text is assumed to consist of a number of words and for each word in the text we shall be required to generate an integer representing the number of occurrences of that word in the text. The result will be a list of pairs of the form

```
( word, count )
```

where count is the number of occurrences of word in the given text. When we have completed the program we shall see how the Treesort program developed in the previous chapter can be extended to sort these pairs in different ways by turning Treesort itself into a higher-order function.

The source text is assumed to consist of sentences separated by full stops where each sentence consists of words separated by one or more space characters. For simplicity a word will be defined as any sequence of characters excluding spaces and full stops. For example, given the text

```
"Hi said Bill. Hi said Ben."
```

we shall generate

```
[ ( "Hi", 2 ), ( "said", 2 ), ( "Bill", 1 ), ( "Ben", 1 ) ]
```

We shall use the function SplitUp which we have already defined in Section 2.6.1 and will assume the definitions of map and reduce given above.

3.4.1 Counting the words

As a first step, we shall have to split the sentence into its component words. We cannot use SplitUp immediately, however, because the text contains full stop characters which separate the sentences and are not processed by SplitUp. We can, however, replace all the full stops by spaces before processing the text by using map (we must replace full stops with spaces rather than remove them altogether so as not to merge the last word of one sentence with the first word of the succeeding sentence when there are no spaces in between):

```
map( lambda c => if c = '.' then ' ' else c, Text )
```

where Text is the text being processed. Having removed the full stops we can now apply SplitUp to take the text apart:

```
SplitUp( map( lambda c => if c = '.' then ' ' else c, Text ) )
```

We are now in a position to build up the required list of (word, count) pairs. What we are going to do is build the list incrementally, starting with the nil list and updating the list each time a new word is encountered in the text. For example if the list contains the pairs

```
[ ( "the", 1 ), ( "day", 1 ), ( "of", 1 ) ]
```

and the next word in the input text is "the", then we will generate a new list of the form

```
[ ( "the", 2 ), ( "day", 1 ), ( "of", 1 ) ]
```

If the next text word is not already in the list then we must create a new entry with an initial count of 1. For example if the next text word after "the" above is "jackal" then we must generate the new list

```
[ ( "the", 2 ), ( "day", 1 ), ( "of", 1 ), ( "jackal", 1 ) ]
```

It will be helpful to define a separate function Update to perform the list update operation in order to make the final program more readable:

```
type word == list( char ) ;
dec Update : word # list ( word # num ) → list( word # num ) ;
--- Update( w, nil ) <= [ ( w, 1 ) ] ;
--- Update( w, ( Entry & ( Word, Count ) ) :: Rest ) <=
        if w = Word
        then ( Word, Count + 1 ) :: Rest
        else Entry :: Update( w, Rest ) ;
```

This leaves us with the job of calling Update for each word encountered in the text. It should be apparent that this can now be done by 'reducing' the list of words in the input text using the Update function:

```
reduce( Update, nil, Wordlist )
```

This builds the expression

$$\text{Update}(\ w_1, \text{Update}(\ w_2, \text{Update}(\ w_3, \ldots \text{Update}(\ w_n, \text{nil}\ ) \ldots)))$$

where the w_i ($1 \leq i \leq n$) are the component words of Wordlist, as required.

Putting things together, we can now define the top-level function WCount which generates the word counts from a text file. Note the use of the predefined function fromfile which, given a file name as a list of characters, returns the contents of that file as a list of characters:

```
type filename == list( char ) ;
dec WCount : filename → list( word # num ) ;
--- WCount( name ) <= reduce( Update, nil, Wordlist )
        where Wordlist == SplitUp( map( RemoveStop, fromfile( name ) ) )
        where RemoveStop == lambda c => if c = '.' then ' ' else c ;
```

As an example of how this program works, suppose the file sample contains the text

```
the dog and the cat.
```

The expression input(sample) delivers the contents of the file sample as a list of characters; mapping the function RemoveStop over the resulting list returns the same list with the full stop at the end removed; the call to SplitUp generates the list of words

```
[ "the", "dog", "and", "the", "cat" ]
```

and finally reducing Update over the result with a base case of nil computes the expression

```
Update( "the", Update( "dog", Update( "and",
          Update( "the", Update( "cat", nil ) ) ) ) )
= [ ( "cat", 1 ), ( "the", 2 ), ( "and", 1 ), ( "dog", 1 ) ]
```

as required.

3.4.2 Sorting the output

It would be nice if, having computed the word counts for each word in the source text, we could sort these counts, for example in order of frequency (most common word first) or based on the textual ordering of the words. Now, we could use the Treesort program developed in Chapter 2 to help us but unfortunately this is defined only to sort lists of integers; here we want it to sort lists of pairs. If we wish to use Treesort here then we must modify the program to sort more general object types.

If we now look back at Treesort we see that the ordering of elements in the intermediate tree is specified by the primitive operator =<. Using this operator the Insert function ensures that all elements in the left subtree of a node are less than or equal to the elements in the right subtree. We can make Treesort more powerful, however, by parameterizing it by this ordering function. This makes Treesort not only higher-order but also polymorphic since we can now sort any object type to which we can attach an ordering. The modifications required are very straightforward. Firstly we must make the tree data type and the associated functions polymorphic; secondly we must add the ordering function as a parameter to Treesort, MakeTree and Insert; finally we must replace the references to the primitive =< in Insert by this new function-valued parameter:

```
type Ordering      == alpha # alpha → truval ;
data tree( alpha )== empty ++ leaf( alpha ) ++
                     node( tree( alpha ) # alpha # tree( alpha ) ) ;
```

```
dec Treesort  : list( alpha ) # Ordering → list( alpha ) ;
dec MakeTree : list( alpha ) # Ordering → tree( alpha ) ;
dec Insert    : alpha # tree( alpha ) # Ordering → tree( alpha ) ;

--- Treesort( UnsortedList, TestFun ) <=
      Flatten( MakeTree( UnsortedList, TestFun ) ) ;

--- MakeTree( List, f ) <=
      reduce( lambda ( n, t ) => Insert( n, t, f ), empty, List ) ;

--- Insert( n, empty, _ ) <= leaf( n ) ;
--- Insert( n, OldLeaf & leaf( m ), f ) <=
      if f( n, m )
      then node( empty, n, OldLeaf )
      else node( OldLeaf, n, empty ) ;
--- Insert( n, node( left, value, right ), f ) <=
      if f( n, value )
      then node( Insert( n, left, f ), value, right )
      else node( left, value, Insert( n, right, f ) ) ;
```

(The definition of Flatten is unaffected by the new ordering function.)

We can make Treesort behave as before by passing it the original ordering function, i.e. =<. For example, the expression

```
Treesort( [ 5, 3, 4, 7, 2, 3 ], =< )
```

will generate the sorted list [2, 3, 3, 4, 5, 7] as before. However, we can now also use the same function to sort our word count pairs. If we want to sort the pairs by word frequency then the required ordering function is based on comparing the frequency counts. The ordering function required looks like this:

```
lambda ( ( _, c1 ), ( _, c2 ) ) => ( c1 >= c2 )
```

If we want to sort the word counts alphabetically, then we compare the word strings, in which case the ordering function will be:

```
lambda ( ( w1, _ ), ( w2, _ ) ) => StringLessEq( w1, w2 )
```

where StringLessEq is the less-than-or-equal function on strings which is easily defined as a recursive function on lists.

So, for example, if we want to sort the word concordance list of our "sample" text file by frequency then we might write

```
Treesort( WCount( "sample" ), OrderingFunction )
  where OrderingFunction == lambda ( ( _, c1 ), ( _, c2 ) ) => ( c1 >= c2 ) )
```

which will yield the sorted list

= [("the", 2), ("dog", 1), ("and", 1), ("cat", 1)]

as required.

Note that an alternative approach to sorting the resulting list is to modify Update so as to maintain the intermediate word count lists in the required order. This could even be done by holding the (word, count) pairs in a sorted tree and ultimately flattening the tree into a sorted list; this will reduce the complexity of the algorithm. Here, however, we have concentrated on developing a clear and simple solution to the problem by separating the generation and sorting operations on the word concordance list. Having produced a clear and correct solution to the problem we can then consider optimization of the program if such optimization is required – ideally this would be performed by the compiler as we discuss in Part III of this book. The alternative solution to the problem outlined here is left as an exercise for the reader.

This concludes our discussion of higher-order functions and the style of progamming which they encourage. It will be noted that in Hope there is no restriction on the number or complexity of such functions which can be defined and this is true of most functional languages. In Chapter 5, however, we shall look at a functional language called FP, in which there is no facility for programmer-defined higher-order functions; instead the language provides a small suite of *built-in* higher-order functions which are treated as program building blocks in much the same way that **let**, **where**, conditional expressions etc. provide the building blocks for Hope programs. In that discussion we shall see again how many recursive programs can be re-expressed non-recursively using applications of the predefined higher-order functions.

Also in Chapter 5 we shall describe a language called Miranda which takes a rather different approach towards higher-order functions. In Hope a function-valued object is created explicitly by means of a lambda expression; in Miranda there is no mechanism for explicitly defining a lambda expression and instead function-valued objects are generated by partially applying existing functions. Some examples illustrating this approach will be given in Chapter 5.

SUMMARY

- Functions themselves can be treated as first-class objects.
- Functions which can take other functions as parameters or which return functions as results are called higher-order functions.
- Higher-order functions can be used to describe common patterns of recursion.

- The use of higher-order functions often leads to very concise and abstract programs.
- Separate higher-order functions may be appropriate to each data type.
- Most functional languages bind variables in function bodies statically.
- Many functions, for example sorting functions, can be generalized by the use of higher-order functions.

EXERCISES

3.1 Define the functions map and ⟨⟩ in terms of the function reduce.

3.2 Suppose a number of Boolean tests are carried out the results of which are stored as a list of truvals. Write down a single expression using reduce which:

(a) returns true if at least one of the tests succeeded (i.e. gave true), i.e. false if they all failed;

(b) returns true if all of the tests succeeded, i.e. false if any one of them failed.

3.3 Define a Hope function of a single parameter n which generates a list of length n where the ith element in the list is a function of one argument which when applied adds i to the number it is given.

3.4 (a) Define a higher-order function compose which given any two functions as arguments returns their composition.

(b) Write down an expression which defines the Treesort function in terms of compose, Flatten and Maketree.

(c) Suppose you are given a list of functions $F = [\, f_1, f_2, \ldots, f_n \,]$ each of type (alpha → alpha); write down a Hope expression, C, using compose and reduce, which composes them together so that $C(F)(x) \equiv f_1(f_2(\ldots(f_n(x))\ldots))$.

3.5 Consider the following infix Hope function

```
infix / : 6 ;
dec / : alpha → ( beta → beta ) # list( alpha ) → ( beta → beta ) ;
--- f / nil   <= lambda y => y ;
--- f / x :: l <= lambda y => f( x )( ( f / l )( y ) ) ;
```

(a) Compare this function with the reduce function on lists.

(b) Define a function sum in terms of / which sums the elements of a given list of numbers.

(c) Define a function add which with the type

```
dec add : num → ( list( num ) → list( num ) ) ;
```

where add(n) returns a function which inserts n into its correct position within any ascending list of numbers.

(d) Write a Hope expression using / and add which sorts the list [4, 2, 7, 3] into ascending order.

3.6 For the following functions

```
--- g( h, n ) <= let x == 5 in h( n + x ) ;
--- f( x )    <= g( lambda y => x + y - 2, 6 ) ;
```

what will be the value of the expression f(1) assuming

(a) static binding,

(b) dynamic binding?

Chapter 4
Evaluation modes

In a language like Pascal the application of a function to an argument results in the argument being evaluated before it is passed to the function. We say that the argument is passed **by-value**, implying that only values are passed into the body of a function, and we talk of the computation rule or calling mechanism of the language being one of **call-by-value**. The advantage of call-by-value is that it is easy to implement efficiently: first we evaluate the argument, then we call the function. The disadvantage is that it may result in redundant evaluation if the argument value is not ultimately required by the called function. An alternative to call-by-value is **call-by-need** in which all arguments are passed to the function in an unevaluated form and are only evaluated when needed inside the function body. The advantage of call-by-need is that no effort will have been wasted if the argument value is not ultimately required. The disadvantage is that it is more expensive to implement than call-by-value because unevaluated expressions must be passed into the function rather than simple values.

In the context of functional languages we generally talk of two evaluation modes, namely **eager** and **lazy** evaluation, although there are some variations. Informally, eager evaluation says 'do anything you can', in other words don't worry about whether the result is ultimately useful. Lazy evaluation on the other hand says 'don't do anything unless you have to'. Eager evaluation therefore corresponds loosely to the call-by-value mechanism in conventional programming terminology and lazy evaluation to the call-by-need mechanism. (They are not precisely equivalent – the exact relationships between the terms will be clarified in Chapter 6.)

Now, although this might suggest that the evaluation mode is merely related to the efficiency of a program and its compilation, the effects of the evaluation mode in functional programming are more far-reaching than initially meets the eye. In this chapter we shall look at the effect of various evaluation modes on the behaviour of a functional program and will see how certain classes of problem rely wholly on the fact that function arguments are left unevaluated at the point of call.

4.1 Strictness

A function which always requires the value of one of its arguments is said to be **strict** in that argument. The primitive function +, for example, cannot be invoked until both of its arguments have been evaluated to yield numbers and so is said to be strict in both arguments. Some functions, however, can produce a result without needing to know the value of one or more of its arguments. As an example, the user-defined function

```
--- f( x, y ) <= if x < 10 then x else y ;
```

does not always require the value of y to be known. It must, however, know the value of x in order that the test 'x < 10' can be performed. We therefore say that f is strict in x but non-strict in y meaning that x is definitely required whereas y might not be.

The consequence of this is that if we evaluate both the arguments at the point of call (i.e. if we pass the arguments by-value, corresponding to eager evaluation) then some of those evaluations may prove redundant. Worse still, if an unwanted argument expression is non-terminating then the whole program will fail to terminate when it might have terminated had the argument been passed by-need. For example, if we evaluate the expression

```
f( 4, ⟨non-terminating expression⟩ )
```

in an eager implementation then the result will be non-termination. If on the other hand we evaluate the same expression in a lazy implementation, we will get the answer 4. Of course, this does not mean that lazy evaluation avoids all non-terminating computations: the expression

```
f( ⟨non-terminating expression⟩, E )
```

for example, will fail to terminate regardless of the evaluation mode because the first argument of f is always required. Turning the argument around, this suggests that the first argument of f can be passed either by-value or by-need since both produce the same behaviour from f. This is an important observation and forms the basis of a number of optimizations to functional language implementations as we shall see throughout the book.

Now, as we have already suggested, call-by-need parameter passing can avoid redundant evaluation as well as non-terminating evaluation. An example of this is the application of reduce given in the previous chapter:

```
reduce( lambda ( next, isthere ) => if next = el then true else isthere,
        false, L )
```

Suppose that the search list L, is the list, of numbers [1, 3, 5, 7] and that we are testing whether 1 is in the list. In an eager implementation 1 is compared with every list element before the result is returned (b denotes the lambda expression above):

```
reduce( b, false, [ 1, 3, 5, 7 ] )
≡ b( 1, b( 3, b( 5, b( 7, false ) ) ) )     (from definition of reduce)
→ b( 1, b( 3, b( 5, false ) ) )
→ b( 1, b( 3, false ) )
→ b( 1, false )
→ true                                      (since b looks for 1s)
```

On the other hand, in a lazy implementation, the value true is returned immediately:

```
reduce( b, false, [ 1, 3, 5, 7 ] )
→ b( 1, reduce( b, false, [ 3, 5, 7 ] ) )
→ true
```

The reason why this stops so quickly is that b does not always require the value of its second argument, i.e. it is *non-strict* in its second argument. If the first argument is equal to the value being tested for membership then the second argument is thrown away; this is the case in the example above where the discarded argument expression is shown underlined.

These discussions might suggest that in order to avoid redundant evaluations and to guarantee 'safe' termination properties, all implementations of functional languages should be lazy. However, there are significant overheads associated with the passing of parameters by-need, as we shall see in Chapter 9 and elsewhere in the book. For this reason, some functional languages are defined to have 'strict semantics', or alternatively 'eager semantics', meaning that all functions are assumed to be strict in all arguments and all parameters are consequently passed by-value. Other languages, however, take the opposite approach and are defined to have 'lazy semantics'; this means that the program behaves as though each parameter is passed by-need. This does not imply that all parameters *have* to be passed by-need since, as we have already seen, a parameter which is always required by a function can be passed in either way without affecting the behaviour of the program. In general, by 'lazy implementation' we simply mean an implementation which preserves lazy semantics rather than one which implements call-by-need everywhere, although, of course, it could.

The reason for adopting eager or lazy semantics is not simply one of efficiency, however, for there are a number of problems which rely on the fact that the underlying implementation is lazy, or at least 'partly' lazy, and so safe in the sense of termination discussed above. In the next three sections we shall give a flavour of the class of problems to which this applies.

4.2 Processing 'infinite' data structures

The following function generates an infinite data structure – in this case, the infinite list of integers x, x + 1, x + 2, ... for a given value of x:

```
dec from : num → list( num ) ;
--- from( x ) <= x :: from( x + 1 ) ;
```

Now, if we use eager evaluation then any application of from will fail to terminate. For example:

```
from( 0 )
→ 0 :: from( 1 )
→ 0 :: ( 1 :: from( 2 ) )
→ 0 :: ( 1 :: ( 2 :: from( 3 ) ) )
etc.
```

If on the other hand we use lazy evaluation then the evaluation will stop as soon as the first constructor has been generated at the top level:

```
from( 0 )
→ 0 :: from( 1 )
```

The arguments to :: are not evaluated at the point of call so because :: has no rule(s) the evaluation stops with the underlined expression denoting an unevaluated call to the from function. The expression will remain in this form until some other function 'forces' the evaluation of the tail of the resulting list. An example of such a function is the following, which computes the sum of the first n elements of a list of numbers:

```
dec sum : num # list( num ) → num ;
--- sum( n, x :: l ) <= if n = 0 then 0 else x + sum( n − 1, l ) ;
```

The evaluation of sum(2, from(1)) proceeds as follows (unevaluated function calls are again shown underlined):

```
sum( 2, from( 1 ) )
```

The pattern matching cannot be done until the structure of the underlined expression is known and so its evaluation is forced to the top-level constructor in order that the match can proceed:

```
→ sum( 2, 1 :: from( 2 ) )
→ 1 + sum( 1, from( 2 ) )
```

Remember that + is strict in both of its arguments so it evaluates the recursive call to sum immediately; this in turn evaluates the call to from, again to enable the pattern matching to proceed:

```
→ 1 + sum( 1, 2 :: from( 3 ) )
→ 1 + ( 2 + sum( 0, from( 3 ) ) )
```

The test n = 0 in sum now evaluates to true so the result 0 is delivered without needing the value of from(3):

```
→ 1 + ( 2 + 0 )
→ 3
```

Now, although this may seem like a fairly useless program there are a number of problems which either rely on infinite data structures or are conveniently expressed as finite explorations of such a structure. A simple example of such a program is the program for computing square roots using the Newton–Raphson algorithm for successive approximation which may be familiar from school mathematics. The program works by making a succession of approximations to the square root of a number N by starting with some initial guess a_0 and by successively refining the guess until the difference between two successive approximations is within some predefined threshold, ε. A new approximation

a_{k+1} is generated from the previous approximation a_k using the rule

$$a_{k+1} = (a_k + N / a_k) / 2$$

To convince ourselves that this generates the required answer, observe that in the limit of convergence, i.e. when we can replace a_{n+1} and a_n by the limit a (assuming this exists), we have that $N = a^2$ as required.

Clearly we do not want to generate more approximations than we require and so one solution to the problem could use a recursive function which only computes the next approximation if the difference between the previous two approximations is greater than the threshold. However a rather clearer solution can be found based on an infinite data structure; indeed this solution is actually a restatement of the problem: 'return the limit of the infinite list of approximations [$a_0, a_1, a_2, \ldots$] where the limit is defined to be the first a_m such that $| a_m - a_{m-1} | < \varepsilon$'. Here it is in Hope:

```
dec Limit : list( real ) # real → real ;
dec Approximations : real # real → list( real ) ;
dec SqRoot : real # real # real → real ;
--- Limit( a1 :: (rest & ( a2 :: _ ) ), epsilon ) <=
        if mod( a1 − a2 ) < epsilon then a2 else Limit( rest, epsilon ) ;
--- Approximations( a, n ) <=
        a :: Approximations( (a + ( n / a ) ) / 2, n ) ;
--- SqRoot( N, Guess, epsilon ) <=
        Limit( Approximations( Guess, N ), epsilon ) ;
```

The application of Approximations here builds the infinite list of approximations starting with the initial Guess, and Limit repeatedly looks at adjacent elements in the resulting list searching for a pair of values within epsilon of one another. It is clear that this program requires lazy evaluation for otherwise the computation of the list of approximations would fail to terminate. An example application of SqRoot tracing the evaluation of SqRoot(4.0, 3.0, 0.2) is shown below.

```
SqRoot( 4.0, 3.0, 0.01 )
→ Limit( Approximations( 3.0, 0.01 ), 0.01 )
→ Limit( 3.0 :: Approximations( 2.17, 0.01 ), 0.01 )
→ Limit( 3.0 :: ( 2.17 :: Approximations( 2.01, 0.01 ) ), 0.01 )
→ Limit( 3.0 :: ( 2.17 :: (2.01 :: Approximations( 2.00, 0.01 ) ) ), 0.01 )
→ Limit( 3.0 :: ( 2.17 :: ( 2.01 :: ( 2.00 ::
        Approximations( 2.00, 0.01 ) ) ) ) ), 0.01 )
→ 2.00
```

Another famous example of a lazy program is the 'Sieve of Eratosthenes' which computes the list of all the prime numbers. The program starts with the infinite list of integers 2, 3, 4, 5 ... and works by removing the number at the front of the infinite list and 'filtering' it through the remainder of the list, striking out all those elements which are divisible by that number. The list of numbers generated (and the numbers which are subsequently filtered) is taken from the head of the list at each recursive step:

```
dec Sieve : list( num ) → list( num ) ;
dec Filter : num # list( num ) → list( num ) ;
--- Filter( n, m :: l ) <= if ( n mod m ) = 0
                           then Filter( n, l )
                           else m :: Filter( n, l ) ;
--- Sieve( n :: l ) <= n :: Sieve( Filter( n, l ) ) ;
```

The list of prime numbers is then computed by the expression

```
Sieve( from( 2 ) )
```

Of course, if we evaluate this expression then it will soon stop because of the application of :: which soon appears at the top level:

```
Sieve( from( 2 ) )
→ Sieve( 2 :: from( 3 ) )
→ 2 :: Sieve( Filter( 2, from( 3 ) ) )
```

We can force more primes to be produced, however, by applying a function which needs more than one value from the resulting list. For example, the following expression computes the sum of the first three prime numbers as shown (the function being applied at each step is shown in boldface):

```
sum( 3, Sieve( from( 2 ) ) )
→ sum( 3, Sieve( 2 :: from( 3 ) ) )
→ sum( 3, 2 :: Sieve( Filter( 2, from( 3 ) ) ) )
→ 2 + sum( 2, Sieve( Filter( 2, from( 3 ) ) ) )
→ 2 + sum( 2, Sieve( Filter( 2, 3 :: from( 4 ) ) ) )
→ 2 + sum( 2, Sieve( 3 :: Filter( 2, from( 4 ) ) ) )
→ 2 + sum( 2, 3 :: Sieve( Filter( 3, Filter( 2, from( 4 ) ) ) ) )
→ 2 + ( 3 + sum( 1, Sieve( Filter( 3, Filter( 2, from( 4 ) ) ) ) ) )
→ 2 + ( 3 + sum( 1, Sieve( Filter( 3, Filter( 2, 4 :: from( 5 ) ) ) ) ) )
→ 2 + ( 3 + sum( 1, Sieve( Filter( 3, Filter( 2, from( 5 ) ) ) ) ) )
→ 2 + ( 3 + sum( 1, Sieve( Filter( 3, Filter( 2, 5 :: from( 6 ) ) ) ) ) )
→ 2 + ( 3 + sum( 1, Sieve( Filter( 3,
          5 :: Filter( 2, from( 6 ) ) ) ) ) )
→ 2 + ( 3 + sum( 1, Sieve( 5 :: Filter( 3,
          Filter( 2, from( 6 ) ) ) ) ) )
```

```
→ 2 + ( 3 + sum( 1, 5 :: Sieve( Filter( 5,
        Filter( 3, Filter( 2, from( 6 ) ) ) ) ) ) )
→ 2 + ( 3 + (5 + sum( 0, Sieve( Filter( 5,
        Filter( 3, Filter( 2, from( 6 ) ) ) ) ) ) ) )
→ 2 + ( 3 + ( 5 + 0 ) )
→ 10
```

We see that each time a function is invoked it produces only a single value and then stops. The calling function then 'consumes' the value, possibly producing a value itself which is passed back to the previous caller, and so on. The net effect of lazy evaluation in this example is that the resulting list of primes is generated one at a time. Only when the previous prime has been consumed and the next prime is required (by +) is the Sieve reinvoked.

The examples we have looked at here rely simply on the fact that the arguments to constructor functions are not evaluated until required and in this sense can be viewed as only partly exploiting lazy evaluation. However one of the most powerful applications of lazy evaluation is in the creation of *circular* structures and it is in this problem domain that the full power of lazy evaluation becomes apparent.

As a simple introduction to the idea of circular structures consider the following function for generating the infinite list [1, 2, 1, 2, 1, 2 . . .]:

```
dec cycle : list( num ) ;
--- cycle <= [ 1, 2 ] <> cycle ;
```

Without lazy evaluation this function will fail to terminate because the argument to the <> function will be evaluated before <> is called. This will involve recursively calling cycle and the process will be repeated indefinitely. Using lazy evaluation the computation will proceed as follows:

```
cycle
= [ 1, 2 ] <> cycle
= 1 :: ( [ 2 ] <> cycle )
```

The evaluation now stops since the constructor :: appears at the top level. We call the definition **circular**, or **cyclic**, because we can view it as a description of the following structure which loops back on itself:

```
→1 :: ( 2 ::  )
```

Indeed we can even implement such a function in this way as we shall see later on in this book.

4.3 Process networks

Using the function from defined in the previous section, we can compute the (infinite) list of non-negative integers by the expression from(0). Another way of computing the same result, however, is to use the function Ints given below:

```
dec IncList : num → list( num ) ;
--- IncList( n :: l ) <= ( n + 1 ) :: IncList( l ) ;
dec Ints : list( num ) ;
--- Ints <= 0 :: IncList( Ints ) ;
```

Thus:

```
Ints
→ 0 :: IncList( Ints )
→ 0 :: IncList( 0 :: IncList( Ints ) )
→ 0 :: 1 :: IncList( IncList( Ints ) )
→ 0 :: 1 :: IncList( IncList( 0 :: IncList( Ints ) ) )
→ 0 :: 1 :: IncList( 1 :: IncList( IncList( Ints ) ) )
→ 0 :: 1 :: 2 :: IncList( IncList( IncList( Ints ) ) )
etc.
```

(In a lazy implementation, of course, the evaluation would continue beyond the second line only if some consumer required more values to be produced.)

Here we have interpreted Ints as a recursively defined function in the usual way. However, the program can also be viewed as a description of a **process network**:

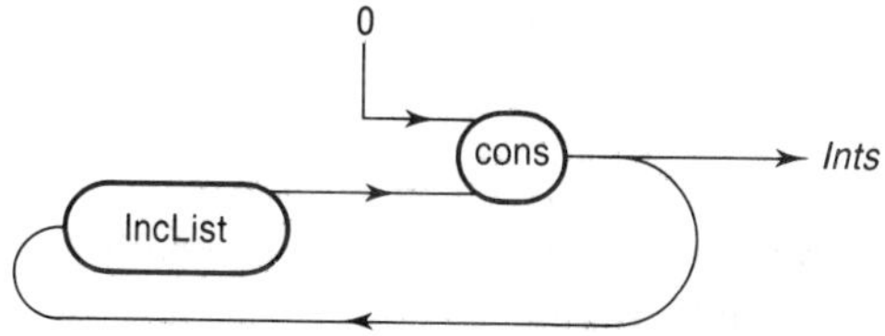

The arcs of this network are infinite lists of integers (often referred to as *streams*) and the IncList node is a process which increments the individual components of its input list. The cyclic connection in the network appears because of the recursive nature of the Ints function. The interesting feature of this network is that we can view each node as a *static* process. For example, although the evaluation sequence shown above reveals that IncList works by making a number of recursive calls to itself we can view it as a static piece of program with a single input 'buffer' and a single output 'buffer', with each output element being the successor of a corresponding input element:

In this respect we can view IncList as an *interactive program*: if we place a number in the input buffer (as part of the input list) then the successor of that number appears in the output buffer regardless of whether any more values exist at the input. If we remove the value from the output buffer and place another value in the input buffer then the same happens again. A static network of processes can be formed by 'connecting' the inputs and outputs of static processes using arcs which correspond to streams of data. This is sometimes loosely termed *knot tying*. The above program is a simple example of knot tying. The 'knot' here refers to the cyclic connection which joins the output arc of Ints to the input arc of the IncList process; this arises from the equation above which defines Ints.

There is another way of expressing the problem which is dependent on making Ints a process itself:

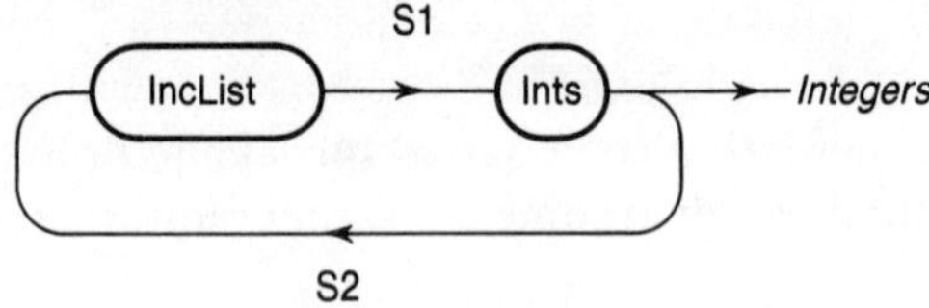

where Ints now has the following definition:

```
dec Ints : list( num ) → list( num ) ;
--- Ints( s ) <= 0 :: s ;
```

Ints no longer ties the knot itself (it is non-recursive!); to do this we must use a recursive **let** or **where** to describe the connections between the two processes, i.e. the streams S1 and S2 above:

```
S2 where ( S1, S2 ) == ( IncList( S2 ), Ints( S1 ) )
```

The result of evaluating this expression is S2 which is the (infinite) list of integers. We see here that the processes themselves are described by functions and the interconnection of those processes by a recursive **where** expression. It is left to the reader to verify that this program will only work if the underlying implementation is lazy.

As an example of a slightly more complicated process network, we shall look at another famous example, namely a program to compute the list of Fibonacci numbers. The Fibonacci numbers, $f_1, f_2, f_3, \ldots$ are given by:

$$f_1 = 1$$
$$f_2 = 1$$
$$f_n = f_{n-1} + f_{n-2} \qquad n > 2$$

However, the sequence can also be expressed as follows:

n	1	2	3	4	5	6	7	...	
f_n	1	1	2	3	5	8	13	...	(S_1)
f_{n+1}	1	2	3	5	8	13	21	...	(S_2)
f_{n+2}	2	3	5	8	13	21	34	...	(S_3)

Reading the elements of each row as streams, S_1, S_2, and S_3, we can compute the value of the nth element of S_3 by summing the nth elements of S_1 and S_2. Because we know f_1 and f_2 we can compute the first element of S_3 at least. But notice now how the second element of S_1 is precisely the first element of S_2 (which we know) and the second element of S_2 is precisely the first element of S_3 (which we now also know). Because we know the second elements of both S_1 and S_2 we can now compute the second element of S_3. The process can therefore continue indefinitely with the complete list of Fibonacci numbers being generated on the stream S_1. This suggests the following process network:

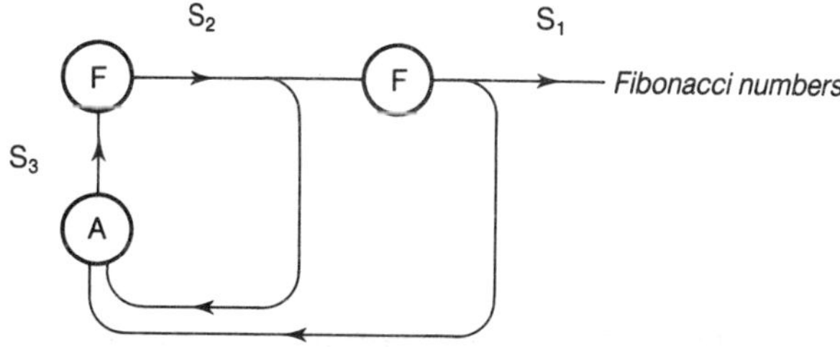

The functions F and A in this diagram are given by:

```
dec F : list( num ) → list( num ) ;
dec A : list( num ) # list( num ) → list( num ) ;
--- F( s ) <= 1 :: s ;
--- A( f1 :: s1, f2 :: s2 ) <= ( f1 + f2 ) :: A( s1, s2 ) ;
```

These specify the processes at the nodes; to specify the interconnection of these processes we have to 'tie a knot' which can again be done using a recursive **where**:

```
S1 where ( S1, S2, S3 ) == ( F( S2 ), F( S3 ), A( S1, S2 ) )
```

Once again we see that the processes have been described by functions and the interconnection of those processes by a recursive **where**.

Although the example programs we have looked at are nothing other than sets of recursive function definitions they can be viewed as specifications of networks of communicating processes. So, although they are quite amenable to being executed on any lazy implementation of the language, we could treat the logical processes in such a network as *physical* processes and even map such processes onto separate hardware components. If we were to do this then the processes would execute in parallel and we would have succeeded in specifying a concurrent system without resort to any additional language features such as channels, buffers or explicit synchronization. The classic paper on this subject is Kahn (1974) and the interested reader is referred to Henderson (1982) and Kelly (1987) for more details of its application to parallel programming.

4.4 Computing with 'unknowns'

To conclude this section on lazy programming techniques we shall look at a style of programming in which the result generated by a function application depends on values which are not known until the evaluation is complete. This may sound impossible, but it can sometimes be done provided the underlying implementation of the language is lazy. We shall consider as an example a function which replaces every element of a list of positive numbers by the maximum element in that list. We shall call this function ReplaceByMax.

Traditionally, we might solve the problem in two parts: first we might compute the maximum element in the list; then we might replace each element of the list by that maximum value. For example (using the functions max, map and reduce defined in previous chapters):

```
dec ReplaceByMax : list( num ) → list( num ) ;
--- ReplaceByMax( l ) <= map( lambda _ => reduce( max, 0, l ), l ) ;
```

This is quite correct and clear enough, but it has the disadvantage that the list must be traversed twice. However, using a recursive **where** (or **let**) statement in conjunction with lazy evaluation we can perform the same operation by traversing the list only once. Here is the function which does it:

```
dec ReplaceByMax : list( num ) → list( num ) ;
--- ReplaceByMax( l ) <= Result
        where ( Result, big ) == reduce( f, ( nil, 0 ), l )
        where f == lambda ( x, ( r, m ) ) =>
                        ( big :: r, if x > m then x else m ) ;
```

The second component of the pair generated by reduce is the maximum element in the original list. The interesting feature of the program, however, is that the elements of the list forming the first component of the pair returned by the function f are all big, but the value of big is not known until the reduce is complete! The reason why this works is that we don't *have* to know the value of big until the reduce is complete. To demonstrate this, let us see what happens if we try to extract one of the elements of the resulting list. For example

```
m where ( m :: _ ) == ReplaceByMax( [ 5, 1, 4 ] )
```

The application of ReplaceByMax proceeds as follows:

```
ReplaceByMax( [ 5, 1, 4 ] )
→ Result where ( Result, big ) == reduce( f, ( nil, 0 ), [ 5, 1, 4 ] )
          where f == lambda ( x, ( r, m ) ) =>
                         ( big :: r, if x > m then x else m )

≡ Result where ( Result, big ) == f( 5, f( 1, f( 4, ( nil, 0 ) ) ) )
→ Result where ( Result, big ) == f( 5, f( 1, ( big :: nil, 4 ) ) )
→ Result where ( Result, big ) == f( 5, ( big :: ( big :: nil ), 4 ) )
→ Result where ( Result, big ) == ( big :: ( big :: ( big :: nil ) ), 5 )
```

Only now can the pattern (m :: _) match and by now the value of big *is* known – it is 5. The result returned is the head of the resulting list, which is therefore also 5.

It should be apparent that this version of ReplaceByMax is far less clear than the previous one and the reader will probably have to study the program in some detail before being convinced that it performs the required calculation. Recall, however, that our only justification for writing the program in this way was to reduce the number of list traversals from two to one, i.e. for optimization purposes. The relative opacity of this version of the program should add weight to the old adage that optimization should be performed only *after* the program is demonstrably correct *if at all*; using this style of programming for mainstream program development is something which should be actively discouraged.

As we have already said, and as we shall see later on throughout the book, supporting laziness can be very costly and much of the effort involved in functional language implementations is dedicated to avoiding it whenever possible. For example, by analysing a lazy functional program we can often determine that a user-defined function is strict in one or more of its arguments. These strict arguments may then be passed by-value, giving improved efficiency without altering the behaviour exhibited by the program under a lazy implementation. This form of optimization, which is known as **strictness analysis**, is discussed in more detail in Chapter 20.

At this point we should make clear the calling semantics of Hope itself. There are in fact two implementations of the Hope language, both of which we shall refer to in the remaining chapters of this book for reasons that will become apparent. In the *standard* implementation of Hope, all functions are called by-value except for constructor functions which are called by-need. This simply means that an argument of a constructor is not evaluated until it is passed on to a non-constructor function as a result of its having been selected by pattern matching. In the *lazy* implementation of Hope all functions are called by-need. This means that strict primitive functions are passed their arguments in an unevaluated form and so must themselves force their evaluation before the primitive can be applied. Therefore, the examples given in Section 4.2 (other than the last one, cycle) will work correctly using either implementation of Hope but the examples of Sections 4.3 and 4.4 will work only using the lazy implementation of Hope. In Chapter 9 we shall see how eager and lazy evaluation can be supported in an interpreter for functional languages written in Hope and will see how the two implementations of Hope produce very different behaviour from that interpreter.

SUMMARY

- Functional languages can be evaluated eagerly or lazily (or using some combination of the two).
- Eager evaluation corresponds to call-by-value, is generally more efficient, but may cause redundant evaluation or unnecessary non-termination.
- Lazy evaluation corresponds to call-by-need and produces termination whenever termination is possible.
- Problems which explore infinite data structures require lazy constructors for their solution.
- Some programs which build circular structures require full lazy semantics in order to terminate.
- Process networks provide an alternative model for the evaluation of some infinitary expressions.
- Lazy evaluation can be used to minimize the number of traversals of data structures but produce complex programs.
- There are two implementations of Hope: a *standard* implementation in which constructor functions are called by-need and all other functions by-value and a *lazy* implementation in which all functions are called by-need.

EXERCISES

4.1 Typically a random number generator consists of a function R which when called with a special value called a **seed** returns a pseudo random number in the range 0 to 1 and a new seed which can be used in any subsequent call to R. Suggest how an infinite list defined using R can be used to replace the multiple calls to R. How is the 'next' random number obtained?

4.2 Suppose that an expression E evaluates to a list of characters which when printed at the terminal covers 20 screens of text. Explain what the user might see when E is evaluated and then printed using a fully eager implementation and then again using a lazy implementation.

4.3 Consider the cycle example given at the end of Section 4.2. An alternative definition of this function is as follows:

```
--- cycle <= 1 :: ( 2 :: cycle ) ;
```

Does this require the full power of lazy evaluation? What is the important difference between the two versions as far as termination is concerned?

4.4 (a) (Refer back to Exercise 3.4(c) before tackling this question.) Define a Hope function pipe using reduce, map and compose which builds a linear pipeline from a given list of functions [$f_1, f_2, \ldots, f_n$]. (*Hint:* A linear pipeline of the functions $f_1, f_2, \ldots, f_n$ describes a 'conveyor belt' processing system in which each element of a stream of arguments is processed in turn by the functions $f_n, f_{n-1}, \ldots$ up to f_1. We can view the f_i as separate physical processing boxes which can operate concurrently; for example, f_1 can be applied to the ith element of the argument stream at the same time that f_2 is being applied to the (i + 1)th element of the stream and so on. Describe how the pipeline will behave using conventional lazy evaluation; in particular describe what will happen if the argument stream is infinite.

(b) Write down an expression which uses pipe to test for intersections between two lists of objects, S and T. The pipeline you should build is the following:

$\ldots s_n\ s_{n-1} \ldots s_2\ s_1 \rightarrow \boxed{t_m} \rightarrow \boxed{t_{m-1}} \rightarrow \ldots \rightarrow \boxed{t_1} \rightarrow$ *intersection* where the t_i $1 \le i \le m$ are the elements of T, the s_i $1 \le i \le n$ are the elements of S and the *intersection* is a stream of values each of which occurs in both S and T. A box containing the value t represents the process which tests the elements of S to see whether they are equal to t. (*Hint:* Assume that the values passed through the pipeline are (value, flag) pairs where the flag indicates whether the value is in the intersection.

4.5 Using a similar technique to that described in Section 4.4 define a function mintips which given a tree of numbers returns an isomorphic tree in which each element is replaced by the minimum element in the original tree using just a single pass over the tree.

Chapter 5
Alternative functional styles

In the previous three chapters we have looked at the style of functional programming which is encouraged by the Hope language. Hope is by no means the only functional language, however, nor is it in any sense the definitive functional language. As we have seen, the important features of a functional language which distinguish it from any other type of language are referential transparency and determinism, the latter feature being the distinguishing factor between functional and *relational* languages such as PROLOG (Colmerauer *et al.* 1973). This leaves considerable scope for variation in areas such as strong typing, user-defined data types, higher-order functions and computation rule, as well as the more cosmetic differences such as language syntax. In this chapter we shall introduce some of the alternative functional styles by taking a brief look at the languages Miranda, LISP and FP. These languages, together with Hope itself, represent a good cross section of the various approaches to functional language design.

Section 5.1 describes Miranda, which is a strongly-typed language, very similar to Hope but differing significantly in its view of functions. Section 5.2 describes LISP which is an untyped list-processing language in which programs and data have a uniform representation. Section 5.3 describes FP which also supports only a single data type (symmetric lists) and is significantly different from other functional languages in that it encourages reasoning at the *function* level, rather than at the object level. This makes FP a very powerful notation for expressing the formal manipulation of functional programs and provides the basis of the program transformation techniques described in Chapter 18.

5.1 Miranda†

The general approach taken in Miranda is similar in many ways to that of Hope: it is a strongly-typed, higher-order language supporting user-defined data types and polymorphism. Miranda is the successor to two earlier languages developed by Turner, namely SASL (Turner, 1976) and KRC (Turner, 1982). The major difference between Miranda and Hope is that Miranda is a curried language meaning that function-valued objects are built by partially applying existing functions rather than by using explicit lambda expressions as we did in Chapter 4. Miranda has lazy semantics so that all functions are called by-need, but strict constructors can be specified by suitably annotating the constructor arguments; this aspect is not discussed here, however.

5.1.1 Miranda program structure

As in Hope, a Miranda program consists of a set of definitions. Unlike Hope, however, the type of each definition is not required to be specified by the programmer. This does not mean that Miranda is untyped; rather, the type of each definition is inferred automatically by a type checker. (In fact the same is true of Hope: the type of each function is determined automatically by a type checker independently of the type equations provided by the programmer. The only difference is that in Hope the inferred types are subsequently checked against the programmer-supplied types.)

As a simple example of a Miranda program, here is the Miranda version of the reverse program given in Hope in Chapter 3 which reverses a given list of objects using an accumulating parameter:

```
rev L = rev2 L [ ]
rev2 [ ] a = a
rev2 ( x : l ) a = rev2 l ( x : a )
```

†Miranda™ is a trademark of Research Software Ltd.

Each definition has a left-hand side and a right-hand side separated by the symbol = (equivalent to <= in Hope). As in Hope, the definitions can contain patterns on the left-hand side; the example above shows the use of pattern matching on lists: [ ] denotes the empty list (equivalent to nil in Hope) and : is the infix list constructor (equivalent to :: in Hope).

As in Hope Miranda provides a shorthand notation for list expressions and lists of characters; the expression

$x_1 : (x_2 : (x_3 : \ldots : (x_n : [\,]) \ldots))$

can be abbreviated to

$[x_1, x_2, x_3, \ldots, x_n]$

and where each of the x_i is a character they can be juxtaposed and enclosed in double quotes, as in

```
"Miranda"
```

However, Miranda takes the shorthand notation further and also provides a mechanism for describing arithmetic series. A finite consecutive sequence of integers can be constructed by specifying the first and last elements separated by '. . .' As an example, the list

```
[ 1, 2, 3, 4, 5 ]
```

can be abbreviated to the expression

```
[ 1..5 ]
```

Using the same notation we can specify infinite lists by simply omitting the upper bound. For example the expression

```
[ 1.. ]
```

delivers the (infinite) list of positive integers (recall that Miranda is a lazy language so that infinite data structures can be expressed without complication).

5.1.2 Currying

It will be noted that in the rev example given above the arguments of each function are separated by spaces and are not collectively enclosed in parentheses. The reason for this notation is that each function in

Miranda is inherently higher-order. When we write a definition in Miranda such as

```
f x y z = ...
```

we might normally interpret f as being a function of three arguments x, y and z or, as in Hope, a function of a single argument triple. However, in Miranda f is actually a higher-order function of just a single argument x. The result of applying f to an argument E_1 which we write

$$f\ E_1$$

is another function, again of only a single argument y. The result of applying this function to a further argument E_2 is yet another function, this time of a single argument z. A complete application of f is written

$$f\ E_1\ E_2\ E_3$$

but its correct reading is as follows:

$$(((f\ E_1)\ E_2)\ E_3)$$

It is a convention that function application associates to the left, however, so that the parentheses can be omitted without changing the meaning of the expression.

This idea of treating a function of n arguments as a concatenation of n single-argument functions is called **currying** after the mathematician H.B. Curry. In Hope a function-valued object is created by using the keyword **lambda**; in Miranda a function-valued object is created by applying a defined function to fewer arguments than appear on the left-hand side of its definition; this is sometimes called **partial application**. As an example of this, the successor function on integers which can be generated in Hope using the lambda expression

```
lambda x => x + 1
```

can be written in Miranda by partially applying the primitive function + to the single argument 1:

```
( + ) 1
```

(The parentheses around the + converts the infix function + into a prefix function.) Both expressions represent the function which ‘adds one to things'. As a further example, consider the map function defined in Hope in Section 3.1. This has the following definition in Miranda:

```
map f [ ]     = [ ]
map f ( x : l ) = ( f x ) : ( map f l )
```

The functions we map over a list can themselves be generated by a partial application. For example, the expression

```
map ( ( + ) 1 )
```

is the function which returns the successor of each element of a given list and the expression

```
map ( max 0 ) L
```

returns the list in which each element of L is replaced by the maximum of 0 and that element. The equivalent Hope definition involves using a **lambda**:

```
map ( lambda n => max( n, 0 ), L )
```

One consequence of the Miranda notation is that all functions must be named. In Hope, we introduce nested functions using **lambda** expressions; in Miranda this is achieved using a normal function definition inside a **where** expression. For example,

```
map ( f 5 ) L where f x y = y + x * x
```

which has the effect of adding 25 to each element of L. Notice that the function introduced can be recursive by virtue of its being named.

Note that it is not necessary for all functions to be curried since Miranda also provides a mechanism for building tuples and decomposing those tuples with pattern matching. The tuple syntax is identical to that of Hope so we could have defined Rev above as follows:

```
rev ( L ) = rev2 ( L, [ ] )
rev2 ( [ ], a ) = a
rev2 ( x : l, a ) = rev2 ( l, x : a )
```

5.1.3 Conditional expressions

Conditionals in Miranda are expressed using *guards* rather than by keywords such as **if**, **then** and **else**. As an example of this, here is the function max which returns the maximum of two numbers m and n:

```
max m n = m,      m > n
          n,      m <= n
```

> and <= (respectively 'greater-than' and 'less-than-or-equal') are examples of primitive Boolean functions which are defined to operate on objects of type num. num is a base type in Miranda as it is in Hope, but unlike Hope it includes both integer and real numbers. The effect of this is that there is a single rule for functions like > and the choice of which of the four cases applies is determined when the function is invoked, i.e. at run-time. This differs from Hope, which determines which rule is applicable before the program is evaluated (i.e. at compile-time). The other base types of Miranda are bool and char which are equivalent to the truval and char base types of Hope.

5.1.4 List abstractions

List abstractions, also called list **comprehensions**, provide an elegant and concise method of describing certain list-processing operations. As an example of this, the following expression computes the (infinite) list of even positive integers by using the expression [1..] as a generator for the infinite list of positive integers and then filtering out those elements which are not divisible by two:

```
[ n | n <- [ 1.. ] ; n rem 2 = 0 ]
```

rem is equivalent to mod in Hope and the symbol <- (which is an approximation to the ∈ symbol) denotes the list membership operator. This expression can therefore be read as follows:

[	n	|	n	<-	[1..]	;	n rem 2 = 0	]
the list of all	n	such that	n	is in	the list [1, 2, 3, . . .]	and	n is divisible by 2	

As an example of how this notation can be used, here is the Miranda function for computing the (infinite) list of prime numbers using the sieve of Eratosthenes as described in Chapter 4:

```
primes = sieve [ 2 . . ]
         where sieve( n : l ) = n : sieve [ m <- l | m rem n ~= 0 ]
```

The list abstraction [m <- l | m rem n ~= 0] has the effect of removing all elements of L which are divisible by n and is identical, therefore, to the Filter function in the Hope equivalent given in Chapter 4.

5.1.5 User-defined data types

We can define our own data types in Miranda in much the same way as we do in Hope. The syntax of type definitions is designed to mimic the BNF notation for describing language syntax. As an example of this, the data type tree which we defined in Hope in Chapter 3 can be defined in Miranda as follows:

```
tree ::= Empty | Tip num | Node tree num tree
```

Note that constructors may also be curried, which explains the syntax of the definition. ::= has the same reading as == in Hope and | has the same reading as ++. Notice that the constructor names start with an upper-case letter, this convention is enforced by the language. The function for flattening trees, which was also defined in Hope in Chapter 3, can now be defined by cases in the usual way:

```
flatten Empty = [ ]
flatten ( Tip n ) = [ n ]
flatten ( Node left value right ) = ( flatten left ) ++ ( value : ( flatten right ) )
```

++ is a primitive function for appending lists and is equivalent to the function <> in Hope.

We can make the definition of tree polymorphic by using type variables. In Miranda the valid type variables are *, **, ***, and so on. A polymorphic definition of trees looks like this:

```
tree * ::= Empty | Tip * | Node ( tree * ) * ( tree * )
```

Also included in the language is a facility for renaming types. The expression

```
string == [ char ]
```

simply attaches the name string to the type [char]. This is equivalent to the Hope **type** declaration:

```
type string == list( char ) ;
```

Also included in the language is the ability to define **unfree** data types. These are simply data types to which 'properties' can be attached, such as the property that each element of an ordered list must be greater than or equal to its predecessor. These properties are expressed as equalities between constructor terms and are ultimately implemented using a form of embedded term-rewriting system. We shall not cover unfree data types further except to say that the requirement for an embedded term-rewriting system adds some complexity to the implementation and introduces issues of completeness and termination which are beyond the scope of this book. The interested reader is referred to Turner (1985) for more details.

5.2 LISP

LISP was the first pure functional language and was designed by John McCarthy in the early 1960s (McCarthy *et al.*, 1962). Although the original LISP language was pure in that it was referentially transparent, the dialects which evolved in subsequent years included many imperative features, most notably constructs for performing destructive assignment which destroyed the inherent simplicity and elegance of the original language. Embedded within all these dialects, however, is a 'pure' subset, which if considered in isolation can be used to write functional programs as we have come to know them. Although the various implementations of LISP differ quite significantly in the choice of keyword names, primitive function names and overall program structure, the underlying principles are the same. The semantic differences between different dialects and implementations of LISP are more significant, however, as we shall see later on. We shall (arbitrarily) base our discussions here on the syntax of the Lispkit dialect of LISP, the full details of which can be found in Henderson *et al.* (1983).

5.2.1 S-expressions

The word 'LISP' stands for 'LISt Processing' and one of the features of LISP which distinguishes it from most other languages (imperative languages included) is that only one composite data type is supported, namely the list. Lists in LISP are untyped so that they may contain arbitrary components and are represented textually using so-called **S-expressions**. An S-expression is either an **atom** or a sequence of other S-expressions separated by spaces and enclosed in parentheses. The latter type of expression is called a **non-atomic** S-expression.

An atom may be either **symbolic** or **numeric**. A numeric atom is a sequence of digits (possibly preceded by a sign character + or −) and a symbolic atom is any sequence of characters beginning with an alphabetic character. Non-atomic S-expressions can be viewed simply as lists. For example, the Hope list

$$[\ e_1,\ e_2,\ \ldots\ ,\ e_n\ ]$$

where the e_i ($1 \leq i \leq n$) are expressions, is represented in LISP by the S-expression

$(e_1\ e_2 \ldots e_n)$

Unlike Hope, however, where each of the e_i must be of the same type, in LISP they can be of arbitrary type. Here are some examples of S-expressions:

```
42
Richard3
( Two on a Tower )
( ( 1 ) ( 2 ) ( 1 2 3 4 ) )
( ( −6 −2 0 ) and ( 2 men in a boat ) are both ( S expressions ) )
```

(Note that the individual atoms are delimited by one or more space characters in non-atomic S-expressions.)

We shall often refer to a non-atomic S-expression of this sort as a list, for obvious reasons. All atoms in LISP are assumed to be non-decomposable, so that we cannot split up a symbolic atom into its component characters. We can, however, decompose a list by applying primitive functions. In Hope we decompose a list by using pattern matching. For example, the following Hope function returns the first element of a list (the *head*) of the list by using a pattern on the left-hand side of the equation:

```
dec head : list( alpha ) → alpha ;
--- head( x :: _ ) <= x ;
```

Similarly,

```
dec tail : list( alpha ) → list( alpha ) ;
--- tail( _ :: l ) <= l ;
```

In LISP there is no pattern matching facility; instead, functions like head and tail given above are provided as primitives of the language and these are used to extract explicitly the required element(s) of a given S-expression. There are four primitives associated with the composition and decomposition of S-expressions:

CAR	equivalent to head
CDR	equivalent to tail (pronounced 'could err')
CONS	equivalent to :: in Hope
ATOM	tests whether its argument is an atom

The primitive ATOM must return some representation of the Boolean values true or false; these are represented by the special atoms T and F respectively (compare this with Hope where truth values are supported as a base type). The decomposition functions have rather curious names which are totally unrelated to the operations which they perform. Their origins go back to the earliest implementation of LISP in which the first element of a non-atomic S-expression (the head) was accessed through a special machine register called the 'address register' and the tail through another special register called the 'decrement register'. The head and tail of an S-expression could then be accessed by referring to the Contents of Address Register and Contents of Decrement Register respectively, hence the names CAR and CDR.

In LISP we represent the application of a function f to a set of arguments $a_1, \ldots, a_n$ by a single S-expression

$$(f\ a_1\ a_2 \ldots a_n)$$

This means that the application as a whole *and* the arguments to the function are represented as lists (S-expressions). It should be noted that most dialects of LISP are defined to have *strict* semantics, meaning that the argument expressions $a_1, \ldots, a_n$ are evaluated before the function f is called. There are exceptions, however: Lispkit LISP, for example, has lazy semantics.

The unfortunate property of the LISP representation of function applications is that the S-expression

```
( 1 2 3 )
```

now has the same format as a function application; as a consequence of this we might read the above expression as the application of 1 to the argument list (2 3), which is not what is intended. To solve this problem, all constants in LISP must be *quoted*. This involves applying the function QUOTE to the (constant) S-expression. The effect of QUOTE is to return its argument unchanged, i.e. without interpreting it as an expression to be evaluated. So, for example, the constant S-expressions

```
62 ( 4–7 ) ( Tom Browns Schooldays )
```

must be written

```
( QUOTE 62 ) ( QUOTE ( 4–7 ) ) ( QUOTE ( Tom Browns Schooldays ) )
```

respectively. Here are some example applications of the primitives given above:

Expression	Result
(CAR (QUOTE (1 2 3)))	1
(CDR (QUOTE (1 2 3)))	(2 3)
(CONS (QUOTE A) (QUOTE (Boys Life)))	(A Boys Life)
(ATOM (QUOTE 1))	T
(ATOM (QUOTE (1 2)))	F
(CAR (CDR (QUOTE (CAR CDR QUOTE))))	CDR

We might now ask what happens if we take the CDR of a list with only one component. The result we obtain is a special atom NIL which is the LISP denotation of the empty list. In this respect NIL denotes the same list as the Hope constructor nil. If we wish to write NIL as part of another expression we must, of course, quote it as above. For example,

Expression	Result
(CDR QUOTE (2))	NIL
(CAR (CDR (QUOTE(−23 NIL NIL (1 4)))))	NIL
(CONS (QUOTE 1) (QUOTE NIL))	(1)
(ATOM (QUOTE NIL))	T

5.2.2 Conditionals and primitive functions

A conditional expression in LISP is simply an S-expression with four components. The first element is the special atom IF; the second is the predicate expression (one which returns either T or F in a valid conditional expression) and the remaining two are the true and false branches of the conditional. For example, the Hope expression

if x = 0 **then** 0 **else** x − 1

is represented in LISP by

```
( IF ( EQ X ( QUOTE 0 ) ) ( QUOTE 0 ) ( SUB X ( QUOTE 1 ) ) )
```

EQ and MIN are further examples of primitive functions. Applications of such functions are written in prefix form rather than infix form as in Hope and Miranda. This makes the syntax of primitive function application identical to that of user-defined function application. The list of primitive functions we shall refer to here is given in Table 5.1, although many others may be supported.

Table 5.1 LISP primitives.

ADD	Arithmetic addition
ATOM	Tests whether its argument is an atom
CAR	Returns the head of a list
CDR	Returns the tail of a list
CONS	Joins head and tail elements to make a new list
EQ	Equality test
GTR	Greater-than test
LESS	Less-than test
MIN	Arithmetic subtraction (minus)
MUL	Arithmetic multiplication

5.2.3 Defining functions

In Hope, we can write down directly an expression which denotes a function by using a lambda expression. For example, the function which increments the value of any given argument can be written:

```
lambda x => x + 1
```

In LISP an identical mechanism exists, only the function is introduced by the special atom LAMBDA rather than with a keyword (**lambda**) as in Hope. A LISP lambda expression is an S-expression with three components: the first is the atom LAMBDA; the second is the list of formal parameter names of the function and the third is the body of the function. For example, the function which increments a given value x is written as follows:

```
( LAMBDA ( x ) ( ADD x ( QUOTE 1 ) ) )
```

The max function referred to earlier, i.e.

```
--- max( m, n ) <= if m > n then m else n ;
```

in Hope, is written as follows in LISP:

```
( LAMBDA ( m n ) ( IF ( GTR m n ) m n ) )
```

Notice that the references to the formal parameters of the function are written using the variables m and n respectively. These are distinct from the atoms m and n which have to be quoted. For example, the function which adds the atom A to the front of a given list can be written

```
( LAMBDA ( A ) ( CONS ( QUOTE A ) A ) )
```

Here we see that quoting has another important effect, namely that of distinguishing atoms from variables.

As in Hope lambda expressions, there is no way in which a LISP lambda expression can be recursive for there is no name to refer to in the function body should the function require to call itself. However, we can name the expression by enclosing the lambda expression within a so-called LETREC (RECursive LET) expression. In Hope there are two methods of writing a recursive function, or a set of mutually recursive functions: either we can declare a new function using **dec** and subsequently provide a definition for that function or we can use a recursive **let** or **where** expression. In LISP all recursive functions are introduced using LETREC. For example, the Hope expression

```
let f == E1 in E2
```

where E1 is an expression containing a reference to f, can be written in LISP as follows:

```
( LETREC E2′ ( f E1′ ) )
```

where E1′ and E2′ are the LISP equivalents of E1 and E2. As an example of this, here is the factorial function in LISP:

```
( LETREC fac
      ( fac ( LAMBDA (x)
            ( IF ( EQ x ( QUOTE 0 ) )
                ( QUOTE 1 )
                ( MUL x ( fac ( MIN x (QUOTE 1 ) ) ) ) ) ) )
      )
)
```

This is actually the LISP version of the Hope expression

```
let fac == lambda x => if x = 0 then 1 else x * fac( x − 1 )
in fac
```

We can use LETREC to define mutually recursive sets of functions by enclosing the definitions of those functions within the same LETREC. For example, the expression which computes the factorial of 3 can be written

```
( LETREC ( f ( QUOTE 3 ) )
      ( f  ( LAMBDA ( x )
          ( IF ( EQ x ( QUOTE 0 ) )
              ( QUOTE 1 )
              ( g x ) ) ) ) )
      ( g ( LAMBDA ( x )
          ( MUL x ( f ( MIN x (QUOTE 1 ) ) ) ) ) )
)
```

which is analogous to the Hope expression:

```
let ( f, g ) == ( lambda x => if x = 0 then 1 else g( x ),
                  lambda x => x * f ( x − 1 ) )
in f( 3 )
```

We can express a set of non-recursive definitions using a LET expression which has the same format as a LETREC expression. For example, the Hope expression

```
let ( a, b ) == (h( x ), h( y ) )
in f( a, b ) + g( b, a )
```

can be written:

```
( LET ( ADD ( f a b ) ( g b a ) )
    ( a ( h x ) )
    ( b ( h y ) )
)
```

5.2.4 Higher-order functions in LISP

Using QUOTE and LAMBDA together we can pass functions (lambda expressions) as parameters to other functions. As an example of this, here is the map function defined earlier which applies a given function f to every element of a list L, and an example application in which the incrementing function is passed as a parameter to map by quoting its defining lambda expression:

```
( LETREC ( map ( QUOTE ( LAMBDA ( x ) ( ADD x ( QUOTE 1 ) ) ) )
               ( QUOTE ( 1 2 3 ) ) ) )
    ( map ( LAMBDA ( f L )
            ( IF ( EQ L ( QUOTE NIL ) )
               ( QUOTE NIL )
               ( CONS ( f ( CAR L ) ) ( MAP f ( CDR L ) ) )
            ) )
    )
)
```

Note that we have to quote the lambda expression, for otherwise it would be interpreted as the application of the function LAMBDA to the argument list ((x) (ADD x (QUOTE 1))). The major problem with the use of QUOTE in this context, however, is that when there are variable references inside the quoted expression which are not 'bound' by the formal parameters of some lambda expression inside it, then a name clash can occur when the lambda expression is eventually applied. For example when we write

```
( LET ( LAMBDA ( x ) ( ADD x n ) )
      ( n ( QUOTE 1 ) )
)
```

it is quite clear that the n in the lambda expression refers to the value 1. However, if we quote this expression and pass it to another function, then the binding of n to 1 may be lost. For example:

```
( LET ( f ( QUOTE ( LAMBDA ( x ) ( ADD x n ) ) ) )
      ( n ( QUOTE 1 ) )
      ( f ( LAMBDA ( g ) ( LET ( g n )
                               ( n ( QUOTE 4 ) ) ) ) ) )
)
```

There are now two possible interpretations of the result: either it is (ADD 4 1) i.e. 5, or it is (ADD 4 4) i.e. 8, depending on how we treat the occurrence of n inside the body of the quoted lambda expression, i.e. depending on whether n is bound *statically* or *dynamically* respectively. It is in the binding strategy that the various implementations of LISP differ most significantly. The first implementations of LISP used dynamic binding but this is now considered to have been a mistake and so the more recent dialects of LISP (such as Lispkit LISP) support static binding. The general mechanism for achieving static binding is described in Chapter 9.

Perhaps the most striking (and attractive) feature of LISP is the simplicity of its syntax. As we have seen, a LISP program is built from only eight types of expression: variables, constants, primitives, conditionals, applications, lambdas, lets and letrecs. 'Special' values like true, false and nil are all represented as atoms. Furthermore, a LISP program is itself just an S-expression, that is, there are no explicit keywords. This results in a uniform representation of programs and data. Although we attach a special meaning to the atoms LET, LETREC, LAMBDA etc. they are nonetheless simple atoms. If these atoms appear in the right position (i.e. at the head of a list) then we can interpret them as keywords. Similarly if the atoms ADD, MIN, CAR etc. appear at the head of a list then we can interpret them as primitive function applications. The net effect of this is that LISP has almost no syntactic rules other than those for forming S-expressions. In this respect LISP is radically different from a language like Hope whosc BNF covers several pages of text.

5.3 FP

Up until now we have concentrated on functional languages in which the user-defined functions are expressed in terms of transformations on explicitly named *objects*. For example, when we write something like

```
--- f( x ) <= 1 + x ;
```

in Hope we are concerned not only with the name of the function f but also the name of the object to which f is ultimately applied, i.e. x. The pattern of function definition in a language like Hope is therefore one of naming the objects being passed to a function and then describing what to do with those arguments once passed. When it comes to writing a program in the first place this approach is the easiest to understand: a function definition takes the form of a set of equations defined over all possible object 'shapes'. We have seen a number of examples of functions defined in this way in the preceding chapters.

One of the most powerful properties of functional languages, however, is that they are amenable to formal manipulation. One form of this is program transformation which exploits the referential transparency of functional programs to 'replace like with like' in such a way as to improve the run-time characteristics of untransformed functions. As we shall see in Part III of this book, formal transformations are often more easily expressed if the object references in the original program can be abstracted out, thereby reducing each function to an object-free (or variable-free) form.

In this section we shall take a brief look at a functional language called FP where each component function is expressed in precisely this way. FP can be used as a programming language in its own right but in this book we shall treat it rather more as an intermediate notation in which formal manipulations can be expressed. This applies particularly in Part III, but in Chapter 13 it is also used to introduce the first-order categorical combinatory logic.

5.3.1 Components of an FP system

An FP system consists of three components: objects, primitives and combining forms.

Objects

Although objects are part of every FP system, there is no mechanism by which a user-defined function can refer to an object directly; objects appear only at run-time as the arguments to, and the results generated by, a function call. A discussion of FP objects is still relevant, however, since in order to define the meaning of various FP functions we must consider what happens when we apply those functions to a given argument object.

There are three object types in an FP system, namely $\perp$ (pronounced 'bottom'), atoms and sequences.

The object $\perp$ is the 'undefined' object and represents an error condition. For example, an attempt to evaluate the expression 1 / 0 will generate $\perp$ since division is undefined when the denominator is zero. When we say that an expression evaluates to $\perp$ we generally mean that in practice an attempt to evaluate the expression will cause the program to abort with a suitable error message or that it will fail to terminate at all.

An atom in FP is any base-type constant. The set of base types supported by an FP system is arbitrary, but typically it includes the set of integers 0, 1, −1, 2, −2 etc., the characters e.g. 'a', 'b', 'c', Boolean constants **T** (true) and **F** (false), real numbers e.g. 11.9, 3.56E − 2, character strings e.g. "Fred", "ATOM" and "so on".

A sequence in FP is a symmetric untyped list. It is symmetric in that for every operation on the front (head-end) of a sequence there is a symmetric operation which operates at the tail-end. Unlike Hope, FP is an untyped language so that there are no constraints on the types of objects that can be passed to a given function or on the types of objects forming a sequence. We write a sequence as a collection of objects separated by commas and enclosed in angle brackets, for example:

⟨⟩	denotes the empty sequence, cf. nil in Hope
⟨1, 2⟩	denotes a sequence of numbers
⟨⟨⟩, ⟨1⟩⟩	denotes a sequence of sequences
⟨1, 'a', ⟨⟩⟩	denotes a sequence of mixed-type objects

Sequences have obvious similarities to the S-expressions of LISP described in the previous section. We say that sequences in FP are *bottom-preserving* meaning that a sequence is undefined if any or all of the sequence components are undefined, i.e.

$$\langle x_1, x_2, \ldots, x_n \rangle = \perp \qquad \text{if for any } i,\ x_i = \perp\ (1 \le i \le n)$$

Primitives

As in Hope the 'primitives' are the predefined functions which are supported directly by the implementation rather than being defined explicitly by the programmer. As with objects the set of primitives which is supported by an FP system is arbitrary. A 'typical' set of primitives (which we assume to exist in our examples here and in later chapters) might be those listed in Table 5.2.

In FP we denote the application of a function f to an argument object x by using the symbol :, i.e.

f : x

Table 5.2 FP primitives.

+, −, ∗, etc.	The arithmetic operators
addk, subk, mulk, etc.	The primitives which respectively add k to, subtract k from and multiply by k a given numeric argument
=, ≠, >, <, . . .	The comparison operators
and, or, not, . . .	The Boolean operators
eqk, neqk, . . .	The 'comparison-with-constant' operators
1, 2, 3, . . .	The sequence 'selector' functions. The application of 'i' to a sequence (of length at least i) yields its ith element, e.g. $3 : \langle x_1, x_2, x_3, x_4 \rangle = x_3$ If the sequence has less than i elements the result is ⊥.
1r, 2r, 3r, . . .	The 'right' selector functions, defined analogously to 1, 2, 3, . . . except that they select from the right-hand end, e.g. $2r : \langle x_1, x_2, \ldots, x_{n-1}, x_n \rangle = x_{n-1}$
hd, tl	The standard head and tail functions on sequences: $hd : \langle x_1, x_2, \ldots, x_n \rangle = x_1$ $tl \; : \langle x_1, x_2, \ldots, x_n \rangle = \langle x_2, \ldots, x_n \rangle$ h : x, t : x = ⊥ if x is not a sequence
hr, tr	The head-right and tail-right functions: $hr : \langle x_1, x_2, \ldots, x_n \rangle = x_n$ $tr \; : \langle x_1, x_2, \ldots, x_n \rangle = \langle x_1, \ldots, x_{n-1} \rangle$ hr : x, tr : x = ⊥ if x is not a sequence
cons	List constructor (equivalent to :: in Hope), defined by $cons \; : \langle x_1, \langle x_2, x_3, \ldots, x_n \rangle\rangle = \langle x_1, x_2, \ldots, x_n \rangle$ cons : x = ⊥ if x is not a sequence of two components the second of which is a sequence
consr	cons right, the right list constructor so that $consr : \langle\langle x_1, x_2, \ldots, x_{n-1} \rangle, x_n \rangle = \langle x_1, x_2, \ldots x_{n-1}, x_n \rangle$ consr : x = ⊥ if x is not a sequence of two components the first of which is a sequence
null	The function which tests whether a sequence is empty (⟨⟩), i.e. $null : \langle\rangle = \mathbf{T}$ $null : \langle x_1, x_2, \ldots, x_n \rangle = \mathbf{F}$ null : x = ⊥ if x is not a sequence

Table 5.2 (*cont.*)

distl	distribute left – this forms a sequence of pairs from an object and a sequence: $\text{distl} : \langle x, \langle y_1, y_2, \ldots, y_n\rangle\rangle = \langle\langle x, y_1\rangle, \langle x, y_2\rangle, \ldots, \langle x, y_n\rangle\rangle$ distl : x = ⊥ if x is not a sequence of two components the second of which is a sequence
distr	distribute right: $\text{distr} : \langle\langle y_1, y_2, \ldots, y_n\rangle, x\rangle = \langle\langle y_1, x\rangle, \langle y_2, x\rangle, \ldots, \langle y_n, x\rangle\rangle$ distr : x = ⊥ if x is not a sequence of two components the first of which is a sequence
ι	iota – given an integer argument n ≥ 0, returns the sequence consisting of the first n positive integers, e.g. $\iota : 4 = \langle 1, 2, 3, 4\rangle$ $\iota : 0 = \langle\rangle$
id	The identity function, id : x = x for all x

If a function takes more than one argument, those arguments are passed to the function in the form of a sequence. Thus if f is a k-argument function then the application of f to the arguments $x_1, x_2, \ldots, x_k$ is written

$$f : \langle x_1, x_2, \ldots, x_k\rangle$$

In this respect all FP functions have an arity of one.

Here are some examples of primitive function applications together with the result of each:

Application	Result
+ : ⟨1,7⟩	8
+ 1 : 3	4
2 : ⟨4, 8, 6⟩	8
2r : ⟨4, 8, 6⟩	8
hr : ⟨1, 2, 3, 4⟩	4
distl : ⟨1, ⟨'a', 'b', 'c', 'd'⟩⟩	⟨⟨1, 'a'⟩, ⟨1, 'b'⟩, ⟨1, 'c'⟩, ⟨1, 'd'⟩⟩

All functions in FP are strict, that is they return ⊥ if the argument to which they are applied is ⊥.

Combining forms

A **combining form** (also called a **functional form** or **program-forming operation** (PFO)) is simply a programming construct, i.e. a building block with which to construct new functions; compare the if... then... else... construct used in most programming languages for example.

In FP there are six combining forms, namely **constant**, **conditional**, **composition**, **construction**, **apply-to-all** and **insert**. A description of each, together with some examples, is given below. Note that a user-defined function is introduced in FP by using the reserved word **def**. For example,

```
def f = ...
```

defines a function f; the body of f is expressed using the combining forms.

1 Constant A constant in FP is simply a function which when applied to any defined object always yields the same answer. We shall use underscores to denote constant functions and in general, for object k,

$$\underline{k} : x = k \quad \text{if } x \neq \bot$$
$$= \bot \quad \text{otherwise}$$

Notice that the underscore distinguishes the constant function $\underline{k}$ from the sequence selector function k. Here are some more examples:

$\underline{\text{"FP"}}$	$\underline{\text{"FP"}} : x = \text{"FP"}$	for defined x
$\underline{F}$	$\underline{F} : x = \mathbf{F}$	for defined x
$\underline{-123}$	$\underline{-123} : x = -123$	for defined x

Note that the values returned are always atoms.

2 Conditional The conditional construct of FP has the following syntax:

$$p \rightarrow q \,;\, r$$

Unlike conditionals in Hope, however, p, q and r here are functions. To understand what $p \rightarrow q ; r$ means we consider what happens when we apply such a conditional to an object, x:

$$(p \rightarrow q ; r) : x = q : x \quad \text{if } p : x = \mathbf{T} \text{ (i.e. true)}$$
$$= r : x \quad \text{if } p : x = \mathbf{F} \text{ (i.e. false)}$$
$$= \bot \quad \text{otherwise}$$

So, for example, $(\underline{T} \rightarrow q ; r) : x$ evaluates to $q : x$ since if x is defined then $\underline{T} : x = \mathbf{T}$ and if $x = \perp$ then both expressions yield $\perp$ since $\underline{T}$ and q are strict. Another example is

$$(\text{eq} \rightarrow 1 ; 2) : \langle 5, 6 \rangle$$

which evaluates to 6 because $\text{eq} : \langle 5, 6 \rangle$ delivers **F** and $2 : \langle 5, 6 \rangle$ returns 6.

The max function used earlier is easily expressed in FP using the conditional construct:

def max = > → 1 ; 2

So, for example,

max : ⟨2, 3⟩
= (> → 1 ; 2) : ⟨2, 3⟩
= 2 : ⟨ 2, 3 ⟩   since > : ⟨2, 3⟩ delivers **F**
= 3

3 Composition In FP the composition of two functions, f and g is written

$$f \circ g$$

with the meaning

$$(f \circ g) : x = f : (g : x)$$

For example, if we wish to apply the primitive + to the first element of a sequence of number pairs (a number pair being a sequence of two numbers) then the solution can be expressed using a composition of two functions, the first of which selects the first element of the sequence and the second of which applies + to the result, i.e.

$$+ \circ 1$$

For example,

(+ ∘ 1) : ⟨⟨3, 4⟩, ⟨1, 5⟩, ⟨7, 2⟩⟩
= + : (1 : ⟨⟨3, 4⟩, ⟨1, 5⟩, ⟨7, 2⟩⟩)
= + : ⟨3, 4⟩
= 7

4 Construction Construction in FP is synonymous with 'build sequence'. A construction of n functions is written

$$[f_1, f_2, \ldots, f_n]$$

The result of applying such a construction to an object x is an n-element sequence in which element i is given by applying f_i to x ($1 \leq i \leq n$), i.e.

$$[\ f_1, f_2, \ldots, f_n\ ] : x = \langle f_1 : x, f_2 : x, \ldots, f_n : x \rangle$$

As an example,

def f = [id, add1, add2]

when applied to a numeric-valued object x yields the 3-element sequence consisting of the numbers x, x + 1 and x + 2. Notice that construction can be used to build the argument sequence for a function application. For example

+ ∘ [id, id]

has the effect of doubling the object it is applied to:

$$\begin{aligned} & (\ + \circ [\ id, id\ ]\ ) : x \\ & = + : (\ [\ id, id\ ] : x\ ) \\ & = + : \langle x, x \rangle \\ & \equiv x + x \end{aligned}$$

5 *Higher-order functions* A distinguishing feature of FP is that there is no facility for expressing user-defined higher-order functions. However, there are other built-in higher-order functions: the PFOs *apply-to-all*, *left insert* and *right insert*. Each of these operate over sequences and the idea is that, for most practical purposes, no other higher-order functions should be needed.

Recall from Chapter 4 that one of the most important applications of higher-order functions is the generalization of structure-processing functions, for example functions defined over lists. The *apply-to-all* construct in FP, usually written α, is precisely the sequence equivalent of the map function defined on lists, that is α f denotes the function which applies f to every element in a given sequence argument:

$$(\ \alpha\, f\ ) : \langle x_1, x_2, \ldots, x_n \rangle = \langle f : x_1, f : x_2, \ldots, f : x_n \rangle$$

As an example of this, α tl maps the tail function over a given sequence of sequences. For example

$$\begin{aligned} & (\ \alpha\, tl\ ) : \langle \langle 1\ 2\ 3 \rangle\ \langle 4\ 5\ 6 \rangle\ \langle 7\ 8\ 9 \rangle \rangle \\ & = \langle\ tl : \langle 1\ 2\ 3 \rangle\ ,\ tl : \langle 4\ 5\ 6 \rangle\ ,\ tl : \langle 7\ 8\ 9 \rangle \rangle \\ & = \langle \langle 2\ 3 \rangle\ ,\ \langle 5\ 6 \rangle\ ,\ \langle 8\ 9 \rangle \rangle \end{aligned}$$

In addition to the map function defined over Hope lists in Chapter 4 we also defined a reduce higher-order function. In FP there are two reduce functionals called *right-insert* (written /) and *left-insert* (written \) which are defined to operate on FP sequences. The right-insert functional is analogous to reduce except that it does not assume any special 'base' case in its basic form:

$$(\,/\,f\,) : \langle x \rangle = x$$
$$(\,/\,f\,) : \langle x_1, x_2, \ldots, x_n \rangle = f : \langle x_1, (\,/\,f\,) : \langle x_2, \ldots, x_n \rangle \rangle$$

The left-insert functional is similar except that the innermost application is $f : \langle x_1, x_2 \rangle$:

$$(\,\backslash\,f\,) : \langle x \rangle = x$$
$$(\,\backslash\,f\,) : \langle x_1, x_2, \ldots, x_n \rangle = f : \langle (\,\backslash\,f\,) : \langle x_1, x_2, \ldots, x_{n-1} \rangle, x_n \rangle$$

We use the word 'insert' rather than 'reduce' because if we imagine a dyadic function as an equivalent infix operator then the / and \ functions have the effect of inserting those operators between each element of a sequence. For example

$$(\,/\,+\,) : \langle x_1, x_2, \ldots, x_n \rangle$$

evaluates to

$$x_1 + x_2 + \ldots + x_{n-1} + x_n$$

There are also variants of the insert combining forms which do have associated base cases. These are shown as subscripts on the / or \ symbols so that, for example,

$$/_0 + : \langle x_1, x_2, \ldots, x_n \rangle \equiv + : \langle x_1, (\,/_0 +\,) : \langle x_2, \ldots, x_n \rangle \rangle$$
$$/_0 + : \langle \rangle = 0$$

This completes the description of the basic components of an FP system. In the next section we briefly discuss the style of programming encouraged by FP. This is largely of academic interest here since we shall be using FP more as a tool for describing transformations than as a tool for software development. However, as we shall see, the FP approach can teach us much about the power of the functional notation, and in particular the expressive power of higher-order functions. Moreover, the characteristic style of programming it encourages makes it a basis for viable functional languages for practical use (Backus *et al.*, 1986).

5.3.2 Some examples of the FP style of programming

Because we can name our own functions using the **def** statement we can write down a recursive function definition by referring to the defined function from within its own body. For example the fac function which computes the factorial of a given number n can be expressed as follows:

$$\textbf{def}\ \text{fac} = \text{eq0} \rightarrow \underline{1};\ * \circ [\ \text{id},\ \text{fac} \circ (- \circ [\ \text{id},\ \underline{1}\ ]\ )\ ]$$

Notice that in this definition there are no object references and so no function application symbols. The body consists entirely of functions and functionals (functions which manipulate functions). When we apply fac to an argument n, however, the expression constructed as a result looks more familiar (at least to the Hope programmer):

$$\text{fac} : \text{n} \equiv \text{eq0} : \text{n} \rightarrow \underline{1} : \text{n}\ ;\ * : \langle \text{n},\ \text{fac} : (\ - : \langle \text{n},\ 1 \rangle\ )\ \rangle$$

As we would expect from the definition of the composition and construction functionals, the compositions (∘) are replaced by applications and the constructions ([..]) are replaced by sequences. Each occurrence of the identity function (id) is also replaced by the object n to which the function is applied. It is important to understand that this expression is constructed only at run-time and is never actually visible to the programmer. The programmer's view of the fac body remains one of a function-valued expression given in terms of functions rather than objects. If the argument, n, in the above application were 3, we would get

$$\begin{aligned} &\text{eq0} : 3 \rightarrow \underline{1} : 3\ ;\ * : \langle 3,\ \text{fac} : (\ - : \langle 3,\ 1 \rangle\ )\ \rangle \\ &= * : \langle 3,\ \text{fac} : (\ - : \langle 3,\ 1 \rangle\ )\ \rangle \end{aligned}$$

precisely the equivalent of 3 ∗ fac(3 − 1) as expected. If the argument were 0 then the base case would apply similarly:

$$\begin{aligned} &\text{eq0} : 0 \rightarrow \underline{1} : 0\ ;\ * : \langle\ 0,\ \text{fac} : (\ - : \langle 0,\ 1 \rangle\ )\ \rangle \\ &= \underline{1} : 0 \\ &= 1 \end{aligned}$$

Any recursive function can be expressed in FP in a similar fashion using the combining forms and primitives of the language. However, many such functions have an alternative definition in FP which makes use of the α, / and \ functions to remove the recursion. As an example of this 'recursion abstraction', the fac function defined above has a non-recursive equivalent expressed using the insert function (with base case value 1):

$$\textbf{def}\ \text{fac} = /_1 * \circ\ \iota$$

This solution is suggested directly from the nature of the factorial problem: the expression fac : n is required to compute the expression $1 * 2 * 3 * .. * (n - 1) * n$. But this expression is precisely the integers 1 to n with a $*$ between each one. Our alternative definition of fac is therefore correct since the primitive ι when applied to n delivers the integers 1 to n and $/ *$ inserts a $*$ between each one!

Here are two further examples of recursive FP programs and their non-recursive equivalents.

EXAMPLE 1: FINDING THE LENGTH OF A SEQUENCE

The recursive definition of the function which computes the length of a sequence suggests itself naturally enough:

$$\textbf{def}\ \text{len} = \text{null} \rightarrow \underline{0}\ ;\ + \circ [\underline{1}, \text{len} \circ \text{tl}\ ]$$

The non-recursive solution, however, is rather cheeky:

$$\textbf{def}\ \text{len} = /_0 + \circ\ \alpha\ \underline{1}$$

This simply says: 'Change each element of the sequence to a 1 and then add up the 1s'! Of course, this example is slightly contrived since it is likely that in practice the len function would be supported as a primitive by the FP system.

EXAMPLE 2: TESTING A SEQUENCE FOR MEMBERSHIP

The following function mem tests whether a given object is a member of a given sequence. The recursive solution looks like this:

$$\textbf{def}\ \text{mem} = \text{null} \circ 2 \rightarrow \underline{F}\ ;\ \text{eq} \circ [\ 1, \text{hd} \circ 2\ ] \rightarrow \underline{T};\ \text{mem} \circ [\ 1, \text{tl} \circ 2]$$

The non-recursive version of mem is very concise:

$$\textbf{def}\ \text{mem} = /_F\ \text{or} \circ \alpha\ \text{eq} \circ \text{dist1}$$

Reading this from right to left, dist1 forms a sequence of pairs from the two arguments of mem, the first item of each pair being the item we are testing for membership and the second being the target sequence member; the αeq applies the primitive eq to each pair yielding a sequence of truth values and /or inserts the or operator between each truth value. Thus, for example,

```
mem : ⟨1, ⟨ 3, 5, 1⟩⟩
= /or : (α eq : (dist1 : ⟨1, ⟨3, 5, 1 ⟩⟩ ) )
= /or : (α eq : ⟨⟨1, 3⟩, ⟨1, 5⟩, ⟨1, 1⟩⟩ )
= /or : ⟨F, F, T⟩
= T
```

These examples, although straightforward, are representative of the style of programming encouraged by FP. In fact, the elegance of the non-recursive solutions are as much a statement of the expressive power of high-order functions as they are about FP. In object-based languages like Hope we can arrive at similar solutions to these problems by using the map and reduce functions described earlier. Although it can be argued that FP is not sufficiently well equipped to be used for serious software development, having no strong typing and only sequences from which to build data structures, there are many advantages to programming in the variable-free manner prescribed. Indeed, there is no reason why these features could not be incorporated into the FP language and this has been initiated in the FL language proposal (Backus *et al.*, 1987) which retains the variable-free programming style.

This concludes our description of the various alternative styles of functional programming. The four languages we have now looked at are still not exhaustive: the interested reader is referred to descriptions of KRC (Turner, 1982) and SASL (Turner, 1976) (which were the predecessors to Miranda), Ponder (Fairbairn, 1985) and Orwell (Wadler, 1985) which are all examples of 'pure' (i.e. referentially transparent) functional languages. ML (Gordon *et al.*, 1979) is another example although this contains certain imperative features which make it referentially opaque. However, as with the impure dialects of LISP, these non-functional features can be easily ignored. Finally, it should be noted that it is also possible to write pure functional programs in an imperative language like Pascal by defining a suitable abstract data type and by writing programs which use only the access functions for that data type. The resulting 'language' has about the same power as a first-order subset of LISP which although limited can teach us much about the principles of functional programming. The interested reader is referred to Bailey (1987) for a more detailed description of this technique.

SUMMARY

- Miranda is a higher-order, strongly-typed, polymorphic functional language which is similar in many respects to Hope.

- Functions in Miranda are curried, meaning that they can be partially applied to create new functions.
- Miranda has list and set abstraction facilities.
- LISP is an untyped higher-order list processing language.
- LISP programs and data are represented uniformly using S-expressions.
- Quoted expressions in LISP can cause problems of variable name clashes.
- FP is an untyped functional language which prescribes programming at the function level rather than at the object level.
- An FP system consists of objects, primitive functions and combining forms.
- All data structures in FP are built using sequences which are symmetrical lists.
- The only higher-order functions of FP are built-in.
- FP programs are built from the combining forms, otherwise known as functional forms or program-forming operations (PFOs).
- Many recursive functions can be re-expressed non-recursively using one or more of the combining forms.

EXERCISES

5.1 Write out the Miranda version of the polymorphic Treesort program given in Chapter 3.

5.2 Consider the curried Miranda function f defined by f $x_1 \ldots x_n$ = E.

(a) Write down the equivalent Hope function using nested **lambda** expressions.

(b) How can f be defined without using tuples by n single-argument Miranda functions combined in a nested **where** expression?

5.3 Fred says: 'Currying is just as powerful as the use of lambda expressions since a partial application of a function can be easily written explicitly as a lambda expression'. Is Fred right?

5.4 What do the following FP functions do?

(a) $\backslash_{\langle\rangle}$ consr

(b) $\alpha + \circ p$ with the definition $p = cons \circ [\,[\,1 \circ 1, 1 \circ 2\,], p \circ [\,tl \circ 1, tl \circ 2\,]\,]$

(c) $\alpha f \circ \iota$ with the definition $f = \alpha \underline{1} \circ \iota$

5.5 (a) Write down a recursive definition of the sequence append function app in FP such that app : $\langle\langle x_1, x_2, \ldots, x_n\rangle, \langle y_1, y_2, \ldots, y_m\rangle\rangle = \langle x_1, x_2, \ldots, x_n, y_1, y_2, \ldots, y_m\rangle$

(b) Now write down a non-recursive definition of app using the PFOs / and $\circ$ and the primitives cons and consr.

Part II
IMPLEMENTATION

Introduction

The first part of this book should have given the reader a thorough grounding in functional programming and we are now in a position to describe the various techniques used for implementing these languages. In order to retain complete generality in our discussions we shall use a special notation for functional expressions which is sufficiently powerful to express all of the features of a functional language yet which is sufficiently simple that the various implementation techniques can be easily described without concern for the idiosyncrasies of a specific source language. The intermediate notation we shall use is called the **lambda notation** and derives from an area of mathematical logic called the **lambda calculus** in which many of the theoretical foundations of functional languages are based. Part II begins with a guided tour of the lambda calculus which describes the syntax of **lambda expressions** as well as the rewriting rules which specify the individual steps required to evaluate, or **reduce**, a given lambda expression. The most important of these is a rule called β-reduction which is the lambda calculus version of function application. Informally, the role of β-reduction is to replace each occurrence of a function's formal parameter by its corresponding actual parameter. In fact it is the order in which successive β-reductions are performed and the conditions under which a reduction sequence ends that underlie the design of any implementation. Broadly speaking, there are two ways of performing β-reduction: either we can leave the formal parameter reference as it is but 'remember' what value it denotes in a separate data structure, or we can perform a substitution which physically replaces the parameter reference by its actual value. The two approaches lead to what are known as **environment-based** and **copy-based** implementations respectively.

The lambda calculus provides the necessary background for the rest of Part II which begins by describing the translation of the source language into an intermediate code based on the lambda notation. Technically, the process begins with lexical and syntax analysis of the source code but as these are well-established techniques we refrain from a detailed discussion, choosing instead to present the parsing rules in an abstract way. Our main coverage of the topic begins in Chapter 7 which describes the type inference or type-checking system which validates (or otherwise) the type structure of a program. Once this has been done and the program has been proven to be type-correct we are in a position to translate the program to the intermediate notation and this translation is described in Chapter 8. As we shall see most source language features translate very easily, the only exception being the translation of pattern matching which requires special consideration.

Having described the intermediate code we proceed to explain how it can be mechanically evaluated by a computer. Our first 'implementation' technique is based on an interpreter for the intermediate code. As well as indirectly providing an implementation of the source language this interpreter will also provide us with an operational semantics of the intermediate language which describes the language by specifying how each language construct is evaluated. We shall see that there are a number of rather subtle issues involved, particularly when we try to implement different evaluation orders. The alternative to the interpretation mechanism is to define an abstract machine to evaluate intermediate code expressions based upon some well-defined computational model and in Chapter 10 we describe one such machine – the SECD machine – which evaluates expressions written in the lambda notation.

Both our interpreter and the SECD machine are environment-based in that the actual parameters of a function are remembered in a separate environment rather than physically substituted into the function body and both are based on viewing the lambda expressions 'textually', i.e. as strings of printed symbols. An alternative to this is to adopt a two-dimensional graphical representation of expressions. An evaluator which reduces expressions in this form to their final values is called a graph reducer and the general computational model is called graph reduction. The model is copy-based in that the application of a function to an argument causes the graph of the function body to be copied with the appropriate argument substitutions made, and it is naturally lazy in that the sub-expressions evaluated are always guaranteed to be required. Alternatively, we say that the computational model is **demand-driven**, which means that the evaluation of an expression is only begun when its value is explicitly demanded. The basic graph reduction model is described in Chapter 11 and various optimizations to the model in Chapters 12 and 13.

As an alternative to graph reduction, in which the evaluation of an expression is initiated only when its value is required, it is possible to conceive of a graphical model in which an expression is evaluated as soon as it can be; in other words a model where function application takes place as soon as the arguments of that function become available. In this way the evaluation is triggered by the availability of argument data rather than the presence of demand and the resulting computational model is called **dataflow**. Dataflow is therefore naturally data-driven and can be viewed as an optimized form of eager graph reduction. Dataflow implementations are described in Chapter 14.

Having by now described the various translations which can be applied to a functional expression and the various computational models which can be used as a basis for evaluating these expressions, it remains only to assemble these to produce a fully compiled system. In Chapter 15 we shall look at basic compilation schemes by considering two example implementations: the first an environment-based implementation based on the optimized SECD machine model and the second a copy-based implementation based on graph reduction. Here we describe the various intermediate codes used in the implementations, the abstract machine architectures involved and the code generation functions required to produce the abstract machine code from a given program. The dynamic use of storage in systems which implement functional (and other) languages results in the accumulation of substantial amounts of unused memory. To complete the picture, therefore, we have only to consider the mechanisms for reclaiming this memory, a technique referred to as **garbage collection**, and in Chapter 16 we conclude Part II by describing the operation of some of the more commonly used types of garbage collectors.

Chapter 6
Mathematical foundations: the lambda calculus

Throughout the remainder of this book we shall make extensive use of a commonly used notation for functional expressions, namely that of the lambda calculus (Church, 1941). The lambda calculus was used as a means of describing, purely syntactically, the properties of mathematical functions, effectively treating them as rules. As we have seen in the preceding chapters of this book, functional programs are built from 'pure' functions, i.e. functions in the mathematical sense, and so the lambda notation is particularly suitable for describing function manipulations formally and even as an intermediate code into which we can translate a source program. Indeed, functional programming languages are often described as 'sugared' versions of the lambda notation in the sense that all functional programs can be translated into equivalent lambda expressions. Although the lambda notation is simple it is sufficiently powerful to describe all of the features of a functional source language. In Chapter 8 we shall define an intermediate code for functional languages based on the lambda notation and will describe how a source program can be translated into that intermediate form.

We begin this chapter by describing the syntax of lambda expressions and will then describe how a lambda expression can be evaluated, or reduced to yield a value. This section will describe the conversion rules of the lambda calculus which are the primitive manipulations used to perform this reduction.

In Section 6.3 we attach a more precise meaning to the word 'value' as used above in the context of a reduction and introduce the idea of a **normal form**. We look at various ways in which we can reach the normal form of an expression which leads us into a discussion on reduction order; this basically tells us 'what to do next' at each stage in the evaluation of an expression. As we shall see in Sections 6.4–6.6, the combination of reduction order and normal form leads to a variety of possible reduction schemes. We describe how these reduction schemes relate to the calling mechanisms often referred to in the context of high-level programming languages. We demonstrate in Section 6.7 how recursive functions can be supported in the lambda calculus. We consider first functions which call only themselves and will then describe how the mechanism can be extended to handle mutually-recursive sets of functions any one of which can call any other.

To conclude the chapter we describe the pure lambda calculus and the canonical lambda calculus. The earlier sections describe an extended version of the lambda calculus in which the existence of a number of predefined constants (atoms and primitive functions) is assumed; e.g. constants like the integers and their associated operations like $+$, $-$ etc. In the pure lambda calculus these constants are not predefined but they can be represented using the smaller set of primitives. We shall look at some of the more comonly used constants and will show how they can be represented as pure lambda calculus expressions. In the canonical lambda calculus all identifiers (names within the lambda calculus) are replaced by integers. We shall explain the benefits of this representation and show how the conversion rules of the lambda calculus translate into the canonical calculus. This notation is referred to again in Chapter 7 where it is used in an implementation scheme called the categorical abstract machine.

6.1 Introduction and syntax

Put simply, the lambda calculus is the calculus of anonymous (unnamed) functions. It provides firstly a method of representing functions and secondly a set of conversion rules for syntactically transforming them.

Let us begin by considering the following simple source function which doubles the value of its argument:

```
--- double( x ) <= 2 * x ;
```

To represent the 'double' function in the lambda notation we drop the name of the function, making the function 'anonymous'. Here it is represented as a lambda expression:

$\lambda x. * 2\ x$

Notice that we write the application of the built-in functions like * in their prefix form. Although we write '$* 2\ x$' in the body of the abstraction, we may read it as 'two times x'. The reason for adopting this notation will soon become apparent. The above expression should be familiar from the earlier chapters on Hope; in Hope we can write down a similar expression using the keyword **lambda** instead of λ and => instead of '.'.

```
lambda x => 2 * x
```

We read the lambda (λ) as 'the function of' and the dot (.) as 'which returns'. Lambda expressions of this form are called **lambda abstractions**.

The x after the λ is called the **bound variable** of the abstraction and corresponds to the idea of a formal parameter in a conventional procedure or function. The expression to the right of the dot is called the **body** of the abstraction and, like conventional procedure or function code, it describes what to do with the parameter once it has been passed.

The body of an abstraction extends as far to the right as possible and can be *any* valid lambda expression. Here is an example:

$\lambda x.\lambda y. * (+ x\ y)\ 2$

This reads as: 'the function of x which returns the function of y which returns $(x + y) * 2$' which is the lambda calculus representation of the following Hope function:

```
lambda x => lambda y => ( x + y ) * 2
```

and also the Miranda function

```
f x y = ( x + y ) * 2
```

Functions in the lambda notation are therefore curried in that they all have just a single argument – recall the description of Miranda given in Chapter 5. All abstractions therefore contain just a single λ and a single bound variable. Strictly, this means that function applications should be bracketed to reflect this, for example

$$(\ldots (((\lambda x_1.\lambda x_2 \ldots \lambda x_n.E)\ x_1)\ x_2) \ldots x_n)$$

However, it is a convention that function application associates to the left so that the parentheses around each nested application can be omitted without changing the meaning of the expression:

$$(\lambda x_1.\lambda x_2 \ldots \lambda x_n.E)\ x_1\ x_2 \ldots x_n$$

(Recall that Miranda also follows this convention.)

We have now seen all of the syntactic features of lambda expressions. For completeness we shall describe the notation more formally as a BNF description:

$\langle exp \rangle$ ::= $\lambda\langle id \rangle.\langle exp \rangle \mid \langle id \rangle \mid \langle exp \rangle\ \langle exp \rangle \mid (\langle exp \rangle) \mid \langle con \rangle$
$\langle id \rangle$ ::= any identifier
$\langle con \rangle$ ::= constant

Note that the set of constants is arbitrary. To avoid any confusion which may arise we list the constants referred to in this chapter in Table 6.1. Here are some more examples of lambda expressions:

42
$(+ 6)$
$\lambda y. * 2\ y$
$(\lambda f.\lambda a.\lambda b.f\ a\ b)\ (\lambda x.(\lambda y.x))$
$\lambda f.\lambda x.COND\ (= x\ 1)\ x\ (* x\ (f(- x\ 1)))$

6.2 The evaluation of lambda expressions

We have seen how the lambda notation can be used to represent functional expressions and we are now in a position to define the **conversion rules** of the lambda calculus which describe how to evaluate an expression, that is, how to transform an expression from its initial state into a final value.

The simplest type of lambda expression is a constant. Constants are **self-defining**, meaning that they cannot be transformed into any simpler expression. The evaluation of the integer constant 5, for example, simply produces 5; similarly for the other constants listed in Table 6.1.

An application of a constant function, however, can be transformed by using the built-in rules for that constant provided there are sufficient arguments. These built-in rules are often referred to as **δ-rules**. The application of any function is written by juxtaposing the function

Table 6.1 The predefined constants assumed.

Constant	*Meaning*
0, 1, −1, 2, −2 ...	The set of integers
TRUE, *FALSE*	The Boolean constants
+, −, ∗, ...	The arithmetic operations
=, ≠, >, <, ...	The Boolean functions
SUCC, *PRED*	The successor and predecessor functions on integers
*EQ*0	The function which returns *TRUE* if a given integer is 0
COND	The conditional function
CONS	The list constructor (cf. :: in Hope)
NIL	The empty list
HD	The function which returns the head of a given list
TL	The function which returns the tail of a given list
IE (or *NULL*)	The function *IsEmpty* (null) which returns *TRUE* if a given list is *NIL*
TUPLE-n	The function which builds an *n*-tuple of expressions
INDEX	The tuple indexing function

and argument expressions so that, for example, the expression

$$+\ 1\ 3$$

involves the application of a constant (the built-in arithmetic function +) to two numbers 1 and 3. This expression can be simplified to the number 4 using the corresponding δ-rule for + which we write as follows:

$$+\ 1\ 3 \rightarrow_{\delta} 4$$

This process of simplification is called **reduction**. The line above may be read: '+ 1 3 *reduces to* 4' with the δ on the arrow (→) indicating that the reduction took place according to one of the δ-rules. In general, however, the arguments to such a function may not be in the required form for the reduction to take place immediately, as in:

$$*\,(+\ 1\ 2)\,(-\ 4\ 1)$$

To reduce this expression we must first reduce the argument expressions of the ∗ function. The evaluation of this expression might proceed as follows:

$$\begin{aligned}
&*\,(+\ 1\ 2)\,(-\ 4\ 1)\\
&\rightarrow_{\delta} *\,(+\ 1\ 2)\ 3\\
&\rightarrow_{\delta} *\ 3\ 3\\
&\rightarrow_{\delta} 9
\end{aligned}$$

We shall drop the δ annotations whenever it is clear that the reduction rule used is a δ-rule.

The most interesting reduction rule describes how to apply lambda abstractions. Consider the following application:

$$(\lambda x. * x\, x)\ 2$$

The situtation is analogous to providing a high-level language procedure or function with an actual parameter to substitute for its formal parameter. In the lambda calculus this substitution is purely textual so we physically substitute occurrences of the bound variable, x, throughout the body of the applied lambda abstraction by the argument expression, 2, returning as a result of the application a modified form of the body. Hence:

$$(\lambda x. * x\, x)\ 2 \rightarrow_{\beta} * \ 2\ 2$$

which can, of course, be reduced to 4 by applying the built-in rule for $*$.

The process of copying the body of an abstraction, replacing all occurrences of the bound variable by the argument expression, is known as **β-reduction**, hence the β symbol on the reduction arrow. It is termed 'reduction' in the sense of simplification since we notionally cancel the λ, the bound variable and the argument expression and return just a modified form of the body. (The terminology is perhaps a little unfortunate in one sense since if the argument expression is very complex and there are multiple occurrences of the bound variable in the abstraction body, then the resulting expression may be longer by far than the original expression, but mathematically it will be simpler!)

The reduction of an abstraction applied to an argument may yield another abstraction, in which case the process may be repeated. For example in the following expression:

$$((\lambda x. \lambda y. + x\, y)\ 7)\ 8$$

we start by substituting 7 for x throughout the body of the outermost abstraction (i.e. $\lambda y. + x\ y$) yielding

$$(\lambda y. + 7\ y)\ 8$$

and end up with the application of another abstraction to an argument expression. This can be reduced similarly to

$$+ \ 7\ 8$$

and hence to 15 by the δ-rule for $+$.

The expression being reduced is called the **redex**, which is short for reducible expression, and for the time being we shall state that the process of reducing a lambda expression consists of repeatedly reducing the redexes of the expression until no more redexes exist. Later on we shall clarify this statement and will look at the implications of using different reduction orders. We shall sometimes qualify the word 'redex' according to the type of rule which can be used to simplify it. A δ-redex therefore corresponds to an expression which can be simplified by using a δ-rule and a β-redex similarly to an expression which can be simplified by a beta reduction. As with δ-reductions we shall usually drop the β from the reduction arrow whenever it is clear that the (sub)expression being simplified is a β-redex.

Now consider the following lambda expression:

$$\lambda x.(\ \lambda x.x\ )\ (\ +\ 1\ x\ )$$

It is clear that the x within the inner abstraction ($\lambda x.x$) refers to a different bound variable to the x in its argument expression ($+\ 1\ x$). If we apply this expression to an argument (1, say), then it would be wrong to perform the β-reduction as follows:

$$\begin{aligned}
&(\ \lambda x.(\ \lambda x.x\ )\ (\ +\ 1\ x\ )\ )\ 1\\
&\rightarrow (\ \lambda x.1\ )\ (\ +\ 1\ 1\ )\\
&\rightarrow 1
\end{aligned}$$

When we perform a β-reduction, we must be careful not to substitute inside an abstraction if the bound variable of that abstraction has the same name as the variable being substituted. If it does then we must leave the (inner) abstraction unchanged. It is possible to avoid this type of name clash by renaming the variables concerned – in this case one of the x's – so as to make each name unique. Such renaming is called α-conversion and expressions which are α-convertible, i.e. equal up to variable renaming, are called **alphabetically equivalent**. This will be considered further in Section 6.4.

As an example of β-reduction at work, here is a worked example of an expression reduction:

$$(\ \lambda f.\lambda x.f\ 4\ x\ )\ (\ \lambda y.\lambda x.\ +\ x\ y\ )\ 3$$

Step 1 Reduce the (only) redex by substituting the argument ($\lambda x.\lambda y.\ +\ x\ y$) for f throughout the body of the abstraction ($\lambda f.\lambda x.f\ 4\ x$)

$$\rightarrow (\ \lambda x.(\ \lambda y.\lambda x.\ +\ x\ y\ )\ 4\ x\ )\ 3$$

Step 2 (Arbitrarily) choose the redex which results in 3 being substituted for x throughout the body expression ($\lambda y.\lambda x.\ +\ x\ y$) 4 x, but do not substitute beyond the λx within the inner abstraction

$\rightarrow$ ($\lambda y.\lambda x.\ +\ x\ y$) 4 3

Step 3 Reduce the (only) redex i.e. ($\lambda y.\lambda x.\ +\ x\ y$) 4

$\rightarrow$ ($\lambda x.\ +\ x\ 4$) 3

Step 4 Reduce the (only) redex

$\rightarrow$ + 3 4

Step 5 Reduce this redex according to the δ-rule for +

$\rightarrow$ 7

Notice that the first reduction involved substituting f with the function ($\lambda x.\lambda y.\ +\ x\ y$). This is quite acceptable; the abstraction containing f corresponds to what would be a higher-order function in the equivalent source program.

An important point to notice is that at step 2 there was a choice of two redexes to reduce and we arbitrarily chose to reduce the outer one first. However, we could have chosen to do a β-reduction on the inner redex first, in which case the evaluation would have proceeded as follows:

($\lambda x.$($\lambda y.\lambda x.\ +\ x\ y$) 4 x) 3
$\rightarrow$ ($\lambda x.$($\lambda x.\ +\ x\ 4$) x) 3
$\rightarrow$ ($\lambda x.\ +\ x\ 4$) 3 (again making an arbitrary choice)
$\rightarrow$ + 3 4
$\rightarrow$ 7

This gives the same result and so seems quite reasonable, but in general we may get very different behaviour from two different reduction orders. This is the subject of the next section.

6.3 Reduction order and normal forms

A lambda expression is said to be in **normal form** if it cannot be further reduced. In other words, it is in normal form if it contains no redexes. Normal form thus corrresponds to the idea of the 'end of computation' in the conventional programming sense. This immediately suggests a naive evaluation scheme:

while there are more redexes **do** reduce one of the redexes **end**
{ expression now in normal form }

The problem with this is that there may be more than one redex within an expression and this begs the question as to which redex to reduce next. To see how significant this decision is, consider the following expression:

$$(\lambda x.\lambda y.y)((\lambda z.z\ z)(\lambda z.z\ z))$$

Here there are two redexes:

$$(\lambda z.z\ z)(\lambda z.z\ z) \qquad \text{and} \qquad (\lambda x.\lambda y.y)((\lambda z.z\ z)(\lambda z.z\ z))$$

If we pick the first of these to reduce next we end up with the following sequence of reductions:

$$\begin{array}{l} (\lambda z.z\ z)(\lambda z.z\ z) \\ \rightarrow (\lambda z.z\ z)(\lambda z.z\ z) \\ \rightarrow (\lambda z.z\ z)(\lambda z.z\ z) \\ \vdots \end{array}$$

which is non-terminating. If on the other hand we choose the second, we get the following reduction:

$$\begin{array}{l} (\lambda x.\lambda y.y)((\lambda z.z\ z)(\lambda z.z\ z)) \\ \rightarrow \lambda y.y \end{array}$$

which terminates in one step. This leads us into a discussion of **reduction order**, which determines which redex to reduce next whenever there is a choice. In order to understand this issue we must first introduce some new definitions:

> The **leftmost** redex is that redex whose λ (or primitive function identifier in the case of a δ-redex) is textually to the left of all other redexes within the expression. (Similarly for the **rightmost** redex.)
>
> An **outermost** redex is defined to be a redex which is not contained within any other redex.
>
> An **innermost** redex is defined to be a redex which contains no other redex.

In the context of functional languages and the lambda calculus there are two important reduction orders to which we shall repeatedly refer in this book:

> **Applicative-order** reduction (AOR) which says:
> reduce the *leftmost innermost* redex first
>
> **Normal-order** reduction (NOR) which says:
> reduce the *leftmost outermost* redex first

Referring back to our example above:

$$(\lambda x.\lambda y.y)((\lambda z.z\ z) (\lambda z.z\ z))$$

the leftmost innermost redex is

$$(\lambda z.z\ z)(\lambda z.z\ z)$$

and the leftmost outermost redex is

$$(\lambda x.\lambda y.y)((\lambda z.z\ z)(\lambda z.z\ z))$$

Applicative-order reduction will therefore evaluate the redex $((\lambda z.z\ z) (\lambda z.z\ z))$ first and will fail to terminate, whereas normal-order reduction will reduce the outermost redex first, i.e. $(\lambda x.\lambda y.y)((\lambda z.z\ z)(\lambda z.z\ z))$, and will terminate in one step.

The function $\lambda x.\lambda y.y$ is a classical example of a function which discards its argument. NOR plays safe in this respect and effectively delays the evaluation of any redexes within the argument expression until there is no alternative redex available, just in case such reductions prove redundant. The leftmost outermost selection policy therefore chooses to substitute for x in $\lambda y.y$ *before* attempting any reductions within the argument expression. It thus yields the normal form $\lambda y.y$ in one reduction step. AOR on the other hand evaluates the argument expression first which in this case leads to non-termination. Although this suggests that we should always choose the leftmost outermost reduction order to ensure that the evaluation terminates whenever possible it turns out that AOR is significantly more efficient when implemented by conventional computer as we shall see throughout this book. The astute reader may have recognized that NOR and AOR are related to *lazy* and *eager* evaluation respectively, as described in the earlier chapters, although they are not directly equivalent. In Section 6.5.2 we shall come back to this issue where we shall attach a more precise meaning to these terms.

6.3.1 Two powerful theorems

As a short aside, note that we have talked about reducing an expression in a variety of different orders under the implicit assumption that if the reduction terminates then we will always end up with the same answer. This is a rather loose assumption but it turns out to be provably correct. Furthermore, it is also possible to prove that normal-order reduction always reduces an expression to its normal form if a normal form exists. These two proofs are embodied in two theorems respectively called the *Church–Rosser* theorem and the *standardization* theorem which are stated informally below:

(Consequence of) Church–Rosser theorem If an expression E can be reduced in two different ways to two normal forms then these normal forms are the same (up to alphabetic equivalence).

Standardization theorem If an expression E has a normal form then reducing the leftmost outermost redex at each stage in the reduction of E guarantees to reach that normal form (up to alphabetic equivalence).

A proof of these theorems may be found in Barendregt (1984).

The uniqueness of the normal form of an expression is a consequence of the Church–Rosser theorem. The theorem itself is concerned with reduction sequences in general and is by no means restricted to β- and δ-reduction.

The **diamond property** for a reduction relation $\rightarrow$ states that if an expression E can be reduced to two expressions $E1$ and $E2$ then there exists an expression N which can be reached (by repeatedly applying $\rightarrow$) from both $E1$ and $E2$. This is illustrated by the following diagram:

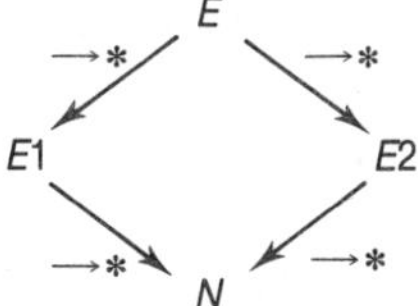

We use the symbol $\rightarrow*$ to denote an arbitrary number, $n \geq 0$, of reductions, i.e. $\rightarrow*$ is the **reflexive transitive closure** of $\rightarrow$. (The 'reflexive' part means that E can be reduced to itself by doing nothing, i.e. $n = 0$.) Formally, therefore, the diamond property states that:

$$E \rightarrow* E1 \text{ and } E \rightarrow* E2 \Rightarrow \exists N : E1 \rightarrow* N \text{ and } E2 \rightarrow* N$$

We say that the reduction relation $\rightarrow$ is Church–Rosser if $\rightarrow*$ satisifes the diamond property and the proof cited above actually demonstrates that β-reduction is Church–Rosser. This, then, is the Church–Rosser theorem, which is usually expressed in the form:

$$X \ cnv* \ Y \Rightarrow \exists N : X \rightarrow* N \text{ and } Y \rightarrow* N$$

where $\rightarrow$ denotes β-reduction and *cnv* denotes the symmetrical β-conversion relation:

$$X \ cnv \ Y \Leftrightarrow X \rightarrow Y \text{ or } Y \rightarrow X$$

(In fact if we include δ-reduction as well as β-reduction in the relation $\rightarrow$ our reduction system may fail to satisfy the diamond property in pathological cases. Nevertheless, a weaker property does hold, namely the weak diamond property. This is similar except that the reductions from E to $E1$ and $E2$ must be **single-step**, i.e. the asterisks on the upper arrows in the diagram are dropped, and the formal statement of the weak diamond property is therefore

$$E \rightarrow E1 \text{ and } E \rightarrow E2 \Rightarrow \exists N : E1 \rightarrow\!\!* \, N \text{ and } E2 \rightarrow\!\!* \, N$$

A reduction relation is said to be weak Church–Rosser if it satisfies the weak diamond property. None of the constant functions we use, however, violate the diamond property.)

The Church–Rosser theorem does not immediately tell us that the normal form of an expression is unique. However, suppose that M and N are two different normal forms of the same expression E. Then we have

$$E \rightarrow\!\!* \, M \text{ and } E \rightarrow\!\!* \, N$$

Now if we apply the Church–Rosser theorem:

$$\exists Z : M \rightarrow^* Z \text{ and } N \rightarrow^* Z$$

But, since M and N are both normal forms this can only be the case if

$$M \cong N \cong Z$$

i.e. the normal form of E is indeed unique. (We use $\cong$ rather than $=$ since the expressions are equal only up to alphabetical equivalence.)

6.4 Beta reduction and the name clash problem

Consider the following expression:

$$\lambda x.\lambda y.x\ y\ y$$

We say that x is **bound** in the whole expression since there is an occurrence of a λx within it. Equivalently, we say that there is a **binding occurrence** of x within the expression. Now let us look at the body of the outermost abstraction:

$$\lambda y.x\ y\ y$$

Although x appears in this expression there is no binding occurrence of x (i.e. there is no λx outside it). We therefore say that the variable x is **free** in the expression. The variable y is still bound, however, by virtue of the λy. If we now consider the body of the innermost abstraction, i.e.

$$x\ y\ y$$

both x *and* y are free. We shall sometimes refer to the set of free variables of an expression E by $FV(\ E\ )$ so that, for example,

$$FV(\ \lambda x.\lambda y.x\ y\ y\ ) = \{\ \}$$
$$FV(\ \lambda x.x\ y\ y\ ) = \{\ y\ \}$$
$$FV(\ x\ y\ y\ ) = \{\ x, y\ \}$$

FV can be defined more formally as follows

$FV(\ k\ )$	$= \varnothing$	k is a constant
$FV(\ x\ )$	$= \{\ x\ \}$	x is a variable
$FV(\ E1\ E2\ )$	$= FV(\ E1\ ) \cup FV(\ E2\ )$	
$FV(\ \lambda x.E\ )$	$= FV(\ E\ ) - x$	

where $S - x$ denotes the set S with any occurrence of x removed. A lambda expression, E, which contains no free variables (i.e. $FV(\ E\ ) = \varnothing$) is said to be **closed**.

Using this notion of bound and free variables we can now formalize the definition of β-reduction:

> To ***β*-reduce** the expression $(\ \lambda x.E\ )\ A$ we return a modified form of E in which all free occurrences of x in E are replaced by A.

Unfortunately this leads to a potential problem with β-reduction which can be illustrated by the following example:

$$\lambda x.\underline{(\ (\ \lambda y.\lambda x.\ +\ x\ y)\ x\ )}$$

This expression contains just a single beta redex which is shown underlined. If we now attempt to reduce this redex we will get:

$$\lambda x.(\ \lambda x + x\ x\ )$$

which is quite clearly wrong.

The problem is that in this example the argument expression contains a free variable which has the same name as one of the bound variables within the abstraction body, i.e.

$$(\ \lambda y.\lambda x.\ +\ x\ y\ )\ x$$

this x is *free* (the final x)

this x is *bound* (the x in the body $+\ x\ y$)

In order that we can safely perform a β-reduction on the redex we must first modify the abstraction so as to make all the bound variable names unique with respect to the free variables within the argument expression. In our example, we must therefore **rename** the bound variable x within the body of the abstraction to some new identifier, say x':

$$(\lambda y.\lambda x. + x\ y) \rightarrow (\lambda y.\lambda x'. + x'\ y)$$

Now the β-reduction can proceed safely:

$$\begin{aligned} &\lambda x.((\lambda y.\lambda x'. + x'\ y)\ x) \\ &\quad \rightarrow \lambda x.(\lambda x'. + x'\ x) \end{aligned}$$

which is correct.

This process of renaming is called **α-conversion** or **α-substitution.** It encapsulates the idea that two expressions such as

$\lambda x.x$ and $\lambda y.y$

denote the same function in that they differ only in the names of their bound variables, in other words that they are alphabetically equivalent. We say that $\lambda x.x$ can be α-converted to $\lambda y.y$ or that $\lambda x.x$ and $\lambda y.y$ are α-convertible and we write:

$$\lambda x.x =_{\alpha} \lambda y.y$$

In general, the expression $\lambda x.E$ can be α-converted to the expression $\lambda x'.E'$ where E' is the same as E with all free occurrences of x replaced by x' provided x' does not itself occur free in E. For example, here is a valid α-conversion:

$$\lambda x.f\,x\,y \rightarrow_{\alpha} \lambda z.f\,z\,y$$

and here is an invalid conversion:

$$\lambda x.f\,x\,y \rightarrow_{\alpha} \lambda y.f\,y\,y$$

The name clash problem places a restriction on the process of β-reduction: we can only safely β-reduce the expression $E1\ E2$ if none of the free variables in $E2$ occurs bound in $E1$ (see Hindley & Seldin (1986) for the required β-reduction rule). Supporting the renaming of the variables in $E1$ is, however, a potentially expensive operation and one which we would like to avoid when we mechanize the reduction by computer. One solution to this problem is to adopt a variable naming convention which avoids the problem (Barendregt, 1986). A second solution involves avoiding β-reduction in the presence of free variables altogether; this is the preferred approach since we require a modification only to our notion of normal form rather than to the reduction scheme or to the variable naming scheme. This approach to solving the name clash problem will be described in Section 6.5 below.

6.4.1 The η-conversion rule

In addition to α- and β-conversion there is a third rule which is known as the **η-conversion** rule. η-conversion encapsulates the idea that the two expressions

$$\lambda x.E\,x \quad \text{and} \quad E$$

denote the same function, provided that x does not occur free in E, because

$$(\,\lambda x.E\,x\,)\,A \rightarrow E\,A$$

for any argument expression A. This is called **functional extensionality**. We write:

$$\lambda x.E\,x \rightarrow_{\eta} E$$

meaning that the expression $\lambda x.E\,x$ η-reduces to the expression E. Similarly, we say that $\lambda x.E\,x$ is an **η-redex**. We call this translation η-reduction since there is an implied simplification of the expression to the left of the arrow. However, we can drive the conversion the other way and so we often use the symbol $=_{\eta}$ as for α-conversion, in which case we say that the two expressions involved are η-convertible.

As a general rule we shall use the terms 'β-reduction' and 'η-reduction', but we do not generally class α-conversion as a reduction since α-conversion does not simplify the structure of the expression being converted. However, we are also perfectly entitled to use the term β-conversion – as in our consideration of the Church–Rosser theorem in Section 6.3.1 for example. X and Y are β-convertible if either $X \rightarrow_{\beta} Y$ or $Y \rightarrow_{\beta} X$; in the latter case we sometimes say that Y is obtained from X by **β-abstraction**.

Although we shall make passing references to η-reduction throughout the book, we shall not be concerned with building η-reduction into any mechanical evaluator of lambda expressions since these can be removed at compile time if necessary. Consequently, when we use the word 'redex' in the context of evaluation we shall usually mean β-redex or δ-redex unless explicitly stated otherwise.

6.5 Avoiding the name clash problem

In Section 6.4 above we saw the problem of name clashes which can occur during β-reduction when the argument expression contains free variables which occur bound in the body of the applied abstraction. This problem can arise whenever we attempt to reduce an expression to its normal form (i.e. a form with no redexes). For example, the expression

$$\lambda x.(\,(\lambda y.\lambda x.\ +\ x\ y\,)\ x\,)$$

is not in normal form so an α-conversion is necessary before the β-reduction can proceed.

It turns out, however, that the name clash problem can be solved without resorting to α-conversion by defining a restricted normal form called **weak head-normal form**. An expression E is said to be in weak head-normal form (sometimes abbreviated WHNF) if:

(1) E is a constant,

(2) E is an expression of the form $\lambda x.E'$ for *any* E',

(3) E is of the form $P\,E_1\,E_2\ldots E_n$ for any constant function P of arity $k > n$.

The third rule states that any partially applied constant function is also a WHNF. This is quite reasonable since we can rewrite an expression such as

$$*\ 3$$

using the η-conversion rule into

$$\lambda x.\ *\ 3\ x$$

which is in WHNF.

Note also that an expression consisting of a single variable is a WHNF but in this discussion we consider only closed expressions.

The advantage of reducing an expression to WHNF rather than to full normal form is that it avoids the need to perform β-reductions in the presence of free variables. The only time we can encounter free variables is if we 'pass through' a λ since all references to the variable it introduces will be free only to the right of the '.'. By stopping the evaluation at the λ we avoid entering the function body so that we don't encounter free variables at all. Using the previous example again

$$\lambda x.\underline{(\,(\lambda y.\lambda x.\ +\ y\ x\,)\ x\,)}$$

we will not attempt to reduce the underlined redex because the expression as a whole is in WHNF. Only when this expression is applied to an argument will any evaluation take place and this evaluation will start by cancelling the leftmost bound variable x according to the rules of normal-order reduction. This will replace the problematic free occurrence of x in $(\lambda y.\lambda x. + y\ x)\ x$ by the argument value (which cannot contain free variables either) and the name clash problem never arises. For example:

$$(\lambda x.((\lambda y.\lambda x. + y\ x)\ x))\ 4$$
$$\rightarrow (\lambda y.\lambda x. + y\ x)\ 4$$
$$\rightarrow \lambda x. + 4\ x$$

Note that a half-way house between normal form and WHNF is **head-normal form** (HNF). An expression, E, is said to be in HNF if either:

(1) E is a constant,

(2) E is an expression of the form $\lambda x_1.\lambda x_2 \ldots \lambda x_n . E'$ where E' is not a redex,

(3) E is of the form $P\ E_1\ E_2 \ldots E_n$ for any constant function P of arity $k > n$.

This definition is included for completeness. Reduction to HNF is not generally practical because it does not succeed in avoiding the name clash problem. Using our example again:

$$\lambda x.((\lambda y.\lambda x. + y\ x)\ x)$$

This is not in HNF because $(\lambda y.\lambda x. + y\ x)\ x$ is a redex. The inner β-reduction will then be performed and the name clash will again occur.

Note that all HNFs are also WHNFs but not vice versa. For example $\lambda x. + 2\ 3$ is in WHNF but not HNF since $+ 2\ 3$ is a redex.

6.6 The effect of sharing

Consider the following expression:

$$(\lambda x. + x\ x)\ E$$

β-reducing this expression we obtain

$$+ E\ E$$

In order to reduce this expression we must first reduce the arguments of the $+$ function and this involves reducing E twice, which is potentially very inefficient.

One way to ensure that an argument is never evaluated more than once is to reduce it *before* doing the β-reduction. This corresponds to applicative-order reduction. Instead of substituting the whole argument expression the argument value is substituted so that repeated occurrences of the bound variable do not cause re-evaluation of the argument. If, however, we wish to implement normal-order reduction then we must somehow 'share' the argument expression after it has been substituted in such a way that the first evaluation of the argument causes the shared copy of the argument expression to be replaced by its value, i.e. by its WHNF.

At this point we depart from the model of reduction suggested naturally by the lambda calculus. The lambda calculus provides a purely textual means of describing the evaluation of expressions. That is, we can write the intermediate expressions forming a reduction sequence by a collection of symbols on the printed page (this is sometimes referred to as **string reduction**). If we wish to study the effect of sharing we have to express somehow the fact that two occurrences of the same identifier refer to the same expression other than by copying that expression out twice. One way to do this is to represent expressions as graphs. This brings us to the idea of **graph reduction**, which will be described in detail in Chapter 11. Here, however, we shall adopt the following convention.

Given an expression of the form

$$(\lambda x. \ldots x \ldots x \ldots)\,E$$

we shall write the resulting reduced expression as follows:

$\ldots x \ldots x \ldots$ **where** x **is** E

to mean that the two occurrences of x in the resulting expression both refer to E. This association between variable names and their values is traditionally known as an **environment** and we say that the reduction mechanism is environment-based rather than copy-based as in the lambda calculus. We shall see more of environments in Chapter 9.

The implication is that when x above (i.e. E) is first evaluated, the reduced form of E not only replaces x in the expression but also the E in the environment. This means that the next time x is required, the reduced form of E will be delivered immediately. For example,

$(\lambda x. + x\,x)\,(+\ 1\ 2)$
$\rightarrow +\ x\,x$ **where** x **is** $(+\ 1\ 2)$
$\rightarrow +\ 3\ x$ **where** x **is** 3
$\rightarrow +\ 3\ 3$
$\rightarrow 6$

and we see that the argument expresssion $(+\ 1\ 2)$ is evaluated only once.

6.6.1 Reduction schemes and calling mechanisms

Now that we have a notion of sharing, we can relate the various possible reduction strategies for evaluating lambda expressions to the **calling mechanisms** often referred to in the context of high-level programming languages. A calling mechanism describes how to pass a parameter to a function or procedure in a high-level language. It is thus closely linked to our previous discussions on reduction orders and sharing.

Given an expression of the form:

$$(\lambda x.E1)\ E2$$

we have seen that one way to simplify the expression is to reduce the argument expression $E2$ first and then to perform the β-reduction, substituting the evaluated form of $E2$ for x throughout $E1$. This corresponds to leftmost-innermost reduction, or applicative-order reduction (AOR) and is equivalent to call-by-value in conventional programming languages for obvious reasons. In the context of functional languages call-by-value is sometimes known as eager evaluation, which we have already seen in Chapter 4. In the context of the evaluation of lambda expressions we can define it as follows:

eager evaluation = AOR to WHNF

As an alternative to AOR we can substitute $E2$ for x throughout $E1$ first, which corresponds to leftmost-outermost or normal-order reduction (NOR). In the lambda calculus, which has no notion of sharing, this substitution is purely textual. It therefore corresponds to the idea of **call-by-textual replacement**. As we have seen, this can lead to name clashes and the re-evaluation of argument expressions. If we avoid the name clash problem (for example by performing α-conversion on each argument expression or by reducing to WHNF only) then the mechanism corresponds to call-by-name. This does not, however, avoid the re-evaluation of arguments.

If we implement normal-order reduction and support sharing (ensuring that arguments are evaluated at most once), then the reduction mechanism corresponds to call-by-need. In traditional languages, call-by-name and call-by-need behave differently only if the argument expression produces side-effects. In a functional language there are no side-effects and so these two calling mechanisms always generate the same result. We can therefore characterize call-by-need as normal-order reduction to WHNF together with sharing of argument expressions. If we combine call-by-need with lazy constructors then we end up with lazy evaluation, which we have already encountered in Chapter 4. By lazy constructors we mean that constructor arguments are assumed to be left unevaluated, i.e. they are not reduced to WHNF. We can therefore describe lazy evaluation in the context of the evaluation of lambda expressions as follows:

lazy evaluation = NOR to WHNF
+ sharing
+ lazy constructors

or alternatively

lazy evaluation = call-by-need + lazy constructors

In fact, constructors (with the possible exception of predefined constructors like the list constructor *CONS*) are usually implemented as tuples, as we shall see in Chapter 8, so that constructor function applications are translated into calls to the predefined function *TUPLE-n* quoted in Table 6.1. The standard implementation of Hope, which is a mixture of eager and lazy evaluation, can be defined as follows:

AOR to WHNF + lazy constructors

If we view (lazy) constructed objects as WHNFs, then we can classify the calling mechanism as 'call-by-WHNF'. This corresponds to calling constructor functions by-need and all other functions by-value, although we have to be careful about our treatment of conditionals. We shall return to these issues in more detail in Chapter 9.

6.7 Expressing recursion

Up until now we have looked only at the representation of non-recursive functions in the lambda calculus. In a high-level language, however, we must be able to write recursive function definitions. We are able to express recursion in a high-level language because we have the facility to name every function we wish to use within the program. These names can then be used anywhere within the program (save for when the name is 'out of scope' in some sense dependent on the language), even within the body of the named function itself.

Now let us consider the problem of supporting recursive functions within the lambda calculus. Functions have no names in the lambda calculus, so if we are to represent recursion then we have to devise a method of allowing a function to call itself other than by referring to itself by name.

Another (rather more convoluted) way to look at recursion is to imagine a recursive function being expressed as a function which takes *itself* as an argument; eventually it may occur bound to one of its own variables and so can be referred to from within its own body.

Consider, for example, the recursive sum function given in Hope by:

```
--- sum( n ) <= if n = 0 then 0 else n + sum( n − 1 ) ;
```

This may be represented as a lambda abstraction in which an extra parameter has been added to enable the function to be passed into itself. We shall call this intermediate version *SUM*:

$$SUM = \lambda s.\lambda n.\ COND\ (\ =\ n\ 0\ )\ 0\ (\ +\ n\ (\ s\ (\ -\ n\ 1\ )\ )\ )$$

All that we have to do now is bind the variable s to the value of the sum function we are trying to define. We can achieve this effect by using a special function known as the ***Y*-combinator**, which is satisfied by the following equation:

$$Yf = f(\ Yf\ )$$

Y is also known as the **fixed point** combinator. A 'fixed point' or 'fixpoint' of a function f is simply an expression which remains unchanged as a result of applying f to it. (We use 'an' rather than 'the' when talking about fixed points because a function may have many fixed points; the identity function, $\lambda x.x$, for example, has an infinite number.)

The expression Yf delivers the **least fixed point** of f. To understand why it is called the least fixed point, we must delve more deeply into the theory of functions. A detailed understanding of this subject is not required here but for the interested reader we include in Appendix B a short tutorial on domain theory which will help to explain what is meant by the term. A more detailed treatment of the subject can be found in Stoy (1977).

Let us now see what happens when we apply *Y* to the *SUM* function above:

$$\begin{aligned}
&Y\,SUM\\
&= Y\ (\ \lambda s.\lambda n.\ COND\ (\ =\ n\ 0\ )\ 0\ (\ +\ n\ (\ s\ (\ -\ n\ 1\ )\ )\ )\ )\\
&\rightarrow (\ \lambda s.\lambda n.\ COND\ (\ =\ n\ 0\ )\ 0\ (\ +\ n\ (\ s\ (\ -\ n\ 1\ )\ )\ )\ )\ (\ Y\,SUM\ )\\
&\rightarrow (\ \lambda n.\ COND\ (\ =\ n\ 0\ )\ 0\ (\ +\ n\ (\ (\ Y\,SUM\ )\ (\ -\ n\ 1\ )\ )\ )\ )
\end{aligned}$$

This appears to be what we want. To see that it is, let us expand the inner expression (*Y SUM*) similarly:

$$\begin{aligned}
\rightarrow (\ \lambda n.\ COND\ (\ =\ n\ 0\ )&\\
&0\\
&(\ +\ n(\ (\ \lambda n.\ COND(\ =\ n\ 0)\ 0(\ +\ n(\ (\ Y\,SUM\ )(\ -\ n\ 1\ )\ )\ )\ )\\
&(\ -\ n\ 1\ )\ )\ )\ )
\end{aligned}$$

We see that this expression behaves in exactly the same way as the original recursive definition of *sum*. The inner occurrence of *Y SUM* constructs a copy of the original *SUM* function placing itself (i.e. *Y SUM*) in place of the *s* within the copy, which is what we require. Therefore the *sum* function is precisely:

$$Y\ SUM \qquad \text{i.e. } Y\,(\,\lambda s.\lambda n.\ COND\,(\,=\,n\,0\,)\,0\,(\,+\,n\,(\,s\,(\,-\,n\,1\,)\,)\,)\,)$$

In general, then, a recursive function f with a defining body E is represented in the lambda notation by the expression

$$Y\,(\,\lambda f.E\,)$$

6.7.1 Mutual recursion

In general we may require to support mutually recursive sets of functions such as the following:

```
--- f1 (...) <= E1 ;
--- f2 (...) <= E2 ;
 :
--- fn (...) <= En ;
```

where the E_i can refer to any (or all) of the f_j ($1 \le i, j \le n$). The trick we use to implement such definitions is one of **tupling**. Put simply, the idea is to package the set of n mutually recursive functions into an n-tuple of functions and then translate the references to f_i into an index to the ith element of that tuple. To do this we shall use the constant functions *TUPLE-n* and *INDEX* which were listed in Table 6.1 and which are defined by:

$TUPLE\text{-}n\ E_1\ E_2 \ldots E_n$ builds the tuple consisting of the expressions E_1, $E_2, \ldots, E_n$ which we shall write here as $\langle\, E_1, E_2, \ldots, E_n \,\rangle$

$$INDEX\ k\,\langle\, E_1, \ldots, E_n \,\rangle = E_k \qquad (1 \le k \le n\,)$$

We first translate the functions $f_1, \ldots, f_n$ into lambda notation, leaving each occurrence of any f_j within the function bodies unchanged; we call these lambda expressions $L_1, \ldots, L_n$. We then build these expressions into an n-tuple using *TUPLE-n*; we call this tuple T, i.e.

$$T = TUPLE\text{-}n\ L_1\ L_2 \ldots L_n$$

We now modify the elements of T, substituting all references to f_i within L_j ($1 \leq i, j \leq n$) by calls to the *INDEX* function, thus:

$$f_i \rightarrow INDEX\ i\ T$$

giving a modified form of L_j say L_j'. Then T is defined by

$$T = TUPLE\text{-}n\ L_1'\ L_2'\ \ldots\ L_n'$$

Notice that this definition is recursive since the L_j' may refer to T itself. So, to complete the definition we must apply the Y-combinator in the same way that we do for any other recursive definition. This gives

$$T \cong Y\ (\ \lambda T.TUPLE\text{-}n\ L_1'\ L_2'\ \ldots\ L_n'\ )$$

as our representation of the set of functions $f_1, \ldots, f_n$.

To see how this works, let us look at a simple example consisting of the two mutually recursive functions:

```
--- f( n ) <= if n = 0 then 0 else g( n ) ;
--- g( n ) <= n + f( n − 1 ) ;
```

These functions can be represented by the following lambda expression:

$$\begin{aligned} &Y\ (\ \lambda T.TUPLE\text{-}2\ (\ \lambda n.COND\ (\ =\ n\ 0\ )\ 0\ (\ (\ INDEX\ 2\ T\ )\ n\ )\ ) \\ &\qquad\qquad (\ \lambda n.\ +\ n\ (\ (\ INDEX\ 1\ T\ )\ (\ -\ n\ 1\ )\ )\ )\ )\ ) \end{aligned}$$

the evaluation of which is set as an exercise at the end of the chapter.

6.7.2 The definition of *Y*

To complete the treatment of recursion we have only to provide a definition of Y. The obvious way to do this is to include Y in the set of constants, i.e. making it a built-in function just like + or *COND*. However, there are two further ways of implementing Y: the first assumes that all lambda expressions are represented in a graphical form; Y is then implemented simply by establishing a circular pointer; we shall come back to this idea in Chapter 12.

Of particular significance here, however, is the observation that Y itself can be written as a lambda expression, which is quite crucial to the pure lambda calculus in which there are no primitive functions. The following rather unlikely-looking expression does the trick:

$$\lambda h.\ (\ \lambda x.h\ (\ x\ x\ )\ )\ (\ \lambda x.h\ (\ x\ x\ )\ )$$

To see that this works, let us apply it to a function f:

$$
\begin{aligned}
& Yf \\
& = (\lambda h.(\lambda x.h(x\,x))(\lambda x.h(x\,x)))\,f \\
& \rightarrow (\lambda x.f(x\,x))(\lambda x.f(x\,x)) \\
& \rightarrow f(\lambda x.f(x\,x))(\lambda x.f(x\,x)) \\
& = f(Yf)
\end{aligned}
$$

Y is seldom implemented this way for reasons of efficiency. Many implementations of the lambda calculus provide extensions to enable the naming of lambda expressions and in Chapter 8 we shall develop a 'sugared' version of the lambda calculus which incorporates this extension.

6.8 The pure lambda calculus

In the preceding sections of this chapter we have described a version of the lambda calculus in which a predefined set of constants was assumed to exist, for example the integers, Booleans and lists, together with their associated functions.

The original texts on the lambda calculus, however, assumed no such rules and an expression E in this so-called 'pure' lambda calculus therefore has the following syntax:

$$\langle exp \rangle ::= \langle id \rangle \mid \lambda \langle id \rangle . \langle exp \rangle \mid \langle exp \rangle \langle exp \rangle \mid (\langle exp \rangle)$$

Although the absence of the δ-rules might suggest that basic arithmetic, list processing etc. are no longer possible, this is far from the truth. In fact every lambda calculus expression we have seen so far can be expressed (albeit somewhat indirectly) in the notation of the pure lambda calculus. In this section we shall provide a flavour of the power of the pure lambda calculus and demonstrate how natural numbers, arithmetic functions, Boolean constants, Boolean operations, lists and list-processing functions can be expressed without recourse to predefined functions. This section is included largely for completeness; we shall not use the pure lambda calculus as a basis for any of the implementations described in this book.

6.8.1 Boolean constants and Boolean operations

When we write an expression like

if P **then** Q **else** R (or $COND\ P\ Q\ R$)

we usually imagine the conditional operator ($COND$) as a built-in function which selects one of Q or R depending on the value of the predicate P. Another way of thinking about conditionals, however, is to view the predicate as a function which itself selects one of Q or R. The expression $COND\ P\ Q\ R$ then translates simply to $P\ Q\ R$ with the rules:

$$TRUE\ x\ y \rightarrow x$$
$$FALSE\ x\ y \rightarrow y$$

This alternative approach provides the basis for the representation of the Boolean constants and their associated operators in the pure lambda calculus. The conditional operator $COND$ is expressed as follows:

$$COND = \lambda p.\lambda q.\lambda r.p\ q\ r$$

and, as we might now expect, $TRUE$ and $FALSE$ are represented as:

$$TRUE = \lambda x.\lambda y.x$$
$$FALSE = \lambda x.\lambda y.y$$

So, for example,

$$\begin{aligned}
&COND\ TRUE\ A\ B \\
&= (\ \lambda p.\lambda q.\lambda r.p\ q\ r\ )\ (\ \lambda x.\lambda y.x\ )\ A\ B \\
&\rightarrow (\ \lambda q.\lambda r.(\ \lambda x.\lambda y.x\ )\ q\ r\ )\ A\ B \\
&\rightarrow (\ \lambda r.(\ \lambda x.\lambda y.x\ )\ A\ r\ )\ B \\
&\rightarrow (\ \lambda x.\lambda y.x\ )\ A\ B \\
&\rightarrow (\ \lambda y.A\ )\ B \\
&\rightarrow A
\end{aligned}$$

as expected. Given this representation of $TRUE$ and $FALSE$ we can now write expressions for computing $A\ OR\ B$, $A\ AND\ B$, $NOT\ A$ and so on. For example, here are AND and OR written as lambda expressions:

$$AND = \lambda x.\lambda y.x\ y\ FALSE$$
$$OR = \lambda x.\lambda y.(\ x\ TRUE\ )\ y$$

The validity of these representations can be established by constructing the appropriate truth tables. For example:

$$\begin{aligned}
&TRUE\ AND\ FALSE \\
&= (\ \lambda x.\lambda y.x\ y\ (\ \lambda x.\lambda y.y\ )\ )\ (\ \lambda x.\lambda y.x\ )\ (\ \lambda x.\lambda y.y\ ) \\
&\rightarrow (\ \lambda y.(\ \lambda x.\lambda y.x\ )\ y\ (\ \lambda x.\lambda y.y\ )\ )\ (\ \lambda x.\lambda y.y\ ) \\
&\rightarrow (\ \lambda x.\lambda y.x\ )\ (\ \lambda x.\lambda y.y\ )\ (\ \lambda x.\lambda y.y\ ) \\
&\rightarrow (\ \lambda y.(\ \lambda x.\lambda y.y\ )\ )\ (\ \lambda x.\lambda y.y\ ) \\
&\rightarrow (\ \lambda x.\lambda y.y\ ) \\
&= FALSE
\end{aligned}$$

6.8.2 Lists in the pure lambda calculus

Now that we have a representation for the Boolean constants *TRUE* and *FALSE* we can use them to define lists.

Traditionally, lists are built using two constructor functions, one which denotes the empty list (*NIL*) and one which builds a new list from an element and an old list (*CONS*). Hope, for example, uses nil and infix :: for this purpose. To represent *CONS* in the pure lambda calculus, the trick we shall use is to treat the expression

$$CONS\ h\ t$$

as a function which takes a selector function as its argument and applies it to the head (h) and tail (t) expression. Hence,

$$CONS = \lambda h.\lambda t.\lambda s.s\ h\ t$$

where h, t and s represent the eventual instantiation of the head, tail and selector functions respectively.

The valid selector functions are those which select one of the first or second arguments of the constructor. These are respectively,

$$\lambda h.\lambda t.h \qquad \text{and} \qquad \lambda h.\lambda t.t$$

which are precisely the definitions of *TRUE* and *FALSE* given above. This means that the functions for extracting the head and tail elements of a list L (i.e. *HD* and *TL* respectively) can be defined as follows:

$$HD = \lambda L.L\ TRUE$$
$$TL = \lambda L.L\ FALSE$$

so that an application of *HD* or *TL* to the expression *CONS a b* results in the appropriate selector being applied to a and b.

Thus, for example (and with some omitted steps):

$$
\begin{aligned}
& HD\ (\ CONS\ a\ b\ ) \\
& = (\ \lambda c.c\ TRUE\ )\ (\ (\ \lambda h.\lambda t.\lambda s.s\ h\ t\ )\ a\ b\ ) \\
& \rightarrow (\ (\ \lambda h.\lambda t.\lambda s.s\ h\ t\ )\ a\ b\ )\ TRUE \\
& \rightarrow (\ \lambda s.s\ a\ b\ )\ TRUE \\
& \rightarrow TRUE\ a\ b \\
& = (\ \lambda h.\lambda t.h\ )\ a\ b \\
& \rightarrow (\ \lambda t.a\ )\ b \\
& \rightarrow a
\end{aligned}
$$

To complete the set of list-processing functions we have only to define the function *isempty* (*IE*) which delivers *TRUE* if applied to an empty list (i.e. *NIL*). The definition of this function will lead us to a suitable representation of the empty list. We begin by looking at the form of the expression *IE* (*CONS a b*):

$$\begin{aligned}
&IE\ (\ CONS\ a\ b\ )\\
&= IE\ (\ (\ \lambda h.\lambda t.\lambda s.s\ h\ t\ )\ a\ b\ )\\
&\rightarrow IE\ (\ \lambda s.s\ a\ b\ )
\end{aligned}$$

Since we expect this expression to deliver *FALSE* for all values of *a* and *b* it is clear that *IE* must be of the form:

$$IE = \lambda c.c(\ \lambda h.\lambda t.FALSE\ )$$

This naturally leads us to an expression for the empty list, defined in such a way that *IE x* yields *TRUE* if $x = NIL$ and *FALSE* otherwise:

$$NIL = \lambda x.TRUE$$

As an example, here is the reduction sequence for the expression *IE* (*TL* (*CONS* 1 *NIL*)):

$$\begin{aligned}
&IE\ (TL\ (\ CONS\ 1\ NIL\ )\ )\\
&= (\ \lambda c.c(\ \lambda h.\lambda t.FALSE\ )\ )\ (\ TL\ (\ CONS\ 1\ NIL\ )\ )\\
&\rightarrow (\ TL\ (\ CONS\ 1\ NIL\ )\ )\ (\ \lambda h.\lambda t.FALSE\ )\\
&= (\ (\ \lambda c.c\ FALSE\ )\ (\ CONS\ 1\ NIL\ )\ )\ (\ \lambda h.\lambda t.FALSE\ )\\
&\rightarrow (\ (\ CONS\ 1\ NIL\ )\ FALSE\ )\ (\ \lambda h.\lambda t.FALSE\ )\\
&= (\ (\ (\ \lambda h.\lambda t.\lambda s.s\ h\ t\ )\ 1\ NIL\ )\ FALSE\ )\ (\ \lambda h.\lambda t.FALSE\ )\\
&\rightarrow (\ (\ (\ \lambda t.\lambda s.s\ 1\ t\ )\ NIL\ )\ FALSE\ )\ (\ \lambda h.\lambda t.FALSE\ )\\
&\rightarrow (\ (\ \lambda s.s\ 1\ NIL\ )\ FALSE\ )\ (\ \lambda h.\lambda t.FALSE\ )\\
&\rightarrow (\ FALSE\ 1\ NIL\ )\ (\ \lambda h.\lambda t.FALSE\ )\\
&= (\ (\ \lambda x.\lambda y.y\ )\ 1\ NIL\ )\ (\ \lambda h.\lambda t.FALSE\ )\\
&\rightarrow (\ (\ \lambda y.y\ )\ NIL\ )\ (\ \lambda h.\lambda t.FALSE\ )\\
&\rightarrow NIL\ (\ \lambda h.\lambda t.FALSE\ )\\
&= (\ \lambda x.TRUE\ )\ (\ \lambda h.\lambda t.FALSE\ )\\
&\rightarrow TRUE
\end{aligned}$$

6.8.3 Natural numbers in the pure lambda calculus

Using the representation of lists developed above we can now define the natural numbers by viewing the number *n* as an *n*-element list of objects of arbitrary value. The number 0 then corresponds to the empty list (*NIL*) and similarly the functions *EQ*0 and *PRED* correspond to the list-processing functions *IE* and *TL* respectively. The successor function, *SUCC*, i.e. the function which adds one to a given number *n*, has only to extend the list representing n by one element and so is defined by

$$SUCC = \lambda n.CONS\ ''any''\ n$$

where $''any''$ is any lambda expression.

There have been a variety of suggested representations for constants like the Booleans, natural numbers and lists; the representations given above are by no means unique. An alternative model for the natural numbers, for example, can be found in Barendregt (1984). The important thing to note is that we have found a way of representing the natural numbers and the operations *SUCC*, *PRED* and *EQ*0. Since we also have the *Y*-combinator (as described in Section 6.7), we can implement any recursive function: a consequence of the theory of recursion (Minsky, 1967). So, although the material in this section is only of academic interest to the rest of the book, it serves to exemplify the expressive power of the lambda calculus, even when the δ-rules, which seemed at first to be so important, are omitted.

6.9 The de Bruijn lambda calculus

In the lambda notation it is quite possible to write down two expressions which are semantically identical yet which are syntactically different by virtue of the variables within the expressions having different names. The basic idea behind the canonical lambda calculus of de Bruijn (1972) is to remove all the variable names from a lambda expression and replace them by integers which represent the number of λs between the occurrence of the variable in the function body and the λ which binds it. In this way such expressions become both syntactically and semantically identical. The numerical denotation of each variable can be viewed as an 'offset' or 'depth of nesting' from its binding occurrence and because of this the binding lambda need contain no information about the name of the variable it binds.

As an example of this, the successor function is written in the de Bruijn lambda calculus as:

$$\lambda .\ +\ L0\ 1$$

The more complex lambda expression

$$\lambda x.\lambda y.\lambda f.f\,(\,\lambda x.x\,)\,(\,+\ x\ y\,)$$

has the canonical representation:

$$\lambda .\lambda .\lambda .L0\,(\,\lambda .L0\,)\,(\,+\ L2\ L1\,)$$

Given that there are now no variable names in an expression, there is no equivalent rule to the α-conversion rule of the lambda calculus, and this begs the question as to whether we can now model β-reduction in the presence of free variables. It turns out that we can perform the equivalent of a β-reduction in the lambda calculus (we shall call this $\beta*$-reduction) without any explicit requirement for renaming, but the $\beta*$-reduction rule is more complicated than the β-reduction rule for the lambda calculus because it has to renumber the canonical variables within the function body even though they may not be required to be substituted; this amounts to much the same thing as α-conversion. The interesting property of $\beta*$-reduction in the presence of free variables, however, is that the rather ill-specified notion of α-conversion, i.e. 'renaming the bound variable in the body to make it unique with respect to the free variables of the argument', becomes a formal algorithm – in fact part of the $\beta*$-reduction rule itself – in the de Bruijn lambda calculus. Full details of the reduction rule may be found in Watson *et al.* (1986).

As far as the reduction of lambda expressions is concerned, the use of the de Bruijn representation of expressions offers little more than a formal definition of the renaming rule. However, the notation of the de Bruijn lambda calculus has been used in an implementation scheme called the **categorical abstract machine** which we consider in Chapter 12.

SUMMARY

- The lambda calculus is the calculus of anonymous functions; it comprises a notation for expressions and a set of conversion rules for manipulating them.
- The conversion rules of the lambda calculus are α-conversion which corresponds to renaming; β-conversion which corresponds to function application and η-conversion which corresponds to functional extensionality.
- The lambda calculus can also be augmented with an arbitrary set of constants such as the integers and their associated functions – these are called δ-rules.
- A subexpression which can be simplified, or reduced, using one of the conversion rules or δ-rules is called a reducible expression or redex; an expression with no redexes is called a normal form.
- When there is a choice of redex to reduce, the one chosen is determined by the reduction order. The two extremes are applicative-order and normal-order reduction corresponding loosely to eager and lazy evaluation respectively.
- Normal-order reduction guarantees to terminate if termination is possible; this is called the standardization theorem.
- If two arbitrary reduction sequences both terminate then they both yield the same result; this is a consequence of the Church–Rosser theorem.

- Recursive functions can be handled in the lambda calculus using a special function called the Y-combinator which finds the least fixed point of a function.
- By removing the δ-rules we obtain the pure lambda calculus; despite the absence of those rules all functions can be expressed in the pure lambda calculus.
- In the de Bruijn lambda calculus all variable names are replaced by integers denoting the binding height of the variable; the β-conversion rule can be adapted to this convention.

EXERCISES

6.1 Identify the bound and free variables of each of the following lambda expressions:

(a) $(\lambda x.x\ y)(\lambda y.y)$

(b) $\lambda x.\lambda y.z\ (\lambda z.z\ (\lambda x.y))$

(c) $(\lambda x.\lambda y.x\ z\ (y\ z))(\lambda x.y\ (\lambda y.y))$

6.2 For each of the following expressions:

(i) $\lambda x.\lambda y.(\lambda z.z)\ x\ (+\ y\ 1)$

(ii) $(\lambda x.\lambda y.x\ (\lambda z.y\ z))(((\lambda x.\lambda y.y)\ 8)(\lambda x.(\lambda y.y)\ x))$

(iii) $(\lambda h.(\lambda x.h\ (x\ x))(\lambda x.h\ (x\ x)))((\lambda x.x)(+\ 1\ 5))$

(a) underline all of the redexes indicating whether they are β, η or δ redexes;

(b) identify the leftmost-outermost and leftmost-innermost redexes;

(c) write down the normal form and weak head-normal form of each showing the reduction steps required to reach them assuming normal-order reduction.

6.3 (a) Consider the expression $F = (\lambda T.T\ T)(\lambda f.\lambda x.f\ (f\ x))$. Show how the name clash problem manifests itself by showing the reduction sequence of this expression assuming normal-order evaluation to normal form.

(b) Show that $F\ succ\ 0$ where $succ = \lambda x.\ +\ x\ 1$ evaluates to 4 under normal-order reduction to WHNF.

6.4 Consider the following expression:

$\lambda x.(\lambda y.y)\ 7$

(a) Show that if the expression ever becomes shared then the redex ($\lambda y.y$) 7 is re-evaluated every time the function is applied (assume normal-order reduction to WHNF). In this sense NOR is not optimal.

(b) Can you suggest a modification to NOR which guarantees that such redexes are evaluated at most once?

6.5 (a) Give an example of a function with

(i) many fixed points,

(ii) exactly one fixed point.

(b) What is the *least* fixed point of $\lambda x. * x\ x$? What are its other fixed points?

(c) Justify the solution to Exercise 6.2 part (c) in the case of expression (iii).

6.6 Consider the mutually recursive Hope functions given earlier:

```
--- f( n ) <= if n = 0 then 0 else g( n ) ;
--- g( n ) <= n + f( n − 1 ) ;
```

which has the lambda calculus equivalent

$$Y\,(\,\lambda T.TUPLE\text{-}2\,(\,\lambda n.COND\,(\,=\,n\,0\,)\,0\,(\,(\,INDEX\,2\,T\,)\,n\,)\,)\\(\,\lambda n.\,+\,n\,(\,(INDEX\,1\,T\,)\,(\,-\,n\,1\,)\,)\,)\,)$$

Show the evaluation sequence for the expression $f(\,1\,)$.

6.7 (a) For the pure λ-calculus representation of the Booleans *TRUE* and *FALSE* suggested in Section 6.8.1

(i) show that *TRUE AND TRUE* = *TRUE*,

(ii) define *NOT* and *EXCLUSIVE-OR*.

(b) For the pure λ-calculus representation of the integers suggested in Section 6.8.3 define *PLUS*.

(c) An alternative way to define the integer $n \geq 0$ in the pure λ-calculus is by

$$n = \lambda x.\lambda y.x(\,x\,(\,\ldots\,x(\,y\,)\,\ldots\,)\,)$$

Define *SUCC* for this representation.

6.8 Show the de Bruijn representations of the following lambda expressions:

(a) $\lambda x.\lambda y.y\,(\,\lambda z.z\ x\,)\ x$

(b) $\lambda x.(\,\lambda x..x\ x\,)\,(\,\lambda y.y\,(\,\lambda z.x\,)\,)$

(c) $(\,\lambda x.\,+\,x\,(\,(\,\lambda y.y\,)\,(\,-\,x\,(\,\lambda z.3\,)\,(\,\lambda y.y\ y\,)\,)$

Chapter 7
Type inference systems and type checking

In Part I of this book we saw the value of strongly-typed functional languages in the program design process. In such languages problems may be solved in terms of mappings on compound data objects which have structures that correspond closely to the logic of the solution rather than some target machine. In addition, polymorphism (introduced in Chapter 2) allows generic functions to be defined which can perform the same operation on several data types, each of which is given by an instantiation of the type variables occurring in some polymorphic type. The alternative to polymorphism in a strongly-typed language is to define explicitly a separate version of each function for every data type to which it is applied; the bodies of these definitions being the same. Moreover, if a typed language is backed up by an implementation which provides compile-time type checking, there is no need to maintain type information at run-time, and the compiled code can be assumed to have no type errors so that, for example, functions will always be applied to arguments of the correct type.

Type checking therefore provides two important services. First it finds a high proportion of programming errors at an early stage – many logical errors result in inconsistently typed expressions – so that often erroneous programs need not be run. Secondly, as we have just observed, run-time performance is greatly enhanced since the concern for types can be removed from the compiled code entirely.

In Section 7.1, we illustrate the main issues in inferring the types of functional expressions by considering two examples, and determining their types by solving sets of simultaneous equations representing the type constraints to be satisfied by all their sub-expressions. The procedure for inferring the most general type of an expression in this way may be formalized as a *proof* in a quite simple logical inference system which has only a small number of rules, and in Section 7.2 we consider such a system. Although the formal description of type inference in this way is rigorous and complete in that it enables any expression to be typed (if a valid type exists), it is not obvious how to choose the appropriate sequence of proof steps and so how to automate the procedure. Type checking schemes are algorithms which infer the most general types of expressions deterministically, and may be thought of as guiding the proofs in a type inference system.

In other words, type checkers may be viewed as theorem provers. They normally involve the unification of pairs of type expressions, and are implemented by applying Robinson's unification algorithm (Robinson, 1965) which finds the most general unifier (a substitution for type variables) of a pair of expressions. We are therefore fortunate in that we can be sure that such a scheme must find the most general type as required, which may be proved in part by appealing to Robinson's results. In Section 7.3 we consider the archetypal type checking algorithm $\mathcal{W}$ (Milner, 1978), which is quite simple and which has important soundness and completeness properties. In Section 7.4 we show how $\mathcal{W}$ may be extended so that functions defined by pattern matching may also be type checked and in the final section we consider some circularly defined types that $\mathcal{W}$ cannot infer.

7.1 An informal introduction to type checking

A type is either a type variable, which we shall denote by a Greek letter, or the application of a type operator to an appropriate number of type arguments. The base types such as *num* (integer type) and *truval* (Boolean type) are therefore type operators of no arguments, and *list* is a type operator of one argument. We also use the binary, infix operators → (the function type operator, equivalent to → in Hope) and × (the Cartesian product type operator, equivalent to # in Hope). Types containing at least one type variable are polymorphic (**polytypes**) and types which contain no type variables are monomorphic (**monotypes**). Thus the base types are monotypes, as are the types of many of the primitive functions, such as *succ* : *num* → *num* and *is_zero* : *num* → *truval*. However, not all primitive functions are monomorphic – for example *hd*: *list* $\alpha \rightarrow \alpha$ is polymorphic since it contains the type variable α. Of course expressions with arbitrarily more complex types may be defined, for example the function *map* whose type expression can be written $(\alpha \rightarrow \beta) \times$ *list* $\alpha \rightarrow$ *list* β. We could include an arbitrary number of base types but for the purposes of this discussion *num*, *truval* and *list* will be sufficient to explain all the principles involved.

In type checking an expression, we wish to find the most general type that it can have in the sense that every valid (monomorphic) type it may acquire is an instantiation of that type, i.e. a type obtained when its type variables are assigned particular monotype values. In other words, we need to construct a type inference system, which will either determine the most general type or else deduce that an expression cannot be typed, i.e. that there is inconsistency and so no most general type. If the source program contains user-supplied type declarations, as would a Hope program, then a subsequent type check is required to ensure that the declared type is consistent with the inferred type. For this to be the case the user-supplied type must be obtainable from the inferred type by applying some substitution (which may be the identity) on its type variables. This may appear to require more work than plain inference but for languages with pattern matching in which a function can be defined by a number of equations, the inferred type of each equation can be type checked against the declared type independently of the other equations. This is potentially more efficient than the corresponding type inference, which would have to unify the types inferred from every equation to obtain the most general type.

7.1.1 Two informal type derivations

The type of a functional expression may often be inferred by heuristic methods and in this section we shall consider two examples, the application of the identity function to the number 3, and the polymorphic function *map*. In particular, we will see that polytypes associated with **let-bound** variables (i.e. variables introduced in qualified expressions), which we call generic, must be handled entirely differently from polytypes associated with non-generic, **λ-bound** variables if we are to avoid assigning a wrong type.

The basic idea may be seen by considering the application of a function f to an expression e. If we know that the type of e is σ, then we can immediately infer that the type of f is $\sigma \rightarrow \rho$ for some type ρ to be inferred. Hence we can type purely applicative expressions recursively, the innermost expressions with known types providing the base cases. If we include qualified expressions then the situation is more complicated since an identifier will be assigned a type twice (i.e. in the qualifier and the resultant), so we must unify these types to find its most general type.

First then, consider the expression E given by

let $f\,x = x$ **in** $f\,3$

which is written in a form of functional 'pseudocode'. For this to be consistent with respect to the types of its sub-expressions, we require the equations below to be satisfied, in which we denote the type of an identifier *ide* by σ_{ide}, and unknown types by $\rho_i\,(\,i > 0\,)$:

$\sigma_3 = num$	(base type)	**(1)**
$\sigma_f = num \rightarrow \rho_1$	(f 3 is an application)	**(2)**
$\sigma_x = \rho_2$	(type of x is unknown)	**(3)**
$\sigma_f = \rho_2 \rightarrow \rho_3$	($f\,x$ is an application)	**(4)**
$\rho_3 = \rho_2$	(two sides of = must have the same type)	**(5)**

(We have omitted an equation for the sub-expression x in $f\,x$. This would give $\sigma_x = \rho_4$, say, and we would then get $\sigma_f = \rho_4 \rightarrow \rho_3$, but from the two equations for σ_x we would have $\rho_2 = \rho_4$, giving the same result.)

The solution to these equations is at once seen to be $\rho_2 = num$, $\rho_1 = \rho_3$ (unifying equations (2) and (4)), $\rho_3 = \rho_2$ (equation (5)), so that $\rho_1 = \rho_2 = \rho_3 = num$, and the type of $f\,3$ is $\rho_1 = num$ as expected. The fact that we can find a solution at all proves the expression E is type-correct.

This also works for polymorphic expressions. Consider the following version of the map function expressed using the primitive selector functions *null*, *nil*, *cons*, *hd* and *tl* rather than by pattern matching:

```
map( f, m ) = if   null( m )
              then nil
              else cons( f( hd( m ) ), map( f, tl( m ) ) )
```

Because the primitive list-processing functions are polymorphic we assign new unknown types, $\tau_1, \tau_2, \ldots$ to their type variables. These type variables are generic in that each occurrence is instantiated with a different unknown type, although in this example there is only one occurrence of each. We therefore begin by making the following assignments:

$$\sigma_{null} = list\ \tau_1 \rightarrow truval$$
$$\sigma_{nil} = list\ \tau_2$$
$$\sigma_{hd} = list\ \tau_3 \rightarrow \tau_3$$
$$\sigma_{tl} = list\ \tau_4 \rightarrow list\ \tau_4$$
$$\sigma_{cons} = (\,\tau_5 \times list\ \tau_5\,) \rightarrow list\ \tau_5$$

Proceeding as in the example above, we now write down equations which ensure the type consistency of every sub-expression in the definition of *map*. Beginning with the left-hand side, we obtain the following equations:

$$\sigma_{map} = \sigma_f \times \sigma_m \rightarrow \rho_1 \quad \text{for some unknown type variable } \rho_1 \tag{1}$$
$$\sigma_{null} = \sigma_m \rightarrow truval \tag{2}$$
$$\sigma_{hd} = \sigma_m \rightarrow \rho_2 \tag{3}$$
$$\sigma_f = \rho_2 \rightarrow \rho_4 \tag{4}$$
$$\sigma_{tl} = \sigma_m \rightarrow \rho_3 \tag{5}$$
$$\sigma_{map} = \sigma_f \times \rho_3 \rightarrow \rho_5 \tag{6}$$
$$\sigma_{cons} = \rho_4 \times \rho_5 \rightarrow \rho_6 \tag{7}$$

Finally, we need equations which ensure that both branches of the conditional expression have the same type, which is also the type of the whole conditional, and that the two sides of the equation defining *map* have the same type. Together, these equations are:

$$\rho_1 = \sigma_{nil} = \rho_6 \tag{8}$$

The above set of eight equations, together with those given for the instantiated primitive identifiers, would in general be solved by the kind of unification-based algorithm we will consider in Section 7.3, but for now we proceed directly. From equation (2) and the equation for *null* we have

$$\sigma_m = list\ \tau_1$$

and from equation (3) and the equation for *hd*

$$\sigma_m = list\ \tau_3 \qquad \text{and} \qquad \rho_2 = \tau_3$$

Proceeding through equations (4)–(7) similarly, we obtain

$$\rho_3 = \sigma_m = list\ \tau_4$$
$$\rho_3 = \sigma_m \ \text{ and } \ \rho_5 = \rho_1 \qquad \text{(comparing the two equations for } \sigma_{map}\text{)}$$
$$\rho_4 = \tau_5$$
$$\rho_5 = list\ \tau_5$$
$$\rho_6 = list\ \tau_5$$

Using these equations and equation (8), we therefore obtain the solution

$$\rho_1 = \rho_5 = \rho_6 = list\ \tau_2 = list\ \tau_5 \qquad \text{so that } \tau_2 = \tau_5$$
$$\rho_2 = \tau_1 = \tau_3 = \tau_4 \qquad \text{(using the equations for } \sigma_m\text{)}$$
$$\rho_3 = \sigma_m = list\ \tau_1$$
$$\rho_4 = \tau_5 = \tau_2$$

Finally, we obtain $\sigma_f = \rho_2 \rightarrow \rho_4$, so that $\sigma_{map} = (\tau_1 \rightarrow \tau_2) \times list\ \tau_1 \rightarrow list\ \tau_2$. Since the types τ_1, τ_2 are arbitrary, we conclude that the polymorphic type of *map* is

$$(\alpha \rightarrow \beta) \times list\ \alpha \rightarrow list\ \beta$$

as expected.

7.1.2 Generic type variables

These examples produced no particular difficulties, but now consider the function *g* given by

$$g = \lambda f.(\ f\ 3,\ f\ true\ )$$

This expression cannot be typed, since we cannot know the polymorphic characteristics of the argument (λ-bound) variable f. The first occurrence of f requires that its instantiated type be $num \rightarrow \alpha$ whereas the second requires $truval \rightarrow \alpha$. The type variables appearing in the type of a λ-bound identifier like f are **non-generic** since, as we can see in this example, they are shared in every occurrence of f in the function body, and some instantiations may conflict. If we gave *g* the type $(\alpha \rightarrow \beta) \rightarrow (\beta \times \beta)$ the expression would evaluate correctly when applied to certain arguments, such as $\lambda x.0$, when the result would be (0, 0). However, the successor function, *succ*, has a type which is an instantiation of $\alpha \rightarrow \beta$ and so is a valid argument to *g*, but will cause a computation to go wrong when it is applied to *true*. This typing is therefore unsound in general, which is why we say that *g* cannot be typed. In fact there are sound extensions to the typing system of Milner that we consider in this chapter, which could type *g*, but these are beyond the scope of this book.

An apparently similar example is the expression

$$\textbf{let}\ f = \lambda x.x\ \textbf{in}\ (\ f\ 3,\ f\ true\ )$$

which we surely must be able to type if polymorphism is to be useful. In fact we can, because now f is a let-bound identifier which is local to the expression, so that we know exactly how it is defined and can use this information to deal with each of its occurrences individually. Here, f has type $\alpha \rightarrow \alpha$, which can be instantiated to $num \rightarrow num$ for the application to 3, and to $truval \rightarrow truval$ for the application to *true*. In the previous example, f acquires its type from the argument to which *g* is applied, and we cannot know exactly how every such argument is defined so that corresponding instantiations are not possible in general. A type variable like α which occurs in the type of a let-bound identifier is called **generic** and has the property of being able to assume different values for different occurrences of the identifier, provided it does not also occur in the type of an enclosing λ-bound identifier. If we try to get round the problem of the previous example by defining

$$\lambda g.\mathbf{let}\ f = g\ \mathbf{in}\ (\ f\ 3,\ f\ true\ )$$

we achieve nothing! Again, an application of this expression to *succ* will go wrong, the reason being that any type variables in the type of f are still not generic, even though f is let-bound, since they appear in the type of the λ-bound identifier g.

To summarize, a type variable occurring in the type of an expression E is generic iff it does not occur in the type of the bound variable identifier of any λ-abstraction of which E is a sub-expression.

Before specifying a type inference system formally in the next section, we should point out how recursive qualified expressions are handled. To do this we rely on the fixed point operator, **fix** (given by the Y-combinator of the lambda calculus) and treat a declaration of the form

$$\mathbf{let}\ f = \ldots f \ldots \mathbf{in} \ldots f \ldots$$

as if the definition of f were expanded to give the non-recursive form

$$\mathbf{let}\ f = \mathbf{fix}\ f.\ \ldots f \ldots \mathbf{in} \ldots f \ldots$$

where **fix** $x.e$ may be considered as $Y\lambda x.e$ although for type inference purposes **fix** need not yield the *least* fixed point.

The complete syntax of the expressions for which we will infer types in the next two sections is therefore as follows:

$$\begin{aligned}\langle exp\rangle ::= {} & \langle id\rangle \mid \mathbf{if}\ \langle exp\rangle\ \mathbf{then}\ \langle exp\rangle\ \mathbf{else}\ \langle exp\rangle \mid \lambda\langle id\rangle.\langle exp\rangle \mid \\ & \langle exp\rangle\langle exp\rangle \mid \mathbf{let}\ \langle id\rangle = \langle exp\rangle\ \mathbf{in}\ \langle exp\rangle \mid \\ & \mathbf{fix}\ \langle id\rangle.\langle exp\rangle \\ \langle id\rangle ::= {} & identifier\end{aligned}$$

7.2 A type inference system

In the preceding discussion, we have abbreviated our notation slightly by omitting the quantifier 'for all', written $\forall$, from type expressions. For example, when we wrote $\alpha \to \beta$ we really meant $\forall\alpha.\forall\beta.\alpha \to \beta$. In Milner's type system on which this chapter is based, all type variables are universally quantified at the top level and quantifiers cannot be nested inside type expressions. Thus we will be concerned exclusively with so-called **shallow** types, where a type is shallow if it is of the form $\forall\alpha_1 \ldots \forall\alpha_n.\tau\ (\ n \geq 0\ )$ and there are no quantifiers in τ. Although the inference system allows the construction of non-shallow types, we do not have a type checking algorithm which can infer them. Of course, since all our types are shallow, we could omit the quantifiers since they are implicit, but we retain them since they explain clearly the distinction between generic and non-generic type variables which correspond exactly to free and quantified type variables respectively.

We now give a set of eight inference rules, due to Cardelli (1984), the first of which is an axiom and the rest of which are proper inferences. The notation $A \vdash e : \tau$ means 'from the set of assumptions A we can deduce that the expression e has type τ' (the $\vdash$ symbol is called **turnstile**). An assumption is an association of a type τ with a variable x, written $x : \tau$, and $A.x : \tau$ denotes the set of assumptions formed by adding $x : \tau$ to A which does not already contain a typing for x.

The notation

$$\frac{A}{B}$$

is read 'from A we can infer B'. Our final piece of notation is that $[\,\sigma / \alpha\,]\,\tau$ is the result of substituting σ for all free occurrences of α in the type expression τ (assuming α does not occur in the scope of a universally quantified variable named σ). The rules are as follows:

Variables $$A.x : \tau \vdash x : \tau \qquad [VAR]$$

Conditionals $$\frac{A \vdash e : \mathit{truval} \quad A \vdash e' : \tau \quad A \vdash e'' : \tau}{A \vdash (\,\mathbf{if}\ e\ \mathbf{then}\ e'\ \mathbf{else}\ e''\,) : \tau} \qquad [COND]$$

Abstractions $$\frac{A.x : \sigma \vdash e : \tau}{A \vdash (\,\lambda x.e\,) : \sigma \rightarrow \tau} \qquad [ABS]$$

Applications $$\frac{A \vdash e : \sigma \rightarrow \tau \quad A \vdash e' : \sigma}{A \vdash (\,e\,e'\,) : \tau} \qquad [APP]$$

Let expressions $$\frac{A \vdash e' : \sigma \quad A.x : \sigma \vdash e : \tau}{A \vdash (\,\mathbf{let}\ x = e'\ \mathbf{in}\ e\,) : \tau} \qquad [LET]$$

Fixed point $$\frac{A.x : \tau \vdash e : \tau}{A \vdash (\,\mathbf{fix}\ x.e\,) : \tau} \qquad [FIX]$$

Generalization $$\frac{A \vdash e : \tau}{A \vdash e : \forall \alpha.\tau} \quad (\alpha \text{ not free in } A) \qquad [GEN]$$

Specialization $$\frac{A \vdash e : \forall \alpha.\tau}{A \vdash e : [\,\sigma / \alpha\,]\,\tau} \qquad [SPEC]$$

As a simple illustration of how these rules may be used to infer the type of an expression, consider the identity function ($\lambda x.x$). The most general type of this expression can be deduced as follows:

$$\cfrac{\cfrac{x : \alpha \vdash x : \alpha \quad [VAR]}{\vdash (\lambda x.x) : \alpha \rightarrow \alpha \quad [ABS]}}{\vdash (\lambda x.x) : \forall\alpha.\alpha \rightarrow \alpha \quad [GEN]}$$

A specialized type for the identity function can be deduced using [*SPEC*] thus:

$$\frac{\vdash (\lambda x.x) : \forall\alpha.\alpha \rightarrow \alpha}{\vdash (\lambda x.x) : num \rightarrow num \quad [SPEC]}$$

The same deduction could have been made more directly had we allocated the type *num* to α in the first place. We would then have obtained

$$\frac{x : num \vdash x : num \quad [VAR]}{\vdash (\lambda x.x) : num \rightarrow num \quad [ABS]}$$

We can infer that the type of ($\lambda x.x$) 3 is *num*:

$$\cfrac{\cfrac{3 : num, x : num \vdash x : num \quad [VAR]}{3 : num \vdash (\lambda x.x) : num \rightarrow num \ [ABS]} \qquad 3 : num \vdash 3 : num \quad [VAR]}{3 : num \vdash ((\lambda x.x)\ 3) : num \quad [APP]}$$

In fact, this system can infer types for expressions which our algorithm will not be able to type. The simplest example is ($\lambda x.x\,x$), which involves the forbidden self-application $x\,x$. Denoting the type $\forall\alpha.\alpha \rightarrow \alpha$ by ϕ we obtain

$$\cfrac{\cfrac{\cfrac{x : \phi \vdash x : \phi \quad [VAR]}{x : \phi \vdash x : \phi \rightarrow \phi \quad [SPEC]} \qquad x : \phi \vdash x : \phi \quad [VAR]}{x : \phi \vdash x\,x : \phi \quad [APP]}}{\vdash (\lambda x.x\,x) : \phi \rightarrow \phi \quad [ABS]}$$

Apart from the initial 'eureka-step' $x : \phi \vdash x : \phi$, the key step in the proof is the use of [*SPEC*] which substitutes $\forall\alpha.\alpha \rightarrow \alpha$ for α producing a non-shallow type. Now let us reconsider our earlier example **let** $f = \lambda x.x$ **in** ($f\,3, f\,true$). It will be convenient for the purposes of this discussion to represent the resultant tuple by an application of the *tuple*-2 function (of type $\alpha \to \beta \to \alpha \times \beta$) introduced in Chapter 6. This is simply because we do not yet have any inference rules for tuples. To this end we shall rewrite the expression as follows:

$$\textbf{let } f = \lambda x.x \textbf{ in } \textit{tuple-2} \; (f \; 3) \; (f \; \textit{true})$$

Let the assumption set $A = \{ 3 : \textit{num}, \textit{true} : \textit{truval}, \textit{tuple-2} : \forall\alpha.\forall\beta.\alpha \to \beta \to \alpha \times \beta \}$ and $\phi = \forall\alpha.\alpha \to \alpha$ as above. The type is given by the following proof:

$$\frac{\dfrac{A.f{:}\,\phi \vdash f{:}\,\phi}{A.f{:}\,\phi \vdash f{:}\, \textit{num} \to \textit{num}} \qquad A.f{:}\,\phi \vdash 3 : \textit{num}}{A.f{:}\,\phi \vdash f\,3 : \textit{num}}$$

$$\frac{\dfrac{A.f{:}\,\phi \vdash f{:}\,\phi}{A.f{:}\,\phi \vdash f{:}\, \textit{truval} \to \textit{truval}} \qquad A.f{:}\,\phi \vdash \textit{true} : \textit{truval}}{A.f{:}\,\phi \vdash f\,\textit{true} : \textit{truval}}$$

$$\frac{\dfrac{\dfrac{\dfrac{A \vdash \textit{tuple-2} : \forall\alpha.\forall\beta.\alpha \to \beta \to \alpha \times \beta}{A \vdash \textit{tuple-2} : \forall\beta.\textit{num} \to \beta \to \textit{num} \times \beta}}{A \vdash \textit{tuple-2} : \textit{num} \to \textit{truval} \to \textit{num} \times \textit{truval}} \qquad A.f{:}\,\phi \vdash f\,3 : \textit{num}}{A.f{:}\,\phi \vdash \textit{tuple-2} \; (f\,3) : \textit{truval} \to \textit{num} \times \textit{truval}} \quad A.f{:}\,\phi \vdash f\,\textit{true} : \textit{truval}}{A.f{:}\,\phi \vdash \textit{tuple-2} \; (f\,3) \; (f\,\textit{true}) : \textit{num} \times \textit{truval}}$$

Finally, using our result for the identity function, we obtain

$$\frac{A \vdash \lambda x.x : \phi \qquad A.f{:}\,\phi \vdash \textit{tuple-2} \; (f\,3) \; (f\,\textit{true}) : \textit{num} \times \textit{truval}}{A \vdash (\textbf{let } f = \lambda x.x \textbf{ in } \textit{tuple-2} \; (f\,3) \; (f\,\textit{true})) : \textit{num} \times \textit{truval}}$$

However, in typing the equivalent expression ($\lambda f.\textit{tuple-2} \; (f\,3) \; (f\,\textit{true})$) ($\lambda x.x$), it is not possible to deduce a shallow type for $\lambda f.\textit{tuple-2} \; (f\,3) \; (f\,\textit{true})$; a non-shallow type derivable by a similar proof (starting with $f{:}\, \alpha \to \beta$) is $(\forall\alpha.\forall\beta.\alpha \to \beta) \to (\forall\gamma.\forall\delta.\gamma \times \delta)$.

We can now clearly distinguish between generic and non-generic type variables. If a variable appears in the type of a λ-bound identifier, it must occur in the assumption set in order that [*ABS*] can be applied subsequently. Hence a variable is generic if it does not appear in the set of assumptions, whereupon we can apply [*GEN*] and introduce a quantifier. There is therefore a precise correspondence between generic variables and quantifiers.

The steps used in the above proofs were certainly not all obvious *a priori*, and for practical type checking we need to automate the proof procedures in this inference system. In fact by extracting an algorithm from it, such as that given in the next section, we may view that algorithm as a **proof heuristic**, i.e. a strategy for determining the order in which to apply the rules. There is a formal way of relating the above inference system to type checking algorithms, and in particular it can be proved that if the algorithm succeeds in finding a type for an expression, then that type can be deduced from the inference system. A closely related analysis is given by Milner (1978).

7.3 The type checking algorithm $\mathcal{W}$

In devising a function for type inference, more commonly known as an algorithm for type checking, there are a number of syntactic and semantic issues that must be considered. First, a syntactic typing scheme must be defined which assigns a unique (most general) type to each valid expression in the syntax; such expressions are called **well typed** and their types are called **well-typings**. Secondly, it should be shown that the typing scheme is **semantically sound**, i.e. every expression which is syntactically well typed is also semantically free from type violation. Thus, when a well typed expression is executed, all its primitive functions are sure to be applied to objects of the appropriate type. Thirdly, the algorithm should be **syntactically sound**, meaning that if it succeeds in finding a type for an expression then that expression is well typed. Finally, we would also like a type checking algorithm to be complete in the sense that if an expression has a well-typing, the algorithm will succeed in finding a typing for it which is at least as general. We will not consider such theoretical aspects in this book, referring the reader to Milner (1978) instead. Our version of the algorithm $\mathcal{W}$ is a slight variant of Milner's, and corresponds more closely with the inference system described in the previous section. We express it in the form of a function.

$\mathcal{W}$ computes the most general type of an expression if a shallow well-typing exists, or else fails. It is based upon Robinson's unification algorithm:

Theorem 7.1 (Robinson, 1965)

There is an algorithm $\mathcal{V}$, which takes any pair of expressions σ, τ (over some alphabet of variables), such that either $\mathcal{V}(\sigma, \tau)$ succeeds, yielding a substitution U with the properties that:

(1) $U\sigma = U\tau$, i.e. U unifies σ and τ

(2) If R unifies σ and τ, then for some substitution S, $R = SU$

(3) U involves only variables occurring in σ and τ

or else $\mathcal{V}(\sigma, \tau)$ fails.

It is property (2) when $\mathcal{U}$ succeeds which ensures that U is the most general unifier. In our case, the expressions are type expressions and the alphabet is the set of type variables. Thus, for example, $\mathcal{U}(\alpha, \alpha)$ succeeds with substitution $U = I$ (the identity substitution) and $\mathcal{U}(\alpha \to \beta, num \to num)$ succeeds with substitution $U = [\,num / \alpha, num / \beta\,]$, where the substitution of the variables α_i by the respective expressions σ_i ($1 \leq i \leq n$) is denoted by $[\sigma_1 / \alpha_1, \ldots, \sigma_n / \alpha_n]$. However, $\mathcal{U}(\alpha \to truval, num \to num)$ fails.

For completeness, we now define a function which implements $\mathcal{U}$, based upon the idea of a **disagreement pair** of type expressions. Informally, given terms e, e' (here type expressions), their disagreement pair, $D(e, e')$ contains the first two sub-terms in e and e' respectively which differ; if $e = e'$, the components are both null, and we denote this pair by $\pi = (\,,\,)$. Thus, for example, $D(num \to num, \alpha \to num) = (num, \alpha)$, $D(\alpha, \alpha \to \beta) = (\alpha, \alpha \to \beta)$, $D(num \to num, num \to num) = \pi$, $D(\gamma \to num \to \beta, (\alpha \to num) \to num) = (\gamma, \alpha \to num)$. Note that the types concerned in the last case cannot be unified. It is simplest to give the precise definition of the disagreement pair in the form of a function. Suppose that every type expression is written in the form $T_i(\sigma_1, \ldots, \sigma_{n(i)})$ ($i \geq 1$) where T_i denotes a type operation of arity $n(i)$, the number of such operations being countable, and σ_j denotes a type expression ($j \geq 1$). Thus, for example, we write $\alpha \to (\beta \times \gamma)$ as $\to(\alpha, \times(\beta, \gamma))$ and a base type such as *num* with arity 0 as *num*.
Our disagreement pair function might therefore be

$$
\begin{aligned}
& D(T_i(\sigma_1, \ldots, \sigma_{n(i)}), T_j(\tau_1, \ldots, \tau_{n(j)})) \\
& \qquad = \textbf{if } T_i \neq T_j \\
& \qquad\quad \textbf{then } (T_i(\sigma_1, \ldots, \sigma_{n(i)}), T_j(\tau_1, \ldots, \tau_{n(j)})) \\
& \qquad\quad \textbf{else if } n(i) = 0 \\
& \qquad\qquad \textbf{then } \pi \\
& \qquad\qquad \textbf{else } D'(1) \\
& \textbf{where } D'(k) = \textbf{if } k = n(i) \\
& \qquad\quad \textbf{then } D(\sigma_k, \tau_k) \\
& \qquad\quad \textbf{else if } D(\sigma_k, \tau_k) = \pi \\
& \qquad\qquad \textbf{then } D'(k+1) \\
& \qquad\qquad \textbf{else } D(\sigma_k, \tau_k)
\end{aligned}
$$

A unification function,

$$\mathcal{U}: term \times term \to substitution$$

may then be defined in terms of the auxiliary function

$$unify : substitution \times term \times term \to substitution$$

as follows:

$$
\begin{aligned}
\mathcal{V}(\, e, e' \,) \quad &= unify(\, I, e, e' \,) \\
unify(\, S, e, e' \,) &= \textbf{if } Se = Se' \\
&\quad \textbf{then } S \\
&\quad \textbf{else let } (\, u, v \,) = D(\, Se, Se' \,) \textbf{ in} \\
&\quad\quad \textbf{if } u \text{ is a variable not occurring in } v \\
&\quad\quad \textbf{then } unify(\, [\, v \,/\, u \,]S, e, e' \,) \\
&\quad\quad \textbf{else if } v \text{ is a variable not occurring in } u \\
&\quad\quad\quad \textbf{then } unify(\, [\, u \,/\, v \,]S, e, e' \,) \\
&\quad\quad\quad \textbf{else } FAIL
\end{aligned}
$$

The composition of two substitutions S and T is denoted by their juxtaposition ST; for example $(\,[\, v \,/\, u \,]S\,)\tau$ is the term obtained by replacing the variable u by the term v in the term $S\tau$. We have omitted the straightforward definitions of the functions which check if u or v is a variable and if so whether u or v occurs in v or u respectively. If neither u nor v is a variable then the unification must fail, but according to the definition it will also fail if u is a variable occurring in v (which could not then be a variable) or v is a variable occurring in u. In either of these situations, there is the possibility of a cyclic substitution resulting in the unification algorithm looping indefinitely and so the unification aborts assuming a failure. This simple check for possible cycles is called an **occurs check**. Although the occurs check prevents non-termination of the unification it can result in a unifier not being found when one does actually exist (in other words the cycle might never happen) and because of this there will be certain perfectly valid circular types which an implementation of $\mathcal{W}$ using this algorithm will fail to infer. We shall return to this issue later on.

We can see how the function works by tracing through the following simple example:

$$
\begin{aligned}
&\mathcal{V}(\, \alpha \to \beta, \beta \to \gamma \,) = unify(\, I, \alpha \to \beta, \beta \to \gamma \,) \\
&\qquad\qquad\qquad\qquad\quad = unify(\, [\, \beta \,/\, \alpha \,], \alpha \to \beta, \beta \to \gamma \,) \\
&\text{since } D(\, \alpha \to \beta, \beta \to \gamma \,) = (\, \alpha, \beta \,) \\
&\qquad\qquad\qquad\qquad\quad = unify(\, [\, \gamma \,/\, \beta \,][\, \beta \,/\, \alpha \,], \alpha \to \beta, \beta \to \gamma \,) \\
&\text{since } D(\, [\, \beta \,/\, \alpha \,](\, \alpha \to \beta \,), [\, \beta \,/\, \alpha \,](\, \beta \to \gamma \,)\,) = D(\, \beta \to \beta, \beta \to \gamma \,) = (\, \beta, \gamma \,) \\
&\qquad\qquad\qquad\qquad\quad = [\, \gamma \,/\, \beta \,][\, \beta \,/\, \alpha \,] \\
&\text{since } [\, \gamma \,/\, \beta \,][\, \beta \,/\, \alpha \,](\, \alpha \to \beta \,) = [\, \gamma \,/\, \beta \,][\, \beta \,/\, \alpha \,](\, \beta \to \gamma \,) = \gamma \to \gamma \\
&\qquad\qquad\qquad\qquad\quad = [\, \gamma \,/\, \beta, \beta \,/\, \alpha \,]
\end{aligned}
$$

Returning now to $\mathcal{W}$, given a set of assumptions A (assigning types to variables as in the previous section) and expression e, if $\mathcal{W}$ succeeds, then $\mathcal{W}(\, A, e \,) = (\, T, \tau \,)$ where τ is the most general type of e and T is the substitution for which TA defines the corresponding type assignments to the type variables in A. In fact T is only returned as part of the result to enable the recursion in the definition of $\mathcal{W}$ to proceed. The complete 'algorithm' is as follows:

$$\mathcal{W}(A, e) = (T, \tau) \text{ where}$$

(a) If e is the identifier x, then $T = I$ and if $x : \forall \alpha_1 \ldots \alpha_n.\sigma \in A$, then

$$\tau = [\beta_1 / \alpha_1] \ldots [\beta_n / \alpha_n]\sigma$$

where $\{ \beta_i \mid 1 \leq i \leq n \}$ are new type variables.

(b) If $e = f\,g$, let

$$\begin{aligned} (R, \rho) &= \mathcal{W}(A, f) \\ (S, \sigma) &= \mathcal{W}(RA, g) \\ U &= \mathcal{V}(S\rho, \sigma \to \beta) \end{aligned}$$

where β is new. Then $T = USR$ and $\tau = U\beta$.

(c) If $e =$ **if** p **then** f **else** f', let

$$\begin{aligned} (R, \rho) &= \mathcal{W}(A, p) \\ U &= \mathcal{V}(\rho, \mathit{truval}) \\ (S, \sigma) &= \mathcal{W}(URA, f) \\ (S', \sigma') &= \mathcal{W}(SURA, f') \\ U' &= \mathcal{V}(S'\sigma, \sigma'). \end{aligned}$$

Then $T = U'S'SUR$ and $\tau = U'\sigma'$.

(d) If $e = \lambda x.f$, let

$$(R, \rho) = \mathcal{W}(A.x : \beta, f)$$

where β is new. Then $T = R$ and $\tau = R\beta \to \rho$.

(e) If $e =$ **fix** $x.f$, let

$$(R, \rho) = \mathcal{W}(A.x : \beta, f)$$

where β is new, $U = \mathcal{V}(R\beta, \rho)$. Then $T = UR$ and $\tau = UR\beta$.

(f) If $e =$ **let** $x = f$ **in** g, let

$$\begin{aligned} (R, \rho) &= \mathcal{W}(A, f) \\ (S, \sigma) &= \mathcal{W}(RA.x : \rho', g) \end{aligned}$$

where $\rho' = \forall \alpha_1 \ldots \alpha_n.\rho$ and $\alpha_1, \ldots, \alpha_n$ are the free variables in ρ which do not appear in RA. Then $T = SR$ and $\tau = \sigma$.

Recalling our discussion in the previous section on the relationship between generic variables and universal quantification, we can see that in (a) the new type variables β_i replace only the generic variables in the type of x, which can therefore be instantiated independently of their occurrences in other types; this corresponds to the use of the inference rule [*SPEC*]. Conversely in (f), all free variables in the type assigned to x which do not occur in the assumptions *RA* are universally quantified since these are generic; this corresponds to the immediate application of [*GEN*] as many times as possible.

Examples illustrating the operation of $\mathcal{W}$ tend to be extremely tedious, and we shall consider the main steps in two: first for the function that we used to demonstrate the difference between generic and non-generic variables in Section 7.2, and then for a recursive function which finds the length of a list, so that all six cases of the algorithm will be required. All βs and subscripted βs will denote new type variables. We will use two different results for the type of a single variable corresponding to the non-generic and generic cases respectively:

$$\mathcal{W}(A.x : \alpha, x) = (I, \alpha)$$
$$\mathcal{W}(A.x : \alpha, x) = (I, \beta)$$

These both follow from case (a), and by (d) we immediately obtain

$$\begin{aligned} &\mathcal{W}(A, \lambda x.x) = (R, (R\beta) \to \rho) \\ &\text{where } (R, \rho) = \mathcal{W}(A.x : \beta, x) = (I, \beta) \\ &\qquad\qquad = (I, \beta \to \beta) \end{aligned}$$

Now consider the expression

$$e = \textbf{let } f = \lambda x.x \textbf{ in } \textit{tuple-}2\ (f\ 3)\ (f\ \textit{true})$$

and the set of assumptions

$$\begin{aligned} &A = \{ 3 : \textit{num}, \textit{true} : \textit{truval}, \textit{tuple-}2 : \varepsilon \to \delta \to \varepsilon \times \delta \} \\ &\mathcal{W}(A, e) = (S_1 R_1, \sigma_1) \\ &\text{where } (R_1, \rho_1) = \mathcal{W}(A, \lambda x.x) = (I, \beta_1 \to \beta_1) \qquad \text{as we have just seen} \\ &\qquad (S_1, \sigma_1) = \mathcal{W}(A_\alpha, \textit{tuple-}2\ (f\ 3)\ (f\ \textit{true})) \\ &\qquad \text{where } A_\alpha = A.f : \forall\alpha.\alpha \to \alpha \qquad \text{by case (f).} \end{aligned}$$

Thus, by repeatedly applying (b), we obtain

$$\begin{aligned} &(S_1, \sigma_1) = (U_1 S_2 R_2, U_1 \beta_2) \\ &\text{where } (R_2, \rho_2) = \mathcal{W}(A_\alpha, \textit{tuple-}2\ (f\ 3)) \\ &\qquad (S_2, \sigma_2) = \mathcal{W}(R_2 A_\alpha, (f\ \textit{true})) \\ &\qquad U_1 = \mathcal{U}(S_2 \rho_2, \sigma_2 \to \beta_2) \end{aligned}$$

$$
\begin{aligned}
&(R_2, \rho_2) = (U_2 S_3 R_3, U_2 \beta_3)\\
&\text{where } (R_3, \rho_3) = \mathscr{W}(A_\alpha, \textit{tuple-2}) = (I, \varepsilon \to \delta \to (\varepsilon \times \delta))\\
&\qquad (S_3, \sigma_3) = \mathscr{W}(IA_\alpha, (f\ 3))\\
&\qquad U_2 = \mathscr{V}(S_3\rho_3, \sigma_3 \to \beta_3)
\end{aligned}
$$

$$
\begin{aligned}
&(S_3, \sigma_3) = (U_3 S_4 R_4, U_3 \beta_4)\\
&\text{where } (R_4, \rho_4) = \mathscr{W}(A_\alpha, f) = (I, \beta_5 \to \beta_5)\\
&\qquad (S_4, \sigma_4) = \mathscr{W}(IA_\alpha, 3) = (I, \textit{num})\\
&\qquad U_3 = \mathscr{V}(S_4\rho_4, \sigma_4 \to \beta_4) = \mathscr{V}(\beta_5 \to \beta_5, \textit{num} \to \beta_4)\\
&\qquad\quad = [\textit{num} / \beta_5, \textit{num} / \beta_4]
\end{aligned}
$$

so that

$$S_3 = U_3, \sigma_3 = \textit{num}$$

and

$$
\begin{aligned}
&U_2 = \mathscr{V}(\varepsilon \to \delta \to (\varepsilon \times \delta), \textit{num} \to \beta_3) = [\textit{num} / \varepsilon, \delta \to (\textit{num} \times \delta) / \beta_3]\\
&R_2 = U_2 U_3 \quad (\text{since } R_3 = I), \rho_2 = \delta \to (\textit{num} \times \delta)
\end{aligned}
$$

Similarly,

$$
\begin{aligned}
&(S_2, \sigma_2) = (U_4 S_5 R_5, U_4 \beta_6)\\
&\text{where } (R_5, \rho_5) = \mathscr{W}(R_2 A_\alpha, f) = (I, \beta_7 \to \beta_7)\\
&\qquad (S_5, \sigma_5) = (I, \textit{truval})\\
&\qquad U_4 = \mathscr{V}(\beta_7 \to \beta_7, \textit{truval} \to \beta_6) = [\textit{truval} / \beta_7, \textit{truval} / \beta_6]
\end{aligned}
$$

so that

$$S_2 = U_4, \sigma_2 = \textit{truval}$$

Thus,

$$U_1 = \mathscr{V}(\delta \to (\textit{num} \times \delta), \textit{truval} \to \beta_2) = [\textit{truval} / \delta, (\textit{num} \times \textit{truval}) / \beta_2]$$

and

$$S_1 = U_1 U_4 U_2 U_3, \sigma_1 = \textit{num} \times \textit{truval}, R_1 = I$$

so that

$$\mathscr{W}(A, e) = (S_1, \textit{num} \times \textit{truval})$$

As with the inference system that we considered in the previous section, note how the generic variable α in the type of f was instantiated to the different types β_5 and β_7, subsequently unified to *num* and *truval* respectively.

For our second example, we express the function *length*, which finds the length of a list, in a non-recursive form that is suitable for the application of $\mathscr{W}$, namely

$$length = \mathbf{fix}\ f.\lambda x.e \text{ where } e = \mathbf{if}\ null\ x\ \mathbf{then}\ 0\ \mathbf{else}\ succ\ (\ f\ (\ tl\ x\ )\ )$$

and we use the set of assumptions

$$A = \{\ null : list\ \alpha_1 \to truval,\ tl : list\ \alpha_2 \to list\ \alpha_2,\ 0 : num,\ succ : num \to num\ \}$$

Then we have, by (e) of $\mathscr{W}$,

$$\begin{aligned} &\mathscr{W}(\ A, length\ ) = (\ U_0R_1,\ U_0\ R_1\beta_1\ ) \\ &\text{where } (\ R_1, \rho_1) = \mathscr{W}(\ A.f : \beta_1, \lambda x.e\ ) \\ &\qquad U_0 = \mathscr{V}(\ R_1\ \beta_1, \rho_1\ ) \end{aligned}$$

Thus,

$$\begin{aligned} &(\ R_1, \rho_1\ ) = (\ R_2, R_2\beta_2 \to \rho_2\ ) \qquad \text{by (d)} \\ &\text{where } (\ R_2, \rho_2\ ) = \mathscr{W}(\ A_2, e\ ) \qquad \text{writing } A_2 \text{ to denote } A.f : \beta_1.x : \beta_2 \\ &\qquad = (\ U_2S_2S_1U_1R_3,\ U_2\sigma_2\ ) \qquad \text{by (c),} \\ &\text{where} \quad \text{(i)} \quad (\ R_3, \rho_3\ ) = \mathscr{W}(\ A_2, null\ x\ ) = (\ U_3S_3R_4,\ U_3\beta_3\ ) \\ &\qquad\qquad \text{by (b)} \\ &\qquad (\ R_4, \rho_4\ ) = \mathscr{W}(\ A_2, null\ ) = (\ I, list\ \alpha_1 \to truval\ ) \\ &\qquad\qquad \text{by (a)} \\ &\qquad (\ S_3, \sigma_3\ ) = \mathscr{W}(\ IA_2, x\ ) = (\ I, \beta_2\ ) \end{aligned}$$

Thus,

$$\begin{aligned} R_3 = U_3 &= \mathscr{V}(\ list\ \alpha_1 \to truval, \beta_2 \to \beta_3\ ) \\ &= [\ list\ \alpha_1 / \beta_2,\ truval / \beta_3\ ] \end{aligned}$$

$$\begin{aligned} &\text{(ii)} \quad U_1 = \mathscr{V}(\ \rho_3, truval\ ) = \mathscr{V}(\ U_3\beta_3, truval\ ) = I \\ &\text{(iii)} \quad (\ S_1, \sigma_1\ ) = \mathscr{W}(\ U_1R_3A_2, 0\ ) = (\ I, num\ ) \\ &\text{(iv)} \quad (\ S_2, \sigma_2\ ) = \mathscr{W}(\ S_1U_1R_3A_2, succ\ (\ f\ (\ tl\ x\ )\ )\ ) \\ &\qquad\qquad = \mathscr{W}(\ U_3A_2, succ\ (\ f\ (\ tl\ x\ )\ )\ ) \\ &\text{(v)} \quad U_2 = \mathscr{V}(S_2\sigma_1, \sigma_2\ ) \end{aligned}$$

Now applying (b) repeatedly, we obtain

$$\sigma_2 = U_4\,\beta_4 \quad \text{and} \quad S_2 = U_4U_5U_6$$
$$\text{where } U_4 = [\ num\ /\ \sigma_4,\ num\ /\ \beta_4\ ],$$
$$U_5 = [\ list\ \alpha_1 \rightarrow \beta_5\ /\ \beta_1\ ],$$
$$U_6 = [\ \alpha_1\ /\ \alpha_2,\ list\ \alpha_1\ /\ \beta_6\ ]$$

(The variables $\sigma_4, \beta_4, \beta_5, \beta_6$ are introduced in the applications of (b) and we will not need all of them.) Thus,

$$\sigma_2 = num$$
$$U_2 = \mathcal{V}(\ \sigma_1, \text{num}\ ) = [\ num\ /\ \sigma_1\ ]$$
$$S_1 = U_1 = I$$
$$R_1 = R_2 = U_2U_4U_5U_6U_3$$
$$\rho_2 = U_2\sigma_2 = num$$
$$\rho_1 = R_2\,\beta_2 \rightarrow \rho_2 = list\ \alpha_1 \rightarrow num$$

Finally,

$$U_0 = \mathcal{V}(\ R_1\,\beta_1, \rho_1\ ) = \mathcal{V}(\ list\ \alpha_1 \rightarrow \beta_5,\ list\ \alpha_1 \rightarrow num\ ) = [\ num\ /\ \beta_5\ ]$$

so that

$$\mathcal{W}(\ A,\ length\ ) = (\ U_0U_2U_4U_5U_6U_3,\ list\ \alpha_1 \rightarrow num\ )$$

For use in practice, $\mathcal{W}$ is not very efficient, and Milner provides an imperative algorithm $\mathcal{J}$ which uses a global environment for the values of type variables, and a procedure *unify* which does not return a result but modifies this environment as a side-effect. In fact it is easy to see that $\mathcal{J}$ simulates $\mathcal{W}$, and this provides the basis of the proof that $\mathcal{J}$ and $\mathcal{W}$ are equivalent.

7.4 Extensions to $\mathcal{W}$ for practical type checking

Efficiency considerations apart, we do not quite have a practical type checker in $\mathcal{W}$ for conventional functional languages such as Hope and Miranda since certain language features have been excluded from the syntax it can check, most notably user-defined compound data types and pattern matching, where the patterns may include tuples. Incorporating compound data types in fact presents no problem since user-defined types may be treated as new primitive type operators (analogous to →, *num* and *list* for example) and their constructor functions as primitive functions defined on those types (analogous to *cons*, *nil* etc.). The user-defined type of each constructor is then simply added into the global set of assumptions. For example given the Hope data definition:

```
data shape == rectangle( num # num ) ++ circle( num ) ;
```

we would add the type assignments:

$$rectangle : num \times num \rightarrow shape \qquad \text{and} \qquad circle : num \rightarrow shape$$

into the global set of assumptions. All types are now treated uniformly, so that if T_1 and T_2 represent constructors, then $\mathscr{V}(T_1(\sigma_1, \sigma_2), T_2(\tau_1, \tau_2))$ must fail if $T_1 \neq T_2$ (for example if $T_1 = rectangle$ and $T_2 = cons$).

As we have already seen, tuples can be treated in a similar way by using the family of tupling primitives, *tuple-n* ($n > 1$) which in general have the following type assignments in the global set of assumptions:

$$tuple\text{-}n : \alpha_1 \rightarrow \alpha_2 \ldots \rightarrow \alpha_n \rightarrow (\alpha_1 \times \alpha_2 \ldots \times \alpha_n)$$

However, it is convenient to treat tuples as special objects because of their role in the definition of non-curried functions of more than one argument. It is fairly straightforward to extend the type checking algorithm to infer the type of a tuple directly, and if we do this we can dispense with the above global assumptions. This requires one further rule for $\mathscr{W}$ which should be obvious in the light of our previous discussions, and we write tuples in their usual bracketed form:

(g) If $e = (e_1, e_2, \ldots, e_n)$, let

$$(R_1, \rho_1) = \mathscr{W}(A_1, e_1)$$
$$(R_2, \rho_2) = \mathscr{W}(A_2, e_2), \ldots, (R_n, \rho_n) = \mathscr{W}(A_n, e_n)$$

where $A_1 = A$ and $A_{i+1} = R_i A_i \; (1 \leq i < n)$.
Then $T = R_n R_{n-1} \ldots R_1$ and $\tau = T_1\rho_1 \times T_2\rho_2 \times \ldots \times T_n\rho_n$ where $T_i = R_n \ldots R_{i+1} \; (1 \leq i < n)$, $T_n = I$.

This modification alone is not sufficient, however, since in our rule for typing lambda abstractions of the form $\lambda x.f$, x was assumed to be a simple variable. This is quite adequate for dealing with (curried) source functions with definitions of the form $g\ x_1\ x_2 \ldots x_n = E$ where the x_i are variables, but not for functions defined over tuples, for example $g(x_1, x_2, \ldots, x_n) = E$. To cater for this possibility we shall include a new expression type which we call a **nu abstraction**, written $\upsilon p.e$, which is like a lambda abstraction except that the 'argument' p can now be an arbitrary pattern (we shall use this idea again in Appendix C).

This new rule subsumes rule (d) of $\mathscr{W}$ since variables are simply special cases of patterns, i.e. $\upsilon x.e \equiv \lambda x.e$ if x is a variable. The corresponding rule for $\mathcal{W}$ is similar to that for lambda abstractions except that now the type of the argument pattern must be inferred in addition to that of the body:

(d′) If $e = \upsilon p.b$, let

$$(R, \rho) = \mathcal{W}(A.x_1 : \beta_1. \ \ldots \ x_n : \beta_n, p)$$

and

$$(R', \rho') = \mathcal{W}(RA.x_1 : R\beta_1. \ \ldots \ x_n : R\beta_n, b)$$

where the β_i $(1 \le i \le n)$ are all new and the x_i $(1 \le i \le n)$ are the variables occurring in p. Then $T = R'R$ and $\tau = R'\rho \rightarrow \rho'$.

Notice that if p is a tuple of k components, a product type, ρ, will be introduced for p by our new rule (g).

The only remaining problem now is how to type a function defined using $m > 1$ equations, each of which in the most general case has the form

$$f\,p_{i1} \ldots p_{in} = e_i \qquad 1 \le i \le m$$

where the p_{ik} $(1 \le k \le n)$ are arbitrary patterns (in Hope, $n = 1$). As we might expect, the ith equation is type-checked as the υ-abstraction

$$f = \upsilon p_{i1}. \ldots \upsilon p_{in} . e_i$$

If we were just checking the type of f against a user-declared type τ, we could now simply perform the unifications $\mathcal{V}(\sigma_i, \tau)$ for each of the m equations separately where σ_i is the type inferred for equation i above $(1 \le i \le m)$. Then, provided none of these failed, the declared type τ would be valid and the type checking would have succeeded.

On the other hand, in order to infer the most general type for the function f which is consistent with all of its m defining equations, we must unify the types inferred from the m individual equations. This yields the new rule (h) for $\mathcal{W}$:

(h) If f is defined by the set of m equations $\{ f\,p_{i1} \ldots p_{in(i)} = e_i \mid 1 \le i \le m \}$, then $\mathcal{W}(A, f) = (Q_m \ldots Q_1 S_1 \ldots S_m, Q_m\sigma_m)$ where $Q_k = \mathcal{V}(Q_{k-1}\,\sigma_{k-1}, \sigma_k)$ $(2 \le k \le m)$, $Q_1 = I$ and for $1 \le i \le m$, $(S_i, \sigma_i) = \mathcal{W}(A, \textbf{fix } f.\upsilon p_{i1}. \ \ldots \ \upsilon p_{in(i)}.e_i)$

We now have all the information necessary to write a type checker for a practical polymorphic functional language such as Hope and leave any further implementation details to published papers on the subject, for example Milner's $\mathcal{J}$ algorithm which is more efficient, and Cardelli's type checker written in ML (Cardelli, 1984).

Finally we consider the question of finding types for a set of *mutually* recursively defined functions. Suppose that functions f and g are defined by mutual recursion. Then, using the **fix** operator, we can express f in terms of g (and g in terms of f) only, possibly using pattern matching in several equations for each. Thus we can find a type for f, given assumptions which associate a type with g, and conversely for g given a type association for f. All we need to do, therefore, is to unify the type inferred for f in the former case with that assigned to the type variable associated with f in the latter. This leads to the following rule:

(i) If $\{ f_i = e_i \mid 1 \leq i \leq n \}$ are a set of mutually recursive equations for function identifiers f_i, let

$$A_i = A.f_1 : \beta_1. \ \ldots \ .f_{i-1} : \beta_{i-1}.f_{i+1} : \beta_{i+1}. \ \ldots \ .f_n : \beta_n$$

and

$$(R_i, \rho_i) = \mathcal{W}(R_{i-1} \ldots R_1 A_i, e_i) \qquad (1 \leq i \leq n).$$

Then for any k, $1 \leq k \leq n$, $\mathcal{W}(A, f_k) = (US_1, \tau)$
where $S_i = R_n \ldots R_i \quad (1 \leq i \leq n)$, $\tau = US_1\beta_k$
and $U = \mathcal{V}(S_{k+1}\rho_k, S_1\beta_k)$.

7.5 The limitations of $\mathcal{W}$

To conclude this chapter we shall now return to the issue of circularly defined types and look at the problems of inferring such types using $\mathcal{W}$.

Suppose we wish to infer a type for the expression $e = \lambda x.cons\ x\ x$. By applying $\mathcal{W}$ to e with assumptions A which include $cons : \alpha \to list(\alpha) \to list(\alpha)$, we obtain:

$$\begin{aligned}
&\mathcal{W}(\text{A}, e) = (R, R\,\beta \to \rho) \\
&\text{where } (R, \rho) = \mathcal{W}(A.x : \beta, cons\ x\ x) \\
&\qquad\qquad\quad = (U_1R_1, U_1\beta_1) \\
&\text{where } U_1 = \mathcal{V}(S_1\rho_1 , \sigma_1 \to \beta_1) \qquad \text{(after some simplification)} \\
&\qquad (R_1 , \rho_1) = \mathcal{W}(A.x : \beta, cons\ x) \\
&\qquad\qquad\quad = ([\alpha / \beta, list(\alpha) \to list(\alpha) / \beta_2], list(\alpha) \to list(\alpha)) \\
&\qquad\qquad\qquad\qquad\qquad \text{(after more simplification)} \\
&\text{and } (S_1 , \sigma_1) = \mathcal{W}(R_1(A.x : \beta), x) \\
&\qquad\qquad\quad = \mathcal{W}((R_1A).x : \alpha, x) \\
&\qquad\qquad\quad = (I, \alpha)
\end{aligned}$$

Thus $U_1 = \mathcal{V}(\, list(\alpha) \to list(\alpha), \alpha \to \beta_1\,)$ and the unification fails because the 'occurs check' observes that the variable α occurs in the other component of its disagreement pair, $list(\alpha)$. If we allow infinite types, we can see that the type of *cons x x* is

$$list(\, list(\, \ldots (\, list(\alpha)\,) \ldots)\,) = list^{\infty}(\alpha)$$

and that the type of $\lambda x.cons\ x\ x$ is therefore $list^{\infty}(\alpha) \to list^{\infty}(\alpha)$. It would not be a serious problem if our type checker failed only to recognize infinite types, but unfortunately the occurs check is more restrictive than this. In particular it will always cause a failed unification when we try to infer the type of an expression which contains a self-application, for example the Y-combinator which has type $(\alpha \to \alpha) \to \alpha$.

To see this we need only consider the expression $x\ x$ which has type τ given by

$$\mathcal{W}(\, x : \beta, x\,x\,) = (\, USR, U\beta'\,) \qquad \text{by rule (b) of } \mathcal{W}$$
$$\text{where } (\, R, \rho\,) = (\, S, \sigma\,) = (\, I, \beta\,)$$
$$\text{and } U = \mathcal{V}(\, S\rho, \sigma \to \beta'\,) = \mathcal{V}(\, \beta, \beta \to \beta'\,)$$

Thus the unification for U fails because the variable β occurs in the type expression $\beta \to \beta'$. Some type checkers are a little more sophisticated than our basic one, however, and do not give up immediately on an occurs check. For example, in the case of the Y-combinator, defined by $Y = \lambda f.(\,\lambda x.f(\,xx\,)\,)(\,\lambda x.f(\,xx\,)\,)$, the following inferences might be made (with several intermediate steps missing):

$$x : \sigma = \sigma \to \tau$$
$$xx : \tau$$
$$f : \tau \to \tau'$$
$$f(\,xx\,) : \tau'$$
$$\lambda x.f(\,xx\,) : \sigma \to \tau'$$

The self application of $(\,\lambda x.f(\,xx\,)\,)$ produces the inference $(\,\lambda x.f(\,xx\,)\,) : \sigma = \sigma \to \tau'$ and so we have the equalities:

$$\sigma = \sigma \to \tau = \sigma \to \tau'$$

from which we can deduce that $\tau = \tau'$ and hence that $f : \tau \to \tau$. The rest is now easy and we conclude that $Y : (\,\tau \to \tau\,) \to \tau$. The deduction that $\tau = \tau'$ was not made as an automatic step in an algorithm, but this is the kind of additional intelligence that is required if the type checker is to handle even the simplest of circular types.

SUMMARY

- Type checking exposes many programming errors at compile-time and enables run-time typing to be avoided in the implementation; this is more efficient.
- A type is inferred for every sub-expression in a program and checked for consistency. User-declared types are also checked against the inferred types.
- Let-bound type variables are generic and can be instantiated to different types in the same expression; lambda-bound variables are non-generic and cannot.
- A logical inference system can deduce the type of an expression formally, but not automatically.
- Milner's algorithm $\mathcal{W}$ infers shallow types by effectively automating the proof procedure of a simple type inference system.
- $\mathcal{W}$ can be extended to handle pattern matching but the 'occurs check' in the unification algorithm may fail to check the types of some well typed expressions such as Y.

EXERCISES

7.1 Use informal arguments to find the most general types for the following Hope functions:

(a) `--- f( a, b, c ) <= if a( b ) then [ c ] else [ b : : c ] ;`

(b) `--- g( x, y ) <= lambda z => if z( x ) then y else z ;`

(c) `--- h( a, b, c ) <= [ lambda x => ( b( x, 2 ), c( b( a, 1 ) ) x ) ] ;`

7.2 Given the assumption pair : $\alpha \rightarrow \beta \rightarrow (\alpha \times \beta)$, use $\mathcal{W}$ to infer the types of the following functions:

$$funpair = \lambda f.\lambda g.\lambda a.\lambda b.(\ f\ a, g\ b\ )$$

$$tagpair = \lambda a.funpair(\ pair\ a, pair\ a\ )$$

7.3 (a) Use the extended version of $\mathcal{W}$ to infer the type of the apply function, defined in Hope by:

```
--- apply ( f, x ) <= f x ;
```

(b) Now suppose that tuples cannot be expressed in the syntax of the source language but instead are represented by explicitly applying the tupling functions. What is the definition of apply now?

(c) Infer the type of the version of apply you defined in (b) assuming that the type assignments of the tupling functions are included in the global assumption set. (You will now not require rule (g)).

7.4 Define a Hope function which curries a function of arity 3, and infer its type using the extended version of $\mathscr{W}$.

7.5 In the new rule (d′) introduced to handle pattern matching, we had to search the argument pattern p for new variables x_i so that a type could be inferred for that pattern. Show how we can avoid this searching by defining the nu rule recursively with the lambda rule for a base case; this will introduce the required variables into the assumption set. Assume that all constructor functions and tupling functions are curried and have their types given in the assumption set. (*Hint*: For the function $f = \upsilon(\ c\ p_1 \ldots p_n\ ).e$, for $n > 0$ consider $\mathscr{W}(\ A,\ \upsilon p_1.\ \ldots\ \upsilon p_n.e\ )$ and define the base cases where p is a variable and the arity of c is 0)

7.6 Show how $\mathscr{W}$ infers that there is no type for the functions:

(a) sum $t\ n$ = **if** $n = 0$ **then** t **else** sum ($t + n$)

(This is a classic example of an 'untyped' function which fortunately could never be valid in Hope. Its type is the union of the types $num \rightarrow num \rightarrow num$, $num \rightarrow num \rightarrow num \rightarrow num$, ... and this may be written as

$$sum : num \rightarrow num \rightarrow (\ FIX\ \tau.(\ num\ {+}{+}\ num \rightarrow \tau\ ))$$

where FIX is the least fixed point operator for type expressions and ++ denotes type union.)

(b) $taut\ 0\ f\ =\ f$
$taut\ (\ n + 1\ )\ f\ =\ taut\ n\ (\ f\ true\ )$ and $taut\ n\ (\ f\ false\ )$
(This function is potentially 'useful'! Given a (curried) predicate preceded by its arity as arguments, it returns the result *true* if the predicate is a tautology and *false* otherwise. Its type is $num \rightarrow bool \rightarrow FIX\ \tau.\ (\ bool\ {+}{+}\ bool \rightarrow \tau\ )$.

7.7 Outline the modifications to $\mathscr{W}$ that are required to support the *overloading* of identifiers.

Chapter 8
Intermediate forms

In this chapter we shall develop an intermediate code for functional languages based upon the notation of the lambda calculus described in Chapter 6. We shall incorporate some simple extensions to the notation to allow us to name expressions; this provides a straightforward mechanism for describing recursive functions and so simplifies the translation of a source program into the intermediate code. The resulting code can be considered as a 'sugared' version of the lambda notation and will be used as the basis of many of the implementation techniques described in the succeeding chapters.

Having described the intermediate code we shall then see how a high-level language can be translated into this intermediate code. The assumption here is that the program has been parsed and subsequently type-checked using the techniques described in the previous chapter so that the (type-correct) program exists in the form of an abstract syntax tree. The translation phase then involves mapping the abstract syntax tree of the source program into the abstract syntax tree of the equivalent intermediate code program, although for the purposes of this discussion we shall view the translation as though it were from source to source. This provides a particularly concise and abstract way of expressing the translation rules. The concrete intermediate code can be produced from the resulting abstract syntax tree if required by flattening it although it is likely that this 'intermediate form' will be further processed according to the techniques described later in this book.

We shall concentrate on the translation rules for Hope as this is our common source language although it should be apparent that the translation of other source languages will follow a similar line.

8.1 An intermediate code for functional languages

The intermediate code we describe here is the lambda notation described in Chapter 6 together with additional facilities for naming expressions. The syntax for intermediate code expressions is given by the label exp in the following BNF description:

```
⟨exp⟩  ::= ⟨id⟩ | λ ⟨id⟩ . ⟨exp⟩ | ⟨exp⟩ ⟨exp⟩ | (⟨exp⟩) | con |
           let ⟨def⟩ in ⟨exp⟩ | letrec ⟨defs⟩ in ⟨exp⟩
⟨defs⟩ ::= ⟨def⟩ | ⟨def⟩, ⟨defs⟩
⟨def⟩  ::= ⟨id⟩ = ⟨exp⟩
⟨id⟩   ::= identifier
⟨con⟩  ::= constant
```

Of the two extensions to the lambda notation, letrec is the more important since let expressions can be defined equivalently using auxiliary functions:

$$\text{let } x = E_1 \text{ in } E_2 \cong (\lambda x.E_2)\, E_1$$

let expressions are included largely for convenience although there are some efficiency advantages to be gained by including them; these will become apparent when we look at functional language compilers in Chapter 15.

The set of constants is again arbitrary. A realistic implementation of a functional language based on this type of intermediate code will very likely use a large number of primitive functions and several base types. The primitive functions we refer to in this chapter will be those listed in Table 6.1 together with a family of CASE selection primitives CASE-1, CASE-2, etc. defined by

$$\begin{aligned} \text{CASE-n } S\ E\ E_0\ E_1\ E_2 \ldots E_{n-1} = {} & E_S && \text{if } 0 \le S \le n-1 \\ & E && \text{if } S < 0 \text{ or } S \ge n \end{aligned}$$

These will be used in the translation of pattern matching described in

Section 8.4. Some examples of expressions in the intermediate notation are given below:

```
13
( + 3 9 )
( λx.λy. f ( + ) 1 ( −x y ) )
CASE-2 ( g x ) 0 ( + x 1 ) ( INDEX 5 T)
let x = 1 in λy. − x y
letrec f = ( λx. + x 1 ), g = ( λx.f (* x x ) ) in ( g 5 )
```

8.2 Abstract syntax trees

The first phase in the translation of a high-level language to intermediate code is the **parsing** phase which translates the source program (a piece of concrete syntax) into an **abstract syntax tree** (a data structure). As we pointed out in the previous chapter, expressions are typically type checked before any subsequent translation or interpretation is performed and we shall assume here that this has been done and that the program is correctly typed. To give the reader a feel for what the abstract syntax tree of a Hope program might look like we include for completeness in Figure 8.1 the data definition for the abstract syntax tree of a Hope program (this is called 'hope_object') expressed itself in Hope syntax. This definition includes one constructor for each type of Hope expression in

```
type string        ==  list( char ) ;
data hope_object   ==  DEF( hope_object # hope_object ) ++
                       APPLY( hope_object # hope_object ) ++
                       FUN( string ) ++
                       PRIM( string ) ++
                       CON( string ) ++
                       VAR( string ) ++
                       INT( num ) ++
                       REAL( real ) ++
                       CHAR( char ) ++
                       TUPLE( list( hope_object ) ) ++
                       COND( hope_object # hope_object # hope_object ) ++
                       QUAL( hope_object # hope_object # hope_object ) ++
                       RECQUAL( hope_object # hope_object # hope_object ) ++
                       LAM( list( hope_object ) ) ++
                       LAMRULE( hope_obj # hope_obj ) ++
                       EQUIV( hope_object # hope_object ) ;
```

(Underscores (_) in patterns are treated as variables in the abstract syntax tree.)

Figure 8.1 The Hope abstract syntax tree data definition.

DEF — A function-defining equation; LHS and RHS denote the left-hand side and right-hand side

H⟦ - - - LHS <= RHS ; ⟧ = DEF(H⟦ LHS ⟧, H⟦ RHS ⟧)

APPLY — Function application

H⟦ F A ⟧ = APPLY(H⟦ F ⟧, H⟦ A ⟧)

FUN — A user-defined function name

H⟦ f ⟧ = FUN(f) f is a user-defined function name

PRIM — A primitive function name; these are distinguished from the user-defined functions so as to simplify their translation to intermediate code (see below)

H⟦ P ⟧ = PRIM(P) P is a primitive function name

CON — A constructor function name; these are distinguished from the other user-defined functions so as to simplify their translation to intermediate code (see below).

H⟦ C ⟧ = CON(C) C is a constructor name

VAR — A variable reference

H⟦ v ⟧ = VAR(v) v is a variable

INT — Integer literals

H⟦ i ⟧ = INT(i) i is an integer literal

REAL — Real number literals

H⟦ r ⟧ = REAL(r) r is a real number literal

CHAR — Character literals

H⟦ c ⟧ = CHAR(c) c is a character literal

TUPLE — Tuple expressions. The components of the tuple are stored as a list of hope-objects in the TUPLE node:

$H\llbracket (E_1, E_2, \ldots, E_n) \rrbracket = \text{TUPLE}([H\llbracket E_1 \rrbracket, H\llbracket E_2 \rrbracket, \ldots, H\llbracket E_n \rrbracket])$

COND — Conditional expressions

$H\llbracket \textbf{if } E_1 \textbf{ then } E_2 \textbf{ else } E_3 \rrbracket = \text{COND}(H\llbracket E_1 \rrbracket, H\llbracket E_2 \rrbracket, H\llbracket E_3 \rrbracket)$

QUAL — Non-recursive qualified expressions i.e. **let** and **where** expressions

$H\llbracket \textbf{let } P == E_1 \textbf{ in } E_2 \rrbracket = \text{QUAL}(H\llbracket P \rrbracket, H\llbracket E_1 \rrbracket, H\llbracket E_2 \rrbracket)$

$H\llbracket E_2 \textbf{ where } P == E_1 \rrbracket = \text{QUAL}(H\llbracket P \rrbracket, H\llbracket E_1 \rrbracket, H\llbracket E_2 \rrbracket)$

RECQUAL — Recursive qualified expressions. These have the same translation rules as for the non-recursive case above except that the constructor is RECQUAL rather than QUAL.

LAM — Lambda expressions

$H\llbracket \textbf{lambda } R_1 \mid R_2 \mid \ldots \mid R_n \rrbracket = \text{LAM}([H\llbracket R_1 \rrbracket, H\llbracket R_2 \rrbracket, \ldots, H\llbracket R_n \rrbracket])$

LAMRULE — Lambda expression rules – these define the R_i above

H⟦ P => E ⟧ = LAMRULE(H⟦ P ⟧, H⟦ E ⟧)

EQUIV — Equivalence in patterns e.g. x & y :: l

H⟦ v & P ⟧ = EQUIV(VAR (v), H⟦ P ⟧)

Figure 8.2 The Hope parsing rules.

just the same way that the data definition for trees, for example, includes one constructor for each different type of tree. In Figure 8.2 the various constructors are described briefly together with a translation (or parsing) rule H which indicates the abstract syntax tree generated by each type of concrete Hope expression. These rules are written

H ⟦ hope expression ⟧ = abstract syntax tree

We use double brackets ⟦ and ⟧ to indicate that the argument to H is a syntactic object.

8.3 Translating Hope into the intermediate code

With the exception of function definitions, **lambda** expressions and qualified expressions (**let** and **where** expressions) which make use of pattern matching, all other Hope expressions translate straightforwardly into the intermediate code. The translation can be viewed as being performed by a translation function T from source expressions to intermediate code expressions. We shall express the rules for T at the concrete level, i.e. at the level of syntactic objects, although in practice the translation will most likely be applied between the abstract syntax trees of the source and intermediate code programs. We shall write each rule in the following way:

T ⟦ source expression ⟧ = intermediate code expression

(The double square brackets (⟦ and ⟧) again indicate that the argument to T is a syntactic object.) The translation rules for the subset of expressions which do not require pattern matching are as follows:

1. *Base-type literals.* (e.g. integers, characters, real numbers etc.). These are unchanged during the translation:

   T ⟦ n ⟧ = n   n is a literal

2. *Identifiers.* If the identifier is one of the built-in Hope functions then we must provide a name mapping to ensure that the correct intermediate code function is selected (the names may be different) otherwise the identifier is unchanged by T. We shall write B_f to mean the intermediate code equivalent of the Hope built-in function f:

   T ⟦ f ⟧ = B_f f is a built-in function identifier
   T ⟦ i ⟧ = i   i is any other identifier

Recall that Hope functions are uncurried and so take only a single argument (which may be a tuple). This means that primitive functions like + in Hope whose argument is a tuple of numbers must be translated into functions which explicitly dismantle that argument, for example B_+ = plus, where plus ≡ λt. + (INDEX 1 t) (INDEX 2 t). The definitions of functions like plus can be included explicitly in the translated program, effectively making them into 'library' definitions. In practice, however, it is quite reasonable to include them in the set of constants. Another solution is to incorporate an optimization to T which looks more closely at the structure of a function application and which uses the curried versions of the primitive functions wherever possible. For example,

$$T[\![+ (E_1 E_2)]\!] = + T[\![E_1]\!] T[\![E_2]\!]$$

For a curried language, of course, the translation is more direct and we would require simply $B_+ = +$.

3. *Conditionals.* These are translated into calls to the built-in function COND. The predicate and the **then** and **else** expressions must themselves be translated into the intermediate code by using T:

$$T[\![\textbf{if } E_1 \textbf{ then } E_2 \textbf{ else } E_3]\!] = \text{COND } T[\![E_1]\!] T[\![E_2]\!] T[\![E_3]\!]$$

4. *Tuple expressions.* These are translated directly into calls to the built-in function TUPLE-n:

$$T[\![(E_1, E_2, \ldots, E_n)]\!] = \text{TUPLE-n } T[\![E_1]\!] T[\![E_2]\!] \ldots T[\![E_n]\!]$$

5. *Function applications.* Because both the function and argument components of an application are expressions we simply apply T to both:

$$T[\![E_1 E_2]\!] = T[\![E_1]\!] T[\![E_2]\!]$$

8.3.1 Representing constructed data

Before we consider the treatment of pattern matching we must decide on a consistent representation for constructed data terms (or *compound* data terms). The technique we are going to use exploits the family of tupling functions TUPLE-0, TUPLE-1 etc. which we introduced for the lambda calculus in Chapter 6. In order to understand this representation, let us look at an example of a Hope **data** type for defining binary trees:

```
data tree == empty ++ leaf( num ) ++ node( tree # num # tree ) ;
```

This definition introduces three new constructors (empty, leaf and node) which can be used during pattern matching to determine which type of tree has been supplied. As part of the pattern matching process we must therefore be able to distinguish applications of the different constructors and to achieve this we attribute a unique *tag* to each constructor within the type. (These tags need only be unique *within* a data type since the strong typing of our source language expressions ensures that when we are expecting a tree, for example, we will always find one.) To this end we shall associate the integers 0, 1 and 2 with the constructors empty, leaf and node respectively – the reason for the numbering convention will become apparent later on. In general, if there are n constructors in the data type then we will use the integers 0, 1, ... , n − 1.

Using these tags, we can now represent an application of a constructor of arity n by an (n + 1)-tuple whose first element is the constructor tag and whose remaining n elements are the arguments of the constructor, for example:

```
empty            → TUPLE-1 0
leaf( n )        → TUPLE-2 1 T ⟦ n ⟧
node( x, y, z )→ TUPLE-4 2 T ⟦ x ⟧ T ⟦ y ⟧ T ⟦ z ⟧
```

Thus for constructor c we define:

$$T [\![c (E_1, \ldots, E_n)]\!] = \text{TUPLE-}(n + 1) N_c \, T [\![E_1]\!] \ldots T [\![E_n]\!]$$

8.4 Translating pattern matching

We now consider those constructs which involve the use of pattern matching, i.e. function definitions, qualified expressions and lambda expressions. There are no translation rules for pattern equivalence (EQUIV in the abstract syntax tree) which merely provides a naming facility. To start with we shall assume that the patterns are non-overlapping, meaning that no two patterns can match with the same argument expression. As we shall see this considerably simplifies the translation process. For completeness, however, we shall consider in Section 8.5 the treatment of best-fit pattern matching, where patterns are allowed to overlap provided they are not collectively ambiguous.

The general situation can be appreciated by looking at a function definition which in the most general case is defined by a set of pattern matching equations. For example, in Hope:

$$
\begin{array}{ll}
\text{---}\; f\; P_0 & \Leftarrow E_0\,; \\
\text{---}\; f\; P_1 & \Leftarrow E_1\,; \\
\vdots & \\
\text{---}\; f\; P_{n-1} & \Leftarrow E_{n-1}\,;
\end{array}
$$

where the P_i are patterns $(0 \le i \le n-1)$. As we shall see later on the treatment of qualified expressions and lambda expressions follows closely the treatment of definitions of this sort. What we are going to do is translate this set of equations into a single rule for f:

f = λa. intermediate code for f

with the complete set of function definitions in the program being packaged into a letrec expression:

```
letrec  f₁ = λa. intermediate code for f₁,
        f₂ = λa. intermediate code for f₂,
        ⋮
        f_N = λa. intermediate code for f_N
in intermediate code for top-level expression
```

Of course, the new argument name a must be chosen so as not to conflict with any existing names in the program.

The intermediate code for each function definition consists of two parts:

(1) code which determines which rule is applicable for a given argument value;
(2) code for each of the function bodies (one for each rule).

In order to determine which rule is applicable we are not interested in the variables which are named in the patterns, only the 'shape' of the argument value. For example, given the rules:

```
--- sum( nil ) <= 0;
--- sum( x :: l ) <= x + sum( l );
```

we are initially interested only in whether the argument is the empty list (nil) or a non-empty list (of the form _ :: _); the code to do this is called the **matching code**. Once the applicable rule has been determined we have to bind the variables named in the matching pattern to the appropriate argument components. For the first rule of sum there are no variables in the pattern and so we translate the body expression directly; in the second rule, we have to generate binding code to bind x and l before translating the right-hand side x + sum(l). The body code therefore consists of a combination of binding code and code for the corresponding right-hand side expression.

The matching code could test each pattern in turn to see whether it matched the argument value but it is more efficient in practice to merge these tests into a single **matching tree**. This matching tree defines a piece of intermediate code which when evaluated returns an integer denoting the rule number whose pattern matches the argument expression or -1 if no match was found. The set of equations defining our template function f above is therefore translated into a single CASE expression which selects the binding code corresponding to the rule number returned by the matching tree code:

```
λa.CASE-n  code for the matching tree
           error
           ( ⟨ binding code for equation 0 ⟩ ⟨ code for E_0 ⟩ )
           ( ⟨ binding code for equation 1 ⟩ ⟨ code for E_1 ⟩ )
           ⋮
           ( ⟨ binding code for equation n − 1 ⟩ ⟨ code for E_{n−1} ⟩ )
```

Notice that if the matching code returns -1 then no match was found and so the program must abort with a suitable error message, hence the error case in the second argument position of CASE-n.

8.4.1 Generating the matching tree

The technique we describe here for generating the matching tree from a set of function-defining equations is a variation on the method described in Hunt (1986) although the details of alternative approaches may be found in Augustsson (1985) and Wadler (1987). The idea is basically this: we first generate a separate matching tree for each equation defining a function and then merge those matching trees into a single matching tree, which is then translated into intermediate code. The result of evaluating this code will be -1 if the argument failed to match any of the patterns in the set of equations and k (≥ 0) if the argument matched the pattern in equation k of the set of definitions. (The equations are assumed to be numbered from 0 to $n-1$ as suggested above.)

Each equation defining a function f in Hope is of the form:

```
--- f P_i <= E_i ;
```

where P_i is a pattern expression which is one of:

(1) a variable e.g. x;

(2) an underscore (_) which for the purposes of the matching tree is the same as a variable;

(3) a constructor term of the form CP where P is a pattern expression (recall that this is represented as a tuple with N_C as its first component); P may be null in which case C is a data *constant.*

(4) a pattern tuple of the form ($P_1, P_2, \ldots, P_m$) where each of the P_i is a pattern expression.

(Equivalences of the form v & P are equivalent to P for the purposes of the matching phase.) In practice we are also permitted to write literals (for example 3) in patterns but including this now will only serve to obscure the nature of the algorithm. We shall see how literal pattern expressions can be handled in Section 8.6.

Whenever a constructor term is encountered in a pattern we are required to test that the argument expression has the required constructor in the corresponding position. This test appears in the matching tree as an internal node which we shall write:

⟨ position, list of matching trees ⟩

The 'position' is a path specification which identifies which component of the argument is being tested. This is written as a list of integer indexes: the empty list [ ] denotes the whole argument expression of the function; [i] denotes the ith element of the argument tuple of the function; [i, j] denotes the jth element of that element; [i, j, k] the kth element of that one and so on. For example, in the equation

--- $g(x, C_1(y_1, y_2), C_2(C_3 (z), n))$ <= . . . ;

where C_1 and C_2 are constructors, [ ] denotes the whole argument tuple; [1] denotes the first element of the argument tuple, i.e. x; [2] denotes the second element of the argument tuple, i.e. $C_1(y_1, y_2)$; [2,1] denotes the first element of the second element of the argument tuple, i.e. the constructor code for C_1 and so on. The path specification always leads to a constructor code (i.e. its last component is always a 1) which is used to select one of the subtrees in the 'list of matching trees' – the number of subtrees in this list is therefore the same as the number of constructors in the corresponding data type. All but one of these subtrees will correspond to a failed match which we shall represent by an *empty* matching tree. The one which does correspond to a match with the constructor code given in the pattern leads to a subtree which is built by repeating the process in a left-to-right (depth-first) fashion over the argument tuple's elements and nested sub-elements. In order to make this more clearly understood, Figure 8.3 shows the matching tree for the following equation (assumed to be the ith) in the definition of the function f:

--- f(empty, node(leaf(x), k, node(empty, y, t)), nil) <= E_i ;

The type of this function has the form tree # tree # list(. . .) → . . . where tree is as defined above. In the figure the list constructors nil and :: are assumed to be encoded as 0 and 1 respectively, with :: being treated as a prefix constructor (remember also that nullary constructors such as empty and nil must be regarded as singleton tuples for consistency).

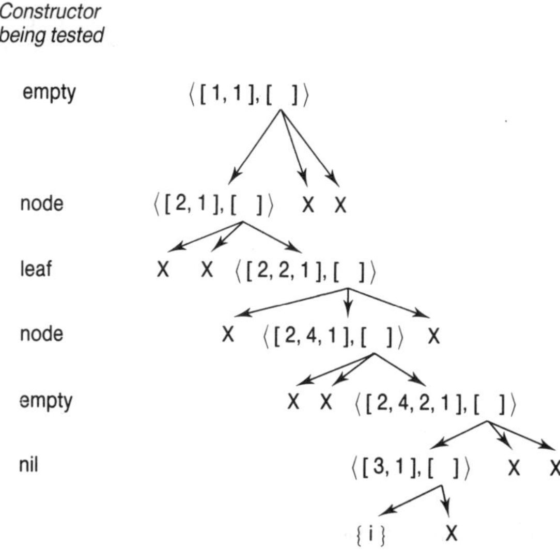

Figure 8.3 The matching tree for equation i.

In this example the order of testing of constructors in the pattern is textually from left to right (i.e. left-to-right depth-first in the abstract syntax tree of the pattern). An X in the diagram denotes an empty matching tree corresponding to 'no match' between the pattern and the argument, and the leaf node { i } indicates a successful match with the pattern in equation i. We shall denote by

G ⟦ P ⟧

the matching tree generated from the pattern P, and by P_m the pattern whose corresponding right-hand side is E_m. The tree of Figure 8.3 is therefore G ⟦ P_i ⟧.

When the matching tree for each equation defining f has been generated, the process is completed by merging these trees into a single matching tree. To illustrate what has to be done here, let us incorporate a second equation into our definition of f:

```
--- f( leaf( x ), leaf( y ), x :: l ) <= Ej ;
```

The matching tree for this (i.e. G ⟦ P_j ⟧) is given in Figure 8.4(a) and the tree resulting from merging this and the existing tree of Figure 8.3 is shown in Figure 8.4(b). We shall call the merging function M so that the tree of Figure 8.4(b) can be expressed more formally as

M(G ⟦ P_i ⟧, G ⟦ P_j ⟧)

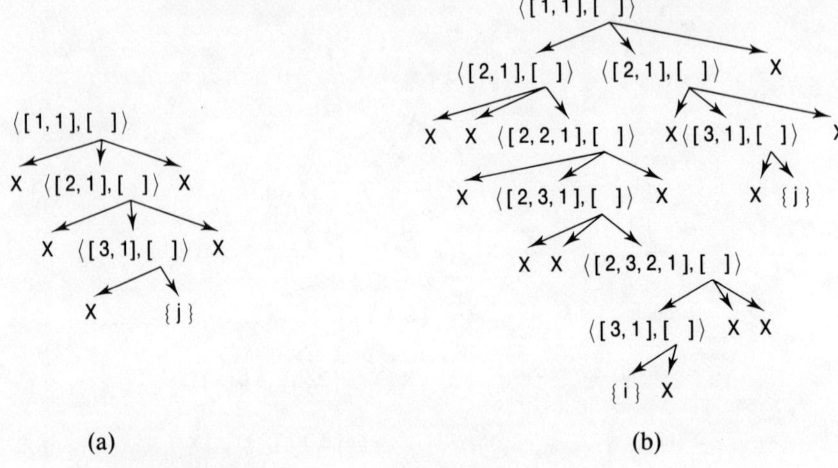

Figure 8.4 Merging trees: (a) the matching tree for equation j; (b) the merged trees.

This merging operation combines together those nodes which test the same argument component. In order to specify the merging operation M we shall have to place an ordering on the 'positions' given in each node of the matching trees so that these nodes can be matched up correctly. This ordering reflects the left-to-right depth-first order of argument component testing as we would expect:

$$[\,] < [1] < [1,1] < [1,1,1] < \ldots < [1,2] < [1,2,1] < \ldots [2] < \ldots .$$

and so on.

The rules for merging two trees T_1 and T_2 (written $M(T_1, T_2)$) are then as follows:

(1) If either T_1 or T_2 is empty (no match) then we return the other. This corresponds to making the matching tree 'more complete' than it was before the merge:

$$M(X, T) = T$$
$$M(T, X) = T$$

(2) If both T_1 and T_2 are nodes then the way in which the merge proceeds is dependent on a comparison of the positions of the two components (p_1 and p_2) being tested at these nodes. If $p_1 = p_2$ then the two nodes are testing the same component of the argument expression and so their matching subtrees are merged pointwise. If

$p_1 < p_2$ then all nodes within T_2 are testing some argument component which is textually to the right of the component specified by p_1; consequently each subtree of T_1 is merged with T_2. If $p_1 > p_2$ then the converse is true and so T_1 is merged with each subtree of T_2:

$$\begin{aligned}
&M(\, T_1 \,\&\, \langle p_1,\, [\, t_{10},\, t_{11}, \ldots,\, t_{1n-1}\,]\rangle,\, T_2 \,\&\, \langle\, p_2,\, [\, t_{20},\, t_{21}, \ldots, t_{2m-1}\,]\rangle\,) = \\
&\quad \langle p_1,\, [\, M(\, t_{10},\, t_{20}\,),\, M(\, t_{11},\, t_{21}\,), \ldots,\, M(\, t_{1n-1},\, t_{2n-1}\,)\,]\rangle \qquad \text{if } p_1 = p_2 \\
&\quad \langle p_1,\, [\, M(\, t_{10},\, T_2),\, M(\, t_{11},\, T_2\,), \ldots,\, M(\, t_{1n-1},\, T_2)\,]\rangle \qquad \text{if } p_1 < p_2 \\
&\quad \langle p_2,\, [\, M(\, T_1,\, t_{20}\,),\, M(\, T_1,\, t_{21}\,), \ldots,\, M(\, T_1,\, t_{2m-1}\,)\,]\rangle \qquad \text{if } p_1 > p_2
\end{aligned}$$

The symbols $=$, $<$ and $>$ are, of course, the Boolean functions on positions rather than integers.

Notice that there is no rule covering leaf nodes explicitly; this is because the patterns are assumed to be non-overlapping, so that leaf nodes will only ever be merged with empty trees, which is covered by case 1. A fuller discussion of this issue is left until Section 8.5 below.

The complete matching tree for a set of patterns $P_1, P_2, \ldots, P_{n-1}, P_n$ is given by

$$M(\, G\,[\, P_1\,],\, M(\, G\,[\, P_2\,], \ldots,\, M(\, G\,[\, P_{n-1}\,],\, G\,[\, P_n\,]\,) \ldots)\,)$$

To complete the discussion we have only to describe the rules for expanding the final matching tree into intermediate code. We shall call the translation rule E. Remember that the result generated by the resulting code must be −1 if there was no match found and n if the argument matched with pattern number n.

We shall need an auxiliary function P which translates a 'position' into intermediate code for selecting the argument component specified by that position. For example

```
P ( a, [ 2, 3, 3 ] ) = INDEX 3 ( INDEX 3 ( INDEX 2 a ) )
```

where a is the argument name. The rules for E are then as follows (a again denotes the argument name):

```
E( a, X ) = −1
E( a, { n } ) = n
E( a, ⟨p, [ t0 , t1, . . . , tn−1 ]⟩ ) = CASE-n P( a, p ) ⊗ E( t0 ) E( t1 ) . . . E( tn−1 )
```

where ⊗ denotes a dummy (error) expression. An error cannot be generated from this CASE expression since the program is known to be correctly typed which guarantees that the selected constructor code lies between 0 and n − 1.

As an aside, note that the reason for wrapping a CASE-n expression around the code for the matching tree in the first place is simply that there may be several occurrences of the same right-hand side number at the leaves of the merged matching tree, in which case the code for that right-hand side will end up being reproduced if we substitute the code for that right-hand side directly. However, we can easily detect when right-hand sides are not referred to more than once, and in such cases we can generate the code for each equation's body directly within the code for the matching tree. This avoids the need for the additional CASE-n function call after the matching phase is complete.

8.4.2 Generating the binding code

The code generated from the matching tree will select one of the equations defining the function based on the structure of the argument expression. But the right-hand side of the matching equation may refer to variables named in patterns on the left-hand side of that equation. It is the purpose of the binding code to extract the named components of the argument in order that they can be used in the right-hand side. This is actually straightforward but it will require an additional component to be associated with the leaf nodes of the matching tree. When the matching tree for each equation is generated we must accumulate a list of bindings of the form 'name/position' where the names are the identifiers referred to in the pattern and the positions are their positions denoted by lists of integers in the manner described above. This extra list can be stored together with the equation number at the leaf of the matching tree and used to generate the binding code when the intermediate code for the corresponding right-hand side is generated. Notice that although 'don't care' patterns (i.e. underscores (_) in Hope) are treated as though they were variables in the matching tree they will not be included in the binding list at the leaf nodes for obvious reasons.

The inclusion of binding lists in the leaf nodes suggests a cosmetic refinement to the rule for E given above:

```
E( a, { n, BindList } ) = n
```

where { n, b } denotes a leaf node comprising the equation number n and the list of bindings b required by E_n.

In order to generate the binding code for equation k we must therefore extract the BindList for equation k and use it to generate code to pick out the named components of the argument expression. Let us consider the general form of the kth equation defining a function f:

```
--- f ( ... x1... x2 ... xn ... ) <= Ek
```

The 'bind list' for equation k (which we write L_k) tells us the positions of the x_i in the argument of f and can be conveniently stored in the leaf node of the matching tree for equation k in the form of a list of pairs:

$$L_k = [\,(x_1, p_1), (x_2, p_2), \ldots, (x_n, p_n)\,]$$

(using the obvious Hope-like notation for lists). The intermediate code for binding each x_i to its corresponding argument component can now take the form of a let expression. Thus, denoting the function to generate the body code by B we obtain the rule:

$$
\begin{aligned}
&B(\,a, E', [\,(x_1, p_1), (x_2, p_2), \ldots, (x_n, p_n)\,]\,) = \\
&\quad \text{let } x_1 = P(\,a, p_1\,) \text{ in} \\
&\quad \text{let } x_2 = P(\,a, p_2\,) \text{ in} \\
&\quad \vdots \\
&\quad \text{let } x_n = P(\,a, P_n\,) \text{ in } E'
\end{aligned}
$$

where a is the argument name and E′ is the intermediate code for the right-hand side of rule k. Of course, if x_i above is referred to only once in the expression E′ then we can remove the auxiliary definition ... let $x_i = P(\,a, p_i\,)$ in ... and instead replace the occurrence of x_i in E by $P(\,a, p_i\,)$ directly. This will produce not only less intermediate code but also, we would hope, more efficient intermediate code since one less binding is then required.

8.4.3 Qualified and lambda expressions

Now that we have seen how to translate pattern matching in a general set of definitions we can define the translation rules for qualified expressions and lambda expressions. Non-recursive qualified expressions can be treated as lambda expressions as we have already seen:

$$
\begin{aligned}
&T[\![\,\textbf{let } P == E_1 \textbf{ in } E_2\,]\!] = T[\![\,(\,\textbf{lambda } P => E_2\,)\,E_1\,]\!] \\
&T[\![\,E_2 \textbf{ where } P == E_1\,]\!] = T[\![\,(\,\textbf{lambda } P => E_2\,)\,E_1\,]\!]
\end{aligned}
$$

where P is a pattern expression. Of course it is not necessary for **let** expressions to be re-expressed as **lambda** expressions before translating them, but the equivalence of the two forms serves to fully specify the translation which is required. The matching and binding code could be produced *in situ* using the translation rules for lambda expressions.

Lambda expressions themselves are simply special cases of function definitions, the major difference being that they are anonymous. Hence:

```
T [[ lambda P0 => E0 | ... | Pn-1 => En-1 ]] =
λa.CASE-n E( a, M( G [[ P0 ]] ..., M( G [[ Pn-2 ]]; G [[ Pn-1 ]] ) ... ) )
          error
          ( B( a, T [[ E0 ]], L0 ) )
          :
          ( B( a, T [[ En-1 ]], Ln-1 ) )
```

where L_i is the bind list for the ith lambda rule P_i => E_i ($0 \leq i \leq n-1$). This brings us to the final rule for T which covers recursive qualified expressions. An example of such an expression is the following:

let (x, 1 :: y) == (1 :: x, x) **in** y

(which binds x and y to the infinite list [1, 1, 1, 1, 1, ...]). Any of the variables introduced on the left-hand side of the == can be referred to in the right-hand side. Because of this there is no equivalence between the expression and a lambda expression as for the non-recursive case above. Instead we must build a letrec expression whose components are the intermediate code for the qualifier, the binding code for each variable in the pattern and also the matching code. Hence, the above expression must be translated into the following intermediate code:

```
letrec  Q  =  intermediate code for ( 1 :: x, x ),
        x  =  INDEX 1 Q
        y  =  INDEX 3 ( INDEX 2 Q )
        m  =  matching code for ( x, 1 :: y )
in COND ( = m -1 ) error y
```

Again the names Q and m must be chosen so as not to conflict with any existing names. The details of the corresponding rule for T are left as an exercise for the reader.

8.5 'Best-fit' pattern matching

The translation algorithm described above is designed to operate on a set of patterns which do not overlap. The best way to understand what this means is to consider the set of argument expressions which match with a given pattern. If we denote the patterns of a set of equations by

$P_1, P_2, \ldots, P_n$

and the set of argument expressions which matches P_i by S_i, $1 \leq i \leq n$, then a set of non-overlapping patterns is characterized by the fact that no two patterns match the same argument expression, i.e.

$$S_i \cap S_j = \emptyset \qquad 1 \leq i, j \leq n, i \neq j$$

The following sets of patterns (drawn across the page) are all examples of non-overlapping patterns:

```
nil         x :: y
empty       node( _, v, _ )   leaf( n )
( nil, x )  ( x :: l, nil )
```

Because the patterns are assumed to be non-overlapping we shall never attempt to merge a leaf node with another leaf node or with an internal node when merging two matching trees according to the rules for M. This is simply because these are the very conditions which lead to two patterns overlapping. Indeed we can even check that the patterns do not overlap by incorporating further rules for M:

$$M(\{m\}, \{n\}) = \text{overlap!}$$
$$M(\{n\}, \langle ... \rangle) = \text{overlap!}$$
$$M(\langle ... \rangle, \{n\}) = \text{overlap!}$$

the implication being that any of these cases will cause an error message to be reported.

Some languages, however, allow overlapping patterns provided that they are unambiguous. (Hope is an example of such a language as we hinted in Chapter 2.) In order to define unambiguity we shall have to introduce the idea of specificity of patterns.

A pattern P_i is said to be a **specialization** of a pattern P_j (or P_i is **more specific** than P_j) if each expression which matches P_i also matches P_j but not vice versa; that is if S_i is a *proper* subset of S_j ($S_j \supset S_i$). Thus for example nil is a specialization of x since x matches with all expressions which match with nil but not vice versa (since x also matches with all non-empty lists). For a set of patterns to be unambiguous, they must satisfy the following condition:

> **Unambiguity:** If any two patterns overlap and neither is a specialization of the other then for each expression, E, that matches both patterns there must be a third pattern which is a specialization of both patterns that also matches with E.

The example patterns given above (i.e. nil and x) are unambiguous because nil is a specialization of x. A more complicated set of patterns is the following:

```
( nil, x )     ( x, nil )     ( nil, nil )
```

The first two patterns overlap and neither is a specialization of the other, but there is a third pattern which is a specialization of them both, i.e. (nil, nil), which matches the only expression which matches both of the first two – hence the patterns are unambiguous. Here is another example:

```
( x, nil )     ( x :: l, y )
```

These overlap since they both match with expressions of the form (a :: b, nil) for any a and b and neither is a specialization of the other. Therefore, because there is no third pattern which is a specialization of them both they are ambiguous. To make them unambiguous we have to add the pattern (x :: l, nil) to cover the expressions with which they both match.

We use the term **best-fit** pattern matching to mean that if the same argument matches two patterns then we choose the pattern which 'fits it best'. We can always find such a pattern provided the set of patterns is unambiguous. Ambiguity occurs when both patterns fit 'equally well' so that we are unable to make a choice without imposing some artificial ordering like lexicographical ordering – the order in which the patterns are written down.

Best-fit pattern matching is very useful in cases when we want to say something like:

> 'if the argument matches this then do this otherwise do that'.

Using non-overlapping patterns 'otherwise' will involve writing down a separate rule for all of the alternatives to 'this'. As a simple example, suppose we wish to define an explicit tree equality function IsEqualTree which takes two trees, t_1 and t_2, and returns true only if $t_1 = t_2$. (This could, of course, be defined using = but we produce the recursive equivalent here for the purposes of the discussion!) Assuming the data definition of trees given above, there will be no less than nine cases to consider:

```
dec IsEqualTree : tree # tree → truval ;
--- IsEqualTree( empty, empty ) <= true ;
--- IsEqualTree( empty, leaf( _ ) ) <= false ;
--- IsEqualTree( empty, node( _,_,_ ) ) <= false ;
:
--- IsEqualTree( node( l1, v1, r1 ), node( l2, v2, r2 ) ) <=
          ( v1 = v2 ) and IsEqualTree( l1, l2 ) and IsEqualTree( r1, r2 ) ;
```

Using best-fit pattern matching, however, we require only four equations:

```
--- IsEqualTree( empty, empty ) <=  true ;
--- IsEqualTree( leaf( m ), leaf( n ) ) <= m = n ;
--- IsEqualTree( node(l1, v1, r1 ), node( l2, v2, r2 ) ) <=
            (v1 = v2) and IsEqualTree( l1, l2 ) and IsEqualTree( r1, r2 ) ;
--- IsEqualTree( t1, t2 ) <= false;
```

The last equation covers the six cases not covered by the first three.

It is possible to adapt the translation algorithm given above for best-fit pattern matching by modifying the merge function M and the structure of each leaf node. Although we shall not go into much detail we shall at least outline the approach; a more detailed treatment of the subject can be found in Field *et al.* (1988).

The first thing we need to be able to do is compare two patterns for specificity and for this we define an ordering function » such that $P_i \gg P_j$ iff $S_j \supset S_i$. Next we modify the structure of the leaf nodes and allow them to contain a list of equation numbers rather than just one. The reason for this is that we may now be required to merge two leaf nodes and in the event that neither pattern corresponding to those leaf nodes is more specific than the other we must leave all of the equation numbers at the merged leaf awaiting a more specific pattern to replace them. If at the end of the whole merge a leaf node still exists with more than one equation number in its component list, then we know that there is ambiguity in the set of patterns. This suggests the following additional rules for M (we shall exclude the binding lists from the leaf nodes for simplicity):

$$
\begin{aligned}
M(\{M\},\{N\}) &= \{[n]\} && \text{if } P_n \gg P_m \text{ for all } m \text{ in the list } L,\ m \neq n \\
&\quad \{L\} && \text{otherwise} \\
&\quad \text{where } L = M <> N
\end{aligned}
$$

where <> is the Hope-like list append function. It is now also possible for internal nodes to be legally merged with leaf nodes (this could not happen with non-overlapping patterns) and so we need two further rules for M to cover these cases. When merging an internal node, N, with a leaf node, L, we observe that the constructor tests specified in N, and in the subtrees of N, simply place further constraints on the argument expression than are specified by the pattern(s) corresponding to L. This means that the equation(s) specified in L will all match wherever those in N do and even where they do not. Consequently the rules for M in these cases must merge L with each leaf node of the subtrees in N, which can be achieved recursively using the rule:

$$
\begin{aligned}
&M(\{L\}, \langle p, [t_1, \ldots, t_n] \rangle)) = \\
&M(\langle p, [t_1, \ldots, t_n] \rangle, \{L\}) = \\
&\langle p, [M(t_1, \{L\}), \ldots, M(t_n \{L\}] \rangle
\end{aligned}
$$

The merging of two internal nodes remains the same as before.

To illustrate how these new rules work in practice, let us consider the following set of definitions. Although the patterns overlap they are unambiguous:

```
--- f( nil, nil ) <= E1 ;
--- f( x, nil ) <= E2 ;
--- f( nil, x ) <= E3 ;
```

The three matching trees are now respectively

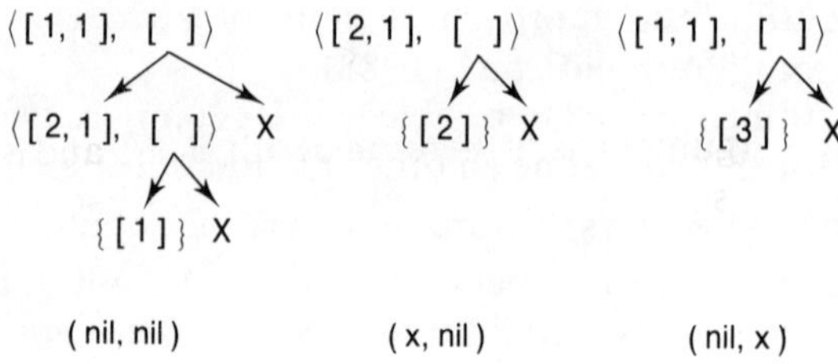

Merging the second and third trees we get:

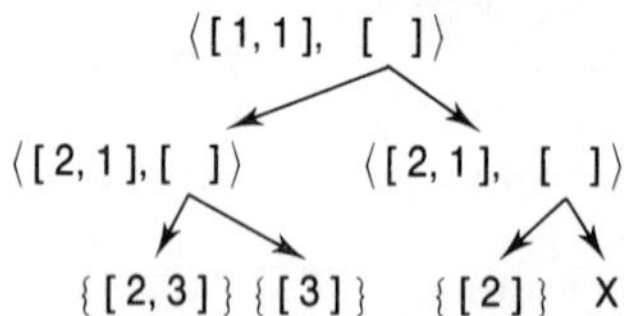

Notice that the result of merging the internal node ⟨[2, 1], [subtrees]⟩ with the leaf node { [3] } from the third equation is obtained by merging it with each of the leaf nodes in *subtrees*. We see that there are now two equation numbers in the leftmost leaf node; this reflects the fact that if both arguments to f are nil then both the second and third equations will match, i.e. they overlap. The 'no match' leaf node in the same tree has been replaced by the leaf node { [3] } reflecting the fact that the third equation matches with all argument tuples whose first component is nil. Merging the resulting tree with the matching tree for the first equation we get:

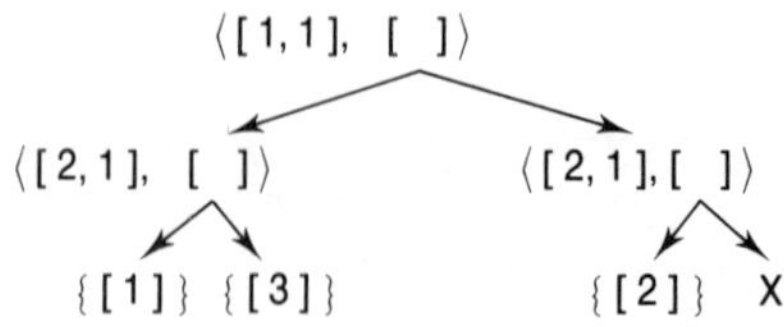

Notice that because the pattern in the first equation is more specific than the patterns of the second and third equations the leaf node { [1] } replaces the node { [2, 3] }. Because none of the leaf nodes now has a component list with more than one element we conclude that the set of patterns is unambiguous.

8.6 Literal patterns

In Hope, and in some other functional languages, we are permitted to write a definition like

```
--- f( 3 )<= E ;
```

which says 'If the argument is 3 then the result is E'; and similarly for other literal patterns such as characters and constant lists. Although our translation algorithm does not allow literal pattern expressions it is straightforward to support such patterns by including a new type of node in the matching tree for each equation. Currently, an internal node of the matching tree specifies a test on the constructor code of a component of the argument expression as given by the 'position' in that node. To allow for literal patterns we must also include internal nodes which specify equality tests on literal argument components, each of which will be ultimately implemented using the primitive EQ in the intermediate code. We shall write such a node as follows:

⟨⟨ literal, position, subtree, subtree ⟩⟩

where the double brackets ⟨⟨ and ⟩⟩ distinguish these literal pattern nodes. The 'position' specifies the argument component being tested as before; the 'literal' specifies the value which the selected argument component must have for the match to succeed and the two (matching) 'subtree's correspond to the test succeeding and failing respectively; the latter is therefore always X. As an example, the matching tree for the Hope equation

```
--- f( 0, x :: l ) <= E ;
```

would now be

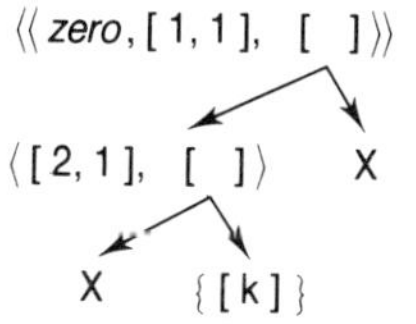

```
⟨⟨zero, [ 1, 1 ],  [    ]⟩⟩
        ↙              ↘
⟨[ 2, 1 ],  [    ]⟩      X
     ↙       ↘
    X      { [ k ] }
```

where k is the associated equation number and *zero* is the intermediate code representation of the literal 0. If this were the only equation for f (so that k = 1) then the intermediate code generated for f would be

```
λa. IF  ( EQ ( INDEX 1 a ) 0 )
        ( CASE-2 ( INDEX 1 ( INDEX 2 a ) )
            error      (cannot occur since program is type-correct!)
            error      (in pattern matching)
            let x = INDEX 2 ( INDEX 2 a ) in
                let l = INDEX 3 ( INDEX 2 a ) in E′ )
        error          (in pattern matching)
```

where again E′ is the intermediate code for E. This assumes, of course, that the additional application of CASE-1 around the code for the matching tree has been removed in the manner described in Section 8.4.1 – the additional CASE operator is not required since only one copy of E′ is guaranteed to be produced.

8.7 On the order of testing

As a short aside notice that throughout our discussions we have assumed a left-to-right, depth-first order of testing on the understanding that the choice of order was unimportant so long as we were consistent. In an eager implementation this is certainly true; however, in a lazy implementation a change in the order of testing can result in a change in the termination characteristics of the program. Let us look at a simple example to illustrate this

```
--- f( x, nil, a :: b ) <= E1 ;
--- f( a :: b, x, nil ) <= E2 ;
--- f( nil, a :: b, x ) <= E3 ;
```

Suppose that we test the arguments in a left-to-right, depth-first order. An application of the form

f(non-terminating expression, nil, E_1 :: E_2) **(1)**

will then cause non-termination but an application of the form

f(nil, E_1 :: E_2, non-terminating expression) **(2)**

will evaluate to E_3 (with the appropriate bindings for a, b and x made). Now suppose that we swap the order of testing and instead test the argument components from right to left. Expressions of the form of (1) above will now evaluate to E_1 whereas expressions of the form of (2) will fail to terminate.

A second assumption we have made is that all patterns which are candidates for a match are tested (notionally) simultaneously, each test possibly eliminating certain patterns from the candidate set. In some languages, however, the patterns are defined to be tested *sequentially* from top to bottom, with each pattern being tested from left to right until either it succeeds, or fails or leads to non-termination; Miranda is an example of such a language. This also affects the termination characteristics of a function; going back to our example, expressions of the form (1) above will then evaluate to E_1 and (2) to E_3. (The translation algorithm we have described can be easily adapted to support this order of testing, specifically by altering the merging function for matching trees – this is left as an exercise for the reader.) The order of testing is therefore significant in lazy languages and this must be borne in mind when using pattern matching in a source program. The differences between matching algorithms are described rigorously by a formal semantics. In Appendix C we provide this for a sequential top to bottom scheme and a correspondingly more complex semantics for best fit matching may be found in Field *et al.* (1988).

This concludes our description of the translation mechanism. It will be noted that each function definition is translated into a lambda abstraction of a single bound variable in the case of Hope. This reflects the fact that Hope functions must be viewed strictly as taking a single tuple of arguments rather than a number of separate arguments. If we translate a curried language like Miranda into the same intermediate code, however, then each function would be represented in the intermediate code in its curried form. For example, the Miranda definition

```
f x y z = E
```

will be translated into the intermediate code expression

$$f \;=\; \lambda x.\lambda y.\lambda x.E'$$

(where E′ is the intermediate code for E) with a surrounding letrec. We could, of course, represent Hope functions on tuples as curried functions of more than one argument but there would be little point since all applications of those functions would be complete, so that we would never require the facility for partial application. The translation of languages like LISP and FP is similar to that of Hope except that there is no pattern matching to remove and these languages exploit the list processing primitives like CONS, HD, TL etc. to build and decompose argument lists rather than using TUPLE-n, INDEX etc. to build and decompose argument tuples as with Hope. Double-ended list processing functions would, of course, be the most suitable primitives for the translation of FP.

SUMMARY

- The sugared lambda calculus provides a good general-purpose intermediate code for functional languages.
- Most high-level language features translate straightforwardly into the intermediate code, the obvious exception being pattern matching.
- Applications of constructor functions are represented as applications of tuple-building functions like TUPLE-n, the first element being the constructor code.
- The translation of pattern matching involves building a matching tree from which efficient case-analysis code can be generated.
- The matching tree for a set of patterns is the result of merging the matching trees of the individual patterns.
- As well as testing the shape of the argument the translated pattern matching code must also bind the variables named in a pattern.
- For languages which do not allow overlapping patterns the translation algorithm can be extended to detect overlapping equations.
- Best-fit pattern matching allows patterns to overlap provided they are not collectively unambiguous.
- Literals in patterns are easily handled by introducing a new node type in the matching tree together with a test on the literal's value.

EXERCISES

8.1 (a) Write out the abstract syntax tree for the Hope equation

```
--- f( node( _, a, empty ) ) <= g( a + 1 ) ;
```

based on the data definition given in Figure 8.1.

(b) In Hope we can pass a constructor as a parameter to a higher-order function (refer back to the discussion of reduce in Chapter 3 for an example). Furthermore, in a curried language constructors can be partially applied. However, we have mentioned nothing about partial tuples in our intermediate code, so does this mean that higher-order constructors are not possible using our translation scheme?

8.2 Write down the definitions of the 'position' comparison operators <, > and = in Hope, assuming that positions have the type list(num).

8.3 Write down a data definition for non-overlapping matching trees in Hope. How might this be extended to accommodate character and integer literals in patterns?

8.4 Consider the following data definition

```
data funny == zero ++ one( funny ) ++ two( funny # funny )
                ++ three( funny # funny # funny ) ;
```

(a) How might the following expressions be represented in the intermediate code?

(i) zero

(ii) two(one(zero), zero)

(iii) three(three(zero, zero, one(zero)), zero, zero)

(b) Draw the matching trees for each equation in the following definition (assuming the merging algorithm for non-overlapping patterns):

```
dec f : funny # funny # funny → num ;
--- f( two( _ , zero ), zero, _ ) <= 7 ;
--- f( two( zero, one( zero ) ), _ , three( _ , _ ,x ) )
        <= g( x ) ;
--- f( _, zero, two( a, b ) ) <= h( a , b , zero ) ;
```

(c) Produce the merged matching tree from the individual matching trees.

(d) What are the bind lists for each equation?

(e) Write down the binding code which will be generated for the third equation of f.

8.5 In Hope we are permitted to write a pattern in which the whole argument tuple of a constructor is named. For example, we can write

```
--- f( . . . , node T, . . . ) <= . . .
```

where node is defined in the tree data type given above and where T denotes the argument tuple of node. Does this facility require special consideration in the translation algorithm? Justify your answer.

8.6 (a) Go through the function IsEqualTree given in the section on best-fit pattern matching and draw the matching trees for each of the four equations.

(b) Merge these trees incrementally and outline the structure of the resulting intermediate code.

(c) Rather than test for specificity (using ») whenever we merge two leaf nodes we could simply accumulate a list of overlapping equation numbers at the leaves and test for specificity (and ambiguity) after the merging is complete. Outline the modifications to the merging function required to do this.

8.7 The definition of unambiguity says that given two overlapping and ambiguous patterns each disambiguating pattern must be a specialization of both patterns and must match with each argument which matches both patterns. Although the merging algorithm tests for specificity explain why it does not need to test for overlap.

8.8 In our earlier discussions we assumed that the constructors nil and :: in Hope were treated as though they were user-defined constructors, i.e. we assumed that they were represented using tuples in the normal way with the constructor code for nil being 0 and :: being 1. Now suppose that nil were mapped to the intermediate code function NIL and :: to the intermediate code function CONS. Outline the changes required to the translation algorithm to accommodate this mapping. What is the major advantage of performing this mapping in the first place?

8.9 (a) What changes must be made to the algorithm for translating pattern matching in order to support curried functions?

(b) Why do curried constructors not present a problem?

Chapter 9
Interpretation techniques

The simplest implementation of a functional language takes the form of an interpreter for that language. In this context an interpreter is simply a function which takes the abstract representation of a program as an argument and which reduces that program to its final value, i.e. to its weak head-normal form according to some well defined reduction order. In this chapter we shall explore the various interpretation techniques using the intermediate code defined in the previous chapter as our subject language and, for consistency, Hope as our defining language. We could, of course, have based our discussions on a source language such as Hope or Miranda rather than the intermediate code but this would have been rather longwinded and would have obscured many of the important aspects of the interpretation mechanism.

The chapter is divided into three main sections. Section 9.1 introduces a Hope data type to represent the abstract syntax trees of intermediate code programs and Section 9.2 describes the basic interpretation mechanism in terms of an eager evaluator for intermediate code programs. In Section 9.3 we modify this interpreter to support call-by-name and describe various techniques for achieving sharing which results in call-by-need and hence lazy evaluation. We conclude the chapter by discussing in more general terms the problems associated with using an interpreter to define the operational semantics of a language.

9.1 An abstract representation of the intermediate code

The abstract syntax tree of an intermediate code program can be represented by a Hope data structure described using a standard **data** definition. This can be generated from the intermediate code by writing a parser or alternatively it can be generated directly from the abstract syntax tree of the source program, the latter approach being the more efficient as it avoids the textual representation of the intermediate code altogether.

We shall name the data type for abstract syntax trees exp to stand for 'expression'. The constructors introduced in this definition reflect the various expression types specified in the BNF description of the intermediate code, together with the various base types we choose to support. For the purposes of this discussion we shall confine ourselves to the integers as our only base type and the integer arithmetic functions + and − as our only primitives. Once we have provided an implementation for these, other base types and primitives can be added sytematically. The Hope data definition for the abstract syntax tree of an intermediate code expression is given in Figure 9.1. Notice that for clarity we have provided an auxiliary type definition for identifiers which are here assumed to be character strings.

Some examples of intermediate code expressions and their corresponding abstract representations are given below.

Expression	Abstract representation
+ 8 x	APP(APP(PRIM("+"), INT(8)), VAR("x"))
λz.z 4	LAM("z", APP(VAR("z"), INT(4)))
let p = + in (f p)	LET("p", PRIM("+"), APP(VAR("f"), VAR("p")))

We recall from Chapter 3 that a function can be applied either eagerly or lazily (i.e. using either call-by-value or call-by-need parameter passing) and to illustrate how these calling mechanisms are supported in practice we shall develop a separate interpreter for each in the next two sections.

In addition to providing an implementation of the intermediate code, the interpreter will also provide an operational semantics for it. This gives meaning to the intermediate code by describing how each feature of that code is implemented. However, we have to be very careful here because in order to define a precise semantics we must first have a detailed understanding of the defining language, i.e. the language in which the interpreter itself is written. In particular, as we shall see, the calling semantics of the defined language (the intermediate code in this

```
type id   == list ( char ) ;
data exp  == VAR( id )                              ++
             LAM( id # exp )                        ++
             APP( exp # exp )                       ++
             LET( id # exp # exp )                  ++
             RLET( list( id # exp ) # exp )         ++
             INT( num )                             ++
             PRIM( id ) ;
```

Figure 9.1 The Hope data type for abstract expressions.

case) is dependent on the calling semantics of the defining language. In the following discussion our defining language will be the standard implementation of Hope in which all constructors are called by-need and all other functions by-value. It is vitally important to bear this in mind because, as we shall see, using the lazy implementation of Hope the interpreter produces a rather different implementation of the intermediate code.

9.2 An eager interpreter

At the heart of most interpreters for functional languages there are two functions called Eval and Apply. Eval is defined to evaluate an argument expression to its weak head-normal form and Apply (which can be viewed as an auxiliary function to Eval) evaluates a function application to its weak head-normal form. The resulting interpreter is often called an Eval / Apply interpreter for obvious reasons; the earliest such interpreter is described in McCarthy (1960).

The interpreter we describe here implements function application (i.e. β-reduction) by leaving the body of the function intact and remembering the bindings for the bound variable in a special structure called an **environment**. This achieves the same effect as the copying (i.e. textual substitution) process suggested naturally by the lambda calculus as described in Chapter 6; indeed we examined briefly the use of environments in our discussions on sharing in Section 6.6. An environment simply provides an association between names (in this case bound variable identifiers) and expressions so that the binding for a given identifier can be determined by looking up the identifier in the current environment and returning the corresponding expression.

The actual representation of the environment is of little concern to us here and so we shall simply view the environment as an abstract data type (called environment) with access functions for adding named expressions and for looking up the expression associated with a given name. It will be helpful, however, to have some concrete way of representing an association and so we shall write

```
( n, e )
```

to mean an association between the name n and the expression e. (This corresponds conveniently to the Hope tuple notation which we shall use in the interpreter itself.) We shall require the following four functions for manipulating the environment:

empty The (constant) function which returns the empty environment.

:+: The infix insert function. ρ :+: (n, e) denotes the environment ρ with the additional association (n, e).

:++: Similar to :+: except that it adds a *list* of associations to the environment.

|| The infix lookup function. ρ || n denotes the value associated with the identifier n in the environment ρ. We require:

$$(\rho :+: (n, e)) \,\|\, n = e$$
$$(\rho :+: (n, e)) \,\|\, m = \rho \,\|\, m \qquad \text{if } n \neq m$$

Note that a lookup returns the most recent binding for a name in the case where two different associations with the same name have been added, so we require one further axiom, namely:

$$((\rho :+: (n, e_1)) :+: (n, e_2)) \,\|\, n = e_2$$

For the sake of simplicity we shall not consider the possibility of the environment being empty when a look up is attempted.

We can now write down the Hope type declarations of Eval and Apply. Eval takes an expression (of type exp as defined in Figure 9.1) and an environment and returns another expression – the weak head-normal form of the argument expression:

```
dec Eval : exp # environment → exp ;
```

Apply takes a function expression and an argument expression and returns the result of applying the function to the argument:

```
dec Apply : exp # exp → exp ;
```

Apply is not required to take the environment as an argument for reasons which will become apparent later on.

In keeping with the Hope programming style described in Part I, we shall now define Eval and Apply by providing one rule for each possible argument expression type, i.e. one rule for each constructor in the exp data type. The important thing to remember at each stage is that the various rules for Eval and Apply must all reduce the given expressions to their weak head-normal forms; so if the expression is already in weak head-normal form then we must return it unmodified, otherwise we must perform the necessary simplifications to reduce it to its weak head-normal form.

9.2.1 Rules for Eval

Initially we begin with seven equations to define the function Eval, corresponding to each of the constructors in the type exp. However, we will also need to introduce two additional constructors as 'internal expression types' to represent function values when we consider the interpretation of primitive functions and lambda abstractions. Here then are the rules:

1. Function application (constructor APP)

Here we first evaluate the function and argument expressions to their weak head-normal form and then use Apply to complete the application:

```
--- Eval( APP( E1, E2 ), env ) <= Apply( Eval( E1, env ), Eval( E2, env ) ) ;
```

Notice that we evaluate the argument expression (E2) *before* applying the function; this corresponds to call-by-value as we require for this interpreter. However, it should be noted that E2 is only evaluated first because in the standard implementation of Hope functions themselves are called by-value. We shall return to this issue in Section 9.3.1.

2. Integers (constructor INT)

Here, we return the integer immediately as it is already in weak head-normal form:

```
--- Eval( e & INT( _ ), _ ) <= e ;
```

(and similarly for any other base-type objects which we choose to support).

3. Identifiers (constructor VAR)

The value associated with an identifier is obtained by looking up the name of that identifier in the environment:

```
--- Eval( VAR( v ), env ) <=env || v ;
```

4. Primitive functions (constructor PRIM)

Primitive functions present an interesting problem to the interpreter because in general we must be able to represent partial applications of them (this cannot be expressed directly in a source language like Hope but it is certainly possible in the intermediate code). We must therefore decide what to return as a result of evaluating an expression like the following:

```
APP( PRIM( "+" ), INT( 1 ) )
```

We cannot apply the primitive until it has all its required arguments (two in the case of "+") and so we have to build a special structure to represent the partial application. This structure will take the form of a triple containing:

(1) the name of the primitive function (so that we know which rule to apply when all the arguments are eventually available). This is the argument of the PRIM constructor.

(2) the number of arguments 'pending' (which tells us how many arguments we still require before the primitive's application can be reduced).

(3) a list containing the arguments which are already available. Initially this list is empty.

Notice that the sum of the length of the list (3) and the number of arguments pending (2) is a constant, the arity of the primitive function concerned. Because this triple is a valid expression, we must augment the data definition of exp to allow for it. We shall label this new expression type by the constructor OP:

```
data exp ==VAR( id ) ++ . . . ++ RLET( list( id # exp ) # exp ) ++
           OP( id # num # list( exp ) ) ;
```

An occurrence of a primitive function symbol can be viewed as a partial application of that primitive to no arguments so that the rule for Eval where the expression is a primitive is as follows:

```
--- Eval( e & PRIM( p ), _ ) <= OP( p, ArityOf( p ), nil ) ;
```

ArityOf is an auxiliary function which returns the arity of the given primitive. Its definition is straightforward:

```
dec ArityOf : id → num ;
--- ArityOf( "+" ) <= 2 ;
--- ArityOf( "−" ) <= 2 ;
```

and similarly for any other primitives we choose to support. Because a partially applied primitive is itself a weak head-normal form (recall the discussion of currying in Chapter 6) we require the further rule:

```
--- Eval( e & OP( _, _, _ ), _ ) <= e ;
```

It is important to understand that OP constructors do not initially exist in the internal form of an intermediate code program; they are only generated by the interpreter as a result of evaluating primitive functions.

5. Qualified expressions (constructor LET)

Here, we evaluate the resultant expression (E2) in the environment augmented by the binding of the new variable (v) to the result of evaluating the qualifier expression (E1):

```
--- Eval( LET( v, E1, E2 ), env ) <= Eval( E2, env :+: ( v, Eval( E1, env ) ) ) ;
```

We often talk of qualified expressions having the effect of 'extending the current environment' to reflect the fact that their evaluation causes additional bindings to be added to the environment. Notice that we again have eager evaluation in that E1 is evaluated before E2. This is precisely what we would expect since, as we have already seen, the expression let $x = E_1$ in E_2 is equivalent to the application $(\lambda x.E_2)\ E_1$.

6. Lambda abstractions (constructor LAM)

This rule is complicated by the fact that the body of the lambda expression may contain free variables. To illustrate this problem, consider the evaluation of the following expression, which is the internal form of the intermediate code expression $\lambda x.\ +\ x\ y$:

```
LAM( "x", APP( APP( PRIM( plus ), VAR( "x" ) ), VAR( "y" ) ) )
```

(plus denotes OP("+", 2, nil) as described above).

The problem here is that the binding for y is given in the environment extant from the point of evaluation. Because the lambda expression is in weak head-normal form we have to return it as it is, but there is a danger that in doing so we may lose the correct binding for the free variable y, which is stored in that environment. (This is called the FUNARG problem by some authors.) For this reason we must return not only the expression but also the environment which provides the correct binding for y. This composite structure is called a **closure** because it represents a closed expression, i.e. an expression which contains no free variables (refer to Chapter 6). What we mean here by 'free variable' is a variable with no associated value. Although it is possible for the body of a closure to contain variables which are strictly speaking free in that they are not bound by a corresponding LAM expression, each of these variables has an associated value in the environment. Hence variables bound to values in the environment of a closure can be viewed simply as alternative representations of those values. Indeed, had we implemented a copy-based interpreter rather than an environment-based interpreter these variables would have been physically replaced by their corresponding argument values and so would not be present at all.

In order to represent closures in our interpreter we must add a further new constructor to the exp data type as follows:

```
data exp == INT( num ) ++ . . . ++ OP( id # num # list( exp ) ) ++
            CLOSURE( exp # environment ) ;
```

The rule for Eval in the case where the expression is a lambda abstraction is then:

```
--- Eval( e & LAM( _,_ ), env ) <= CLOSURE( e, env ) ;
```

Because closures represent functions and because functions are themselves weak head-normal forms, we must also include a rule for Eval in the case where the expression is a closure:

```
--- Eval( e & CLOSURE( _, _ ), _ ) <= e ;
```

As with partially applied primitives (constructor OP), closures do not initially exist in the internal form of an intermediate code program and are only generated by the interpreter as a result of evaluating lambda abstractions.

Notice that the use of closures guarantees that variables are bound statically as described in Chapter 3. If we were to omit closures then the interpreter would implement dynamic binding since the environment argument of Eval can only grow allowing new (dynamic) bindings to replace the correct static ones.

7. Recursive let expressions (constructor RLET)

The treatment of recursive definitions forms the trickiest part of the interpreter. For simplicity we shall assume that every definition is a lambda abstraction (i.e. a function) so that we must build a closure from each definition in turn and add the appropriate bindings to the environment (this can be relaxed slightly – see the exercise at the end of the chapter). The problem we encounter with these definitions can be understood by looking at a simple example:

```
letrec f = λy.g x, g = λz.h f z
in f 1
```

The closures for f and g must contain not only the bindings for the free variables x and h which must exist in the environment when the expression is evaluated but also the bindings for both f and g themselves. Consider, then, the closure for f. The environment for this closure must be the current environment augmented with the bindings (f, C_f) and (g, C_g) where C_f is the closure for f and C_g is the closure for g. However, the environment inside C_f must also contain the bindings for f and g, which are themselves closures. Therefore, these closures must also contain an environment which includes the bindings for f and g, and so on. The process continues indefinitely.

The solution to this problem is suggested by its circularity: a circular environment is needed, i.e. an environment which notionally 'loops back' on itself. We have seen how to build circular ('knot-tied') structures in Chapter 4 by using recursive **let** or **where** expressions and we use the same technique here:

```
--- Eval( RLET( defs, E ), env ) <= Eval( E, NewEnv )
      where NewEnv == env :++: map ( lambda ( n, e ) =>
                              ( n, CLOSURE (e, NewEnv ) ), defs ) ;
```

The call to map in this rule has the effect of building a closure from each function in the list of definitions (defs). The environment for each closure is NewEnv, hence the circularity. The result of the map is a list of name/closure pairs which are added to the environment env using the access function :++:. This relies on the fact that the value of NewEnv is not immediately required, by virtue of the fact that the arguments to the constructor CLOSURE are not evaluated at the point of call.

Now, it should be apparent that we are exploiting the fact that Hope constructors are lazy in the standard implementation of Hope in order that the circular environment can be constructed. The astute reader might now ask what happens if we use a strict language such as strict LISP or FP as the defining language. Using these languages it is not possible to construct a circular environment without some form of lazy evaluation – in this case just lazy constructors – without the program looping indefinitely. In the absence of a circular environment the only way to ensure that bindings are not incorrectly superseded is to rename the variables introduced in RLET expressions to make them unique with respect to the other variables in the program, this being done once and for all before the interpreter is invoked. The binding of a given variable can then only be superseded by a binding of the same variable which, of course, is quite safe because of referential transparency (cf. normal recursion). The rule for Eval in the case of RLET expressions would then be

```
--- Eval( RLET( defs, E ), env ) <= Eval( E, env :++: defs ) ;
```

We have now considered all the expression types, so completing the definition of Eval. We shall now move on to the definition of Apply.

9.2.2 Definition of Apply

To define Apply, we give one equation for each possible type of function. There are, in fact, only two types of function to consider -- closures and primitives – this being apparent from the right-hand sides of the above rules for Eval.

To apply a closure (containing a lambda expression and an environment) to an argument value, we simply evaluate the body of the lambda expression in the closure environment updated to include the binding of the bound variable (v) to the argument value (A):

```
--- Apply( CLOSURE( LAM( v, B ), env ), A ) <= Eval( B, env :+: ( v, A ) ) ;
```

Notice that Apply is not required to take the environment as an argument. This is as a result of evaluating both the function and the argument expressions before calling Apply. The only evaluated expressions which can contain (free) variables in this interpreter are lambda abstractions and the bindings for these variables are given in the corresponding closure. Notice that to evaluate a function application we have to use Eval rather than Apply directly.

This leaves us with the rule for handling primitives which are labelled by the constructor OP (see the rule for evaluating primitives above). If the pending argument count (PAC) of the primitive operator is 1, then the application will serve to complete the argument list for the function and the primitive rule (the delta rule) can be applied. If the PAC is greater than 1, then we have to form a new primitive whose PAC is one less than before and whose arglist is appropriately extended; this says that the result of partially applying a primitive function is itself another

```
type id    == list( char ) ;
data exp   == INT( num ) ++ VAR( id ) ++ PRIM( id ) ++
              APP( exp # exp ) ++ LAM( id # exp ) ++ LET( id # exp # exp ) ++
              RLET( list( id # exp ) # exp ) ++ OP( id # num # list( exp ) ) ++
              CLOSURE( exp # environment ) ;

dec Eval    : exp # environment → exp ;
dec Apply   : exp # exp → exp ;
dec ArityOf : id → num ;
dec FunOf   : id → ( list( exp ) → exp) ;

--- Eval( APP( E1, E2 ), env )        <= Apply( Eval( E1, env), Eval( E2, env ) ) ;
--- Eval( e & INT(_), _ )             <= e ;
--- Eval( VAR( v ), env )             <= env || v ;
--- Eval( PRIM( p ), _ )              <= OP( p, ArityOf( p ), nil ) ;
--- Eval( e & OP( _, _, _ ), _ )      <= e ;
--- Eval( LET( v, E1, E2 ), env )     <= Eval( E2, env :+: ( v, Eval( E1, env ) ) ) ;
--- Eval( e & LAM( _, _ ), env )      <= CLOSURE( e, env ) ;
--- Eval( e & CLOSURE( _, _ ), _ )    <= e ;
--- Eval( RLET( defs, E ), env )      <= Eval( E, NewEnv )
      where NewEnv = = env :+ +: map( lambda ( n, e ) =>
          ( n, CLOSURE ( e, NewEnv ) ), defs ) ;

--- Apply( CLOSURE( LAM( v, B ), env), A ) <= Eval( B, env :+: ( v, A ) ) ;
--- Apply( OP( p, PAC, args ), A ) <=
      ( if PAC = 1 then ( FunOf( p ) )( arglist ) else OP( p, PAC − 1,arglist ) )
      where arglist == args <> [ A ] ;

--- ArityOf( "+" ) <= 2 ;
--- ArityOf( "−" ) <= 2 ;

--- FunOf( "+" )  <= lambda [ INT( a ), INT( b ) ] => INT( a + b ) ;
--- FunOf( "−" )  <= lambda [ INT( a ), INT( b ) ] => INT( a − b ) ;
```

Figure 9.2 The eager interpreter.

primitive function:

```
--- Apply( OP( p, PAC, args ), A )
      <= ( if PAC = 1 then ( FunOf( p ) )( arglist )
           else OP( p, PAC-1, arglist ) )
               where arglist == args <> [A] ;
```

FunOf is a higher-order function which returns the Hope function required to implement the given primitive (another useful application of higher-order functions). Its type declaration looks like this:

```
dec FunOf : id → ( list( exp ) → exp ) ;
```

The returned function must be written to accept the primitive's arguments in the form of a list of expressions because the argument 'accumulator' (args) is itself a list. We can use the full power of Hope pattern matching here to help us:

```
--- FunOf( "+" ) <= lambda [ INT( a ), INT( b ) ] => INT( a + b ) ;
--- FunOf( "−" ) <= lambda [ INT( a ), INT( b ) ] => INT( a − b ) ;
```

Note that we are certain that the arguments of these functions are evaluated (i.e. in the form INT(x)) because of the call-by-value nature of the interpreter – this explains why only a single pattern is required in each lambda expression.

The complete Hope listing of the interpreter is given in Figure 9.2. The simplicity of the final program further demonstrates the expressive power of the functional notation.

9.2.3 Conditional handling

The interpreter defined here implements call-by-value for every function. This means that if we implement conditional expressions in terms of the COND function then we will end up evaluating both branches of the conditional and the predicate expression each time it is applied, which will almost certainly cause the program to fail. The traditional way to solve the problem is to treat conditionals as a special case and include an additional constructor in the definition of exp to accommodate them:

```
data exp == INT( num ) ++ ... ++ CLOSURE ( exp # environment )
            ++ COND( exp # exp # exp ) ;
```

This means that for the purposes of this interpreter the intermediate code expression

cond E_1 E_2 E_3

should be translated to the following abstract syntax tree:

COND(E_1', E_2', E_3')

rather than

APP(APP(APP(PRIM("cond"), E_1'), E_2'), E_3')

where E_k' is the abstract representation of E_k. If we assume here that true and false are represented by the integers 1 and 0 respectively (in practice truth values might be supported as an additional base type), then the additional rule for Eval will look like this:

```
--- Eval( COND( E1, E2, E3 ), env ) <=
        if Eval( E1, env ) = INT( 1 ) then Eval( E2, env ) else Eval( E3, env ) ;
```

Note that this additional constructor is only required in an eager implementation; in a lazy implementation (such as the one described below) conditional expressions can be translated into calls to the primitive function cond without complications.

9.3 A lazy interpreter

We shall now modify the eager interpreter of Section 9.2 to support normal-order evaluation. To start with we shall implement call-by-name but in Section 9.3.1 we shall see various ways in which sharing and hence call-by-need can be supported.

The first, and most obvious change we have to make is to the rule for Eval when the expression argument is an application. We still require the function to be either a closure or a primitive before we can complete the application so we still need to evaluate the function before calling Apply; however, we now also want to delay the evaluation of the argument until its value is actually required. We could simply pass the argument expression to Apply intact but this again brings us back to the problem that the argument may contain references to variables. Consequently we must use a similar structure to a closure in order to remember both the argument expression and the environment which contains the correct bindings for the variables in that expression. We shall call this structure a **suspension** to reflect the fact that it represents a 'suspended' expression evaluation, although it is often referred to as a **recipe** since it represents a recipe for computing a value. To this end we modify the data definition of exp in the following way:

```
data exp == INT( num ) ++ . . . ++ CLOSURE( exp # environment )
                ++ SUSP( exp # environment ) ;
```

The rule for Eval when the expression is an application now becomes:

```
--- Eval( APP( E1, E2 ), env ) <= Apply( Eval( E1, env ), SUSP( E2, env ) ) ;
```

However, now we must also include a rule for Eval in the case that the argument expression is a suspension. This will involve evaluation of the expression inside the suspension to its weak head-normal form by invoking Eval recursively:

```
--- Eval( SUSP( E, env ), _ ) <= Eval( E, env ) ;
```

Because of the equivalence of let x = E_1 in E_2 and ($\lambda x.E_2$) E_1 we must also modify the rule for Eval for LET expressions in an analogous fashion to that of APP expressions:

```
--- Eval( LET( v, E1, E2 ), env ) <= Eval( E2, env :+: ( v, SUSP( E1, env ) ) ) ;
```

We observe that it is now possible for the environment to contain suspensions, so when we look up an identifier in the environment we are no longer guaranteed to be returned an expression in weak head-normal form. Consequently, we must apply Eval to each value we look up:

```
--- Eval( VAR( v ), env ) <= Eval( env || v, env ) ;
```

To complete the modifications to Eval we shall now extend the evaluation rule for RLET. Now that we have suspensions we can allow any set of mutually recursive definitions (i.e. not only mutually recursive functions) by building a suspension from each definition in turn instead of assuming them to be functions and building a closure for each, as above. The modification to Eval in the case of RLET is therefore straightforward:

```
--- Eval( RLET( defs, E ), env ) <= Eval( E, NewEnv )
        where NewEnv == env :++: map( lambda ( n, e ) =>
                                  ( n, SUSP( e, NewEnv ) ), defs ) ;
```

The only other rules we have to change are those for the primitive functions. Once again the argument(s) to a primitive function may be suspensions so they must be evaluated before the primitive operation can be completed:

```
--- FunOf( "+" ) <= lambda [ x, y ] => INT( a + b ) ;
                    where ( INT( a ), INT( b ) ) ==
                          ( Eval( x, empty ), Eval( y, empty ) ) ;
--- FunOf( "−" ) <= lambda [ x, y ] => INT( a − b ) ;
                    where (INT ( a ), INT( b ) ) ==
                          ( Eval( x, empty ), Eval( y, empty ) ) ;
```

Notice that Eval is called with an empty environment in each case; this is because the environment for the evaluation of each argument is contained within its corresponding suspension. The complete listing of the modified interpreter is given in Figure 9.3.

As an aside, note that it is possible to represent suspensions by using closures. Given an argument expression, E, we can use β-abstraction to translate E into the expression

$$(\lambda x.E) \ y$$

```
type id      == list( char ) ;
data exp     == INT( num ) ++ VAR( id ) ++ PRIM( id ) ++
                APP( exp # exp ) ++ LAM( id # exp ) ++ LET( id # exp # exp ) ++
                RLET( list( id # exp ) # exp ) ++ OP( id # num # list( exp ) ) ++
                CLOSURE( exp # environment ) ++ SUSP(exp # environment) ;

dec Eval    : exp # environment → exp ;
dec Apply   : exp # exp → exp ;
dec ArityOf: id → num ;
dec FunOf  : id → ( list( exp ) → exp ) ;

--- Eval( APP( E1, E2 ), env )        <= Apply( Eval( E1, env ), SUSP( E2, env ) ) ;
--- Eval( e & INT(_), _ )             <= e ;
--- Eval( VAR( v ), env )             <= Eval( env || v, env ) ;
--- Eval( PRIM( p ), _ )              <= OP( p, ArityOf( p ), nil ) ;
--- Eval( e & OP( _, _, _ ), _ )      <= e ;
--- Eval( LET( v, E1, E2 ), env )     <= Eval( E2, env :+: ( v, SUSP( E1, env ) ) ) ;
--- Eval( e & LAM( _,_ ), env )       <= CLOSURE( e, env ) ;
--- Eval( e & CLOSURE( _,_ ), _ )     <= e ;
--- Eval( SUSP( E, env ), _ )         <= Eval( E, env ) ;
--- Eval( RLET( defs, E ), env )      <= Eval( E, NewEnv )
     where NewEnv == env :++: map( lambda ( n, e ) =>
                                    ( n, SUSP( e, NewEnv ) ), defs ) ;

--- Apply( CLOSURE( LAM( v, B ), env), A ) <= Eval( B, env :+: ( v, A ) ) ;
--- Apply( OP( p, PAC, args ), A ) <=
     ( if PAC = 1 then ( FunOf( p ) )( arglist ) else PRIM( OP( p, PAC − 1,arglist ) ) )
     where arglist == args <> [ A ] ;

--- ArityOf( "+" ) <= 2 ;
--- ArityOf( "−" ) <= 2 ;

--- FunOf( "+" )  <= lambda [ x, y ] => INT( a + b )
                     where ( INT ( a ), INT ( b ) ) == ( Eval ( x, empty ), Eval ( y, empty ) ) ;
--- FunOf( "−" )  <= lambda [ x, y ] => INT( a − b )
                     where ( INT ( a ), INT ( b ) ) == ( Eval( x, empty ), Eval( y, empty ) ) ;
```

Figure 9.3 The modified interpreter.

for any y provided neither x nor y occurs free in E. Indeed, if we allow the idea of 'void' parameters, written ⊗ and 'dummy' expressions, written ?, then we can write this as:

(λ⊗.E) ?

without having to worry about naming problems. With this done, we can form a closure from the resulting function (i.e. λ⊗.E) and so mimic the behaviour of suspensions. This leads to the following equivalence:

SUSP(E, env) ≅ CLOSURE(LAM(⊗,E), env)

The story isn't quite complete, however, because, unlike suspensions, we have to explicitly 'force' the evaluation of E whenever the value of E is required. To do this we have to apply the closure for E to a dummy argument. This forcing is only required to be done where the value of the expression is actually needed, i.e. during the interpretation of strict primitives such as + and −. So, for example, we define instead

```
--- FunOf( '+') <= lambda [ x, y ] => INT( a + b )
        where ( INT( a ), INT( b ) ) == ( Eval( APP( x, ? ), empty ),
                                          Eval( APP( y, ? ), empty ) ) ;
```

To see that the two mechanisms are equivalent let us see the effect of Eval in both cases. Firstly, for suspensions we have:

```
Eval( SUSP( E, env1 ), env2 )
→ Eval( E, env1 )
```

And now for the closure representation:

```
Eval( APP( CLOSURE( LAM( ⊗, E ), env1 ), ? ), env2 )
→ Apply( Eval( CLOSURE( LAM ( ⊗, E ), env1 ), env2 ),
         CLOSURE( LAM( ⊗,? ), env2 ) )
→ Apply( CLOSURE( LAM( ⊗, E ), env1 ),
         CLOSURE(LAM( ⊗,? ), env2 ) )
→ Eval( E, env1 :+: ( ⊗, CLOSURE( LAM( ⊗, ? ), env2 ) )
≅ Eval( E, env1 )
```

since ⊗ is the void identifier and so does not extend the environment upon insertion.

Notice, however, that if an argument is referred to more than once inside a function body, then a separate evaluation of the suspension or application of the corresponding closure to a dummy parameter must be performed. This has the effect of re-evaluating the argument each time it is required and so the calling mechanism achieved is actually call-by-name. To implement lazy evaluation we have to support call-by-need, which requires us to share not only the argument expressions but also the argument results. The mechanisms for achieving this are described in the next section.

9.3.1 Implementing call-by-need

In Chapter 6, we saw the following lambda expression:

$$(\lambda x.\ +\ x\ x)\ E$$

and showed how, using environments, we avoid creating two copies of E.

We get the same effect in our interpreter so that after the first application there will be two references to the same expression within the environment and the expression is shared.

The problem with the interpreter at the moment, however, is that when E is eventually reduced to its weak head-normal form (after the evaluation of the leftmost argument of +, say) the environment is not updated. This means that the evaluation of the rightmost argument of + will cause E to be evaluated a second time. So, despite the fact that we create only a single copy of the argument expression, we still end up repeating the evaluation of E so that the interpreter implements call-by-name. Now, although this might suggest that we require some form of destructive assignment operator in order to effect the replacement of a suspension by its final value in the environment, a more satisfactory (i.e. referentially transparent) solution exists which again exploits the fact that constructors in the standard implementation of Hope are themselves called by-need. The trick here is to embed a call to the Eval function within each suspension as it is created:

```
--- Eval( APP( E1, E2 ), env ) <= Apply( Eval( E1, env ),
                                         SUSP( Eval( E2, env) ) ) ;
```

(requiring an obvious modification to exp to accommodate the change to the SUSP constructor). The argument to the SUSP constructor is now an expression but this will not be evaluated until its value is actually required, after which that value will be shared. This only occurs in the corresponding rule for Eval, which must now be modified as follows:

```
--- Eval( SUSP( E ), _ ) <= E ;
```

Now let us return to our simple example given above. The first time the value of the closure for E is required (i.e. during the evaluation of one of the arguments of +) the expression within the suspension will be evaluated; when the second argument to + is evaluated the suspension is again retrieved from the environment, but this time the expression contained within it will be found in its weak head-normal form. So, although we have to retrieve the closure twice from the environment we only have to perform the evaluation of the argument expression once. This gives us call-by-need.

Now consider what would have happened if we had used the lazy implementation of Hope instead of the standard implementation. Let us return to the eager interpreter of Section 9.1 and to the rule for Eval where the expression is an application:

```
--- Eval( APP( E1, E2 ), env ) <= Apply( Eval( E1, env), Eval( E2, env) ) ;
```

We noted that E2 would be evaluated before applying the function because in the standard implementation of Hope functions themselves are called by-value. Using the lazy implementation of Hope, however, E2 will not be evaluated immediately because the expression Eval(E2, env) is a parameter to the Apply function and so is itself passed by-need. The effect of this is that the environment contains 'suspended' calls to the Eval function. These calls will only be completed when actually required, i.e. during the interpretation of the strict operators, as in

```
--- FunOf( "+" ) <= lambda [ INT( a ), INT( b ) ] => INT( a + b ) ;
```

When this function is applied (in ApplyPrim) the argument expressions must be evaluated in order for the pattern matching to succeed, and it is at this point that the suspended calls to Eval will be completed. Furthermore, these suspended calls will be automatically replaced by their values (INT(a) and INT(b) respectively), so implementing call-by-need. So, although the rule for Eval above looks as though it implements call-by-value it would actually implement call-by-need!

This observation about the behaviour of the interpreters exposes an interesting question: how *do* we implement call-by-value using a lazy defining language? The answer is that we can't unless we use some trick to 'force' the evaluation of the argument, like comparing it with itself:

```
--- Eval( APP( E, A ), env ) <=
        let E == Eval( A, env ) in
        if E = E then Apply( Eval( F, env ), E) else Apply( Eval( F, env ), E ) ;
```

However, even this will not work if the implementation uses the fact that E = E is always true without requiring E to be evaluated (If we define = to be a strict function then $\perp = \perp$ must deliver $\perp$ rather than true. In other words, both arguments of = will then be fully evaluated and the forcing trick referred to will work.)

These points are very subtle indeed and are well worth summarizing: Using a fully eager defining language (without even lazy constructors) we can interpret call-by-value without complication (although we cannot build a circular environment sufficient to support arbitrary recursive definitions); we can also interpret call-by-name by having explicit suspensions, but we cannot effect call-by-need because we cannot explicitly overwrite the environment. If the defining language supports lazy constructors and eager functions (like the standard implementation of Hope) then we can implement call-by-value, call-by-name and call-by-need by using the eager properties of functions and the lazy properties of constructors. If the defining language is lazy throughout (like the lazy implementation of Hope) then we can interpret call-by-name (using the original version of the SUSP constructor given above) and call-by-need, but call-by-value is only possible if we explicitly force the evaluation of expressions using a strict operator like =.

This is one sense in which an interpreter can be very misleading as a means of describing a language. We can learn much from the interpreter so long as we have a detailed understanding of the semantics of the defining language. However, if we have any doubts or misconceptions about this language then we can get a totally false idea of the semantics of the defined language. This situation is worsened considerably if the interpreter for a language, L, say, is written in L itself (such an interpreter is called **metacircular**) for then we can look at the rule for evaluating function applications and have no idea at all which calling mechanism is intended or being implemented. This is not peculiar to function-calling semantics – each of the defined language constructs is necesssarily implemented in terms of the defining language constructs, so that if we have misunderstood any of these then we will have little chance of fully understanding the semantics of the language being defined. It is for this reason that the semantics of a programming language is often expressed in non-operational terms. In short the idea is to get away from the idea of defining a language in terms of another language and instead give the semantics independently in terms of precise mathematical concepts – a particularly appropriate medium for functional languages. This takes us away from operational semantics and into the realms of **denotational** semantics, which defines a language by explicitly stating the mathematical value denoted by each language construct, the values being drawn from some well specified domain. In order to provide a basic feel for the subject we provide in Appendix C of this book a short tutorial on denotational semantics. As we might expect, this material assumes a limited understanding of domain theory and so follows on quite naturally from the material in Appendix B.

SUMMARY

- An intermediate code program can be represented in abstract form as a data structure.
- An interpreter reduces the abstract representation of an intermediate code expression to its weak head-normal form.
- The values of all free variables in an expression are stored in a separate structure called an environment.
- Different calling mechanisms can be implemented by modifying the rule for evaluating function applications.
- Closures are used to represent functions; they remember the values of free variables in function bodies by maintaining an environment.
- Closures guarantee static binding; without them we obtain dynamic binding.
- Suspensions are used to represent unevaluated expressions in a lazy implementation.

- Suspensions also remember environments and can be simulated using closures.
- The interpretation of letrec expressions relies on the use of circular environments.
- The operational semantics of the defined language inevitably depends on the semantics of the defining language.

EXERCISES

9.1 For each of the following expressions:

(i) (λx.λy.x y y)(λx.λy.y)

(ii) (let x = 4 in λy. + x 7) 5

(iii) (λf.λg.λx.f g (+ x 1) 2) * (λx.x)

(a) write down the abstract representation of the expression as a Hope constructed data term (of type exp as given above);

(b) trace the evaluation of the expression using the eager interpreter of Section 9.2.

9.2 (a) Suppose 'environment' has the type list(identifier # exp). Write down the declarations and definitions of the access functions empty, :+:, :++: and ||.

(b) Define :++: in terms of :+: using the reduce function on lists.

(c) What will be definitions of empty, :+: and :++: if the environment is represented as a function with type identifier → expression?

9.3 Extend the interpreter to include the base type truval, the Boolean function > and the logical operator not. Write down the abstract representation of the expression (if (not (> 1 3)) (λx.x) (λx. + 1 x)) 5 and trace its evaluation.

9.4 It is clearly not necessary to form a suspension when an argument expression is in weak head-normal form or, indeed, an existing suspension. Suggest an optimization to the interpreter which would avoid these redundant suspensions.

9.5 In our interpreters we have represented partial applications of primitive functions by special triples as described in Section 9.2.

(a) Can you suggest another representation which uses closures instead?

(b) As far as the user of the interpreter is concerned what is the advantage of the special representation? (*Hint*: consider the case where the result of a program is a partially applied primitive.)

9.6 Go back and look at the rule for Eval in the case of RLET expressions in the eager interpreter of Section 9.2. Here we have assumed that each of the definitions introduces a function (we have entered only closures in the circular environment constructed). In what sense is this an over restrictive assumption, in other words what is the general rule which governs the type of expression which can occur in each definition in an eager interpreter? Use your answer to write down an alternative definition for Eval in this case.

9.7 (a) Consider the 'family' of tupling functions tuple-n, n ≥ 0, which were used in the previous chapter to represent constructed data. Remembering that n may assume any value (≥ 0) suggest how these functions might be represented in the abstract syntax tree of an intermediate code program and suggest how applications of them might be handled in the interpreter. (*Suggestion*: Introduce a new data type AllPrims which contains one constructor for each primitive, e.g.

```
data AllPrims == plus ++ minus ++ . . . ; )
```

(b) Write down the (new) rule for FunOf for the primitive tuple indexing function index for your chosen representation of tuples.

(c) Explain how lazy constructors can be incorporated into the eager interpreter of Figure 9.1. (*Hint*: Consider an additional family of primitives lazytuple-n (n ≥ 0) which is similar to the tuple-n family except that each such function is non-strict in all arguments.)

Chapter 10
Stack-based implementations – the SECD machine

The first part of this book should have provided a good understanding of functional language concepts and an introduction to their mathematical foundations. Some of the properties required of a system which evaluates functional expressions should also be apparent, for example the preservation of referential transparency and the correct realization of the evaluation order chosen for the language. In the previous chapter we considered the interpretation of functional languages, and looked at interpreters which were also written in a functional language. This gave us a good idea as to how to go about constructing an implementation for a functional language from the point of view of providing a rigorous high-level specification, but the operational characteristics of such interpreters rely on the facilities which support the execution of the language in which the interpreter itself is written – recall the discussion on achieving eagerness or laziness in an interpreter written in an eager or lazy language. In this chapter, we begin our discussion of suitable abstract machines for executing functional languages, using an **environment-based** computational model.

We shall consider the most general environment-based implementation which interprets expressions of the λ-calculus. As we have seen, the λ calculus has sufficient power to represent any functional language and so provides a good basis on which to build practical implementations. We have also seen how to translate functional languages into this form, so that it would also be possible to adopt the λ-calculus, or some variant, as a suitable intermediate code for their implementation. The first interpreter of this type was introduced by Landin (1964), and uses four 'stacks', labelled *S*, *E*, *C* and *D*, to provide mechanical evaluation of λ-expressions. In Section 10.1 we consider the eager version of this so-called SECD machine and go on to describe the modifications necessary to implement a lazy version of it in Section 10.2. Finally, a proof of its correctness is given in Section 10.3. To establish the correctness of an implementation requires at least a formal proof that the semantics of its computational model is equivalent to the semantics of the language. (In general, it is also necessary to prove that a formal specification of the implementation is consistent with the model's semantics, but this is a relatively simple task if the interpreter is written in a functional language which can itself express the model's semantics. Hence we will not be concerned with the latter proofs.) The correctness proof, due to Plotkin (1975), therefore entails providing a formal semantics for the SECD machine's operation, and then showing its equivalence with the semantics of β-reduction. It is given for the eager machine, but the modifications required for the lazy version are straightforward.

10.1 The SECD machine

Landin's SECD machine uses four explicit stacks to evaluate λ-expressions. Its operation is very easy to describe informally and also to define rigorously by prescribing the states of the machine in terms of the contents of its four stacks, and the transitions between these states. The importance of this implementation lies in its generality and in the fact that it does involve many techniques which can be adopted in practical implementations. However, without optimization, it is clearly not the most efficient means for implementing a functional language.

We begin with an eager system in which parameters are passed by value, i.e. one which uses applicative order evaluation of lambda expressions, and then in the next section show how the implementation can be generalized to provide lazy evaluation. The eager and lazy versions of the SECD machine are often termed **data-driven** and **demand-driven** respectively. Recall that expressions in the λ-calculus have the following BNF syntax:

$$\langle exp\rangle ::= \lambda\langle id\rangle.\langle exp\rangle \,|\, \langle id\rangle \,|\, \langle exp\rangle\langle exp\rangle \,|\, (\,\langle exp\rangle\,) \,|\, \langle con\rangle$$

where ⟨*id*⟩ represents identifiers and ⟨*con*⟩ an arbitrary set of constants such as atoms and primitive functions.

We shall also need to consider closures as a means of representing lambda abstractions together with their associated free variable bindings (cf. Chapter 9). These will be written [*id*, *exp*, *env*], where *id* is the bound variable identifier of the lambda expression, *exp* is the body of the lambda expression and *env* is an environment which assigns values to the free variables of the body. Each entry in the environment is a pair of form (*id*, *value*), where for the eager SECD machine the values are expressions in WHNF.

The state of the SECD machine is a 4-tuple, (S, E, C, D) where

- S is a stack of objects, used in recursive expression evaluation;
- E is an environment, i.e. association list of identifier–object pairs;
- C is the control string, i.e. remaining part of the expression currently being evaluated;
- D is the dump, i.e. a previous state, used on return from function invocation.

The operation of the machine is described in terms of state transitions, which we specify by a state transition function in the next section. This function can be used to define formally the operational semantics of the implementation, and is given for applicative order evaluation. We show the modifications required to support lazy evaluation and so to define lazy semantics in the next section, and the operation of each type of machine is illustrated with examples.

Before giving the definition of the state transition function, we first define some notation. The selector functions *bv*, *body*, *rator* and *rand*, which refer to components of the composite expression types, are defined as follows:

$$bv(\ \lambda x.E\ ) = x$$
$$body(\ \lambda x.E\ ) = E$$
$$rator(\ E_1\ E_2\ ) = E_1$$
$$rand(\ E_1\ E_2\ ) = E_2$$

Each of the state components S, E, C, D may be viewed as either a stack or a list, where *push* corresponds to *cons* (which we write using the infix function ::) *TOS* to *hd* and *pop* to *tl* (perhaps together with assignment of the head of the list to some accumulator). We adopt the list interpretation, and in the examples showing sequences of state transitions, the lists grow to the left in the conventional way of the *cons* operation. Under the stack interpretation, therefore, stacks also grow to the left, with top-of-stack leftmost on the page.

10.1.1 The state-transition function

We now give a specification for the state-transition function of an applicative-order SECD machine, *transition* : *state* → *state*, from which a Hope program, shown in Figure 10.1, follows immediately as a runnable interpreter. Given the current state (S, E, C, D), the next state is determined by the current control string C, and there are two cases to consider, the first of which divides into a number of sub-cases, as follows:

(1) If the control string is non-empty, and has the item X at the front, i.e. $X = hd(\ C\ )$, then we have the following four sub-cases:

(a) X is a constant or an identifier. The value of X in the current environment is pushed onto the stack S, and the object X is removed from the control string, C. In the case of a constant, the value is the constant itself, and in the case of an identifier the value is 'looked up' in the current environment. Thus the next state is

$$(\ valueof(\ X, E\ ) :: S, E, tl(\ C\ ), D\ )$$

($valueof(\ K, E\ ) = K$ for constant K in all environments E).

(b) X is a λ-abstraction. In this case we form a closure from the abstraction consisting of the bound variable of the expression, the body of the abstraction and the current environment which remembers the values of the free variables in the body (the mechanism is exactly the same as that of the interpreter given in the previous chapter). The next state is therefore

$$(\ [\ bv(\ X\ ), body(\ X\ ), E\ ] :: S, E, tl(\ C\ ), D\ )$$

Note that in a correct implementation for closed expressions (with no free variables), all of the free variables occurring in the body must have entries in the current environment because we are reducing to weak head-normal form. Of course, if there are no free variables, there is no need to create an explicit closure in this way – the lambda expression could be applied directly to its argument if one is present (or else returned as the result immediately). However, recall that the purpose of the SECD machine is not to provide an implementation for efficient practical use. The necessary optimization is left as a straightforward exercise.

(c) $X = F\,A$, i.e. X is the application of the expression F, a function, to the expression A, its argument. In the eager implementation, the expressions A and F are first evaluated,

```
type identifier      == char ;
data exp             == ID ( identifier ) ++
                        LAM ( char # exp ) ++
                        APP ( exp # exp ) ++
                        @ ;

data WHNF            == INT ( num ) ++
                        PRIM ( WHNF → WHNF ) ++
                        CLOSURE ( exp # char # list( char # WHNF ) ) ;

type Stack           == list ( WHNF ) ;
type Environment     == list ( char # WHNF ) ;
type Control         == list ( exp ) ;
type Dump            == list ( Stack # Environment # Control ) ;

type State           == ( Stack # Environment # Control # Dump ) ;

dec  LookUp : identifier # Environment → WHNF ;

---  LookUp( i1, ( i2, W ) :: E )
     <= if i1 = i2 then W else LookUp( i1, E ) ;

dec  Evaluate : State → WHNF ;

---  Evaluate ( Result :: S, E, nil, nil )
     <= Result ;

---  Evaluate ( x :: S, E, nil, ( S1, E1, C1 ) :: D1 )
     <= Evaluate ( x :: S1, E1, C1, D1 ) ;

---  Evaluate ( S, E, ID( x ) :: C, D )
     <= Evaluate ( LookUp( x, E ) :: S, E, C, D ) ;

---  Evaluate ( S, E, LAM( bv, body ) :: C, D )
     <= Evaluate ( CLOSURE( body, bv, E ) :: S, E, C, D ) ;

---  Evaluate ( CLOSURE( body, bv, E1 ) :: ( arg :: S ), E, @ :: C, D )
     <= Evaluate ( nil,
                   ( bv, arg ) :: E1,
                   [ body ] ,
                   ( S, E, C ) :: D ) ;

---  Evaluate ( PRIM( f ) :: ( arg :: S ), E, @ :: C, D )
     <= Evaluate ( f( arg ) :: S, E, C, D ) ;

---  Evaluate ( S, E, APP( fun, arg ) :: C, D )
     <= Evaluate ( S, E, arg :: ( fun :: ( @ :: C ) ), D ) ;
```

Figure 10.1 State-transition function for the applicative-order SECD machine.

and the value of F is then applied to the value of A. This is accomplished by replacing the item $F\ A$ at the front of the control string by the three items A, F, @ where @ is the special *apply* symbol which (as we will see next), when it appears at the head of the control string, causes the top element on the stack to be applied to the element beneath it.

The next state is therefore

$$(S, E, A :: (F :: (@ :: tl(C))), D)$$

(d) $X = @$, the special symbol *apply*. The *rator* at the top of the stack, f say, must either be a primitive function or else a closure, according to the previously defined state transitions. If the stack, $S = f :: a :: S'$, we have two further subcases:

(i) If f is a primitive function, it is applied to a (the head of the tail of S) and replaces the *rator* and *rand* there. The @ is removed from the control string and the next state is therefore

$$(f(a) :: S', E, tl(C), D)$$

(ii) If f is the closure [V, B, E'], then the body expression, B, is evaluated in the environment E augmented with the binding of V to a. Before this can be done, however, the state of the machine must be remembered in order that the evaluation can resume when the evaluation of B is complete. This state consists of the current state (which is a 4-tuple), with the top element of the control string and top two elements of the stack removed. The new stack is empty, the new environment is that of the closure to be applied, extended with the association of its bound variable identifier with the *rand* taken from the stack, and the new control string consists of the single item B. The next state is therefore

$$(( ), (V, a) :: E', B, (S', E, tl(C), D))$$

(2) Otherwise the control string C is empty, so the current (sub-) expression evaluation must be complete, its result being the single element on the stack S (for syntactically correct expressions). The state at the head of the dump D is then restored, and the result just evaluated is pushed onto the new stack. If $D = (S', E', C', D')$, the next state is then

$$(hd(S) :: S', E', C', D')$$

From this specification, it is a simple task to write a basic implementation of the eager SECD machine by defining a data type to represent the state of the machine and by defining a function to implement each of the state transitions. The Hope program that is shown in Figure 10.1 provides a specification which is not only clear and concise, but also executable.

Note that in this program identifiers are represented by single characters for simplicity. Note also that the data type representing the dump is defined as a list of triples rather than a recursive quadruple. The latter alternative would also be perfectly correct, provided an empty dump constructor is included in the corresponding data definition (cf. the nil constructor of lists). The result of the program is actually a WHNF rather than a 'final' state. Because of the tail-recursive nature of the Evaluate function, however, the type of object returned by Evaluate is dependent wholly on the first defining equation (the 'base' case) so that if this were to return the whole state rather than just the top of the evaluation stack Evaluate would assume the type State → State.

We can now illustrate the operation of the machine by showing the sequence of state transitions which occur in the evaluation of the expression corresponding to *twice succ* 0. We will then go on to extend the capacity of the machine to enable it to handle other primitive constructs which are necessary in practical functional programming languages – conditional expressions and recursion. Since the latter can be expressed in the lambda calculus using the *Y*-combinator, it would appear that we already have enough to evaluate applications of recursively defined functions. However, we will see that this approach poses some problems for the eager version of the SECD machine.

10.1.2 An example evaluation

The example we shall consider makes a call to the function *twice* defined by $twice = \lambda f.\lambda x.f(\,fx\,)$. Taking the function *succ* to be primitive (the successor function defined on the integers), our expression *twice succ* 0 becomes

$$(\,\lambda f.\lambda x.f(\,fx\,)\,)\; succ\; 0$$

and the initial state of the SECD machine has this as the single item on its control stack, with empty *S*, *E* and *D* stacks. Subsequent states of the machine are shown in Figure 10.2, each entered successively according to the specification given for the state-transition function in the previous section.

10.1.3 Special primitive operations in the SECD machine

The pure untyped lambda calculus is complete in the sense that it can express and reduce to its normal form any expression written in a functional programming language. However, for practical purposes it does require augmenting with certain primitives – at least a primitive

S	E	C	D
( )	( )	$((\lambda f.\lambda x.f(fx))\,succ\,0)$	( )
( )	( )	$0, ((\lambda f.\lambda x.f(fx))\,succ), @$	( )
0	( )	$((\lambda f.\lambda x.f(fx))\,succ), @$	( )
0	( )	$succ, \lambda f.\lambda x.f(fx), @, @$	( )
$succ$, 0	( )	$\lambda f.\lambda x.f(fx), @, @$	( )
$[f, \lambda x.f(fx), ()], succ, 0$	( )	@, @	( )
( )	$(f = succ)$	$\lambda x.f(fx)$	(0, ( ), @, ( ))
$[x, f(fx), (f = succ)]$	$(f = succ)$	( )	(0, ( ), @, ( ))
$[x, f(fx), (f = succ)], 0$	( )	@	( )
( )	$(x = 0, f = succ)$	$f(fx)$	((),(),(),())
( )	$(x = 0, f = succ)$	$fx, f, @$	((),(),(),())
( )	$(x = 0, f = succ)$	$x, f, @, f, @$	((),(),(),())
0	$(x = 0, f = succ)$	$f, @, f, @$	((),(),(),())
$succ$, 0	$(x = 0, f = succ)$	$@, f, @$	((),(),(),())
1	$(x = 0, f = succ)$	$f, @$	((),(),(),())
$succ$, 1	$(x = 0, f = succ)$	@	((),(),(),())
2	$(x = 0, f = succ)$	( )	((),(),(),())
2	( )	( )	( )

Figure 10.2 State transitions in the evaluation of *twice succ* 0 by an applicative-order SECD machine.

conditional expression, some primitive data types (e.g. the integers), primitive functions (e.g. +, − etc.) and perhaps a means for representing recursion other than the Y-combinator. The alternative representations as lambda expressions are not only obscure to the programmer, but also inefficient in execution – in contrast to the single (abstract) machine operation required for a primitive. For example, recall from Chapter 6 that the conditional function is normally represented by $\lambda x.\lambda y.\lambda z.xyz$, with 'truth values' $\lambda x.\lambda y.x$ and $\lambda x.\lambda y.y$ to represent *true* and *false* respectively.

Strict primitive functions of one argument pose no problems and primitive functions of more than one argument are conventionally regarded as being curried. A partial application of a function of n arguments ($n > 1$) to $m < n$ objects simply results in a closure, the instantiated body not being evaluated until all arguments are available. This machinery is all available in the SECD machine as currently described, apart from the addition of the appropriate primitive operations, and indeed for a lazy machine it is all we require. However, certain problems do arise in the eager implementation concerning both conditional expressions and recursion. We consider these next.

Evaluation of conditional expressions

Under applicative order evaluation, a conditional expression which has a defined value may not terminate. For example, the expression **if** $a \neq 0$ **then** $1/a$ **else** a is defined on all integers a, but is not defined when $a = 0$ under applicative-order evaluation, since the **then** branch expression, $1/a$, (as well as the **else** branch expression) is always evaluated, whatever the result of the predicate. Moreover it is not only relatively pathological cases such as this which cause the problem – any conventionally defined recursive function will also exhibit it. For example, in the evaluation of a factorial expression, where the factorial function is defined by $fac(\ n\ ) =$ **if** $n = 0$ **then** 1 **else** $n * fac(\ n - 1\ )$, the **else** branch will always be evaluated on every recursive call, causing an infinite sequence of calls and so non-termination.

One solution to the problem is to transform conditional expressions by the use of dummy functions of either no arguments or equivalently a dummy argument if we wish to be consistent with our lambda style of syntax in which all functions have exactly one argument. This is a standard technique which can be used to provide normal-order semantics for expressions which are to be evaluated using applicative-order reduction. In particular, the conditional expression above has equivalent form

(**if** $a \neq 0$ **then** $\lambda dummy./\ 1\ a$ **else** $\lambda dummy.a$) *any*

where *any* can be any object. (Note that in this expression we have reverted to the normal (curried) prefix notation for the division of 1 by a.) This certainly removes the possibility of (incorrect) non-termination and can of course be more efficient than the applicative-order counterpart – for example when the branch which is not required is a complex, expensive expression – in the limiting case non-terminating! The technique is similar to that described in Chapter 9 for implementing call-by-name.

A more practical approach to the problem is to define a new type of expression:

⟨*exp*⟩ ::= ... | *cond* ⟨*exp*⟩ ⟨*exp*⟩ ⟨*exp*⟩

where the arguments of *cond* are respectively the **then** branch expression, the **else** branch expression and the predicate expression. The reason for the strange ordering is to allow a conditional expression of the form *cond T E P* to be treated like any other application, so that when it appears at the head of the control string, it is replaced by the three items *P*, *cond T E*, @. Then, eventually, the value of the predicate expression, *P*, will be at the top of the stack, whilst the item *cond T E* will be at the head of the control string.

We can now extend the specification of the state transition function to include one extra sub-case in case (1) for the head of the control string X:

(e) If $X = cond\ B\ A$ then the next state is

$$(tl(S), E, B :: tl(tl(C)), D) \quad \text{if } hd(S) = true$$
$$(tl(S), E, A :: tl(tl(C)), D) \quad \text{if } hd(S) = false$$

(There are no other alternatives in a properly type-checked system.)

Thus, during execution of an expression of the form $cond\ B\ A\ P$, where B, A, P are themselves expressions, when the value of P is at the top of S, the control string C will consist of $cond\ B\ A$, @, . . . and it is then easily seen that the above extended state-transition function evaluates the conditional expression correctly (assuming correctly typed P). Alternatively, the extra case could be tested for as the sub-case $F = cond\ B$ when a general application, $F\,A$, is at the head of the control string; the details are similar to the above.

Evaluation of expressions containing recursive functions

We consider two methods of handling recursion in an applicative-order SECD machine; using a form of the Y-combinator and via **labelled expressions**, which we introduce below. It is tempting to use Y in the usual way to remove the explicit recursion from an expression that involves a recursive function, and then simply to feed the resulting lambda expression into the SECD machine; it was after all specifically designed to evaluate such expressions! Thus, if the recursive function f is defined by the equation $f(x) = E(f, x)$ for some expression E, we would write

$$f = Y\, \lambda g.\lambda x.E(g, x)$$
$$\text{where } Y = \lambda h.(\lambda x.h(xx))(\lambda x.h(xx))$$

Then, for example, we might write a version of the factorial function as

$$fac = Y\, \lambda f.\lambda n.\mathbf{if}\ (= n\ 2)\ \mathbf{then}\ 2\ \mathbf{else} * n\ (\ f\ (\ pred\ n\ )\ )$$

where *pred* is the primitive predecessor function defined on the integers. Mutually recursive definitions can be implemented by packaging the definitions into a recursively defined tuple (or list, even) as described in Chapter 6.

So can we implement recursive functions directly as least fixed points? The answer is *not if we use applicative-order reduction*. The problem is that the self-application of the closure corresponding to the term xx fails to terminate – try it! However, we can modify the definiton of Y to avoid this problem, and define instead the Y' combinator:

$$Y' = \lambda h.(\ \lambda x.h(\ \lambda y.xxy\ )\ )\ (\ \lambda x.h(\ \lambda y.xxy\ )\ )$$

which is equivalent to Y under η-conversion ($Y' \leftrightarrow_\eta Y$). Now using Y' instead of Y to remove the explicit recursion, the self application is only evaluated when it is itself applied to an argument, specifically the one corresponding to y, for example the integer to which the invocation of *fac* is applied. If the application of the function corresponding to h, for example *fac* to this argument value involves no recursive call, the self-application will not be evaluated. Try this too! It may have been noticed that this method of avoiding non-termination in applicative-order reduction uses essentially the same approach as we saw in Chapter 9 for achieving normal-order semantics. Of course, there is no problem in using the normal Y-combinator with the lazy SECD machine which will not attempt to evaluate the self-application until absolutely necessary. The use of Y or Y' to handle recursion in SECD machines tends to be complex and inefficient, although some optimizations are given in Burge (1975). We do not pursue this here, and now go on to consider an alternative method.

First, we add the new syntactic type 'labelled expression' to the expression syntax:

$$\langle exp \rangle ::= \ldots \mid \langle\!\langle\ \langle id \rangle,\ \langle id \rangle.\langle exp \rangle\ \rangle\!\rangle$$

We now extend the state-transition function's specification in two places, first to include a further test on the head of the control string X as follows:

(e) If X is the labelled expression $\langle\!\langle\ N, L\ \rangle\!\rangle$, then the λ-abstraction L is associated with the name N and added into the current environment. X is then replaced at the front of the control string by its λ-abstraction L, and the next state is therefore

$$(\ S,\ (\ N, L\ ) :: E,\ L :: tl(\ C\ ),\ D\ )$$

A labelled expression may be regarded as a standard λ-abstraction, together with an extension to the current environment which associates the name in the first component of the labelled expression with this λ-abstraction. Thus, when a labelled expression is at the head of the control string, it can be replaced by the λ-abstraction in its second component if the environment is updated appropriately. Any subsequent occurrences of its name at the head of the control string (during an application of its λ-abstraction) will then cause its λ-abstraction to be pushed on to the stack through this addition to the environment. We therefore have to introduce a new transition rule corresponding to states in which the head of the control string is @ and there is a λ-abstraction at the top of the stack S: the λ-abstraction must be converted into a closure before it can be applied since it may have some free variable occurrences. Thus we extend the specification of the transition function further by adding a new sub-case when the head of the control string $X = @$ and the stack $S = f :: a :: S'$, giving:

(1) (d) (iii) If f is a λ-abstraction, push it onto C so that the next transition will form a closure on S. The new state is then

$$(\, a : S', E, f :: C, D \,)$$

The required closure is therefore formed in two steps. This is clearly not the most efficient implementation of recursion by labelled expressions; in particular, the closure corresponding to the λ-abstraction is known at the time the labelled expression first appears at the head of the control string.

10.2 The lazy SECD machine

In order to implement normal-order reduction, it must be possible to represent unevaluated sub-expressions or suspensions, which essentially freeze argument expressions until they are needed in the evaluation of an instantiated function body. As in the previous chapter, a suspension consists of an expression together with an environment which gives meanings to the free variables of the expression. Suspensions form another type in the expression syntax and we shall write them as expression–environment pairs enclosed in braces, for example $\{\, e, E \,\}$, where e is an expression and E an environment.

The state-transition function for the eager SECD machine defined in Section 10.1.1 requires modification in three places in order to provide an implementation with normal-order semantics, which may be realized either by the call-by-name or the call-by-need computation rules. In the case of the former rule, the transition function can be defined purely functionally, but as we have seen, this rule is inefficient, involving repeated evaluation of the argument-expressions corresponding to parameters with multiple occurrences in a λ-body. To obtain lazy semantics via a call-by-need rule requires that argument expressions be shared, which can only be done by means of an assignment to the suspensions representing the unevaluated arguments. In either case, the modifications needed in the transition function correspond to states having the following three characteristics:

(a) *Application at the front of the control string, C* When an application ($F\ A$) is at the front of C, rather than initiating evaluation of the argument A, the suspension representing A is created and pushed onto S. F is then evaluated and applied to this suspension as before.

(b) *Function at the top of S with @ at the front of C* If the function is a suspension or a strict primitive applied to a suspension, evaluation of the suspension must be initiated, the current state being saved on the dump. After the suspension has been evaluated, the function can be re-applied. This type of return must be distinguished from the usual type of return from a closure application, and since such 'control' information is a part of the current state, it is most appropriately stored in the dump. Thus, every dump is specially tagged – either as an application-dump or as a suspension-dump. This is all that is necessary for the call-by-name computation rule.

In a lazy implementation, however, suspensions on the object-stack are represented by pointers to their actual locations, and the location of a suspension must also be saved when its evaluation is initiated. Then, on completion of its evaluation, its value can be stored in that location, permitting further references to the suspension to share its *evaluated* version. This location is also a part of the current state, and so too is stored in (an extension to) the dump. Such an extended dump (a suspension-dump) is often called an **assigning-dump** (Burge, 1975).

(c) *When C is empty* For the call-by-name computation rule, if the dump is a suspension-dump, the state saved in it is restored with the suspension's value (the result currently at the top of S) pushed onto the restored object-stack. The application that forced the evaluation of the suspension will then be executed. This enables the purely functional specification of the transition function to be retained, but on a subsequent reference, the same suspension will be re-evaluated. For the call-by-need computation rule, if the dump is a suspension-dump, so that the result at the top of S is the value of a suspension, the location saved in the dump is overwritten with this result. The state is then restored from the rest of the dump as above.

Thus, in the lazy implementation, both a suspension and any eventual value computed for it occupy the same location (which must therefore be tagged to indicate which is the case), all accesses to it being indirect. Then all (shared) references are updated simultaneously on return from the evaluation of the suspension. We shall see in Chapter 11 that this corresponds in the graph reduction computational model to the *overwriting* of redex-nodes in a graph by the results of subgraph reductions. Thus in the lazy SECD machine there is no duplication of the evaluation of an argument because β-reduction is performed through the substitution of bound variables by their values in the current environment. A revised specification for a state-transition function which provides normal-order semantics is therefore as follows:

(1) If the control string is non-empty, and $X = hd(C)$, then there are four sub-cases:

(a) If X is a constant or an identifier, the next state is

$$(\, valueof(X, E) :: S, E, tl(C), D\,)$$

exactly as in Section 10.1.1.

(b) If X is a λ-abstraction,the next state is

$$(\,[\, bv(X), body(X), E\,] :: S, E, tl(C), D\,)$$

exactly as in Section 10.1.1.

(c) If $X = F\,A$, for call-by-name semantics, the suspension of A is constructed and pushed onto S and the next state is therefore

$$(\{\, A, E\,\} :: S, E, F :: (\,@ :: tl(C)\,), D\,)$$

In the case of call-by-need semantics, the suspension is stored off the stack and a pointer to it is pushed onto S instead.

(d) If $X = @$, and $S = f :: a :: S'$, we now have three sub-cases:

(i) If f is the closure $[\, V, B, E'\,]$, there is no change to the eager specification and the next state is

$$(\,(\,), (\,V, a\,) :: E', B, (\,S', E, tl(C), D\,)\,)$$

(ii) If f is a strict primitive function and a is the suspension $\{\, B, E'\,\}$ (or a pointer to it in the call-by-need implementation) the next state is

$$(\,(\,), E', B, (\,s, (\,S', E, f :: C, D\,)\,)\,)$$

Notice the use of a suspension dump, indicated by the first field s. For call-by-name semantics, this field will merely be the tag indicating the type of dump and for call-by-need it will contain the location of the suspension, i.e. a.

(iii) If f is the suspension $\{\, B, E'\,\}$ the next state is

$$(\,(\,), E', B, (\,s, (\,a :: S', E, C, D\,)\,)\,)$$

(iv) Otherwise f is primitive and can be applied to a immediately, whether or not it is a suspension, so that the next state is (for call-by-name semantics)

$$(f(a) :: S', E, tl(C), D)$$

as before. For call-by-need semantics, the application $f(a)$ should be replaced by $f(a\uparrow)$ where $a\uparrow$ denotes the contents of the location pointed to by a.

(2) If C is empty, we now have two sub-cases:

(a) If D is the assigning dump $(y, (S', E', C', D'))$, in the case of call-by-name semantics the next state is simply

$$(hd(S) :: S', E', C', D')$$

For call-by-need, the location y of the associated suspension must be overwritten with its value and the next state is

$$(y :: S', E', C', D')$$

with $y := hd(S)$ – a non-functional destructive assignment.

(b) Otherwise $D = (S', E', C', D')$, an ordinary dump, and the next state is

$$(hd(S) :: S', E', C', D')$$

as in the eager machine.

We can now illustrate the operation of the lazy SECD machine by considering the sequence of state transitions which occur in the evaluation of the head of a lazy list, which in general may be infinite and so fail to terminate in the eager implementation. Recall also that simple recursive functions such as factorial can now be applied without recourse to use of the modified Y-combinator, and that conditional functions need less elaborate mechanisms. To represent lists, we use the constants *nil* and *cons* and we will abbreviate the list

$$cons\ a_1 (cons\ a_2 (cons\ a_3 \ldots (cons\ a_n\ nil) \ldots))$$

by $\langle a_1, \ldots, a_n \rangle$. We also use the selector function *hd* which returns the head of a list. (Of course we could represent lists directly in the pure lambda calculus as described in Chapter 6 without relying on additional primitives.) The state transitions undergone by the lazy SECD machine in its evaluation of the expression $hd(cons\ x\ y)$, where x and y are arbitrary, possibly infinite expressions, are shown in Figure 10.3.

In the figure, $L1$, $L2$ and $L3$ denote the locations of the suspensions stored off the stack when their expressions appeared as arguments in applications at the front of C. Notice that *cons* is a non-strict function and so can be applied to any argument immediately,

S	E	C	D
( )	E0	(hd(cons x y))	D0
L1	E0	hd, @	D0
hd, L1	E0	@	D0
	E0	(cons x y)	D1
L2	E0	cons x, @	D1
L3, L2	E0	cons, @, @	D1
cons, L3, L2	E0	@, @	D1
cons L3, L2	E0	@	D1
⟨L3, L2⟩	E0	( )	D1
L1	E0	hd, @	D0
hd, L1	E0	@	D0
L3	E0	( )	D0

L1 : { (cons x y), E0 } := ⟨L3, L2⟩
L2 : { y, E0 }
L3 : { x, E0 }

where D1 = (L1, ((hd, L1), E0, @, D0))

Figure 10.3 Transitions in the lazy SECD machine evaluation of *hd*(*cons*(*x*, *y*)).

yielding an unevaluated result.

In the first two sections of this chapter we have considered the classical SECD machine, the archetypal implementation of functional programming languages, which maintains an *explicit environment* to hold the values of the free variables of sub-expressions. Many enhancements exist, ranging from a simple machine for first-order languages which requires no more than a stack for its environment, through the more general FPM compiler (Chapter 15) to the categorical abstract machine (Chapter 13). In the next chapter we shall see that there are alternative methods of representing the environment, there being no definitive answer as to which approach is optimal.

10.3 Correctness of the SECD machine implementation

The operation of the SECD machine has been defined in a semi-formal way, in terms of a state and a function, *trans*, which defines the one-step transitions between states. The machine evaluates expressions of a language, denoted here by Λ, which is the pure λ-calculus extended to include an arbitrary set of constants. In order to show that it provides a correct implementation of Λ, it is necessary to define mathematically the operational semantics and prove that this is equivalent to the accepted (denotational) semantics of Λ, defined in terms of β- and δ-reduction. For this we adopt a proof method based on that of Plotkin (1975). We first give formal definitions for the constituents of the SECD machine, and then define an operational evaluation function, *Eval*, for it. When applied to an expression of Λ, this function returns as its result the value computed by the SECD machine for the same expression. The evaluation function for Λ, *eval*, is then defined in terms of substitution (corresponding to β-reduction and δ-reduction), and the two functions *Eval* and *eval* are proved to be equal up to α-conversion, i.e. are alphabetically equivalent. The proof is straightforward, but rather detailed, and the proofs of two lemmas are postponed to the end of this section.

10.3.1 Notation and definitions

We first define some naming conventions to avoid having to make tedious explicit references to sets.

M, N	terms of Λ
x, y	variables
a, b	data constants
f, g	primitive function constants

The set of all terms in Λ is denoted by *Terms*, and $FV(M)$ is the set of free variables occurring in the term $M \in \Lambda$. Alphabetic equivalence of terms M and N is denoted by $M =_\alpha N$ and is defined in Chapter 6.

The SECD machine is given by a set, *Dumps*, of states together with a transition function denoted in infix form by $\Rightarrow$. The set *Dumps* comprises 4-tuples, the first three components of which are members of the sets *Stacks*, *Environments* and *Control-strings* respectively. *Stacks* and *Environments* are both defined in terms of another set, *Closures*. *Closures* and *Environments* are defined inductively by:

(1) If $x_1, \ldots, x_n$ are distinct variables ($n \geq 0$) and Cl_i ($1 \leq i \leq n$) are members of *Closures*, then $E = \{ \langle x_i, Cl_i \rangle \mid 1 \leq i \leq n \}$ is a member of *Environments*. We then write $Dom(E) = \{x_i \mid 1 \leq i \leq n\}$ and $E(x_i) = Cl_i$ ($1 \leq i \leq n$).

(2) If E is an environment (i.e. a member of *Environments*) and M is a term such that $Dom(E) \supseteq FV(M)$, then $\langle M, E \rangle$ is a closure.

In the base-case, the environment, $E = \varnothing$, i.e. $n = 0$ in (1), and the closure $\langle M, E\rangle$ represents a constant, since M can have no free variables. In fact, in our formal specification of the SECD machine the constant a is represented by $\langle a, \varnothing\rangle$. The evaluation of a closure, to yield a Λ-term, is represented by the function $Real : Closures \rightarrow Terms$ which is defined inductively by

$$Real(\langle M, E\rangle) = [\, Real(E(x_1))/x_1\,] \ldots [\, Real(E(x_n))/x_n\,]\, M$$
$$\text{where } FV(M) = \{\, x_i \mid 1 \leq i \leq n \,\}$$

In the sequel, we extend our naming conventions to include Cl as a closure, and we denote by $E\{ Cl / x\}$ the unique environment E' such that $E'(y) = E(y)$ if $y \neq x$ and $E'(x) = Cl$. We also define inductively the notions of a value-closure and value-environment, which are essentially the closures and environments we used in our informal description of the eager SECD machine.

(1) A closure $\langle M, E\rangle$ is a value-closure if and only if M is a λ-abstraction or a constant, and E is a value environment.

(2) An environment E is a value-environment if and only if for every variable $x \in Dom(E)$, $E(x)$ is a value-closure. Thus the empty environment is a value-environment.

We can now define:

$$Stacks = Closures^*, \text{ the set of all sequences of closures,}$$
$$Control\text{-}strings = (\, Terms \cup \{ @ \}\,)^*$$

Dumps is then defined inductively by:

(1) $nil \in Dumps$

(2) If $S \in Stacks$, $E \in Environments$, $C \in Control\text{-}strings$, $D \in Dumps$ and $Dom(E) \supseteq FV(C)$, then $\langle S, E, C, D\rangle \in Dumps$.

We can now define the transition function, $\Rightarrow : Dumps \rightarrow Dumps$, which was actually specified quite formally before as the function trans. However, since we are going to analyse the behaviour of the SECD machine essentially as a term-rewriting system, we now give another definition of the transition function in the form of a set of rewrite rules. In fact this definition bears a strong resemblance to the Hope program given in Section 10.1. There are seven cases:

(a) $\langle Cl :: S, E, nil, \langle S', E', C', D'\rangle\rangle \Rightarrow \langle Cl :: S', E', C', D'\rangle$
(b) $\langle S, E, x :: C, D\rangle \Rightarrow \langle E(x) :: S, E, C, D\rangle$
(c) $\langle S, E, a :: C, D\rangle \Rightarrow \langle\langle a, \varnothing\rangle :: S, E, C, D\rangle$
(d) $\langle S, E, (\lambda x.M) :: C, D\rangle \Rightarrow \langle\langle(\lambda x.M), E\rangle :: S, E, C, D\rangle$

(e) $\langle\langle(\lambda x.M), E'\rangle :: Cl :: S, E, @ :: C, D\rangle \Rightarrow$
$\langle nil, E'\{Cl / x\}, M, \langle S, E, C, D\rangle\rangle$

(f) $\langle\langle f, E'\rangle :: \langle a, E''\rangle :: S, E, @ :: C, D\rangle \Rightarrow \langle\langle f(a), \varnothing\rangle :: S, E, C, D\rangle$

(g) $\langle S, E, (MN) :: C, D\rangle \Rightarrow \langle S, E, N :: M :: @ :: C, D\rangle$

The function $\Rightarrow$ may be regarded as defining rewrite rules, or single-step term reductions, and we extend the notation by defining $\Rightarrow^t$ to denote t-step reduction, i.e. the transitions corresponding to t applications of the rewrite rules. Thus $\Rightarrow^t$ is defined by $\Rightarrow^1 \equiv \Rightarrow$ and $\Rightarrow^t(D) = \Rightarrow(\Rightarrow^{t-1}(D))$ for dump D, $t > 1$. We also write $\Rightarrow^*$ to represent an arbitrary positive number of transitions, i.e. to denote the application of $\Rightarrow$ any number of times. Thus $\Rightarrow^*$ is interpreted as '$\Rightarrow^t$ for some t'.

10.3.2 The equivalence theorem

We are at last in a position to be able to give the evaluation function, *Eval*, for the SECD machine. Intuitively, this function represents the loading of the machine with a term in its control string, allowing it to run until it finishes, and then unloading the result from its stack. Thus, *Eval* is defined formally in terms of two auxiliary functions, *Load* and *Unload*, as follows:

$$Eval(M) = N$$

if and only if

$$Load(M) \Rightarrow^* D, \qquad \text{and} \qquad N = Unload(D)$$

for some dump D where *Load* and *Unload* are defined by

$$Load(M) = \langle nil, \varnothing, M, nil\rangle$$
$$Unload(\langle Cl, \varnothing, nil, nil\rangle) = Real(Cl)$$

It is much easier to define the semantic function, *eval*, for the abstract evaluation of terms using β-reduction and the δ-rules.

$$\begin{array}{lll} eval(a) & = a & \text{if } a \text{ is a constant} \\ eval(\lambda x.M) & = \lambda x.M & \\ eval(MN) & = eval([N'/x]M') & \text{if } eval(M) = (\lambda x.M') \text{ and } eval(N) = N' \\ & \quad f(a) & \text{if } eval(M) = f \text{ and } eval(N) = a \end{array}$$

In order to compare evaluation functions, we must be able to relate the values of expressions, given by the semantic function *eval*, to the state-transition sequences of the SECD machine. We define the value of a closed term to be its WHNF (another, unique term), together with an integer related to the number of reductions required to reach that normal form. This number, called a **time**, is equal to one more than twice the number of reduction steps. Thus, for example, the value of a WHNF is itself at time 1, and in general we define the predicate 'M has value N at time t' by induction on t for closed terms M and N as follows:

(1) a has value a at time 1 and $(\lambda x.M)$ has value $(\lambda x.M)$ at time 1.

(2) If M has value $(\lambda x.M')$ at time t, N has value N' at time t' and $[N'/x]M'$ has value L at time t'', then (MN) has value L at time $t + t' + t'' + 1$.

(3) If M has value f at time t and N has value a at time t', then if $f(a)$ is defined, (MN) has value $f(a)$ at time $t + t' + 1$.

Otherwise, a term has no value.

Thus it can be seen (formally by induction) that if M has values N, N' at times t, t' then $N = N'$ and $t = t'$. Hence the definition:

$$eval(M) = N \quad \text{if and only if } M \text{ has value } N \text{ at some time}$$

is well-defined.

We will use the ordering induced by the t of the predicate 'M has value N at time t' in the inductive proofs of the lemmas and theorem below, in which reduction sequences are related to SECD machine state-transitions. Since variable names are not changed in the definition of the predicate, it is clear that if $M =_\alpha M'$, then M has value N at time t if and only if for some $N' =_\alpha N$, M' has value N' at time t. It is also clear that if $eval(M)$ exists, it is a closed value. The statement of the correctness of the SECD implementation is now given by the following:

Theorem 10.1 For any term M, $Eval(M) =_\alpha eval(M)$.
The proof of this theorem uses two lemmas which we now state, the proofs being given in Section 10.3.3.

Lemma 10.1 Suppose E is a value-environment, $\langle M, E\rangle$ is a closure and M'' is the value of $Real(\langle M, E\rangle)$ at time t. Then, for all S, E, C, D with $Dom(E) \supseteq FV(C)$, and some $t' \geq t$,

$$\langle S, E, M :: C, D\rangle \Rightarrow^{t'} \langle\langle M', E'\rangle :: S, E, C, D\rangle$$

where $\langle M', E'\rangle$ is a value-closure and $Real(\langle M', E'\rangle) =_\alpha M''$.

Notation If for some $t \geq 1$, $D \Rightarrow^t D'$ where D' is not of the form $\langle Cl, \varnothing, nil, nil\rangle$ and there does not exist a dump D'' such that $D' \Rightarrow D''$, then D is said to hit the **error-state** D'.

Lemma 10.2 Suppose E is a value-environment and $\langle M, E\rangle$ is a closure. If $Real(\langle M, E\rangle)$ has no value at any time $t' \leq t$ ($t \geq 1$), then for all S, C, D with $Dom(E) \supseteq FV(C)$, either $\langle S, E, M :: C, D\rangle$ hits an error-state or $\langle S, E, M :: C, D\rangle \Rightarrow^{t} D'$ for some D'.

Proof of the theorem Suppose that $eval(M) = M''$. Then M'' is the value of M at some time t. By Lemma 10.1,

$$\langle nil, \varnothing, M, nil\rangle \Rightarrow^{t'} \langle\langle M', E'\rangle, \varnothing, nil, nil\rangle \qquad \text{for some } t' \geq t,$$

where $Real(\langle M', E'\rangle) =_\alpha M''$. Thus $Eval(M) =_\alpha M''$.

If instead M has no value at any time, by Lemma 10.2, either $\langle nil\ \varnothing, M, nil\rangle$ hits an error-state or else for every t there is a dump, D_t, such that $\langle nil, \varnothing, M, nil\rangle \Rightarrow^{t} D_t$, i.e. the evaluation does not terminate. In either case, $Eval(M)$ is not defined.

10.3.3 Proofs of the lemmas

The lemmas used in proving the correctness of the eager SECD machine are now restated and proved by induction on the notion of 'time' introduced in the definition of the predicate 'term M has value N at time t'. This section may be omitted by the less mathematically inclined reader.

Lemma 10.1 Suppose E is a value-environment, $\langle M, E\rangle$ is a closure and M'' is the value of $Real(\langle M, E\rangle)$ at time t. Then, for all S, E, C, D with $Dom(E) \supseteq FV(C)$, and some $t' \geq t$,

$$\langle S, E, M :: C, D\rangle \Rightarrow^{t'} \langle\langle M', E'\rangle :: S, E, C, D\rangle$$

where $\langle M', E'\rangle$ is a value-closure and $Real(\langle M', E'\rangle) =_\alpha M''$.

Proof There are four cases to consider for the form of M, the third of which, application, divides into two sub-cases which are proved by induction on t.

Case (1) M is a constant. Here $FV(M) = \varnothing$, so that $M'' = Real(\langle M, E\rangle) = M$ and $t = 1$. Since $\langle S, E, M :: C, D\rangle \Rightarrow \langle\langle M, \varnothing\rangle :: S, E, C, D\rangle$, we can take $\langle M', E'\rangle = \langle M, \varnothing\rangle$ and $t' = 1$.

Case (2) M is an abstraction. Here $M'' = Real(\langle M, E\rangle)$ and $t = 1$. Since $\langle S, E, M :: C, D\rangle \Rightarrow \langle\langle M, E\rangle :: S, E, C, D\rangle$, we can take $\langle M', E'\rangle = \langle M, E\rangle$ and $t' = 1$.

Case (3) M is a variable. Here $M'' = Real(E(M))$ and $t = 1$. Since $\langle S, E, M :: C, D\rangle \Rightarrow \langle E(M) :: S, E, C, D\rangle$, we can take $\langle M', E'\rangle = E(M)$ and $t' = 1$.

Case (4) $M = (M_1M_2)$ is an application. Here $Real(\langle M, E\rangle) = N_1N_2$ where $N_1 = Real(\langle M_1, E\rangle)$ and $N_2 = Real(\langle M_2, E\rangle)$, and there are two sub-cases.

Sub-case (i) Let N_1 have value $(\lambda x.N_3)$ at time u, N_2 have value N_4 at time v. Then M'' is the value of $[N_4 / x]N_3$ at time w, and $t = u + v + w + 1$. By the inductive hypothesis, there exist $u' \geq u$ and $v' \geq v$ such that

$$
\begin{aligned}
&\langle S, E, (M_1M_2) :: C, D\rangle \Rightarrow \langle S, E, M_2 :: M_1 :: @ :: C, D\rangle\\
&\Rightarrow^{v'} \langle\langle M_2', E_2'\rangle :: S, E, M_1 :: @ :: C, D\rangle\\
&\Rightarrow^{u'} \langle\langle M_1', E_1'\rangle :: \langle M_2', E_2'\rangle :: S, E, @ :: C, D\rangle
\end{aligned}
$$

where $Real(\langle M_1', E_1'\rangle) =_\alpha (\lambda x.N_3)$ and $Real(\langle M_2', E_2'\rangle) =_\alpha N_4$, and the $\langle M_i', E_i'\rangle$ are value-closures.

Here $M_1' = (\lambda y.M_3')$ for some term M_3', and it is easy to see that $Real(\langle M_3', E_1'\{\langle M_2', E_2'\rangle / y\}\rangle) =_\alpha [N_4 / x] N_3$. Therefore since $[N_4 / x]N_3$ has value M'' at time w, $Real(\langle M_3', E_1'\{\langle M_2', E_2'\rangle / y\}\rangle)$ has value M_3'', say, at time w, where $M_3'' =_\alpha M''$. Now,

$$
\begin{aligned}
&\langle\langle M_1', E_1'\rangle :: \langle M_2', E_2'\rangle :: S, E, @ :: C, D\rangle\\
&\Rightarrow \langle nil, E_1'\{\langle M_2', E_2'\rangle / y\}, M_3', \langle S, E, C, D\rangle\rangle\\
&\Rightarrow^{w'} \langle\langle M', E'\rangle, E_1'\{\langle M_2', E_2'\rangle / y\}, nil, \langle S, E, C, D\rangle\rangle
\end{aligned}
$$

for some $w' \geq w$ by the inductive hypothesis, where $\langle M', E'\rangle$ is a value-closure such that $Real(\langle M', E'\rangle) =_\alpha M_3'' =_\alpha M''$,

$$\Rightarrow \langle\langle M', E'\rangle :: S, E, C, D\rangle$$

Thus

$$\langle S, E, M :: C, D\rangle \Rightarrow^{t'} \langle\langle M', E'\rangle :: S, E, C, D\rangle$$

where $t' = u' + v' + w' + 3 > t$.

Sub-case (ii) Let N_1 have value f at time u, N_2 have value a at time v. Then $f(a) = M''$ and $t = u + v + 1$. By the inductive hypothesis, there exist $u' \geq u$, $v' \geq v$ and value environments E_1, E_2 such that

$$
\begin{aligned}
&\langle S, E, (M_1M_2) :: C, D\rangle \Rightarrow \langle S, E, M_2 :: M_1 :: @ :: C, D\rangle\\
&\Rightarrow^{v'} \langle\langle a, E_2\rangle :: S, E, M_1 :: @ :: C, D\rangle\\
&\Rightarrow^{u'} \langle\langle f, E_1\rangle :: \langle a, E_2\rangle :: S, E, @ :: C, D\rangle\\
&\Rightarrow \langle\langle M'', \varnothing\rangle :: S, E, C, D\rangle
\end{aligned}
$$

Taking $t' = u' + v' + 2 > t$ and $\langle M', E'\rangle = \langle M'', \varnothing\rangle$ concludes the proof.

Lemma 10.2 Suppose E is a value-environment and $\langle M, E\rangle$ is a closure. If $Real(\langle M, E\rangle)$ has no value at any time $t' \leq t\,(t \geq 1)$, then for all S, C, D with $Dom(E) \supseteq FV(C)$, either $\langle S, E, M :: C, D\rangle$ hits an error-state or $\langle S, E, M :: C, D\rangle \Rightarrow^{t} D'$ for some D'

Proof This is also by induction on t, and for $t = 1$ the result is trivial.

For $t > 1$, $Real(\langle M, E\rangle)$, and so M, must be λ-applications, which follows from the definition of the predicate giving the value of a term at time t in the previous section. Let $M = M_1M_2$. Then

$$\langle S, E, (M_1M_2) :: C, D\rangle \Rightarrow \langle S, E, M_2 :: M_1 :: @ :: C, D\rangle$$

If $Real(\langle M_2, E\rangle)$ has no value at any time $\leq (t-1)$, the result follows by applying the inductive hypothesis to $\langle M_2, E\rangle$. (We are proving the result for *all* closures with the stated properties, so $\langle M_2, E\rangle$ is certainly eligible.)

Otherwise, suppose that M_2'' is the value of $Real(\langle M_2, E\rangle)$ at time $v \leq (t-1)$. By Lemma 10.1,

$$\langle S, E, M_2 :: M_1 :: @ :: C, D\rangle \Rightarrow^{v'} \langle\langle M_2', E_2'\rangle :: S, E, M_1 :: @ :: C, D\rangle$$

where $v' \geq v$, $\langle M_2', E_2'\rangle$ is a value-closure and $Real(\langle M_2', E_2'\rangle) =_\alpha M_2''$. If $v' \geq t-1$, we are finished, since we would then have, for $1 \leq s \leq v'+1$, $\langle S, E, M :: C, D\rangle \Rightarrow^{s} D_s$ for some D_s, and we could choose $s = t$. Suppose therefore that $v' < t-1$.

Again, if $Real(\langle M_1, E\rangle)$ has no value at any time $\leq (t-1-v')$, the result follows by applying the inductive hypothesis to $\langle M_1, E\rangle$. Otherwise, suppose that M_1'' is the value of $Real(\langle M_1, E\rangle)$ at time $u \leq (t-1-v')$. By Lemma 10.1,

$$\langle\langle M_2', E_2'\rangle :: S, E, M_1 :: @ :: C, D\rangle \Rightarrow^{u'} \langle\langle M_1', E_1'\rangle :: \langle M_2', E_2'\rangle :: S, E, @ :: C, D\rangle$$

where $u' \geq u$, $\langle M_1', E_1'\rangle$ is a value-closure and $Real(\langle M_1', E_1'\rangle) =_\alpha M_1''$. If $u' \geq t-1-v'$, we are again finished, and so we suppose that $u' < t-1-v'$. We now have three possible cases:

Case (1) $M_1' = (\lambda x.M_3')$. We now have

$$\langle\langle \lambda x.M_3', E_1'\rangle :: \langle M_2', E_2'\rangle :: S, E, @ :: C, D\rangle \Rightarrow$$
$$\langle nil, E_1'\{\langle M_2', E_2'\rangle / x\}, M_3', \langle S, E, C, D\rangle\rangle$$

If $t = u' + v' + 2$ we are finished as before, so suppose otherwise, and let $E_3' = E_1'\{\langle M_2', E_2'\rangle / x\}$. If $Real(\langle M_3', E_3'\rangle)$ has no value at any time $\leq (t - u' - v' - 2)$, the result follows from the induction hypothesis applied to $\langle M_3', E_3'\rangle$. Otherwise, suppose that $Real(\langle M_3', E_3'\rangle)$ has value M_3'' at time

$w \leq (t - u' - v' - 2)$. Then, as in the proof of Lemma 10.1, $Real(\langle M, E \rangle)$ has value $M'' =_\alpha M_3''$ at time $u + v + w + 1 \leq u' + v' + (t - u' - v' - 2) + 1 < t$, contradicting the original hypothesis of the lemma.

Case (2) M_1' and M_2' are function- and data-constants respectively. Here, $Real(\langle M, E \rangle)$ has a value at time $u + v + 1 \leq (u' + v' + 1) < t$, also a contradiction.

Case (3) For all other possibilities for M_1' and M_2', an error-state occurs.

SUMMARY

- The SECD machine is a stack-based implementation for the lambda calculus which uses an environment to maintain variable bindings and so perform β-reduction.
- Its operation is described by a function which describes the transitions of the machine's state; this state is a tuple comprising four 'stacks'.
- There are both eager and lazy variants of the SECD machine, the most natural being eager.
- Recursion is implemented using the *Y*-combinator or a new type of expression called a labelled expression.
- Special forms of the conditional operator and the *Y*-combinator are required in the eager machine to avoid non-termination.
- Normal-order semantics can be obtained under the call-by-name computation rule by modifying the eager machine's transition function, but call-by-need semantics requires the use of assignments and off-stack storage to provide sharing of arguments.
- The functional specification of the machine's operation is conducive to formal proofs of its correctness.
- The operational semantics given by the state transition function is equivalent to the substitution semantics of β-reduction and δ-reduction in the lambda calculus.

EXERCISES

10.1 (a) Show the state-transition sequence in the eager SECD machine for the evaluation of the lambda expression $(\lambda x.\lambda y. + y\ x)\ 2\ 3$. How would this change in the lazy implementation?

(b) Show the state-transition sequence in the lazy SECD machine for the evaluation of

$$hd\ (\mathit{from}\ 1\ )$$

where the function *from* is defined by

$$\mathit{from}\ x = \mathit{cons}\ x\ (\ \mathit{from}\ (\ +\ 1\ x\ )\ ).$$

10.2 Explain why the implementation of recursion in the eager SECD machine using the Y-combinator directly results in non-termination. Given the function definition

$$f(n) = \mathit{cond}\ 2\ (\ *\ n\ \underline{f(\ -\ n\ 1)}\ )\ (\ =\ n\ 2\ )$$

where *cond* is the conditional operator defined in Section 10.1.3, consider the evaluation of the expression $f(\ 3\ )$:

(a) Justify your explanation above and show that by using Y' (defined in Section 10.1.3) instead of Y the correct result is computed. Sketch the state-transition sequence. (This will take some time!)

(b) Illustrate the evaluation of $f'(\ 3\ )$, where f' is the labelled expression which is equivalent to f.

10.3 Modify the Hope program (Figure 10.1) that implements the eager SECD machine so as to incorporate the primitive conditional operator, *cond*, and labelled expressions defined in Section 10.1.3.

10.4 Suggest an optimization for the implementation of labelled expressions which requires fewer transitions in the SECD machine.

10.5 Labelled expressions are adequate to represent recursion expressed in the syntax used in this chapter but do not properly implement static binding in general if mutually recursive definitions are allowed. Given the recursive qualified expression:

$$\begin{aligned}
&\textbf{let}\ f = \lambda x.\mathit{cond}\ 1\ (\ g\ x\ )\ (\ =\ x\ 0\ )\\
&\quad\ \ g = \lambda f.h\ f\\
&\quad\ \ h = \lambda y.f\ (\ -y\ 1\ )\\
&\textbf{in}\ f\ 132
\end{aligned}$$

write down the labelled expressions representing the functions f, g, h and show that in the application f 132 the occurrence of f in the body of h is bound incorrectly. How could this problem be rectified?

10.6 Modify the Hope program of Figure 10.1 to implement normal-order reduction:

(a) using the call-by-name computation rule;
(b) using the call-by-need computation rule.

10.7 The proof of correctness of the SECD machine given in Section 10.3 assumes eager semantics. Suggest how this proof could be adapted to show that the implementation specified for normal-order reduction with the call-by-name computation rule is similarly correct.

Chapter 11
An introduction to graph reduction

In the previous chapter we looked at a stack-based abstract machine for evaluating functional expressions written in the lambda notation. As we saw, this machine is most naturally suited to supporting applicative-order evaluation corresponding to the call-by-value computation rule. Extending the machine to support call-by-need required additional structures to be introduced for explicitly representing suspensions. In this chapter we shall look at a rather different approach to lambda expression evaluation in which we assume the expressions to be represented as graphs rather than as linear text strings. The resulting computational model is termed **graph reduction** for obvious reasons. One immediate advantage of the graphical representation is that sharing is then easy to express; we require no additional structure, such as an environment, to store the (shared) variable bindings since a (shared) subgraph can be referred to any number of times using pointers. A second advantage of the representation is that normal-order evaluation is both easy to express and relatively efficient to implement. This makes graph reduction a particularly natural vehicle for supporting call-by-need and hence lazy evaluation in functional languages.

Section 11.1 describes how an expression written in a λ-

calculus based notation, such as the intermediate code we introduced in Chapter 8, can be represented by a graph. In Section 11.2 we describe the various rules for reducing these graphs using normal-order evaluation. This is concerned in particular with the rule for locating the next redex and then applying the graphical equivalent of β- or δ-reductions to these redexes as required. These rules are summarized in the form of a graph reduction algorithm which is presented in Section 11.3. In Section 11.4 we consider the problem of free variables in expressions and suggest various ways in which these free variables can be transformed out during the compilation of the program. This provides us with a lead into combinator implementations which are the subject of Chapters 12 and 13.

11.1 Representing lambda expressions as graphs

Up until now we have considered only expressions written in textual form, i.e. in the form of a linear string of text symbols. Whilst this is perfectly adequate for expressing the conversion rules of the lambda calculus we noted certain problems with the representation, in particular the fact that the sharing of argument expressions is hard to express. In Chapter 6 and later in Chapters 9 and 10 we used an environment to store the bindings of each variable in an expression; two references to the same variable then simply caused the same binding to be retrieved from the environment, so avoiding the need to duplicate it. A second method of achieving sharing of this sort, however, is to adopt a graphical representation of the expression so that multiple references to the same argument expression can be represented simply by multiple arcs into a single shared copy of the corresponding argument graph. In this section we describe how the various types of lambda expression can be represented in graphical form and will later show how such expressions can be reduced to yield weak head-normal forms (WHNFs). As in the previous chapter we shall base our discussions on the lambda calculus and will assume that let and letrec expressions in our intermediate code have been transformed out. In fact the treatment of recursive definitions is deferred until the next chapter.

We shall now consider each of the possible expression types showing how each of these is represented as a **directed graph**. A 'directed' arc from a source node A to a destination node B in the graph is normally denoted by an arrow between the two:

$$A \rightarrow B$$

but here we shall omit the arrowhead and use the convention that every arc leads *downwards* from its associated source node and likewise into its destination node. For example we might draw the previous arc as follows:

In fact each of the graphs in this chapter will be a **directed acyclic graph**, or DAG. By 'acyclic' we mean that there are no cycles in the graph so that it is not possible to return to a node by following any of the arcs emanating from that node. The latter restriction will be lifted later on in Chapter 12, however, in order to provide an efficient treatment of recursive definitions. There are four expressions types to be considered:

(1) Constants are represented simply as trees consisting of a single node containing the value of the constant; in other words constants appear in the graphical representation of an expression as leaves.

(2) Function applications of the form $E_1\, E_2$ are represented by a special type of node called an **apply-node** which is labelled by the symbol @:

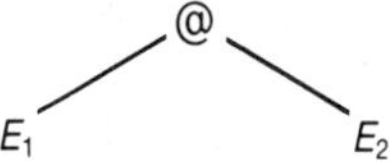

It should be noted that primitive functions of more than one argument are written in their curried form as described in Chapter 6. For example, the expression + 1 3 is interpreted as (+ 1) 3 where the result of applying the function + to the argument 1 is a new function equivalent to the successor function on integers. The expression graph for this function is shown below:

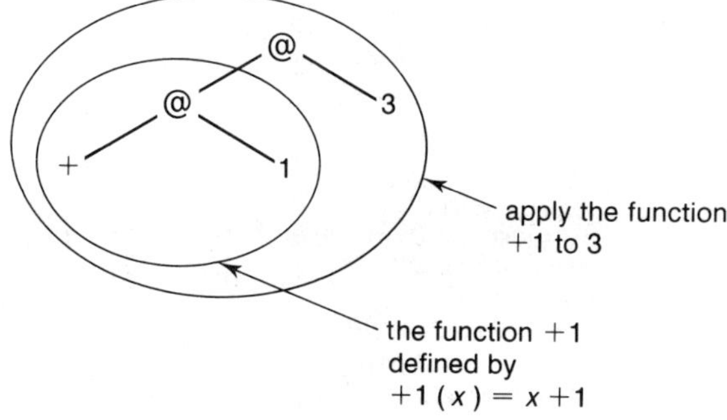

(3) Lambda abstractions of the form $\lambda x.B$ are represented by a second special type of node, the λ node, with the bound variable associated with the (leaf) node on the left outgoing arc, and the subtree representing the body expression attached to the right outgoing arc:

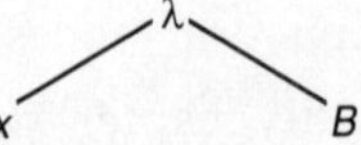

The body-expression will in general include occurrences of the bound variable, and possibly also occurrences of the bound variables of other (outer) lambda abstractions as free variables. All such variable references are represented, as we would expect, by leaf nodes. As an example of this, the following graph represents the expression $\lambda x.\lambda y. + x\,(\,*\,y\,y\,)$:

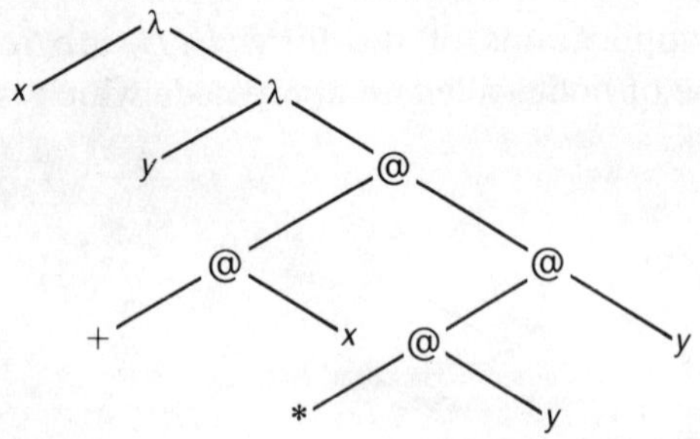

As another example, here is the graph for the expression let $x = 1$ in x which as we noted earlier is assumed to be transformed to the expression $(\,\lambda x.x\,)\ 1$:

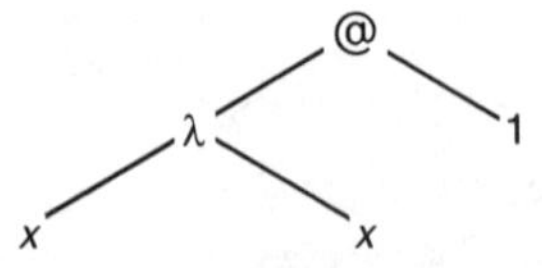

We could, of course, introduce a further new node type for let expressions of this form but this is unnecessary and serves only to obscure the inherent simplicity of the graph reduction mechanism. The treatment of recursive letrec expressions is handled similarly but also uses the Y-combinator (which has its own graph transformation rule); we defer this until Chapter 12 although we shall briefly consider the problem in Section 11.2 below.

(4) A further possible node type is one representing constructed data built from constructor functions such as *cons*. Without any special consideration for these functions we would expect them to be treated like any other function with applications of them being represented using explicit @-nodes. The difference is that they have no associated graph transformation rules since any application constitutes a weak head-normal form. For example, the expression *cons E nil* might be represented as

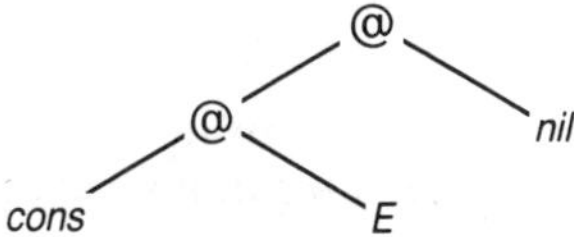

where *cons* and *nil* are provided in the predefined set of constants. We could even resort to the pure lambda calculus definition of *cons*, namely $\lambda x.\lambda y.\lambda c.c\ x\ y$, thereby obviating the need for any special type of node, but this is a rather esoteric solution. We choose instead to use an alternative, more efficient representation for constructor applications by introducing a new type of node :: as follows:

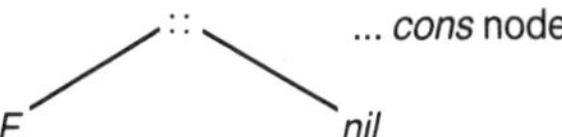

It is now possible to determine that the graph represents a constructed term without having to traverse the left spine to locate the occurrence of *cons* as before. The same idea can be applied to any other constructors which are supported as primitives. For example, if we were to view the family of tupling functions introduced in Chapter 6 as constructor functions then we could rewrite applications of the function *TUPLE-n* using special nodes of the form T_n as in

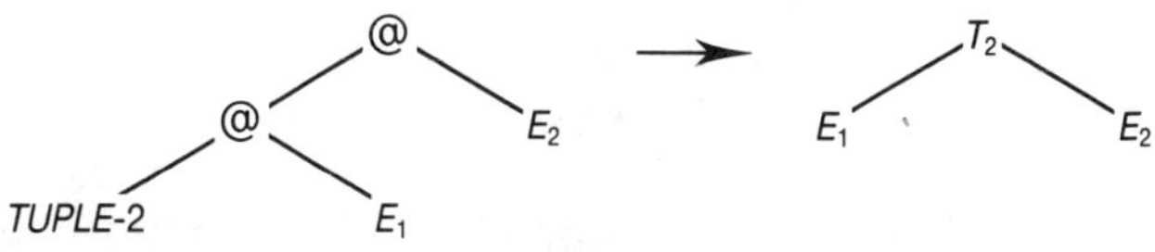

Different sized tuples now have a similar format, differing only in the number of arcs emanating from the *T* node, this being indicated by the subscript on the *T*. The corresponding tuple

indexing function is then easily defined – indexing into the nth element of a tuple built using T_m ($m \geq n$) simply delivers the nth subgraph attached to the T_m node.

It should be noted that this treatment of primitive constructors could be extended to user-defined constructors. Recall from Chapter 8 that constructed terms can be represented as ($n + 1$)-*tuples* where n is the arity of the constructor and where the first element of the tuple is the constructor code. For example if C is a three-argument user-defined constructor with code c then an application of C is translated as follows:

$$C(x, y, z) \rightarrow \mathit{TUPLE}\text{-}4\ c\ x'\ y'\ z'$$

where e' is the translated version of e. However, we could also choose to store the constructor at a special 'user-defined constructor' node:

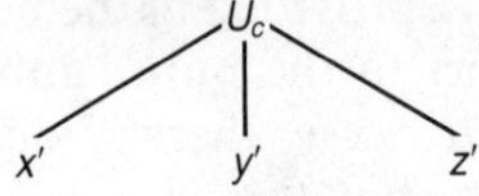

The U here is simply a 'tag' which distinguishes it from the other types of node. The constructor code, which would ordinarily be accessed by indexing into the first element of the constructed tuple, will now be accessed by extracting c from this special tagged node. We shall assume this representation in the ensuing discussions although we will use the constructor name instead of a subscripted U in order to simplify the understanding of the graphs. This means that if an internal node is not one of @ or λ then it can be assumed to be the name of a constructor.

However, use of these special nodes presents a minor complication when we consider *partial applications* of constructors since we have no means of labelling the resulting special node as being a function and no means of getting the pending arguments of that function into their correct positions. To solve this problem we can either go back to the original curried representation of the partial application or we can wrap additional λ nodes 'outside' the special constructor node. As an example, consider the expression *cons* 7 i.e. the partial application of the list constructor *cons* to the number 7. The curried version of the application will be

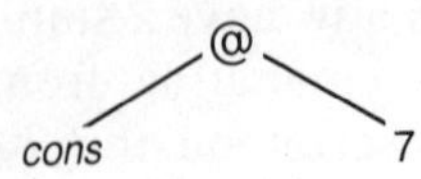

The alternative is to use a special :: node using an additional λ node outside it:

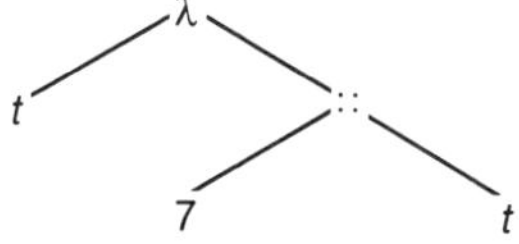

This is the optimized graphical representation of the expression $\lambda t.cons$ 7 t which as the reader may observe is equivalent to *cons* 7 by the rules of η-conversion. The extra λ node required in such cases constitutes the 'penalty' paid for representing constructors in this fashion.

It should be noted that the same sort of trick could be used for applications of primitive non-constructor functions such as + although we choose to represent them here in their curried form. We choose a different representation for constructors simply to emphasize the fact that they are functions with special properties, namely that they have no associated rules.

Having given the representation of every expression type in our language, we can now proceed to define the graph transformations corresponding to expression reduction in the lambda calculus, specifically to β-reduction and the application of primitive functions according to the delta rules. As in our previous discussions we shall assume that all expressions are to be reduced to their weak head-normal form (WHNF).

11.2 Rules for graph reduction

We begin our discussion of graph reduction by viewing the reducer as an interpreter of function expression graphs. Before a reduction can take place it is first necessary to locate the next redex node in a graph and to determine whether the redex is a β or a δ redex. Now, the most general expression in our intermediate language may be written in the form $Ge_1 \ldots e_n$ for some non-negative integer n, where the expression G is not an application. This expression has the graphical representation shown in Figure 11.1. The sequence of application nodes together with the root of the graph representing G, found by taking successive left branches from the root node (marked †), is called the **(left) spine** of the graph.

It should be apparent that locating the outermost redex according to normal-order reduction simply involves traversing the left spine of the graph until the traversed node is not an @-node. At this point the function represented by G can be one of four things:

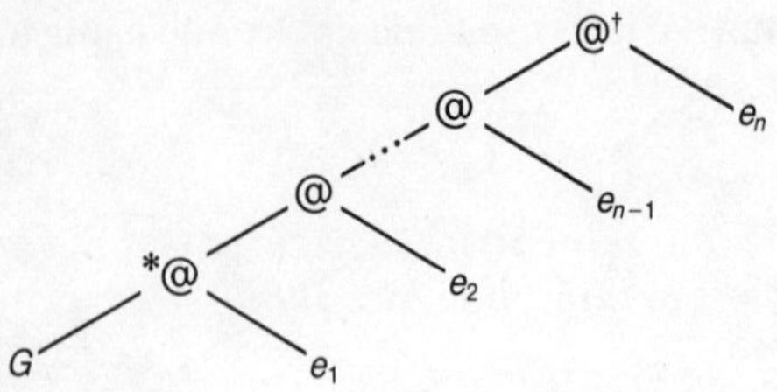

Figure 11.1 Expression graph for $Ge_1 \ldots e_n$.

(1) G may be an atomic data object, for example a number. In this case, if $n = 0$, the expression is in WHNF, and no further reductions can be performed. Of course the case $n > 0$ constitutes a type error since we have an expression in which we are trying to apply a data object to arguments. However, we shall assume here that the original program (and hence the equivalent expression graph) has been type-checked in the manner described in Chapter 7, so that this type of expression will never arise.

(2) G may be a composite data object, that is the sub-graph represented by G has a (primitive) constructor cell at its root. As in case (1), if $n = 0$ the expression will be in WHNF since there is no reduction rule for constructors; again, the case $n > 0$ will constitute a type error.

(3) G may be a lambda abstraction. In this case, if $n = 0$, then there is no outer @-node so that the expression as a whole is in WHNF. If $n \geq 1$, then the sub-expression Ge_1 must be reduced, that is the node marked $*$ constitutes the next redex node.

(4) G may be a primitive function of arity k. Now, if $k > n$, the expression represents a partial application of that primitive which, as we noted in Chapter 6, is a WHNF: the primitive's application cannot be reduced until it is applied to $k - n$ more arguments. If $k \leq n$, then the sub-expression $Ge_1 \ldots e_k$ is reduced using the delta rule for the primitive function G. For example, if $k = n$ the next redex node is the root of the whole graph, marked † in Figure 11.1. If $k < n$, then the result of the application of the primitive function must itself be another function – that is the primitive function G must be higher-order.

Having determined how to find the next redex node in a graph at each stage in a computation, we must now define the **graph transformations** corresponding to sub-expression reductions which preserve the representation of the graph, i.e. which are such that the graph represents correctly its associated expression both before and after any transformation. We have already seen that all redexes are application nodes, and also that every transformation must represent either a β-reduction or an application of a δ-rule. In other words, there are just two types of graph transformation that we must consider: application of a lambda abstraction sub-graph to an argument sub-graph, or λ-application, and application of a primitive function node of arity k to k argument sub-graphs.

11.2.1 λ-application

The application of a lambda abstraction sub-graph to an argument sub-graph constitutes the graphical representation of a β-redex. The result of the λ-application is therefore a version of the lambda abstraction sub-graph (the function graph) in which each leaf node representing the bound variable is somehow replaced by the argument (sub-)graph. To effect the sharing of argument graphs we replace each pointer to a bound variable leaf within the function graph with a pointer to the root node of the argument graph, producing as a result the modified copy of the function graph. The redex node is then overwritten by the result, i.e. with the root node of the modified function graph. In order to illustrate this mechanism Figure 11.2 shows the graph transformation resulting from the β-reduction of the expression $(\lambda x.succ\ x)\ 3$, where *succ* is the (primitive) successor function on integers. The original graph is shown on the left and the transformed one on the right.

Henceforth, when referring to the sub-graphs representing particular types of expression, such as argument, function body, bound variable, we will drop the words 'sub-graph', 'graph' or 'leaf' and refer to just the expression type. We shall now consider in more detail the individual modifications to the graph which arise from the substitution of the argument, the overwriting of the redex and the copying of the body respectively.

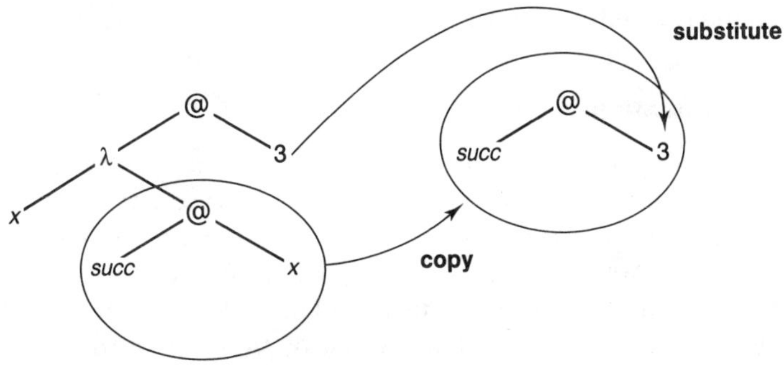

Figure 11.2 Simple λ-application graph transformation.

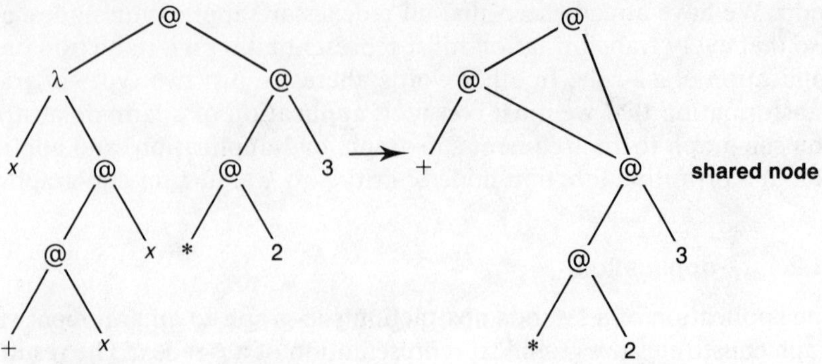

Figure 11.3 Graph transformation corresponding to the β-reduction ($\lambda x.\ +\ x\ x$) ($*\ 2\ 3$) $\rightarrow$ + ($*\ 2\ 3$) ($*\ 2\ 3$).

11.2.2 Substitution of arguments

As we stated above the substitution of a bound variable with an argument is achieved by replacing the variable reference by a pointer to the argument graph. This means in the event that the function body contains multiple references to the bound variable, multiple pointers to a single shared copy of the argument graph will be established. An example of this is given in Figure 11.3 which shows the graph transformation corresponding to the reduction

$$(\lambda x.\ +\ x\ x)\,(*\ 2\ 3) \rightarrow +\,(*\ 2\ 3)\,(*\ 2\ 3)$$

in which the sub-expression ($*$ 2 3) is shared.

The graphical representation therefore enables expressions to be shared in a natural way, without the need for an explicit environment, and it is this which makes graph reduction a viable model for the implementation of functional languages; this observation was first made by Wadsworth (1971).

11.2.3 Overwriting the root of a redex

After performing argument substitution to implement β-reduction, the redex is physically overwritten by the result of its reduction, either by an atom or the root node of the simplified (reduced) expression. If the redex node is itself shared, then each subsequent reference to that node will find the node in its reduced form and it is this overwriting operation which gives the implementation its call-by-need semantics. As in the updating of a suspension associated with an assigning dump in the lazy SECD machine, the overwriting of the redex node is meaning-preserving in that it replaces one graph by another graph with the same value. The

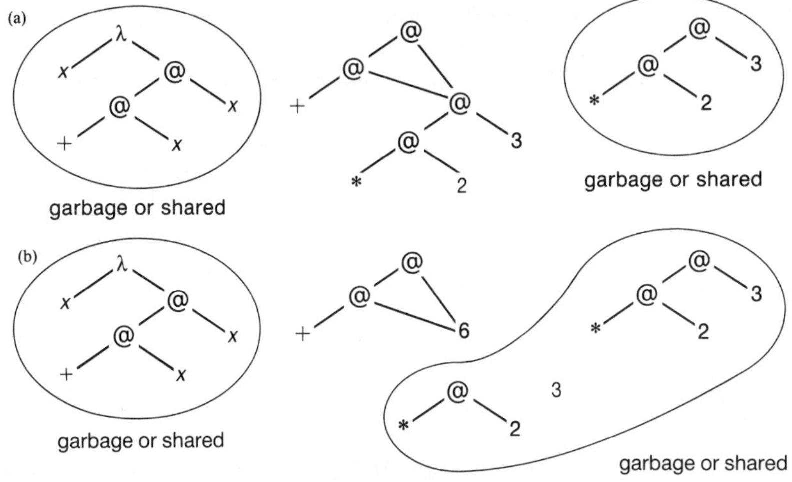

Figure 11.4 Graph transformation showing potential garbage cells ($\lambda x. + x\, x$) ($*$ 2 3) $\rightarrow$ + ($*$ 2 3) ($*$ 2 3) $\rightarrow$ + 6 6.

other nodes in the redex will be unaffected by the overwrite but will be 'disconnected' from the root node as a result. If these nodes are not shared (i.e. if they are no longer required in the evaluation) then they constitute what is aptly named **garbage** and the space which they occupy can legitimately be reclaimed using a so-called **garbage collector**. The various types of garbage collector and their method of operation are described in Chapter 16. In the examples shown so far in Figures 11.2 and 11.3, these potential garbage nodes are not shown. Figure 11.4 illustrates in part (a) the reduction of Figure 11.3 again, this time showing all of the disconnected cells which may have become garbage, as well as the next reduction in part (b).

11.2.4 Copying the λ-body

The introduction of sharing in argument substitution implies that a lambda abstraction may be shared by virtue of its being an argument itself in some λ-application. Thus in a λ-application we must make the substitutions for the bound variable nodes within a *copy* of the body of the applied lambda abstraction. The copy of the body requires new graph nodes for every node other than its root node, which is written into the redex node as required.

This is precisely the way in which the β-reductions have been implemented in the above examples, illustrated in Figures 11.2–11.4. To be more precise, we should also have shown the detached lambda abstraction sub-graph representing $\lambda x.succ\ x$ in Figure 11.2, since these cells are still there after the reduction and may be needed by some other part of the computation. However, the corresponding cells are shown in Figure 11.4, for the lambda abstraction ($\lambda x. + x\ x$) after this has been applied to the expression $*\ 2\ 3$.

Here is a more complex example which illustrates the main points of this section, namely the graph reduction of the intermediate code expression:

$$\text{let } twice = \lambda f.\lambda x.f\ (\ f\ x\ ) \text{ in } twice\ (\ \lambda x. + x\ 1\ )\ 2$$

which by expanding the definition of twice is equivalent to

$$(\ \lambda f.\lambda x.f\ (\ fx\ )\ )\ (\lambda x. + x\ 1\ )\ 2.$$

The graph transformations are illustrated in Figure 11.5. Garbage cells are not shown, and the root node of the next redex is marked $*$ in each graph. The node at the top of each graph is always the same, being the root of the original expression, which will eventually hold the result, 4. In the first graph, (a), the redex is a λ-application in which the body has two occurrences of the bound variable, x. The substitution leads to the graph (b), where the sharing of the argument expression is clear. In the next reduction, the body has only one occurrence of the bound variable, y, yielding the graph (c). The next reduction involves both a λ-body with more than one occurrence of the bound variable and a shared lambda abstraction. The importance of copying is quite clear here: the same lambda abstraction is used to provide the template for the result as well as part of the argument substituted into it. The last three reductions involve rules for the application of primitive functions, and parts (d)–(g) may be looked at after the reader has read the next section if desired. However, the graph transformations are very simple and quite obvious: the redex in graph (d) is chosen to be the first argument of the strict primitive function, +, and the next two reductions are just primitive function (+) applications to constant arguments.

The astute reader may feel that the rules for reducing λ-applications force us unnecessarily to copy λ-bodies as a consequence of sharing: why should we not share λ-bodies provided that we copy every argument which is a lambda abstraction? The objection to this idea lies in the implementation of recursion. This is normally achieved using cyclic graphs (considered in the next chapter) so that the same functions may be applied several times to different arguments, each application therefore requiring a fresh copy of the body. Thus the alternative scheme would not work. An alternative approach might be to use the Y-combinator directly, which produces perfectly good lambda expressions and, with our normal-order graph reducer, has no problem with non-terminating computations (see the corresponding discussion on the eager SECD machine in the

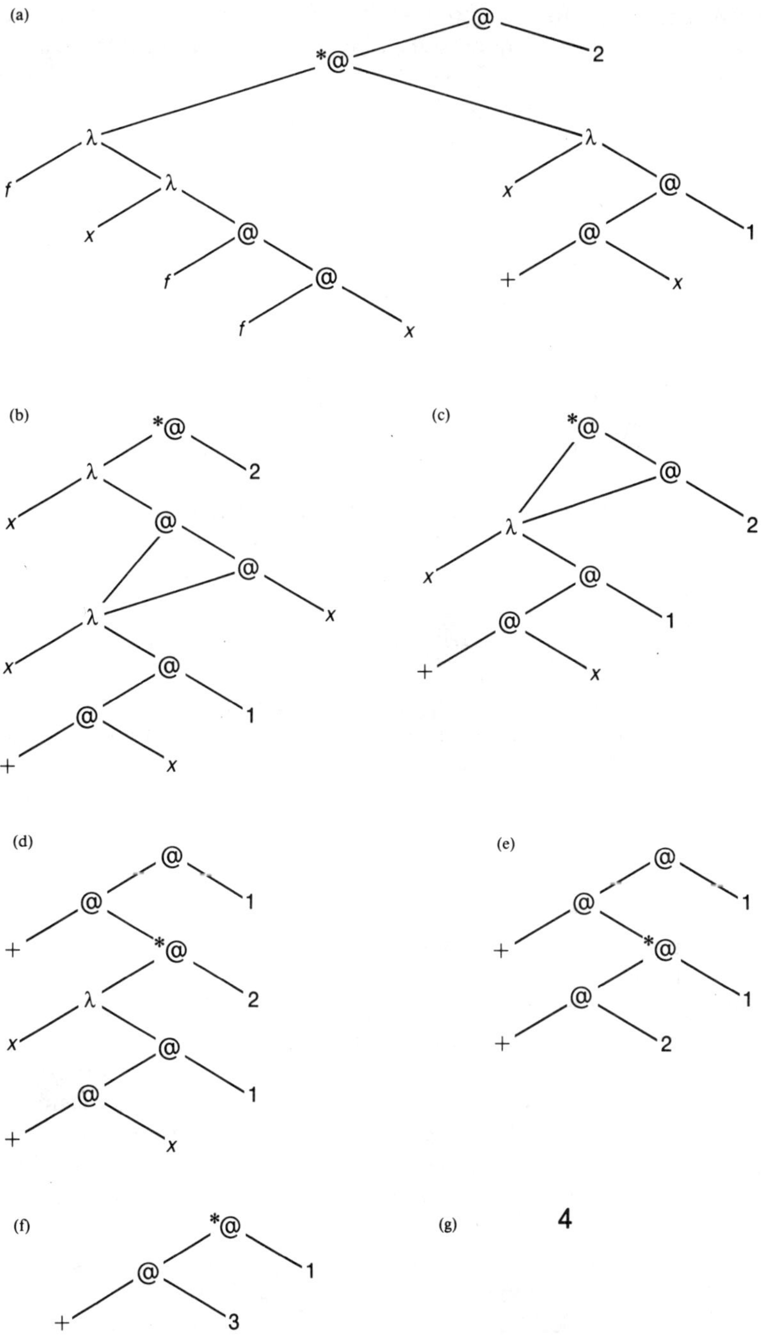

Figure 11.5 Graph reduction of the expression *twice* ($\lambda x.+ x\ 1$) 2.

previous chapter). However, the whole point of using the *Y*-combinator in this way is to implement self-application, involving many lambda abstractions as arguments, which would be copied anyway in the proposed alternative scheme. In fact we shall see in the next chapter that a more efficient implementation of *Y*-combinator applications also makes use of a cyclic graph. The preferred method for implementing λ-applications is therefore the one we have presented.

11.2.5 Primitive function application

The rules for transforming a graph corresponding to the application of a primitive function are given by the delta rules of the function. These include information indicating in which arguments the function is strict, i.e. which ones must be evaluated before the function can be applied, together with some built-in function which computes the result of the application when the required arguments have been evaluated.

Given the delta rules, which cannot be specified in more detail in general, we can now quite simply define the transformation of a graph corresponding to the reduction of a primitive function application redex. For a primitive function of arity k:

(1) Evaluate the strict arguments of the primitive function, as specified in the delta rules, by recursively applying the graph reducer to the appropriate graphs from those labelled $e_1, \ldots, e_k$ in Figure 11.1 – i.e. from those having their root nodes connected to the application nodes on the spine.

(2) Execute the primitive function application using the delta rule and the evaluated arguments, generating a graph as the result.

(3) Overwrite the redex node with the graph representing the result. This operation will detach sub-graphs from the redex node, creating garbage unless the cells are shared, in exactly the same way as we saw for λ-applications.

We now give two examples of the graph transformations arising from primitive function applications: the first for the arithmetic function + which is strict in both its arguments and the second for the conditional function – *cond* in the intermediate code.

EXAMPLE 1

Consider the primitive function application + 1 (*succ* 2) where, as before, *succ* is the successor function on integers. This has the graph representation shown in Figure 11.6(a) The redex is the

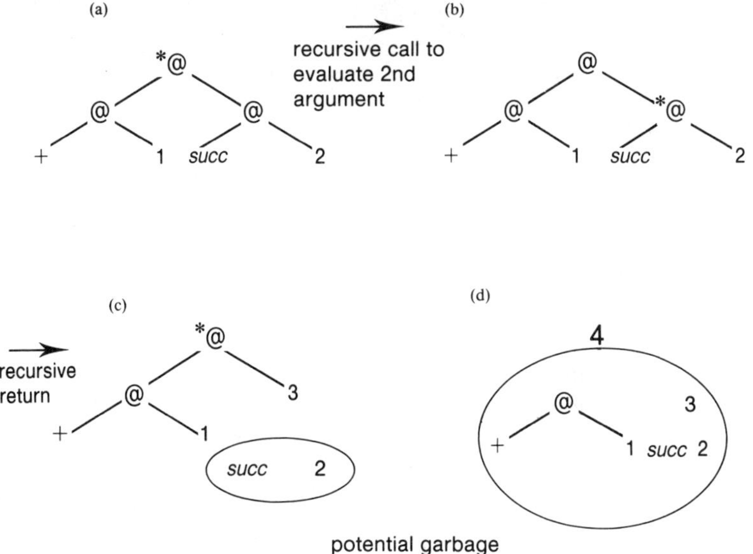

Figure 11.6 Reduction of the expression + 1 (*succ* 2).

root node of the graph, corresponding to the application of +. Since + is strict in both its arguments, but only the first is in WHNF, the graph reducer is called recursively to reduce the second, which is the right sub-graph of the redex node. On return, the result 3 overwrites the argument redex node as in Figure 11.6(c), and the primitive function + can be applied, giving the result 4 in the original redex node, as in Figure 11.6(d).

EXAMPLE 2

Next we consider the expression ($\lambda x.cond$ ($neg\ x$) 0 ($square\ x$)) 3, where *neg* and *square* are given by

$$neg \quad = \lambda x. < x\ 0$$
$$square = \lambda x. * x\ x$$

In fact the expression is a λ-application, and it is left to the reader to arrive at the graph of Figure 11.7(a) after one reduction step (the expansions of *neg* and *square* are not shown).

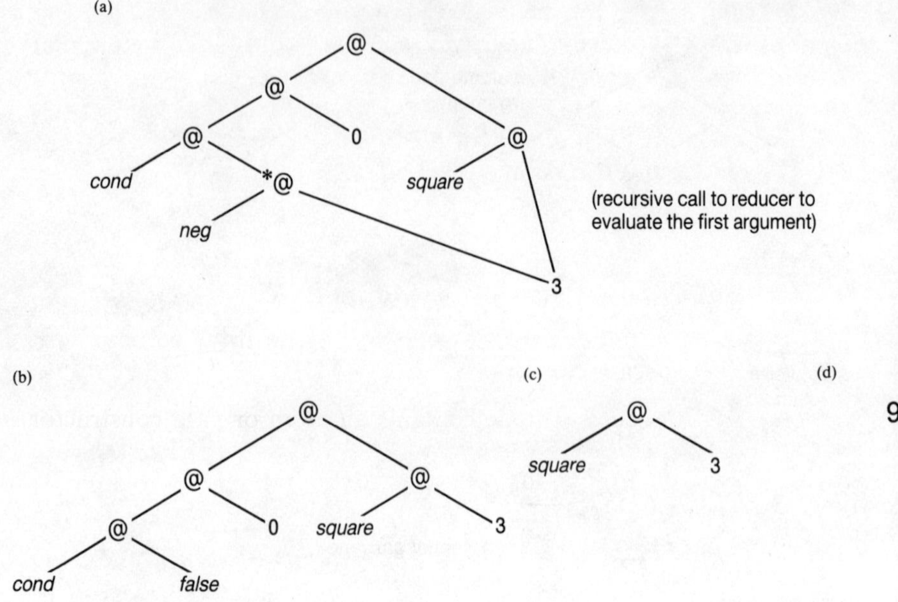

Figure 11.7 Reduction of the expression ($\lambda x.cond$ (*neg x*) 0 (*square x*)) 3.

It should be noted that *cond* is strict in its first argument so that the transformation giving the graph (b) from (a) in the figure is performed by recursive invocation of the reducer to evaluate the expression *neg* 3. The evaluation of this expression yields *false* and so the delta rule for *cond* selects the sub-graph of the second argument for the result of the application, hence giving the graph of Figure 11.7(c). Finally, the square of 3 is evaluated according to the reduction of *square* 3, giving the result 9 as shown in Figure 11.7(d). (Notice that *false* is asumed here to be a constant although it could equally well be encoded in some other way, for example as an integer.)

11.3 Interpreters based on graph reduction

We are now in a position to design an evaluator which reduces any lambda expression to WHNF, and below we give an informal algorithm for doing this which is based on the graph template shown in Figure 11.1. The presentation is at a sufficiently abstract level that the detailed graph manipulations are hidden in higher-level operations. For example certain problems introduced by selector functions are resolved in the statement 'overwrite redex node'. Similarly, the explicit management of the recursive calls needed for the evaluation of the arguments of primitive functions is not specified. These two issues are considered below. For completeness we include the tests which would detect type errors, although as we noted earlier these will not be required if the expressions have been previously type checked.

To reduce an expression graph:

REPEAT

(1) Successively move down the left branch of the graph (*unwind* the left spine) to the first non-@ node.

(2) Perform the following actions depending on the type of current node being scanned:

(a) If the current node contains an atom or data constructor then
if current node is the root of the graph (i.e. 0 arguments)
then Expression in WHNF
else Type error

(b) If the current node contains a primitive function of k arguments then
if $k >$ number of @-nodes scanned on the spine
then Expression in WHNF
else Find which arguments must be evaluated from the corresponding delta rule; recursively reduce those arguments sub-graphs to their WHNF; execute the primitive function, producing a new sub-graph; overwrite the redex node, which is the kth @-node up the spine from the current node with the result, i.e. replace it by the root of the new sub-graph; (*rewind* the spine)

(c) If the current node is a λ-node then
if current node is the root of the graph
then Expression in WHNF
else Make a copy of the λ-body substituting the shared argument sub-graph for the bound variable nodes (the bound variable name hangs off the left branch of the λ-node); overwrite the redex node (first @-node up the spine) with the result, i.e. replace it by the root of the substituted λ-body copy.

UNTIL Expression in WHNF

11.3.1 Projection functions and synonym nodes

In this section we consider a particular complication in our graph reduction scheme which is caused by the application of **projection** (or

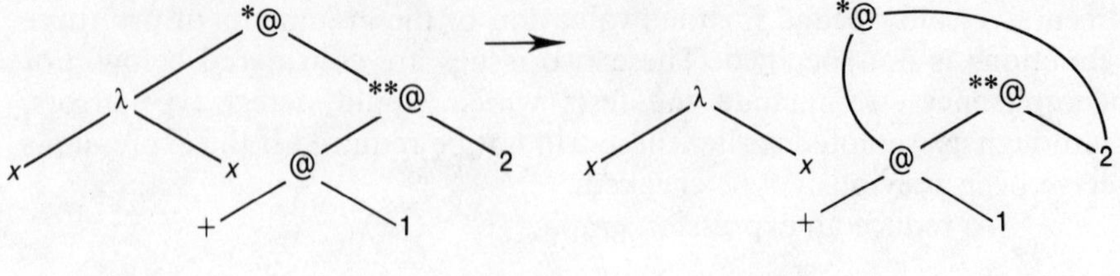

(a) $(\lambda x.x)(+1\ 2)$

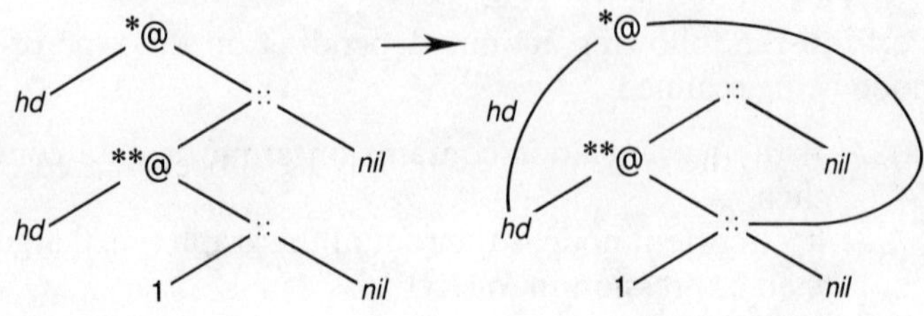

(b) *hd* (*cons* (*hd* (*cons* 1 *nil*)) 3)

Figure 11.8 Graph reductions of projection function applications by 'copying'.

projector) functions. A projector function is defined as any function which returns as the result of its application to an argument expression a component of that expression, i.e. an unchanged sub-graph of the unreduced graph. For example, the identity function, $\lambda x.x$, which we shall refer to as I, is a projection function since it returns its argument graph unchanged. A further class of examples is provided by all the primitive selector functions defined on compound data objects; for example, the primitive functions *hd* and *tl* which respectively select the head and tail of a list.

The problem with the implementation we have so far described is that the redex node is overwritten by the root node of the (unchanged) result sub-graph, so that there then exist two copies of this sub-graph in which all nodes other than the root nodes are shared. Since each root node can subsequently become a redex, duplicated reduction of the sub-graph may occur. Figure 11.8 illustrates the graph transformations corresponding to the two projection function applications

(a) $I(+\ 1\ 2)$
(b) *hd* (*cons* (*hd* (*cons* 1 *nil*)) 3)

The redex-nodes are again marked $*$.

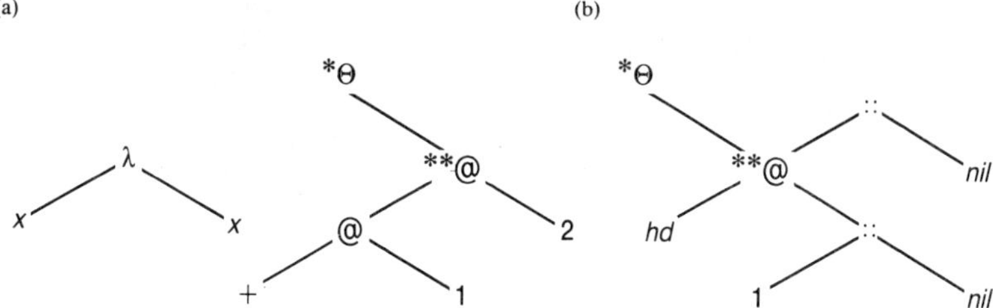

Figure 11.9 Graph reductions of projection function applications by 'indirection'.

In each case, the node marked ** may have been shared, so that after the reduction the node is not garbage, but may become a redex. This could result in recomputation of the expression + 1 2 (the corresponding sub-graph in case (b) is in WHNF), which could have been arbitrarily more expensive to evaluate. There are two solutions to this problem, the first of which relies on the use of so-called **indirection nodes** or **synonym** nodes labelled by Θ in a graph. The interpretation of these nodes is that the expression represented by the graph with an indirection node at its root is the same as that represented by the graph having the referenced node as its root. A projection function application, with redex node *PA* and result redex node *PR*, may then be represented by making *PA* a synonym node pointing to *PR*, as shown in Figure 11.9 for the examples (a) and (b) of Figure 11.8.

The trouble with this idea is that synonym nodes can occur anywhere, i.e. wherever a projection function has been applied, so that chains of indirections can form – a potential source of inefficiency. In general we cannot know whether or not *PR* will itself become a synonym node after reduction of the result sub-graph, and if so whether the node it points to will be a synonym node and so on. This leads to the second solution to the problem. This uses the observation that after the application of the projection function, the next redex to be chosen will be *PR*, if *PR* is not already in WHNF. This follows by definition of *NOR*: if *PR* were not the outermost redex after the reduction of *PA*, then *PA* could not have been when it was selected for reduction. Thus we conclude that *PR* can be reduced to WHNF *before* selecting *PA* as the next redex and *PR* can then be copied to *PA* (i.e. the reduced form of ** can be copied to * in Figure 11.9) without risk of later duplicated reductions.

This suggests that, if we select the redex-node *PR* for reduction first, the copying method, which requires no other change to the graph reduction algorithm, will be superior. However, the indirection method can also make use of the same change in the selection order of redexes, for if *PR* is reduced first, it will be known at the time that *PA* is overwritten

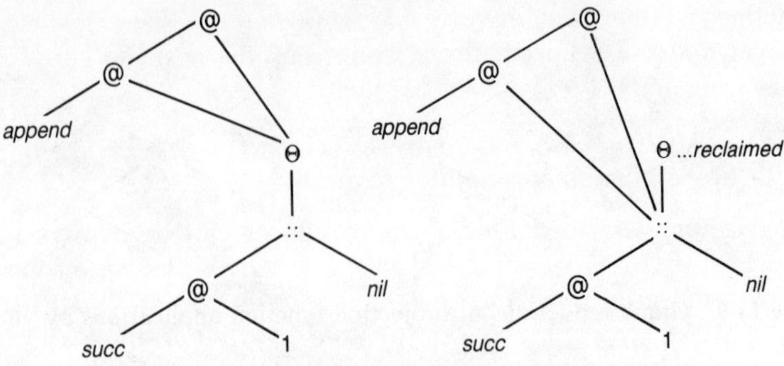

Figure 11.10 Garbage collection of synonym nodes.

whether or not *PR* is a synonym node. In this way we can ensure we only have only single-step indirections, since if *PR* is a synonym node, it is copied into *PA* (as in normal graph reduction) and if it is not *PA* becomes a synonym node pointing to *PR*.

The performance of the indirection method (with only single-step indirections) is similar to that achieved by copying. The same number of reductions are performed since in both implementations the result sub-graph (with root *PR*) is reduced to WHNF only once. Moreover, the storage requirement is the same in both cases since both schemes generate just one redundant node: an indirection node and a duplicated redex node respectively. The disadvantage of the single-step indirection method is that each subsequent reference to *PA* requires a second node access to obtain the contents of *PR*. However, these indirection nodes can be short-circuited by the garbage collector, which is responsible for locating and reclaiming unused cells. An example of this short-circuiting is illustrated in Figure 11.10 which shows a graph representing the expression *append* (*cons* (*succ* 1) *nil*) (*cons* (*succ* 1) *nil*) where *append* is equivalent to ⟨ ⟩ in Hope.

The disadvantage of using indirection is that any node may be a synonym node, and must be tested (by examining a tag-field) before its contents can be used, introducing a small but persistent run-time overhead. However, there is one other more subtle advantage which indirection has over copying, namely that it facilitates the 'memoizing' optimization more easily. Memoizing will be discussed in Chapter 19, and essentially means 'remembering argument–result pairs' for a function, so that recomputation can be avoided when the function is applied more than once to the same argument value. If there are two copies of a sub-graph representing the same function, as could occur in the copying method of handling projector applications, the argument–result association list ought to be shared or possibly two separate copies could be maintained. Either way involves a significant overhead, whereas if synonym nodes were used, there would only be a single copy of the function sub-graph, so the problem would not arise.

11.3.2 Spine access and pointer-reversal

We have now described how a graph reducer can be constructed to evaluate expressions in our extended lambda calculus which includes constants and primitive functions. However, one point which was not elaborated on was the unwinding of the spine upon application of a primitive function and conversely rewinding (moving back up the spine) which is required in the evaluation of a primitive function's arguments and upon completion of its application (i.e. function 'return'). One reason for not spelling out all of the implementation details was that a straightforward stack-based method works adequately, as we shall see. However, in reducing a graph, we already have a data structure within which we can also maintain a stack to manage spine unwinding and rewinding, namely the graph itself. The technique which enables the encoding of the stack in the graph is called **pointer reversal** and relies on performing a simple local transformation of the graph each time the spine is unwound or rewound one step.

Unwinding and rewinding using a stack

In the evaluation of a primitive function application, the spine of a sub-graph is unwound until a non-application node is found, as shown in Figure 11.1. To implement this using a stack we simply follow the left spine pushing each @-node onto the stack (in practice we push the address of each @-node onto the stack) until a λ node or a primitive function node is encountered. With this done the argument subgraphs and the redex node can be located in constant time by simply indexing from the top of the stack. Note that such a stack is not strictly necessary except for reasons of efficiency. Assume the location of the redex node of the application is known, and that the number of @-nodes unwound, n, has been counted, then the ith argument sub-graph may be accessed through the $(n - i)$th @-node down the spine from the redex node.

Evaluating the top-level expression involves simply unwinding the spine of its graph to find the first redex and then reducing it. It is this reduction which generates further reductions, possibly involving recursive calls to the reducer. We now outline a suitable stack-management scheme by listing the operations performed on unwinding the spine of a (sub-)graph, initiating reduction of an argument sub-graph and completing the reduction of a (sub-)graph, as follows:

(1) Unwinding is the first operation to be performed when reducing

the graph representing the top-level expression or a new sub-graph, and it therefore uses a new segment of the stack, called a **stack frame** which is defined to start at the current top-of-stack (*TOS*), and so is built on top of the previous stack frame. During unwinding, the stack position of the base of the new stack frame is remembered for later use, and pointers to each @-node on the left-spine of the (sub-)graph are pushed successively onto the stack. The number of @-nodes on the spine is therefore the depth of the stack frame at the end of unwinding.

(2) If the next node, after unwinding, is a λ-node, the corresponding reduction proceeds as described in the previous sections of this chapter, using the *TOS* to locate the redex-node. Alternatively, if it is a primitive function application, with arity n which is less than or equal to the depth of the current stack frame (i.e. the number of available arguments), then the delta rules for that function are inspected to find out which arguments must be evaluated. If there are none, the reduction of the redex is performed according to these rules and the reduction is completed as described in (3) below.

If there is at least one strict argument, its evaluation is initiated by restarting the evaluator recursively, after preserving the current *state* on the stack by pushing the position of the base of the current stack frame (which was remembered above) and the relevant status information. Specifically, the status information must include the identifier of the primitive function currently being applied together with the current position in the execution of its delta rules, e.g. which arguments have been evaluated. If the required argument is the ith ($1 \leq i \leq n$), its root-node is pointed to by the right outgoing arc from the @-node pointed to by the stack element i positions below the *TOS* (before pushing the status information). The evaluator will then begin reducing the sub-graph by pushing the address of this node.

(3) When the reduction is complete, the evaluator returns having overwritten the redex node with the result, which may be atomic or the root of another sub-graph (for example in the case of a selector or the conditional function). The stack is popped down to the base of the current stack frame and if this is the bottom of the stack, the evaluation is complete, the newly reduced sub-graph representing the weak head-normal form of the top-level expression. Otherwise, the previous stack frame and status information are popped and the evaluation is resumed from the (saved) calling point in the delta rules of the primitive function which required the argument result. This operation is sometimes called **rewinding**.

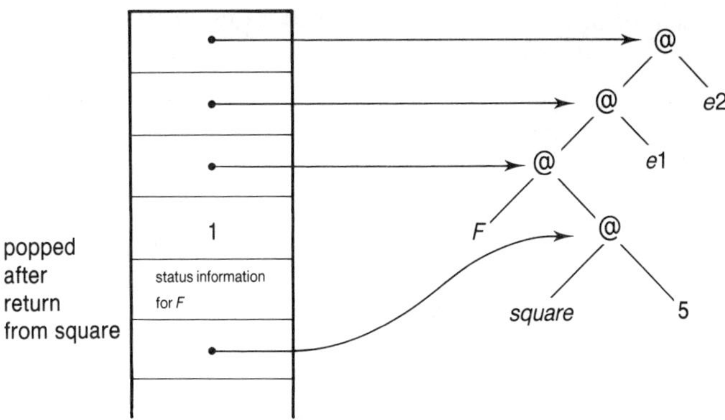

Figure 11.11 Evaluation stack after a recursive call to the graph reducer.

As an example, Figure 11.11 shows the state of the stack in the evaluation of the expression

F (*square* 5) *e*1 *e*2

where *F* is a primitive function which is strict in its first argument and *e*1 and *e*2 are arbitrary expressions. Immediately after initiating the evaluation of the first argument the stack and graph will look as shown in Figure 11.11.

Unwinding and rewinding using pointer reversal

The stack used for controlling access to the spine of a (sub-)graph during the evaluation of arguments of primitive function applications may be located physically in the nodes of the graph itself, with the obvious implication for the efficiency of the implementation in terms of storage. From the discussion in the previous section, it will be clear that at any stage in the evaluation of an expression, it is only necessary to be able to access the current node being scanned (and so the sub-graph accessible via its outgoing arcs) and the previous node scanned. In this way it is possible to backtrack to find argument sub-graphs and rewind on completion of a primitive function application. It is the validity of this 'one-step' mode of operation of a stack which enables the spine-stack to reside on the spine itself by reversing the incoming pointer of a node as it is scanned – from either direction. Thus, when unwinding, the node just arrived at will contain, in general, the following pointers:

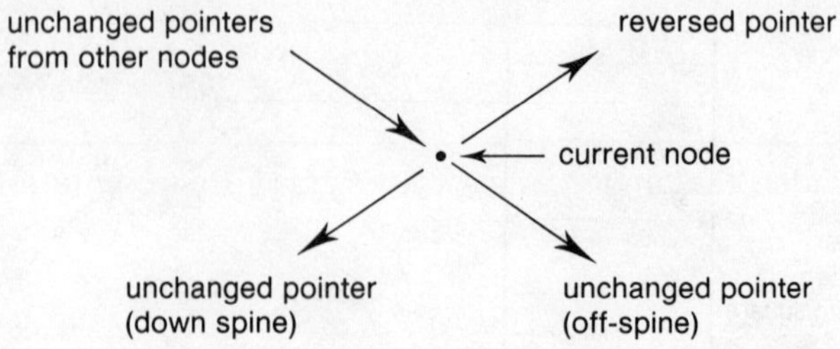

Note that, after unwinding and rewinding, a spine will have had the pointers in all of its nodes reversed twice, leaving the graph unchanged on return from a call to the evaluator (except for the reduction of the appropriate redex node to its weak head-normal form). We now show how pointer reversal works in graph reduction by outlining algorithms and giving two examples to illustrate their main features. It should then be straightforward to extend the reduction algorithm given above to incorporate it.

Spine unwinding and rewinding uses the nodes of the spine together with three dynamic pointers, FORE, AFT and TEMP, and a special, unique pointer value, NULL, to indicate the end of a chain. Initially, prior to the unwinding operation which is the first to be performed by the evaluator, we assign AFT := NULL and FORE := redex node-pointer. We use LEFT(n) and RIGHT(n) to denote the left and right pointers in a node n. The unwinding algorithm then consists of the following:

```
UNWIND:
        while FORE points to an application node
            TEMP        := FORE ;
            FORE        := LEFT(FORE) ;    (point FORE to next node
                                              down spine)
            LEFT(TEMP)  := AFT ;           (reverse pointer in
                                              previous node)
            AFT         := TEMP ;          (update head of reverse-
                                              pointer chain)

        end
```

At the end of unwinding, FORE points to the first non-@ node on the spine, *G* in Figure 11.1, AFT points to the last @-node on the spine, and the left-pointer in each of the @ nodes on the spine points to the previous one, except for the redex node, for which the left pointer is NULL. Rewinding is essentially the reverse of unwinding, the roles of FORE and AFT being interchanged in the UNWIND algorithm. The loop terminates after a given number of steps in the case of finding the redex node of an argument expression, or when AFT becomes NULL on rewinding to the redex of the primitive function application after its evaluation is complete.

EXAMPLE

Consider the unwinding of the graph representation of the expression + 1 2, i.e.

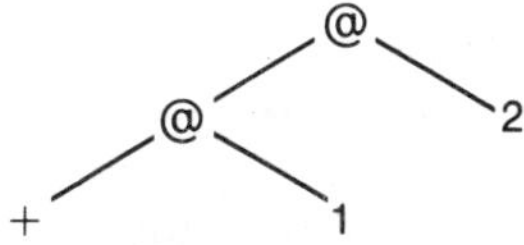

As the spine unwinds, its successive states, together with the values of the pointers FORE and AFT, are shown in Figure 11.12.

To initiate evaluation of the *i*th argument of a primitive function application, we simply rewind through *i* nodes up the spine (from the first non-@ node), and then move into the argument's spine by taking the right arc to its redex node, using pointer reversal to establish the path back to the previous spine as follows:

```
       TEMP := FORE;
       FORE := RIGHT(AFT);
RIGHT(AFT) := TEMP;
```

Notice that the pointer AFT does not change, indicating the @-node to be returned to after evaluation of the argument. Similarly, the left pointer of this node still points up the left spine towards the redex node of the

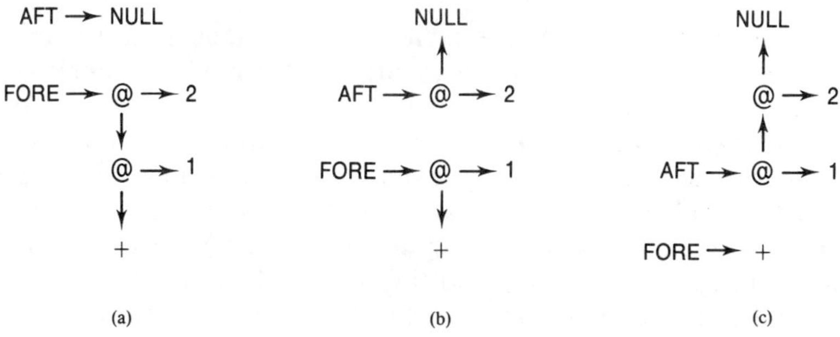

Figure 11.12 Unwinding of the spine of the graph for the expression + 1 2: (a) initial state; (b) one step down spine; (c) end of unwind.

primitive function's application, but the right pointer is set to point down this spine. The argument to be evaluated next, if any, will be determined by the delta rules of the primitive function being applied and the current state of the evaluation of those delta rules.

We can now call the evaluator to reduce the argument sub-graph but can no longer use the special NULL pointer to indicate the end of rewinding, since the AFT pointer has already been used. We suggest two ways of solving this problem. The first, and the one we consider throughout the rest of this section, is to use one extra bit to *mark* the @-node on the spine pointed to by AFT when entering the spine of the argument sub-graph. This mark is tested on rewinding after the argument has been evaluated and the evaluator wishes to overwrite the redex and return; this replaces the test for AFT having the value NULL. The other method involves keeping a separate small stack, similar to the one described in the previous section, but not containing the node-pointers, i.e. essentially just storing link information. The pointer to the @-node on the previous spine (i.e. the value of AFT above) could be stacked, thus enabling AFT to be initialized to NULL as before. Alternatively, the number of @-nodes on a spine could be stacked after unwinding, so that the number of rewind steps necessary to reach the redex node will always be known. Details of these methods are left as exercises.

EXAMPLE

To illustrate argument evaluation using pointer reversal, we consider the expression + (+ 1 2) 3, and show in Figure 11.13 the state of its graph representation after unwinding, upon entering the spine of its first argument expression and at the beginning of unwinding the new spine. The marked node is annotated with a +.

Finally, we consider the actions necessary on return from the evaluator after reduction of a redex node to WHNF. If the pointer AFT is NULL, the evaluation is complete, but otherwise we only know that we have just evaluated *some* argument in *some* primitive function application. In order to resume a primitive function application which caused a call to the evaluator, it is necessary to find out the identity of the primitive function, and which argument has just been evaluated. In theory at least, we can deduce this information by unwinding the spine again to the primitive function node: if the number of steps required to do the unwind is k, then we know that the kth argument was the one just evaluated. However, it is simpler and more efficient in execution time to stack the identities of the primitive function and its argument, as well as

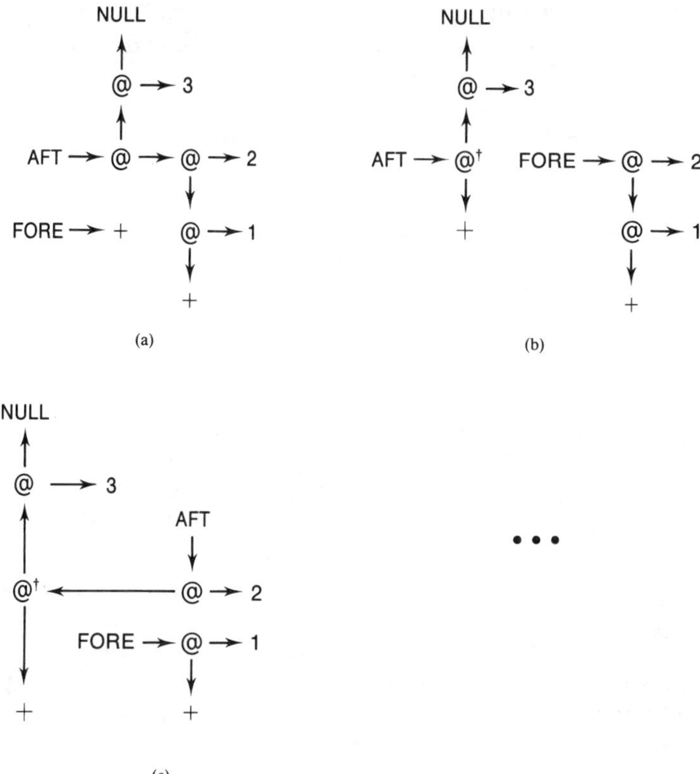

Figure 11.13 Argument evaluation using pointer reversal: (a) after unwinding; (b) enter argument-spine; (c) begin unwinding new spine.

the state of execution of the delta rules, on entry into that argument's spine. When the argument evaluation is complete this information can be restored and used to resume the execution of the delta rule.

11.4 The problem of free variables

We conclude this chapter by identifying a quite serious impediment to efficiency which is posed by the existence of free variables in function-bodies. In any closed expression, which is what we are considering, free variables are the bound variables of 'outer' lambda abstractions in an enclosed lambda abstraction, as discussed in some detail in Chapter 6. In fact the problem identified here is just an instance (in a graph-representation) of its earlier, more abstractly presented form. Consider the expression ($\lambda x.\lambda y.x$) $E1$ $E2$, where $E1$ and $E2$ are arbitrary expressions. This is represented by the following graph, in which the first redex node is a λ-application marked (1) and the graph is also shown after one reduction step (without garbage-nodes).

So far there has been no copying of sub-graphs, except for the template of the λ-body with the bound variable appropriately substituted for $E1$. Now consider the next reduction corresponding to the redex marked (2). This is also a λ-application which, following the rules given earlier in this chapter, involves making a copy of the sub-graph representing the λ-body $E1$, and overwriting node (2) with its root – there being no occurrence of the bound variable to replace. It is clearly desirable to share the sub-graph representing $E1$; $E1$ may be arbitrarily complex, requiring a large copying overhead, and duplicated reduction of its redexes may also occur subsequently if both copies are referenced. This problem has arisen because the body of the lambda abstraction $\lambda y.x$ is independent of y. We have seen this situation before in the context of projection functions, which suggests that we might try to solve the problem in the same way. Thus we might reduce a λ-body which has no occurrence of its bound variable to its WHNF before its lambda abstraction is applied to an argument, safe in the knowledge that it would have been the next redex after the application in any case. Then the reduction of $(\lambda x.E)E'$ where x does not occur in E might be:

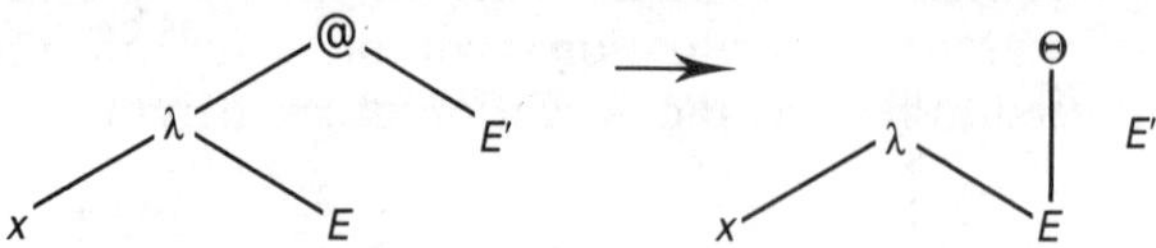

This solution therefore works nicely, and the pre-evaluation of the λ-body also improves efficiency if the lambda abstraction is shared. However, it requires some analysis by the evaluator to detect whether or not a λ-body contains references to its bound variable.

Unfortunately, there is a more general free variable problem which loses efficiency that the above method cannot recover. Consider the reduction sequence

$$(\lambda x.(\lambda y. + x\ y)\ 1)\ 2 \rightarrow (\lambda y. + 2\ y)\ 1 \rightarrow +\ 2\ 1$$

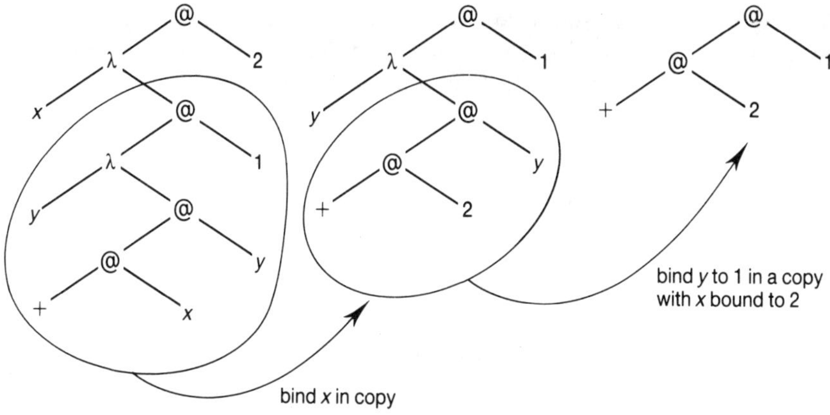

Figure 11.14 The problem of free variables in graph reduction.

These reductions are as shown graphically in Figure 11.14.

The problem is that copies of the body $\lambda y.\ + x\ y$ are different for different bindings of x. Therefore no sharing is possible and, more seriously, there is no fixed sequence of instructions that can be used to generate the copies, making it difficult to compile the copying routine. The significance of this remark relates to the compilation of functional expressions for execution on an abstract machine having graph reduction as its computational model. A detailed example of this is provided by the G-machine, which is considered in Chapter 15.

So are there any solutions to this free variable problem? Fortunately the answer is 'yes'. There are two approaches that we can take. The first is to implement a mechanism which provides direct access to free variables, that is one that maintains an explicit environment. This leads to the SECD type of abstract machine, which was considered in the previous chapter. The alternative approach is to transform out the explicit free variables in some way at compile-time – their presence becoming implicitly distributed throughout the computation. One way of doing this is to translate lambda expressions into *combinatory logic* – see for example Hindley and Seldin (1986) – and define a graph reduction machine for combinator graphs. A second method is to treat all free variables as arguments to additional lambda abstractions; this technique is called **lambda lifting** and applies equally well to nested higher-order functions (with global parameter references) in a conventional functional language. There are also more sophisticated methods, for example using **super-combinators** (Hughes, 1984), and we consider the combinator-based approaches to finding efficient implementations for graph reduction in the next two chapters. An additional benefit that can be gained by solving the free variable problem in this way is that unnecessary copying and duplicated reduction can be avoided, leading to the property of so-called **full laziness** in the implementation.

11.5 Parallel graph reduction

The reader may have noticed that during the reduction of an expression graph it is quite possible for a number of redexes to be present within that graph at any time. Now, because of referential transparency we know that these redexes will always evaluate to the same thing regardless of where or when the evaluation takes place and because of this it is quite possible to evaluate them at the same time by allocating them to separate processors. Each processor can then go to work on reducing their respective redexes, possibly generating further redexes and so more parallel tasks in the process. The fact that the graph is now being reduced by several processors simultaneously means that there are additional factors involved in the reduction process such as the representation and synchronization of tasks and the prevention of repeated evaluation of the same redex by two processors. However, these problems can be overcome and the interested reader is referred to Clack and Peyton Jones (1986) for a fuller discussion of the issues involved.

Although parallel graph reduction is in its infancy it represents a very exciting and novel approach to parallel computation. At the time of writing research into parallel graph reduction and parallel reduction machine design is being actively pursued by a number of groups worldwide. The machines described in Keller (1985), Darlington *et al.* (1987), Hudak (1985) and Peyton Jones *et al.* (1985) are all either pure graph reduction machines or machines which rely on many of the graph reduction principles for their operation. The ALICE reduction machine described in Darlington *et al.* (1987) has actually been constructed and first became operational in February 1986.

SUMMARY

- Lambda expressions can be represented as graphs.
- Applying the reduction rules of the lambda calculus to the graphical representation of lambda expressions is called **graph reduction**.
- Sharing is easy to express using a graphical representation.
- Graph reduction is naturally lazy; the next redex is found by unwinding the left spine of the graph until a function node is found.
- Lambda applications involve copying the graph of the function body, substituting argument graphs for bound variables and overwriting the redex node with the result.

- Primitive function applications involve (recursively) reducing the strict argument(s) of the primitive and then carrying out the primitive operation according to its delta rules.
- Projection functions return an unmodified component of their argument; without special consideration they can cause duplication of redexes and hence repeated evaluation.
- The projection function problem can be solved by indirection nodes and/or by reducing the selected argument component before overwriting the redex.
- The unwinding of the left spine can be done either using a stack or by using pointer reversal.
- Free variables in function bodies can lead to unnecessary copying; this problem can be solved either by using an environment or by transforming out the free variables.
- Graph reduction can be implemented in parallel by allocating separate redexes to separate processors for evaluation.

EXERCISES

11.1 For each of the following expressions:

(i) $(\lambda x.\lambda y.y\,(\lambda h.h\,x))\;7\;(\lambda x.x)$

(ii) $(\lambda f.(\lambda y.f\,y))\,(\lambda x.+\,2\,x)\;3$

(iii) $(\lambda T.T\,T)\,(\lambda f.\lambda x.f\,(f\,x))\;S\;0$ where $S = \lambda x.+\,1\,x$

(a) draw the graph representing the expression;

(b) label each node on the graph and then reduce the graph to WHNF indicating at each stage which nodes are new and which nodes become potential garbage. Identify the redex node in each reduction.

11.2 Assume that the expression *cons x y* is represented by the special node

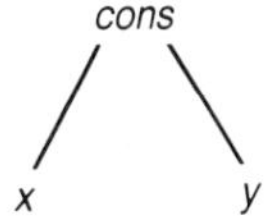

as described in the text. Show the normal-order graph reduction of the expression $(\lambda g.(\lambda s.+\,1\,(hd\;s))\,(g\,(cons\;4)))\,(\lambda f.f\;nil)$.

11.3 Given the usual definition of the Y-combinator,

$$Y = \lambda h.(\lambda x.h (x\, x)) (\lambda x.h (x\, x))$$

(a) draw the graph representation of Yf using sharing to represent the self application in the body of Y;

(b) show that $Yf = f(Yf)$ by successive transformations of the graph, again using sharing wherever possible.

11.4 Consider the lambda calculus expression

$$E = (\lambda a. + ((\lambda x.x) \, a) \, a) ((\lambda y.y) \, 7)$$

(a) Draw the graph of E.

(b) Reduce the graph of E using the normal rules for graph reduction and show that the evaluation of the expression $(\lambda y.y) \, 7$ is performed twice.

(c) Show how indirection nodes can be used to avoid the redundancy in this example.

11.5 (a) Suggest a concrete representation for each node type in a graph. You should consider the following nodes types: @ nodes; λ nodes; identifiers; constants; *tuple-n* nodes and *cons* nodes. For your chosen representation draw the concrete graph of *tuple*-3 ($\lambda x.$*cons* (+ 1 x)) 2.

(b) What are the main advantages and disadvantages of the special *tuple-n* representation proposed in Section 11.1?

11.6 Suggest how the graph reduction algorithm given in Section 11.3 can be modified to implement applicative-order evaluation.

11.7 Trace the reduction of the expression + (− 3 1) (($\lambda x.x$) 1)

(a) using a stack;

(b) using pointer reversal.

For (a), indicate the state which has to be stored on the stack each time a primitive argument evaluation is initiated. To what extent is it true that the whole state of the evaluation is held within the graph when pointer reversal is used?

Chapter 12
Combinator reduction

In the previous chapter we looked at the graph reduction model of computation in the context of the λ-calculus and showed how normal-order reduction could be implemented by reducing the leftmost-outermost redex using graph transformation rules which correspond to the reduction rules of the lambda calculus. Also in that chapter we identified a problem affecting the efficiency of the scheme which arises when free variables occur within a nested lambda abstraction. The presence of the free variables means that each application of the function must cause the function body to be copied in order to bind those variables to their correct values.

In this chapter we shall look at combinator implementations and in particular the graph reduction of combinator expressions. Here, each λ-expression is transformed into an equivalent expression built only from applications of primitive functions and combinators, each of which is a closed expression, i.e. an expression with no free variables. The heart of the translator is therefore a function which abstracts the free variables of an expression leaving behind a trail of combinator applications.

In Section 12.1 we look at some of the theory underlying this type of implementation, namely the combinatory logic (Curry and Feys, 1958). In theory only two combinators called S and K are required to represent any λ-expression, although the resulting implementation is inefficient due to the very large number of such combinators (and their associated applications) which are required. However, we can augment this set with additional combinators, which reduce the complexity of the resulting combinator expressions, and in Section 12.2 we shall look at the effect some of these have on the efficiency of the resulting implementation. We shall then see how recursive definitions can be handled by using the Y-combinator in a variety of different ways. In a graphical framework Y has a particularly efficient representation which leads to a very elegant treatment of arbitrary recursive definitions; furthermore recursion may be supported in the same way in other forms of graph reduction such as we saw in the previous chapter. To conclude we give another view of fixed combinator implementations, namely director strings. This provides a particularly intuitive feel for how fixed combinators work as well as suggesting a more efficient way of representing them.

12.1 Basic combinatory logic and reduction

A **combinator** is a λ-expression in which there are no occurrences of free variables. For example, the *identity* function $\lambda x.x$ is a combinator and is usually referred to by the identifer I. Another example is the *fixed-point* combinator introduced in Chapter 6, which is defined by

$$Y = \lambda h.((\lambda x.h(xx))(\lambda x.h(xx)))$$

Two further examples are the *cancellator* K given by $K = \lambda x.\lambda y.x$ and the distributor S given by $S = \lambda f.\lambda g.\lambda x.fx(gx)$. (Incidentally, the names for these are K and S rather than C and D because they were invented by Germans.)

Now, as we shall see, any λ-expression E can be converted into an **applicative expression**, i.e. an expression built entirely from function applications, lambda abstractions thereby being absent. To achieve this we require at least the two combinators (functions) S and K to be included in the expression syntax as additional constants. In fact, the λ-calculus and the combinatory logic (CL) defined on these combinator expressions are equivalent in the following sense. There is a set of axioms, as may be found in Hindley and Seldin (1986), which determine when two combinatory expressions M_{CL} and N_{CL} are equal, which we shall write $M_{CL} =_{CL} N_{CL}$. Similarly in the λ-calculus, the equality of expressions, written $=_{\lambda}$, is interpreted as the reflexive transitive closure of the conversion rules which were given in Chapter 6. Then if E_{CL} and E_λ represent the same expression in the two respective logics, it can be shown that $M_{CL} =_{CL} N_{CL}$ if and only if $M_\lambda =_\lambda N_\lambda$. In this way combinatory logic may be viewed as a *model* of the λ-calculus.

In our presentation we shall also use the identity combinator I although it should be noted that it can be defined in terms of S and K using the identity $I = S\,K\,K$. This identity follows from the axioms in *CL* and it is easy to verify in the λ-calculus; this exercise is left to the reader.

Expressions in the combinatory logic have the following syntax:

⟨*CLexp*⟩ ::= ⟨*identifier*⟩ | ⟨*CLexp*⟩ ⟨*CLexp*⟩ | (⟨*CLexp*⟩) | ⟨*con*⟩
⟨*con*⟩ ::= 1 | 2 | . . . | + | − | . . . | *S* | *K* | *I*

Observe that the only mechanism for combining expressions is that of function application – hence the term 'applicative expression' used to denote the expressions of CL.

The constants (combinators) S, K and I are defined by the reduction rules

$$
\begin{aligned}
&S\,e\,f\,g \rightarrow e\,g\,(f\,g)\\
&K\,e\,f \rightarrow e\\
&I\,e \rightarrow e
\end{aligned}
$$

With this syntax, every expression is in purely applicative form and so can be represented as a graph in which the only type of internal node is an @- node. Strictly speaking, we should say that there are no abstraction nodes, i.e. λ-nodes, since we may still admit data constructor nodes. However, the only reduction rules which involve such nodes are applications of constructor and selector functions. In the former case a new constructor node will be created and the application of a selector function is represented in the same way as the application of any other primitive function or combinator. No copying is involved and the only special action is the optimization, which changes the selection order of redexes and which might introduce synonym nodes as we discussed in the previous chapter. We need give no special consideration, therefore, to the presence of constructor cells. (In fact we can retain the purely applicative structure of a combinator graph by representing constructor functions as special primitive combinators which are applied to arguments like any other combinator (via @-nodes), but for which there is no reduction rule. We also considered this option at the beginning of the previous chapter, and it is the approach suggested in Turner (1979) where a pairing combinator P is introduced to represent lists.)

Thus all we have to do is define the rules for transforming the graph corresponding to applications of S, K and I, and combine these with the rules for applying the primitive functions to obtain a simplified graph reducer. As with graph reduction the resulting implementation is naturally lazy in that the leftmost outermost redex is always chosen as the next redex.

Before specifying these graph transformations, we first show how λ-expressions may be translated into combinator form. This translation is performed by successively abstracting the variables from sub-expressions, and we first define an **abstraction function**, *abs*, which has the property that for variable x and combinator expression E,

$$abs(\ x, E\ )\ x = E$$

That is, if the result of abstracting x from E is applied back to x, this result reduces to E. We therefore define *abs* as follows:

$abs(\ x, x\ )$	$= I$	
$abs(\ x, k\ )$	$= Kk$	if k is a constant (e.g. S or K)
$abs(\ x, y\ )$	$= Ky$	if y is a variable not equal to x
$abs(\ x, E_1\ E_2\ )$	$= S\ abs(\ x, E_1\ )\ abs(\ x, E_2\ )$	for λ-expressions E_1, E_2
$abs(\ x, (\ E\ )\ )$	$= (\ abs(\ x, E\ )\ )$	for λ-expression E

The expression $abs(\ x,\ E\ )$ is often abbreviated to $[\ x\ ]\ E$ so that, for example, we may write the third rule for *abs* as

$$[\ x\ ]\ y = Ky$$

The translation function, *comb*, which maps λ-expressions to their equivalent combinator form, is now defined by:

$comb(\ v\ )$	$= v$	for variable v
$comb(\ c\ )$	$= c$	for constant c
$comb(\ \lambda x.E\ )$	$= [\ x\ ]\ comb(\ E\ )$	for expression E
$comb(\ E_1\ E_2\ )$	$= comb(\ E_1\ )\ comb(\ E_2\ )$	for expressions E_1, E_2
$comb(\ (\ E\ )\ )$	$= (\ comb(\ E\ )\ )$	for expression E

It is not difficult to show that this translation is 'correct' in the sense that if the combinators S and K are substituted by their defining lambda expressions in $comb(\ E\ )$, then the result, $sub(\ comb(\ E\ )\ )$, is equal to E (up to α- and β-conversion). This follows by induction on the structure of the lambda expression E, and the only tricky step is to prove that $sub(\ [\ x\ ]comb(\ E\ )\ ) = \lambda x.E$ for all variables x and lambda expressions E. This proof is set as an exercise at the end of the chapter.

Consider as an example of the abstraction process at work the combinatory logic version of the expression $\lambda x.(\ \lambda y.\ +\ x\ y\ )$. Applying the translation function, *comb*, to this expression we obtain

$$
\begin{aligned}
&comb(\,\lambda x.(\,\lambda y.\ +\ x\ y\,)\,)\\
&\quad = [\,x\,]\ comb(\,\lambda y.\ +\ x\ y\,)\\
&\quad = [\,x\,][\,y\,]\ comb(\,+\ x\ y\,)\\
&\quad = [\,x\,][\,y\,]\ comb(\,+\ x\,)\ comb(\,y\,)\\
&\quad = [\,x\,][\,y\,]\ comb(\,+\,)\ comb(\,x\,)\ y\\
&\quad = [\,x\,][\,y\,] + x\ y\\
&\quad = [\,x\,]\,S\,[\,y\,](\,+\ x\,)\,[\,y\,]y\\
&\quad = [\,x\,]\,S(\,S\,[\,y\,]+\ [\,y\,]x\,)\,I\\
&\quad = [\,x\,]\,S(\,S(\,K+\,)(\,Kx\,)\,)\,I\\
&\quad = S\,[\,x\,](\,S(\,S(\,K+\,)(\,Kx\,)\,)\,)\,[\,x\,]I\\
&\quad = S(\,S\,[\,x\,]S\,[\,x\,](\,S(\,K+\,)(\,Kx\,)\,)\,)(\,KI\,)\\
&\quad = S(\,S(\,KS\,)(\,S\,[\,x\,](\,S(\,K+\,)\,)\,[\,x\,](\,Kx\,)\,)\,)(\,KI\,)\\
&\quad = S(\,S(\,KS\,)(\,S(\,S\,[\,x\,]S\,[\,x\,](\,K+\,)\,)(\,S\,[\,x\,]K\,[\,x\,]x\,)\,)\,)(\,KI\,)\\
&\quad = S(\,S(\,KS\,)(\,S(\,S(\,KS\,)(\,S\,[\,x\,]K\,[\,x\,]+\,)\,)(\,S(\,KK\,)\,I\,)\,)\,)(\,KI\,)\\
&\quad = S(\,S(\,KS\,)(\,S(\,S(\,KS\,)(\,S(\,KK\,)(\,K+\,)\,)\,)(\,S(\,KK\,)\,I\,)\,)\,)(\,KI\,)
\end{aligned}
$$

This is an amazingly complicated way of writing a function to add two numbers, with efficiency to match. A much better, equally correct representation would be +! Nevertheless, let us see how this 'plus-combinator' works in expression reduction by applying it to an argument, say 2, using the notation => to denote combinator reduction, or alternatively β-reduction in any number of steps. Some steps have been omitted and some of the more obscure sub-expressions are underlined.

$$
\begin{aligned}
&S(\,S(\,KS\,)(\,S(\,S(\,KS\,)(\,S(\,KK\,)(\,K+\,)\,)\,)(\,S(\,KK\,)\,I\,)\,)\,)(\,KI\,)\,2\\
&\quad \Rightarrow S(\,KS\,)(\,S(\,S(\,KS\,)(\,S(\,KK\,)(\,K+\,)\,)\,)(\,S(\,KK\,)\,I\,)\,)\,2\,(\,(\,KI\,)\,2)\\
&\quad \Rightarrow K\,S\,2\,(\,S(\,S(\,KS\,)(\,S(\,KK\,)(\,K+\,)\,)\,)(\,S(\,KK\,)\,I\,)\,2\,)\,I\\
&\quad \Rightarrow S(\,S(\,KS\,)(\,S(\,KK\,)(\,K+\,)\,)\,2\,(\,K\,K\,2\,(\,I\,2\,)\,)\,)\,I\\
&\quad \Rightarrow S(\,K\,S\,2\,(\,S(\,KK\,)(\,K+\,)\,2\,)(\,K\,2\,)\,)\,I\\
&\quad \Rightarrow S(\,S(\,K\,K\,2\,(\,K+\,2\,)\,)(\,K\,2\,)\,)\,I\\
&\quad \Rightarrow S(\,S(\,K+\,)(\,K2\,)\,)\,I
\end{aligned}
$$

This expression represents the partial application of the function + to the argument 2, i.e. + 2. Note how the atom, 2, has become attached to the combinator *K*, waiting for the application to the second argument, whereupon it will be inserted in the right place, as we shall see shortly. The same applies to the constant primitive function, +, and in general an expression bound to a free variable becomes the first (or only) argument of an application of *K*. In this way, the environment is distributed over an expression's graph, the values associated with variables being connected to *K* nodes. To complete the example, we can apply the combinator-representation of the partial application + 2 to the integer 3, as follows:

$$
\begin{aligned}
S(\,S(\,K+\,)(\,K2\,)\,)\,I\,3 &\Rightarrow S(\,K+\,)(\,K2\,)\,3\,(\,I\,3\,)\\
&\Rightarrow K+3\,(\,K\,2\,3\,)\,3\\
&\Rightarrow +\ 2\ 3\\
&\Rightarrow 5
\end{aligned}
$$

The main appeal of the combinator approach is its mathematical elegance and its computational simplicity which arises from the existence of only three graph transformation rules (excluding those associated with primitive functions). Because the most natural implementation is by graph reduction, the computational model is inherently lazy and since there are no variables, there is no need to be concerned with an environment or with variable naming. Unfortunately, even very simple lambda expressions have complex combinator expressions in CL and although there are now no variables, the use of an environment has effectively been replaced by the passing of argument expressions as parameters; this has its own overheads. Thus, this raw approach is impractical without optimization on the grounds of efficiency, and in the next section we seek such optimization by enlarging the set of fixed combinators S, K and I.

12.2 Curry's optimization and Turner's combinator-graph reduction

Although the complexity of the CL expressions which use only the S, K and I combinators is unacceptably high for use as a viable implementation technique, certain sub-expression structures have much simpler forms, which are equivalent under the equality of CL, $=_{CL}$. Moreover, a much larger number of expressions may be simplified similarly if we introduce two further primitive combinators into the fixed set, using corresponding new identities. The new combinators in question are called the **compositor**, denoted by B, and the **permutator**, denoted by C, and are defined in the λ-calculus by $B = \lambda f.\lambda x.\lambda y.f\ (\ x\ y\ )$ and $C = \lambda f.\lambda x.\lambda y.f\,y\,x$. The following equations then hold in the combinatory logic which now has S, K, I, B and C for its primitive combinators.

$$S\,(\,K\,E1\,)\,(\,K\,E2\,) =_{CL} K\,(\,E1\ E2\,) \qquad \text{(rule 1)}$$
$$S\,(\,K\,E1\,)\,I =_{CL} E1 \qquad \text{(rule 2)}$$
$$S\,(\,K\,E1\,)\,E2 =_{CL} B\,E1\,E2 \qquad \text{(rule 3)}$$
$$S\,E1\,(\,K\,E2\,) =_{CL} C\,E1\,E2 \qquad \text{(rule 4)}$$

These equations were introduced by Curry (Curry and Feys, 1958), and each provides a rule for simplifying applications of S. The first two provide the major enhancements, in particular the 'full laziness' property which ensures that there are no repeated computations of sub-expressions. They may be derived by appealing to the equivalence between the λ-calculus and combinatory logic and showing that the left-hand side of each converts under β-reduction to the right-hand side when the appropriate λ-expressions are substituted for the combinators. For example, reading cnv_β as β-conversion:

$$
\begin{aligned}
S(K\,E1)(K\,E2) &\cong \lambda x.K\,E1\,x(K\,E2\,x) \qquad \text{where } K \text{ stands for } \lambda x.\lambda y.x \\
&\to_\beta \lambda x.E1\,(K\,E2\,x) \\
&\to_\beta \lambda x.E1\,E2 \\
&\cong K(E1\,E2)
\end{aligned}
$$

Alternatively, we can prove that the equations are extensionally true directly in the combinatory logic; we say that M is extensionally equal to N if $Mx = Nx$ for arbitrary x, i.e. if the behaviour of M and N *as functions* is the same. We therefore apply both sides of each proposed equation to an arbitrary CL expression, apply the rewrite rules for the combinators involved and arrive at the same result. Thus, for the first equation we would obtain for the left-hand side

$$
\begin{aligned}
S(K\,E1)(K\,E2)\,X &\Rightarrow_S K\,E_1\,X(K\,E_2\,X) \\
&\Rightarrow_K E_1\,E_2
\end{aligned}
$$

and for the right-hand side

$$K(E1\,E2)\,X \Rightarrow_K E_1\,E_2$$

(the annotation on each arrow => denotes the combinator being used). These optimizing equations may easily be built in to the abstraction function, which is now defined by the equations:

$[x]x = I$
$[x]y = Ky$ if y is a constant or a variable not equal to x
$[x]E_1E_2 =$ **if** $[x]E_1 = K\,M$
  then if $[x]E_2 = I$
    then M
    else if $[x]E_2 = K\,N$
      then $K(M\,N)$
      else $B\,M\,[x]E_2$
  else if $[x]E_2 = K\,N$
    then $C\,[x]E_1\,N$
    else $S\,[x]E_1\,[x]E_2$
$[x](E) = ([x]E)$

for λ-expressions $E1$, $E2$, E.

It is easier to illustrate the application of the new abstraction function to a λ-expression if we use strict rather than lazy evaluation and since *every* λ-expression has a corresponding CL expression, each evaluation order gives a computation which terminates with the same result. Thus the above example in which we translated the λ-expression $\lambda x.\lambda y. + x\ y$ into a combinator expression containing only applications of S, K and I now becomes

$$comb(\ \lambda x.\lambda y. + x\ y\ ) = [\ x\ ]\,[\ y\ ] + x\ y$$ (by exactly the same steps as above)

$$= [\ x\ ]+ x$$ (because $[\ y\ ](\ + x\ ) = K(\ + x\ )$, since $[\ y\ ]+\ = K+$, $[\ y\ ]x = Kx$ and $[\ y\ ]y = I$)

$$= +$$ (because $[\ x\ ]+\ = K+$ and $[\ x\ ]x = I$)

Thus we actually obtain the optimal form of the function *plus* in this simple example, using only the optimization rules 1 and 2. A more complicated example is shown in Section 12.2.2 after we have defined the graph transformation rules for combinator application. First, we consider in the next two sub-sections an optimal property of the enhanced system which further simplifies the translation of λ-expressions into combinator form, and a further optimization of Turner's.

12.2.1 Applicative sub-expressions

In this section we establish an important optimality property of the enhanced fixed-set combinator representation of λ-expressions. This is the *preservation of applicative sub-expressions* which actually requires only the optimization rule 1 of the previous section and not the additional B and C combinators. In the unoptimized $\{\ S, K, I\}$ representation, this property does *not* hold – consider, for example, the expression $\lambda x. + 1\ 2$, which is translated into the CL expression $S\,(\ S\,(\ K+\ )\,(\ K1\ )\,)\,(\ K2\ )$ by application of *comb*. The components of the constant sub-expression $+\ 1\ 2$ become distributed over the expression. However, if the first optimization given above is applied, the resulting CL expression becomes $K\ (\ +\ 1\ 2\ )$, leaving the sub-expression $+\ 1\ 2$ intact. The preservation of constant sub-expressions is especially important in the case of constant redexes and it is this which facilitates their sharing during expression evaluation. As a result, it is possible to avoid repeating the evaluation of these redexes. This promotes 'full laziness', which is a term sometimes used to mean that no computation is performed more than once in the execution of a functional program.

In fact, applicative sub-expressions (defined by the syntax of CL expressions in Section 12.1) are preserved in general in the optimized combinator representation. Thus in the lambda expression $\lambda x. + y\ 2$, the sub-expression $+\ y\ 2$ would be preserved by the application of *comb*, but it would not if it occurred in the expression $\lambda y. + y\ 2$, in which y is bound.

The preservation of applicative sub-expressions is not immediately obvious and so a more formal proof is appropriate. This requires the following two lemmas:

Lemma 12.1 For applicative expression, E, in which the variable x does not occur free,

$$[\,x\,]E = K\,E$$

The proof of this lemma is by induction on the number of applications in the expression E. In the base case, E is either a constant or a variable not equal to x, and the result is then true by definition. If $E = E_1E_2$, then both E_1 and E_2 have fewer applications than E and no occurrences of x. Thus by the inductive hypothesis,

$$[\,x\,]E = S\,[\,x\,]E_1\,[\,x\,]E_2 = S\,(\,K\,E_1\,)(\,K\,E_2\,) = K(\,E_1\,E_2\,) = K\,E$$

Lemma 12.2 If E' is a sub-expression of the applicative expression E, then it is also a sub-expression of the expression $[\,x\,]E$ for all variables x which do not occur in E'.

The proof is again by induction on the number of applications in the expression E. First, if $E' = E$, then $[\,x\,]E = K\,E$ by Lemma 12.1, which has E' as a sub-expression by hypothesis. This establishes the base case in particular, when E is a constant or a variable. For the inductive step, we consider the case where $E = E_1E_2$ and where $E' \neq E$ so that E' is a sub-expression of one of E_1 or E_2. Without loss of generality we shall assume that E' is a sub-expression of E_1. Thus, by the inductive hypothesis, E' is a sub-expression of $[\,x\,]E_1$ and hence also of $[\,x\,]E = S\,[\,x\,]E_1\,[\,x\,]E_2$. Note that if $E = (\,E''\,)$, $[\,x\,]E = (\,[\,x\,]E''\,)$, and the result follows similarly.

Proposition 12.1 If E' is an applicative sub-expression of the λ-expression E, then E' is preserved by *comb*, i.e. E' occurs also as an applicative sub-expression of *comb*(E).

The proof of this proposition is by structural induction on the expression E. First, if $E' = E$ then E is an applicative expression so that $E' = E =$ *comb*(E) and the result follows.

The base case follows immediately since if E is an identifier or a constant, its only sub-expression is itself, i.e. $E' = E$.

For the inductive step we need only consider the case that $E' \neq E$ and there are three cases to consider:

Case (1) $E = E_1E_2$
If $E' \neq E$, then E' must be a sub-expression of either E_1 or E_2.

Thus by the inductive hypothesis, E' is a sub-expression of either $comb(E_1)$ or $comb(E_2)$. But

$$comb(E) = comb(E_1E_2) = comb(E_1)comb(E_2)$$

so that E' also occurs as a sub-expression of $comb(E)$.

Case (2) $E = (E'')$
E' must be an applicative sub-expression of E'' and so E' is a sub-expression of $comb(E'')$ by the inductive hypothesis. But since $comb(E) = (comb(E''))$, E' is a sub-expression of $comb(E)$.

Case (3) $E = \lambda x.E''$
E' must be an applicative sub-expression of E'' and so E' is a sub-expression of $comb(E'')$ by the inductive hypothesis. But $comb(E'')$ is an applicative expression, and so by Lemma 12.2, E' is a sub-expression of $comb(E) = [x]comb(E'')$.

Before leaving the issue of optimality properties, it should be noted that optimization rule 2 models η-reduction. This follows because

$$\begin{aligned} comb(\lambda x.E\,x) &= [x]comb(E\,x) = [x](comb(E)\,comb(x)) \\ &= [x](comb(E)\,x) = S\,[x]comb(E)\,[x]x \end{aligned}$$

But, if x does not occur in E then it does not occur in $comb(E)$ either, so by Lemma 12.1, $[x]comb(E) = K\,comb(E)$. Thus,

$$comb(\lambda x.E\,x) = S\,(K\,comb(E))\,I = comb(E) \qquad \text{by rule 2}$$

which would also have been obtained if we had first used $\lambda x.E\,x \rightarrow_\eta E$.

12.2.2 Graph reduction rules for combinator expressions

An applicative combinator expression may be represented by a graph containing only apply nodes as defined in the previous chapter. Thus it remains only to give the graph transformation rules corresponding to each of the primitive combinators which might be applied, namely S, K, I, B and C.

These rules are shown in Figure 12.1, where the rule corresponding to application of combinator A is labelled by $\rightarrow_A$ for $A = I, K, S, B, C$.

The capital letters F, G, X and Y denote the (root nodes of the) sub-graphs that represent the argument expressions to which the appropriate combinator is applied. Notice that in the rules for I and K, no new nodes are created, the redex node (top @-node) simply being overwritten with the contents of the root node, X. Thus, for I, two of the original nodes may become garbage and for K four of the original nodes may become garbage. In the case of the S rule, there are just two new nodes created (the

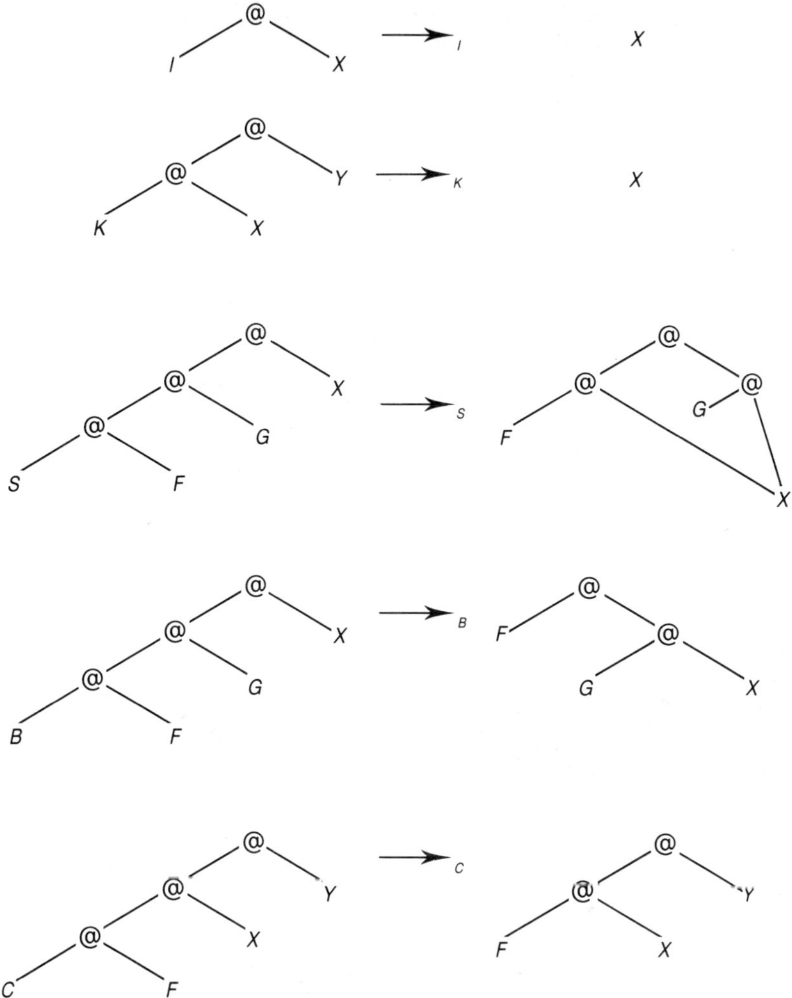

Figure 12.1 Graph transformation rules for combinator reduction.

lower @-nodes), the top @-node being the original redex node, and up to three garbage cells may be produced. Similarly, only one new node is created in each of the rules for B and C.

Any graph representing a partial application, i.e. which contains too few @-nodes to permit the reduction to be applied, is in WHNF, for example

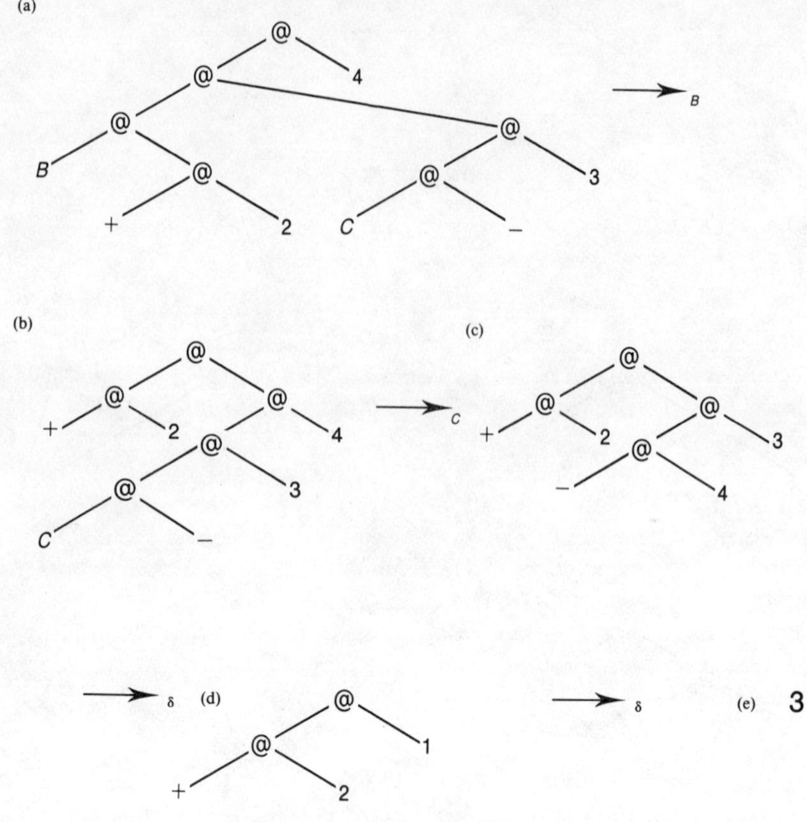

Figure 12.2 Combinator graph reduction of $\lambda x. + 2 (- x\ 3)$.

which represents the function which when applied to the argument n gives the result $n + n^2$.

In the case of the rule for the S combinator, it will be observed that the sub-graph denoted by X, representing the last argument, is shared, and that this is the only situation in which sharing is introduced so far in the combinator implementation. However, it has already been seen that S appears in several places in the combinator forms of many lambda expressions, and moreover it is applications of S that model β-reduction, i.e. the application of λ-abstractions. This is where the sharing of argument sub-graphs was introduced in basic graph reduction, and so similar gains in efficiency can be expected from this simple optimization in the reduction rule for S.

Let us now consider a more complex example, the translation of the λ-abstraction $\lambda x. + 2 (- x\ 3)$ and the graph transformations which occur in the reduction of its application to the constant 4.

$comb(\ \lambda x.\ +\ 2\ (\ -\ x\ 3\ )\ )$
$= [\ x\ ]comb(\ +\ 2\ (\ -\ x\ 3\ )\ )$
$= [\ x\ ](\ +\ 2\ (\ -\ x\ 3\ )\ )$ since the argument of *comb* is applicative
$= S\ [\ x\ ](\ +\ 2\ )\ [\ x\ ](\ -\ x\ 3\ )$
$= S\ (\ K(\ +\ 2\ )\ )\ (\ S\ [\ x\ ](\ -\ x\ )\ (\ K3\ )\ )$ since $+\ 2$ is applicative
$= S\ (\ K(\ +\ 2\ )\ )\ (\ S\ (\ S(\ K-\ )\ I\ )\ (\ K3\ )\ )$
$= S\ (\ K(\ +\ 2\ )\ )\ (\ S\ -\ (\ K3\ )\ )$ by optimization rule 2
$= S\ (\ K(\ +\ 2\ )\ )\ (\ C\ -\ 3\ )$ by optimization rule 4
$= B\ (\ +\ 2\ )\ (\ C\ -\ 3\ )$

Denoting the λ-abstraction $\lambda x.\ +\ 2\ (\ -\ x\ 3\ )$ by A, the application of A to the constant 4 is represented by the combinator expression $B\ (\ +\ 2\ )\ (\ C\ -\ 3\ )\ 4$ (formally because $comb(\ A\ 4\ ) = comb(\ A\ )comb(\ 4\ )$ and $comb(\ 4\ ) = 4$). The reduction of this application is represented by the sequence of graphs shown in Figure 12.2.

This example illustrates the translation into optimized combinator form, and the operation of the graph transformation rules. However, we have not yet considered recursive functions. This is addressed in Section 12.3, where a much more complicated example of combinator graph reduction is given which should clarify all of the principles involved. To conclude this section, we take a second look at the free variable problem, which the approach of this chapter was intended to solve in the first place.

12.2.3 Further optimizations

There is a multitude of optimizations, of varying magnitude, which can be achieved by adding new combinators to the Curry/Turner set; the combinator set defined in Turner (1981) contains over twenty.

Commutative operators

We first point out a very simple optimization relating to commutative primitive functions and the C combinator. This is given by the equation $C\ p =_{CL} p$, for commutative primitive function p. This equation can be verified, as for Curry's optimization, by using the equivalence between CL and the λ-calculus, since $C\ p =_{\beta} \lambda x.\lambda y.p\ y\ x = \lambda x.\lambda y.p\ x\ y$ (since p is commutative) $=_{\eta} p$. Alternatively, for any CL expressions X and Y, $C\ p\ X\ Y \Rightarrow_C p\ Y\ X = p\ X\ Y$, so that $C\ p$ is extensionally equal to p. This optimization is very easily incorporated into the abstraction function, *abs*, provided it is known which primitive functions are commutative, and some occurrences of C can thereby be removed.

Multiple variable abstraction

A more subtle optimization concerns the successive abstraction of several variables from an expression. Although Curry's optimization generally produces compact expressions when a single variable is abstracted from an applicative expression, this is not the case when several variables are abstracted successively. For example, consider the abstraction of the variables x, y and z from the applicative expression E_1E_2, where E_1 contains occurrences of x, y and z. For expression E, we denote by E', E'', E''' the abstractions $[\,x\,]E$, $[\,y\,][\,x\,]E$, $[\,z\,][\,y\,][\,x\,]E$. Then we obtain on successive abstractions:

$$
\begin{aligned}
[\,x\,]E_1E_2 &= S\,E_1'\,E_2' \\
[\,y\,][\,x\,]E_1E_2 &= S\,(\,B\,S\,E_1''\,)\,E_2'' \\
[\,z\,][\,y\,][\,x\,]E_1E_2 &= S\,(\,B\,S\,(\,B\,(\,B\,S\,)\,E_1'''\,)\,)\,E_2'''
\end{aligned}
$$

The size of the expression (i.e. the total number of combinators in it) which represents the abstraction of the nth variable is in general at least quadratic in n. This explosion in size can be avoided if we introduce the new combinator S', which is defined by the rule

$$S'\,k\,x\,y\,z = k\,(\,x\,z\,)\,(\,y\,z\,)$$

S' is similar to S except that it leaves intact an additional term applied to an application of three more terms. We can now introduce a further equation in the definition of the abstraction function, namely

$$[\,x\,]AE_1E_2 = S'\,A\,[\,x\,]E_1\,[\,x\,]E_2 \qquad \text{if } x \text{ does not occur in } A.$$

The validity of this equation may be seen by applying both sides to an expression X, giving $[\,X\,/\,x\,]AE_1E_2$ on the left and $A[\,X\,/\,x\,]E_1[\,X\,/\,x\,]E_2$ on the right, which is the same expression if there is no occurrence of x in A. (Remember that $[\,E\,/\,x\,]E_1$ means E_1 in which all free occurrences of x have been replaced by E; this should not be confused with the abstraction function, e.g. $[\,x\,]E$.) A variable is abstracted from an application of *two* terms as before, using S, but from an application of three terms using S' if the variable does not occur in the first. It is often the case that the first term has been constructed previously as a constant expression involving only combinators, during the abstraction of another variable, so that S' can then certainly be used. In our example, we would obtain:

$$
\begin{aligned}
[\,x\,]E_1E_2 &= S\,E_1'\,E_2' \\
[\,y\,][\,x\,]E_1E_2 &= S'\,S\,E_1''\,E_2'' \\
[\,z\,][\,y\,][\,x\,]E_1E_2 &= S'\,(\,S'\,S\,)\,E_1'''\,E_2'''
\end{aligned}
$$

and if we wished to abstract a fourth variable, w, we would obtain

$$[\,w\,][\,z\,][\,y\,][\,x\,]E_1E_2 = S'\,(\,S'\,(\,S'\,S\,)\,)\,E_1''''\,E_2''''$$

Thus we see that the sizes of the successive expressions from which n variables have been abstracted are now only linear in n, the constant expression at the front simply increasing by one occurrence of S' on each abstraction.

A further, similar refinement can be applied in the event that the abstracted variable occurs in only one of the sub-expressions of an application. We define the modified B and C combinators:

$$B'\ k\ x\ y\ z = k\ x\ (\ y\ z\ )$$
$$C'\ k\ x\ y\ z = k\ (\ x\ z\ )\ y$$

These induce the following optimizations, compare with Curry's at the beginning of Section 12.2:

$$S\ (\ B\ A\ E_1\ )\ E_2 =_{CL} S'\ A\ E_1\ E_2$$
$$B\ (\ A\ E_1\ )\ E_2 \quad =_{CL} B'\ A\ E_1\ E_2$$
$$C\ (\ B\ A\ E_1)\ E_2 =_{CL} C'\ A\ E_1\ E_2$$

Functions of several arguments

We have already seen, in Chapter 6, that a function of more than one argument is easy to express in an equivalent curried form. However, we also considered 'tupled languages' in their own right, where functions are applied to single arguments which are tuples, their components being accessed through tuple selector functions. A similar approach can be adopted in the combinator representation of functional expressions if we introduce the 'untupling' combinator, U, defined by

$$U f\ (\ x\ ) \qquad\qquad = f x$$
$$U f\ (\ x_1, \ldots, x_n\ ) = f x_1\ (\ x_2, \ldots, x_n\ ) \qquad (\ n \geq 2\ )$$

where $(\ x_1, \ldots, x_m\ )$ is an abbreviation for the expression $T_m\ x_1 \ldots x_m$ and T_m is the 'tupling' combinator for constructing m-tuples ($m \geq 1$) equivalent to the *TUPLE-m* function introduced in Chapter 6.

Then the function f defined by the equation $f(\ x_1, \ldots, x_n\ ) = e$, where the variables $x_1, \ldots, x_n$ may occur in e, has combinator form

$$comb(\ f\ ) = U\ (\ [x_1\ ](\ U\ (\ [\ x_2\ ](\ \ldots\ (\ U\ (\ [\ x_n\ ]comb(\ e\ )\ )\ )\ \ldots\ )\ )\ )\ )$$

12.2.4 The free variable problem revisited

One of the motivating factors which led us to consider combinator implementations for functional languages was the free variable problem explained at the end of the last chapter. In this section we first re-state the problem and then decide whether the solution we have obtained is satisfactory.

Consider the λ-expression $(\lambda x.\lambda y.E)\,A_1\,A_2$, in which A_1, A_2 are argument expressions and E contains an occurrence of x as a free variable. The graph reduction system considered in the previous chapter required that different copies of the graph representing the sub-expression $\lambda y.E$ be created for different values of A_1 bound to x if the λ-abstraction $\lambda x.\lambda y.E$ is shared. Now, this expression is translated into

$$comb(\,(\lambda x.\lambda y.E)\,A_1\,A_2\,) = comb(\,\lambda x.\lambda y.E\,)\;comb(\,A_1\,)\;comb(A_2)$$

and if the λ-abstraction $\lambda x.\lambda y.E$ is shared in an enclosing expression (as the argument to some other function), then so would be the sub-expression $comb(\,\lambda x.\lambda y.E\,)$ in the corresponding combinator graph. However, the latter sub-expression would not be copied during evaluation of the applications since it contains no variables, and only one version is necessary. The only penalty is that incurred in general from any increased complexity of the combinator representation over that of the λ-calculus. It is not difficult to see that the same conclusion is valid in any situation where a shared λ-abstraction containing a free variable is applied to different arguments and so necessitates copying, and we have indeed solved the free-variable problem. However, there was one smaller problem which we encountered in the previous chapter, not only in the context of free variables, namely projection functions. This arises in the current example when $E = x$, whereupon, as we saw, the λ-abstraction became a projector, returning an existing sub-graph when applied to an argument sub-graph. In this case, $comb(\,\lambda x.\lambda y.x\,) = K$ as expected, but K is a projector also, as will be seen by inspection of its graph transformation rule. Thus the projector problem is also present in combinator implementations – in applications of both K and I. The possible solutions suggested in Chapter 11, for example using synonym nodes, apply equally well here.

12.3 Representation of recursion

As we noted in Chapter 11, recursion can be represented in the lazy graph reduction computational model by direct application of the Y-combinator, which is a perfectly good λ-expression. To apply this technique in the combinator implementation, we would have to apply the CL expression corresponding to the defining λ-expression for Y, viz. $comb(\,\lambda h.(\,\lambda x.h(\,xx\,)\,)(\,\lambda x.h(\,xx\,)\,)\,)$. The complexity of the resulting expression is prohibitive, even in the extended fixed-set combinator representation, although a slightly more efficient approach expresses Y in terms of the combinator $W = \lambda h.\lambda x.h\,x\,x$, for which a new reduction rule is defined; this approach is the subject of an exercise at the end of this chapter. We therefore reject the direct use of Y in the form of a λ-expression as a practical implementation technique for recursion on the grounds of efficiency, and we now give two alternative approaches. One approach uses the Y-combinator as a primitive, introducing an additional graph transformation rule which involves a cycle, and is both efficient and generally applicable. The other approach also involves cyclic graphs, and is rather more simple, but less general. We describe this approach first.

12.3.1 Top-level recursion

Consider a set of mutually recursive definitions of the form

$$\begin{aligned} \text{letrec } & f_1 = E_1, \\ & f_2 = E_2, \\ & \vdots \\ & f_n = E_n \\ \text{in } E & \end{aligned}$$

The most straightforward way of representing the recursion in these definitions is to construct the n graphs which represent each function body and link any arc directed to one of the functions to the root node of its graph. More precisely, let the defining expression of the function f_i be denoted by E_i; then each f_j may occur any number of times in E_i as a free variable (or equivalently, a constant), for $(1 \leq i, j \leq n)$. Thus, each f_j may occur any number of times in the corresponding combinator-expression, $comb(E_i)$. The graph which represents this system of mutually recursive function definitions is then the union of the n separate graphs representing the expressions $E_1, \ldots, E_n$, in which every arc directed to a node representing the variable f_j is redirected to the root-node of the graph representing E_j. In the case of a single recursive function definition, the resulting graph structure is illustrated in Figure 12.3.

As a concrete example, consider the expression

$$\begin{aligned} \text{letrec } f &= \lambda x.cons\ x\ (g\ x), \\ g &= \lambda x.cons\ (*\ x\ x)\ (f\ x) \\ \text{in } f\ 2 & \end{aligned}$$

This generates the infinite list [2, 4, 2, 4, . . .]. In combinator form, these definitions become

$$f = comb(\lambda x.cons\ x\ (g\ x)) = [x](cons\ x\ (g\ x)) = S\ cons\ g$$
$$g = [x](cons\ (square\ x)\ (f\ x)) = S\ (B\ cons\ square)\ f$$

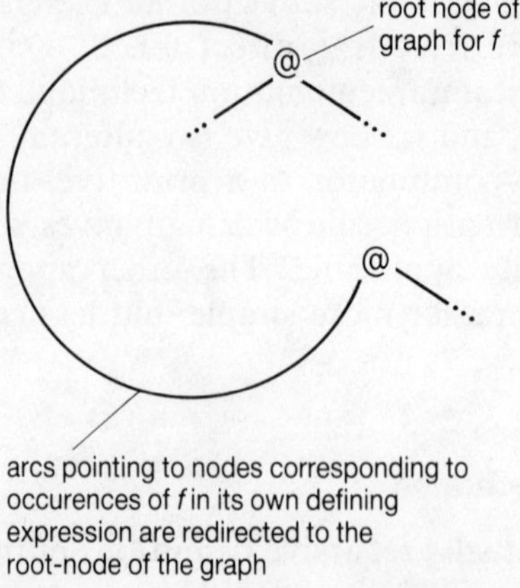

Figure 12.3 Representation of the recursive function defined by $f = \ldots f \ldots$.

These expressions are therefore represented by the graph shown in Figure 12.4.

Incidentally, note that with the optimization of Section 12.2.3, the combinator form of the function g is simply S' *cons square* f.

In Figure 12.5, we show the graph representation of the definition of factorial given in combinator form as

$$factorial = S\,(\,C\,(\,B\,cond\,(\,=\,2\,)\,)\,2\,)\,(\,S\,*\,(\,B\,factorial\,(\,C\,-\,1\,)\,)\,)$$

(see the exercise at the end of the chapter). Then in Figure 12.6, the transformations performed in the reduction of the expression factorial 3 are shown.

The marked nodes will be pointed to by arcs in the graphs of Figure 12.6, which illustrates the application of factorial, as represented by the graph of Figure 12.5, to the constant 3. This constant physically occupies only one node, marked # in the figure, although it is sometimes replicated to simplify the sketches.

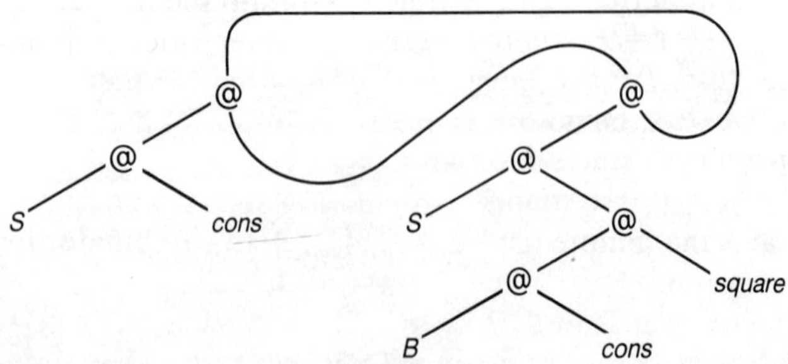

Figure 12.4 Representation of a pair of mutually recursive functions.

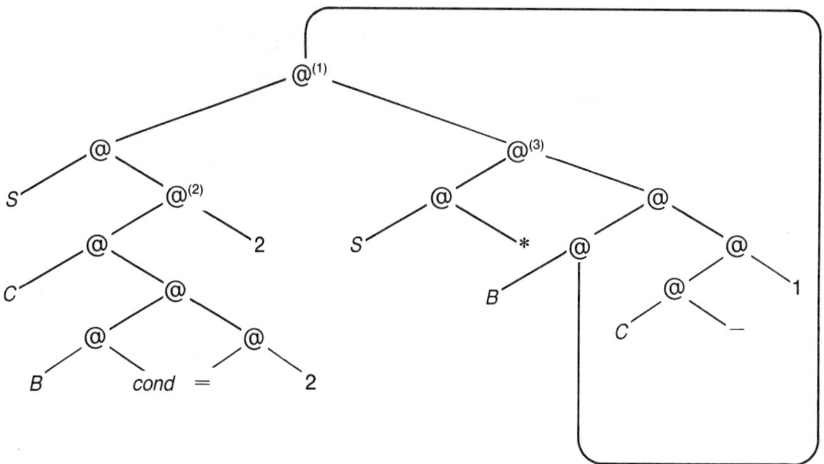

Figure 12.5 Combinator-graph representation of factorial.

Note that at stage (h) in the reduction sequence shown in Figure 12.6, the sub-expression $C - 1\ 3$ would not have been reduced in a lazy implementation. However, the reduction is eventually needed, and was made at the earlier stage only to simplify the graphs in the figure.

This representation of recursion is fine for a flat, or non-nested, set of user-defined functions, but recursive auxiliary functions (defined in recursive let or where clauses) cannot be represented directly in this way. We therefore appeal in such cases to the fully general method which employs the Y-combinator, together with a new primitive graph transformation rule for it, as we now describe.

12.3.2 Efficient representation of recursion via the *Y*-combinator

We saw in Chapter 6 how any recursive expression written in a functional language can be expressed in the λ-calculus using the Y-combinator. In particular, if a function f is defined without the use of qualified expressions by $f(x) = E$, where E is an expression which contains an occurrence of f, then f is the least fixed point of the λ-expression $\lambda f.\lambda x.E$, i.e. $f = Y(\lambda f.\lambda x.E)$. Thus f has the equivalent combinator expression $Y[\,f\,][\,x\,]comb(\,E\,)$ since $comb(\,Y\,) = Y$.

Similarly, suppose that f is defined using a recursive qualified expression, for example by

$$f = \lambda x.\text{letrec } g = E_1 \text{ in } E_2$$

where g occurs in E_1, f occurs in E_2 and x occurs in both E_1 and E_2.

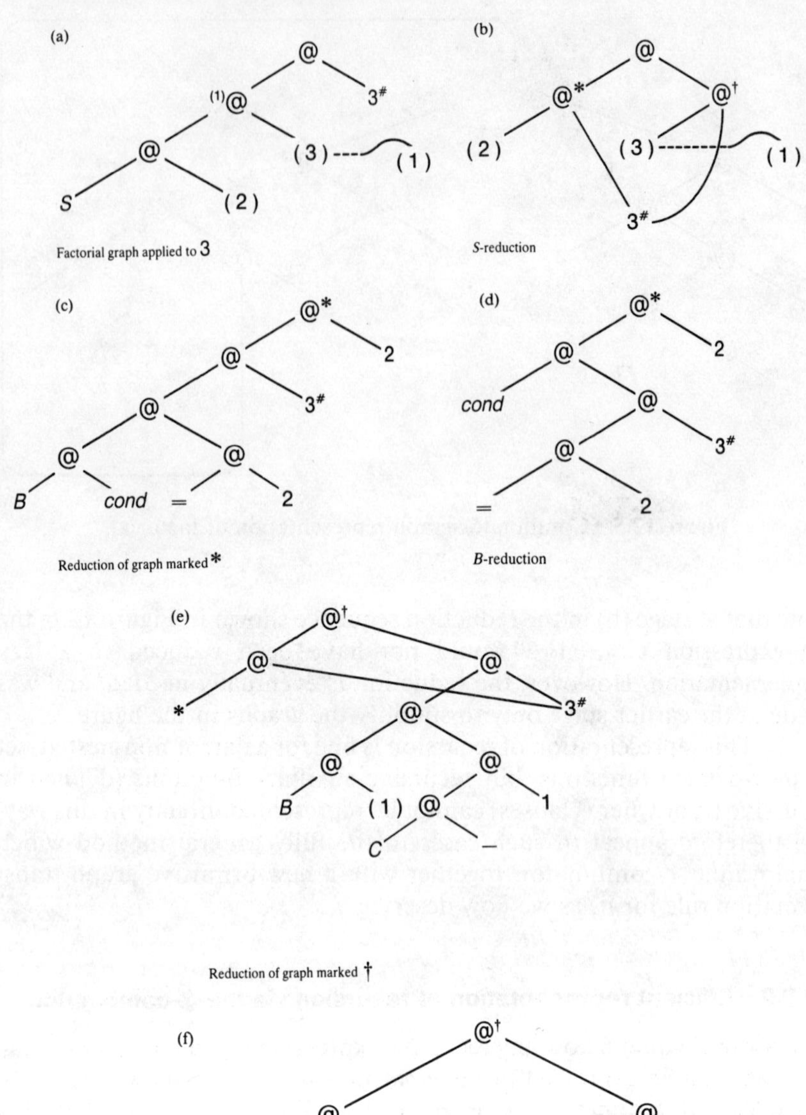

Figure 12.6 Combinator graph reduction sequence for factorial 3.

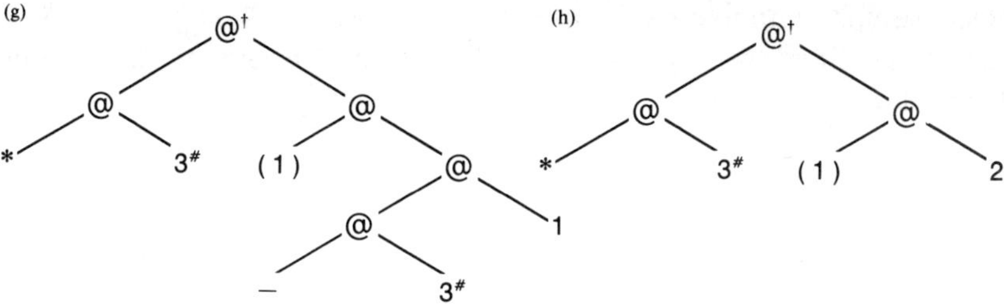

Premature *C*-reduction

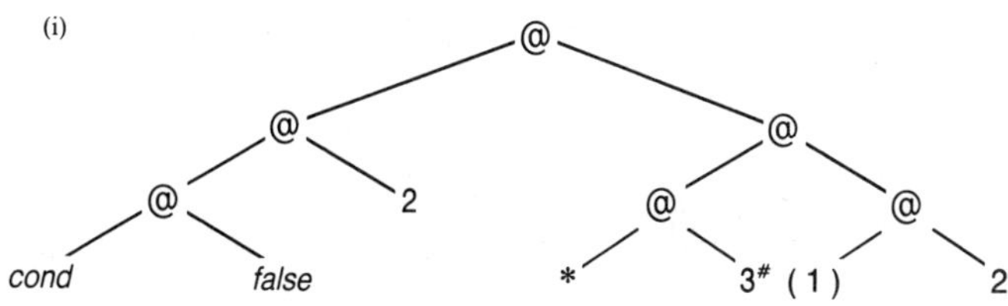

Whole graph for factorial (3) after evaluation of predicate of *cond*

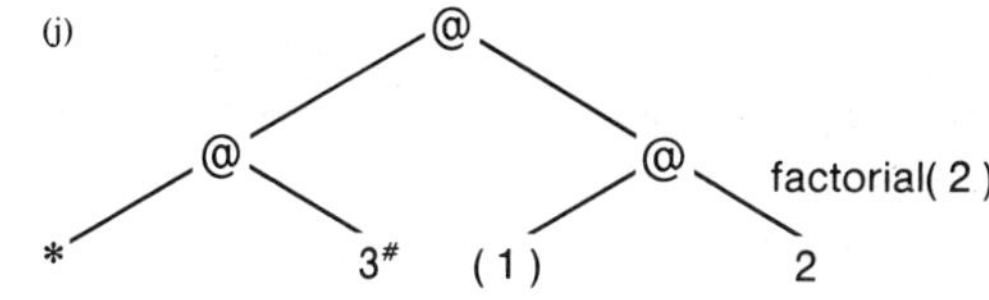

Application of *cond*

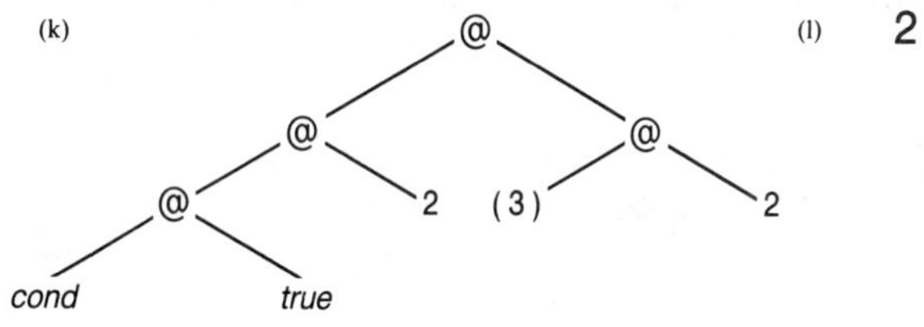

End of reduction of factorial 2

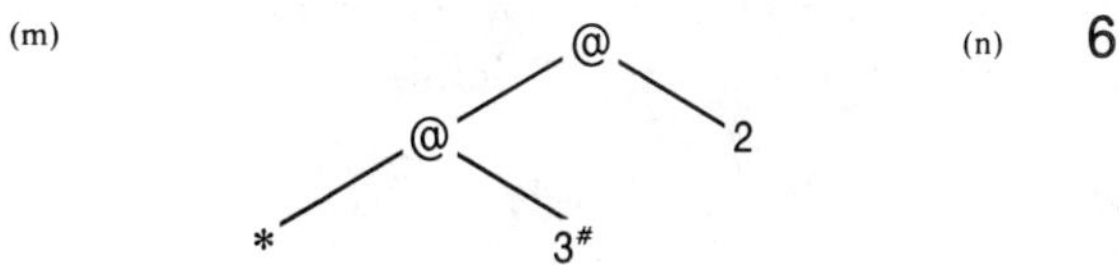

End of reduction sequence

Because g is recursive its defining expression using Y is $g = Y\lambda g.E_1$ so that f is defined by $f = Y\lambda f.\lambda x.(\lambda g.E_2)(Y\lambda g.E_1)$. Thus the combinator form of f is

$$comb(f) = Y[f][x]([g]comb(E_2))(Y[g]comb(E_1))$$

Mutual recursion may be represented by successively expressing the defined functions in non-recursive form (using Y) and substituting in the defining expressions of all of the others. However, this method substitutes for every occurrence of a function's name in the right-hand side of each equation (excluding its own). Thus several occurrences of Y may be introduced on the right-hand sides of the equations. For example, the two definitions of the form

$$\begin{aligned} f &= \ldots f \ldots g \ldots \\ g &= \ldots f \ldots f \ldots g \ldots \end{aligned}$$

would be transformed into the non-recursive forms

$$\begin{aligned} f &= Y\lambda f. \ldots f \ldots (Y\lambda g. \ldots Y\lambda f.E \ldots Y\lambda f.E \ldots g \ldots) \ldots \\ g &= Y\lambda g. \ldots (Y\lambda f.E) \ldots (Y\lambda f.E) \ldots g \ldots \end{aligned}$$

where $E = \ldots f \ldots g \ldots$.

An alternative method, described in Chapter 6, is to package the mutually recursive functions into a single recursive tuple, accessing the individual component functions by tuple indexing functions. We could use the same technique here and the abstraction would proceed without complication. Without the family of tupling functions *TUPLE-n*, and the indexing function *INDEX*, an alternative approach would be to make use of the 'untupling' combinator U defined in Section 12.2.3. If we have the set of mutually recursive definitions of the form

$$\begin{aligned} \text{letrec}\quad f_1 &= E_1, \\ f_2 &= E_2, \\ &\vdots \\ f_n &= E_n \\ \text{in } E \end{aligned}$$

we package the E_i into a tuple which can be expressed in combinator form using U. We therefore obtain the definition:

$$(f_1, \ldots, f_n) = (E_1, \ldots, E_n)$$

We may write this equation in the form

$$(f_1, \ldots, f_n) = U(\lambda f_1.(U(\lambda f_2.(\ldots(U(\lambda f_n.(E_1, \ldots, E_n)))\ldots))))(f_1, \ldots, f_n)$$

so that

$$(f_1, \ldots, f_n) = Y(U(\lambda f_1.(U(\lambda f_2.(\ldots (U(\lambda f_n.(E_1, \ldots, E_n))) \ldots)))))$$

From the definition of the tupling combinator T_n in Section 12.2.3, we can derive the combinator form of a tuple as follows:

$$\begin{aligned} comb((e_1, \ldots, e_n)) &= comb(T_n\, e_1 \ldots e_n) \\ &= T_n\, comb(e_1) \ldots comb(e_n) \\ &= (comb(e_1), \ldots, comb(e_n)) \end{aligned}$$

for arbitrary expressions $e_1, \ldots, e_n$ and $n \geq 1$. Hence we obtain

$$comb((f_1, \ldots, f_n)) = Y(U([f_1] (U([f_2](\ldots (U([f_n] \\ (comb(E_1), \ldots, comb(E_n))))) \ldots)))))$$

The right-hand side of this definition has n occurrences of U and only one of Y. In our example above, assuming the right-hand sides of the equations are applicative expressions for simplicity, we therefore obtain the much simpler combinator form

$$\begin{aligned} &comb((f, g)) \\ &\quad = Y(U([f](U([g](\ldots f \ldots g \ldots, \ldots f \ldots f \ldots g \ldots))))) \end{aligned}$$

It now remains to define an efficient graph transformation to represent application of the Y-combinator. Fortunately this is not difficult, and follows from the definition of a fixed point, i.e. for all λ-expressions, X, $Y\,X = X(\,Y\,X\,) = X(\,X(\,X \ldots X(\,Y\,X\,) \ldots)\,)$. Thus a cyclic graph provides the correct representation, as shown in Figure 12.7

The only question we might now ask is: does this represent the least fixed point of X? The answer is 'yes', but a rigorous proof of the claim is outside the scope of this book. However, notice that in the semantic domain of lambda expressions (see Appendix B), the least fixed point of (the value denoted by) X is the limit of the infinite sequence formed by repeatedly applying X to the undefined element, i.e. $X^{\infty}\bot$. Although it is clear that the cyclic graph for YX represents X^{∞} it has no $\bot$ so that we cannot see immediately that it represents the least fixed point of X.

If the recursive function f has the defining combinator expression

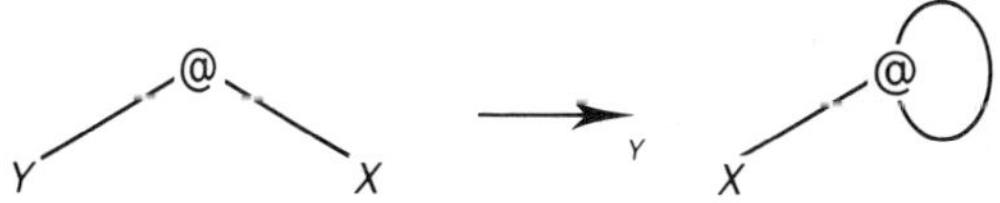

Figure 12.7 Graph transformation rule for applications of Y.

Y F, then the expression *f k* for expression *k* (which we take to be a constant for the sake of simplicity) has graph representation:

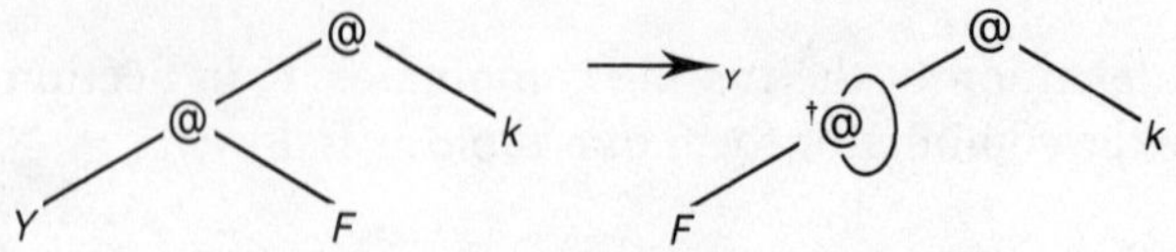

The next graph transformation is determined by the structure of the sub-graph representing *F*. The resulting graph will contain arcs directed to the node marked † which perpetuates the cyclic behaviour – *Y* is never applied again!

This completes our discussion of fixed-set combinator implementations of graph reduction. The approach is certainly mathematically elegant, avoids the problems associated with free variables, and can be made relatively efficient. Turner's set of combinators renders the approach viable for some practical implementations of functional languages, and various further extensions to the fixed set of combinators have achieved significant improvements in performance. An inherent problem with the fixed-set of combinators approach is the small size of the **grain** of computation. Grain size is a measure of the complexity of primitive operations, i.e. of applications of the fixed, primitive combinators in performing graph reductions. Thus the grain size is extremely small in the case of the $\{S, K, I\}$ representation and small grain results in excessively high computational overheads. Grain size is still small even when we extend the set of primitive combinators, and an alternative approach is to generate more complex combinators tailored to the particular expression to be evaluated. These combinators are generated by the compiler and lead to a variable-set combinator implementation, as we discuss in the next chapter.

12.4 Director strings

The reader unfamiliar with the idea of combinators might have found the general combinator approach somewhat unusual and rather 'mystical' in nature. At first reading it is often very hard to see what is actually going on during the abstraction process and later when the resulting combinator expressions are applied to arguments. There is, however, a very intuitive interpretation of the reduction rules of the fixed combinators which not only serves to explain what combinators achieve but also naturally suggests an alternative and more efficient representation of combinator expressions. The idea is due originally to Kennaway and Sleep (1982) although a more detailed discussion of the implementation issues can be found in Stoye (1985).

First, let us go back and consider the expression $S\ E_1\ E_2$, the application of the S combinator to two combinator expressions E_1 and E_2. Another way to view this expression is as an annotated application of E_1 to E_2, the annotation reflecting the presence of the S combinator, and we represent this by the graph:

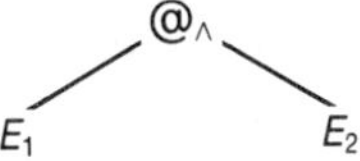

(The reason for choosing the annotation ^ will soon become apparent.)

Similarly we annotate the graph of the application $C\ E_1\ E_2$ with a / to reflect the fact that the applied combinator is C, and we get

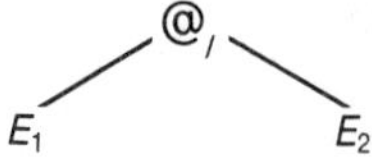

For B, we annotate with a \ so that the graph representing the expression $B\ E_1\ E_2$ appears as:

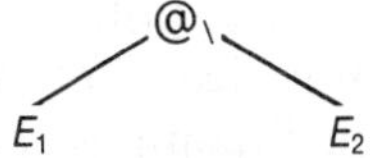

By comparing these graphs with those obtained by applying the rules given in Section 12.2.2 when the three expressions are applied to an argument x, we see a pattern emerging: the annotations on the @-nodes in these graphs can be viewed as argument *feeders*. In other words when an expression with an annotated @-node at its root is applied to x, the annotation describes which way x should be passed through the @-node: the ^ annotation, corresponding to the S combinator, feeds x to both the function and argument subgraphs; the / annotation, corresponding to the C combinator, feeds the argument to just the function subgraph leaving the argument intact and the \ annotation, corresponding to the B combinator, conversely feeds x to the argument subgraph leaving the function graph intact. These annotations are called **directors** for obvious reasons. In fact to complete the picture we also require a director – corresponding to the K combinator which discards the incoming argument; this is required when a bound variable is not referred to within a function body, as in

$\lambda x.\ +\ 1$

for example. The graph for this expression looks like this:

Now, of course, the reason for feeding the argument through the graph is to get it to its intended position, that is to where it would ultimately end up using conventional β-reduction, and to this end we require a special type of node which acts like a 'hole' into which any incoming argument is placed, corresponding, as we might expect, to the I combinator in the equivalent combinator graph. As a simple example let us consider the expression $\lambda x.x\ x$. As can be verified by the reader, this has the combinator representation $S\ I\ I$ and hence an alternative graph representation using the director $^\wedge$ and I:

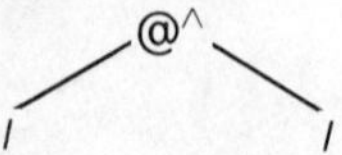

Applying this to an argument expression E will cause E to be fed into both arms of the @-node, where it will replace the two occurrences of I. This constructs the expression $E\ E$ as we would expect.

Whilst these directors work quite satisfactorily when only a single bound variable is involved, it is clear that when there are multiple bound variables, and hence multiple incoming arguments, a single director on each @-node is insufficient. This is simply because the directions for each incoming argument will be different as they are required to be sent to different parts of the graph. To solve this problem we must extend the director annotations on each node and allow instead arbitrary director *strings*. The director at the head of the string indicates where the first argument should be sent; the next director in the string indicates where the second argument should be sent and so on. To illustrate this mechanism, consider the following example:

$$\lambda x.\lambda y. * (+ x\ x)\ y$$

The director-annotated graph of this expression looks like this:

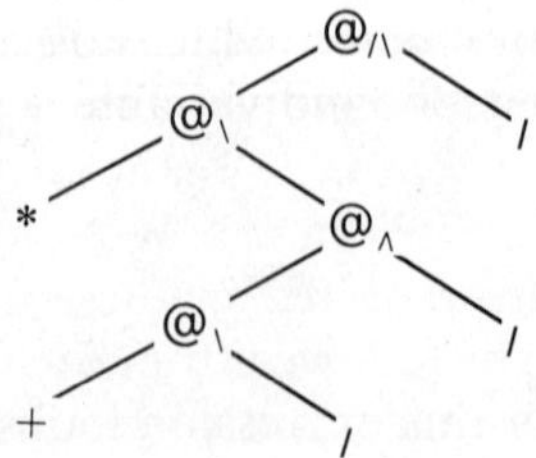

Now imagine the first argument (x) being passed to the root node of the graph. The first director / (i.e. the first director in the string / \) causes the argument to be passed to the left branch of the @-node only. From there on it is fed into the inner application of +, where it replaces both occurrences of I. The second incoming argument (y) now obeys the director \ (the second director in the string / \) and so replaces the topmost I immediately. Because this second argument is never passed to the left branch of the topmost @-node, only a single director is required on each @-node in that branch. Because there are only two bound variables a maximum of two directors is required in each string.

We can express the effect of directors more formally by providing reduction rules corresponding to an arbitrary director string $d_1 d_2 \ldots d_n$ in an expression graph of the form:

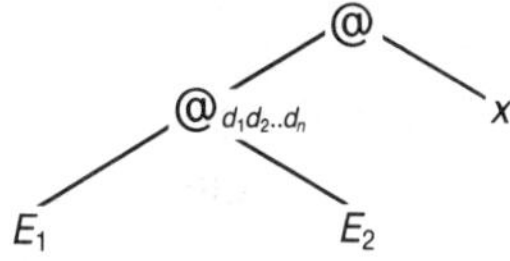

which we write

$$(@_{d_1 d_2 \ldots d_n} E_1\ E_2)\ x$$

The reduction rules are expressed recursively by writing down the expressions obtained for each possible director at the head of the string as follows:

$$\begin{aligned}
(@_{\wedge d_2 \ldots d_n} E_1\ E_2)\ x &= @_{d_2 \ldots d_n} (E_1\ x) (E_2\ x) \\
(@_{/ d_2 \ldots d_n} E_1\ E_2)\ x &= @_{d_2 \ldots d_n} (E_1\ x)\ E_2 \\
(@_{\backslash d_2 \ldots d_n} E_1\ E_2)\ x &= @_{d_2 \ldots d_n} E_1 (E_2\ x) \\
(@_{- d_2 \ldots d_n} E_1\ E_2)\ x &= @_{d_2 \ldots d_n} E_1\ E_2
\end{aligned}$$

Apart from providing an alternative representation for fixed combinator graphs, these directors also provide us with an insight into how the translation function *comb* of Section 12.1 for fixed combinators can faithfully model β-reduction. In short the translation function removes (abstracts) variables from expressions, leaving behind a sort of 'route map', encoded in the form of combinators, which describes how an incoming argument can be fed back to the original location(s) of the abstracted variable. We now see in a pragmatic way why only a fixed number of combinators are required in theory: there are only a fixed number of paths which can be followed from each node in the graph. Furthermore we now also have an intuitive justification for the optimizations of Section 12.2 which yield the combinators B and C: if we send an argument to both branches of an @-node (S) and then in one branch throw it away (K), then as an optimization we can avoid sending it down the K branch altogether, instead directing it only where it is required.

As the reader may have noticed, another interesting property of director strings is that they preserve the original structure of the graph (with the λs removed, of course). The information which is otherwise embodied within a complex combinator expression is now contained within the original @-nodes as annotations. This is particularly significant from the point of view of space: because there are only four types of director, each can be encoded in two bits. A director string can then be formed from 'words' of multiples of two bits with a possible 'escape' mechanism to allow longer strings than can be stored within one such word to be built by chaining several words together. Without this, a limit must be placed on the number of 'nested' bound variables allowed in order that the director strings can all be located in a single word.

Director strings therefore behave rather like optimized fixed combinators; indeed the strings themselves can be viewed as explicit combinators by simply rearranging the graphs:

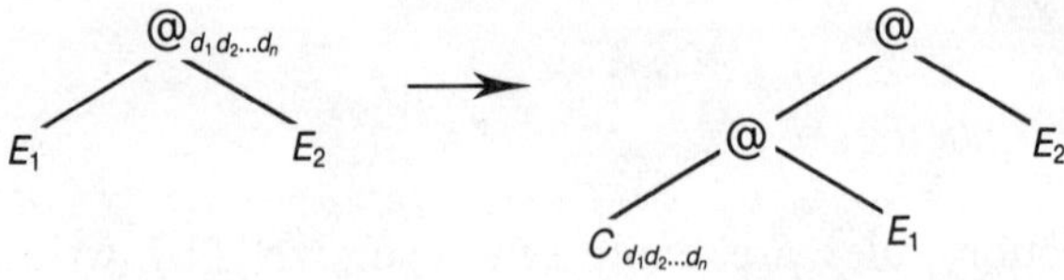

where $C_{d_1d_2\ldots d_n}$ is some combinator. The reduction rules for the implied set of combinators

$$\{ C_{d_1d_2\ldots d_n} \mid d_i \in \{ \wedge, /, \backslash, -, \}, 1 \leq i \leq n \}$$

are then simple re-expressions of the four (recursive) reduction rules given above. For example,

$$C_{/\backslash}\, a\, b\, c\, d = (\, a\, c\,)\,(\, b\, d\,)$$

Although in theory the value of n here is unbounded, in practice n may be limited in which case the implied combinator set would itself be 'fixed' and finite.

SUMMARY

- Applicative expressions can be implemented efficiently and have no problem with free variables.

- Combinatory logic (CL) provides a model of the lambda calculus in which expressions are applicative and built using only the S and K combinators (together with constants).
- CL expressions are very complex but can be optimized using Curry's identities and introducing the combinators B and C.
- By using the first of these identities the constant sub-expressions in a lambda expression can be preserved, so facilitating sharing and promoting laziness.
- Further enhancement may be obtained by adding additional combinators to the set.
- Recursion may be implemented by cyclic graphs or by using the Y-combinator, which is represented by a pointer from a node to itself.
- Directors provide a model of combinator reduction, in which the flow of combinator arguments through the graph is represented explicitly.

EXERCISES

12.1 Translate the following lambda expressions into *S-K-I* combinator form:

(a) $\lambda x. + x\ 1$

(b) $\lambda x.x\ (\ \lambda x.x\ )\ 1$

(c) $\lambda x.cond\ (\ =\ x\ 0\ )\ 1\ (\ -\ x\ 1\ )$

12.2 Prove Curry's four identities on the extended set of combinators S, K, I, B and C. Translate the expressions given in Exercise 12.1 into optimized combinator code.

12.3 Given the following definitions:

$$X = (\ \lambda x.\lambda y.y\ (\ x\ x\ y\ )\ )\ (\ \lambda x.\lambda y.y\ (\ x\ x\ y\ )\ )$$

$$S = \lambda x.\lambda y.\lambda z.x\ z\ (\ y\ z\ )$$

$$B = \lambda x.\lambda y.\lambda z.x\ (\ y\ z\ )$$

$$K = \lambda x.\lambda y.x$$

(a) show that X is a fixed point operator;

(b) prove $SKK \cong I$ by showing that I is the normal form of SKK in Λ or by using the reduction rules for applications of S and K, assuming extensionality in CL;

(c) show that $S\ (KS)\ K \cong B$.

12.4 For combinator expression E and variable x, prove by induction on the applicative structure of E that $sub([\,x\,]E) =_{\alpha,\beta} \lambda x.sub(E)$ where $sub(E)$ denotes the lambda expression obtained from E by substituting S, K and I by their defining lambda expressions. Hence show that

$$sub([\,x\,]comb(E)) =_{\alpha,\beta} \lambda x.E$$

and that

$$sub(comb(E)) =_{\alpha,\beta} E$$

12.5 Modify the variable abstraction function, *abs*, to incorporate the optimization which uses the combinator S' in place of S when abstracting from a triple application whenever possible. Optimize *abs* further by incorporating B' and C' similarly.

12.6 Given the lambda calculus definition of the Y-combinator

(a) draw the graph representation of Yf using sharing to represent the self-application in the body of Y;

(b) show that $Yf = f\,(\,Yf\,)$ by successive transformation of the graph.

12.7 Given the definition

$$factorial\,(\,n\,) = cond\,(\,=\,2\;n\,)\,2\,(\,*\,n\,(\,factorial\,(\,-\,n\;1\,)\,)\,),$$

(a) show that an equivalent combinator definition is

$$factorial = S\,(\,C\,(\,B\,cond\,(\,=\,2\,)\,)\,2\,)\,(\,S*\,(\,B\,factorial\,(\,C\,-\,1\,)\,)\,)$$

(b) show that an equivalent non-recursive definition is

$$factorial = Y\,(\,B\,(\,S\,(\,C\,(\,B\,cond\,(\,=\,2\,)\,)\,2\,)\,)\,(\,B\,(\,S*\,)(\,C\,B\,(\,C\,-\,1\,)\,)\,)\,)\,)$$

(c) show the graph reduction sequence for the evaluation of the expression *factorial* 3 where *factorial* is represented by the expression given in (b).

12.8 The combinator W is defined by the reduction rule $W\,h\,x = h\,x\,x$.

(a) Translate W into optimized combinator form (using the combinators S, K, I, B, C) and show the graph reductions corresponding to evaluation of the expression $W + 2$.

(b) Define a suitable primitive graph transformation rule for W, exploiting sharing.

(c) Draw the graph for $E = S\,(\,B\,W\,B\,)\,(\,B\,W\,B\,)$.

(d) Show that E is equivalent to Y by illustrating that successive transformations on the graph representation of Ef produces the graph representation of $f(\,Ef\,)$.

12.9 Develop an abstraction algorithm for generating director strings from an arbitrary pure lambda calculus expression. (*Hint:* Use the *FV* function given in Chapter 6 which returns the set of free variables of a given expression.)

12.10 (a) Consider the expression $\lambda x.\lambda y.7$. The body cannot be annotated with the director '–' because there is no @-node in it. Suggest a method of solving the problem.

(b) Why do '–' directors only appear on the *root* node of a subgraph representing a lambda abstraction?

12.11 Draw the director-annotated graph of the lambda calculus expression for the Y-combinator.

Chapter 13
Advanced combinator implementations

The appeal of combinator implementations is that all of the expressions to be evaluated are in purely applicative form, in fact **constant applicative form** (which we shall often write CAF) meaning an applicative form in which there are no variables. Thus only two types of transformation are involved in combinator graph reduction, representing the application of either a combinator or a primitive function to a sub-expression, also in CAF. Each combinator is therefore a 'pure' function in that an application of it depends solely on the value of its arguments and not in addition on the value of any free variables in its body. In this way each combinator can be viewed as a constant in precisely the same way as can each primitive function such as $+$.

In this chapter we are going to look at a rather different approach to combinators in which each lambda expression is translated into CAF using new combinators which are generated directly from the lambda abstractions involved. The effect of this is to generate a different set of combinators from each program rather than relying on a fixed set, such as the Turner combinators described in the previous chapter. Despite the fact that the set of combinators we consider is now unbounded the advantages of the combinator approach are retained. Each combinator is a pure function and so can be viewed as another constant and all expressions are in CAF so that the implementation is still environment free. In fact the new approach has certain advantages over the fixed combinator approach in that each combinator produced is almost certain to be 'larger' than the fixed combinators so that fewer applications are required to do the same amount of work. We say that the **grain size** of each combinator is increased.

The simplest transformation of this type is called **λ-lifting** and works by abstracting the free variables from each λ-body, producing one new combinator in the process. However, this is not the most efficient implementation in that the number of applications contained in the resulting expressions generated (and so graph reductions required during their evaluation) can be reduced, and the grain size of the combinators can be increased. More seriously, full laziness may be lost in that the same sub-expression may be evaluated more than once during expression evaluation. In Section 13.2 we describe an enhancement to simple λ-lifting based on so-called **super-combinators**. This approach abstracts whole sub-expressions which contain free variables, rather than just the free variables themselves, and does not lose full laziness; furthermore, it increases the complexity of the (super-)combinators and reduces the number of function applications which are ultimately required. Some further optimizations for the super-combinator implementation are given in Section 13.3.

Finally, in Section 13.4, we consider a more recently developed implementation which is based on **categorical combinatory logic**. The abstract machine for this type of combinator reduction, called the CAM (for categorical abstract machine), is based on sound mathematical foundations which facilitate a good degree of optimization. Interestingly, its operation is defined in terms of transitions between states, very much akin to the operational semantics of the SECD machine.

13.1 Free variable abstraction by simple λ-lifting

The simplest abstraction scheme 'lifts out' (abstracts) the free variables from one λ-body at a time. The λ-abstraction is then replaced by the partial application of a new combinator which has one more parameter than the number of free variables abstracted, the extra one corresponding to the bound variable of the λ-abstraction. To illustrate this consider the λ-abstraction $L = \lambda x.E$, where E is in applicative form, and let the set of free variables in the expression E, i.e. $FV(E)$, be $\{v_1, \ldots, v_n\}$. We now define the combinator α by $\alpha\ v_1\ v_2 \ldots v_n\ x = E$ and may replace L by the expression $\alpha\ v_1\ v_2 \dots v_n$ since for any argument expression, E', we have $LE' = \alpha\ V_1\ V_2 \dots V_n\ E'$ in any environment in which v_i is bound to the expression $V_i\ (1 \le i \le n)$, x being bound to E'. If we now regard the combinator α as a new primitive, we have succeeded in replacing the λ-abstraction L by an applicative expression. We do still have to define the graph transformation rule corresponding to its application to $n + 1$ argument expressions, this rule being environment-independent by construction, whereupon α becomes just like any other combinator such as S, K, I etc. The rule itself must be defined solely in terms of applications involving the argument expressions, primitive functions and previously generated combinators. In this way, we can transform a whole expression into CAF by abstracting the variables from the innermost λ-abstraction and working outwards. After each step, the bound variable no longer appears in the transformed expression, and eventually all variables will be removed to form a closed expression. This variable removal operation is performed by the function *lift*, which maps open λ-expressions to purely applicative expressions and is defined by:

$lift(\ E\ ) = E$	if E is in applicative form
$lift(\ \lambda x.E\ ) = \alpha\ v_1 \dots v_n$	if E is an applicative expression with $FV(\ \lambda x.E\ ) = \{v_1 \dots v_n\}$
where α is defined by $\alpha\ v_1 \dots v_n\ x = E$	
$lift(\ \lambda x.E\ ) = lift(\ \lambda x.lift(\ E\ )\ )$	if E is not an applicative expression
$lift(\ E_1\ E_2\ ) = lift(\ E_1\ )\ lift(\ E_2\ )$	for λ-expressions E_1, E_2
$lift(\ (\ E\ )\ ) = (\ lift(\ E\ )\ )$	for λ-expression E

A more general λ-lifting function is defined in Section 13.3.4 which lifts the free variables from several nested λ-expressions at a time.

To illustrate the λ-lifting mechanism we shall consider the following function (taken from Hughes, 1984) for selecting the nth element of a given list:

$$element = \lambda n.\lambda s.cond(\ =\ n\ 1\ )\ (\ hd\ s\ )\ (\ element\ (\ -n\ 1\ )\ (\ tl\ s\ )\ )$$

The recursion (which would otherwise be captured by embedding the definition within a letrec expression) can be expressed explicitly using the Y-combinator as follows:

$$element = Y(\ \lambda el.\lambda n.\underline{\lambda s.cond(\ =\ n\ 1\ )\ (\ hd\ s\ )\ (\ el\ (\ -n\ 1\ )\ (\ tl\ s\ )\ )}\ )$$

We first show, in an algorithmic way, how the variable-free form is obtained by abstracting the variables from the innermost λ-abstraction (underlined in the above expression) and working outwards. We then show how the same transformation is arrived at by application of the function *lift*. In fact the former method essentially shows the computation sequence that corresponds to an eager application of *lift* to the argument *element*. Denoting the innermost λ-abstraction by $E_1 = \lambda s.cond\ (= n\ 1)\ (hd\ s)\ (el\ (-\ n\ 1)\ (tl\ s))$, we first generate the combinator α, given by

$$\alpha\ n\ el\ s = cond(=\ n\ 1)\ (hd\ s)\ (el\ (-\ n\ 1)\ (tl\ s))$$

so that

$$lift(\ E_1\ ) = \alpha\ n\ el$$

and now

$$element\ =\ Y(\ \lambda el.\underline{\lambda n.\alpha\ n\ el}\ )$$

The new innermost λ-abstraction, with applicative body, is again underlined and we denote it by E_2. Repeating the lifting operation, we generate the combinator β, given by

$$\beta\ el\ n\quad = \alpha\ n\ el$$

so that

$$lift(\ E_2\ ) = \beta\ el$$

and now

$$element\ =\ Y(\underline{\lambda el.\beta\ el}\ )$$

Finally, the single remaining λ-abstraction is denoted by E_3, and we generate the combinator γ, given by

$$\gamma\ el\quad = \beta\ el$$

so that

$$lift(\ E_3\ ) = \gamma$$

and we are finished, having now obtained:

$$element\ =\ Y\ \gamma$$

where

$$\begin{aligned}
\gamma\ el &= \beta\ el \\
\beta\ el\ n &= \alpha\ n\ el \\
\alpha\ n\ el\ s &= cond\ (=\ n\ 1)\ (hd\ s)\ (el\ (-\ n\ 1)\ (tl\ s))
\end{aligned}$$

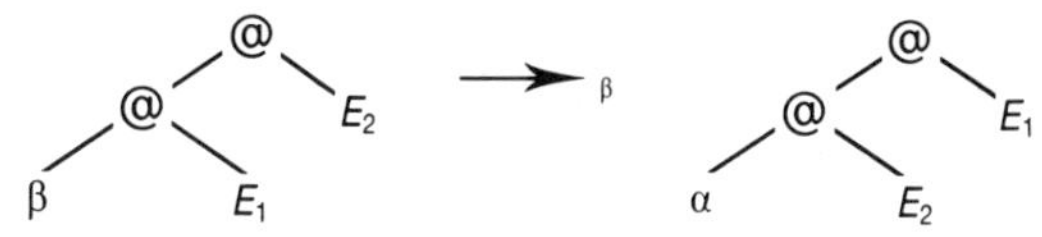

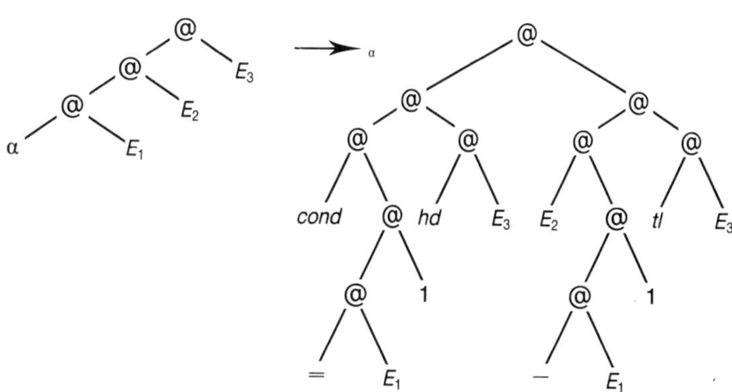

Figure 13.1 Graph transformation rules for the combinators α and β.

It now only remains to define the graph transformation rules that represent the applications of α, β and γ to 3, 2 and 1 arguments respectively. Clearly, we define $\gamma = \beta$, and the graph transformations representing the expressions $\beta\ E_1\ E_2$ and $\alpha\ E_1\ E_2\ E_3$, for argument expressions E_1, E_2, E_3 are shown in Figure 13.1.

The increased grain size is now quite clear in the complexity of the reduction rule for α. The rather intuitive, algorithmic description of the variable lifting process does indeed give the same result as that obtained by applying the function *lift* to the expression *element*, which executes as follows:

$$
\begin{aligned}
\mathit{lift}(\mathit{element}) &= \mathit{lift}(\ Y\ )\ \mathit{lift}(\ \lambda el.\lambda n.\lambda s.\mathit{cond}\ (\ =\ n\ 1\ )\ (\ hd\ s\ )\ (\ el\ (\ -\ n\ 1\ )\ (\ tl\ s\ )\ )\ )\\
&= Y\ \mathit{lift}(\ \lambda el.\mathit{lift}(\ \lambda n.\lambda s.\mathit{cond}\ (\ =\ n\ 1\ )\ (\ hd\ s\ )\ (\ el\ (\ -\ n\ 1\ )\ (\ tl\ s\ )\ )\ )\\
&= Y\ \mathit{lift}(\ \lambda el.\mathit{lift}(\ \lambda n.\mathit{lift}(\ E1\ )\ )\ )\\
&= Y\ \mathit{lift}(\ \lambda el.\mathit{lift}(\ E_2\ )\ )\\
&= Y\ \mathit{lift}(\ E_3\ )\\
&= Y\ \gamma
\end{aligned}
$$

where E_1, E_2, E_3 and γ are as defined above.

Although this method is quite elegant and also increases the grain size as we observed for the combinator α, it is certainly not optimal. Clearly, the new combinators β and γ are equal, and there was no need to generate γ. A little less obvious is that β need not be defined either because of its similarity with α; these combinators are equal up to ordering of parameters. Much less clearly, the simple λ-lifting technique may result in duplicated reduction of constant sub-expressions; that is, full laziness has been lost. Consider, for example, the partial application, *element* 2, which evaluates as follows:

$$\begin{aligned} element\ 2 &= \lambda s.cond\ (\ =\ 2\ 1\ )\ (\ hd\ s\ )\ (\ element\ (\ -\ 2\ 1\ )\ (\ tl\ s\ )) \\ &= \lambda s.cond\ false\ (\ hd\ s\ )\ (\ element\ 1\ (\ tl\ s\ )\ ) \\ &= \lambda s.element\ 1\ (\ tl\ s\ ) \end{aligned}$$

where the constant sub-expressions $=$ 2 1 and $-$ 2 1 have been evaluated for the first and only time. (In a lazy implementation, the moment of evaluation would be postponed of course, but the result could still be shared.) However, applying the λ-lifted version yields:

$$\begin{aligned} element\ 2 =\ & Y\ \gamma\ 2 & \\ \Rightarrow_Y\ & \gamma\ element\ 2 & \text{by definition of } Y \\ \Rightarrow_\gamma\ & \beta\ element\ 2 & \text{by definition of } \gamma \\ \Rightarrow_\beta\ & \alpha\ 2\ element & \text{by definition of } \beta \end{aligned}$$

No further reduction is possible until the expression, *element* 2, is applied to an argument (to which to bind s in the reduction rule for α). Thus if the partial application *element* 2 is shared, the two constant sub-expressions would be evaluated on each application. Now, in this example the duplicated effort will be fairly trivial. In general, however, the re-evaluated sub-expressions may be arbitrarily complex. For example, consider the general expression

$$f = \lambda x.\ \lambda y.\ +\ (\ BIG\ x\ )\ (\ *\ y\ x\ )$$

where *BIG* is a computationally complex function. λ-lifting this expression gives the following combinators

$$\begin{aligned} f\ \ &= \beta \\ \beta\ x\ \ &= \alpha\ x \\ \alpha\ x\ y &= +\ (\ BIG\ x\ )\ (\ *\ y\ x\ ) \end{aligned}$$

A partial application of f to the argument A, say, will yield $\alpha\ A$ – a partial application of α. Each subsequent application of this function to an argument, B say, will then build the expression $+\ (\ BIG\ A\ )\ (\ *\ B\ A\ )$ so that the sub-expression *BIG A* will be evaluated each time.

Fortunately, this repeated expression evaluation can be avoided quite easily: any non-constant sub-expression of a λ-body which has no occurrence of the bound variable will be a candidate for this redundancy. We call this type of expression a **free expression** (abbreviated to fe), and this source of duplicated expression reduction leads us to consider fe's rather than just variables as our 'units' of abstraction.

13.2 Super-combinators

As we have seen in the previous section, when using simple λ-lifting to transform a λ-expression into CAF, the free variables of applicative λ-bodies become represented by the parameters of the newly generated combinator. These isolated free variables are the minimal non-constant fe's of λ-bodies, in that they contain no proper sub-expressions. In contrast to this, we could instead define similar new combinators, the parameters of which represent the non-constant maximal fe's (abbreviated to mfe's) of the corresponding λ-bodies. The combinators obtained in this way are called **super-combinators**, and were first introduced by Hughes (1984) with a view to overcoming some of the difficulties associated with simple λ-lifting discussed above. In particular, full laziness will be preserved, as this was only lost when a free variable occurring in a larger fe was lifted from a λ-body. Since, in this enhanced implementation, all free expressions are represented as (sub-expressions of) parameters of the super-combinators, their computed values are guaranteed to be shared; recall that argument sub-graphs are not copied in a graph-reduction implementation of function application. We now present the super-combinator transformation of λ-expressions into CAF, and illustrate the technique by reconsidering the element function of the previous section.

The super-combinator representation of a λ-abstraction with applicative λ-body is obtained by the following procedure:

(1) Successively find the largest sub-expressions containing free variables, but not the bound variable of the λ-abstraction, using a standard 'bracket-counting' method, remembering the 'invisible' brackets associating to the left by convention. In other words, find the mfe's. A recursive function, *mfes*, which returns the set of mfe's when applied to an applicative λ-body with bound variable named *bv*, may be defined as follows:

$$
\begin{aligned}
&mfes(E) &&= \varnothing \quad \text{if } FV(E) = \varnothing \quad \text{or } FV(E) = \{bv\} \\
&mfes(E) &&= \{E\} \quad \text{if } bv \notin E \ \&\ FV(E) \neq \varnothing \\
&mfes(E_1E_2) &&= mfes(E_1) \cup mfes(E_2) \quad \text{if } bv \in E_1E_2 \\
&mfes((E)) &&= mfes(E)
\end{aligned}
$$

(2) Successively replace each occurrence of an mfe in the λ-body by a new parameter name, i.e. a new super-combinator bound variable. If an mfe is the same as a previously replaced mfe, replace it with the corresponding previous parameter name.

The function, *mfelift*, which lifts mfe's from λ-bodies and generates super-combinator expressions is therefore a modification of the *lift* function given in the previous section, and is defined on λ-expressions as follows:

$mfelift(\ E\ )$	$= E$	if E is in applicative form
$mfelift(\ \lambda x.E\ )$	$= \alpha\ m_1 \ldots m_n$	if E is an applicative expression with $mfes(\ E\ ) = \{\ m_1 \ldots m_n\ \}$, $n \geq 0$
	where α is defined by $\alpha\ p_1 \ldots p_n x = [\ p_1\ /\ m_1, \ldots, p_n\ /\ m_n\ ]E$	
$mfelift(\ \lambda x.E\ )$	$= mfelift(\ \lambda x.mfelift(\ E\ )\ )$	if E is not an applicative expression
$mfelift(\ E_1 E_2\ )$	$= mfelift(\ E_1\ )\ mfelift(\ E_2\ )$	for λ-expressions E_1, E_2
$mfelift(\ (\ E\ )\ )$	$= (\ mfelift(\ E\ )\ )$	for λ-expression E

Note that the substitution, $[p_1\ /\ m_1\ , \ldots , p_n\ /\ m_n]\ E$, is not totally trivial to implement. In the algorithm that determines the mfe's, each mfe may be substituted for upon its detection and duplications can be handled by explicit comparison with the current list of mfe's so far found. It is left as an exercise to modify the function *mfes* to create a function which performs the desired substitution.

There is also a more subtle problem with multiple occurrences of mfe's. Suppose that a copy of an mfe, m_1, occurs as a proper sub-expression of another mfe, m_2. Then two parameters p_1, p_2 are created corresponding to m_1, m_2 respectively – even if there are no free variable occurrences in m_2 other than those in its sub-expression equal to m_1. For example, we might have $m_1 = -\ n\ 1$ and $m_2 = \text{cond}\ (\ =\ (\ -\ n\ 1)\ 1)$. We will return to this issue when we consider optimizations in the next section.

Let us now return to our *element* example of the previous section, and see how the super-combinator approach preserves full laziness. We show the transformation of the defining expression into CAF using the algorithmic (or applicative-order) description which is simpler to read than the trace of function calls occurring in the equivalent application of *mfelift*. We begin with the definition:

$$element = Y(\ \lambda el.\lambda n.\lambda s.\underline{cond\ (\ =\ n\ 1\ )}\ (\ hd\ s\ )\ (\ \underline{el\ (\ -\ n\ 1\ )}\ (\ tl\ s\ )\ )\ )$$

The mfe's of the innermost λ-body are underlined and we associate them with parameters p and q of the super-combinator α which is defined by

$$\alpha\ p\ q\ s = p\ (\ hd\ s\ )\ (\ q\ (\ tl\ s\ )\ )$$

so that

$$element = Y(\,\lambda el.\lambda n.\alpha\,(\,cond\,(\,=\,n\;1\,)\,)\,(\,el\,(\,-n\;1\,)\,)\,)$$

There is only one mfe, *el*, in the new innermost λ-body and we generate the super-combinator β which is defined by

$$\beta\;u\;n = \alpha\,(\,cond\,(\,=\,n\;1\,)\,)\,(\,u\,(\,-\,n\;1\,)\,)$$

so that

$$element = Y(\,\lambda el.\beta\;el\,)$$

Finally, we generate γ, given by

$$\gamma\;el = \beta\;el$$

and obtain $element = Y\gamma$ where $\gamma\;el = \beta\;el$, $\beta\;u\;n = \alpha\,(\,cond\,(\,=\,n\;1\,)\,)\,(u\,(\,-\,n\;1\,)\,)$, $\alpha\;p\;q\;s = p\,(\,hd\;s\,)\,(\,q\,(\,tl\;s\,)\,)$.

We can see that this version of the *element* function is fully lazy by looking at the result of applying it to the integer 2, as we did with the simple λ-lifted version.

$$\begin{aligned} element\;2 &= Y\,\gamma\;2 \\ &= \gamma\;element\;2 \\ &= \beta\;element\;2 \\ &- \alpha\,(\,cond\,(\,=\,2\;1\,)\,)\,(\,element\,(\,-\,2\;1\,)\,) \end{aligned}$$

On the first call to the function *element* 2, i.e. the first time that *element* 2 is applied to an argument, the sub-expressions $=\;2\;1$ and $-\;2\;1$ will be evaluated. If this evaluation is performed using graph reduction, then the root nodes of these subexpressions will be overwritten by the values *false* and 1 respectively. Any subsequent shared applications of *element* 2 will then find these values in the graph already so that the original sub-expressions need never be re-evaluated. The difference between this and λ-lifting is that here the shared sub-expressions occur as *arguments*, which are naturally shared in graph reduction.

13.3 Optimization of super-combinator implementations

There are two potential sources of optimization in the super-combinator transformation scheme. The first is in the selection of the mfe's of an applicative λ-body, and the second is in the assignment of sequence numbers to the parameters of the super-combinators generated. The two are not unrelated either: the abstraction of a particular mfe influences the structure of the residual λ-body, and so the set of remaining mfe's. A rather trivial optimization which we have already assumed is that constant sub-expressions are not mfe's. If they were considered as mfe's, the transformed super-combinator expression would certainly be correct, but each constant sub-expression so abstracted would become a constant argument during expression evaluation, resulting in unnecessary parameter-passing overhead. Of course it is not difficult to ensure that the compiler selects only sub-expressions which do contain free variables as mfe's.

We begin with a second look at the potential problem posed by the occurrence of a copy of one mfe as a sub-expression of another. We then consider orderings of the parameters of the super-combinators with a view to maximizing the size of each mfe and hence the final grain-size. At the same time we shall aim to minimize the number of such parameters and so minimize the function application overhead. The elimination of redundant parameters and combinators is considered in Section 13.3.3 and we show that the ordering which maximizes mfe-size is also optimal for eliminating this redundancy. Finally, we consider a further optimization of the super-combinator implementation which can be used when partially applied functions are not shared. In such cases several nested λ-abstractions may be transformed together to form a single new combinator.

13.3.1 Multiply occurring mfe's

Suppose, as in Section 13.2, that a copy of mfe m_1 occurs as a proper sub-expression of mfe m_2, and that the corresponding two parameters p_1, p_2 are created. Call this implementation scheme A. As we have seen already, this may be inefficient, generating a redundant parameter. As an optimization, we could substitute all instances of m_1 by the parameter p_1 in the whole λ-body after detection of m_1, and treat p_1 in the same way as the bound variable when finding the remaining mfe's, so that it cannot be included in an mfe. Call this implementation scheme B. If then $[\,p_1 / m_1\,]m_2$ has no free variables, only the parameter p_1 would be generated, but not p_2, which is the optimal solution with respect to numbers of parameters, although in general not to sharing. On the other hand, it may be the case that $[\,p_1/m_1\,]m_2$ has two non-constant mfe's, for example if $m_1 = q$ and $m_2 = p\,q\,r$ where p, q, r are all free variables. In this case, three parameters would be generated in total, so that scheme B would actually generate less efficient code than the straightforward scheme A.

13.3.2 Parameter order and maximal free expressions

In general, where we have a choice, we would like to generate mfe's which are as large as possible, and of which there are as few as possible. The larger an mfe is, the more free sub-expressions it will contain, and so the more possibilities there will be for sharing – each instance of such a free sub-expression will be available for evaluation as soon as its variables are bound. Moreover, since there corresponds one super-combinator parameter to each mfe, the fewer mfe's are created the lower will be the parameter passing overhead.

To illustrate the effect of changing the sequencing of the super-combinator parameters on the numbers and sizes of the mfe's generated, we consider two examples. First, suppose we are transforming the following sub-expression of the expression E:

$$E = \ldots (\, \lambda n.\alpha \,(\, hd\ s\,)\ n\ (\, tl\ s\,)\,) \ldots$$

where α is the previously defined super-combinator which has three parameters. There are two mfe's, $\alpha\,(\, hd\ s\,)$ and $(\, tl\ s\,)$. However, if α had been defined with its second and third parameters interchanged – an arbitrary decision – the expression E would have become

$$E = \ldots (\, \lambda n.\alpha \,(\, hd\ s\,)\,(\, tl\ s\,)\ n\,) \ldots$$

in which there is only one mfe, $\alpha\,(\, hd\ s\,)\,(\, tl\ s\,)$, which is larger than each of the two obtained under the alternative parameter ordering for α. Parameter ordering therefore has important repercussions on mfe-creation, although the choice of ordering is arbitrary from the point of view of the correctness of the implementation. Our second example is a little more explicit. Suppose now that we are transforming the innermost λ-body in the expression, E, defined by

$$E = \ldots (\, \lambda z. +\ y\,(\, *\ x\ z\,)\,) \ldots$$

We may define either

$$\alpha\ p\ q\ z = q\,(\, p\ z\,) \quad \text{with} \quad E = \ldots \alpha\,(\, *\ x\,)\,(\, +\ y\,) \ldots$$

or:

$$\alpha'\ p\ q\ z = p\,(\, q\ z\,) \quad \text{with} \quad E = \ldots \alpha'\,(\, +\ y\,)\,(\, *\ x\,) \ldots$$

Suppose that x is 'freer' than y, i.e. that y is abstracted before x as we work outwards. Then in the body of the λ-abstraction that binds y, $\alpha\,(\, *\ x\,)$ will be an mfe if we define α, whereas $(\, *\ x\,)$ will be an mfe if we define α'. We should therefore define α to maximize the size of our mfe's. Conversely, if y is freer than x, we should choose to generate α' and obtain the mfe $\alpha'\,(\, +\ y\,)$ when abstracting x. Thus, intuitively, to get the largest mfe's which are also fewest in number, we should assign the 'freest' mfe's to the leftmost parameter positions. Before showing that this is indeed the optimal ordering, we first give a more rigorous definition of the 'freeness' of mfe's.

Formally, the depth of nesting of a sub-expression is given by the **level numbers** of the variables which occur in it. Assuming that all variables have unique names (so that the definition is well defined), the level number of a variable, x, which occurs in the λ-expression, E, is denoted by $\mathit{level\_number}(x, E)$, where the function *level_number* is defined as follows:

$$
\begin{array}{lll}
\mathit{level\_number}(x, x) & = 0 & \\
\mathit{level\_number}(x, \lambda y.E) & = 1 & \text{if } x = y \\
 & = 1 + \mathit{level\_number}(x, E) & \text{if } x \neq y \\
\mathit{level\_number}(x, E_1\, E_2) & = \mathit{level\_number}(x, E_1) & \text{if } x \text{ occurs in } E_1 \\
 & = \mathit{level\_number}(x, E_2) & \text{if } x \text{ occurs in } E_2 \\
\mathit{level\_number}(x, (E)) & = \mathit{level\_number}(x, E) &
\end{array}
$$

where E, E_1, E_2 are λ-expressions. Constants and free variables are defined to have level number zero, i.e. $\mathit{level\_number}(x, E) = 0$ if x is a constant or a variable that does not occur in E.

A sub-expression, for example an mfe, is now defined to have a level number equal to the maximum of the level numbers of the variables occurring in it. If this number is greater than zero, then it is equal to the level number of the bound variable of the innermost λ-abstraction in which the sub-expression is not free.

The 'freest-first' selection order for mfe's is therefore not uniquely defined, since two mfe's might have the same level number. However, it is sufficient for our purposes if the ordering of two mfe's with equal level numbers is arbitrary. With this definition, it can be shown that the freest-first ordering produces the largest mfe's which are fewest in number (Hughes, 1984).

13.3.3 Redundant parameters and combinators

In our *element* example, the transformation into super-combinator form generated the combinator γ defined by $\gamma\ el = \beta\ el$, where β is a previously generated combinator. It is not difficult to see, in this blatant case of redundancy, that $\gamma = \beta$ (technically, by using η-conversion). More generally, suppose that the super-combinator β is defined by

$$\beta\, p_1 \ldots p_n = \alpha\, e_1 \ldots e_m \qquad (n, m \geq 1)$$

and that

$$p_n = e_m,\ p_{n-1} = e_{m-1}, \ldots, p_{k+1} = e_{k+m-n+1}$$

but

$$p_k \neq e_{k+m-n} \qquad \text{for } n \geq k \geq \mathit{max}(0, n - m)$$

Then the parameters $p_{k+1}, \ldots, p_n$ are all redundant and we can omit them by giving an equivalent definition for β, namely

$$\beta\ p_1 \ldots p_k = \alpha\ e_1 \ldots e_{k+m-n}$$

For example, if we have $\beta\ a\ b\ c\ x\ y\ z = \alpha\ e1\ e2\ x\ y\ z$ for arbitrary expressions $e1$ and $e2$, then we can 'cancel' the x, y and z from both sides and obtain instead $\beta\ a\ b\ c = \alpha\ e1\ e2$. Note that if $k = n - m \geq 0$, we would have $\beta\ p_1 \ldots p_{m-m} = \alpha$, but α contains no free variables, and so $n = m$ (and $k = 0$), for otherwise there would be free variables in the left-and side of the equation. Similarly, if $k = 0$, the equation becomes $\beta = \alpha\ e_1 \ldots e_{m-n}$ and since there are no free variables in the left-hand side, we must have $m = n$. Thus the range of valid values for k is $n \geq k > max(0, n - m)$ or alternatively $k = 0$ and $n = m$, whereupon the combinator β itself is redundant, a situation we have already encountered for the *element* function.

We therefore see that the ordering defined for the parameter sequence numbers of the super-combinators is again important; clearly only some orderings will allow the cancellation of equal parameters in the defining equations. In fact it can be shown that the freest-first ordering allows the maximum number of parameters and hence combinators to be eliminated from combinator definitions, as well as generating the fewest and largest mfe's as we saw in the previous section (Hughes, 1984).

To see how this works, consider the application of *mfelift* to the sub-expression $\lambda x.A$ of some expression E, where

$$A = \beta\ e_1 \ldots e_k \qquad (k \geq 0)$$

has been produced by a previous call to *mfelift* in the translation of some expression. β is a previously defined combinator and $e_1, \ldots, e_k$ have non-decreasing level number in E. Using *mfelift* we will define the new super-combinator α given by

$$\alpha\ p_1 \ldots p_n\ x = [\ p_1 / m_1, \ldots, p_n / m_n\ ]\ (\ \beta\ e_1 \ldots e_k\ ) \qquad \text{for some integer } n \geq 0$$

where $m_1, m_2, \ldots, m_n$ are the mfe's of A. Now, unless $e_k = x$ and x does not occur in e_j for $1 \leq j < k$, no parameter can be eliminated and so there is no scope for optimization. Let us assume that these conditions do hold, then, so that the parameter x can be eliminated. There are now two cases to consider, $k > 1$ and $k = 1$:

- If $k > 1$, then $\beta\ e_1 \ldots e_{k-1}$ is the only mfe and we define $\alpha\ p\ x = p\ x$, so that $\alpha = I$ and can be eliminated. The result of the application of *mfelift* is $\beta\ e_1 \ldots e_{k-1}$.

- If $k = 1$, then $\alpha\, x = \beta\, x$ so that $\alpha = \beta$ and again α can be eliminated. The result of the application of *mfelift* is then β, and in both cases all parameters and the new combinator α can be eliminated.

Although this ordering of mfe's is optimal for eliminating redundancy, the decision to select mfe's in the first place is not in general optimal in this respect, and the (rejected) alternative of simple λ-lifting of variables (minimal free expressions) is more successful. To see this, suppose that we have defined the new combinator α as above by

$$\alpha\, p_1 \ldots p_n\, x = [\, p_1 / m_1, \ldots, p_n / m_n]\, (\, \beta\, e_1 \ldots e_k\,)$$

and that $e_k = x$. Now, the only impediment to the cancellation of the last parameter, x, is the occurrence of x in the expressions $e_1, \ldots, e_{k-1}$. If we lifted only variables, then not only would we always have $e_k = x$ if x occurred in $\beta\, e_1 \ldots e_k$, but we would also be sure that $e_j \neq x$ for all $j < k$, permitting elimination of the combinator α entirely. Unfortunately, we have already seen that simple λ-lifting provides inadequate sharing of sub-expressions and it was the resulting loss of laziness that motivated the super-combinator implementation in the first place. However, the super-combinator technique can be refined somewhat to alleviate this situation.

First, it is not worth lifting certain mfe's in favour of the variables they contain, even from the point of view of sharing. In particular, there is no advantage in lifting partially applied combinators or strict primitive functions as sub-expressions, since they cannot be evaluated until they have been applied to sufficient arguments to permit reduction of the whole function application. Thus, there can be no evaluated sub-expression to share. For example, suppose that in some sub-expression there are several applications of $+\ x$ to different argument expressions containing the variable y which is less free than x. Then if x is bound to the constant 2 at run-time, the mfe $+\ 2$ cannot be evaluated and so its sharing achieves no gain in efficiency.

Another possibility might be to ensure that any mfe which is a variable, v say, does not occur in any of the other mfe's of the expression, E say, being lifted by application of the function *mfelift*. This can be easily implemented, as noted in Section 13.3.1, at the expense of searching E for v when v has been identified as an mfe; at least this is faster than searching for an arbitrary mfe, however. In this way, if $e_k = x$, then it cannot occur in the expression $\beta\, e_1 \ldots e_{k-1}$, and so the elimination can be performed.

13.3.4 General λ-lifting and refined super-combinators

At the end of the previous section, we noticed a conflict between two desirable features of a super-combinator implementation: allowing the possibility of sharing, i.e. full laziness, and the elimination of redundant combinators. However, it is often the case that there is no need to optimize for full laziness: those sub-expressions which can be shared are sub-expressions of mfe's and these can be evaluated only after they have had their free variables instantiated, i.e. after an application. Thus, if a function is never partially applied there is no need to be concerned with sharing at all.

We can generalize the simple λ-lifting technique described in Section 13.1 so that several nested λ-abstractions can be transformed together to form a single new combinator; we call this transformation general λ-lifting. A λ-abstraction which is not the body of another immediately enclosing λ-abstraction is transformed into the same combinator by both simple and general λ-lifting. However, a λ-abstraction which is the body of another is transformed by general λ-lifting into a combinator which has an additional parameter corresponding to the bound variable of the outer λ-abstraction, and this extends inductively to an arbitrary nesting of λ-abstractions. A λ-abstraction of m arguments (i.e. m nested λ-abstractions) that contains occurrences of n distinct free variables is transformed into a combinator with $n + m$ parameters, applied to the n free variables as arguments. For the sake of brevity, we denote the nested λ-abstraction $\lambda x_1.\lambda x_2 \ldots \lambda x_m.E$ where E is not a λ-abstraction, by $\lambda x_1 \ldots x_m.E$. The general 'lifting' function, which we denote by *glift*, therefore has the following definition:

$glift(\ E\ ) = E$ if E is in applicative form

$glift(\ \lambda x_1 \ldots x_m.E\ ) = \alpha\ v_1 \ldots v_n$ if E is an applicative expression and $\{v_1, \ldots, v_n\} = FV(\ E\ ) \setminus \{x_1, \ldots, x_m\}$

where α is defined by $\alpha\ v_1 \ldots v_n\ x_1 \ldots x_m = E$

$glift(\ \lambda x_1 \ldots x_m.E\ ) = glift(\ \lambda x_1 \ldots x_m.\ glift(\ E\ )\ )$ if E is neither an applicative expression nor a λ-abstraction

$glift(\ E_1\ E_2\ ) = glift(\ E_1\ )\ glift(\ E_2\ )$ for λ-expressions E_1, E_2

$glift(\ (\ E\ )\ ) = (\ glift(\ E\ )\ )$ for λ-expression E

Now let us apply general λ-lifting to our *element* example:

$$element = Y(\ \lambda el\ n\ s.cond\ (\ =\ n\ 1\ )\ (\ hd\ s\ )\ (\ el\ (\ -\ n\ 1\ )\ (\ tl\ s\ )\ )\ )$$

This involves a triple-nested λ-abstraction, so that

$$glift(\ element\ ) = Y\alpha$$

where

$$\alpha\ el\ n\ s = cond\ (\ =\ n\ 1\ )\ (\ hd\ s\ )\ (\ el\ (\ -\ n\ 1\ )\ (\ tl\ s\ )\ )$$

This involves one, more complex, combinator than the two obtained under the (optimized) super-combinator transformation, the gain in efficiency being obtained at the expense of loss of sharing potential, which may or may not be desirable. It should be noted here, however, that simple lambda lifting together with the freest first ordering of combinator parameters is equivalent to general lambda lifting. Although several combinators are generated by simple lambda lifting (one for each bound variable) all but the first one is redundant under this parameter ordering.

A more general example is a variant *sqelement*, of the *element* function which computes the square of a selected element:

$$sqelement = Y(\lambda el\ n\ s.cond\ (=n\ 1)\ ((\lambda x.*\ x\ x)\ (hd\ s))\ (el\ (-\ n\ 1)\ (tl\ s)))$$

Now

$$glift(\lambda x.*\ x\ x) = \alpha \quad \text{where } \alpha\ x = *\ x\ x$$

and so

$$\begin{aligned} glift(\ sqelement\ ) &= Y\ glift\ (\lambda el\ n\ s.cond\ (=n\ 1)\ (\alpha\ (hd\ s))\\ &\quad (el\ (-\ n\ 1)\ (tl\ s)))\\ &= Y\beta \end{aligned}$$

where

$$\beta\ el\ n\ s = cond\ (=n\ 1)\ (\alpha\ (hd\ s))\ (el\ (-\ n\ 1)\ (tl\ s))$$

and

$$\alpha\ x = *\ x\ x$$

Although the super-combinator approach suffers the disadvantages indicated above if sharing is not required, it does still possess certain other advantages. For example, it may generate fewer parameters in certain situations through lifting mfe's rather than variables. Lambda lifting and translating into super-combinators represent two extremes in the compilation of expressions into CAF with different objectives; namely to minimize the number of combinators and to maximize sharing respectively. However, some partial applications of a lambda abstraction may be shared whereas others may not. For example, in the expression

$$\text{let } f = \lambda x.\lambda y.\lambda z.E \text{ in } g\ (f\ 2\ 3)\ (f\ 2\ 5\ 7)$$

where g is some function, the partial application $f\ 2$ is shared but neither $f\ 2\ 3$ nor $f\ 2\ 5$ is shared.

This leads to the idea of *refined* super-combinators, which are generated by abstracting maximal free sub-expressions from a number of nested λ-abstractions at the same time. This technique is, of course, the extension of the general λ-lifting transformation which is analogous to the extension of the simple λ-lifting transformation to the super-combinator scheme. It therefore requires that just one defining equation of the function *glift* be changed to give the extended definition – of the function *mfeglift*, say – as follows:

$$mfeglift(\ \lambda x_1 \ldots x_k.E\ ) = \alpha\ m_1 \ldots m_n$$

if E is an applicative expression with

$$mfes(\ \lambda x_1 \ldots x_k.E\ ) = \{\ m_1\ , \ldots , m_n\}$$

where α is defined by

$$\alpha\ p_1 \ldots p_n\, x_1 \ldots x_k = [\ p_1\ /\ m_1, \ldots , p_n\ /\ m_n\ ]E$$

The CAF generated by applying *mfeglift* to a lambda expression produces the smallest number of super-combinators which preserves full laziness provided we know that no partial application of the abstraction can ever become shared.

13.4 Categorical combinators

The idea of a functional language without variables was put forward by Backus (1978), who introduced the language called FP, introduced in Chapter 5. We have also seen the advantages of implementations which do not represent variables explicitly: expressions are applicative, and their evaluation can be prescribed by sets of transformation rules for the applications of operators which are either combinators or primitive functions. In fact FP was proposed primarily as the basis of a programming language for practical use, the claim being that it provided a natural means for specifying solutions. Moreover, the formal, variable-free definition of the language induces a 'functional algebra' which simplifies formal reasoning about programs and facilitates optimization through program transformation, as we discuss in Chapter 18.

FP has a fairly conventional set of primitive functions, and a small number of primitive *functionals* – the 'program forming operations' (PFOs) introduced in Chapter 5 – which manipulate functions, each defining a new function according to its particular rewrite rules. These functionals too therefore constitute a fixed set of combinators. In this section, we consider initially the first-order subset of FP, and identify informally a set of combinators which is natural for defining functional expressions. From this informal presentation, we turn to results from category theory to define a set of 'categorical combinators' which is complete in the sense that its associated logic is a model of the λ-calculus in the same way as the classical combinatory logic, CL. On the more practical side, it is straightforward to translate any functional language such as Hope into categorical combinator form. In Chapter 18, a description of the translation into FP may be found for first-order functions which use both pattern matching and user-defined compound data types; the extension to categorical combinators and higher-order functions is immediate.

13.4.1 The fixed combinators of FP

FP requires only three primitive functionals, *composition, construction* and *conditional,* together with a representation for *constant* functions, to express first-order recursive functions. The composition functional is precisely the 'compositor' combinator B defined in Chapter 12. The notation of FP is defined in Chapter 5, but in this section we denote a constant function by a 'quote' followed by the constant's name, rather than by an underscore as in the rest of the book. This then conforms with Curien (1986), and for object k, we define $'k\ x = k$ for all objects x.

To enrich FP to accommodate higher-order functions we first introduce the *apply* function, *app*, as an additional primitive. This is defined by $app\langle f, x\rangle = f x$ for function f and object x and we therefore have the rule $(app \circ [f, g])\, x = (f\, x)(g\, x)$ so that *app* is equivalent to the S-combinator.

In fact some form of the primitive function *app* is fundamental in any model of the λ-calculus, and since it has two arguments, the construction functional – or at least a pairing operation – is also a natural primitive. Again, every such model involves pairing in some form or another; for example in CL it takes the rather obscure form of currying. We will find that the above intuition has a sound mathematical basis in the next section.

In fact *app* almost gives us enough power to express any function definable in the λ-calculus, but unfortunately we still cannot express the K-combinator – if we could, we would have the power since we would then be able to represent both S and K, and hence the whole of CL. One possibility is to augment FP with K itself, but this defeats the object of seeking a more natural representation than CL. Instead, we turn to the theory of closed Cartesian categories, and the work of Curien (1986) to provide the new combinator we seek. We will then be in a position to present a formal description of an evaluation mechanism, based on de Bruijn's notation introduced in Chapter 6, which utilizes these theoretical results. The following section may be omitted if the reader is not concerned with the theoretical origins of some of the rewrite rules used for the reduction of categorical combinator expressions. These rules will be found to be quite intuitive anyway.

13.4.2 Categorical combinators (Curien, 1986)

In this section we outline the results from category theory which are necessary for the sequel. A **category**, $\underline{C}$, is a collection of **objects**, $obj(\underline{C})$, such that

(1) Given $A, B \in obj(\underline{C})$, there is a collection of arrows from A to B, denoted by $A \to B$, and if f is in $A \to B$, we say that the **domain** of f is A, and the **codomain** of f is B, or $dom(f) = A$, $cod(f) = B$.

(2) For all objects A, B, C there is a **composition** operation, $\circ$, defined on arrows which is associative, i.e. if f is in $B \to C$ and g is in $A \to B$ then $f \circ g$ is in $A \to C$, and $(f \circ g) \circ h = f \circ (g \circ h)$ for all arrows f, g, h such that $cod(h) = dom(g)$, $cod(g) = dom(f)$.

(3) For each object A, there is an **identity** arrow, id^A in $A \to A$, such that for all arrows f, g with $cod(f) = dom(g) = A$, $id^A \circ f = f$ and $g \circ id^A = g$.

For example, the objects of a category might be sets, and the arrows mappings between those sets. We shall refer to a category defined in this way as a **basic** category.

In a **Cartesian category**, $\underline{C}$, there is a **product** construction, defined as follows.

For all objects A, B, there exists an object $A \times B$ and arrows $Fst^{A,B}$: $A \times B \to A$, $Snd^{A,B} : A \times B \to B$, called **projections**, with the property that for any object C and arrows $f: C \to A$, $g : C \to B$, there exists a *unique* arrow of $C \to A \times B$, denoted by $\langle f, g \rangle$ and called the **pair** of f and g, with the property that $f = Fst \circ \langle f, g \rangle$, $g = Snd \circ \langle f, g \rangle$. (We have dropped the superscripts on Fst and Snd where there is no ambiguity. The angle brackets are not to be confused with the sequence delimiters of FP.)

This is most easily seen in a diagram, such as that in Figure 13.2.

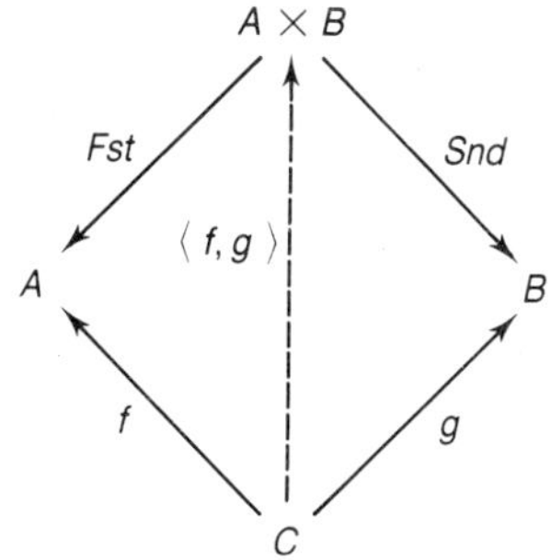

Figure 13.2 The product construction in a Cartesian category.

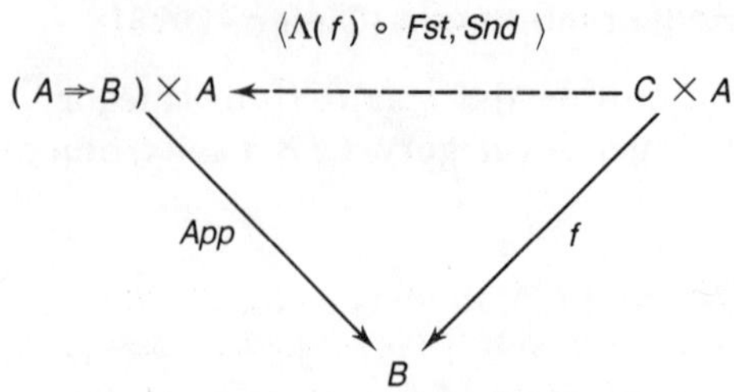

Figure 13.3 The exponential construction in a Cartesian closed category.

The (binary) product of A and B is defined by the triple ($A \times B$, $Fst^{A,B}$, $Snd^{A,B}$), and provides a formal description of the 'construction' of two functions, together with the associated selector functions denoted by 1 and 2, as introduced in the previous section. In particular, it follows that $\langle f, g \rangle \circ h = \langle f \circ h, g \circ h \rangle$ for all arrows h with $cod(h) = C$, and this will be one of the axioms used for reduction in the next section. It is the uniqueness of the product construction which ensures that an heuristic notion of function pairing really is well defined.

The representation of the λ-calculus is completed by introducing two further constructs into Cartesian categories, namely application and currying, which leads to the following definition:

> A **Cartesian closed category** (CCC) is a Cartesian category in which for all objects A, B, there exists an object, $A \Rightarrow B$, and an arrow $App^{A,B}$: $(A \Rightarrow B) \times A \rightarrow B$, called **application**, with the property that for any object C and arrow $f : C \times A \rightarrow B$, there exists a *unique* arrow of $C \rightarrow A \Rightarrow B$, denoted by $\Lambda(f)$, and called **currying** of f, such that $f = App \circ \langle \Lambda(f) \circ Fst, Snd \rangle$.

This is illustrated in Figure 13.3. Composing with $\langle Id^C, g \rangle$ on the right yields $f \circ \langle Id^C, g \rangle = App \circ \langle \Lambda(f), g \rangle$ which is an axiom of the logic we introduce in the next section.

The object $A \Rightarrow B$ represents the **function space** defined on A and B, and the pair ($A \Rightarrow B$, $App^{A,B}$) defines the **exponential** of A and B. The equation satisfied by the unique arrow defining $\Lambda(f)$ implies that for a data item, (x, y) in $C \times A$, $f(x, y) = App(\Lambda(f)\, x, y) = \Lambda(f)\, x\, y$, which is the usual definition of currying. Again, it is the uniqueness of the exponential which ensures that the heuristic notion of currying really is well defined.

The two uniqueness properties given above for products and exponentials are respectively equivalent to the following two equations, where f is any appropriately typed arrow:

$\langle Fst \circ f, Snd \circ f \rangle = f$ (surjective pairing) (since $Fst \circ \langle Fst \circ f, Snd \circ f \rangle = Fst \circ f$, and similarly for Snd) or equivalently $\langle Fst, Snd \rangle = id$

and

$$\Lambda(App \circ \langle f \circ Fst, Snd \rangle) = f \qquad \text{(surjective currying)}$$

(since $\Lambda(f') = \Lambda(App \circ \langle \Lambda(f') \circ Fst, Snd \rangle)$ and we let $f = \Lambda(f')$).

A further equation may be derived by expanding $f \circ g$ first as $\Lambda(App \circ \langle f \circ Fst, Snd \rangle) \circ g$, and then as $\Lambda(App \circ \langle f \circ g \circ Fst, Snd \rangle)$, where f and g are any appropriately typed arrows. Now, by the rules for products, $\langle f \circ Fst, Snd \rangle \circ \langle g \circ Fst, Snd \rangle = \langle f \circ g \circ Fst, Snd \rangle$, and so we deduce that $\Lambda(App \circ \langle f \circ Fst, Snd \rangle) \circ g = \Lambda(App \circ \langle f \circ Fst, Snd \rangle \circ \langle g \circ Fst, Snd \rangle)$. Appealing to uniqueness, we then obtain

$$\Lambda(f) \circ g = \Lambda(f \circ \langle g \circ Fst, Snd \rangle)$$

for all appropriately typed f, g. In fact this equation provides an alternative definition of the exponential, and is an immediate consequence of the adjunction theorems of category theory.

The equations given in this section facilitate a purely equational description of CCCs. In the next section, we will use them to define the rewrite rules for expression reduction in terms of categorical combinatory logic (CCL), analogously to the classical CL, defined in terms of the rules for S and K. To summarize, the categorical framework provides the mathematical rigour needed for a formal model of the λ-calculus which is defined in terms of natural constructs, expressed in variable-free form as combinators – as categorical combinators.

13.4.3 Expression evaluation using de Bruijn's notation and CCL

The mechanism presented in this section evaluates expressions written in de Bruijn's notation using categorical combinators as primitives, CCL as the basis for the rewrite rules, and an explicit environment. The reader might well sense the flavour of the SECD machine returning; the analogy will become stronger as this section develops, culminating in the definition of the categorical abstract machine in terms of state transitions. Before continuing, the reader should be sure to fully understand de Bruijn's notation for the λ-calculus as described in Chapter 6.

In de Bruijn's notation, variables are referred to by their 'freeness' relative to the level of the λ-body in which they occur. Consequently, during the evaluation of any expression, the lowest variable number is always zero, referring to the bound variable, and the numbers increase up to the maximum value which is the current level of nesting of the λ-body involved in the reduction. An environment which associates a value with each free variable can therefore be implemented as a simple list, which we take to have its head at the right. Thus an environment, ρ, takes the form $(\ldots (( ), v_n) \ldots, v_0)$, where v_i is the value of variable number i. That is, $( )$ is the empty environment, and if ρ is an environment, so is (ρ, d) where d is a data value.

The evaluation of a de Bruijn λ-expression is therefore given by the following semantic function, *eval*, which maps expression – environment pairs to values and is defined as follows:

$$
\begin{aligned}
&eval[\![L0, (\rho, d)]\!] &&= d \\
&eval[\![L(n+1), (\rho, d)]\!] &&= eval[\![Ln, \rho]\!] \\
&eval[\![k, \rho]\!] &&= k \qquad \text{(where } k \text{ is a constant)} \\
&eval[\![MN, \rho]\!] &&= eval[\![M, \rho]\!]\, eval[\![N, \rho]\!] \\
&eval[\![\lambda.M, \rho]\!]\, d &&= eval[\![M, (\rho, d)]\!]
\end{aligned}
$$

To begin with, three combinators are introduced:

(1) S which is equivalent to the usual distributor combinator;
(2) Λ i.e. 'curry' as discussed above;
(3) $'$ i.e. 'quote' which denotes constant functions.

To these are added the infinite set of combinators $\{ n! \mid n \geq 0 \}$ which are used to index the environment. The translation function, *comb*, is then defined by:

$$
\begin{aligned}
&comb(Ln) &&= n! \\
&comb(k) &&= {'k} \qquad \text{(where } k \text{ is a constant object)} \\
&comb(MN) &&= S(comb(M), comb(N)) \\
&comb(\lambda.M) &&= \Lambda (comb(M))
\end{aligned}
$$

and the reduction rules for the combinators are:

$$
\begin{aligned}
&0!\,(x, y) &&= y \\
&(n+1)!\,(x, y) &&= n!\; x \\
&('x)\; y &&= x \\
&S(x, y)\; z &&= x\, z\, (y\, z) \\
&\Lambda(x)\; y\; z &&= x\, (y, z)
\end{aligned}
$$

Now, we can represent all of these combinators in terms of the categorical combinators introduced in the last section, whereupon all of the machinery of CCCs will become available to us, for example in optimization and proving equivalence theorems between alternative sets of reduction rules. Thus we may regard $S(x, y)$ as an abbreviation for $App \circ \langle x, y \rangle$ and $n!$ as an abbreviation for $Snd \circ Fst^n$ (where $Fst^0 = Id$, the identity function and $Fst^{n+1} = Fst \circ Fst^n$), and we arrive at the following axioms of combinatory logic:

$$
\begin{array}{lll}
(\,ass\,) & (\,x \circ y\,)\,z & = x\,(\,y\,z\,) \\
(\,fst\,) & Fst\,(\,x, y\,) & = x \\
(\,snd\,) & Snd\,(\,x, y\,) & = y \\
(\,dpair\,) & \langle x, y\rangle\,z & = (\,xz, yz\,) \\
(\,d\Lambda) & \Lambda(\,x\,)\,y\,z & = x\,(\,y, z\,) \\
(\,app\,) & App\,(\,x, y\,) & = x\,y \\
(\,quote\,) & (\,'x\,)\,y & = x
\end{array}
$$

Notice that the S-rule is now represented by the three rules *app*, *dpair* and *ass*. We also note that in fact the rule (*quote*) is redundant, since $\Lambda(\,x \circ Snd\,)\,y\,z = (\,x \circ Snd\,)\,(\,y, z\,) = x\,z$ for all x, y, z by ($d\Lambda$), (*ass*) and (*snd*). Thus we may regard $'M$ as an abbreviation of $\Lambda(\,M \circ Snd\,)$, to which it is equal up to η-conversion.

The reduction steps of this categorical combinator expression evaluator are illustrated in the following example, which shows the (normal-order) reduction sequence for

$$M = (\,\lambda x.x\;4\,(\,(\,\lambda x.x\,)\;3\,)\,)\,+$$

In the de Bruijn notation this becomes $M = (\lambda.L0\;4\,(\,(\,\lambda.L0\,)\;3\,)\,)\,+$. We then obtain the combinator form:

$$M' = comb(\,M\,) = S\,(\,\Lambda\,(\,S\,(\,S\,(\,0!, '4\,), S\,(\,\Lambda\,(\,0!\,), '3\,)\,)\,), '+\,)$$

Since M' is a closed expression we apply it to the empty environment giving the reductions as follows:

$$
\begin{array}{ll}
M'(\,) \rightarrow_S & \Lambda(\,S(\,A, B\,)\,)\,(\,)\,(\,'+\,(\,)\,) \\
\multicolumn{2}{l}{\text{where } A = S(\,0!, '4\,) \text{ and } B = S(\,\Lambda(\,0!\,), '3\,)} \\
\rightarrow_\Lambda & S(\,A, B\,)\,C \\
\multicolumn{2}{l}{\text{where } C = (\,(\,), (\,'+\,(\,)\,)\,)} \\
\rightarrow_S & S(\,0!, '4\,)\,C\,(\,S(\,\Lambda(\,0!\,), '3\,)\,C\,) \\
\rightarrow_S & 0!\;C\,(\,'4\;C\,)\,(\,S(\,\Lambda(\,0!\,), '3\,)\,C\,) \\
\rightarrow_{0!} & +\,(\,'4\;C\,)\,(\,S(\,\Lambda(\,0!\,), '3\,)\,C\,) \\
 & \text{since } C \rightarrow_{'} (\,(\,), +\,) \\
\rightarrow_{'} & +\;4\,(\,S(\,\Lambda(\,0!\,), '3\,)\,C\,) \\
\rightarrow_S & +\;4\,(\,\Lambda(\,0!\,)\,C\,(\,'3\;C\,)\,) \\
\rightarrow_\Lambda & +\;4\,(\,0!\,(\,C, (\,'3\;C\,)\,)\,) \\
\rightarrow_{0!} & +\;4\,(\,'3\;C\,) \\
\rightarrow_{'} & +\;4\;3 \\
\rightarrow_+ & 7
\end{array}
$$

The rules given above in fact define the **weak categorical combinatory logic**, WCCL, which is weak in the sense that it cannot reduce all λ-expressions (or more precisely the result of applying *comb* to their de Bruijn versions) to their normal form. This can be seen by considering the λ-expression $Q = \lambda x.(\lambda x.x)\, x$ which is in WHNF and which has the normal form $\lambda x.x$. The de Bruijn version of Q is $\lambda.(\lambda.L0)\, L0$, and its combinator form is $Q' = comb(\lambda.(\lambda.L0)\, L0) = \Lambda(S(\Lambda(0!), 0!))$. Thus there is no weak reduction rule which can be applied to $Q'\,()$, since the $d\Lambda$-rule requires two arguments for its application. The same will be true of all WHNFs of the form $\lambda x.e$. In general, WCCL cannot evaluate through lambdas, and moreover depends on application of its expressions to an environment to drive the reduction process.

There is, however, a *strong* categorical combinatory logic, CCL, which takes as its axioms results from the theory of Cartesian closed categories, as discussed in the previous section. These axioms are essentially a more abstract form of the rules of WCCL, in the sense that applications of functions to variables representing environments are replaced by compositions with other function variables. This requires the introduction of an identity function, *Id*, together with two axioms corresponding to its composition on the left and on the right. This representation would still be equivalent to WCCL, and to provide full normal-order evaluation we add two axioms to model general β-reduction, which are properties of the exponential construction discussed in the previous section. The axioms of CCL are therefore the following, where the labels now begin with a capital letter and the origin of each rule in either basic categories, Cartesian categories or CCCs is indicated by C, CC and CCC respectively.

(*IdL*)	$Id \circ x$	$= x$	(C)
(*IdR*)	$x \circ Id$	$= x$	(C)
(*Ass*)	$(x \circ y) \circ z$	$= x \circ (y \circ z)$	(C)
(*Fst*)	$Fst \circ \langle x, y \rangle$	$= x$	(CC)
(*Snd*)	$Snd \circ \langle x, y \rangle$	$= y$	(CC)
(*DPair*)	$\langle x, y \rangle \circ z$	$= \langle x \circ z, y \circ z \rangle$	(CC)
($D\Lambda$)	$\Lambda(x) \circ y$	$= \Lambda(x \circ \langle y \circ Fst, Snd \rangle)$	(CCC)
(*Beta*)	$App \circ \langle \Lambda(x), y \rangle$	$= x \circ \langle Id, y \rangle$	(CCC)

The reduction of the above expression $M = (\lambda x.x\; 4\; ((\lambda x.x)\; 3))\; +$, which has the combinator form

$$\begin{aligned} M' &= App \circ \langle \Lambda(X), \Lambda(+ \circ Snd) \rangle \\ \text{where } X &= App \circ \langle Y, Z \rangle \\ Y &= App \circ \langle Snd, \Lambda(4 \circ Snd) \rangle \\ Z &= App \circ \langle \Lambda(Snd), \Lambda(3 \circ Snd) \rangle \end{aligned}$$

now proceeds by direct rewriting, without the application to the empty environment, beginning as follows:

$$
\begin{aligned}
M' &\rightarrow_{Beta} X \circ \langle Id, \Lambda(+ \circ Snd)\rangle \\
&\rightarrow_{Beta} App \circ \langle Y, Snd \circ \langle Id, \Lambda (3 \circ Snd)\rangle\rangle \circ \langle Id, \Lambda(+ \circ Snd)\rangle \\
&\rightarrow_{Snd} App \circ \langle Y, \Lambda(3 \circ Snd)\rangle \circ \langle Id, \Lambda(+ \circ Snd)\rangle \\
&\rightarrow_{DPair} App \circ \langle Y \circ \langle Id, \Lambda(+ \circ Snd)\rangle, \Lambda(3 \circ Snd) \circ \langle Id, \Lambda(+ \circ Snd)\rangle\rangle \\
&\rightarrow_{D\Lambda} App \circ \langle Y \circ \langle Id, \Lambda(+ \circ Snd)\rangle, \Lambda(3 \circ Snd \circ \langle\langle Id, \Lambda(+ \circ Snd)\rangle \circ \\
&\qquad Fst, Snd \rangle)\rangle \\
&\rightarrow_{Ass, Snd} App \circ \langle Y \circ \langle Id, \Lambda(+ \circ Snd)\rangle, \Lambda(3 \circ Snd)\rangle \\
&\rightarrow_{DPair, Snd} App \circ \langle App \circ \langle \Lambda(+ \circ Snd), \Lambda(4 \circ Snd) \circ \langle Id, \Lambda(+ \circ Snd)\rangle\rangle, \\
&\qquad \Lambda(3 \circ Snd)\rangle \\
&\rightarrow_{D\Lambda, Ass, Snd} App \circ \langle App \circ \langle \Lambda(+ \circ Snd), \Lambda(4 \circ Snd)\rangle, \Lambda(3 \circ Snd)\rangle \\
&\rightarrow_{Beta} App \circ \langle + \circ Snd \circ \langle Id, \Lambda(4 \circ Snd)\rangle , \Lambda(3 \circ Snd)\rangle \\
&\rightarrow_{Snd} App \circ \langle + \circ \Lambda(4 \circ Snd), \Lambda(3 \circ Snd)\rangle \\
&= S(+ \circ '4, '3) = S(S('+,'4), '3) = comb(+ \; 4 \; 3)
\end{aligned}
$$

Moreover, now the expression Q with combinator form $Q' = \Lambda (App \circ \langle \Lambda (Snd), Snd\rangle)$ may also be reduced:

$$Q' \rightarrow_{Beta} \Lambda(Snd \circ \langle Id, Snd\rangle) \rightarrow_{Snd} \Lambda(Snd)$$

Thus the strong rules reduce Q' to the CCL form of the λ-expression $\lambda x.x$, which also results from β-reduction of the original λ-expression Q. However, as we noted above, Q is in WHNF and so could not be reduced by the weak rules.

In fact Curien (1986) shows that WCCL and CCL are equivalent in the sense that every WCCL-reduction has an equivalent CCL-reduction, and the converse is also true up to a form of η-reduction. In other words, CCL $\vdash$ WCCL and WCCL+$\eta \vdash$ CCL.

13.4.4 The categorical abstract machine

The systems of combinatory logic defined in the previous section provide a basis for the evaluation of λ-expressions in much the same way as did the combinators *S*, *K*, *I*, *B*, *C* in Chapter 12. Similarly, the implementation may be based on graph reduction, by defining the graph transformation rules corresponding to applications of each of the combinators $\circ$, *Fst*, *Snd*, *Id*, *App*, Λ, $\langle , \rangle$. However, the representation of λ-expressions in categorical combinator form is not only 'natural' in the sense that the meaning of such expressions is clear, but also in that the primitive operations required of an evaluation mechanism correspond quite closely to the particular combinators forming an expression. An evaluator is therefore most easily defined in terms of the transitions undergone by some state, representing the partially evaluated expression, as an expression is scanned. This is indeed the basis of the categorical abstract machine (CAM), (Curien, 1986; Mauny and Suarez, 1986), the specification of which is reminiscent of the SECD machine considered in Chapter 10.

The state of the CAM is a triple, (T, C, S), where T is a term which represents the part of an expression currently being manipulated (corresponding to the elements near the top of the stack of the SECD machine), C is a categorical combinator code-sequence (corresponding to the control string of the SECD machine) and S is a stack (corresponding to a combination of the stack and the dump of the SECD machine). Code is represented in the form given in Section 13.4.3 for the weak CCL, with the exception of compositions, $x \circ y$, for function-valued expressions x, y. In the evaluation of the application $(x \circ y)\, v$, for expression v, x must be applied to $y\, v$, so that since expressions are scanned from left to right, the application must be compiled into the form $v\,(y\, x)$; i.e. the composed functions must be reversed. Therefore, the translation function, *comb*, for translating λ-expressions into CAM-code now becomes:

$$
\begin{array}{lll}
comb(\,Ln\,) & = Fst^n\, Snd & \\
comb(\,k\,) & = {}'k & \text{(where } k \text{ is a data-constant)} \\
comb(\,f\,) & = \Lambda(\,Snd\ f\,) & \text{(where } f \text{ is a primitive function)} \\
comb(\,MN\,) & = \langle comb(\,M\,), comb(\,N\,)\rangle\ app & \\
comb(\,\lambda.M\,) & = \Lambda(\,comb(\,M\,)\,) &
\end{array}
$$

The new postfix operator, *app*, now has a lower-case initial letter to distinguish it from *App*.

We can now formally describe the operation of the weak CAM in terms of the state transition function, $\Rightarrow : (\,term \times code \times stack\,) \rightarrow (\,term \times code \times stack\,)$ defined in infix form as follows:

$$
\begin{array}{llll|llll}
(\,(\,s, t\,) & Fst :: C & S &) \Rightarrow & (\,s & C & S &) \\
(\,(\,s, t\,) & Snd :: C & S &) \Rightarrow & (\,t & C & S &) \\
(\,s & 'c :: C & S &) \Rightarrow & (\,c & C & S &) \\
(\,s & \Lambda(\,C\,) :: C1 & S &) \Rightarrow & (\,(\,C\,s\,) & C1 & S &) \\
(\,s & \langle :: C & S &) \Rightarrow & (\,s & C & s :: S &) \\
(\,t & , :: C & s :: S &) \Rightarrow & (\,s & C & t :: S &) \\
(\,t & \rangle :: C & s :: S &) \Rightarrow & (\,(\,s, t\,) & C & S &) \\
(\,(\,C\,s, t\,) & app :: C1 & S &) \Rightarrow & (\,(\,s, t\,) & C \langle\rangle C1 & S &) \\
(\,m & + :: C & S &) \Rightarrow & (\,+\,m & C & S &) \\
(\,(\,m, n\,) & + :: C & S &) \Rightarrow & (\,add(\,m, n\,) & C & S &)
\end{array}
$$

where *add* denotes the δ-rule for integer addition. It will be observed that these transition rules implement applicative-order evaluation in that the argument(s) of a function are evaluated before the function is applied. This is solely for the sake of efficiency, however, and not an inherent property of the underlying theory.

The symbol ⟨⟩ denotes *append*, so that in the third last equation the code sequences C and $C1$ are joined together. The last equation gives a rule for applying the primitive function '*plus*'; there clearly must be at least one additional equation for each new primitive function introduced. The operation of the CAM is illustrated with the weak CCL reduction of the expression M given above, applied to the empty environment. The code generated for M is

$$M'' = \langle \Lambda\,(\,\langle A, B\rangle\, app\,),\, \Lambda(\,Snd\, +\,)\,\rangle\, app$$
$$\text{where } A = \langle Snd, '4\rangle\, app \quad \text{and} \quad B = \langle \Lambda(\,Snd\,), '3\rangle\, app$$

The machine enters the following sequence of states. (For notational convenience the stack items are separated by semi-colons or by spaces when there is no ambiguity. Therefore, the code sequence $a\ b\ c\ d$ is shorthand for $a :: (\,b :: (\,c :: (\,d :: nil\,)\,)\,)$. The empty sequence is written [ ].)

( )	⟨Λ (⟨*A*, *B*⟩ *app*), Λ(*Snd* +)⟩ *app*	[ ]
( )	Λ (⟨*A*, *B*⟩ *app*), Λ(*Snd* +)⟩ *app*	( )
⟨*A*, *B*⟩ *app* ( )	, Λ(*Snd* +)⟩ *app*	( )
( )	Λ(*Snd* +) ⟩ *app*	⟨*A*, *B*⟩ *app* ( )
+″	⟩ *app*	⟨*A*, *B*⟩ *app* ( )

where +″ = *Snd* + ( )

(⟨*A*, *B*⟩ *app* ( ), +″)	*app*	[ ]
(( ), +″)	⟨*A*, *B*⟩ *app*	[ ]
(( ), +″)	*A*, *B* ⟩ *app*	(( ), +″)
(( ), +″)	*Snd*, '4 ⟩ *app*, *B* ⟩ *app*	(( ), +″); (( ), +″)
+″	, '4 ⟩ *app*, *B* ⟩ *app*	(( ), +″); (( ), +″)
(( ), +″)	'4 ⟩ *app*, *B* ⟩ *app*	+″ ; (( ), +″)
4	⟩ *app*, *B* ⟩ *app*	+″ ; (( ), +″)
(*Snd* + ( ), 4)	*app*, *B* ⟩ *app*	(( ), +″)
(( ), 4)	*Snd* +, *B* ⟩ *app*	(( ), +″)
4	+, *B* ⟩ *app*	(( ), +″)
+4	, *B* ⟩ *app*	(( ), +″)
(( ), +″)	*B* ⟩ *app*	+4
(( ), +″)	Λ(*Snd*), '3 ⟩ *app* ⟩ *app*	(( ), +″); +4
Snd (( ), +″)	, '3 ⟩ *app* ⟩ *app*	(( ), +″); +4
(( ), +″)	'3 ⟩ *app* ⟩ *app*	*Snd* (( ), +″); + 4
3	⟩ *app* ⟩ *app*	*Snd* (( ), +″); + 4
(*Snd* (( ), +″), 3)	*app* ⟩ *app*	+4
((( ), +″), 3)	*Snd* ⟩ *app*	+4
3	⟩ *app*	+4
(+ 4, 3)	*app*	[ ]
(4, 3)	+	[ ]
7	[ ]	[ ]

We have described a machine which operates very simply by applying the axioms of WCCL as rewrite rules. The strong rules could also have been used as the basis for a similar system, but even in the weak version they have an important role in the optimization of certain code sequences. For example, the Beta rule provides an optimization for auxiliary expressions such as **let** $x = N$ **in** M, which should not be compiled as $(\lambda x.M)N$ since this would be implemented by first constructing a closure and then immediately applying it. The details may be found in Cousineau *et al.* (1985).

We have not mentioned recursion, this being handled in ways similar to those given in Chapter 10 for the SECD machine, for example using the Y-combinator. A neat optimization is given in Mauny and Suarez (1986) which employs 'cyclic environments', resembling the method described in Chapter 9 for representing environments in an interpreter. We have in a sense completed the circle of environment-based and copy-based implementations discussed in the introduction to Part II.

13.5 Enhancements to the CAM

The operation of the CAM described in terms of state transitions in the previous section may be made more efficient in a number of ways for the purposes of practical implementation of functional languages. In particular, certain commonly occurring rewrite sequences may be represented by new rules and it may be shown that other existing rules will then never be applied in practical situations. In addition, the way the environment is accessed through the combinators *Fst* and *Snd* is inefficient, and although the 'quote rule' was shown to be technically redundant, its alternative involves three rewrites rather than one.

In the next section we give Lins' optimizations (Lins, 1986) for the leftmost-outermost reduction of CCL expressions, which restore a direct rule for constant functions, provide more direct access to the environment, combine certain rules into a new rule and eliminate rules which become redundant. This results in a new compilation function and set of rewrite rules which are listed in Section 13.5.2.

13.5.1 The optimized set of rules

The first optimization simply restores the quote rule for constants in its strong form as follows:

$$'c \circ x = 'c \qquad \text{where } c \text{ is a constant object}$$

Each function defined on constants will have its own laws, as we saw in the previous section. For example in the case of integer addition we would have the extra law:

$$App \circ \langle App \circ \langle add, x \rangle , y \rangle = x + y$$

For the three other optimizations, we need to distinguish between those CCL expressions which are direct translations of λ-expressions and those which are not – called **λ-equivalent** and **intermediate** expressions respectively. Intermediate expressions arise in the rewriting of CCL expressions.

In a λ-equivalent expression, the combinators *Fst* and *Snd* are only used to represent variables, and for a variable with level number $n \geq 0$ we write

$$n^* = (\ldots((Snd \circ Fst) \circ Fst) \circ \ldots \circ Fst)$$

in which there are n occurrences of *Fst*. By checking the interactions between such variables and the set of rules, it may be shown that the rules (*Fst*) and (*Snd*) may be replaced by

$$n^* \circ \langle x, y \rangle = (n - 1)^* \circ x \qquad (n > 0)$$
$$0^* \circ \langle x, y \rangle = y$$

which are the strong versions of the rules originally introduced in Section 13.4.3.

The third optimization combines the rules ($D\Lambda$) and (*Beta*) by noting that

$$App \circ \langle \Lambda(x) \circ y, z \rangle = x \circ \langle y, z \rangle$$

by successively applying the rules ($D\Lambda$), (*Beta*), (*Ass*), (*Dpair*), (*Ass*), (*Fst*), (*IdR*), (*Snd*).

We may therefore introduce this rule into the rewriting system – saving seven rewrites every time it is applied. Moreover, it can actually replace ($D\Lambda$) for all practical purposes. This claim is justified by the observation that in practice expressions evaluate to *base types*, i.e. to values which are neither functions nor contain functions as embedded subexpressions. Thus, for each Λ in a CCL expression there must also be a corresponding *App* which enables it to be removed, since there are no Λs in the fully rewritten result. It therefore follows that whenever a subexpression $\Lambda(x) \circ y$ can be rewritten, it must occur in a (sub-)expression of the form $App \circ \langle \Lambda(x) \circ y, z \rangle$. Hence we may dispense with the rule ($D\Lambda$).

In a λ-equivalent expression *App* can only appear composed with a pair, and by inspecting the rules involving *App*, it can be seen that *App* either disappears – via (*Beta*) or the new rule just introduced above – or else must be rewritten by (*Ass*) and then (*Dpair*), giving

$$(\, App \circ \langle x, y \rangle \,) \circ z = App \circ \langle x \circ z, y \circ z \rangle$$

Thus *App* always appears composed with a pair in all CCL expressions, and if the expression being reduced is not itself of a product type, the rule (*Dpair*) cannot be applied in any other situation. Thus, denoting $App \circ \langle x, y \rangle$ by $\langle\langle x, y \rangle\rangle$, we may replace (*Dpair*) by the similar rule:

$$\langle\langle x, y \rangle\rangle \circ z = \langle\langle x \circ z, y \circ z \rangle\rangle$$

Finally, it can be shown that the first three rules (*IdL*), (*IdR*) and (*Ass*) can never be applied in the leftmost-outermost reduction of λ-equivalent expressions. This may be proved by showing that their left-hand sides cannot occur in either λ-equivalent expressions (trivial from the compilation function given in the next section) or in the right-hand sides of the other rules (Lins, 1986).

13.5.2 The new compilation function and rules of CCL

We can now define the optimized system for the leftmost-outermost reduction of CCL λ-equivalent expressions of ground, non-product type. Firstly, the compilation function, *comb′*, is defined by:

$$
\begin{aligned}
comb'(\,\lambda.M\,) &= \Lambda(\,comb'(\,M\,)\,)\\
comb'(\,MN\,) &= \langle\langle comb'(\,M\,), comb'(\,N\,)\rangle\rangle\\
comb'(\,Ln\,) &= n^*\\
comb'(\,k\,) &= {}'k \qquad \text{where } k \text{ is a constant}
\end{aligned}
$$

The reduced set of rewrite rules is:

$$
\begin{array}{lll}
(\,\text{Opt.1}\,) & n^* \circ \langle x, y \rangle & = (\,n - 1\,)^* \circ x \qquad (\,n > 0\,)\\
(\,\text{Opt.2}\,) & 0^* \circ \langle x, y \rangle & = y\\
(\,\text{Opt.3}\,) & \langle\langle x, y \rangle\rangle \circ z & = \langle\langle x \circ z, y \circ z \rangle\rangle\\
(\,\text{Opt.4}\,) & \langle\langle \Lambda(\,x\,), y \rangle\rangle & = x \circ \langle Id, y \rangle\\
(\,\text{Opt.5}\,) & \langle\langle \Lambda(\,x\,) \circ y, z \rangle\rangle & = x \circ \langle y, z \rangle\\
(\,\text{Opt.6}\,) & {}'k \circ x & = {}'k \qquad \text{(where } k \text{ is a constant object)}
\end{array}
$$

It may be shown that this set of rules is minimal by considering the reduction of the CCL form of the λ-expression $(\,(\,(\,\lambda x.\lambda y.(\,xy\,)\,)\,(\,\lambda z.c\,)\,)\,u\,)$ where c is a constant. This reduction, which gives result c, involves all of the six rewrite rules and is left as an exercise for the reader.

SUMMARY

- Free variables may be 'lifted' from a lambda expression to produce a constant applicative form (CAF) containing combinators from a variable set.
- The graph transformation rules for each combinator are more complex than for the fixed combinator implementation but must be compiler generated.
- Simple lambda lifting abstracts free variables from lambda bodies; it does not preserve full laziness.
- Translating into super-combinator form abstracts maximal free expressions (mfe's) from lambda bodies and guarantees full laziness.
- The 'freest first' parameter selection order results in the fewest and most complex mfe's, and eliminates the maximum number of redundant parameters and super-combinators.
- General lambda lifting abstracts free variables from nested lambda abstractions, producing fewer combinators; again, however, it does not ensure full laziness.
- Using refined super-combinators produces the smallest number of combinators which preserve full laziness.
- Categorical combinators provide an alternative (fixed) set of combinators resembling the constructs of FP.
- A set of rewrite rules based on categorical combinatory logic reduces the categorical forms of lambda expressions to WHNF and forms the basis of the categorical abstract machine.

EXERCISES

13.1 (a) Use simple lambda lifting to transform the following definition into constant applicative form:

$$mult = Y\lambda m.\lambda x.\lambda y.cond\,(\,=\,x\;1\,)\;y\,(\,m\,(\,-\,x\;1)\;y\,)$$

(b) Explain how your solution to part (a) may cause the same sub-expression to be evaluated more than once. Under what circumstances will this redundancy not arise? Give an example to support your answer.

(c) Derive the super-combinator form of *mult* and explain how this representation overcomes the redundancy of part (b).

(d) Show the graph transformation rules for each of the combinators of part (c) in the style of Figure 13.1.

13.2 Express the function

$$f = \lambda x.\lambda y.cond\ (<x\ y)\ x\ (f(-\ x\ y)\ y)$$

in super-combinator form. What benefits related to sharing are available in this example? Justify your answer.

13.3 Consider the function f with the nested definition:

$$\ldots \textbf{let}\ f\ x_1\ x_2 \ldots x_n = E\ \textbf{in} \ldots$$

for some expression E in which the variables $v_1, v_2, \ldots, v_m$ occur free.

(a) Express this definition of f in the form of a partial application of a combinator and define this combinator.

(b) What are the advantages of this type of translation with regards to the efficiency of higher-order functions?

(c) Under what circumstances is full laziness preserved and what analysis does the compiler have to do in order to detect this?

13.4 Under what conditions is general lambda lifting equivalent to freest-first simple lambda lifting? Give an example in which this is not the case.

13.5 In what sense does a combinator correspond to 'pure code'? What are the implications of this for compiled combinator implementations?

13.6 For the following expressions

(i) $(\lambda f.\lambda x.f\ x\ (+\ 1\ x)) + 2$

(ii) $(\lambda x.\lambda y.\lambda z. *\ (x\ z)\ (x\ (y\ z)))\ (\lambda x.x)\ (\lambda y.-\ y\ 1)\ 4$

(a) translate the expression into the de Bruijn notation;

(b) translate the resulting de Bruijn expression into categorical combinators;

(c) reduce to WHNF the resulting combinator expressions using the axioms of CCL.

13.7 Show that $App \circ \langle \Lambda(x) \circ y, z \rangle = x \circ \langle y, z \rangle$ using the axioms of CCL. Translate the expressions given in the previous question into the optimized CAM code of Section 13.5.

Chapter 14
Dataflow implementations

The principles of operation of most conventional computers are normally described in terms of sequences of instructions which manipulate data, residing in the machine's registers or store, in some way. The execution sequence of instructions is controlled through the program counter, a special register. In more general, abstract terms, such architectures have a computational model defined in terms of control flow, and we have already seen such a model in this book for functional languages. The transition function used to describe the SECD machine in Chapter 10, for example, performs transformations on the machine state given by the 4-tuple (Stack, Environment, Control_string, Dump), the process being driven by the Control_string, whose contents control the state transformations.

In Chapter 11 we looked at an alternative model of computation, namely that of graph reduction, in which the basic expression reduction rules of the lambda calculus are implemented directly on a graphical representation of the expression. The various graph transformations might represent the substitution of an argument for a parameter, as in β-reduction, or the application of a primitive function with built-in rules, as in δ-reduction. The model can be extended to allow fixed or variable combinators, for each of which there will be an associated rule as we saw in the previous two chapters.

An alternative approach to defining a model of computation is to view the data as the dynamic or active entities, which flow amongst a collection of passive transformers that perform the appropriate manipulations whenever sufficient data has arrived. In this way, the operational characteristics of an architecture are specified in terms of the availability of operands for a given set of operators, and the passage of data amongst them. In other words the computational model is defined in terms of *dataflow* rather than control flow or graph reduction and programs are notionally represented by dataflow graphs.

In this chapter, we first describe in Section 14.1 a basic dataflow abstract machine for the evaluation of functional expressions. In this model, an expression is represented by a set of nodes representing operators, together with connecting arcs representing the passage of data between them, organized in a directed acyclic graph. Although we have already seen the use of the DAG to represent functional expressions by graphs in the previous two chapters, its use here is rather different, in that arcs now model the dynamic flow of data items rather than provide (statically) information about the arguments of function applications, data constructors or λ-abstractions. We will also see that the acyclic property is significant, even when handling recursion; having consumed the data on its incoming arcs and sent output on its outgoing arcs, a node can be discarded, and the storage it occupies reclaimed by the garbage collector, on which the unoptimized model would heavily depend. The basic dataflow machine is said to be data-driven, implementing eager evaluation using the call-by-value computation rule. In Section 14.2 we describe how the machine can be modified to yield a demand-driven version which implements lazy evaluation using the call-by-need computation rule. In Section 14.3, we summarize the dataflow model and compare it to the graph reduction model described in Chapter 11.

14.1 Applicative-order functional dataflow

The most natural dataflow implementation for functional languages is *data-driven*, which gives applicative-order semantics, and this is the computational model we consider first.

Functional expressions will be given here in terms of primitive and user-defined functions, rather than the λ-calculus, which has been predominant in the previous implementations we have considered, and are represented by directed acyclic graphs (DAGs) which we call **dataflow graphs**, abbreviated to DFGs. It is assumed that the equivalent of λ-

lifting has been applied, so that all user-defined functions exist at the top level, possibly defined in terms of auxiliary combinators. All function-valued objects will then be represented by partial applications of existing functions. This simplifies considerably the definition of the dataflow implementation, without losing any of the expressive power of the source language, at the expense of a little additional compilation effort.

14.1.1 Dataflow graphs

A DFG is simply a graph in which the nodes represent operators and the arcs between the nodes represent the data dependencies between those operators. In more practical terms the arcs can be viewed as communication links along which the data flows from the output of one operator to the input of the next, as determined by the data dependency. As a simple example here is the DFG for the expression (2 * 3) + (1 * 4).

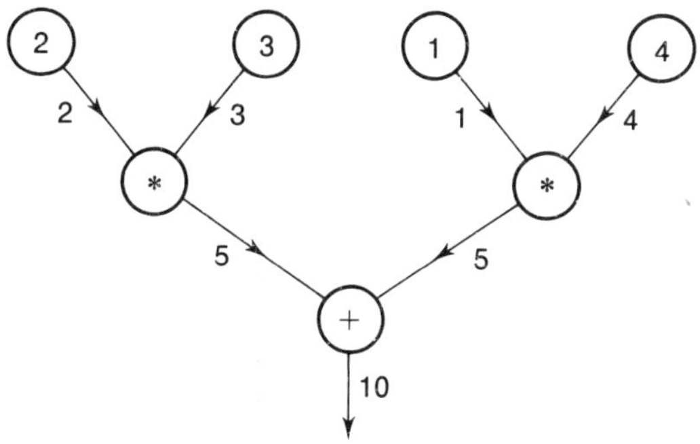

In the dataflow model we describe here there are six different types of node, five of which represent the primitive dataflow operations, the other representing the (infinite) set of values which comprises user-defined functions, primitive functions and constants such as the integers. Associated with each node type is a set of rules that specify on which incoming arcs there must be data available before the associated operator can compute a result (corresponding to the arguments in which the operator is strict) and that define the data values to be placed on the outgoing arcs in terms of these data. For the primitive operators, these rules are equivalent to the delta rules of the lambda calculus. In the case of a *value* node, there are no incoming arcs, and data is always available on its outgoing arc. Nodes representing data constructors, i.e. *constructor* nodes, may be represented as a special node type as in Chapter 11 for graph reduction.

An arc directed from node A to node B represents the passing of the result produced by the operator at node A as an argument to the operator at node B. Any arguments required by node A will have been provided similarly to enable the result to be produced, and will have been sent along the appropriate incoming arcs to A. The graph representing a functional expression is acyclic, so that no arc can transmit data more than once. Therefore, once a node has generated data and placed them on its outgoing arcs, it can never again be activated by data on its incoming arcs, and so can be discarded, the storage occupied being reclaimed by the garbage collector; see Chapter 16. (Of course, one could invent pathological nodes which performed more than one computation using independent inputs and outputs, for example by coalescing two primitive nodes into one. However, we shall assume no such nodes.)

The body, or defining expression, of a user-defined function is represented by a DFG which has one external incoming arc for each of the function's formal parameters, and one external outgoing arc corresponding to its result. The function is referred to in the DFGs of other functions by means of a value node which will be described shortly.

We now define the operations associated with each of the six different node types. This requires minimal explanation in every case other than the *apply* node, which is the one that may involve the substitution of a DFG representing a user-defined function, and the one that must build and apply partial applications, which we again refer to as *closures* for consistency. Having defined all of the constituents of a DFG, we show the DFGs for two functions as examples: the first-order function for computing Fibonacci numbers and the higher-order function map which applies a given function to every element of a given list.

The nodes of a DFG are defined as follows:

(1) A *primitive function* node has one incoming arc for each parameter of the primitive function, and one outgoing arc. When there is data on each of the incoming arcs corresponding to the strict arguments of the function (the ones it requires), the result of applying the function to the arguments with those respective values is placed on the outgoing arc. The node is labelled by its type, together with the identifier of the associated primitive function. The strict arguments and the result of the application are determined by the function's delta rule. For example, the arithmetic function + has two incoming arcs, both of which must have data on them before the application can proceed, whereupon the sum of these data items (assumed to be a number) is placed on its output arc. For example

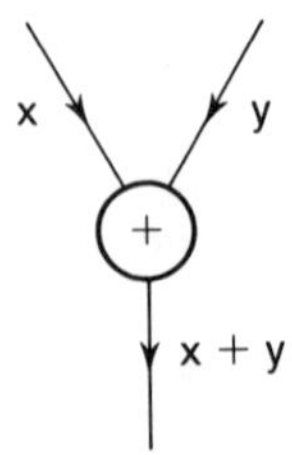

(2) The *copy* node has one incoming arc and any number of outgoing arcs. It is used to duplicate the incoming data, which is always required, so that several operators in a DFG can refer to the same value. For example, as we will see, any argument which appears more than once in a function body must be so duplicated.

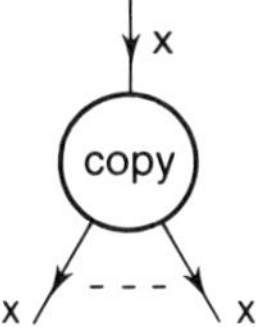

(3) The *value* node has no input arcs, but an associated value which may be either a constant data item (or structure) or a primitive or user-defined function represented as a closure in the manner described below. This value, or some representation of it such as an address or pointer to it, is placed on the single output arc. Here, for example, is the value node for the literal 3:

(The reason for including primitive value nodes is to allow primitives to be partially applied. This will become apparent as we proceed.)

(4) The *switch* node is used to control the flow of data through a DFG according to the Boolean-valued data item on its 'control' arc, which is conventionally drawn on the left-hand side of the node, as shown below. Both of the inputs are required to permit the switch operation to be performed, and there are two outgoing arcs, labelled T and F.

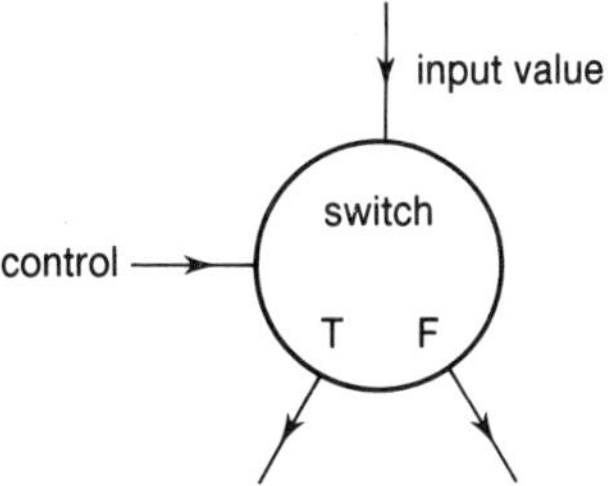

If the value true (more precisely the value representing true) is on the incoming control arc, the value of the data on the second incoming arc, i.e. 'input value', is placed unchanged on the outgoing arc labelled T. Similarly, if the control input is false, the input value is placed on the output arc emanating from F. (We assume that the source program is type-correct so that no other input value is possible.)

(5) The *merge* node is complementary to the switch node. There is again a control input, conventionally the first numbered incoming arc, two further incoming arcs labelled T and F, and a single outgoing arc. Data is required on the control input, and on one of the other inputs depending on the value on the control arc.

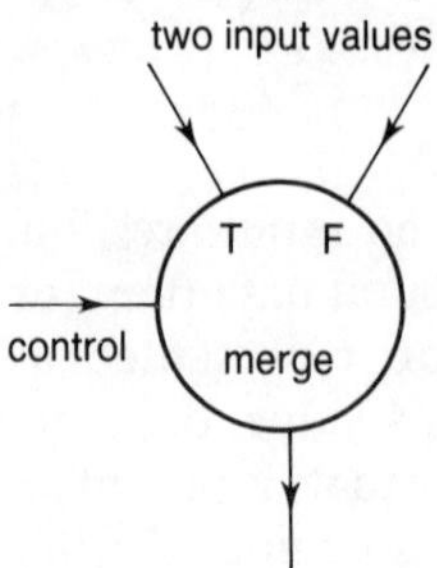

If the control input data has the value true, the value of the data on the incoming arc marked T is placed on the outgoing arc, and similarly if it is false the value on the F arc is placed on the outgoing arc.

(6) The *apply* node performs the most complex operation, this being the dataflow equivalent of β-reduction in the lambda calculus. There are two incoming arcs, the first corresponding to a function to be applied, again conventionally drawn on the left-hand side, and the second corresponding to the argument, as shown below. The data is required on both incoming arcs in the data-driven model, but only on the function input in the lazy, demand-driven model. The result of the application is eventually placed on the outgoing arc, sometimes after substitution of the sub-DFG representing the body of the user-defined function associated with the function input.

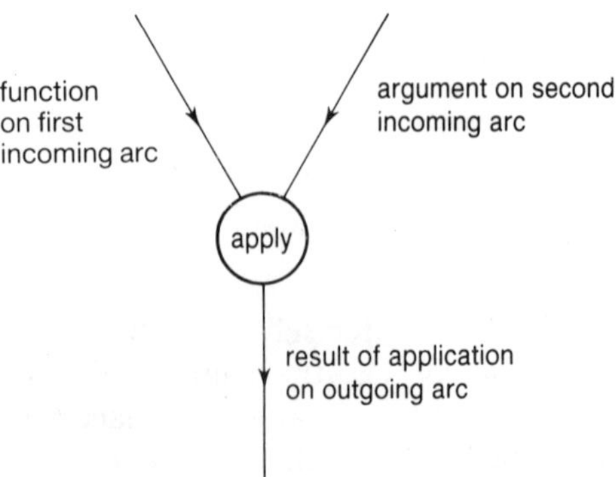

The applied function in this case is always a closure which we shall represent by the pair [B, E], where B is the body of the closure (a DFG) and E is an environment. The environment initially consists of a list of arc identifiers (corresponding to argument identifiers) but these are bound whenever the corresponding argument value is supplied, producing as a result a list of identifier/value pairs of the form $(i_1 = v_1, \ldots, i_n = v_n)$. When all the arcs have associated values the DFG of the closure body can be evaluated by conceptually replacing each input arc by a value node representing the corresponding argument. In this way all closure bodies are static and so can be created at compile-time – only the environment is dynamic, being constructed during expression evaluation. The result of applying a closure is therefore dependent on the *arity* of the closure, which is the number of arguments to which the closure must be applied to provide a binding for each identifier in the environment.

(a) If the closure has an arity of 1, then the application will serve to complete the identifier bindings in the environment, and the function contained in the closure will be applied by placing values on the input arcs of the function's DFG as described above.

(b) If the arity of the closure is greater than 1, then a new closure is returned with arity one less than before, i.e. with one further binding in the environment.

To illustrate the closure application mechanism consider the function (combinator)

```
f x y z = + ( + x y ) z
```

The DFG for the body of f, B_f say, will then be

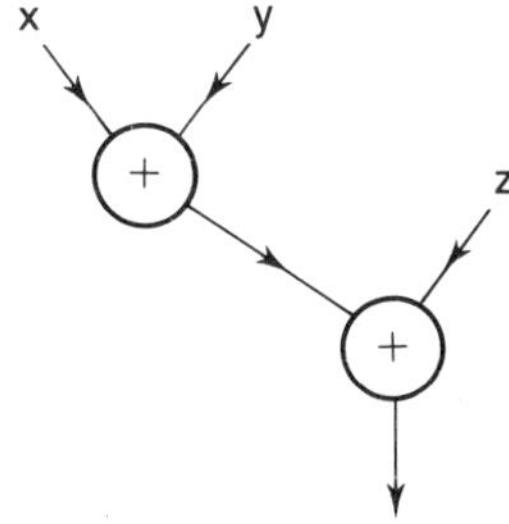

The initial closure for f looks like this:

$$f - [B_f, (x, y, z)]$$

and it is this closure (or rather a pointer to it) which is delivered on the outgoing arc of the value node whose associated value is f.

Partial applications of f are represented by closures in which one or more of the arc identifiers x, y and z are bound to their corresponding values X, Y and Z, say:

$$\begin{aligned} f\,X &= [\,B_f, (x = X, y, z)\,] \\ f\,X\,Y &= [\,B_f, (x = X, y = Y, z)\,] \\ f\,X\,Y\,Z &= [\,B_f, (x = X, y = Y, z = Z)\,] \\ &= +\,(+\,X\,Y)\,Z \end{aligned}$$

The DFG of the expression + (+ X Y) Z is equivalent to the original DFG for B_f with the input arcs x, y and z attached to value nodes containing the values of X, Y and Z. It should be apparent that the closures used here are simply generalizations of the closures used in the SECD machine in that they model partial applications of multiple-argument combinators instead of single-argument curried functions. In short, B_f is not instantiated until all of its argument values are available.

14.1.2 Examples

In order that the basic dataflow mechanism can be more clearly understood we shall now consider two example functions, namely the function fib for computing Fibonacci numbers and map for applying a function to every element of a given list. These functions have the following definitions:

```
fib x     = cond ( < x 2 ) 1 ( + ( fib ( − x 1 ) ) ( fib ( − x 2 ) ) )
map f s  = cond ( null s ) s ( cons ( f ( hd s ) ) ( map f ( tl s ) ) )
```

Their DFGs are shown respectively in Figures 14.1 and 14.2. In these figures each node is given a sequence number providing a convenient means of referring to the various parts of the DFG.

In the case of the function fib, it will be noticed that there is no outgoing arc from the T output position of the switch node numbered 5. This is because that output is not required in the result of the application of fib, which would be the constant 1. If the function were as follows

```
fib x = cond ( < x 2 ) x ( + ( fib ( − x 1 ) ) ( fib ( − x 2 ) ) )
```

then there would be an arc from this T output to the T input of the merge node numbered 17, and no value node, 15.

The function map is an example of a function of more than one argument, and so requires a curried application, involving the construction of a closure and its application.

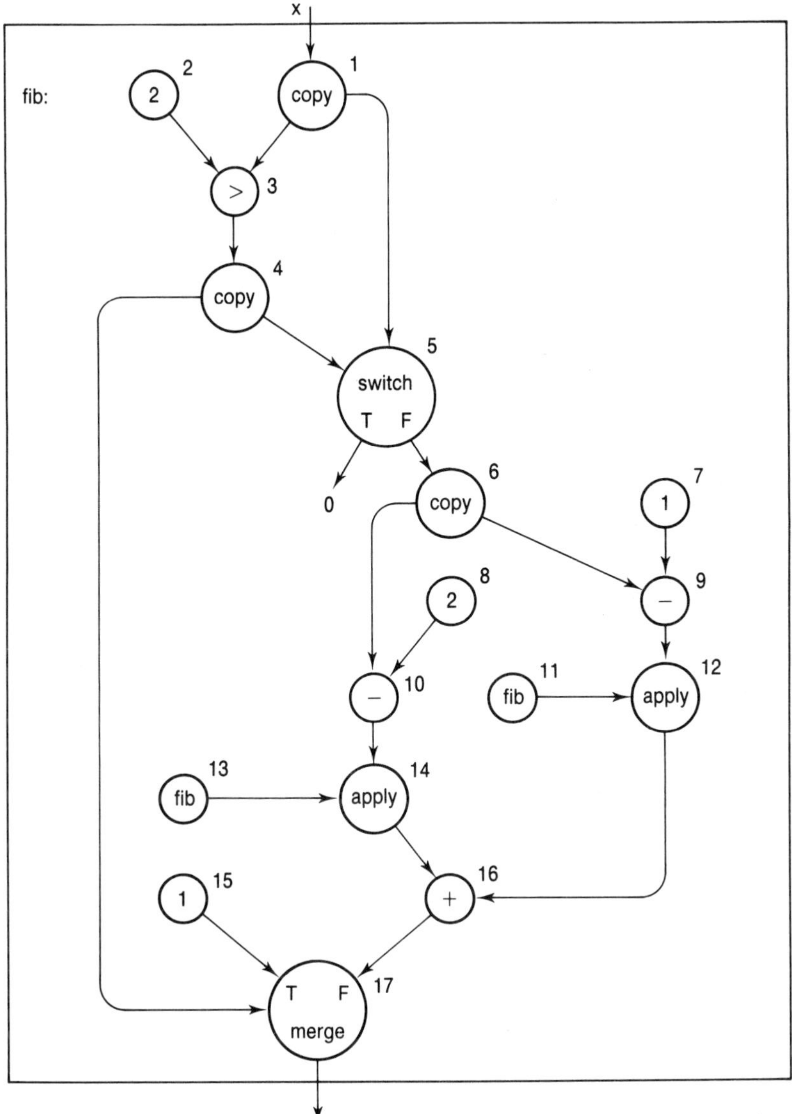

Figure 14.1 The DFG for the function fib.

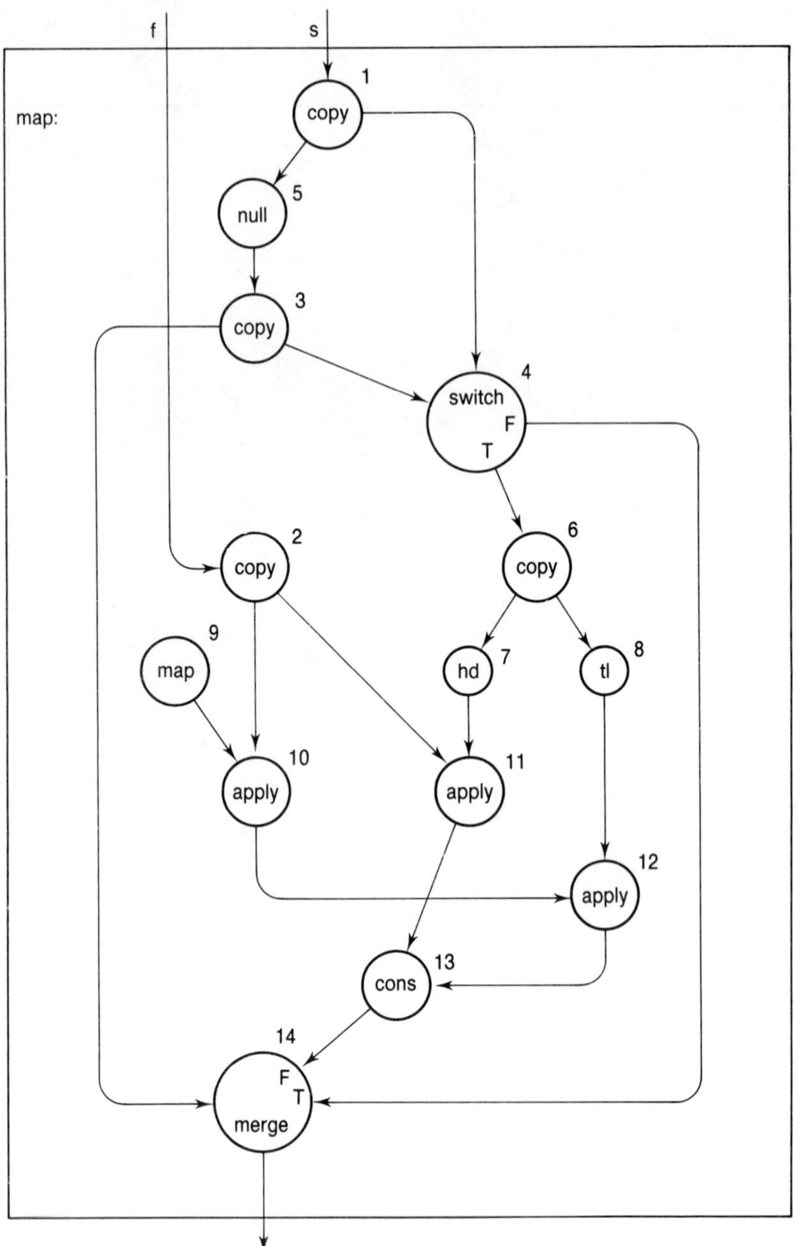

Figure 14.2 The DFG for the function map.

14.1.3 Operation of the data-driven abstract machine

In the abstract machine we now describe, each node in a dataflow graph corresponds to an *instruction* in a dataflow program. A dataflow instruction has four fields, namely:

(1) an *identifier*, for example the sequence number of the associated node in the dataflow graph, or an address in memory in a computer implementation;

(2) an *input list* which represents the sequence of values on the incoming arcs to the corresponding node;

(3) the *node type*, i.e. copy, value, merge, etc.;

(4) an *output list*, each element of which is a pair comprising a node identifier and an input position. In our definition of the DFG, only copy and switch nodes may have more than one element in their output lists, with the possible addition of some as-yet unspecified primitive functions.

Note that it is the output list field (together with any external inputs) which determines the connectivity of the corresponding dataflow graph, by indicating where each output should be sent. We can now write down the dataflow instructions which represent any given dataflow graph – the instruction sequence for the Fibonacci function given earlier is shown in Table 14.1. Those for the map function are just as easily obtained and this is left as an exercise.

Table 14.1 Dataflow instructions for the Fibonacci function.

Identifier	*Input list size*	*Type*	*Output list*
1	1	copy	(3.2, 5.2)
2	0	value : 2	(3.1)
3	2	prim : >	(4.1)
4	1	copy	(17.1, 5.1)
5	2	switch	(null, 6.1)
6	1	copy	(10.1, 9.1)
7	0	value : 1	(9.2)
8	0	value : 2	(10.2)
9	2	prim : −	(12.2)
10	2	prim : −	(14.2)
11	0	value : fib	(12.1)
12	2	apply	(16.2)
13	0	value : fib	(14.1)
14	2	apply	(16.1)
15	0	value : 1	(17.2)
16	2	prim : +	(17.3)
17	3	merge	(output)

In the output list field, the list item i.k denotes the kth input field of the instruction with identifier i. For instructions of type value, the associated constant is also specified in the type field, and similarly for instructions of type prim. The value fib in this example refers to the initial closure for fib which will be [body of fib, 1.1 = ?]. Here, body of fib now represents the dataflow instructions for fib rather than its DFG and the ? symbol indicates that no value has been bound to the input variable, this being done upon the application of (the initial closure of) fib to its argument.

The operation of the data-driven dataflow machine is now given by the following informal algorithm:

```
REPEAT
  Choose any instruction with all required arguments in its input list ;
  Execute the instruction ;
  Delete the instruction ;
UNTIL instructions exhausted
```

Notice that DFGs are acyclic since an instruction, which corresponds to a node in a DFG, may be deleted when it has been evaluated since it can never again have a data value on its incoming arcs. Notice also that the set of 'all required arguments' refers to the inputs of the corresponding node in a DFG which must be present (as data values) in order that the node's operation may be executed. These inputs are given by rules specific to each instruction type, for example all inputs in the cases of the instruction types copy, switch and apply (but only in the data-driven machine in the last case). In the case of merge, the first (control) input is required, and also the second (T) or the third (F) input depending on whether the value of the first is true or false respectively. In the case of a primitive function, the required inputs correspond to the strict arguments of the primitive function concerned, which are given by the delta rule of that function. Thus, in every case, all of the required input list items are known. Note that several instructions might have all of their required arguments at the beginning of a new cycle of the algorithm. Because functional expressions are referentially transparent and DFGs are acyclic, any such instruction or instructions may be selected for execution, and indeed any number of identical algorithms may be executed concurrently, which is very conducive to a parallel implementation.

To conclude this section we consider the most complex of the operations that are performed in the algorithm, namely 'execute instruction'. This is quite straightforward in all cases except that of the apply instruction, being determined entirely locally by the characteristics of the instruction type concerned. For example a merge instruction with all required inputs would simply transfer the appropriate input (determined by the value of the control input) to the input field addressed in the singleton output list. The operation of an apply node in a DFG depends on the closure which is present on its first input arc.

If the application is sufficient to complete the closure then a copy of the function's body is generated, i.e. the set of instructions representing its DFG. The second input list item of the apply instruction is then stored in the input field of the body's copy as specified in the closure itself and the output list item of the apply instruction is stored in the output field of the body's copy. (Recall that in the example program for fib given earlier the output field for that body occurred in the output list of the final merge instruction in the program.) In this way, the function is applied to the intended argument, and its result is directed to the intended destination. We adopt the convention that the output field of a function body corresponds to the output field of the *last* instruction of the body, as we saw in the fib example earlier. The procedure for generating copies of function bodies is discussed below and some limitations of our convention are noted. Notice that in the case of a partially applied primitive function such as +, the body of the closure will consist of just a single node, which will replace the corresponding apply node when the closure is eventually complete.

If, on the other hand, the closure has an arity greater than 1, then the argument value (the second input list item of the apply instruction) is assigned to the next variable which has not been bound in the closure's environment. The result is then a copy of the old closure augmented with the new binding.

14.1.4 A stack-based optimized implementation

The trouble with the implementation described in the previous section is that the new 'instances' of the function bodies generated by function application must be 'knitted-in' explicitly into a DFG. Such knitting is expensive and can be avoided in a stack-based implementation, so that all addressing of instructions is then relative to the address of the instruction being executed. In this way, there are no absolute addresses in the bodies of functions or closures, and so no address transformation is necessary. This idea leads to the following stack-based implementation which is based on the material in Glaser and Hayes (1986).

The instructions that constitute the dataflow program for evaluating a functional expression are placed on a stack and each instruction on this stack has two fields: a data field and an operation field. The data field consists of a pair of operands or inputs, and the operation field consists of an opcode (corresponding to the type of a DFG node) and two relative offsets from the instruction into the stack, indicating where to place the result of its execution. An offset of $+ m.n$ ($n = 1, 2$) in the opcode field of the instruction at position i on the stack refers to the nth operand in the data field of the instruction m positions below i, that is at position $n + i$. Initially all of the data fields are 'holes', waiting for data to arrive from preceding instructions (instructions higher on the stack), and the stack only contains the instructions used in the 'top-level' expression to be evaluated, i.e. none from the bodies of any user-defined functions that might be involved. Evaluation proceeds by executing the instruction at the top of the stack, popping it, and repeating the cycle until the stack is empty. The execution of each type of instruction is defined in exactly the same way as we saw for DFGs and our previous instruction formats, but some elaboration in the case of the apply instruction illustrates the difference in this implementation (and its improved performance). Just before executing an apply instruction the item at the top of the stack will be of the form

| f | a | apply | + m.n |

where f is the closure to be applied and a is its argument. The destination of the result of the application is m positions below the top-of-stack, in the nth operand position. The apply instruction is first popped from the stack, and the rules for performing the application are then analogous to those described above. Before stating those rules it should be noted that the environment of a closure is assumed to consist of a list of argument values, rather than a list of pairs comprising an arc identifier and a corresponding value as before. This is simply because in the optimized implementation the arguments of a function are defined to correspond to the input fields of the first instructions in the instruction list; we shall call these the **input instructions**. This all relates to the use of a stack to hold function parameters as should soon become apparent. The application rules are as follows:

> If the closure of f is of arity 1 then a copy of its body is loaded, unmodified, onto the top of the stack. The argument value a is then stored in the first operand field of the instruction at the top of the stack and the offset +m.n is stored in the output field of the last instruction in the copy (in other words it is restored to its position in the original apply instruction!).
>
> If on the other hand f is a closure of arity p > 1 then a new closure (of arity p − 1) is constructed whose environment is augmented with the value of the argument a.

We close this section with an example to illustrate the salient points of the operation of the optimized dataflow implementation. Consider the expression succ (f 3) where succ is the primitive successor function on integers and the user-defined function, f, is defined by f x = + x x. The body of f has the following dataflow instructions:

```
copy        +1.1    +1.2
prim : +    (output)
```

and its initial closure consists of the body together with an empty environment. The top-level expression is given by the initial stack:

(1)	–	–	value : 3	+2.2
	–	–	value : f	+1.1
	–	–	apply	+1.1
	–	–	prim : succ	(output)

The following stacks are then obtained:

(2)	–	–	value : f	+1.1
	–	3	apply	+1.1
	–	–	prim : succ	(output)

(3)	[f, ( )]	3	apply	+1.1
	–	–	prim : succ	(output)

(Although the closure [f, ( )] is drawn in the apply input list a pointer to the closure would be used in practice.)

(4)	3	–	copy	+1.1	+1.2
	–	–	prim : +	+1.1	
	–	–	prim : succ	(output)	

(Notice how the output field of the new copy of the function body, i.e. +1.1 is the same as the output field of the original apply instruction.)

(5)	3	3	prim : +	+1.1
	–	–	prim : succ	(output)

(6)	6	–	prim : succ	(output)

(7) output = 7

It should now be apparent that using this approach, the code for each function (the operand fields and output lists of each instruction) are unaltered during the evaluation of a function. This suggests that it is not necessary to copy the body of the applied function onto the stack – rather we can step through a *shared* copy of the function code using a conventional 'program counter'. Applying a function now consists simply of allocating sufficient space on top of the stack to hold all the inputs of the instructions in the function body and 'calling' the function code as though it were a conventional subroutine. Placing the result of the application in the 'output' field of the function body then corresponds to leaving the result on top of the stack so that the position of the result 7 in the diagram above becomes significant. In this way it is now possible to compile the dataflow instructions into conventional machine code in which the primitive operations all take their inputs from the top of the stack.

It will also be noted that conditional expressions in the source program will be translated into sequences of instructions for the predicate, the true branch and the false branch, with a switch node effectively selecting one of the two branches depending on the value of the predicate. Unfortunately, the scheme described so far requires that all the instructions for such conditionals be processed by successively popping them from the stack, whereas we only need to process those corresponding to the 'success' branch. For this reason we must incorporate the idea of a *kill token*, which when sent to the input(s) of an instruction causes that instruction to be deleted without being executed. When the predicate value is known kill tokens must be sent to the inputs of each instruction in the failed branch, so that when those instructions are encountered by the evaluator they are simply ignored. This notional 'broadcasting' of kill tokens can be achieved incrementally by having each instruction propagate any kill token appearing on its strict inputs through to its output(s). The killing off of the failed branch can then be initiated by placing a single kill token on the 'failed' output arc of the corresponding switch node. As a further optimization, in the sequential implementation of the dataflow model described here it will be noted that the instructions for each branch are contiguous and so it is possible to achieve the effect of kill tokens by simply skipping over the whole of the failed branch by updating the stack pointer and program counter. This is the dataflow analogy of a 'jump' instruction in a conventional computer.

14.2 Normal-order functional dataflow

The implementation considered in the previous section operates on the principle that the nodes in a dataflow graph, or instructions in a dataflow program, are executed whenever data is available on the required inputs – whether or not the result of the execution is actually needed by another part of the computation, i.e. by another node in the DFG as an input. This data-driven mode of execution therefore performs applicative-order reduction corresponding to the call-by-value computation rule. In order to achieve normal-order semantics, a function application must be completed only when it is explicitly *demanded*. This demand must be propagated in the event that the evaluation of the demanded application requires the result of another application. This propagation of demand eventually reaches an atomic node or arc in the DFG, i.e. a value node or an external input to a function, whereupon a node can execute. The resulting implementation mode is called **demand-driven** dataflow and in this section we describe the modifications needed in the data-driven version to support it. As usual, for reasons of efficiency, we need to ensure that argument expressions are not evaluated more than once, i.e. we require the call-by-need computation rule, rather than call-by-name. This is obtained free in the dataflow implementation since an argument is shared by being distributed by a copy node, which sends its result on all of its output arcs when any output is demanded.

14.2.1 Operation of the demand-driven dataflow machine

The principle of operation of the demand-driven machine is that a dataflow instruction is executed when and only when its output has been demanded and all of its required inputs have been evaluated and have arrived. Conceptually, this is achieved by maintaining a 'required list' of all the instructions from which output has been requested, but physically this might be implemented by *tagging* each instruction to show whether or not it had received a demand. This immediately introduces the need for an additional instruction field which contains a list of identifiers of instructions from which output must be demanded (as input to the instruction) which we shall call the **source list** field. The source list therefore has one entry for each input position in which the instruction is strict, the respective instruction identifier being that residing at the other end of the incoming arc. To start the ball rolling we have to demand the output instruction associated with the top-level expression which propagates the demand in the opposite direction to the direction of the subsequent data flow. Physically, the instructions required by the top-level expression will be signalled, using the identifiers on the appropriate source list, and their demand tags set. Again, having been executed, an instruction is deleted (since DFGs are acyclic) and so if tagged, also removes itself from the implicit 'required list'. The main cycle of the demand-driven dataflow machine now becomes:

```
REPEAT
  Choose any instruction whose output has been requested, by testing its
  tag;
  if All required arguments are in the input list field;
  then Execute this instruction;
       Delete this instruction;
       Acknowledge the signalling instruction (whose identifier is con-
       tained in the output list of the instruction)
  else Signal the appropriate instructions in the source-list for output;
       Change status, i.e. reset the tag to indicate 'not requested'
UNTIL instructions exhausted
```

Not necessarily all of the instructions with identifiers on the source list need be signalled prior to execution of a requested instruction; this depends on the particular type of instruction concerned. The term 'appropriate' is determined by the instruction 'owning' the source list, and excludes any instructions from which input has already arrived. For copy and switch instructions all of the instructions in the source list must be signalled. For the merge instruction the first instruction in the source list must be signalled, i.e. that instruction having its output arc connected to the control input, and either the second or the third instruction depending on whether the value of the first input turns out to be true or false respectively. The second signal is sent on a subsequent selection of the merge instruction for execution, following the arrival of the Boolean result from its first source list instruction. For a primitive function instruction, the instructions in the source list that must be signalled when the instruction is selected for execution correspond to the strict parameters of the function. Finally, in the case of the apply instruction, only the instruction with identifier first in the source list (corresponding to the applied function) is signalled. That function will itself send a request for its argument as necessary, using its own copy of the second element of the source list of the apply instruction; this will become apparent from the description of the operation of the apply instruction given below.

After the execution of an instruction has been completed, the instruction can be deleted, since DFGs are acyclic as we have already noted. Also, an acknowledgement is sent to signal the signalling instruction, which thereby becomes 'requested', and will subsequently attempt to re-execute with the input on which it was waiting now available. Of course, if there are several such required inputs, that instruction may still be unable to execute and have to deschedule itself again, but a more elaborate scheduling system which does not re-activate a waiting instruction until all of the inputs it has requested have arrived is not difficult to devise.

14.2.2 Execution of the apply instruction

As with the data-driven machine, the key to the operational principles of the demand-driven version is the way in which the apply instruction executes. On the first selection of an apply instruction, the source of the function to apply (the first input) is signalled, as described in the previous section, and on its second selection the actions performed are as follows:

- If the first input is a closure of arity greater than 1, a new closure is generated as in the data-driven case, except that the values assigned in the environment are now pointers to the source instructions which will ultimately generate the required values. In the general, unoptimized case, each binding will consist of an arc identifier/source instruction pair, although as we have seen it is possible to rely on a positional ordering of the input arcs when using a stack. The resulting closure is then the result of the application, and is stored in the input list entry specified in the output list of the apply instruction in the usual way.

- If the first input is a closure of arity 1, a suitably instantiated copy of the closure function body is generated, in much the same way as with the data-driven machine. Firstly, all instructions of the function body are reproduced with new, unique identifiers, with all items in the output lists and source lists of the instructions, other than the external output, updated. Of course, if a stack implementation such as that given in Section 14.1.4 is used, then the address translation is not required for the reasons given above. The following four 'knitting' operations are now performed:

  (1) The output list item of the apply instruction is placed in the output field of the body's copy as before.

  (2) The source list entry for each input arc of the body is replaced by the corresponding binding given in the environment. This associates with each input arc a pointer back to the instruction which will ultimately yield the value on that arc.

  (3) The output list item of each source instruction referenced in the environment is changed to point to the input instruction corresponding to that environment entry (this is just the opposite of (2) above).

  (4) The output instruction of the body's copy is tagged to make it 'requested' – this is the demand that will drive the evaluation of the newly created function application.

The astute reader will have noticed that we now need to make the minor restriction that if the output list of an instruction contains an item which is the second input list entry of an apply node, then it can contain no other items, i.e. it must be a singleton list; otherwise in (3) it would not be known which list item to change. However, this restriction could be avoided by making each source list entry a pair comprising a source instruction and an output list position.

14.3 Comparison with other models

Like the other computational models considered in this book, namely the SECD machine and graph reduction, the functional dataflow model gives a representation of β-reduction and of the delta rules of the primitive functions supported. These primitive functions include the conditional, which although treated separately through the switch and merge nodes, could equally well have been considered in terms of just two more primitive functions and their delta rules. Moreover, the redex of such an application may be considered to be overwritten in the sense that incoming arcs to its apply node are redirected into the function body.

There is therefore a direct correspondence between the operational principles of the functional dataflow and graph reduction computational models, and this also extends to the graphical representation of expressions, although this may not be obvious at first sight. An arc in a DFG indicates the flow of data from a source node to the node which transforms that data, whereas in graph reduction an arc points to the source of an argument (and, indeed, the source of the function). Thus the arcs point in opposite directions in the two computational models and for this reason dataflow is often termed 'upside-down graph reduction'. In fact, when we considered the demand-driven dataflow model, we found that the demand signals, i.e. the requests for output, were propagated backwards in the opposite direction to that of the dataflow arcs, i.e. in the same direction as the arcs in the corresponding reduction graph. In the same way that a reduction graph can contain many redexes, so a DFG can contain many executable instructions, i.e. instructions which have data on all of their required inputs. For this reason the dataflow model is also a particularly natural vehicle for exploiting parallelism. The interested reader is referred to Watson and Gurd (1979) and Arvind *et al.* (1980) which describe the application of dataflow techniques to the parallel implementation of *single-assignment* languages, which resemble strict first-order functional languages. More general surveys of parallel dataflow techniques can be found in Dennis (1980) and *IEEE Computer* (1982).

The only significant difference that is found between a reduction graph and an inverted DFG is the splitting and combining performed by the switch and merge nodes. This too could be avoided by discarding the switch node type and treating the merge node as a 'conditional' node, with the usual three inputs: predicate, consequent and alternative. This would lead to redundant sub-expression evaluations, in the data-driven model, since only one of the consequent and alternative inputs would ever be required. The reason for the existence of the switch node is to ensure that only the required computations are performed. However, in the demand-driven model, an instruction is executed only if it is specifically signalled, i.e. definitely required, so switch nodes are unnecessary, and the inverted DFG looks exactly like a reduction graph of the kind discussed in Chapter 11. The role of the switch node is played by the delta rules of the merge node in the demand-driven model, and we conclude that graph reduction and upside-down demand-driven dataflow are essentially the same.

SUMMARY

- Programs can be expressed graphically by dataflow graphs (DFGs).
- The nodes of a DFG represent operators and the arcs between the nodes represent data dependencies.
- The most natural implementation of dataflow is *data-driven* meaning that operators 'fire' as soon as all their required inputs are available.
- DFGs can be represented by sets of instructions, where there is one instruction for each node in the DFG.
- These instructions can be executed sequentially on a conventional computer, thereby implementing the operations specified by the DFG; the instruction inputs can be held on a stack.
- The dataflow model can be extended to perform *demand-driven* evaluation which corresponds to normal-order reduction; this significantly complicates the model.
- Dataflow can be implemented on a parallel machine by executing different dataflow instructions on different processors.

EXERCISES

14.1 Consider the following functions

(i) f x y g = + (* 2 x) (g y y x)

(ii) g x y = − x (cond (= x 0) 0 (g (− y 1) (− x 1)))

(iii) h x = f (− x 3) (+ x)

(a) Draw the DFG for each function.

(b) For each of the DFGs produced write down the sequence of dataflow instructions required to implement the function.

14.2 For a function F of the form F x_1 x_2 . . . x_n = E we could conceivably represent an application of F by linking the output arcs of the instructions generating the values of x_i to the ith input arc of the DFG of F directly. In this way we would represent applications of F by directly knitting in its DFG rather than by forming an initial closure from F and then applying it using a cascade of apply nodes. What limitation does this impose on the way F can be used? Justify your answer.

14.3 (a) In what way can the expression + x y be expressed as a DFG in both curried and uncurried form?

(b) According to our definition of value nodes, the value node for a primitive function with corresponding DFG node P delivers the closure [P, ( )]. Now suppose that it instead delivered a corresponding function symbol p. Extend the rules for function application given in Section 14.1 to allow for the function arc of an apply node to hold such a primitive function symbol.

14.4 Consider the top-level expression E = f (g 3) 7 where f and g are given by

```
f h x = + ( h x ) x
g a b = − a 1
```

(a) Draw the DFGs for E, f and g.

(b) Write down the corresponding dataflow instructions for E, f and g using the notation of Section 14.1.4.

(c) Show the intermediate dataflow instruction stacks obtained by the stack-based evaluation of E (assume that function application is implemented by instruction copying).

14.5 Explain why sending a kill token to the failed arm of the DFG of a conditional expression does *not* cause a kill token to appear at the output of that DFG. Explain your answer by making reference to the DFG for map, given in Figure 14.2.

14.6 Refer back to the example evaluation of Section 14.1.4, which shows the intermediate stacks in the evaluation of succ (f 3). How can the output field (output) be expressed in the form +m.n?

14.7 Suppose that the input fields of an instruction can be allowed to hold either a value or the identifier of the instruction which will ultimately deliver that value. Describe how this facility can be used to implement an optimized demand-driven implementation of dataflow.

Chapter 15
Compiling functional languages

The objective of this chapter is to describe how a functional program expressed in an intermediate form can be translated into a sequence of low-level instructions for a conventional, sequential computer. Part of the exercise here is to see how the various techniques we have already described can be combined to form a complete and efficient implementation of the source language and in many respects this chapter completes the picture of the implementation of functional languages, for it provides the final link between a source program and the hardware of a target machine.

The diversity of translation techniques we have covered presents many options for the compiler writer and the final implementation developed is invariably only one of many that could have been pursued. Fortunately, however, many of the basic compilation techniques for each are similar in nature, so that a good understanding of the subject can be acquired by examining one or two particular implementations as examples. Therefore, in addition to describing compilation at a general level (Section 15.1) the bulk of this chapter is taken up with two case studies of functional language compilers, concentrating particularly on code generation and the abstract machines to which they target a compiled program. These examples have been chosen since they represent two extremes in functional language implementations, respectively the implementation of strict languages based on an optimized SECD machine and the implementation of lazy languages based on an optimized graph reducer. These will be discussed in Sections 15.2 and 15.3. Both of these example implementations have been used as the basis of real compilers, namely a compiler for a strict subset of the Hope language described in Part I of this book and for a lazy dialect of the functional subset of ML, a description of which may be found in Augustsson (1984).

15.1 The structure of a compiled implementation

Figure 15.1 illustrates the basic structure of a typical functional language compiler.

The translations appearing in the top half of the diagram should be familiar from previous chapters. In Part I we looked at source programming languages and how to use them. In Chapter 7 we described an intermediate form based on the sugared lambda calculus, showing how to translate from the source program to such a form. Finally in Chapters 12 and 13 we considered combinator representations and how to obtain them by variable abstraction into a fixed combinator set, or by lambda (or mfe) lifting into a set of super-combinators – producing the 'Intermediate form 2'. The code-generation phase of the compiler is concerned with the translation of these (super-)combinators into 'pure' code sequences, as suggested in Chapter 13. The assumption is, therefore, that the intermediate form of the program is submitted to the code generator in the form:

⟨definition of combinator 1⟩
⟨definition of combinator 2⟩
⋮
⟨definition of combinator N⟩
⟨expression to be computed⟩

This is based on the premise that the (possibly partial) application of combinators is always more efficient than implementing β-substitution by copying, as in the lambda calculus and in the graph reduction scheme described in Chapter 11. Certainly this should be the case if the target machine is a conventional sequential computer, for then each combinator becomes a sequence of machine instructions which, once invoked, implement directly the operations specified by that combinator. Of course, had the target machine been designed at the outset with copying in mind, then special facilities built into the hardware of that machine might make the approach more efficient – for example by exploiting

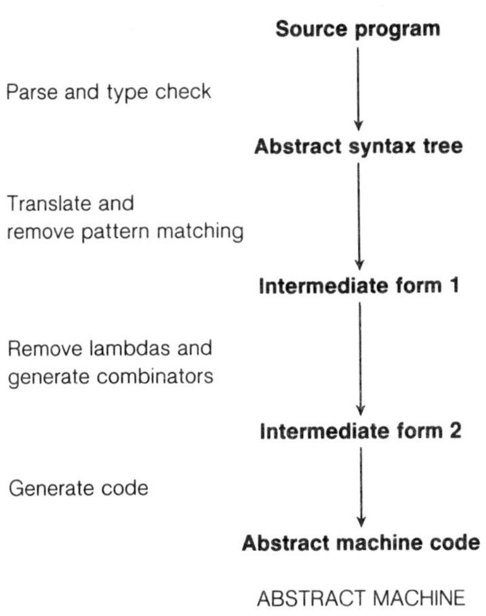

Figure 15.1 A typical compilation route.

parallelism to do the substitution concurrently. The fact that we refrain here from considering graph copying in the context of sequential compilers does not, however, rule out the use of graph reduction, as we shall see later on.

Note that if a program is translated into a fixed combinator set the intermediate form of the program still has the structure of Figure 15.1 and the number N above will be constant for all programs.

Although Figure 15.1 implies that each intermediate form exists explicitly during the compilation of a program, in practice this may be relaxed. For example, we could choose to generate the second intermediate form directly from the abstract syntax tree, omitting the first intermediate form, or even omit both intermediate forms altogether and generate the machine code directly. The final output of a compiler is a sequence of machine code instructions which are represented as binary code inside the main memory of a target computer and so we could write 'real machine' in Figure 15.1 in place of 'abstract machine', a real machine being, for example, a VAX or a specific make of microcomputer. The disadvantage of committing to one type of target machine is that the compiler is then tailored specifically to that machine and is not easily 'ported' onto other machines without rewriting much, or all of the code generator. For this reason we talk about abstract machines rather than concrete machines and try to define an abstract machine architecture and instruction set which is sufficiently general to enable the same compiler to be used on a variety of target machines. This implies the need for an extra layer of translation, which converts the individual abstract machine instructions into concrete machine instructions. These concrete machine instructions manipulate concrete data structures which represent the components of the abstract machine architecture, for example a stack; these structures are themselves stored in the target machine's memory.

In both of the case study implementations we describe in the next two sections, the starting point is a set of (possibly recursive) combinator definitions derived from an intermediate form of the source program by lambda lifting, as described in Chapter 13. The major difference between the two lies in the nature of their abstract machines and in the function calling semantics they support. In our first case study, namely the FPM system, the abstract machine is based on the strict SECD machine, which was introduced in Chapter 10, and the compiled code for that machine implements eager evaluation. As we shall see, there is a close correspondence between the abstract and concrete machine architectures, so that most expressions translate directly into the underlying physical machine-code instruction sequences, resulting in very efficient code. In the second case study, namely the G-machine, the abstract machine supports normal-order (lazy) graph reduction. Here, expressions are translated into code which manipulates a graph, namely the graph representing the top-level expression. This graph is transformed from its initial state into a state representing an expression in WHNF, the final value of the program. The disparity between the computational models of the G-machine and the target machine (graph transformation and instruction execution respectively) means that G-machine programs are partly 'interpreted' in that the compiled code explicitly manipulates a data structure representing an expression.

15.2 The FPM system

FPM is an acronym for functional programming machine. The FPM abstract machine is stack-based and can be viewed as an optimized version of the SECD machine as we shall see later on. There is a code generator which translates programs expressed in an intermediate form called FC[†] into FPM abstract machine instructions (F-code). Source programs are translated into FC by first removing pattern matching as

[†] This code was invented by R. Bailey under the name FP/M (Functional Programming/ Microprocessors) (Bailey, 1985).

described in Chapter 8 and then lambda lifting each user-defined function to produce a set of combinators.

Since we are not using the lambda calculus directly, by 'lambda lifting' we mean the removal of nested functions. A nested function is translated into a 'global' function by appending to the front of its parameter list all of the formal parameters of its textually enclosing functions that occur in its body (the free variables of its body). Each reference to the nested function is then replaced by the application of its transformed version to the additional arguments corresponding to these parameters. The transformed functions are then defined at the same level as all other functions so that in the end there are no nested function definitions. As an example, the nested function definition in the following Hope function

```
dec f : num # num → (num → num) ;
--- f( x, y ) <= lambda z => z * y + x ;
```

is ultimately translated into the partial application of a compiler-generated function g:

```
f x y    = g x y
g a b c = + ( * c b ) a
```

Notice that we write f as a curried function here, although in practice it should strictly be defined as a function of a single 2-tuple as described in Chapter 7. Similarly g should strictly be defined as a curried function of two arguments: the pair (a, b), corresponding to the argument of f, and the parameter c, corresponding to the bound variable z of the lambda expression.

In other languages such as Miranda, nested functions may occur in qualified expressions, for example in the definition of f:

```
f x y = x * y * ( g y ) where g z = x + z
```

g is a nested definition. Although g is not an explicit lambda expression, it is still lambda lifted to yield the equations

```
f x y   = * x ( * y ( g' y x ) )
g' u v = + v u
```

The FPM system was originally developed to support the original Edinburgh version of Hope (Burstall *et al.*, 1980) which we shall call E-Hope. There are two important differences between E-Hope and the Hope language used in this book which affect the underlying code generator. Firstly E-Hope is a strict language so that both user-defined

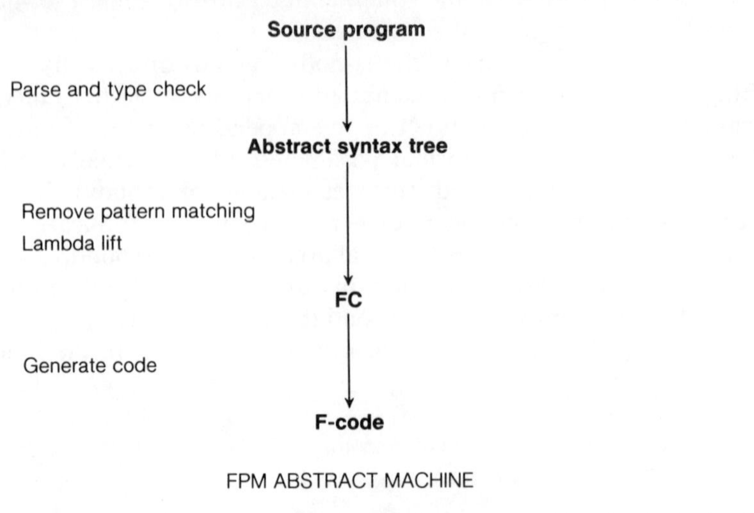

Figure 15.2 FPM compilation route.

functions and constructors are called by-value and secondly real numbers are not supported as a base type. The complete compilation route is shown in Figure 15.2.

The FC → F-code translator contains a number of optimizations, many of which are too detailed to be listed here. Therefore, we shall describe a stripped-down version of the compiler which performs only very few optimizations; this will help to explain all of the salient features of the FPM system and, indeed, the general techniques of strict language compilation without getting bogged down in unnecessary detail.

15.2.1 The intermediate code FC

An FC program is represented as an S-expression (see Chapter 5). At the top level, a program consists of a list of combinator definitions (comblist) and a top-level expression (exp) which describes what the result of the program should be. Each combinator definition (combdef) comprises the arity of the combinator (argcount), which is an integer, and the expression defining the combinator. There are six types of expression: constants (cv); local values (lv); make-tuple expressions (mt); temporary values (tv); conditionals (if) and function applications (af). There are three classes of function: built-in functions (bi) i.e. primitives; user-defined functions (ud) which are the program's combinators; and function-expressions (fe) which are expressions that deliver closures as their results. The formal syntax is as follows:

```
⟨program⟩  ::= ( ⟨comblist⟩ ⟨exp⟩ )
⟨comblist⟩ ::= ( ⟨combdef⟩ * )
⟨combdef⟩  ::= ( ⟨argcount⟩ ⟨exp⟩ )
⟨exp⟩      ::= ( cv ⟨con⟩ ) | ( lv ⟨argnum⟩ ) | ( mt ⟨exp⟩+ ) |
               ( tv ⟨arity⟩ ⟨exp⟩ ⟨exp⟩ ) | ( if ⟨exp⟩ ⟨exp⟩+ ) |
               ( af ⟨funtag⟩ ⟨exp⟩ * )
⟨con⟩      ::= ⟨integer⟩ | '⟨character⟩' | ⟨conlist⟩ | ⟨contup⟩
⟨conlist⟩  ::= ( ⟨con⟩ * )
⟨contup⟩   ::= [ ⟨con⟩ * ]
⟨funtag⟩   ::= ( bi ⟨code⟩ ) | ( ud ⟨funnum⟩ ) | ( fe ⟨exp⟩ )
⟨argcount⟩ , ⟨argnum⟩ , ⟨arity⟩ , ⟨code⟩ , ⟨funnum⟩ , ⟨tag⟩
             ::= integers 0, 1, 2, . . .
```

M∗ denotes zero or more occurrences of M and M^+ denotes one or more occurrences of M. It should be noted that the reason for splitting up the expression syntax explicitly into smaller tagged expressions is to enable FC programs to be interpreted efficiently. An FC interpreter is included in the overall FPM system but is not described here.

We now explain the most significant points of the six expression types informally.

Constants (cv)

FC constants are either atoms, lists of constants represented as S-expressions or tuples of constants represented as S-expressions delimited by square brackets. Lists and tuples in FC are untyped but in practice all list elements will be of the same type by virtue of the source language being strongly typed. Atoms are either integers or characters and constant lists of characters can be written in double quotes as a shorthand. For example:

```
( cv 12 )         ( cv 'x' )        ( cv "Hope springs eternal" )
( cv [ 1 'a' ] )  ( cv ( 1 2 3 ) )  ( cv ( 2 "for" [ 't' 'e' 'a' ] ) )
```

Local values (lv)

The expression (lv n) refers to the nth parameter of the combinator in which the expression occurs. For example, for the source function

```
--- f( x, y ) <= . . . x . . . y . . . ;
```

the equivalent FC combinator will have an arity of 2 and x and y will be referred to by (lv 1) and (lv 2) respectively. The actual parameters of a combinator are stored in a special structure called the **local environment** which is described below.

Make tuple (mt)

mt expressions are used to build tuples which are constant-access-time data structures. These form the building blocks for user-defined data structures as described below. For example,

```
( mt ( cv 1 ) ( lv 3 ) ( cv "Bill" ) )
```

builds the 3-tuple whose first element is the number 1, whose second is the value of the third argument of the combinator currently being evaluated and whose third is the constant list of characters "Bill".

Temporary values (tv)

tv expressions are used to introduce new local values and correspond to **let** statements. For example, the FC expression

$$(\text{tv}\ k\ E_1\ E_2)$$

is equivalent to the expression

$$\textbf{let}\ (x_1, x_2, \ldots, x_k) == E_1\ \textbf{in}\ E_2$$

If $k > 1$ then E_1 must evaluate to a k-tuple (built using mt) and the elements of that tuple are added componentwise to the local environment. If the local environment contained n entries before evaluation of the tv expression then it will be extended by k values (giving a total of $n + k$) for the evaluation of E_2. The first element of the tuple is referred to from within E_2 by the expression (lv n+1), the second element by (lv n+2) and so on. In this way tv expressions can be used to decompose a tuple into its components.

Conditional (if)

Conditionals in FC are *multibranch* conditionals, meaning that a single conditional expression can have an arbitrary number of outcomes, rather than just two. For a conditional expression

$$(\text{if}\ S\ E_1\ E_2 \ldots E_n)$$

The selector expression S is first evaluated to yield an integer which must be in the range 0 to $n - 1$. If the result of evaluating S is k, then the value of the expression is the value of E_{k+1}. In a standard two-branch conditional false is encoded as the integer 0 and true as the integer 1. Note that if is not supported as a built-in function because of the strict function-calling semantics of FC.

Apply function (af)

Function applications have the following format

```
          ( bi c )
( af      ( ud m )     E1 E2 . . . En )
          ( fe E )
```

$E_1, \ldots, E_n$ denote the argument expressions to which the function in the second field is applied. Because FC is a strict language these expressions are evaluated before the function is called. If the function is built in (bi) then c denotes the function code. The built-in function codes we shall refer to in this chapter are given in Table 15.1. If the function is user-defined (ud) then m denotes the mth combinator in the list of combinators defined in the program.

We shall use the terms 'user-defined function' and 'combinator' interchangeably although it should be remembered that some of the combinators will be compiler-generated as a result of lambda lifting; by 'user-defined' we really mean 'not built-in'. If the function is neither built-in nor user-defined, then the expression E denotes a function-valued expression (fe) which must always evaluate to a closure. A closure is generated as the result of partially applying a function, that is by applying a function to fewer arguments than its arity. The arity of each user-defined function is included in its definition; the arities of the various built-in functions are predefined and so are 'known' by the compiler; the arity of an existing closure is contained within the closure itself as we shall see shortly. As an example of partial application, the successor function on integers can be expressed by partially applying the + function (built-in function code 1).

```
( af ( bi 1 ) ( cv 1 ) )
```

Table 15.1 A subset of the FC built-in functions.

Code	*Name*	*Arity*	*Description*
1	plus	2	
2	mult	2	
3	greater	2	
4	empty	0	Returns the empty (nil) list
5	cons	2	List constructor function
6	head	1	Returns the head of a given list
7	tail	1	Returns the tail of a given list
8	isempty	1	Returns true (1) if given list is empty; false (0) otherwise
9	index	2	Returns a tuple component. The first parameter is the tuple; the second is the index of the component

This expression denotes the function which 'adds 1 to things'; when evaluated it returns a closure.

Here is an example of an FC program which defines the map function on lists from Chapter 3 and an example application of map which increments each element in a list of numbers. The equivalent E-Hope definition is also supplied (the comments in braces { , } are *not* part of FC):

```
dec map : ( alpha → beta ) # list( alpha ) → list( beta ) ;
--- map( f, nil ) <= nil ;
--- map( f, x :: l ) <= f( x ) :: map( f, l ) ;
dec succ : num → num ;
--- succ( n ) <= n + 1 ;
map( succ, [ 1, 2, 3 ] ) ; ! Top-level expression !
```

```
(                                          { EXAMPLE PROGRAM }
(2                                         { map( f, l ) =   }
  ( if ( af ( bi 8 ) ( lv 2 ) )            { if not isempty( l )   }
     ( af ( bi 5 )                         { then cons(            }
        ( af ( fe ( lv 1 ) )               {       f( head( l ) ),  }
           ( af ( bi 6 ) ( lv 2 ) ) )      {                        }
        ( af ( ud 1 )                      {       map( f, tail( l ) ) ) }
           ( lv 1 )                        {                        }
           ( af ( bi 7 ) ( lv 2 ) ) )      {                        }
     )                                     {                        }
     ( af ( bi 4 ) )                       { else nil               }
  )
)
( 1                                        { succ( n ) =            }
  ( af ( bi 1 ) ( lv 1 ) ( cv 1 ) )        { n + 1                  }
)
)
( af ( ud 1 ) ( af ( ud 2 ) ) ( cv ( 1 2 3 ) ) )   { map( succ, [ 1, 2, 3 ] )}
)
```

Notice that lists are supported in FC by means of the built-in functions empty (code 4), isempty (code 8), cons (code 5), head (code 6) and tail (code 7). The E-Hope to FC translator recognizes applications of the E-Hope list processing functions and translates them directly into applications of the corresponding FC functions. For more complex user-defined data types, constructed data terms are represented as tuples. In keeping with the approach described in Chapter 8 the constructor functions within each data type are encoded as integers 0, 1, . . ., N − 1 where N is the number of constructors in the type. The application of constructor number k to arguments $E_1, E_2, \ldots, E_n$ is then represented by the FC expression

(mt (cv k) E'_1 E'_2 . . . E'_n)

where E'_i is the FC representation of E_i. The E-Hope → FC translator uses the pattern matching translation algorithm given in Chapter 8 and exploits the FC multibranch conditional to implement the CASE-n function using the constructor code as the branch selector. For example, in the following skeleton E-Hope program

```
data T1 == C1( . . . ) ++ C2( . . . ) ++ . . . ++ Ck( . . . ) ;
dec f : T1 → . . . ;
--- f( C1( . . . ) ) <= E1 ;
--- f( C2( . . . ) ) <= E2 ;
⋮
--- f( Ck( . . . ) ) <= Ek ;
```

the pattern matching in f is achieved using a single FC conditional expression:

(if (af (bi 9) (lv 1) (cv 1)) E'_1 E'_2 . . . E'_k)

As a general rule we shall write E'_i to mean the FC representation of E_i. The call to the tuple index function (code 9) with parameters lv 1 and cv 1 returns the first element of the tuple given by lv 1 which corresponds to the constructor code of the argument to f. If this is 0 (constructor C1) then E'_1 is evaluated; if it is 1 (constructor C2) then E'_2 is evaluated and so on, as required. Having selected the correct rule for f the argument can be decomposed using one or more tv expressions as indicated above.

Although FC is generated in the FPM system directly from an E-Hope program we can write other FC generators. For example, the rules for translating the intermediate code of Chapter 8 into FC are given in Table 15.2. C_P denotes the FC built-in function code for the primitive P, N_F denotes the number of the combinator (user-defined function) corresponding to F and L_x denotes the local value number associated with the identifier x – for example its position in the parameter list of its associated combinator.

15.2.2 The FPM abstract machine

The FPM abstract machine has four components: a *program store* which contains the compiled code for each combinator; an *evaluation stack* which is used to hold the arguments to a combinator and any temporary

Table 15.2 Summary of intermediate code → FC translation rules.

Intermediate code expression		*Equivalent FC expression*
C	C is constant	(cv C′)
x	x is an identifier	(lv L_x)
$\lambda x_1.\lambda x_2 \ldots \lambda x_n.E$		lambda-lifted to FC combinator
let x = E_1 in E_2		(tv 1 E_1' E_2')
letrec $x_1 = E_1, x_2 = E_2, \ldots, x_n = E_n$ in E		E′ The recursive definitions are lambda-lifted to FC combinators
TUPLE-n $E_1, E_2, \ldots, E_n$		(mt E_1' E_2' ... E_n') or (cv [E_1' E_2' ... E_n']) if the E_i are all constants
IF E_1 E_2 E_3		(if E_1' E_2' E_3')
P E_1 $E_2 \ldots E_n$	P is primitive (not TUPLE-n)	(af (bi C_P) E_1' E_2' ... E_n')
F E_1 $E_2 \ldots E_n$	F is user-defined	(af (ud N_F) E_1' E_2' ... E_n')
E E_1 $E_2 \ldots E_n$	E is a function expression	(af (fe E′) E_1' E_2' ... E_n')

values introduced using tv; a *call stack* which holds return addresses for combinator calls and a *heap* which stores the data structures built by the program and any closures generated by partially applying a function.

The program store

The code generator, which is described below, translates each user-defined function into a sequence of abstract machine instructions and these are stored contiguously in the program store. The starting address of each piece of code is given a label: FUN_1 labels the start of the code for user-defined function 1, FUN_2 for the second, and so on. As in a conventional computer, a program counter always points to the instruction being executed. The set of compiled function definitions corresponds to the global environment of the program.

The evaluation stack

When a function is called the arguments to that function are evaluated and placed on the evaluation stack. The required function is then called by executing the compiled code for that function. If the function is the nth user-defined function then this corresponds to executing the code

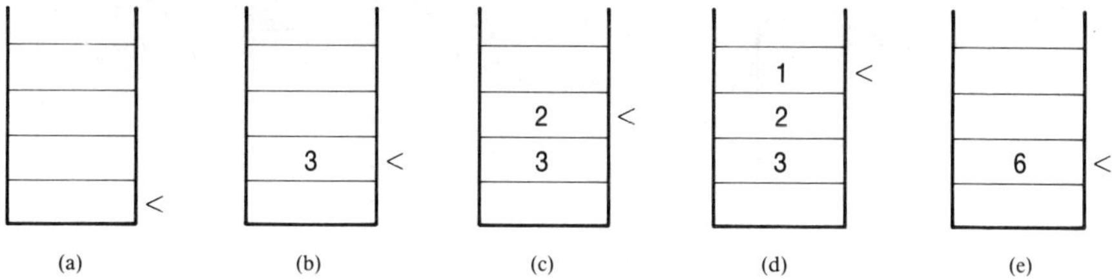

Figure 15.3 Calling a function.

starting at the label FUN_n in the program store. If the function is built in then a predefined instruction is invoked according to the built-in function code. The set of arguments built on the evaluation stack corresponds to the local environment of the called function. The local environment of the called function is replaced by the result computed by the function (this corresponds to overwriting the redex in graph reduction).

To illustrate the operation of the evaluation stack, suppose that user-defined function 4 takes three arguments and returns their sum. An example application of the function to 1, 2 and 3 proceeds as in Figure 15.3. The FC representation of this application will be

```
( af ( ud 4 ) ( cv 1 ) ( cv 2 ) ( cv 3 ) )
```

The intial stack is shown in Figure 15.3(a); the top of stack pointer is shown as an arrow (<) and the stack is drawn so that it grows towards the top of the page. The values of the three arguments to the function are pushed in turn onto the stack (Figures 15.3(b)–(d)). Note that the arguments are pushed right to left; the reason for this will become clear after the discussion of closures below. Figure 15.3(d) shows the completed local environment for the function being called. Calling the function has the effect of replacing the local environment with the computed value, in this case $1 + 2 + 3 = 6$ (Figure 15.3(e)).

Local values (function parameters) are referenced by indexing into the local environment from the top of the stack. The local environment may be 'extended' by use of a tv expression in FC in which case the new value, or values, introduced will be pushed onto the evaluation stack. For example, the E-Hope expression

let x == 1 **in** E ≅ (tv 1 (cv 1) E′)

compiles to code which pushes the value 1 onto the evaluation stack (Figure 15.4):

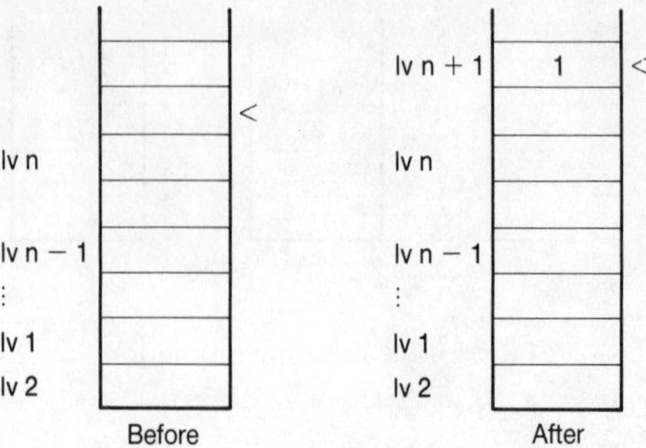

Figure 15.4 The effect of a tv.

During the evaluation of this expression, we assume we are currently applying a combinator of arity 2 and that n − 2 additional local variables have already been created by tv, beginning at lv 3. However, note that these local variables do not necessarily occupy consecutive stack locations; for example if they are generated in **let** expressions occurring as the arguments of functions in other **let** expressions.

All references to lv n+1 within E will be compiled to stack indexes to the value 1. When the evaluation of E is complete, the result replaces the temporary value (1) on the stack.

The call stack

The call stack is equivalent to a conventional subroutine call stack. When a function is called the address of the instruction to be executed after the call is pushed onto the call stack. When the called function completes, the address at the top of the call stack is popped and replaces the program counter. This has the effect of resuming the execution of the program at this address.

The heap

The heap is used to store all data structures generated during the evaluation of the program. There are three types of heap object or cell: cons cells built by calling the built-in list constructor function (built-in function code 5); tuples generated by FC mt expressions and closures which are built whenever a function is partially applied. It is also possible to extend the abstract machine to allow for recipes, or suspensions, to enable lazy evaluation to be supported, in which case we would require a further type of heap cell. We shall return to this issue briefly later on. The

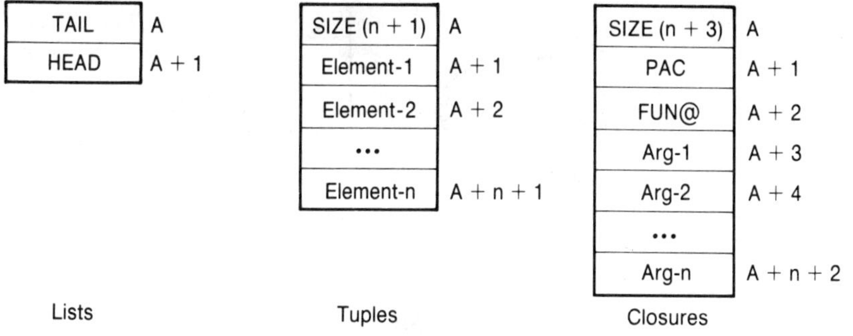

Figure 15.5 Heap cell structures.

three structures have the format shown in Figure 15.5. The SIZE fields in tuple and closure cells indicate the number of words within that cell (including the SIZE field itself). List cells always contain two words, representing the tail and head of the list respectively.

New cells are added to the heap by pushing their component words; in other words the heap behaves like a push-only stack, cells being accessed directly by their address and never being popped. A top-of-heap pointer points to the top of the heap and is updated each time a word, or cell, is pushed. If the heap is ever exhausted a garbage collector is invoked, which reclaims unused cells from the heap; various garbage-collection techniques are explained in Chapter 16.

An n-tuple is stored as a contiguous array of n + 1 words; the first indicates the size of the cell (n + 1 words) and the (i + 1)th represents the ith tuple component ($1 \leq i \leq n$). A closure always denotes the partial application of either a built-in function or a user-defined function. The PAC field denotes the 'pending argument count' of the closure (its arity) which is an integer representing the number of arguments to which the closure must be applied before the corresponding function can be called; i.e. PAC is the difference between the arity of the function and the number of arguments to which it has been applied so far. The compiled code for this function is located at the address FUN@. The remaining fields in the closure cell define the 'partial' local environment of the function at FUN@. This environment will be completed if the closure is applied to PAC arguments, at which point the completed environment is placed on the evaluation stack and the function at FUN@ is called. If fewer than PAC arguments are supplied (k, say) then a new closure is formed in which the pending argument count is PAC−k and the partial environment is the old partial environment with the k arguments added to it. As an example, if user-defined function 7 requires three arguments, then the FC expression

```
( af ( ud 7 ) ( cv 1 ) )
```

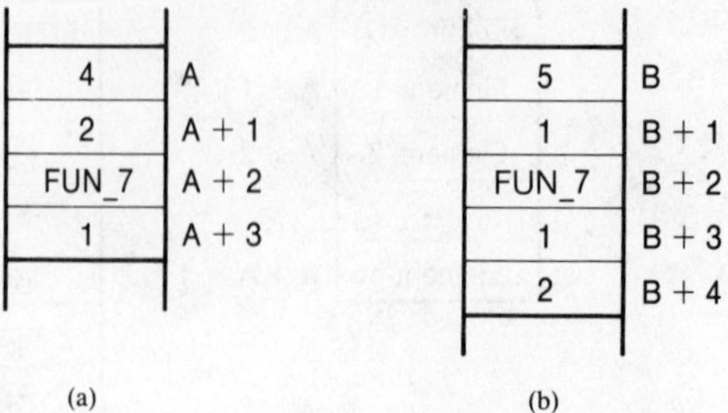

Figure 15.6 Forming and applying closures.

will cause the closure shown in Figure 15.6(a) to be constructed – at address A, say. If this closure is applied to a single argument, for example

```
( af ( fe ⟨expression returning above closure⟩ ) ( cv 2 ) )
```

then a new closure must be constructed (Figure 15.6(b)) – at B say. If this new closure is now applied to a further argument (on the stack) then the function (user-defined function 7) is called by offloading the partial environment in the closure onto the evaluation stack and executing the code starting at address FUN_7. Notice that doing this builds the complete environment with the first argument nearest the top of the stack. This is why, in general, function arguments are evaluated right to left.

Every function returns a value on the evaluation stack in the form of a single word which is either an integer, a character, or an address of a heap cell in the event that the result is a tuple, a constructed term or a closure. Because the original E-Hope programs are strongly typed, and we assume they have been successfully type checked, the compiled program does not need to distinguish these word types explicitly. However, the garbage collector needs to recognize the difference between atoms (integers or characters) and heap cell pointers, as we shall see in the next chapter. For this reason each word on the evaluation stack and heap has associated with it a tag. Each tag is two bits in length with the following meaning:

00 = integer
01 = heap cell pointer (address)
10 = character
11 = ⟨unused⟩

List cells on the heap can therefore be distinguished from tuple and closure cells because of the pointer tag (01) attached to the first word in the list cell. The size field at the top of each tuple and closure cell carries a tag of 00 because the size of the cell is itself an integer. The distinction between characters and integers is not important as far as code generation is concerned.

Notice that when a tv expression introduces more than one value, then those values will be located in the heap in the form of a tuple. In this case the tuple must be unpacked and its components pushed onto the evaluation stack.

Relationship to the SECD machine

The connection between FPM and the SECD machine defined in Chapter 10 should now be apparent: the program store together with the program counter of FPM corresponds to the control stack of the SECD machine. Here, however, the program is stored as compiled code rather than as lambda expressions. The call stack serves to remember the state of a computation at the point of a function call and restore that state when the called function has completed. In this respect it performs a similar role to the dump stack of the SECD machine. The evaluation stack of FPM is precisely a combination of the stack and environment of the SECD machine. In the latter, function parameters retain their names and the bindings of names to values is recorded in the environment. However, in FPM all function parameter references are compiled directly into stack offsets which obviates the need to maintain a name/value association list. Finally, the FPM heap is just a storage area for structures and closures. For example, whereas in Chapter 10 we talked of pushing closures directly onto the S stack of the SECD machine, in FPM we build the closure in the heap and push a pointer to the closure onto the stack, which amounts to the same thing. In fact we saw a closer resemblance when we considered the lazy SECD machine where suspensions really were viewed as heap objects, accessed indirectly through pointers. So, although the SECD machine may have appeared rather inefficient for practical purposes, we see that it is important in that it defines a general implementation scheme for functional languages which can be adapted in a variety of ways; FPM is just one of many implementations based on the SECD machine.

15.2.3 A simple code generator for FPM

We shall now describe a code generator for FC expressions which produces sequences of F-code instructions: for simplicity we shall consider a stripped-down version of the full F-code instruction set consisting of ten basic instructions and one instruction for each built-in function; we shall call this subset 'SIMPLE'. These instructions are listed in Table 15.3.

Notionally there is a SIMPLE assembler which translates SIMPLE instructions into executable binary code for the FPM abstract machine.

Table 15.3 SIMPLE instructions.

Instruction	*Operand(s)*	*Comments*
PUSH	#N	Pushes integer literal N onto the evaluation stack
	$C	Pushes character literal C onto the evaluation stack
	@A	Pushes address A onto the evaluation stack
	%N	Pushes value N words from top of stack onto stack
	*n	Pushes the nth entry in the table of constants onto the evaluation stack
TABLE	k	Pops the stack and puts the result in position k of the constants table
COPY	n	Builds a heap cell by copying the top n elements of the stack onto the heap together with the integer n + 1 which forms the size field of the cell. A pointer to the heap cell replaces the items on the stack
DROP	m, n	Moves the m values on top of the stack down n words and updates the top of stack pointer accordingly
UNPACK		Unpacks the components of the tuple pointed to from the top of the stack which is popped and pushes them onto the stack. The number of elements in the tuple is held in the size field of the tuple
CASE	n	Pops the stack and uses the value as an index into a table of addresses (a jump table) located after the CASE instruction. Instruction execution continues at the indexed address
JUMP	A	Forces instruction execution to continue at address A
CALL	A	Calls function at address A. (Return address is saved on the call stack)
RET		Return from function call (resume address is popped from the call stack)
APPLY	n	Applies the closure pointed to by the top of stack to the n arguments beneath that pointer on the stack
ADD, SUB, EMPTY etc.		Built-in operations which take their argument(s) from the top of the stack. The result replaces the arguments on the stack

In addition to the instruction mnemonics there are three assembler directives:

ADDR A	which is assembled as the address A.
LABEL L	which labels a piece of code. An occurrence of L as an operand of an instruction/ADDR directive is then replaced by the address of that piece of code.
RESERVE N	which reserves the N consecutive words of store which forms the constants table (see below).

In practice, SIMPLE instructions are treated as macros and are macro-expanded into sequences of concrete machine code instructions – specifically into VAX machine code instructions. The definitions of each macro are stored in a macro library for this purpose.

The bulk of the FC → SIMPLE compiler is described in terms of five compilation schemes D, E, F, C and S which respectively compile function definitions, expressions, function calls, constants and structured constants. The D compilation scheme compiles a user-defined function definition into a sequence of SIMPLE instructions. The generated code must adhere to the function-calling conventions of FPM: when a function is entered the arguments to that function will always be at the top of the evaluation stack and the result computed by the function must always replace these arguments. To express what each of the compilation schemes does in a concise manner we shall use a semi-functional shorthand notation. To compile the kth user-defined function we write:

D ⟦ (n e) ⟧ k = LABEL FUN_k ; ⟨compiled body expression, e⟩; DROP 1, n ;
RET

(Again, the double brackets are used to delimit *syntactic* objects.) D is a function which given an FC function definition and the function number, k, returns the compiled code for that function as a sequence of SIMPLE instructions (the ; between each instruction can be construed as a form of append function on instruction sequences). We shall use a similar notation when we describe the G-machine in Section 15.3. The D rule states that to compile the kth function definition we first label the function code FUN_k; we then compile the body of the function e using the E-scheme, which generates code that leaves the value computed by e on top of the stack; we then generate code to overwrite the argument frame (the local environment) with this result using the DROP instruction and finally return to the caller of the function using RET.

To compile the body expression we use the E-scheme. This is complicated slightly by the fact that the local environment in which the

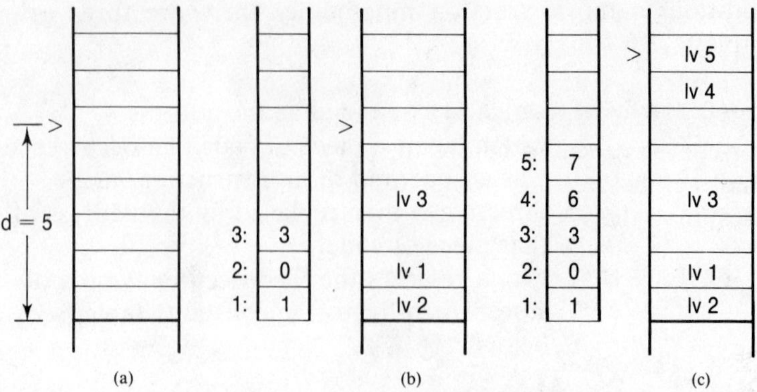

Figure 15.7 Local value index maps.

expression is being evaluated is accessed by indexing from the top of the evaluation stack. Whenever we push an item onto the stack (for instance, when we are building the local environment for a nested function call) the 'distance' from the top of the stack to the local environment frame increases by one word. For this reason we must parameterize E by d, which is the number of words between the top of stack and the base of the local environment (Figure 15.7(a)). Furthermore, the local environment may be extended by using a tv expression, and this may result in the local environment entries being scattered over the stack. For this reason we must also parameterize C by an *index map* I which indicates the number of words between the base of the local environment frame and each local value; an example with three local values is shown in Figure 15.7(b). Whenever we add to the local environment using tv this map is updated to include the offsets of the new local value(s) using the parameter d. If I maps n local values then I ++ [k, m] will be used to denote the extension of I which also maps local value $n + 1$ to the offset $m + 1$ (from the base of the local environment), local value $n + 2$ to the offset $m + 2$ and so on up to local value $n + k$ which is mapped to the offset $m + k$. Figure 15.7(c) shows the state of the parameter map after two new local values have been added to the stack of Figure 15.7(b). It is important to understand that the parameter map shown is a compile-time structure, not a run-time structure.

When we invoke the E rule to compile the body of an expression we must initialize the index map with the offsets of the initial local values (function arguments). Thus in the initial index map, which we write I^k, local value i has an offset of $k - i$ from the base of the local environment frame ($1 \leq i \leq k$). The full rule for D now becomes

$$D [\![(n\ e)]\!]\ k = \text{LABEL FUN\_k} ; E [\![e]\!]\ n{-}1\ I^n ; \text{DROP } 1, n ; \text{RET}$$

There is one E rule for each type of FC expression. If the expression is a constant then we use the C-scheme to compile it. If the constant is an atom then code is generated to push the value of the constant onto the stack. Structured constants are lifted out and compiled into initialization code which is executed before the code for the top-level expression is entered i.e. before the mainstream program execution begins; this ensures that they are evaluated only once. The initialization code evaluates the constant and leaves a pointer to it in a constants table which forms part of the program store – see Figure 15.8. The kth table entry points to the kth constant lifted from the program. The S-scheme which generates this intialization code is described later on. Hence we have:

E ⟦ (cv k) ⟧ d I = C ⟦ k ⟧

C ⟦ 'c' ⟧ = PUSH $c
C ⟦ n ⟧ = PUSH #n (if n is an integer)
(C ⟦ "abcd . . ." ⟧ ≅ C ⟦ ('a' 'b' 'c' 'd' . . .) ⟧)
C ⟦ (E_1 E_2 . . . E_n) ⟧ = C ⟦ [E_1' E_2' . . . E_n'] ⟧
= ⟨lift out the constant to be compiled later⟩ ;
PUSH ∗k (if this is the kth constant lifted)

Notice that the final rule suggests the need for an additional parameter to C (the current constant number, k) and additional result to be delivered by C (the list of constants to be compiled later); however, these are omitted for clarity.

If the expression being compiled under the E-scheme is a local value reference then we use the parameters d and I to compute the offset of the required local value from the top of the stack. This value is then pushed onto the stack:

E ⟦ (lv n) ⟧ d I = PUSH % (d − I_n)

(the nth entry in the index map I is written I_n).

If the expression is an mt expression, then the tuple elements are first evaluated and placed on the stack. This creates copies of the required tuple cell elements on the stack; these are then transferred to the heap using the COPY instruction. Code is generated to check whether there is sufficient space to store the tuple and to add the size field to the tuple cell automatically if so. The elements on the stack are replaced by a pointer to the tuple in the heap and we have

E ⟦ (mt E_1 E_2 . . . E_n) ⟧ d I = E ⟦ E_n ⟧ d I ; E ⟦ E_{n-1} ⟧ d+1 I ; . . . ;
E ⟦ E_1 ⟧ d+n−1 I ,
COPY n

If there is insufficient space on the heap to store the tuple then a garbage collector is invoked to reclaim any unused heap space – see Chapter 16.

If the expression is a tv expression then one or more new local values are added to the local environment; this involves updating l for the evaluation of the resultant expression as follows:

$$
\begin{aligned}
\mathsf{E}[\![(\mathsf{tv\ n\ E_1\ E_2})]\!]\ \mathsf{d\ l} = {} & \mathsf{E}[\![\mathsf{E_1}]\!]\ \mathsf{d\ l}\ ; \\
& \textbf{if}\ \mathsf{n > 1}\ \textbf{then}\ \mathsf{UNPACK}\ ; \\
& \mathsf{E}[\![\mathsf{E_2}]\!]\ \mathsf{d + n}\quad \mathsf{l ++ [\,n, d\,]\ ;\ DROP\ 1, n}
\end{aligned}
$$

Notice that if the number of local values being defined is greater than 1, then the result of evaluating E_1 will be a tuple and so must be unpacked onto the stack using the UNPACK instruction. Because the original language is strongly typed we are certain that n matches the size field of the tuple. The arity test is performed by the compiler and is not part of the generated code.

If the expression is a multibranch conditional, then we must generate code to evaluate the predicate, build the jump table and then compile each 'arm' of the conditional. The last instruction in each arm (except the last arm) must be a JUMP instruction which skips over any remaining arms to an 'exit label'. To ensure that the label numbers generated by the compiler are unique we must allocate sufficient label numbers to compile the expression before beginning the compilation. In this way we can be sure that any labels issued in the compilation of the code for each arm will also be unique. The statement ⟨Claim n⟩ reserves n unique label numbers for this purpose. Labels have the format L_⟨label number⟩. We therefore define:

$$
\begin{aligned}
\mathsf{E}[\![(\mathsf{if\ P\ E_1\ E_2 \ldots E_n})]\!]\ \mathsf{d\ l} = {} & \mathsf{E}[\![\mathsf{P}]\!]\ \mathsf{d\ l\ ;\ CASE\ n}\ ; \\
& \langle \mathsf{Claim\ n + 1} \rangle \qquad (\text{assume } \mathsf{b, b + 1, \ldots, b + n} \text{ allocated}) \\
& \mathsf{L\_b + 1\ ;\ ADDR\ L\_b + 2\ ;\ \ldots\ ;} \\
& \mathsf{ADDR\ L\_b + n}\ ; \\
& \mathsf{LABEL\ L\_b + 1\ ;\ E}[\![\mathsf{E_1}]\!]\ \mathsf{d\ l\ ;\ JUMP\ L\_b}\ ; \\
& \mathsf{LABEL\ L\_b + 2\ ;\ E}[\![\mathsf{E_2}]\!]\ \mathsf{d\ l\ ;\ JUMP\ L\_b\ ;\ \ldots\ ;} \\
& \mathsf{LABEL\ L\_b + n\ ;\ E}[\![\mathsf{E_n}]\!]\ \mathsf{d\ l}\ ; \\
& \mathsf{LABEL\ L\_b}
\end{aligned}
$$

Finally, if the expression is a function application, we first generate code to evaluate all the function's arguments and then generate code to call the function using the A-scheme. If the function being applied is a closure then we generate an APPLY instruction. If the number of arguments in the argument list is less than the arity of the function, we form a closure by pushing the function address and the pending argument count onto the stack and then using COPY to transfer the closure to the heap; otherwise we call the specified function. In order to test whether we must form a closure from the application, A must be parameterized by the number of arguments supplied to the function. We denote the arity of a function f by A_f and the instruction mnemonic corresponding to a built-in function c by M_c. For example, M_1 delivers ADD, M_2 delivers SUB and so on. Hence we define:

```
E ⟦ ( af F E₁ E₂ . . . Eₙ ) ⟧ d l = E ⟦ Eₙ ⟧ d l ; E ⟦ Eₙ₋₁ ⟧ d+1 l; . . . . ;
                                    E ⟦ E₁ ⟧ d+n−1 l ;
                                    A ⟦ F ⟧ d+n l n

A ⟦ ( fe E ) ⟧ d l n  = E ⟦ E ⟧ d l ; APPLY n
A ⟦ ( bi c ) ⟧ d l n  = if n = A_c
                        then M_c
                        else PUSH @BI_c ; PUSH A_c − n ; COPY n + 2
A ⟦ ( ud k ) ⟧ d l n = if n = A_k
                        then CALL FUN_k
                        else PUSH @FUN_k ; PUSH A_k − n ; COPY n + 2
```

Notice that if the function being partially applied is built in, the function address stored in the resulting closure is the address associated with the label BI_c where c is the numeric FC code for the built-in function. So, in addition to there being an instruction for each built-in function c, there must also be a piece of code at label BI_c which performs the same operation as that single instruction. For example,

```
LABEL BI_1 ; ADD ; RET
LABEL BI_2 ; SUB ; RET
etc.
```

These code sequences are the same for each program compiled and so may be viewed as a library of definitions. In fact they are stored in the *kernel* of the FPM system, which will be described later on. It is important to understand that these code sequences will only be referred to when a built-in function is partially applied; if the function is provided with all of its arguments at once then the single instruction associated with it will be invoked. This all follows from the fact that the function address field of a closure (i.e. FUN@) must be an address; we cannot place an instruction in that field directly.

To complete the code generator we have only to define the S-scheme which generates (initialization) code to build a constant list or tuple and which leaves a pointer to it in the constants table. The initialization code is preceded by the constants table itself, the space for which is reserved by the RESERVE assembler directive. If a total of N constants is lifted from the program then the directive RESERVE N will be inserted in to the code sequence prior to the initialization code.

S is applied to each lifted constant in turn. To compile the kth constant, C_k, we first generate code to build the constant and then place the pointer to the constant in the constants table at position k:

$$S[\![C_k]\!] ; \text{TABLE } k$$

S is given by

$$\begin{aligned}
S[\!['c']\!] &= \text{PUSH \$c} \\
S[\![n]\!] &= \text{PUSH \#n} \quad \text{(n is an integer)} \\
(S[\!["abcd \ldots"]\!] &\cong S[\![('a' \, 'b' \, 'c' \, 'd' \ldots)]\!]) \\
S[\![(E_1 \ldots E_{n-1} \, E_n)]\!] &= \text{EMPTY} ; S[\![E_n]\!] ; \text{CONS} ; \\
&\quad S[\![E_{n-1}]\!] ; \text{CONS} ; \ldots ; \\
&\quad S[\![E_1]\!] ; \text{CONS} \\
S[\![[E_1 \, E_2 \ldots E_n]]\!] &= S[\![E_n]\!] ; S[\![E_{n-1}]\!] ; \ldots ; S[\![E_1]\!] ; \text{COPY } n
\end{aligned}$$

(Note that EMPTY has the effect of pushing the empty list (nil) onto the stack.)

To compile the top-level expression we have only to invoke E suitably parameterized to indicate that the local environment for the top-level expression is empty:

$$E[\![\text{top-level expression}]\!] -1 \; l^0$$

The following examples illustrate the compilation rules in action. Note that we write l^n explicitly as a sequence of ⟨local value, stack offset⟩ pairs delimited by square brackets:

$$l^n = [\langle 1, n-1 \rangle, \langle 2, n-2 \rangle, \ldots, \langle n, 0 \rangle]$$

EXAMPLE 1

The function f(m, n) <= ∗ m (+ nm), which we shall assume is the *third* user-defined:

```
D⟦ ( 2 ( af ( bi 2 ) ( lv 1 ) ( af ( bi 1 ) ( lv 2 ) ( lv 1 ) ) ) ) ⟧ 3
= LABEL FUN_3 ;
  E⟦ ( af ( bi 2 ) ( lv 1 ) ( af ( bi 1 ) ( lv 2 ) ( lv 1 ) ) ) ⟧ 1 [ ⟨1, 1⟩, ⟨2, 0⟩ ] ;
  DROP 1, 2 ; RET ;
= LABEL FUN_3 ; E⟦ ( af ( bi 1 ) ( lv 2 ) ( lv 1 ) ) ⟧ 1 [ ⟨1, 1⟩, ⟨2, 0⟩ ] ;
  E⟦ ( lv 1 ) ⟧ 2 [ ⟨1, 1⟩, ⟨2, 0⟩ ] ; MUL ; DROP 1, 2 ; RET ;
```

```
= LABEL FUN_3 ; E ⟦ ( lv 1 ) ⟧ 1 [ ⟨1, 1⟩ , ⟨2, 0⟩ ] ;
  E ⟦ ( lv 2 ) ⟧ 2 [ ⟨1, 1⟩ , ⟨2, 0⟩ ] ;
  ADD ; E ⟦ ( lv 1 ) ⟧ 2 [ ⟨1, 1⟩, ⟨2, 0⟩ ] ; MUL ; DROP 1, 2 ; RET ;
= LABEL FUN_3 ; PUSH %0 ; PUSH %2 ; ADD ; PUSH %1 ; MUL ;
  DROP 1, 2 ; RET ;
```

EXAMPLE 2

The function f(x) = **if** x > 4 **then** 2 * x **else** x, which we assume is the *seventh* in the list of user-defined functions:

```
D ⟦ ( 1 ( if ( af ( bi 3 ) ( lv 1 ) ( cv 4 ) ) ( lv 1 ) ( af ( bi 2 )
   ( cv 2 ) ( lv 1 ) ) ) ) ) ⟧ 7
= LABEL FUN_7 ;
  E ⟦ ( if ( af ( bi 3 ) ( lv 1 ) ( cv 4 ) ) ( lv 1 ) ( af ( bi 2 ) ( cv 2 )
  ( lv 1 ) ) ) ⟧ 0 [ ⟨1, 0⟩ ] ;
  DROP 1, 1 ; RET
= LABEL FUN_7 ; E ⟦ ( af ( bi 3 ) ( lv 1 ) ( cv 4 ) ) ⟧ 0 [ ⟨1, 0⟩ ] ;
  CASE 2 ; ADDR L_2 ; ADDR L_3 ; { assume label numbers 1, 2 and 3 allo-
  cated }
  LABEL L_2 ; E ⟦ ( lv 1 ) ⟧ 0 [ ⟨1, 0⟩ ] ; JUMP L_1
  LABEL L_3 ; E ⟦ ( af ( bi 2 ) ( cv 2 ) ( lv 1 ) ) ⟧ 0 [ ⟨1, 0⟩ ] ;
  LABEL L_1 ; DROP 1, 1 ; RET ;
= LABEL FUN_7 ; PUSH #4 ; PUSH %1 ; GTR ;
  CASE 2 ; ADDR L_2 ; ADDR L_3 ;
  LABEL L_2 , PUSH %0 ; JUMP L_1
  LABEL L_3 ; E ⟦ ( lv 1 ) ⟧ 0 [ ⟨1, 0⟩ ] ; E ⟦ ( cv 2 ) ) ⟧ 1 [ ⟨1, 0⟩ ] ; MUL ;
  LABEL L_1 ; DROP 1, 1 ; RET
= LABEL FUN_7 ; PUSH #4 ; PUSH %1 ; GTR ; CASE 2 ;
  ADDR L_2 ; ADDR L_3 ;
  LABEL L_2 ; PUSH %0 ; JUMP L_1 ;
  LABEL L_3 ; PUSH %0 ; PUSH #2 ; MUL ;
  LABEL L_1 ; DROP 1, 1 ; RET
```

EXAMPLE 3

The function f(a, g) = **let** (x, b) == g(a) **in** (b, b), which we assume is the *first* user-defined function.

```
D ⟦ ( 2 ( tv 2 ( af ( fe ( lv 2 ) ) ( lv 1 ) ) ( mt ( lv 4 ) ( lv 4 ) ) ) ⟧ 1
= LABEL FUN_1 ;
  E ⟦ ( tv 2 ( af ( fe ( lv 2 ) ) ( lv 1 ) ) ( mt ( lv 4 ) ( lv 4 ) ) ) ⟧ 1
  [ ⟨1, 1⟩, ⟨2, 0⟩ ] ;
  DROP 1, 2 ; RET
```

```
= LABEL FUN_1 ; E ⟦ ( af ( fe ( lv 2 ) ) ( lv 1 ) ) ⟧ 1 [ ⟨1, 1⟩, ⟨2, 0⟩ ] ;
  UNPACK ; E ⟦ ( mt ( lv 4 ) ( lv 4 ) ) ⟧ 3 [ ⟨1, 1⟩, ⟨2, 0⟩ ] ++ [ 2, 1 ] ;
  DROP 1, 2 ; DROP 1, 2 ; RET
= LABEL FUN_1 ; E ⟦ ( lv 1 ) ⟧ 1 [ ⟨1, 1⟩, ⟨2, 0⟩ ] ;
  A ⟦ ( af ( fe ( lv 2 ) ) ⟧ 2 [ ⟨1, 1⟩, ⟨2, 0⟩ ] 2 ;
  UNPACK ; E ⟦ ( mt ( lv 4 ) ( lv 4 ) ) ⟧ 3 [ ⟨1, 1⟩, ⟨2, 0⟩, ⟨3, 2⟩, ⟨4, 3⟩ ] ;
  DROP 1, 2 ; DROP 1, 2 ; RET
= LABEL FUN_1 ; PUSH %0 ; PUSH %2 ; APPLY ; UNPACK ;
  PUSH %0 ; PUSH %1 ; COPY 2 ; DROP 1, 2 ; DROP 1, 2 ; RET
```

There are clearly a great many optimizations which can be built into the code generator to improve the quality of the resulting code. Typically, these optimizations are concerned with minimizing data movement to and from the stack and rely on making the F-code instruction set orthogonal in order that certain function arguments can be compiled directly into instruction operands rather than into stack pushes. In this respect they are rather low-level optimizations more akin to peephole optimizations and are rather machine specific in that they assume certain properties of the underlying concrete machine instruction set. However, there are some rather higher-level optimizations which can be applied. One of the simpler ones, which is the subject of an exercise at the end of the chapter, is to avoid building redundant heap cells. This attempts to deduce when it is safe to leave a tuple's components on the stack after the execution of an mt instruction.

Another commonly used optimization is one which handles tail-recursion. Recall that a tail-recursive function is one whose result (in the non-base case) is determined by a recursive call to itself as in

```
--- f( x, a ) <= if x = 0 then a else f( x - 1, a + x ) ;
```

In fact the optimization is more general in that it can be applied regardless of whether the recursive call is to f or to some other function, g say.

The first thing we need to know is whether the expression being compiled constitutes the result of the function whose code we are in the process of generating. To this end we add an extra parameter to the E-scheme which is Y if this is the case and N otherwise. In the case of function applications this extra parameter must be inspected: for user-defined functions if the extra parameter is Y then a jump to the called function can be made instead of the usual call. Before this can be done, however, the arguments of the function being called must be dropped down over the arguments of the current function, which are no longer required. This prevents the stack from growing on each recursive call:

$$
\begin{aligned}
A[\![(ud\ k)]\!]\ d\ I\ n\ Y = {} & \textbf{if}\ n = A_k \\
& \textbf{then}\ \mathrm{DROP}\ n, d - n + 1\ ;\ \mathrm{JUMP\ FUN\_k} \\
& \textbf{else}\ \mathrm{PUSH\ @FUN\_k}\ ;\ \mathrm{PUSH}\ A_k - n\ ; \\
& \qquad \mathrm{COPY}\ n + 2\ ;\ \mathrm{DROP}\ 1, d - n
\end{aligned}
$$

The extra parameter must be appropriately propagated through each of the compilation schemes. Each of the rules for E must ensure that when the parameter is Y the compiled code for the given expression replaces the current stack frame by the result and returns to the calling function. This obviates the need for the DROP and RET instructions in the rule for D which now looks like this:

$$D[\![(n\ e)]\!]\ k = \mathrm{LABEL\ FUN\_k}\ ;\ E[\![e]\!]\ n - 1\ I^n\ Y$$

The extensions to E required to support the extra parameter are left as an exercise.

15.2.4 The FPM kernel

We have now described all of the basic ingredients of the FPM system and it only remains to put them all together. The components of the FPM abstract machine together with all of the supporting code is contained in the FPM kernel which comprises:

(1) An implementation of the abstract machine structures, namely the call stack, the evaluation stack and the heap. The program store comprises the executable binary code generated by the compiler and is combined with the kernel by using a system-dependent (i.e. VAX) linker.

(2) A garbage collector. For reasons of efficiency this is hand-coded in the assembly language of the underlying concrete machine (in this case a VAX). The FPM garbage collector is a so-called *copying* collector which is described in detail in Chapter 10.

(3) A set of library definitions. These include subroutines for implementing some of the more complicated built-in functions, for example I/O and complex list-processing functions, and support code for instructions like APPLY.

(4) Built-in function definitions which are called when built-in functions are partially applied as described above. This again constitutes a library of definitions, this time of the form:

```
LABEL BI_1 ; ADD ; RET ;
LABEL BI_2 ; SUB ; RET ;
```

and so on.

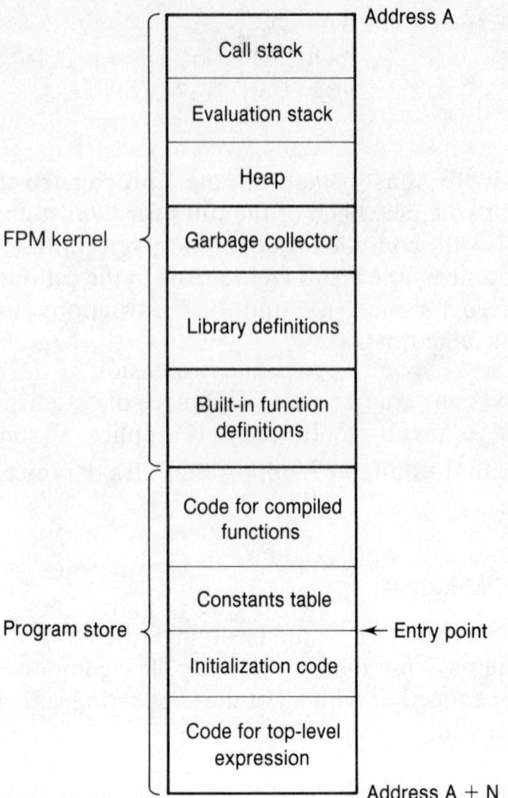

Figure 15.8 FPM run-time system structure.

The entry point to the whole system (i.e. the piece of code which is executed when the program is first entered) is the first instruction of the compiler-generated initialization code which builds the table of structured constants (if there are any such constants). This is followed by the compiled code for the top-level expression which starts the evaluation going. The overall structure of the combined program and kernel is shown in Figure 15.8.

15.2.5 Extensions for laziness

As we have already suggested, it is possible to extend the FPM system to handle lazy evaluation by including suspensions in the set of heap cell types. Indeed the extensions required reflect the extensions to the SECD machine needed to make it lazy as we described in Chapter 10. As will have been apparent from our discussion of interpreters in Chapter 9, suspensions are very similar to closures except that they represent complete applications of functions rather than partial applications. This suggests that their representation should be identical to that of a closure except for the PAC field which is not required (since it would always be zero) and, of course, a separate tag to enable suspensions to be distinguished from the other cell types. To make the compiled FC code fully lazy the compiler must be modified to construct a suspension from each of a function's arguments instead of evaluating them before calling the function, and the built-in functions must be modified to test that their strict arguments are fully evaluated rather than in the form of suspensions before applying their reduction rules. A further piece of kernel code must be included which forces a suspension by unloading its arguments onto the stack and calling the suspended function and which subsequently replaces the first word of the suspension by the result to give us the call-by-need computation rule. This piece of code is invoked only in the event that a primitive function is applied to one of its strict arguments which is in the form of a suspension. An additional tag is then required to distinguish evaluated and unevaluated suspensions.

Of course, the number of suspensions which must be constructed, tested for, forced and ultimately garbage-collected can be drastically reduced if we know in advance the strictness of each function. For then we can safely evaluate some or all arguments prior to calling the function since we can be sure that if this evaluation fails to terminate then so would the evaluation of the function's application. This effectively turns a call-by-need parameter into a call-by-value one. Fortunately the strictness of each primitive function is known and so we can at least avoid constructing and passing a suspension to strict primitives, choosing instead to evaluate the argument before the call. However, the strictness of the user-defined functions is not immediately identifiable and it is at this point that we see the need for a so-called *strictness analyser*. For a large number of functions it is possible to detect automatically whether a function is strict in one or more of its arguments. Using the information from such an analyser together with the information concerning the strictness of the primitives we can significantly boost the performance of the compiled code by using call-by-value parameter passing wherever we can. We shall return to this subject in Chapter 20, where we shall describe a general analysis technique called *abstract interpretation*, one application of which is strictness analysis.

15.3 The G-machine

In this section we describe a compiled lazy implementation for a functional language, the computational model for which is graph reduction, hence the name 'G-machine' (Johnsson, 1984). The system is still partly interpretive in that the graphs representing expressions reflect closely the structure of the source language but are represented and interpreted using conventional machine instructions. As in the FPM system the executable code is ultimately VAX assembler, which is generated by macro expansion from a compiler target language comprising macros defining an imperative stack-based machine. However, the code which builds and transforms the graphs at run-time is compiled from the top-level expression and the function-defining expressions and if the target machine had been custom-designed to transform expression graphs, rather than a conventional computer, the system would have been unarguably 'fully compiled'. It is for the same reason that the FPM implementation of the previous section can claim to be fully compiled, its abstract machine being stack-based and hence close in structure to the target machine.

A number of the low-level features considered in the FPM system are equally applicable in other abstract machines and so in this discussion of the G-machine we will not be concerned with them. For example we will not consider the physical representation of the (run-time) data structures, the organization of the heap or the construction of the table of constants during initialization.

The syntax of the functional language that we will compile in this section, corresponding to intermediate code 2 in Figure 15.1, is as follows:

```
⟨expression⟩      ::= ⟨constant⟩ | ⟨identifier⟩ | ⟨function-name⟩ |
                      ⟨expression⟩ ⟨expression⟩ | ⟨qual-expression⟩
⟨qual-expression⟩ ::= let ⟨local-def-list⟩ in ⟨expression⟩ |
                      letrec ⟨local-def-list⟩ in ⟨expression⟩
⟨local-def-list⟩  ::= ⟨local-def⟩ | ⟨local-def⟩, ⟨local-def-list⟩
⟨local-def⟩       ::= ⟨variable-name⟩ = ⟨expression⟩
```

We have omitted bracketed expressions which are not crucial in the implementation. Note that again the constants can include any base types and primitive functions although here we shall restrict ourselves to integers, Booleans and lists, together with their associated functions, in order to simplify our discussions. The major difference between this language and FC, which formed the basis of the FPM system, is the inclusion of recursive qualified expressions (letrec expressions). Technically, these are not required since all recursive definitions can be 'lifted' to the top level, i.e. as additional combinators, but they are included to allow cyclic structures to be created at run-time. As a simple example we could replace the expression

```
letrec cycle = cons a cycle
```

where a is a free variable, by the expression C a, where C is an auxiliary function defined by

```
C x = cons x ( C x )
```

However, this will work by the normal recursion mechanism, so that the cycle will not be established. The reason why such expressions do not occur in FC is simply that FC is a strict language; the cycle function will fail to terminate regardless of whether or not it is lifted to form a new combinator!

A function definition has the syntax:

⟨function-def⟩ ::= ⟨function-name⟩ ⟨param-list⟩ = ⟨expression⟩

⟨param-list⟩ ::= ⟨empty⟩ | ⟨variable-name⟩ ⟨param-list⟩

As with the FPM system, this syntax implicitly assumes that all expressions have been previously translated into some form of combinators as described in Chapter 13.

In fact the syntax is very close to that of the intermediate code described in Chapter 8 (which itself corresponds to 'intermediate code 1' in Figure 15.1). The most significant difference is, of course, that lambda abstractions are assumed to have been lifted out so that an intermediate code expression

$$f = \lambda x_1.\lambda x_2 \ldots \lambda x_n.E$$

will be translated here into the function (combinator) definition

$$f\ x_1\ x_2 \ldots x_n = E$$

Notice also that let expressions in this code comprise a *list* of local definitions rather than just a single definition as in the intermediate code of Chapter 8. This is only a cosmetic difference, however, since

$$\text{let } x_1 = e_1,\ x_2 = e_2, \ldots, x_n = e_n \text{ in } E \cong$$
$$\text{let } x_1 = e_1 \text{ in let } x_2 = e_2 \text{ in} \ldots \text{let } x_n = e_n \text{ in } E$$

Conditional expressions can be treated as applications of the primitive function cond because of the lazy semantics of the G-machine. This is in contrast to the FPM system which relies on treating conditionals as a special case (see also Chapter 9 for a discussion of this issue).

The only remaining syntactic types which are not covered are tuples and constructed data. A tuple of length $n \geq 0$ can also be represented as the application of a tupling function like TUPLE-n of Chapter 8, which is treated in the same way as any other application. Constructed data may also be represented in terms of tupling functions as described in Chapter 7, and the optimization given in Chapter 11, whereby constructors are represented by special nodes in a graph, could be used; we do not consider this here, however.

The G-machine implementation is divided into the following four compilation schemes which can be specified in a similar manner to the compilation schemes of the FPM system:

(1) the C-scheme, which generates the code to *construct* graphs representing expressions;
(2) the E-scheme, which generates the code to *evaluate* expressions represented by the graphs constructed by code generated by the C-scheme, leaving a pointer to the result at the top of an evaluation stack;
(3) the F-scheme, which generates the *function-bodies* of the user-defined functions, i.e. the code that reduces the graph (constructed by code produced by the C-scheme) corresponding to the general function application, $f\ e_1 \ldots e_n$, to yield its value;
(4) the B-scheme, which is similar to the C-scheme, but compiles code to evaluate integer- and Boolean-valued expressions, leaving their results at the top of another stack called the *dump*. This separates out the handling of primitive-function applications which require strict semantics, and improves the efficiency of the basic arithmetic, logical and conditional operations which take their arguments from the top of the dump, so avoiding the overheads associated with graph construction.

Notice that the dump contains values of atomic data and, as we will see later, state information preserved on a function call, whereas the stack contains only pointers into the graph of the expression currently being reduced. The sub-expressions represented by these pointers may also be (indirectly accessed) atoms but more generally could be lists or partially evaluated function applications.

The execution of a compiled G-machine program is based upon the computational model described in Chapter 11. It uses the pointer stack to unwind and rewind the spine of a graph and, together with the dump, to evaluate function applications. The only additional feature that we have here is the application of user-defined functions, the 'body graphs' of which must be appropriately instantiated with their argument graphs. This is done according to rules analogous to those for implementing β-reduction given in Chapter 11, by copying the template generated by the F-scheme for the applied function, all references to arguments being indirect through stack pointers. This type of 'knitting-in' will also be reminiscent of the dataflow model of computation covered in Chapter 14.

In the next section we define some notation and the (abstract) primitive instructions of the G-machine in the form of macros. We then go on to describe the four compilation schemes introduced above in the three sections that follow; the E-scheme and B-scheme are considered together. In fact the combined E- and F-schemes form an eval/apply implementation of the sort we first looked at in Chapter 9.

15.3.1 The G-machine macros and general notation

The primitive operations required in the abstract machine may be considered in four classes: stack and dump manipulation, creation and updating of graph nodes (and so graphs), function call and return, and the evaluation of applications of the primitive functions. Each such operation is expressed as a macro in the G-machine code generated by the compiler and these macros constitute the *instruction set* for the abstract machine, which could be implemented on any target computing system having a programming language which is adequate to implement them. For example, the PUSH and SLIDE macro-instructions require only the use of instructions with indexing. The macro-based intermediate language is therefore conducive to portability, and might be implemented in a conventional programming language or the machine language of the chosen computer.

The macros corresponding to primitive function applications simply implement the appropriate delta rule of the primitive, and the complete set of macros for stack and dump management, graph manipulation and function call/return is defined in the three subsections below. However, their operation should become clear as each is introduced in the sequel, and these definitions may be omitted on a first reading and used solely for reference purposes as required. First, however, we define some more general notation.

General notation

- The top-of-stack pointer is abbreviated to TOS, and the current depth of the stack, i.e. the number of pointers in it, is denoted by n. Thus TOS is the nth stack pointer. We also denote the item m positions below TOS, i.e. the item at position (n − m), by TOS − m.
- The environment, which associates expressions with variable names, will be denoted by r, which is a set of name/integer pairs. The empty environment, containing no pairs, is denoted by r_0, and we write r{ p / x }, for non-negative integer p, to denote the environment r updated to include the association x := p.
- The pth stack location then points to the graph node representing the expression associated with the variable x in the environment r – i.e. p refers to the pointer in the pth stack location. Thus, for example, in the environment r_0{ n / x }, the variable x refers to the graph having its redex node pointed to by the TOS. The stack-position associated with the variable x in the environment r is denoted by r(x), e.g. r(x) = p above.
- Finally, we use double square brackets to denote the syntactic constructs which are compiled by the four schemes. For example, E⟦ + 2 3 ⟧ denotes the code generated to add the constants 2 and 3, leaving a pointer to the constant node containing its result (i.e. 5) at the top of the stack.

Table 15.4 Macros for stack manipulation.

PUSH m	Push onto the stack the mth stack item below the TOS. Thus, if m = 0, PUSH 0 means 'copy TOS'
PUSHFUN f	Push the pointer to the root node of the body (defining expression) of f
PUSHINT i	Push the pointer to a new node containing the integer i
PUSHBOOL b	Push the pointer to a new node containing the Boolean b
PUSHNIL	Push the pointer to a new node containing the empty list
SLIDE m	Copy TOS to stack position (n − m), i.e. m below TOS. (TOS has 'slid down m places')

Macros for stack management

There are six stack operations, the macros for which are defined in Table 15.4.

Of course, the macros PUSHINT, PUSHBOOL, PUSHNIL can be augmented to include corresponding macros for any additional data type, for example PUSHCHAR.

Table 15.5 Macros for manipulating graphs.

MKAP	Construct an apply node (@-node) with TOS and TOS − 1 for its left and right pointers respectively; pop the stack twice; push the pointer to the new @-node on to the stack (i.e. replace the two pointers by the pointer to the @-node).
UPDATE m	Copy the contents of the node pointed to by TOS into the node pointed to by TOS − m; pop the stack.
ALLOC m	Allocate m 'holes' (i.e. create m new nodes with contents unspecified); successively push the m pointers to them on to the stack.
CONS	Construct a new cons node with TOS and TOS − 1 for its left (head) and right (tail) pointers respectively; pop the stack twice; push the pointer to the new cons node on to the stack.
MKINT MKBOOL	Construct a new constant node, the value in which is taken from the top of the dump; pop the dump; push the pointer to the new constant node on to the stack.
GET	Dereference TOS, i.e. fetch the contents of the node pointed to by TOS and pop the stack; push the fetched contents on to the dump.

Table 15.6 Macros for function call and return.

EVAL	Push on to the dump the remainder of the expression currently being evaluated (i.e. the symbols following this EVAL in the expression string) and the current stack *excluding* its TOS; create a new stack with the current TOS as its only item; evaluate the new expression consisting of the single macro UNWIND;
UNWIND	**while** TOS points to an @-node **do** push its argument (right) pointer on to the stack; push its function (left) pointer on to the stack; **end_while** **if** TOS points to a user-defined function node **then if** number of parameters on the stack ≥ arity of function **then** set expression currently being evaluated to the function's body (i.e. defining expression) **else** restore environment (current expression and stack) by popping the dump (i.e. return since the partial application is in WHNF) **else if** TOS points to a primitive function node **then** apply primitive function according to its delta rules (e.g. first initiate evaluation of its arguments) **else** type-error
RET m	pop m stack-elements; **if** TOS points to an @-node or a function-node **then** UNWIND (result is a function, e.g. a partial application) **else** pop and save TOS; restore environment (current expression and stack) by popping the dump; push saved TOS (i.e. a normal function return leaving the result of the called function at TOS)

Macros for graph manipulation

The graph-manipulation macros are used in the generation of graphs for function bodies and constructed data and in the interaction between the E- and B-schemes. The definitions of these macros are given in Table 15.5.

Macros for function call and return

These are given in Table 15.6.

It is these macros which drive the graph reduction. The macro EVAL initiates the evaluation of an expression which, in a lazy system, is already the required result until its computation is specifically forced. Thus EVAL instructions evaluate the top-level expression (see Section

15.3.3) and user-defined function applications (see Sections 15.3.4 and 15.3.3). The execution of UNWIND or RET always corresponds to some execution instance of EVAL. Primitive function applications are handled by the B-scheme as discussed in Section 15.3.3.

15.3.2 Code generation for expression-graph construction – the C-scheme

The C-scheme compiles the code that constructs the graph representing an expression, and leaves a pointer to its redex (root) node at the top of the stack. We denote the compiled code of an expression e as C⟦ e ⟧ r n when the environment is the association list r, defined in the previous section, and the depth of the stack is n. At run-time, any variable in r is a formal parameter of a user-defined function and must have a corresponding pointer in the stack to its argument sub-graph. The argument pointers are accessed by the PUSH macro, where PUSH i pushes a copy of the pointer at stack position i onto the TOS. It is because argument pointers are accessed relative to the top of the stack that the depth of the stack, n, must also be a parameter of C. We can now define C by a case analysis over the syntactic types of expressions, defined at the beginning of Section 15.3.

For each basic type, c-type, we define a macro, PUSHCTYPE, which when applied to a constant argument of type c-type, creates a node containing that constant as its value and pushes a pointer to the node on to the stack. Thus we have in general for constant c of type c-type,

C⟦ c ⟧ r n = PUSHCTYPE c

and in particular

C⟦ i ⟧ r n	= PUSHINT i	for integer i
C⟦ b ⟧ r n	= PUSHBOOL b	for Boolean b
C⟦ nil ⟧ r n	= PUSHNIL	for the empty list, nil

(In the last case there is no need for PUSHNIL to have an argument since we only define one list constant.)

A function is also a constant, whether primitive or user-defined, and may be considered as a combinator as in Section 15.2. In the latter case its 'value' is its set of graph transformation rules given by the code compiled for it by the F-scheme, together with its arity; this 'value' is stored in the global environment. Thus we have for a function-name f,

C⟦ f ⟧ r n = PUSHFUN f

A variable is represented by its associated expression in the current environment, which is pointed to by the corresponding stack pointer, as described above. Thus, for variable x,

$$C[\![x]\!]\, r\, n = \text{PUSH}\,(\, n - r(x)\,)$$

where $r(x)$ is the position of the stack pointer to the expression-graph associated with x in the environment r.

The compiled code for a general application of the form $e_1\, e_2$ consists of three parts. First code is generated which evaluates the argument expression e_2, leaving a pointer to the root node of the resulting graph at the top of the stack, the depth of which is increased by one. This is then followed by the code for the function-valued expression e_1 and an instruction to perform the application. Thus we have,

$$C[\![e_1\, e_2]\!]\, r\, n = C[\![e_2]\!]\, r\, n\, ;\, C[\![e_1]\!]\, r\,(n + 1)\, ;\, \text{MKAP}$$

where the macro MKAP creates an apply node (@-node) with the top two stack pointers popped to provide its left and right pointers respectively (i.e. pointing to the graphs representing the expressions e_1 and e_2 respectively), and then pushes the pointer to the new @-node (replacing the popped pointers to the graphs of e_1 and e_2). Note that this does not mean that we have eager evaluation. Although the code to build the graph of the argument expression is generated, this graph will be reduced only when its root becomes a redex, as determined by the EVAL macro used in the E-scheme. We will see in the next section that this does not initiate argument evaluation, except for strict primitive functions.

In the case of constructor functions (cons being the only one we consider here) the situation is similar. First code is compiled corresponding to the two arguments representing the head and tail of a list, so as to push the appropriate pointers to the graphs they build onto the stack. However, instead of creating an @-node, a specially tagged cons node is then created, again with its left and right pointers popped from the stack, and the pointer to the new cons node is pushed onto the stack. Thus we have

$$C[\![\text{cons}\; e_1\, e_2]\!]\, r\, n = C[\![e_2]\!]\, r\, n\, ;\, C[\![e_1]\!]\, r\,(n + 1)\, ;\, \text{CONS}$$

Finally, we come to qualified expressions, for which we first consider the simpler, non-recursive case. In the expression let $x_1 = e_1$ in e, the variable x_1 can be regarded as a formal parameter in the expression e, and can be referenced in the same way, namely by pushing a pointer to the graph of e_1 and updating the current environment by assigning the new TOS to the variable x_1. After the code for e has been executed, the pointer to the qualified expression's graph should be popped from the stack before the pointer to the graph generated for e is pushed to replace it. Thus a non-recursive qualified expression is compiled according to

$$\begin{aligned} C[\![\,\mathbf{let}\; x_1 = e_1, \ldots, x_m = e_m \;\mathbf{in}\; e \,]\!]\, r\, n = {} & C[\![e_1]\!]\, r\, n\, ;\, C[\![e_2]\!]\, r\,(n+1)\, ; \ldots ; \\ & C[\![e_m]\!]\, r\,(n+m-1)\, ; \\ & C[\![e]\!]\, r'\,(n+m)\, ;\ \mathrm{SLIDE}\ m \end{aligned}$$

where $r' = r\{(n+1)/x_1\}\ldots\{(n+m)/x_m\}$.

Now consider the expression **letrec** $x_1 = e_1$ **in** e, with the single, recursively defined qualified expression, e_1, in which there is at least one occurrence of the variable x_1. In the graph generated for the expression e, x_1 can again be referenced through an updated environment, just as in the non-recursive case. However, since e_1 contains references to itself through occurrences of x_1, the graph of e_1 must also contain corresponding pointers to its redex node. Some rather clever code is generated to construct such a graph. The trick is to first allocate a node – a 'hole' – which will eventually become the redex of the graph e_1, but leave the hole empty, to be filled in after the code generation for e_1 is complete. The pointer to the hole is pushed on to the stack, and the environment is updated to associate its pointer (i.e. the new TOS) with the variable x_1 in the code compiled for e_1. This code is almost that generated by the C-scheme with the updated environment and stack, except that its redex node, pointed to by the TOS, is not the hole allocated for this purpose. Nevertheless, references to x_1 do indeed compile into pointers to the hole according to the environment given above, so all that remains to be done is to copy the contents of the node pointed to by the TOS into the hole, which is pointed to by the next-to-TOS, and pop the stack. This is done by the UPDATE macro, where UPDATE m is defined to overwrite the contents of the node pointed to by TOS − m with the contents of the node pointed to by TOS, and pop the stack. The allocation of holes is performed by the ALLOC macro, where ALLOC m allocates m holes and pushes their pointers on to the stack. We therefore have

$$\begin{aligned} C[\![\,\mathbf{letrec}\; x_1 = e_1 \;\mathbf{in}\; e \,]\!]\, r\, n = {} & \mathrm{ALLOC}\ 1\, ;\, C[\![e_1]\!]\, r'\,(n+1)\, ; \\ & \mathrm{UPDATE}\ 1\, ;\, C[\![e]\!]\, r'\,(n+1)\, ;\ \mathrm{SLIDE}\ 1 \end{aligned}$$

where $r' = r\{(n+1)/x_1\}$.

The corresponding G-machine code for expressions with more than one recursive qualified definition is left as an exercise for the reader. Note that it is always correct to use the recursive version, even if the qualified expressions are not recursive. Thus, the code $C[\![\,\mathbf{letrec}\; x_1 = e_1, \ldots, x_m = e_m \;\mathbf{in}\; e \,]\!]\, r\, n$ is fully general, giving the correct graph whether or not any of the m qualified expressions are mutually recursively defined.

We conclude this section with two examples which illustrate the significant parts of the C-scheme.

EXAMPLE 1: let x = 5 in + x x

Given environment r and a stack of depth n, successive application of the equations defining the function C yields:

$$
\begin{aligned}
C[\text{let } x = 5 \text{ in } + x x]\, r\, n &= C[\![5]\!]\, r\, n \,;\, C[\![(+ x) x]\!]\, r\{(n+1)/x\}(n+1)\,; \\
&\quad \text{SLIDE } 1 \\
&= \text{PUSHINT } 5 \,;\, C[\![x]\!]\, r\{(n+1)/x\}(n+1)\,; \\
&\quad C[\![+ x]\!]\, r\{(n+1)/x\}(n+2)\,;\, \text{MKAP}\,; \\
&\quad \text{SLIDE } 1 \\
&= \text{PUSHINT } 5 \,;\, \text{PUSH } 0\,; \\
&\quad C[\![x]\!]\, r\{(n+1)/x\}(n+2)\,; \\
&\quad C[\![+]\!]\, r\{(n+1)/x\}(n+3)\,;\, \text{MKAP}\,;\, \text{MKAP}\,; \\
&\quad \text{SLIDE } 1 \\
&= \text{PUSHINT } 5 \,;\, \text{PUSH } 0\,;\, \text{PUSH } 1\,;\, \text{PUSHFUN } +\,; \\
&\quad \text{MKAP}\,;\, \text{MKAP}\,;\, \text{SLIDE } 1
\end{aligned}
$$

The execution of this code would proceed as follows. After the execution of the first four macro-instructions, the stack and graph configuration appears as:

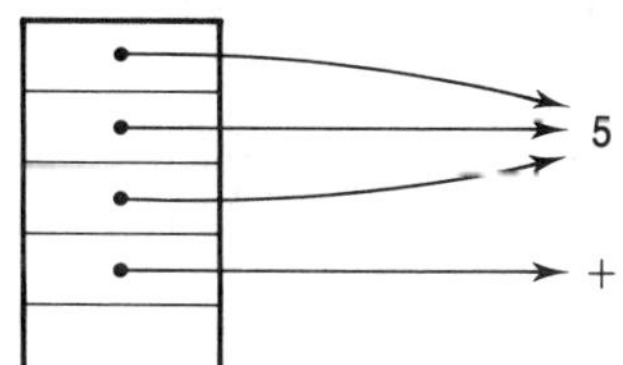

Notice that we draw the stack 'upside down' here so that it grows downwards; the reason for this is simply that the stack then grows in the direction of the unfolding expression graph.

Execution of the next instruction, MKAP, yields:

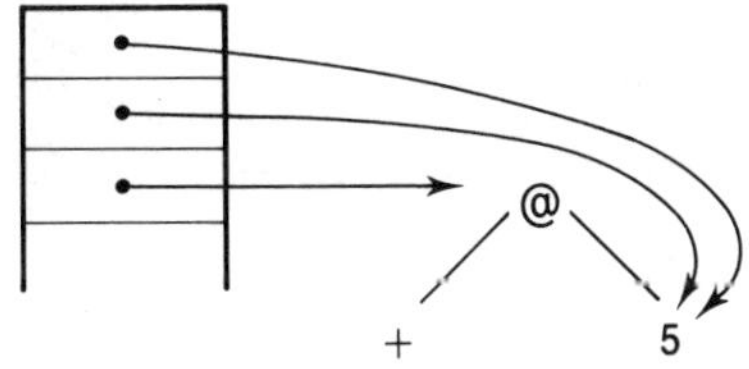

Execution of the second MKAP macro yields:

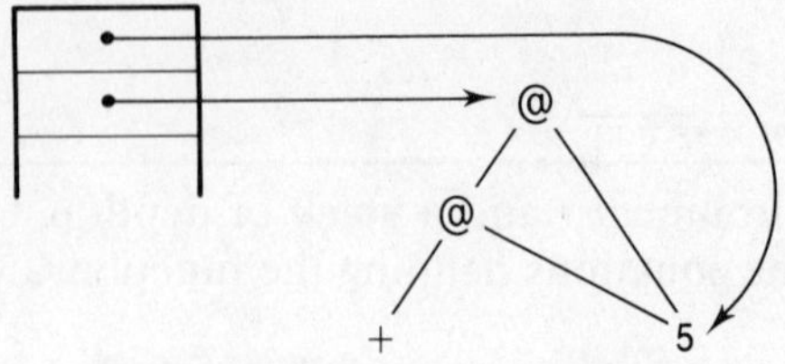

and finally, the SLIDE 1 instruction yields the result:

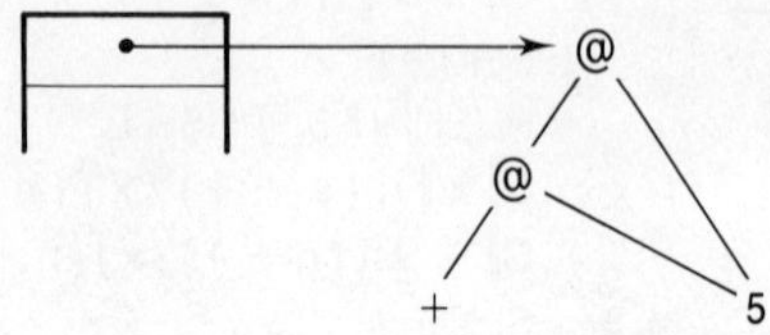

EXAMPLE 2: **letrec** x = f x **in** x x

Again, given environment r and a stack of depth n, successive application of the equations defining the function C yields:

C⟦ **letrec** x = f x **in** x x ⟧ r n
 = ALLOC 1 ; C⟦ f x ⟧ r{ (n + 1) / x } (n + 1) ; UPDATE 1 ;
 C⟦ x x ⟧ r{(n + 1) / x } (n + 1) ; SLIDE 1
 = ALLOC 1 ; C⟦ x ⟧ r{ (n + 1) / x } (n + 1) ;
 C⟦ f ⟧ r{ (n + 1) / x } (n + 2) ; MKAP ;
 UPDATE 1 ; C⟦ x ⟧ r{ (n + 1) / x } (n + 1) ;
 C⟦ x ⟧ r{ (n + 1) / x } (n + 2) ; MKAP ; SLIDE 1
 = ALLOC 1 ; PUSH 0 ; PUSHFUN f ; MKAP ; UPDATE 1 ; PUSH 0 ;
 PUSH 1 ; MKAP ; SLIDE 1

After the execution of the first three macro-instructions, the stack and graph configuration appears as:

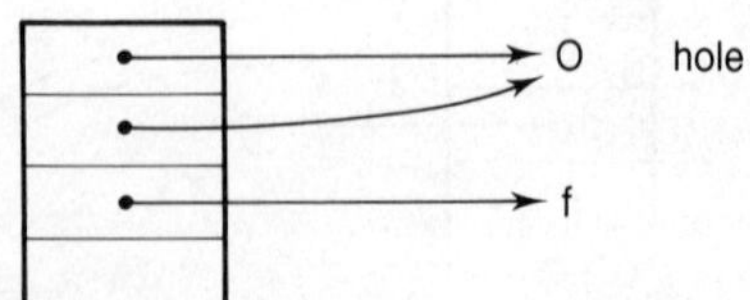

The next instruction, MKAP, then yields:

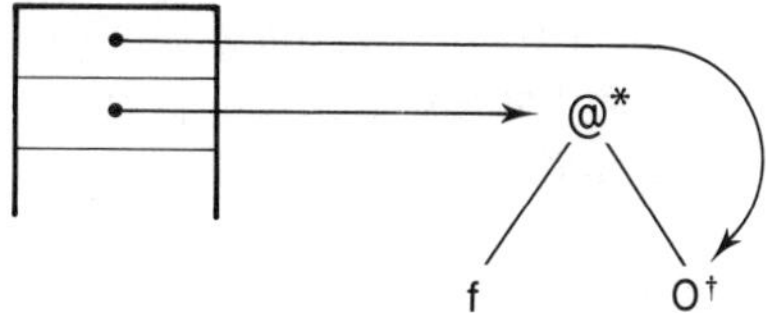

The UPDATE 1 instruction then copies the contents of the node marked * (pointed to by the TOS) into the hole marked † (pointed to by the next-to-TOS), to yield:

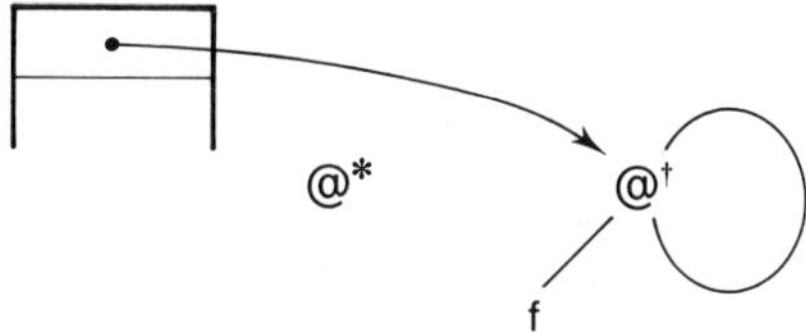

The node marked * has now become detached, and may be recovered by the garbage collector since it is not shared. Execution of the next two instructions, PUSH 0 and PUSH 1, then gives:

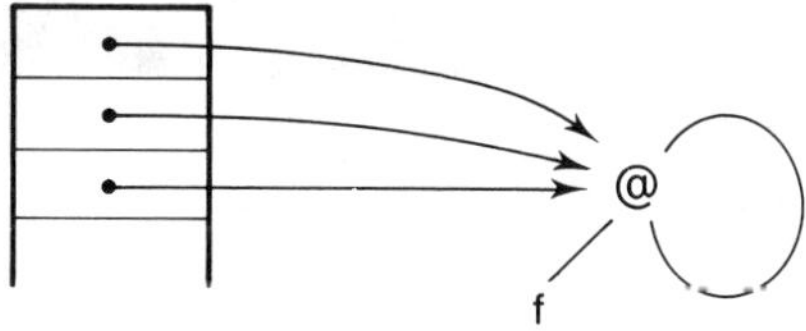

and the next two instructions, MKAP and SLIDE 1, give the result:

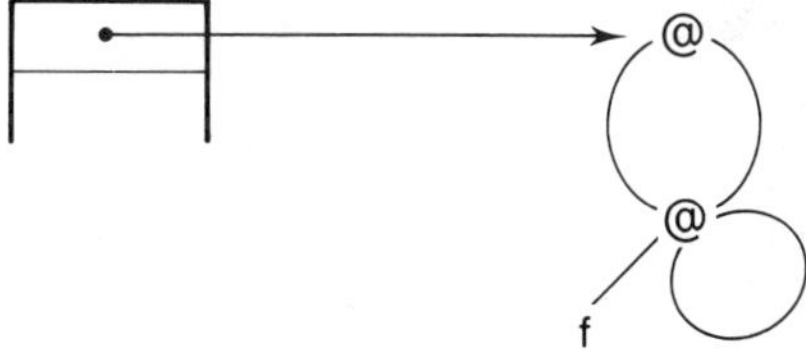

15.3.3 Code generation for expression evaluation – the E-scheme

The E-scheme compiles code to evaluate an expression, represented by a graph, and leave a pointer to the result, a graph representing an expression in WHNF, at the top of the stack. Given the C-scheme, this is a very simple compilation. First, the code to construct the graph representing the expression to be evaluated, say e, is compiled for the arbitrary environment r and stack depth n, giving the code C⟦ e ⟧ r n. At run-time, having constructed the graph, it is then necessary to reduce it, using the macro instruction EVAL, which initiates the unwinding of the spine of the graph and performs any appropriate graph reduction according to the rules given in Chapter 11. This actually gives a complete definition of the E-scheme, namely

E⟦ e ⟧ r n = C⟦ e ⟧ r n ; EVAL

so that, for example,

E⟦ x ⟧ r n = PUSH (n − r(x)) ; EVAL   for variable x

However, if the expression e is in WHNF, then the execution of the EVAL macro has no effect, as can be seen by inspecting its definition given in Section 15.3.1. It is therefore redundant in such cases, and although it cannot be determined in general at compile-time whether or not an expression is in WHNF, this is certainly true of the syntactic types constant, function name and (lazy) constructor function (i.e. cons in our syntax). We can therefore define

E⟦ c ⟧ r n = C⟦ c ⟧ r n = PUSHCTYPE c

for constant c of type c-type, and in particular,

E⟦ i ⟧ r n = PUSHINT i   if i is an integer
E⟦ b ⟧ r n = PUSHBOOL b   if b is a Boolean
E⟦ nil ⟧ r n = PUSHNIL
E⟦ f ⟧ r n = PUSHFUN f   if f is a function name

Similarly, we have

E⟦ cons e_1 e_2 ⟧ r n = C⟦ cons e_1 e_2 ⟧ r n = C⟦ e_2 ⟧ r n ; C⟦ e_1 ⟧ r (n + 1) ; CONS

In fact, there is one more type of expression we might consider separately, namely those involving the primitive functions. Again, we could quite reasonably consider that such functions have already been included in the system described, appearing in leaf nodes in expression graphs, and their application to arguments being initiated by the UNWIND macro. The appropriate delta rules could then be applied exactly as described in Chapter 11. However, in the G-machine implementation, all applications of the strict primitive (or 'basic') functions are evaluated under the B-scheme using the dump as a separate stack. This scheme improves the efficiency of the machine's operation by avoiding the overhead of graph construction. In contrast to the E-scheme, the evaluation of expressions built from the B-scheme has strict semantics, so that the arguments of a primitive function are available on top of the dump in evaluated form, i.e. as constants, when that function is applied. We therefore add to the definition of the compilation function E, equations of the form

$$\mathrm{E}[\![+ e_1\, e_2]\!]\, r\, n = \mathrm{B}[\![+ e_1\, e_2]\!]\, r\, n\,;\ \mathrm{MKINT}$$
$$\mathrm{E}[\![\mathrm{not}\ e_1]\!]\, r\, n = \mathrm{B}[\![\mathrm{not}\ e_1]\!]\, r\, n\,;\ \mathrm{MKBOOL}$$

where there is one such equation for each primitive function. The macro MKINT (respectively MKBOOL) creates a new node in the graph containing the constant which it pops from the top of the dump, and pushes a pointer to the new node on to the stack.

For each strict primitive function, there is a macro instruction denoted by the same name as the function, but in capital letters; for example the macros ADD and NOT correspond to the primitive functions + and not. As in the E-scheme, there is one equation in the B-scheme for each primitive function, of the form

$$\mathrm{B}[\![+ e_1\, e_2]\!]\, r\, n = \mathrm{B}[\![e_1]\!]\, r\, n\,;\ \mathrm{B}[\![e_2]\!]\, r\, (n+1)\,;\ \mathrm{ADD}$$
$$\mathrm{B}[\![\mathrm{not}\ e]\!]\, r\, n = \mathrm{B}[\![e]\!]\, r\, n\,;\ \mathrm{NOT}\ \text{etc.}$$

For any other expression, e, which is not a primitive function application,

$$\mathrm{B}[\![e]\!]\, r\, n = \mathrm{E}[\![e]\!]\, r\, n\,;\ \mathrm{GET}$$

where the macro GET dereferences the TOS (i.e. it fetches the contents of the node to which the TOS points), pops the stack and pushes the contents of the node on to the dump. Thus, the B-scheme calls upon the E-scheme to evaluate the expression e, and the E-scheme may subsequently call upon the B-scheme in a similar fashion.

15.3.4 Compilation of function-bodies – the F-scheme

In Chapter 11 we saw how the next redex node in an expression graph is selected by unwinding the graph's left spine, and in the G-machine implementation, the state of the stack after the graph of the expression $G\ e_1 \ldots e_m$ has been fully unwound is shown in Figure 15.9. Unwinding is performed by execution of the UNWIND instruction which was described

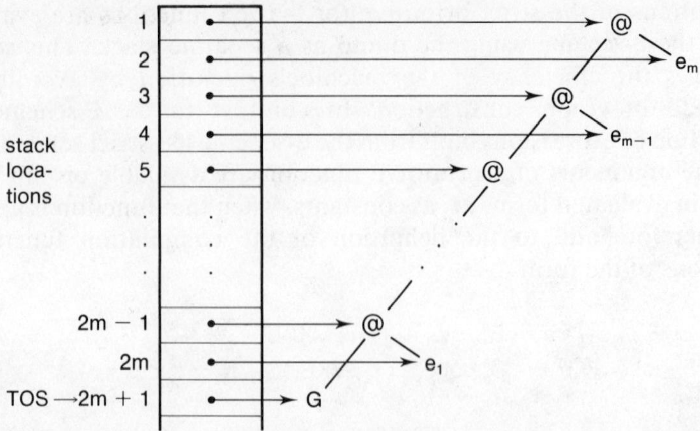

Figure 15.9 Stack-state after unwinding the expression $G\ e_1 \ldots e_m$.

fully in Section 15.3.1. Prior to unwinding, the only item on the stack is a pointer to the redex node of the expression's graph, and during unwinding, successive argument/function pointer pairs are pushed on to the stack until there are no further @-nodes on the spine.

An application of a user-defined function f of arity m is reduced only when f is applied to m arguments, an application of f with less than m arguments being in WHNF already, and the F-scheme generates code that reduces the unwound graph representing the application $f\ e_1 \ldots e_m$ for arbitrary expressions $e_1, \ldots, e_m$. Now, the root node of e_i $(1 \leq i \leq m)$ is pointed to by the pointer in stack position $2(m - i + 1)$, as shown in Figure 15.9. Thus, given the function definition $f\ x_1 \ldots x_m = e$, where the expression e may contain occurrences of formal parameters, i.e. the variables, $\{ x_i \mid 1 \leq i \leq m \}$, the result of reducing the above application, $f\ e_1 \ldots e_m$, is the value of e in the environment

$$r = r_0\{ 2m / x_1 \}\{ 2m - 2 / x_2 \} \ldots \{ 2 / x_m \}$$

with a stack depth $(2m + 1)$. This result would be computed by the code $E[\![e]\!]\, r\, (2m + 1)$, and stored in a new node addressed by a pointer pushed on to the stack, i.e. by the pointer at stack position $(2m + 2)$. However, on return from the invocation of the function f, the result must overwrite the redex node of the function application, according to the normal rules of graph reduction, and this redex node is pointed to by the stack pointer immediately below that pointing to the last argument of the application, i.e. by the pointer at position 1 on the stack. This pointer is therefore $2m + 1$ positions below the TOS, so the redex node is correctly overwritten using the macro instruction UPDATE $(2m + 1)$; recall that UPDATE also pops the stack.

It then remains to pop the top 2m pointers off the stack, leaving the TOS pointing to the root node of the resulting graph, and execute the function return. If the result is a function or an application (a partially applied function), then the return consists of executing an UNWIND instruction to search for the next redex. Otherwise, the stack and expression to be evaluated must be restored from the dump, and the result pointer pushed on to this stack. This constitutes a 'normal' function return. These operations are accomplished by the macro instruction RET 2m, which was also defined fully in Section 15.3.1.

Thus we define the F-scheme by

$$F[\![f\ x_1 \ldots x_m = e]\!] = E[\![e]\!]\ r\ (2m + 1)\ ;\ \text{UPDATE}\ (2m + 1)\ ;\ \text{RET}\ 2m$$

EXAMPLE: f x = cons x (f x)

An eager application of the function f defined by this equation always fails to terminate, but the lazy semantics of the G-machine permits finite parts of the infinite result of the application to be explored. The F-scheme generates the following code for f:

$$F[\![f\ x = \text{cons}\ x\ (f\ x)]\!] = E[\![\text{cons}\ x\ (f\ x)]\!]\ r_1\ 3\ ;\ \text{UPDATE}\ 3\ ;\ \text{RET}\ 2$$

since in the above notation, m = 1 so that $r_1 = r_0\{ 2 / x \}$

$$\begin{aligned} &= C[\![f\ x]\!]\ r_1\ 3\ ;\ C[\![x]\!]\ r_1\ 4\ ;\ \text{CONS}\ ;\ \text{UPDATE}\ 3\ ;\ \text{RET}\ 2 \\ &= C[\![x]\!]\ r_1\ 3\ ;\ C[\![f]\!]\ r_1\ 4\ ;\ \text{MKAP}\ ;\ \text{PUSH}\ (4 - r_1(x))\ ; \\ &\quad \text{CONS}\ ;\ \text{UPDATE}\ 3\ ;\ \text{RET}\ 2 \\ &= \text{PUSH}\ 1\ ;\ \text{PUSHFUN}\ f\ ;\ \text{MKAP}\ ;\ \text{PUSH}\ 2\ ; \\ &\quad \text{CONS}\ ;\ \text{UPDATE}\ 3\ ;\ \text{RET}\ 2 \end{aligned}$$

As with the FPM system, each combinator f_i has an entry in the global environment, E_0 say, which is the pair consisting of the function's arity and the code generated for it by the F-scheme. Thus for example we might have:

$$\begin{aligned} E_0 = \{\ & f_1 : (\ n(1),\ F[\![f_1\ x_1 \ldots x_{n(1)} = e_1]\!]\ ), \\ & \vdots \\ & f_m : (\ n(m),\ F[\![f_m\ x_1 \ldots x_{n(m)} = e_m]\!]\ ) \\ & + : (\ 2,\ F[\![+\ x_1\ x_2 = \text{ADD}\ x_1\ x_2]\!]\ ) \\ & - : (\ 2,\ F[\![+\ x_1\ x_2 = \text{SUB}\ x_1\ x_2]\!]\ ) \\ & \vdots \\ \} & \end{aligned}$$

The primitive functions + , −, not etc. appear in two forms due to the fact that they occur in expressions to be reduced under the E-scheme, but when applied to sufficient argument expressions, their applications are compiled to be executed under the B-scheme which is what 'knows' their delta rules. The use of capital letters distinguishes the truly primitive functions, which only ever arise in redexes, and not in partial applications which are in WHNF. Indeed, if all occurrences of the primitive function + , say, in the top-level expression and function bodies were applied to two arguments, the E-scheme would compile code involving the instruction ADD directly in each case, and the entry for + in the global environment would never be accessed at run-time.

15.3.5 Optimizations

The G-machine as described in this chapter provides a good basis for a realistic implementation of a functional language. However, there are several optimizations that can be made. Some of these are generally applicable to functional language implementations in general, and are provided by the transformation and abstract interpretation techniques considered in Part III. For example, applications of linear functions may be converted into loops, avoiding the overheads involved in function calls, and the optimization for tail recursive functions in particular was planned by Johnsson, who proposed new instructions MOVE, to copy data into loop accumulators, and JFUN, to perform the jumps, for this purpose. Secondly, the G-machine has lazy semantics, resulting in a considerable overhead from constructing and maintaining the graphs representing unevaluated argument expressions (these correspond directly to suspensions). However, many arguments will eventually be required in evaluated form anyway, and so the use of a suspension in such a case could be avoided, the argument being passed by value. A considerable performance improvement can therefore be gained if such strict arguments are detected at compile-time, and the appropriate code generated to pass them by value. This is the purpose of *strictness analysis*, discussed in Chapter 20, which attempts to achieve the best of both of the lazy and eager worlds, giving lazy semantics with efficiency closer to that of an eager system.

Finally, there are more specific optimizations that could be made to this particular implementation. For example, in graph-construction the number of nodes created can be reduced by introducing certain additional macro-instructions. One instance of this arises in code that constructs graphs representing user-defined function applications and recursive qualified expressions. These code sequences terminate with an UPDATE m instruction for some positive integer m, which causes any node that may have been created by the instruction immediately preceding it to become inaccessible, its contents being copied into some redex node elsewhere in the graph. Thus we may define the macros UPCONS and UPMKAP such that the instructions UPCONS m and UPMKAP m replace the pairs of instructions CONS ; UPDATE (m + 1) and MKAP ; UPDATE (m + 1) respectively, but do not create the intermediate node. Applications for these two optimizations have been seen in the examples in Sections 15.3.4 and 15.3.2 respectively.

SUMMARY

- Functional programs expressed in some suitable combinator form can be translated into code for an abstract machine.
- The abstract machine can be implemented on any physical machine by interpreting the instructions of the abstract machine as macros.
- FPM is an example of an eager abstract machine and can be viewed as an optimized version of the SECD machine.
- In FPM source programs are first compiled into a low-level functional code called FC; they are then translated into FPM machine code using a number of translation schemes.
- The G-machine is an example of a lazy abstract machine; it is based on the graph reduction of combinator expressions.
- In the G-machine source programs are compiled into an intermediate code which resembles the intermediate code of Chapter 8; this is then translated into G-machine code again using a number of compilation schemes.
- The G-machine code produced explicitly manipulates a graphical form of the top-level expression; an instruction called UNWIND always locates the leftmost-outermost redex.

EXERCISES

15.1 Write down the FC equivalents of each of the following functions (assume that the function is the first user-defined function in each case):

(a) f = λx. + x (∗ x x)

(b) f = λx.cond (= x 0) 1 (f (− x 1))

(c) f = λx.λy.let s = (+ x 1) in (tuple-3 s s y)

(d) f = λx λy.λg.case-3 (g x 1) 0 y (− x 1) (∗ x y)

(e) f = λx.λg.cond (= x 0) (g (λy. ∗ x (g y))) (f (− x 1) (+ x y))

In case (e) you will have to lambda lift the inner λ-abstraction producing one auxiliary function (combinator); assume that this function ends up being the eighth user-defined function in the list.

15.2 In what sense does FC implement a limited form of pattern matching? What is the advantage of FC in this respect? (*Hint:* Consider expressions of the form

$$\textbf{let } x_1 = E_1 \textbf{ in let } x_2 = E_2 \textbf{ in} \ldots \textbf{let } x_n = E_n \textbf{ in } E$$

where the E_i refer to elements of the same tuple).

15.3 Write down the compiled code sequences for each of the following FC functions (an n : preceding the function indicates that the function number is n):

(a) 3 : (1 (af (bi −) (cv 1) (lv 1)))

(b) 5:(2(tv5(lv1)(mt(cv4)(lv2)(lv7)(af(bi+)(lv3)(lv5)))))

(c) 6 : (2 (if (af (bi <) (lv 1) (lv 2)) (cv 0) (af (ud 6) (af (bi −) (lv 1) (cv 1)) (lv 2)))))

15.4 Consider the following FC expression

(tv 3 (mt E_1 E_2 E_3) E)

(a) Write down the compiled code (F-code) for this expression denoting the compiled code for e by e′.

(b) It will be noted that the compiled code constructs a tuple on the heap and then immediately copies it back onto the stack. As an optimization it would be more efficient to leave the tuple elements on the stack and bypass the heap altogether. What property of the mt expression enables this to be done?

(c) Suggest a modification to the compilation rules which will perform this optimization. (*Hint:* Add an additional parameter to E which indicates the number of elements which the code for the expression being compiled must leave on the stack.)

15.5 The conditional function, cond, has not been considered in the compilation schemes for the G-machine. It is a primitive function of three arguments which is strict only in its first argument, which is Boolean-valued. Define the G-machine code for the evaluation of an expression of the form cond E_1 E_2 E_3 in the environment r when the depth of the stack is n. (*Hint:* look at the code generated for cons and use the B-scheme for the evaluation of the first argument. You will need a new macro COND to select the appropriate branch of the conditional.)

15.6 Give the G-machine code for the function from defined by

from n = cons n (from (succ n))

and show the graph constructed for the expression from (succ 0).

15.7 Work through the evaluation of the G-machine code E⟦ hd (tl (from 1)) ⟧ r_0 0 using the additional rules:

E⟦ hd e ⟧ r n = E⟦ e ⟧ r n ; HD ; EVAL

and

E⟦ tl e ⟧ r n = E⟦ e ⟧ r n ; TL ; EVAL

where HD and TL are the primitive head and tail macro instructions, with the obvious definitions; from is the function defined in Exercise 15.6. Show the behaviour of the stack and graph during the evaluation.

15.8 An application of the Y-combinator can be expressed in λ-lifted form as Y f, where

Y x_1 = D x_1 (D x_1)
D x_1 x_2 = x_1(x_2 x_2)

Derive the code for Y f (in environment r with stack of depth n) and show that it generates the graph representing the expression f (Y f) when it is executed.

Chapter 16
Garbage collection

One of the major benefits of functional languages is that they relieve the programmer from having to think about how or where the program or its data is stored within the memory of the host computer. We define data types at an abstract level with no concern as to how they are represented internally in the machine, this being done automatically. For example, to build a data structure we simply apply constructor functions to build new data objects in terms of already existing objects and we never have to worry about where or how the new object is constructed. Furthermore, the lifetime of the object is also unimportant as far as the programmer is concerned and so we do not have to worry about when (if ever) an object ceases to be required by the program. The price we pay for this high level of abstraction is, of course, the increased complexity of the underlying memory manager. Space for new cells has to be automatically allocated and old cells which are no longer required have to be automatically reclaimed in order that the cell storage area is not rapidly exhausted by the program.

In general most of the complexity of the cell management system is concerned with reclaiming unwanted cells, a process which is commonly known as **garbage collection** and in this chapter we shall look at the more commonly used garbage collectors and will describe the environments in which they are most often used. Some of these collectors aim to minimize the time taken to reclaim the unwanted areas of store; some aim to minimize the size of the memory required; some are concerned with keeping useful data together, i.e. in adjacent store cells, so as to maximize locality for virtual memory systems, whilst others are specifically aimed at the garbage collection of a distributed memory system as might be found in a multiprocessor.

There are three major classes of garbage collector, namely *mark–scan*, *copying* and *reference count* collectors and these are described in Sections 16.2–16.4. Before this, however, Section 16.1 describes some 'typical' memory organizations, which will be referred to in the remaining sections.

16.1 Memory organization

The execution of a functional program will generate a number of run-time data structures. These will include structures built explicitly by the program (such as lists and trees) and structures built by the implementation (such as closures, suspensions or function graphs). These structures are generally constructed in an area of the computer's memory called the **heap**.

In general the heap consists of a collection of memory *words*. The run-time structures of a program will be built on the heap as a collection of distinct *cells*, which are themselves collections of heap words. These cells may be of fixed size, as in a conventional list store (Figure 16.1(a)) or

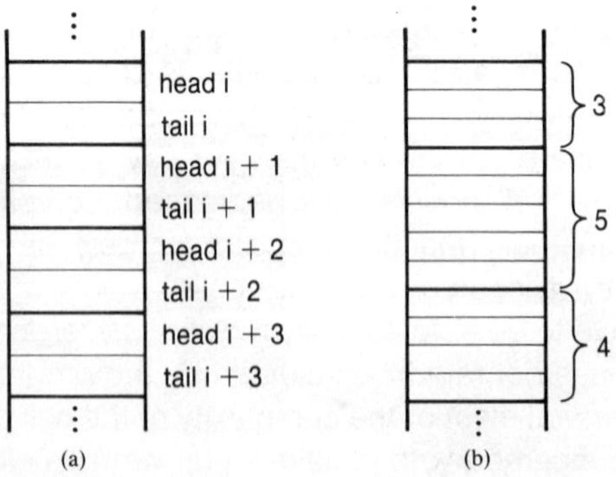

Figure 16.1 Possible list-based heap organizations.

alternatively they may be of variable size (Figure 16.1(b)). In Figure 16.1(a) there is a cell boundary after every second word; in Figure 16.1(b) this boundary must be made explicit by either placing the size of the cell in the first word of the cell or alternatively by placing the address of the next cell in the same word – this amounts to much the same thing.

The advantage of a list-based heap is the simplicity of the corresponding store manager. Each cell is of a fixed size and so the boundaries between cells are easily determined. The disadvantage is that all run-time structures have to be stored as lists. Although this is particularly suitable for a language such as LISP it is rather less appropriate for a language like Hope which allows arbitrarily large user-defined tuples and constructor terms. By using variable size cells for the latter, tuple elements (and hence constructor arguments) can be extracted in constant time using standard indexing techniques rather than having to traverse a list to locate the required element.

16.1.1 Finding the free space

Before we can allocate a heap cell we must know which part(s) of the heap are currently unused. One way of doing this is to maintain a **free list**, which is a chain of free cells pointed to from a free list register. Figure 16.2(a) shows a list-based heap with a free list register pointing to the list of free cells which are chained together through the tail words of each free cell. The shaded cells are those which are currently allocated. If the heap allows variable-size cells, then we can maintain a number of free lists, one for each size of cell. Figure 16.2(b) shows a variable-cell heap supporting

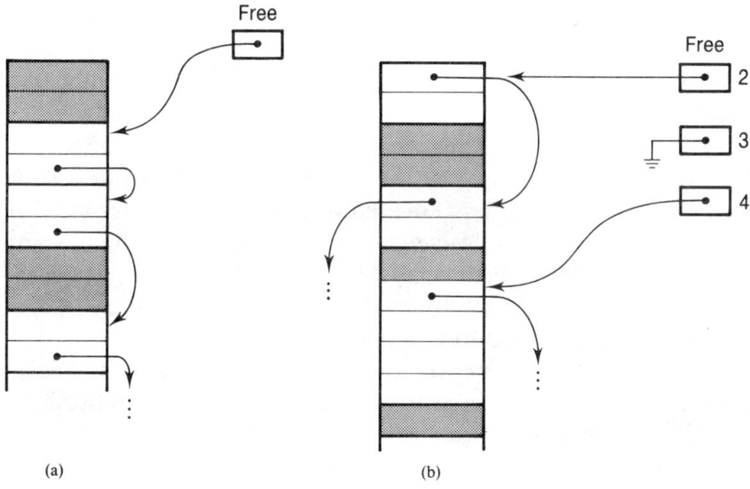

Figure 16.2 Free lists.

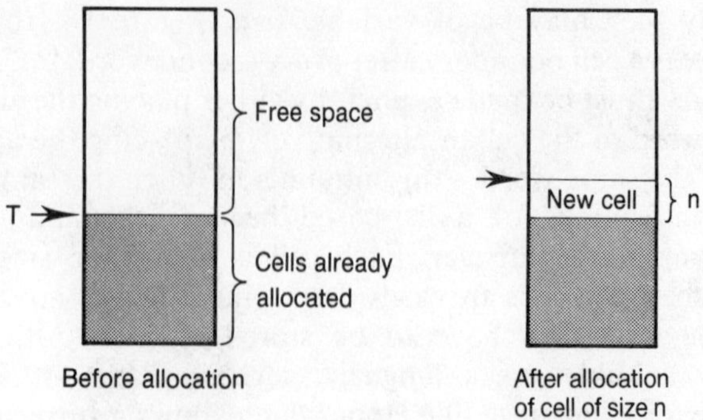

Figure 16.3 Heaps as push-only stacks.

cells of size 2, 3 and 4 only. In general there will be a vector of such pointers in which the ith element points to the list of free cells of the ith size.

When a free cell is required by the program, the appropriate free list is selected (determined by the size of the cell required) and the cell at the front of the list is allocated for use. The corresponding free list register is then updated to point to the next free cell in the list. Each cell must carry with it its own size in order that it can be placed back on the appropriate free list when it is garbage collected.

As an alternative to using a free list to keep track of the free cells, we can organize the heap as a push-only stack in which new cells are always allocated at the top. Each component word of a cell is then added to the heap by pushing it in the same way that words are pushed onto a conventional stack. Here, we require a register, T, which always points to the 'top' of the already allocated cells. When a new cell of size n is allocated the component words of the cell are placed at successive addresses above T and T is updated by n accordingly. This is illustrated in Figure 16.3.

We can divide the heap cells into three categories: those cells which are currently 'in use' by the program are called the *active* cells; those cells which have been allocated but are no longer required by the program are called the *garbage* cells and, as we have already implied, those cells which have yet to be allocated at all are called the *free* cells. It is the job of the garbage collector to locate and recapture the garbage cells, effectively turning them into free cells.

In order to determine which cells are active we have to analyse the current state of the computation. This state may be represented by anything from an evaluation stack (as in an SECD-style machine) to a single pointer referencing the top-level cell of an evaluation graph (as in a graph reduction implementation). The current state, and hence the set of active cells, is indicated by one or more words external to the heap which

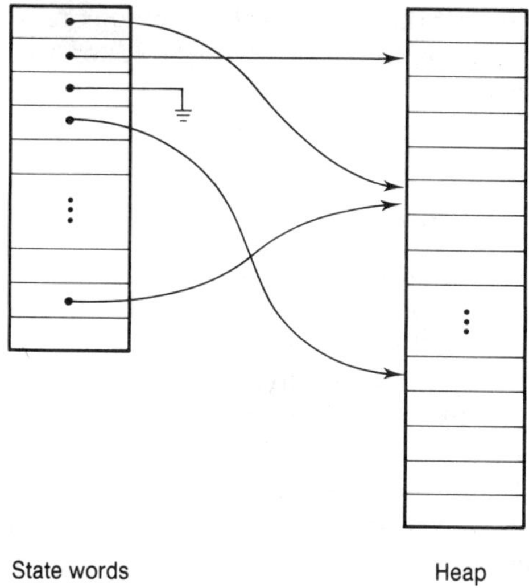

Figure 16.4 State words and heap pointers.

we shall call the **state words**. The set of active cells will consist of the heap cells referred to from these state words together with all those cells accessible from them. In general, we have the situation depicted in Figure 16.4 which shows a single heap and a number of state words, some of which are pointers into the heap.

Each state word and each heap word may contain either an atom (i.e. non-pointer values such as integers, characters etc.) or a pointer to a cell contained in the heap. Since we are interested in tracing the active cells from the state words we must be able to distinguish an atom from a pointer. Traditionally this is done by including a *tag* within each word of the machine. This tag may be used to distinguish a number of different word types, for example numbers, characters, Booleans, pointers and so on, but the garbage collector requires only to distinguish atoms from pointers. We shall therefore assume that there is a single bit within each word which is set to 0 if the word represents an atom and 1 if the word represents a heap pointer.

In summary, garbage collection consists of:

(1) detecting which heap cells are garbage, and
(2) making those cells available for further use.

The process can be intermittent or continuous: an intermittent garbage collector requires the user process (often referred to as the *mutator*) to suspend whilst the garbage collector runs and a continuous garbage collector allows the mutator and garbage collector to proceed concurrently, or at least in an interleaved fashion. For obvious reasons the former is called a *stop/start* garbage collector and the latter a *concurrent* or *real-time* garbage collector.

16.2 Mark–scan garbage collection

In order to describe the basic operation of a mark–scan garbage collector, we shall assume that we have a single list-based heap space with a free list register which points to the start of a chain of free cells in the heap.

We shall assume that the free list is terminated by a nil pointer which is represented by a pointer word to a non-existent cell at address 0. The allocation of a new cell involves using the cell pointed to from the free list register F and then updating F to point to the next cell in the chain. If F contains the address 0 when the allocation is attempted, then the free list is empty and at this point we must invoke the garbage collector to build a new free list from the garbage cells on the heap. If no garbage cells can be found, then the heap is genuinely exhausted and the program must be aborted.

The cell allocation algorithm, which assigns the address of the next free cell on the free list to a variable N can be expressed informally as follows:

```
if F = 0 then garbage collect ;
N := F ; F := tail( F )
```

Note that tail(F) delivers the next free cell in the free list. The imperative nature of the algorithms we describe in this chapter reflect the fact that the garbage collector is part of the abstract machine underlying the implementation; the primitive operations of the abstract machine are naturally imperative since they affect its state.

When the garbage collector is invoked each state word is examined. If it is a pointer to a heap cell, then the referenced cell is *marked*, indicating that it is an active cell. This process is now applied recursively to the head and tail words of the cell. If we encounter a cell which is already marked then the process stops, since we know that all cells which can be traced from that cell must already have been marked. Similarly the recursion terminates if we encounter an atomic cell. When each state word has been examined all the active cells in the heap will have been marked, and conversely all the garbage cells will be left unmarked. The *scan* phase (sometimes referred to as the *sweep* or *collect* phase) now traverses each heap cell and builds up a new free list from all those cells which were left unmarked after completion of the mark phase.

The marking of a cell is usually achieved by including an extra mark bit in each cell. Notice that unlike the tag bits on each word which

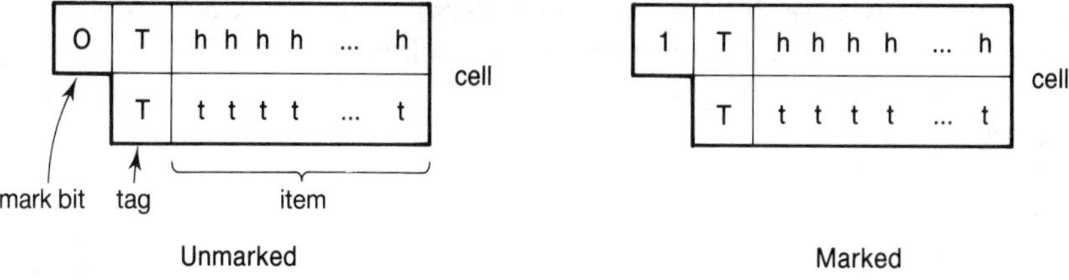

Figure 16.5 Mark bit formats.

distinguish atoms from pointers, the mark bit is attached to the cell as a whole (Figure 16.5).

As we scan the heap rebuilding the free list, the mark bit of each cell must be reset in case the garbage collector is invoked again.

An informal description of the marking algorithm therefore looks like this:

```
To mark a cell C:
  if C is not already marked
  then begin
         set mark bit of C to 1 ;
         if head word of C is a pointer
         then mark cell pointed to by head of C ;
         if tail word of C is non-nil
         then mark cell pointed to by tail of C
       end
```

The scan phase involves constructing a new free list, resetting all mark bits to 0:

```
Initialize the free list to nil ;
For each heap cell:
  if mark bit is 1
  then set mark bit to 0
  else add cell to free list ;
```

One of the problems with the mark phase of the garbage collector is that it involves tracing all the active cells recursively. Encoding the recursion is relatively straightforward, even if the garbage collector is expressed in a low-level language like machine code or microcode. The main problem is that it requires extra space in the form of a recursion stack. The recursion stack must be at least as large as the depth of the deepest structure in the heap which is bounded only by the total size of the heap. Recall from Chapter 11, however, that it is possible to visit every node on a graph using pointer reversal with just two registers FORE and AFT and the same technique can be used in garbage collection to visit every active cell from the set of state words. This obviates the need for the recursion stack.

Although mark–scan garbage collection is straightforward to implement, there are three disadvantages to the scheme. Firstly, it is a stop/start collector requiring the mutator to be suspended whilst garbage collection takes place. Whilst this is satisfactory for batch processing systems it is less so for real-time or interactive systems where a significant pause in the execution of the program is often observed. Secondly, all active cells are visited twice (once during the mark phase and then again during the scan phase) and all garbage cells once (to build up the free list) making it expensive in terms of execution time. Thirdly, it results in the free list and hence component cells of a structure being scattered arbitrarily across the heap. This is not a serious problem in a real-memory system, although the benefits of cacheing might be lost. In a virtual-memory system, however, this fragmentation may prevent any locality between connected cells of a structure and so may result in 'thrashing', i.e. the excessive swapping of pages to and from backing store. However, mark–scan collectors are capable of collecting cyclic data structures, and in many implementations this is an important requirement – an example being in graph reduction which uses cyclic pointers to implement recursion.

16.3 Copying garbage collectors

As we pointed out above, one of the major problems with the mark–scan algorithm is its tendency to fragment the heap store, distributing the active cells of a structure somewhat randomly over the set of heap addresses. In a **copying** garbage collector, the intention is to compact the active cells into a contiguous area of the heap, leaving the free space in a contiguous block of memory. This results in successive cells being allocated in successive heap addresses which helps to localize the adjacent cells of a data structure within the heap. The inherent locality of reference which results is of particular benefit if the target machine is based on virtual memory.

In this section we shall describe four types of copying collector: the first divides the heap into two semispaces and operates by successively moving the active cells of one semispace into the other semispace. The second is an enhancement to this scheme which allows the collector and the mutator to operate concurrently by interleaving them, and this is itself optimized in the third scheme we describe. The fourth algorithm performs the same compacting operation but this time using just a single heap space.

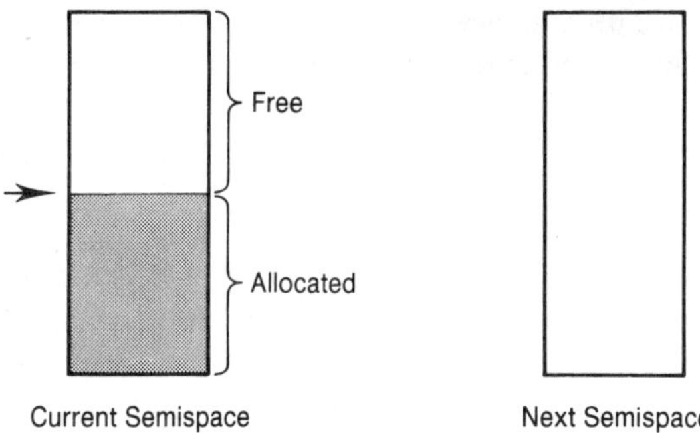

Figure 16.6 Semispace organization.

16.3.1 Two-space compaction

For the purposes of this discussion, and to make the garbage collector as general as possible, we shall assume that the heap contains cells of varying size, each cell containing a size field which indicates the number of words contained in that cell. The trick here is to divide the heap area into two equal-sized semispaces. We shall call these two spaces SPACE1 and SPACE2. The addresses of the topmost and bottommost words of each space are respectively labelled TOP1, BASE1, TOP2 and BASE2. (We maintain all four addresses only for convenience; we could easily compute TOPi given BASEi knowing the size of the semispace.) During the evaluation of the program all new cells are allocated in one of the two semispaces; this semispace is labelled the *current* semispace and the other semispace the *next* semispace. The boundary addresses of the current semispace are given by CURTOP and CURBASE, and those of the next semispace are similarly given by NEXTTOP and NEXTBASE.

The current semispace acts like a push-only stack; new cells are simply allocated on top of the contiguous block of currently active cells and are accessed through pointers rather than the pop operation. The address of the topmost cell in the current semispace is given by a register T. We shall use a notation in which heaps are always drawn growing towards the top of the page in the direction of *decreasing* memory addresses; pushing then corresponds to decrementing T. When there is insufficient space at the top of the current semispace to allocate a new cell, the garbage collector is invoked. This condition can be detected by comparing T with CURTOP prior to the allocation of the next cell, but in these discussions we shall assume that there is an additional register (NFW) which holds a count of the number of free words of heap space currently available. The situtation is shown in Figure 16.6.

The successive words of a newly allocated cell are pushed on the heap in the current semispace, decrementing the T register, but before this can be done we must check to see that sufficient space exists above T to store the cell. If the cell is to contain N words, then we must do the following:

```
NFW := NFW − N ;
if NFW < 0 then garbage collect
```

The garbage collector works by stepping through the state words locating references to active heap cells. However, instead of simply marking those cells, as in the mark–scan collector, they are physically moved into the other semispace – above any cells which have already been moved. The current semispace is referred to as the FROMSPACE and the other semispace as the TOSPACE for obvious reasons. This requires a second register (called T′) to point to the topmost word of the TOSPACE; this is initialized to the value of NEXTBASE before the copying cycle begins and is incremented each time a cell word is placed in the TOSPACE. The original reference to each cell moved and the first word of the old copy of the cell (in the FROMSPACE) are then set to point to the new location of the cell in the TOSPACE. The address left behind in the old copy of the cell is called a **forwarding address** or **invisible pointer** and is used to update any other reference to that cell which may be encountered subsequently. Such a reference is replaced by the forwarding address, i.e the address of the new copy of the cell, as required. This ensures that shared references are preserved during garbage collection. We must be able to distinguish a forwarding address from other types of cell words for this to work and this requires an extra tag bit in the first word of each cell to indicate a forwarding address, rather like the mark bit of the mark–scan collector. Figure 16.7 shows the state of the heap and state word W before and after a cell of size N has been moved into the TOSPACE.

Once the cell has been moved the relocation is applied to all cells referenced from within that cell by recursively invoking the collector as in the mark–scan collector and the pointer reversal trick can be applied equally well. We shall see another method of avoiding this recursion in Section 16.3.2 below. An informal description of the garbage collector is as follows:

```
To garbage-collect:
  For each state word S:
    TRACE S

To TRACE a word W:
  if W is a pointer to cell C
  then if first word of C is the forwarding address F
         then W := F
         else COPY C
```

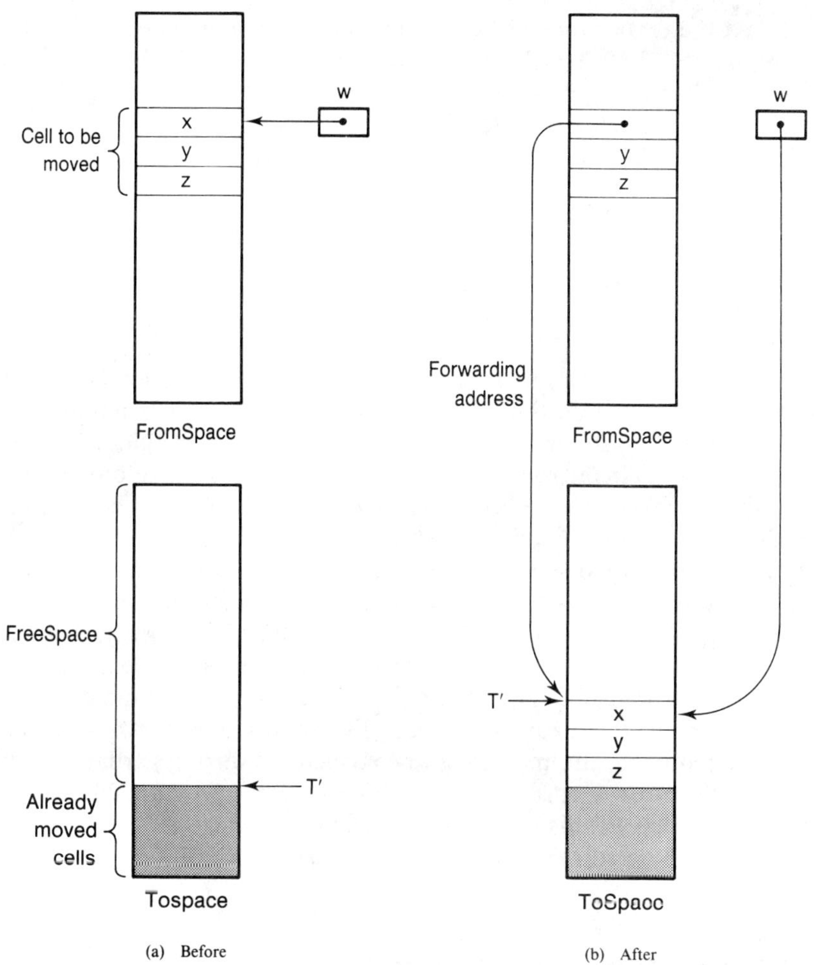

Figure 16.7 Relocating a cell.

```
To COPY a cell C:
  push each word of C on TOSPACE ;
  W := T′ ;
  first word of C ( in FROMSPACE ) := ↑ T′ ;
  for each word W′ in C:
    TRACE W'
```

Note that ↑ A denotes a forwarding address to the cell at address A, i.e. the address A appropriately tagged.

At the end of the garbage collection all the active cells present in the FROMSPACE will have been moved into the TOSPACE. The area above these cells forms the new free space. The number of free words in this area is now assigned to NFW (this is easily computed from the final value of T′ and NEXTTOP) and the two semispaces are swapped:

```
NFW := T′-NEXTTOP
T := T′
Swap NEXTBASE and CURBASE
Swap NEXTTOP and CURTOP
```

Aside from the advantages which derive from compacting the active cells, notice that the number of visits made to each active cell is reduced from 2 in the mark–scan collector to just 1 here. Note also that the garbage cells in FROMSPACE are never accessed at all. In other words the garbage collection time is dependent only on the number of state words and active cells. Of course, the cost of this is measured by the amount of additional space required. The heap must be exactly twice as large as that in a mark–scan collector and the utilization is never better than 50%. However, we must remember that this collector is now rather better suited to virtual memory systems so that in practice the additional space requirement may not be such a serious objection. One emphatic disadvantage of the algorithm is that, like mark–scan, it is a stop/start collector requiring the mutator to be suspended during garbage collection. In the next section we shall describe Baker's algorithm which, although similar to this one, has the added advantage that the mutator and collector can run together in an interleaved fashion.

16.3.2 Baker's algorithm (Baker 1978)†

As in the previous garbage collector, the heap is divided into two semispaces. The mutator proceeds in the usual fashion until the current semispace is exhausted, whereupon the garbage collector is invoked. Unlike the previous algorithm, however, where the garbage collector is run to completion once invoked, the collector now relocates a fixed number (k) of cells and then passes control back to the mutator to continue processing. The next time the mutator requires a new cell to be allocated (for example as a result of calling CONS) another k cells are relocated before the allocation is completed. The process of mutation and partial relocation continues until all active cells in the FROMSPACE have

†The garbage collector we describe is actually a generalization of the one reported in Baker (1978). However, the principles are essentially the same.

been moved to the TOSPACE, whereafter the mutator resumes its operation uninterrupted until the new semispace is again exhausted. The algorithm can be expressed informally as follows:

```
To allocate a cell:
  if the garbage collector is not running
  then if space left then allocate cell else set garbage collector running ;
  if garbage collector running
  then relocate k cells (or all remaining cells if fewer than k left) ;
       allocate space for the new cell ;
       if all cells relocated then stop garbage collector
```

Using this scheme it is now possible for the mutator to encounter references to cells in the FROMSPACE before they have been relocated. However, these cells will only be accessed by the primitive functions like head, tail, index etc. and so we can create the illusion that they are already in the TOSPACE by relocating them whenever they are encountered. If the result of applying one of these primitives is also a cell reference, then that cell must also be relocated and the new address of that cell (in the TOSPACE) returned to the mutator. This gives the mutator the impression that all the active cells have been instantaneously relocated in the TOSPACE after the initial call to the garbage collector. Hence:

```
To take the tail of a cell C1:
  if garbage collector is running
  then if C1 is in FROMSPACE
       then relocate C1 in TOSPACE ;
       if tail of cell points to a cell C2 in FROMSPACE
       then relocate C2 ;
  return the tail of C1
```

and similarly for head, index etc.

When the garbage collector is set running it first swaps over the two semispaces and initializes T′ in such a way that any new cells created by the mutator will be placed in the TOSPACE, the opposite semispace to the one before the garbage collector was invoked. This operation is called FLIP. When this has been done, the state words are searched for references into the heap. When such a reference is found the cell pointed to is relocated into the TOSPACE and a forwarding address is placed in the old copy of the cell as before. Unlike the previous collector, however, the descendants of the relocated cell are not immediately traced. Instead, a second pointer S is set to scan each word in the TOSPACE from the base to the top (i.e. in the direction of allocation) relocating any cells in the FROMSPACE which it finds referenced from the TOSPACE. The cells lying between S and T′ have therefore all been moved but their component

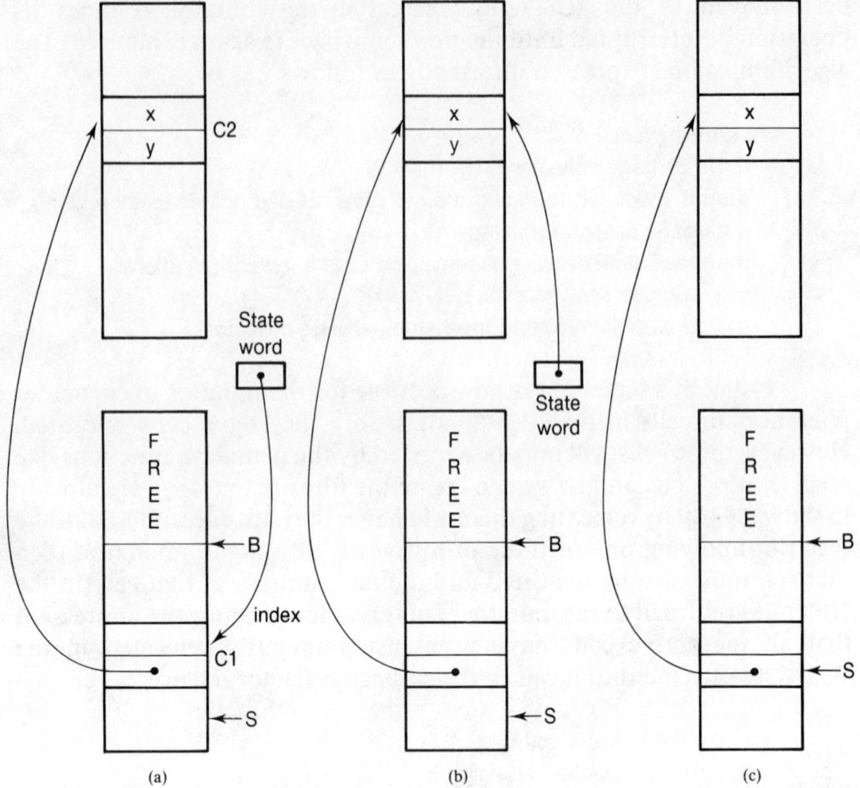

Figure 16.8 Moving a cell.

fields have not yet been updated. This will be done as S works its way up the TOSPACE towards T′. All the cells lying below S will have been moved as will have all their direct descendants. When S < T′ we know that all the active cells in the FROMSPACE will have been moved into the TOSPACE and that the FROMSPACE will contain only garbage. Therefore, the statements 'all cells relocated' and 'relocate k cells' in the cell allocation procedure above should be refined as follows:

```
all cells relocated → S < T′

relocate k cells    → iteration := 1 ;
                      while S ≥ T′ and iteration ≤ k do
                         if word pointed to by S is a pointer to a cell C
                         then relocate C ;
                              iteration := iteration + 1 ;

                         S := S - 1
                      end
```

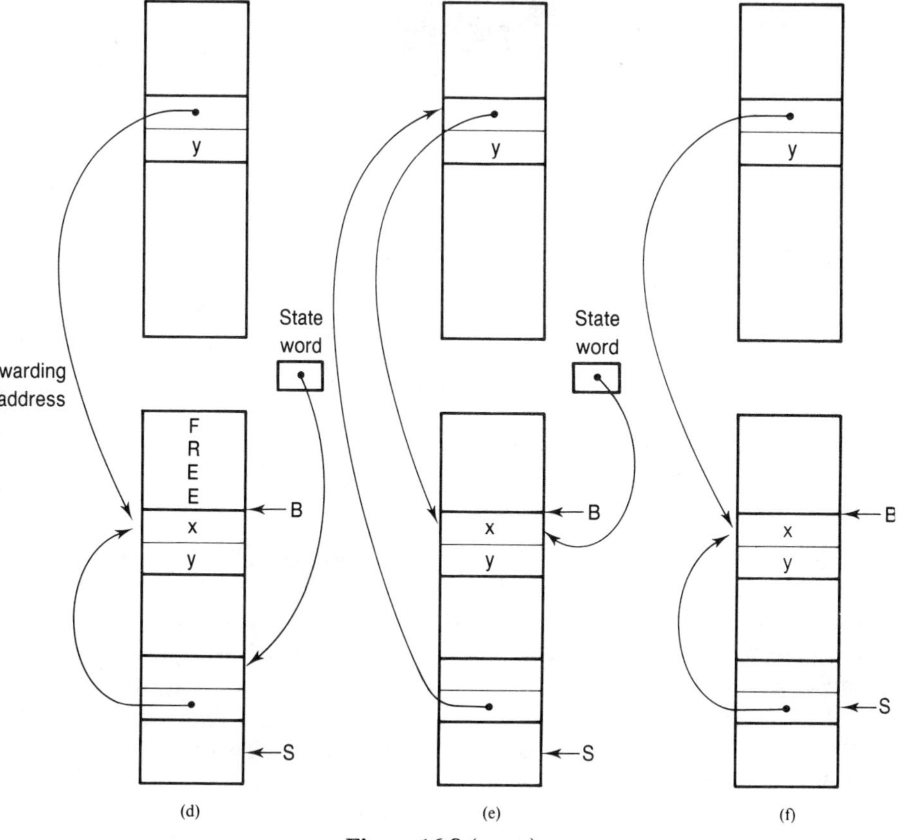

Figure 16.8 (cont.)

By using S and T′ in this way we avoid the need to recursively invoke the collector. What we are doing here is using the FROMSPACE as a collector queue rather than employing a separate area of store as a collector stack as above. For this reason all structures in the FROMSPACE will be copied into the TOSPACE in a breadth-first manner rather than in a depth-first manner as is the case with the recursive collector.

To summarize the operation of the collector, Figure 16.8 shows three example set-ups when a cell C2 is about to be moved. C2 will be moved for one of three reasons: either because the mutator requires to index a cell C1 which contains a reference to C2 (Figure 16.8(a)), or because a reference to C2 has been found while searching the state words after the FLIP operation (Figure 16.8(b)) or because the collector register S has come across a reference to C whilst traversing the TOSPACE (Figure 16.8(c)). Figures 16.8(d–f) show the set-ups which result from Figures 16.8 (a–c) respectively after C2 has been moved.

The allocation of all new cells is done in the TOSPACE. This results in new cells being interleaved with old cells relocated by the collector. When these new cells are visited by the S register nothing will happen

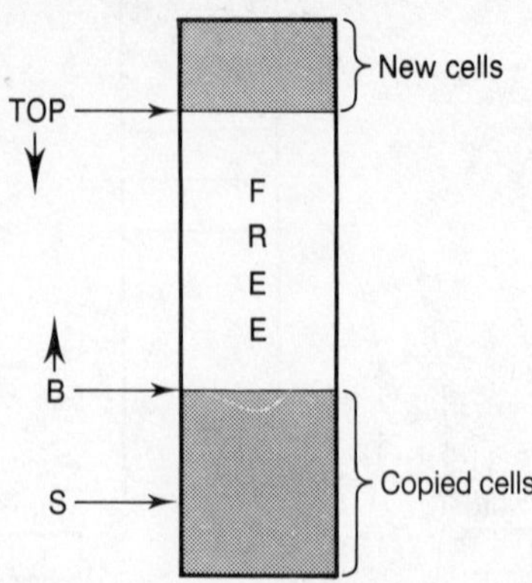

Figure 16.9 Allocating new cells at the top.

since any pointers in these cells will be either to new cells or to cells which have already been moved into the TOSPACE. It is therefore not necessary for S to traverse these cells at all and to do so only slows down the collector. This redundancy can be avoided by allocating all new cells at the topmost end of the heap, i.e. growing down towards T′. This requires an extra pointer TOP to point to the current top of the free area. This will be incremented each time a new cell is allocated in this area. This set-up is shown in Figure 16.9.

Given that the mutator and the collector now place new cells in TOSPACE in an interleaved fashion, we might ask how much space is required in order to guarantee that the TOSPACE is not exhausted before all the accessible cells in the FROMSPACE have been relocated. Alternatively, we might ask how large k should be for a given size of heap space to guarantee the same thing.

For simplicity, let us suppose that each cell is of a fixed size and that after the semispaces have been flipped there are N accessible cells. This means that during garbage collection N cells will be moved from the FROMSPACE to the TOSPACE and N / k cells (rounded up to the next integer) will be newly created by the mutator; remember that each new cell allocation causes k active cells to be relocated in the TOSPACE. This requires a total semispace capacity of $N + N / k$ cells, i.e. a total heap space capacity of $2N(1 + 1 / k)$ cells. For example if one old cell is relocated each time a new cell is allocated (i.e. if $k = 1$) then we will require a total of 4N cells in the heap. This figure can be reduced by increasing k, although with diminishing returns. Turning the argument around, if we now suppose that the program has a maximum cell requirement of N cells and that each semispace contains space for M cells, then the parameter k must be at least $N / (M - N)$.

16.3.3 Multiple heap spaces

An obvious problem with the previous two algorithms is that no more than 50% of the available heap space will be in use at any time. Additionally, every active cell is relocated during each garbage collect cycle. An important empirical observation about the behaviour of functional programs, however, is that

> the most recently allocated heap cells almost invariably contain the most garbage

in other words, the older a cell is the more likely it is to be active.

This suggests that we can overcome the major problems with Baker's algorithm by dividing the heap into a larger number of smaller spaces (instead of using just two) and by garbage collecting (condemning) one region at a time, with younger regions being condemned more frequently than older regions (Lieberman and Hewitt, 1983).

The heap is then divided into n equal-sized regions, n - 1 of which are active, the remaining one being 'spare' for the purposes of relocation. Each region is now given a generation number which indicates when that region came into use – i.e. when the mutator first started using it. The higher the generation number the younger the region. The idea is that the younger regions (which should contain relatively more garbage than older regions) are condemned more often than the older regions. Condemning a region consists of relocating the active cells therein into the spare region in the manner prescribed by Baker's algorithm. A **condemnation frequency function** determines which region to condemn next, i.e. which region to designate as the next FROMSPACE. For example, we could condemn the region with generation number g twice as often as that of generation number g - 1, and so on. We may attach another parameter to a region to help us here, namely a version number which is incremented each time the region is condemned whilst its generation number remains unchanged.

The implementation of this scheme would be straighforward enough were it not for the fact that there may be references to cells in the designated FROMSPACE from the other regions in the heap. However, there is another important empirical observation which helps us here:

> most references across region boundaries tend to be to older regions

This says that in most cases the pointer components of a new cell will be pointers to cells which already exist. To avoid the need to search through all the older regions, we therefore maintain an **entry table** with each region which contains the complete set of pointers into that region from older regions. (All pointers from older regions are directed through these

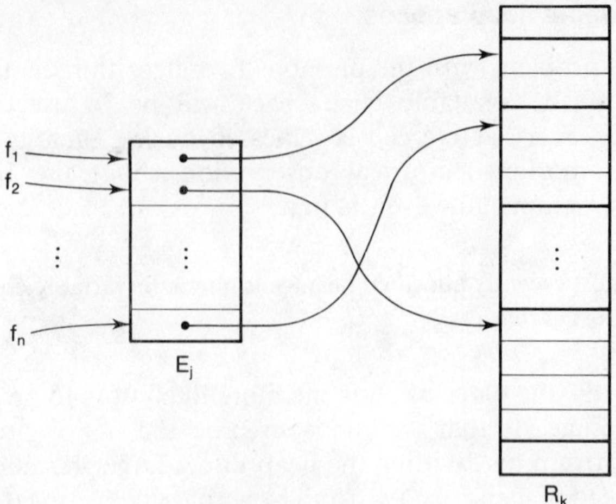

Figure 16.10 Entry tables.

entry tables, giving an extra level of indirection in the mutator for such addressing.) Now the only regions we have to search completely for pointers into the condemned region are the younger regions. Since younger regions are condemned more frequently than older regions the number of regions younger than the condemned region will, on average, be small. Figure 16.10 shows a region R_k and its corresponding entry table E_j (we will see below that entry tables may move between regions so that j and k are not necessarily the same).

The set of forward pointers $f_1, f_2, \ldots, f_n$ from older regions are directed into R_k via the entry table E_j. If we now condemn region R_k and apply Baker's algorithm to relocate the active cells in R_k into the spare region, say R_s, then we have only to update the pointers in E_j to resolve the complete set of forward references.

When the relocation is complete, R_k becomes the spare region. Therefore, we have to record the fact that entry table E_j is now associated with R_s, rather than R_k as before, and so we must also maintain a mapping table which records which entry tables are associated with which regions. Using mapping tables in this way, the external forward references $f_1, f_2, \ldots, f_n$ need never be changed.

This presents us with only one problem, namely how large to make the entry tables. An elegant solution to this problem (and one which also obviates the need for the mapping table) involves locating the entry table for a region *within* that region in the form of a stack which grows from the top of the region downwards with the cells being allocated at the bottom of the region (Davies, 1985). Because the entry tables are no longer separate from the regions themselves, the entry table associated with a

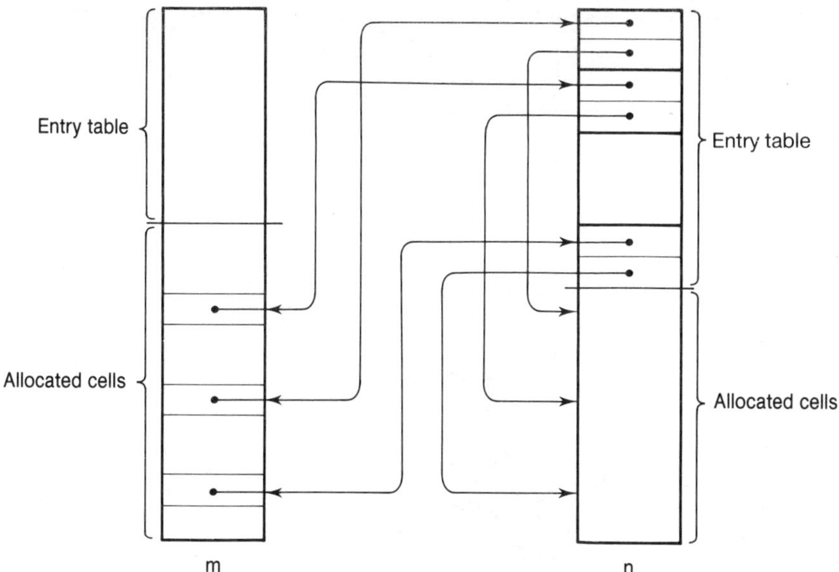

Figure 16.11 Entry tables as stacks.

region must be relocated along with the cells in that region whenever the region is condemned. Consequently those cells in older regions which point into the entry table of the region being condemned must also be updated, which requires that the elements of the entry table also contain pointers back to these older cells. This requires each entry table element to contain two pointers: one into the condemned region and one to the addressing cell in the older region. An example set-up is illustrated in Figure 16.11. This shows region n together with the forward pointers from region m which point into the entry table for region n.

In the worst case the region will be full of active cells each of which is accessed from an older region and so the entry table is required to contain as many entries as there are cells within the region. For example, if each cell comprises two words and if the capacity of the region is to be N cells then the total size of the region must be 4N words.

16.3.4 Morris's algorithm

In the previous sections we have seen how compaction can be achieved by relocating active heap cells from one region of the heap to another 'spare' region. The primary objective of Morris's garbage collection algorithm is to perform this compaction in the same heap area as the one in which these cells originally reside (Morris, 1978).

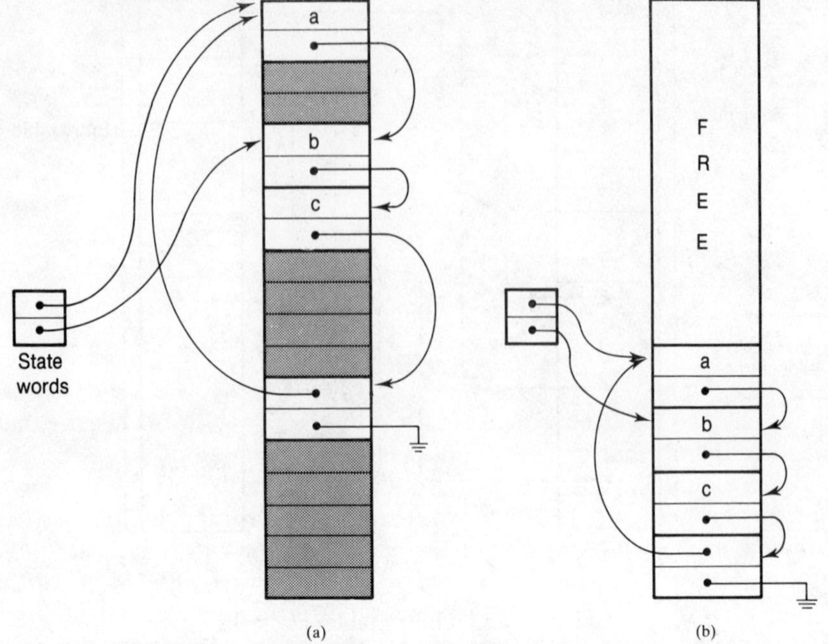

Figure 16.12 The effect of Morris's algorithm.

In order to understand the subtleties of the algorithm it is worthwhile looking at the heap before and after the compaction has taken place. Figure 16.12 shows a simple arrangement in which two external pointers (state words) reference two heap structures with shared descendants and a circular pointer.

Notice that after the compaction the direction of each pointer is preserved, i.e. if C1 is above C2 in the heap before the compaction then it will be above C2 after the compaction. What we are doing here is 'closing up the garbage gaps' (these are shown shaded in Figure 16.12(a)) and pushing the active cells together in the direction of the base of the heap.

For this process to work we have to keep track of all those cells referencing a particular cell C so that when C is relocated all the pointers to C can be updated. The problem, of course, is to do this using no extra space (except possibly a small number of registers). The trick is again to use the pointer reversal technique described in Chapter 11 and referred to earlier in this chapter. Suppose we have the set-up shown in Figure 16.13(a). Cells A, B and C all reference a shared cell S which contains an item I in its first word. To remember all those cells which point to S we turn all the pointers around and form a chain with I contained in the last pointer field

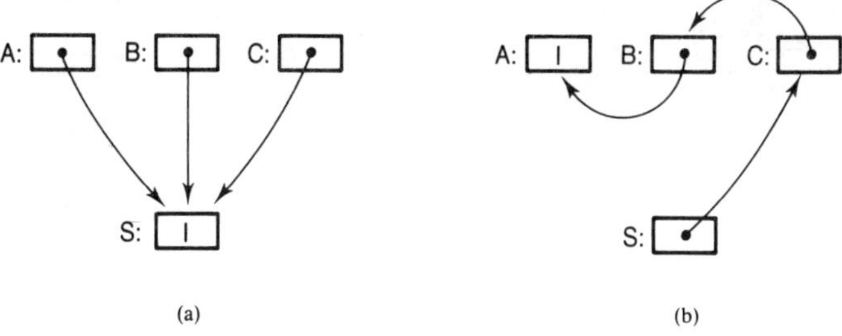

Figure 16.13 Pointer reversal.

in the chain. This arrangement is shown in Figure 16.13(b). Observe that we lose no information as a result of this transformation.

To achieve this is actually quite simple: when we encounter a pointer as in Figure 16.14(a), we 'reverse the pointer' by storing the contents of the cell pointed to in the pointer cell and storing the address of the pointer cell in the cell it pointed to, as shown in Figure 16.14(b). Notice that in order to be able to detect the start and end points of a reverse pointer chain we must annotate each reverse pointer as such which requires one extra tag bit in each pointer field. This annotation is shown in Figure 16.14 by a shaded triangle within the pointer field. Notice also that each reverse pointer points to an individual word within a cell rather than to the cell as a whole. This is because we may wish to build several pointer chains, each 'passing through' different words of the same cell.

The operation of the collection phase of the garbage collector assumes that all active cells have previously been marked by tracing

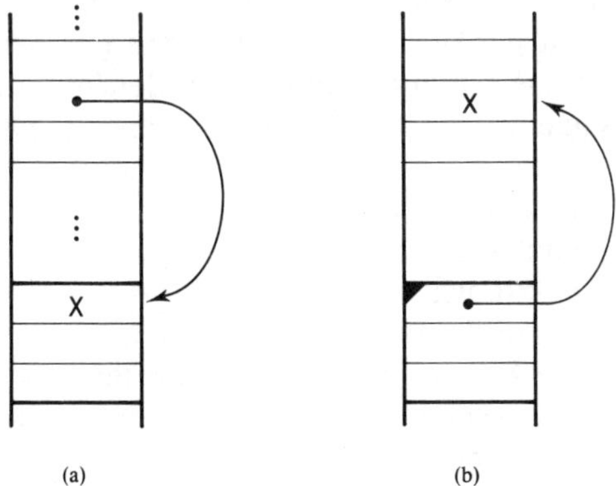

Figure 16.14 One pointer reversal step.

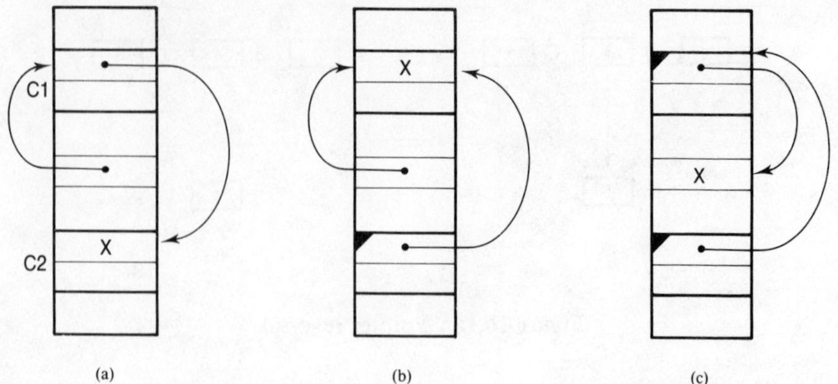

Figure 16.15 Forward and backward pointer conflict.

pointers from the state words. During the mark phase the total number, A, of active words (i.e. words contained within active cells) must be counted in order that the number of words of garbage, which we shall call G, can be computed – this is easily obtained by subtracting A from the total heap size. The idea is to use G to compute the eventual addresses of each cell after they have been relocated. If the topmost word of the heap is located at the address T, then the first active cell nearest T will eventually end up at the new address $T + G$, the next cell after that will end up at $T + G + S_1$ (where S_1 is the size of the first active cell), the third will end up at $T + G + S_1 + S_2$, and so on.

Once the active cells have been counted and marked (as in mark–scan collection) the collector proceeds in two phases. The first phase replaces all forward references (i.e. references to cells further down the heap than the pointer itself) by the eventual addresses of those cells. The second phase does the same thing only with backward pointers (i.e. pointers to cells further up the heap than the pointer itself) and also moves the cells to their final locations. In order to understand why it is necessary to 'resolve' these references in two separate passes consider the set-up shown in Figure 16.15(a), and observe what happens if we try to resolve the references in just a single pass.

When we encounter a reference to cell C2 we will form a new reverse pointer as shown in Figure 16.15(b). When we reach the backward pointer to cell C1 we will similarly generate another reverse pointer as shown in Figure 16.15(c). We can interpret this diagram as meaning that all the references are to C2, which is clearly wrong. The problem is that we have built a reverse pointer to a word which represents the end of an already existing reverse pointer chain. Establishing the new pointer has the effect of extending the original pointer chain, which is not

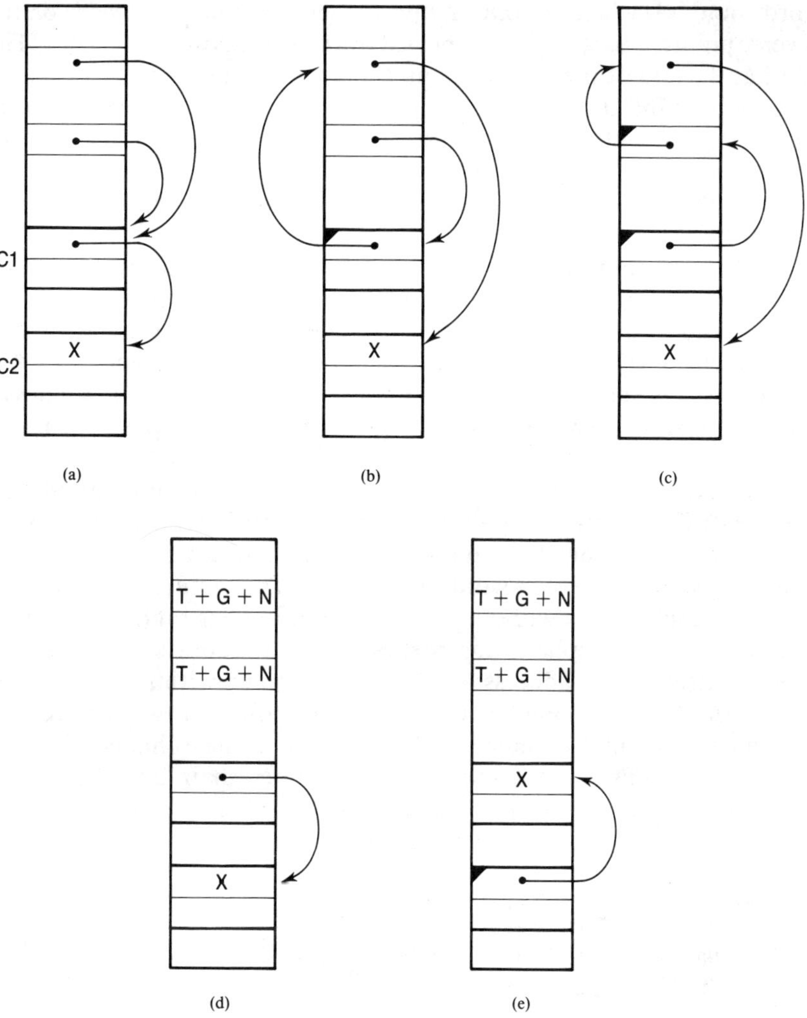

Figure 16.16 Morris's algorithm at work.

what we required. We have therefore to avoid building reverse pointers to cells which have already been processed, which explains why the collector must operate in two passes.

On the first pass down the heap we again count the active words as we process them in order that the eventual address of each cell can be determined as it is encountered (remember from above that we require to know the size of each cell, S_1, S_2, ..., or more precisely the accumulated cell sizes $S_1 + S_2 + \ldots$ in order to compute these addresses, which is exactly what we achieve by counting the active words). So, if the active word count is N when we come across a reverse pointer, each word on the reverse pointer chain must be replaced by the new address T + G + N. The word at the end of the pointer chain (indicated by the absence of the reverse pointer bit) then replaces the word at the start of the reverse pointer chain. If this replacement should happen to restore another forward pointer to its original position, a further pointer reversal will be required immmediately. To illustrate this scheme Figure 16.16 shows a simple example.

Initially there is a shared cell C1 whose first field points to another cell C2, lower down the heap (Figure 16.16(a)). The collector walks down the heap and on encountering the first reference to C1 starts a reverse pointer chain (Figure 16.16(b)). When the second reference to C1 is encountered we extend the chain (Figure 16.16(c)). Each time we pass a marked word we increment the active word counter. Suppose, then, that when we reach the first word in cell C1 this counter contains the value N. This tells us that the eventual location of cell C1 will be at address T + G + N. Thus, when we find the reverse pointer in C1 (marked as such by the shaded triangle) we follow the pointer chain placing the new address T + G + N in each word in the chain. This pointer chasing stops when we reach a word without the reverse pointer flag bit (no shaded triangle). This field replaces the first word in the pointer chain and is replaced itself by the address T + G + N. We end up with the situation in Figure 16.16(d). To complete the picture, we note that this replacement restores the original pointer to cell C2 from C1. Since this is a forward reference we must start another reverse pointer chain and the process continues. This is shown in Figure 16.16(e). The algorithm for the forward traversal can be expressed informally as follows:

```
N := 0 ; W := address of first word in heap ;
while W ≤ address of last word in heap do
  if W↑ is marked as active
  then if W↑ is a forward pointer, P
         then t := P↑ ;      {start reverse pointer chain}
              P↑ := ← W ;
              W↑ := t ;
              W := W + 1
         else if W↑ is a reverse pointer
              then chase( W, T + G + N, W ) ;
         N := N + 1
  else W := W + 1
end
```

A↑ denotes the value at address A and ←A denotes a reverse pointer to A (i.e. a pointer with a shaded triangle). chase(C, A, W) chases the reverse pointer chain starting at C, setting each word in the chain to A, and replaces the word at W to the last value in the chain:

```
chase( C, A, W ) =
   if C↑ is a reverse pointer
   then next := C↑ ;
         C↑ := A ;
         chase( next, A, W )
   else W :=C↑
```

Once the sweep from the top to the bottom of the heap has been completed the process is repeated, this time from bottom to top, to resolve all the backward references. During this pass we perform the relocation of the active cells. Again this requires us to maintain an active cell counter, only this time we use it to move the cells to their final destinations. The counter starts off at A, the total number of active cells, and is decremented each time we process an active word. Each active word is moved to its final location T + G + N (where N is the current value of the counter). Any reverse pointer chains which must be started from this word will then be established after the word has been moved (this simply guarantees that the new copy of the cell will be updated when this reverse pointer chain is eventually unwound). At the end of the second sweep, all of the active cells will have been compacted at the bottom end of the heap and all pointers adjusted accordingly. The algorithm for the reverse sweep can be expressed informally as follows:

```
N := A ; W := address of the last heap cell
while W ≥ address of first cell in heap do
   if W↑ is active
   then copy word to address T + G + N;
         if W↑ is a backward pointer, P
         then ( T + G + N )↑ := P↑
               P↑ := ← ( T + G + N );
               W := W − 1
         else if W↑ is a reverse pointer
               then chase( W, T + G + N, W )
         N := N − 1
   else W := W − 1
end
```

Notice that when we talk of a 'reverse pointer' we actually mean a pointer in the opposite direction to the direction of the scan.

The cost of performing this compaction in the same heap space is that it requires two full passes through the heap (scanning both active and garbage cells) plus a 'partial' traversal of the heap to mark the active cells in the first place. It is therefore rather more costly in execution time than the copying collectors so far described. Also, it is not possible to implement Morris's collector in real time because the mutator has nowhere to put new cells until the whole process is completed. Of particular significance to some language implementations, however, is the fact that the order of the active cells remains unchanged as a result of garbage collection.

16.4 Reference count garbage collection

In the garbage collectors we have encountered so far, determining the active cells in the heap has been carried out by a logically separate process from that of the mutator. The tracing operation starts at the state words and progresses into the heap by chasing pointers. An alternative to this two-process model of garbage collection is a unified approach in which the active status of a cell is continuously updated as part of the user process. Unlike the garbage collectors described above, where we are interested only in whether a given cell is active, here we maintain within each cell a counter which records the number of references to that cell; whenever this count is greater than zero, that cell is by definition active.

Each cell in the heap therefore contains an additional integer-valued field called the **reference count** field. If there are n references to a cell from the state words and from other active cells in the heap, then the reference count of that cell will be n. When a cell is first allocated, therefore, its reference count is set to one, and each time a new reference to that cell is created its reference count will be increased by one. Conversely, each time a reference to it is destroyed its reference count is reduced by one. When the reference count reaches zero, we know that there are no longer any references to the cell so that it can be recycled. Before we can recycle it, however, we must also decrement the reference count of each cell pointed to from within that cell (destroying this cell has the effect of removing one reference from each cell it points to). The reference counts of these cells may also be reduced to zero as a result and so the process will be repeated on these cells, notionally in a recursive manner. Notice that using this scheme the heap cells are not relocated as the result of garbage collection. For this reason reference count collectors normally work in conjunction with a free list. When a cell is recovered, by virtue of its reference count dropping to zero, it can be added to the free list.

An important feature of this type of collection is that the user program is not required to stop while the garbage collector runs; garbage collection takes place continuously as part of the user program. Another advantage of the scheme is its suitability for use in a distributed environment. Here, decrementing the reference count of a cell can take place within one memory module while useful computation continues elsewhere.

The major disadvantages of the scheme are that it requires additional space within each cell to hold the reference count and that, as with the mark–scan algorithm, it tends to fragment the heap since the active cells are not relocated. A further disadvantage is that it does not naturally enable cyclic structures to be collected since such a structure always has a reference count of at least one (it points to itself). However, the scheme can be extended to get round this problem by associating a reference count with each *maximal cyclic structure* (a cyclic structure which is not a component of some other cyclic structure). A graph of such structures is then guaranteed to be acyclic, which means it is conducive to standard reference count techniques. The main problem is identifying these maximal cycles – the full details of the scheme can be found in Hughes (1985).

16.4.1 Lazy garbage collection

One problem with standard reference counting is that dereferencing the top-level cell of a large data structure may cause the whole structure to become garbage (because none of the internal nodes are shared) whereupon there may be a delay in the user process whilst these cells are reclaimed. The use of a separate processor (or maybe even multiple processors) can help here. However, the problem can also be solved on a single processor implementation by modifying the organization of the free list. Instead of 'chasing' all the references from a garbage cell as described above, we can use a so-called 'to be decremented' stack (TBD stack) which holds the addresses of all cells which are due to have their reference counts decremented (Glaser and Thompson, 1985). Incrementing the reference count of a cell proceeds in the usual way. To decrement the reference count of a cell, however, we need do no more than push the address of that cell onto the TBD stack. The tricky part comes when we want to allocate a new cell. To do this we pop the TBD stack and inspect the reference count of the addressed cell. If this is 1 then we know that the cell is garbage (its reference count is due to be reduced to 0). Consequently the cell can be allocated immediately after pushing all the pointer fields in it onto the TBD stack; these are also due to be decremented. The allocated cell even has the correct initial reference count, i.e. 1! If, on the other hand, the reference count is greater than one, then it is decremented in the usual way and the next entry is popped from the TBD stack. This process continues until the allocation is successful or the TBD stack is exhausted, whereupon the free list is used. Hence, assuming for now that there is at least one entry on the TBD stack with a reference count of one:

To allocate a cell:

```
while cell not allocated do
  P := pop TBD stack ;
  if Rp = 1
  then push all pointer fields of P↑ onto TBD stack ;
       ALLOCATE P
  else Rp := Rp − 1
end
```

To duplicate a pointer C:

```
Rc := Rc + 1
```

To destroy a pointer C:

```
push C onto the TBD stack
```

Although the garbage collection now takes place in a lazy fashion, it is still possible for there to be a large number of addresses at the top of the stack each of whose corresponding cells has a reference count greater than 1. However, this is less likely than there being a long chain of references to be 'chased' in the previous scheme as a consequence of another important empirical observation concerning the behaviour of functional programs:

most cells have a reference count of 1 (Stoye *et al.*, 1984)

In other words, most cells are not shared. This observation prompts another reference count technique which is described in the next section.

Despite this observation, however, it is still possible, in pathological cases, for there to be a long chain of shared cells referenced at the top of the TBD stack. To get round this problem we can combine the TBD stack with a conventional push-only heap and then set a limit on the number of times we allow the TBD stack to be popped without finding a garbage cell. If we set this limit to k, say, then if k successive pops of the TBD stack all fail to find a garbage cell, or if the TBD stack is exhausted, then we can simply push a cell onto the heap in the usual way. This improves the real-time performance of the collector. However, if the push-only heap is ever exhausted, then we have no choice but to continue the popping of the TBD stack until a garbage cell is found. If both the heap and the TBD stack are exhausted then the program must, of course, abort.

16.4.2 Single-bit reference counts

The single-bit reference count scheme is based on the observation that most cells are not shared and so have a maximum reference count of 1. As the name implies the reference count of each cell is just a single bit instead of a whole word. If this bit is 0 then there is just a single reference to that cell. If a new reference to that cell is created (i.e. if that cell ever becomes shared) then the reference count bit is set to 1. Once this has been done the bit cannot be reset to 0 because we cannot be sure that there are only two references to that cell – there may be many more. For this reason it will be necessary to employ a second type of garbage collector in the event that all the cells in the heap acquire a reference count bit of 1. However, because of the predominance of single references, this garbage collector will be invoked considerably less often than if used on its own.

A particularly ingenious optimization to this scheme places the reference count bit within the pointer to a cell rather than in the cell itself. If this bit is 0 then we know that the pointer is the only pointer to that cell. Whenever we duplicate a pointer to the cell (the way in which sharing is realized) we have only to set the bit to 1 within the original pointer and the new pointer to obtain the required effect. If we ever destroy a pointer whose reference count reads 0, then we know that this is the only pointer to the referenced cell and so that cell can be immediately reclaimed. The pointers within the referenced cell must then be inspected similarly; if any have a reference count of 0 then their referenced cells can be reclaimed and so on. Now observe that the duplication of a pointer requires no access to the referenced cell; it is here that we see the advantage of storing the reference count in the pointers to cells rather than in the cells themselves. In a sequential implementation this saves one memory access per copy; in a distributed environment it saves one (possibly remote) communication with the corresponding cell.

16.4.3 'Weighted' reference counts

The idea of placing the reference count of a cell within the pointer(s) to that cell can be extended to schemes allowing reference counts greater than unity. The scheme described here, which is sometimes called the **weighted** reference count technique, was developed independently by Thomas (1981) and Bevan (1985).

The idea is that each cell carries a standard reference count and each pointer a weight such that at all times the sum of the weights of the pointers to a cell is equal to the reference count in the cell. Thus, a pointer with a weight of W can be viewed as being equivalent to W pointers each with a weight of 1. Now, as in the single-bit reference count scheme, when a pointer is duplicated it is not necessary to access the referenced cell – rather the weight of the pointer can be equally divided between

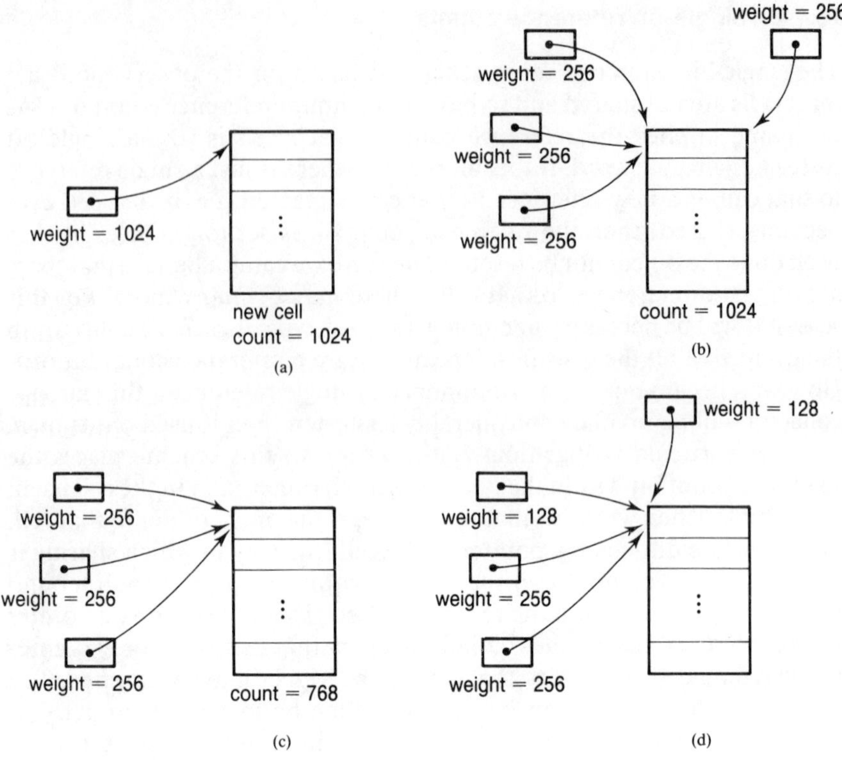

Figure 16.17 Weighted reference counts.

itself and the new pointers, the reference count of the cell remaining unchanged. When a pointer is destroyed, however, the pointer weight must be decremented from the reference count of the cell in order to preserve the ground rule that the sum of the weights must equal the reference count of the cell.

An example of the operation of the scheme is shown in Figure 16.17. Here, a cell has been created with an initial reference count of 1024 and there is initially a single pointer to the cell with a matching weight of 1024 (Figure 16.17(a)). Figure 16.17(b) shows the situation when three new references to the cell are created. The reference count of the cell remains the same but the weight of the original pointer is now equally divided among the four pointers. Each pointer now has a weight of 256 preserving a total weight of 1024. No 'communication' with the cell is required.

Figure 16.17(c) shows what happens when one of the four pointers to the cell is deleted: the reference count of the cell itself is decremented by the weight of the deleted pointer (i.e. 256) and so is reduced to 768. This number reflects the total of the pointer weights now remaining. Figure

16.17(d) shows the situation assuming that one of the remaining pointers is further duplicated. This restores the total number of pointers to four but the weights of the copied pointer and new pointer are now halved to 128 – preserving the total weight of 768. It should be apparent that only when all pointers to a cell have been deleted will the reference count of that cell be reduced to zero and at this point the cell can be garbage collected in the usual way.

As with the single-bit reference count scheme the major advantage of storing a weight within each pointer is that we require no access to a cell when we increase the number of pointers to it. We do need to modify the reference count of the cell when we destroy references to it, but in this situation we would normally be dereferencing the pointer cell so that the cell pointed to would be accessed anyway. It is for this reason that the weighted reference count scheme is particularly well suited to distributed implementations of functional languages where communication is so often the limiting factor in performance.

SUMMARY

- Garbage collection is the process of locating and reclaiming unused cells.
- There are three major classes of garbage collector: mark–scan, copying and reference count.
- A garbage collector which requires the program to halt whilst it runs is called a stop/start collector; the alternative is called a concurrent garbage collector.
- The mark–scan collector is a stop/start collector; it is simple but inefficient since it requires between one and two full passes through the heap.
- Copying collectors perform relocation and compaction of active cells; this makes them better suited to virtual memory systems than mark–scan collectors.
- The simplest copying collector is stop/start in nature; it uses two semispaces and works by copying active cells from one semispace to the other.
- More sophisticated schemes run concurrently, use multiple spaces or use a single space; this is particularly effective for machines with small memories.
- Reference count collectors work concurrently by keeping track of the number of references to each cell, but require other methods to reclaim cyclic structures.

- Lazy reference count garbage collectors delay collection of a structure for as long as possible and do so in bits rather than all at once.
- Single-bit reference counts are efficient and can be stored in the pointers to cells: duplicating a pointer to a cell requires no access to that cell. This is good for distributed systems.
- The weighted reference count scheme is a generalization of the single-bit scheme.

EXERCISES

16.1 Fred says: 'Using a copying collector the relative amount of time spent garbage collecting decreases (ultimately to zero) as the size of the heap increases.' What does Fred mean? Why would Fred's remark be invalid for mark–scan garbage collectors?

16.2 (a) Why do all pointers in a call-by-value implementation of a functional language point 'back in time' i.e. to older cells? What are the advantages of this when it comes to implementing a multiple heap version of Baker's algorithm?

(b) Explain how 'forward' references, i.e. references to younger cells can be created in a lazy implementation of a functional language.

16.3 In Morris's garbage collector what is the problem with handling self-referencing pointers? Suggest how this problem can be overcome.

16.4 (a) Suggest how the 'Read-Modify-Write' mode of memory operation can be used to reduce the number of heap memory accesses using the TBD stack. (This part need only be attempted by the hardware specialist!)

(b) Explain how a TBD stack can be combined with single-bit reference count garbage collection to avoid all access to a cell during a pointer copy/destroy operation.

16.5 For the weighted reference count garbage collector

(a) suggest a method of copying pointers whose pointer weight is 1;

(b) discuss the advantages of the scheme if the number of references initially allocated to a cell is a power of two;

(c) consider the following set up:

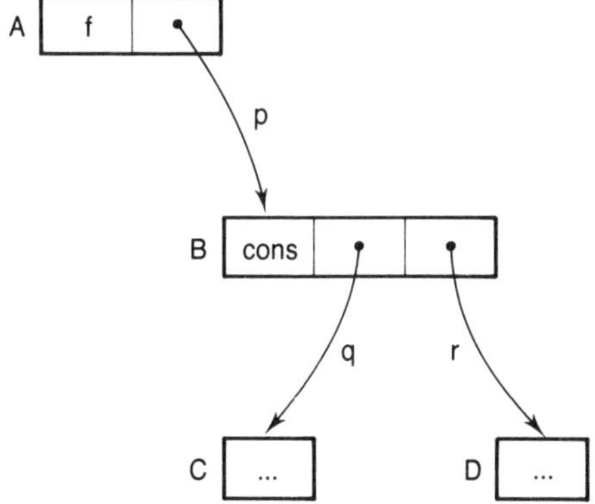

where A, B, C and D are cells; p, q and r are pointers and where f has the equivalent Hope definition

```
--- f(x :: y ) <= g ( y ) ;
```

Describe how a weighted reference count garbage collector would modify the reference counts of each cell and each pointer as a result of applying f.

Part III
OPTIMIZATION

Introduction

By now we have seen a variety of implementations of functional languages; interpreted and compiled, with strict and lazy semantics, based on computational models that use an explicit environment, graph-reduction and combinators of various forms. In each case there has been scope for enhancement of the run-time performance, in terms of both execution time and utilization of storage. The latter type of enhancement has been addressed up to a point by our consideration of garbage collectors in the previous chapter, but this type of solution to the problem is a little like 'closing the stable door after the horse has bolted', since we would really like to reduce the need for any garbage collection to a minimum in the first place. Similarly, we noted certain 'local' optimizations that could be made in particular implementations, many of them in the context of the FPM compiler such as the compilation of tail-recursion into loops, others including the use of a stack in the 'TUKI'-style of dataflow machines, addition of extra combinators into the fixed SKIBC-set and the introduction of extra macros in the G-machine. In fact some of the implementations we considered were specifically introduced to overcome some of the performance problems inherent in their predecessors which were initially put forward as a close representation of some idealized computational model. For example, the free variable problem in the graph reduction model for evaluation of lambda expressions led to the combinator implementations considered in Chapters 12 and 13; certainly the use of lambda lifting and super-combinators was motivated by precisely this problem.

Part III of this book is concerned with rather more fundamental forms of optimization than the local type referred to in the previous paragraph. On the one hand, we will consider program **transformation**, in which the whole structure of a functional program might be modified, and on the other, the way in which a program executes may be controlled by the use of annotations derived by **abstract interpretation**. Unfortunately, optimizing compilers have a history of producing code which does not always compute the results intended by the source program, i.e. they change a program's semantics. However, for functional languages which have a precise mathematical semantics, transformation and abstract interpretation are two techniques that are available to provide the semantically correct type of optimization we require. As a matter of terminology, there are some who consider transformation to mean any semantically correct optimization, so that abstract interpretation would then be viewed as just one piece of the transformation tool kit. At the same time the converse view would maintain that any formally based static analysis of a program, including transformation, is abstract interpretation.

There are a number of glaring limitations on performance in

unoptimized implementations of functional languages – certainly on sequential architectures of the von Neumann type. For example, the evaluations of many function applications exhibit behaviour which is 'linear' in the size of the argument (defined formally in Chapter 18), and would invariably be expressed as a loop in an imperative language. We have already seen instances of this in tail recursion, which is relatively easy to convert into a loop at compile-time as described in Chapter 15, but the classical examples are functions of the factorial class, which are not tail recursive but certainly are linear and equally certainly are programmed using loops in favour of recursion in imperative languages. Similarly, one would rarely expect an application of the Fibonacci function to be evaluated using a number of function calls which is exponential in the argument when two accumulators successively added and switched provide the same result in linear time and constant space in an imperative loop. The question of whether this would be immaterial in a customized, presumably parallel architecture is largely irrelevant. For one thing, von Neumann machines are surely here to stay for the immediate future and longer, but in any case parallel machines comprise a collection of sequential processors, each of which is best employed executing non-trivial computations. Otherwise function calling overheads become prohibitive – i.e. the grain of the computation becomes too small. Thus, optimization is not simply a desirable optional extra in the way that it tends to be in imperative languages, but an essential component of any viable implementation of a functional language.

Fortunately, such imperative-style implementations can often be obtained semi-automatically (requiring some assistance from the programmer), and sometimes fully automatically, from the definitions of the functions involved. The process of deriving more efficient versions of functional programs in a meaning-preserving way falls into the first category of the optimizations that we are about to consider, namely transformation, where the internal structure of functions and functional expressions are modified. Some transformations simply generate new programs in the same language which are equivalent semantically but execute more efficiently. This is called **source-to-source** transformation, and typically the target program is tail recursive, which is considered equivalent to a loop because of the relative ease with which one can compile an application of a tail recursive function into iterative, imperative form. Alternatively, the target program may not be expressed in a functional language at all, but directly in an imperative language, for example. However, we will normally take the term 'transformation' to refer to its source-to-source variety.

A second important application of program transformation concerns the efficient implementation of **abstract data types**, which define the data structures used in the problem-oriented, high-level specifications of the solutions to problems. The expressive power of user-defined data types in writing functional programs was explained in the first part of this book, and many functional languages support them, including Hope. However, in general they must be represented in a computer by blocks of memory which are linked together by pointer fields, so that all references to the items contained in a structure are indirect, as we saw in Chapter 15. This is not the most efficient way of accessing the contents of storage locations in machines with direct or indexed addressing, for which the ideal data structure is linear, occupying a contiguous block of store which can be traversed sequentially. Similarly, in a parallel architecture, the optimal data structure might be organized as a binary tree, enabling different parts of it to be accessed independently by different parts of a distributed computation. Thus, if we consider the simplest example of an abstract data type, the *list*, we might wish to transform its representation on sequential von Neumann and on parallel machines by vectors and trees respectively. However, the programmer should ideally only have to define functions on his own **abstract** types, leaving the (concrete) definitions on the corresponding **implementation** types (e.g. vectors or trees) to the compiler. The synthesis of such concrete definitions may also be provided by transformation techniques.

Although this brief overview of transformation emphasizes execution time, some economies in storage utilization may also be obtained as a secondary optimization. For example, since loops employ destructive assignment to an accumulator (or more than one accumulator), clearly they are also efficient with respect to use of storage. Nevertheless, transformation schemes have also been developed with storage optimization as the primary objective, for example by deriving an equivalent set of functions, for some given set, which generate fewer intermediate data structures (Bellegarde, 1984). This is the subject of current research, however, and we do not address it further in this book.

The second approach that we will consider for making functional programs run more efficiently uses abstract interpretation to control the way in which a program executes, without modifying its definition. Such control is formalized by annotating a particular program so as to specify its operational semantics more precisely than can be done by only defining the semantics for the language as a whole. For example, we have already encountered on several occasions the 'eager evaluation' and 'lazy evaluation' semantics for functional languages, in which parameters are always passed by value and by need respectively. However, there is no reason why some function applications may not be eager, their arguments being passed by value, and others lazy, their arguments passed by need. It requires only a one-bit annotation for each parameter of a functions definition to indicate which semantics is required for every compiled function application, but the real problem lies in making the right choice in the first place. Ideally, we would like a functional language to have lazy semantics for reasons of correctness and perhaps the ability to work with data structures of unbounded size, as we have discussed in Chapter 4. Unfortunately, lazy implementations are in general less efficient than their strict counterparts because of the need to maintain suspensions to represent unevaluated expressions. In addition, a strict implementation can exploit any available parallelism by evaluating the arguments concurrently with the function application. However, for many parameters, the eager and lazy semantics of a function application are the same, each yielding the same result or each failing to terminate. Thus, to get the best of both worlds, we would like to identify at compile-time which applications must be evaluated lazily (to preserve the correct semantics) and which may be evaluated strictly (to gain efficiency) by analysing the way in which functions' parameters are accessed in their defining expressions.

This type of compile-time analysis is called 'strictness analysis', and we will use it to illustrate the more general technique of abstract interpretation which, very briefly, deduces certain properties of a program's execution by working with an 'abstract domain' which is much simpler than the (standard) semantic domain of the expressions being analysed. A second application of abstract interpretation might be considered to arise in type inference systems, which form the basis of type checking algorithms, although the term 'abstract interpretation' had not been coined at the time the first type checkers were written. Compile-time type checking is clearly an optimization, but has already been considered in Chapter 7.

A third type of optimization is **memoization**, which might be viewed as a combination of both the transformation and abstract interpretation techniques. The idea behind this is very simple indeed. Each function is implemented as a corresponding **memo function**, which evaluates the results of applications of the function to new arguments in the usual way, but also saves the argument–result pairs of values in a table, called the **memo table**, so that on a second application of the function to the same argument, the result can be obtained by a simple table look-up. (Functions of more than one argument may be handled in the same way by regarding the arguments as a single tuple.) The technique relies on the property of referential transparency in functional languages, and could provide large performance enhancements were it not for the potentially explosive growth of the memo-table at run-time, which might not only occupy an undue amount of storage, in the extreme taking up all of the available main store, but also incur an access time which is comparable with that of re-evaluating the function's application. Thus, the main problem in implementing memoization is in managing the memo table, i.e. in determining when an entry will no longer be needed and so can be deleted, or which entry is the most suitable for replacement if a fixed size table becomes full. The use of an equivalent function, the memo function, may therefore be regarded as the result of program transformation. Similarly, any prediction of the usage patterns of argument values for the purposes of table management could be regarded as a form of abstract interpretation; certainly any formal proof of the semantic correctness of an implementation of memoization with a given table entry replacement strategy would require techniques of this type.

In the next chapter, we first consider an operational view of program transformation, and describe a methodology for incrementally converting a function's definition into a more efficient version, whilst preserving its meaning, using rules from a set of six different rule types. We then show how this methodology may be applied in the transformation of data types. In Chapter 18, we give an alternative algebraic approach to transformation in which equivalent functions are obtained for generic classes of functions, enabling the transformation process to be reduced to identifying an instance of a 'theorem' (stating such an equivalence) and then applying the theorem to the function being transformed. The latter approach uses an analysis of variable-free expressions written in the FP-style, as described in Chapter 5 for example. Such a so-called **function-level** analysis is based on Backus's 'functional algebra', the relevant results of which are introduced at the beginning of the chapter. We consider memoization in Chapter 19, addressing the main issues arising in the management of memo tables, and giving several examples of its application, including source-to-source transformation. Finally, in Chapter 20, we discuss abstract interpretation, introducing the basic idea informally with a simple numeric example, and then using strictness analysis as the archetypal example of its practical application.

Chapter 17
Program transformation and the operational approach

The objective that a program be correct and easily understandable often conflicts with the parallel requirement that it should execute efficiently, i.e. in as short a time and using as little storage space as possible. Thus ideally we would like to develop initial solutions to problems, concentrating on clarity and correctness, largely disregarding their efficiency, and then transform these solutions into efficient forms using manipulations that guarantee to preserve the meaning of the program. Such a transformational approach is particularly well suited to functional languages in that these languages are purely declarative, possessing the property of referential transparency as discussed in the first part of this book. Thus it is relatively easy to derive meaning-preserving transformations by use of the natural equality relation; the same syntactic expression always takes the same value, i.e. is semantically the same, in all contexts. Imperative languages, on the other hand, are not referentially transparent because of the presence of global variables and destructive assignment, so that expresssions may take different values when they appear in different contexts, and the mathematical use of equality is made much more difficult.

There are two distinct types of transformation that we will consider. First, in this chapter, we look at the **transformation**

methodology of Burstall and Darlington (1977) which prescribes a small set of meaning-preserving rules for generating new recursion equations. These equations may then be used to define new functions or to redefine existing functions in a different, hopefully more efficient, way. The choice of the sequence of rules to apply is not precisely specified in the methodology, the next rule to apply in any transformation process being selected by the program designer, perhaps under the guidance of some informal transformation heuristic. The transformation methodology therefore has very great flexibility, allowing a wide range of optimizations to be performed, each one of which is guaranteed to be correct semantically. It might be considered as presenting an operational description of program transformation. In contrast to this, the second transformation style that we will consider (in the next chapter) is algebraic in nature, and is based on a collection of theorems which state generic equivalences, i.e. semantic equalities, between classes of functions. Then in a functional program, expressions may be rewritten by more efficient, equivalent expressions which are given by one of these theorems. In this way, the process of transformation becomes that of the identification and application of instances of theorems, and the algebraic approach is therefore particularly conducive to mechanization.

However, given intelligent user interaction, the transformation methodology is more flexible, allowing a large class of transformations to be expressed as sequences of its primitive rules – including those that can be expressed as an instance of an algebraic theorem. Algebraic approaches require a new theorem for each new class of transformations to be invented before their own advantages become apparent. In order to develop a practical transformation system based on the operational approach, it is necessary to introduce a *meta-language* in which the sequences of steps required in the transformation of a program can be specified by the user in meta-programs or *scripts*. Moreover, scripts could equally well be used to provide a user interface for algebraic transformation too – the theorems would become new, high-level primitive steps – producing a unified transformation system. The use of meta-programming for the unfold/fold methodology is the subject of Section 17.2.

In Section 17.3, we consider the transformation of abstract data types into concrete types that can be implemented efficiently. We use the unfold/fold approach, and give two examples to illustrate the techniques involved. Again, we will see that the methodology has great flexibility, but that it is even more difficult to mechanize in general. Although the corresponding algebraic approach does introduce a good degree of automation, the increased complexity of the transformations requires more advanced theoretical results, and we will not cover it in this book.

17.1 The 'unfold/fold' transformation methodology

Before giving the set of rules that define this methodology, let us first give an extremely simple example to illustrate the type of optimization we have in mind. Suppose we have the following naive Hope definition of the function, g, that sums a list of doubled numbers:

```
dec sum : list( num ) → num ;
--- sum( nil ) <= 0 ;
--- sum( x :: l ) <= x + sum( l ) ;

dec double : list( num ) → list( num ) ;
--- double( nil ) <= nil ;
--- double( x :: l ) <= (2 * x ) :: double( l ) ;

dec g : list( num ) → num ;
--- g( l ) <= sum( double( l ) ) ;
```

This is clearly an inefficient solution to the problem in that two lists must be traversed: the original list in which each element is doubled and the result of this which is summed. We can derive a new version of g which traverses the list only once by application of just three rules (named in italics as they are used) as follows:

`--- g( nil ) <= sum( double( nil ) ) ;`	by substitution in the definition of g, *instantiation*
`<= sum( nil ) ;`	by the first recursion equation for the function double, *unfolding*
`<= 0 ;`	*unfolding*
`--- g( x :: l )<= sum( double( x :: l ) ) ;`	*instantiation*
`<= sum( ( 2 * x ) :: double( l ) ) ;`	*unfolding*
`<= ( 2 * x ) + sum( double( l ) ) ;`	*unfolding*
`<= ( 2 * x ) + g( l ) ;`	by the recursion equation for the function g, *folding*

Note that the rules of 'unfolding' and 'folding' each consist of the substitution of one side of a recursion equation for the other, the right for the left in the case of unfolding and the left for the right in the case of folding. The new program that we have obtained, i.e. the semantically equivalent definition of g, is therefore

```
dec  g : list( num ) → num ;
---  g( nil ) <= 0 ;
---  g( x :: l ) <= ( 2 * x ) + g( l ) ;
```

In fact the unfold/fold system of Burstall and Darlington (1977) consists of six rules that allow new equations to be introduced which are consequences of existing equations. In these rules, we will use the term 'instance of an expression' which refers to any expression obtained from the said expression by substituting expressions, e.g. constants, for each of its variables. The rules of the unfold/fold system are then as follows:

(1) *Definition.* Introduce a new recursion equation in which the left-hand expression is not an instance of the left-hand expression of any existing equation. The new recursion equation therefore defines a new function, or extends the domain of an existing function, typically introduced previously by this same rule.

(2) *Instantiation.* Introduce a substitution instance of an existing equation, i.e. an equation obtained by substituting particular expressions (e.g. constants) for the variables occurring in the existing equation.

(3) *Unfolding.* If E <= E′ and F <= F′ are equations and there is some occurrence of an instance of E in F′, replace that occurrence by the corresponding instance of E′ to obtain F*, and then add the equation F <= F*. Thus $F^* = [\, E'/E \,]^{I} F'$,the superscripted I denoting the substitution instance in the equation E <= E′.

(4) *Folding.* If E <= E′ and F <= F′ are equations and there is some occurrence of an instance of E′ in F′, replace that occurrence by the corresponding instance of E to obtain $F^{\dagger}$, and then add the equation F <= $F^{\dagger}$, where $F^{\dagger} = [\, E / E' \,]^{I} F'$ in similar notation to (3).

(5) *Abstraction.* Introduce a **where** clause (qualified expression) by deriving from an existing equation E <= E′ a new equation

$$E \Leftarrow [\, u_1 / F_1, \ldots, u_n / F_n \,]E' \ \textbf{where}\ (\, u_1, \ldots, u_n \,) = (\, F_1, \ldots, F_n \,)$$

(6) *Laws.* We may transform an equation by using on its right-hand expression any laws we might have about the primitives contained in it, for example associativity, commutativity, etc. The new equation is again obtained by application of a mathematical

equality – between expressions which are equal under the law, e.g. $x + (y + z) = (x + y) + z$.

Each rule is an equality, so that the meaning of any functional program transformed according to the unfold/fold methodology is indeed guaranteed to be preserved – at least partially as we will discuss shortly.

Let us first consider a slightly more complicated example, a function which finds the average of a list of numbers, in the transformation of which we use all of the first five rules. The initial, naive, but clear and clearly correct solution is:

```
dec average : list( num ) → num ;
--- average( l ) <= sum( l ) div length( l ) ;

--- sum( nil ) <= 0 ;
--- sum( n :: l ) <= n + sum( l ) ;

--- length( nil ) <= 0 ;
--- length( n :: l ) <= 1 + length( l ) ;
```

As in the first example, there are two list-traversals, this time of the same list from which the sum and number of elements are obtained separately and then divided in the function average. We would like to perform the two operations together on the same pass of the list, and can derive a semantically equivalent functional program which does this, using the unfold/fold methodology as follows:

```
dec av : list( num ) → num # num ;
--- av( l ) <= ( sum( l ), length( l ) ) ;                definition

--- av( nil ) <= ( sum nil, length nil ) ;                instantiation
              <= ( 0, 0 ) ;                               unfolding

--- av( n :: l ) <= ( sum( n :: l ), length( n :: l ) ) ; instantiation
                 <= ( n + sum( l ), 1 + length( l ) ) ;   unfolding
                 <= ( n + u, 1 + v )
                    where ( u, v ) == ( sum( l ), length( l ) ) ;
                                                          abstraction
                 <= (n + u, 1 + v)
                    where ( u, v ) == av( l ) ;           folding

--- average( l ) <= sum( l ) div length( l ) ;
                 <= u div v
                    where ( u, v ) == ( sum( l ), length( l ) ) ;
                                                          abstraction
                 <= u div v
                    where ( u, v ) == av( l ) ;           folding
```

This gives the following final, transformed program:

```
dec average : list( num ) → num ;
dec av : list( num ) → num # num ;
--- average( l ) <= u div v
                  where ( u, v ) == av( l ) ;
--- av( nil ) <= ( 0, 0 ) ;
--- av( n :: l ) <= ( n + u, 1 + v )
                  where ( u, v ) == av( l ) ;
```

As intended, when executed, an application of the function average to a list of numbers, as defined by the final program, only traverses the list once, accumulating the sum and length of the list as the evaluation progresses, and having reached the end of the list, divides them. An example with much more spectacular gains in efficiency is the transformation of the Fibonacci function, which is non-linear, requiring a number of function calls that is exponential in the magnitude of its argument (actually proportional to its result). The function can be defined by:

```
dec fib : num → num ;
--- fib( 0 ) <= 1 ;
--- fib( 1 ) <= 1 ;
--- fib( n + 2 ) <= fib( n + 1 ) + fib( n ) ;
```

In this definition we use a non-standard syntax for patterns: the pattern n + k simply specifies that the argument must be k or greater (n being 0 or more). It should be appreciated that this is not standard Hope, although some Hope compilers have been extended to allow such definitions. In general a definition such as this would have to be defined using overlapping patterns. The third equation for fib would then use the pattern n, exploiting the fact that both 0 and 1 are more specific than n (see Chapter 8) causing the first equation to be selected if the argument were 0 and the second if the argument were 1.

The non-linearity in the definition of fib arises because of the two recursive calls in the right-hand expression of the third defining equation, giving binary trees as representations of partially evaluated applications. The transformed version, however, runs in linear time, or more precisely requires a number of function calls that is linear in the magnitude of its argument. The unfold/fold methodology yields the following transformation:

```
dec g : num → num # num ;
--- g( n ) <= ( fib( n + 1 ), fib( n ) ) ;        definition

--- g 0 <= ( fib( 1 ), fib( 0 ) ) ;               instantiation
        <= ( 1, 1 ) ;                             unfolding
```

```
--- g( n + 1 ) <= ( fib( n + 2 ), fib( n + 1 ) ) ;          instantiation
               <= ( fib( n + 1 ) + fib( n ), fib( n + 1 ) ) ;
                                                             unfolding
               <= ( u + v, u )
                    where ( u, v ) == ( fib( n + 1 ), fib( n ) ) ;
                                                             abstraction
               <= ( u + v, u )
                    where ( u, v ) == g( n ) ;               folding

--- fib( n + 2 ) <= fib( n + 1 ) + fib( n ) ;
                 <= u + v
                      where ( u, v ) == ( fib( n + 1 ), fib( n ) ) ;
                                                             abstraction
                 <= u + v
                      where ( u, v ) == g( n ) ;             folding
```

This gives the following transformed version of the Fibonacci function:

```
dec fib : num → num ;
dec g : num → num # num ;
--- fib( 0 ) <= 1 ;
--- fib( 1 ) <= 1 ;
--- fib( n + 2 ) <= u + v
                      where ( u, v ) == g( n ) ;

--- g( 0 ) <= ( 1, 1 ) ;
--- g( n + 1 ) <= ( u + v, u )
                    where ( u, v ) == g( n ) ;
```

Clearly the execution time of the application g(N), and so of fib(N), is of the order O(N); i.e. the transformed Fibonacci function is indeed linear in the size of its argument. There are many more examples of functions that can be transformed in this way, some of which can be found as exercises at the end of this chapter. We give no further examples in this section, but a similar methodology will be used in the transformation of data types in Section 17.3.

The key steps in the above transformation are the choice of the definition of g in terms of fib, followed by the **where** abstraction and fold in the derivation of the recursion equation for g(n + 1). A pair of successive steps comprising a **where** abstraction and a fold are sometimes regarded as a composite step and referred to as **forced folding**. In general, and certainly in this example, ingenuity is required on the part of the programmer to choose appropriate definitions (of g in our example) and tuples to abstract in forced folding, (f(n + 1), f(n)) in our example. As a result, such steps have been referred to as *Eureka* steps, in common with others requiring creative acts of intelligence, exogenous to the transformation system, and we will also use the term. Thus, whilst certainly being very generally applicable, the unfold/fold methodology requires precise guidance from the programmer, and its use resembles program design in the conventional sense. Full automation would appear difficult, although it may be possible for various collections of standard rule sequences to be maintained in a 'transformation library' and applied as higher-level transformation tactics. Before taking this point further in the next section, we first address the correctness and completeness issues of the unfold/fold transformation system.

Since the rules of the unfold/fold methodology are based solely on equational reasoning, i.e. the use of mathematical equality, 'wrong' results, i.e. an inconsistent set of new functions, cannot be derived. However, it is possible to generate new functions which do not terminate. For example, from the equation

```
--- f( x ) <= x ;
```

we may obtain, by folding, the transformed equation

```
--- f( x ) <= f( x ) ;
```

which clearly will not terminate. In fact it can be shown that the unfold/fold system preserves *partial correctness*; whenever the transformed program terminates, it is guaranteed to return the same results as the original program (for appropriate underlying domains of objects). This is because the functions defined by the original set of recursion equations are the least solutions of these equations, given by the least fixed points of a corresponding set of functional equations. Since all transformed equations are derived by successively substituting subexpressions occurring in existing equations by equal expressions, these solutions must also *satisfy* the resulting set of equations. In other words, they are also solutions of the set of equations defining the transformed functions, but they are not necessarily the *least* solutions of these equations. Thus the function defined by the transformed equations is weaker than (in the associated function space) the corresponding function defined by the original equations.

If f is a function between domains D and C of objects and C is *flat*, i.e. $x < y$ if $x = \perp$ or $x = y$ for $x, y \in C$, we can immediately see that we have partial correctness as follows, even though the function space $[D \rightarrow C]$ will not be flat in general. If the transformed version of f is f', which has to be weaker than f, then for all objects $x \in D, f'\ x < f x$ so that if $f'\ x$ terminates, i.e. $f'\ x \neq \perp$, we must have $f x = f'\ x$. If further f is defined on the same set of objects as its transformed version, f', i.e. $f x = \perp$ if and only if $f'\ x = \perp$ for objects $x \in D$, *total* correctness is ensured, since $f'\ x <$

$f\,x$ and so either $f'\;x = \perp = f\,x$, by hypothesis, or $f'\;x = f\,x$. These conditions are sufficient for the total correctness of the unfold/fold methodology, but they are clearly not necessary, and formal analyses of correctness may be found in Kott (1978). It may worry some readers that there appears to be a lack of symmetry in this argument, in that all transformation steps are applications of mathematical equality and so any solution for a function defined by the transformed equations must also be a solution for the original equations, and so greater than their least solution. This would yield equal transformed functions and so total correctness. However, the converse argument does not hold in general, since the transformation rules are not reversible. That is, it is not always possible to define a meaning-preserving transformation which recovers an equation from one obtained by applying one of the six rules to it, as we saw in the above example yielding non-termination. In other words, the asymmetry arises from that of the unidirectional transformation rules themselves.

Total correctness may be established by a separate demonstration of the termination of the final, transformed program, or ensured by imposing certain restrictions on the application of the folding and unfolding rules. In the latter case, it was shown by Kott that, loosely speaking, a transformation involving more unfolds than folds is 'safe', i.e. preserves total correctness.

Regarding completeness, the unfold/fold transformation system is formally incomplete, in that certain equivalent sets of recursion equations exist which cannot be converted one to the other by successive application of the rules. For example, the equations

```
--- f( 0 ) <= 0 ;
--- f( x + 1 ) <= 1 + f( x ) ;
```

are equivalent to the equation

```
--- f( x ) <= x ;
```

but there is no way the latter equation can be obtained from the first pair by applying the six rules of the unfold/fold methodology. However, such examples tend to be rather pathological in nature, and it is claimed that the methodology is complete for all practical purposes. Its real problem is that it is only, at best, semi-automatic, requiring guidance by an intelligent programmer, so that it is essentially a program design tool. There is here an analogy with theorem proving, where the axioms, or rules, used by the prover are very simple, and typically require a great deal of database searching for the appropriate sequence of proof steps, or else user assistance. Although the alternative algebraic approach to program transformation holds out a better prospect for automation, the unfold/fold approach offers greater flexibility through its near-completeness – it is certainly more generally applicable than the set of theorems currently available. Thus it is important to develop a meta-language system through which the programmer can specify the transformation steps he desires as a meta-program. Such a system would facilitate the development of the final implementation of the user's application program, and so should be regarded as an integral part of a functional programming support environment. This is the subject of the next section, and we will see a further application of the unfold/fold methodology in the transformation of data types in Section 17.3.

17.2 Control of the unfold/fold system – a transformation meta-language

A function written in the meta-language – a **meta-function** or **meta-program** – operates on programs written in the functional language which are to be transformed and such programs are the objects of the meta-language. One obvious example of a meta-function is a program editor, which has the type

```
program # list of commands → program
```

where the type program refers to some abstract representation of the program (see for example Chapter 8 which gives the data definition for Hope abstract syntax trees in Hope itself).

We may express transformations as meta-functions of type program → program, where for a functional language such as Hope a program's type is set of equations and an equation's type is given in terms of some abstract syntax tree. The transformation meta-functions are in turn defined as compositions of other first-level meta-functions which operate on the equations and expressions forming a program. Thus, to express the unfold/fold transformations using a meta-language we need to define six first-level meta-language functions – one for each of the transformation rules. The programmer expresses the transformation steps required using meta-language expressions and the rule sequences generated by the meta-program will be similar to those shown in the examples of the previous section.

Unfortunately, the unfold/fold methodology as we have presented it requires a substantial amount of programming at the meta-level by the user – in fact probably more than is required to obtain the initial solution in the first place. Of course this is not altogether surprising since the original program represents a 'high-level' specification of the solution to a problem which we like to think can be expressed clearly and concisely, but without regard for efficiency. However, the onus of this amount of meta-programming is prohibitive, and we must look for more effective ways of applying the transformation rules, or for an alternative basis for transformation.

The trouble with the methodology described in this chapter is that its rules operate at too low a level of detail, being concerned with the individual equations that define functions. Thus one approach to developing a practical meaning-preserving transformation system is to try to build structured meta-programs, in the top-down fashion that has been advocated for many years by the software engineers. Higher-level meta-functions might then be able to generate the lower-level transformation steps necessary to achieve the goal of the transformation, but the complexity of these step sequences would be hidden from the user. Certainly many functions with similar structure will require similar sets of steps for their transformation, and such structural similarities may identify generic classes of functions that can be transformed by the same meta-functions.

However, it will be insufficient in general for a higher-level meta-function to be simply a macro, i.e. a fixed sequence of the primitive rules, suitably parameterized in terms of the function names, variable names and constants occurring in the equations of the program being transformed. For this to be sufficient, it would be necessary for the functions in a generic class to be isomorphic, not merely 'similar'. In practice, the higher-level meta-functions would not only include explicitly defined transformation descriptions – in terms of sequences of rules of the unfold/fold methodology known *a priori* – but also apply heuristic searching tactics to try various possible rule sequences in the hope of finding suitably optimized function definitions. They would also have to be capable of responding to 'advice' provided by the user, ideally interactively, in the form of a script of suggested meta-functions to apply, since the methodology is not conducive to automation. Algebraic schemes offer much better prospects for the automatic transformation of certain functions, and these schemes could be integrated as second-level tactics into the type of meta-system suggested in this section. In fact it turns out that 'linearize' (refer to Chapter 18) would be a prime example, as would 'convert to iterative form' which attempts to generate tail recursive versions of functions.

17.3 The transformation of data types

The use of the abstract data type (ADT) is well established in programming languages, both functional and imperative, since it provides the programmer with great expressive power, allowing the objects manipulated by a program to be described in a way most natural to the problem being solved. Such advantages are well known and in particular the benefits of a strongly typed functional language were made clear in the first part of this book. We will not repeat these arguments here. Unfortunately, the structure inherent in an abstract type rarely matches the typically very restricted structure of the storage areas in a computer's memory, and so its implementation is inefficient, in terms of both the memory space required for objects of that type and the time taken to select items from such objects. The unoptimized representation of a compound data object in memory simply organizes the words of memory according to the precise structure of the object's type, using pointers and a heap as discussed in Chapter 15. However, many data structures are ordered in some way and are accessed sequentially with respect to that ordering – lists being the most obvious example. In such cases, it would clearly be most efficient to exploit the natural ordering of conventional computer memories by assigning sequential abstract objects to contiguous blocks of storage, so speeding up both the storing operation, typically implemented by a MOVE machine operation, and the operation of selecting an item which could use indexing. Of course contiguous storage allocation is not necessarily optimal for all computers. In a parallel architecture, for example, a more appropriate structure for a run-time object might be a binary tree which would facilitate independent, simultaneous access to its components by several processors. For structured data with components that can be processed in any order, this would indeed be optimal, and we might therefore wish to represent a list by such a tree.

The trouble is that if a programmer wishes to improve the run-time performance of a program by exploiting the properties of the architecture of the underlying machine, he has no alternative but to define all of his data types in a machine-oriented way, and write all of his functions to manipulate objects of these types. Ideally, however, the programmer should have to define only a set of abstract types, a set of concrete types in which objects of the abstract types are to be represented at run-time and mappings between corresponding concrete and abstract types. It should then be sufficient to define functions that manipulate the abstract types only, leaving the compiler to synthesize the corresponding functions that manipulate the concrete types. In this way, there would be no need to represent the abstract types explicitly at run-time at all, whilst at the same time the programmer would retain the benefits of programming at the problem level. Thus, by 'data type transformation' we really mean the synthesis of concrete functions defined on concrete types corresponding to abstract functions defined on abstract types.

Such an idealistic situation does not come cheaply, and to generate automatically such an implementation of an abstract program manipulating concrete objects with maximum efficiency demands a lot of the compiler's transformation system, if indeed it is possible. However, such transformation schemes can be derived in certain cases by both the unfold/fold and algebraic approaches. Unfortunately, the sequences of steps required are even more obscure than those we saw in Section 17.1, and this application of the methodology needs additional user interaction.

The unfold/fold methodology can be applied to the transformation of data types without change, other than the addition of new 'laws' corresponding to the properties of the types concerned, from the scheme described in Section 17.1, driven by a meta-system such as the one outlined in Section 17.2. As we have already noted, the steps required in the transformation process are somewhat more obscure, particularly the definition, fold and abstraction steps, but the scheme is practicable in relatively simple applications, guaranteeing that any transformation it derives is (partially) correct. Here we give two examples to illustrate present capabilities, but point out that no such system has been implemented at the time of writing.

EXAMPLE 1: REPRESENTATION OF TREES BY ARRAYS

Suppose we have the usual polymorphic Hope definition of the tree data type:

```
data tree( alpha ) == leaf( alpha ) ++ node( tree( alpha ) # alpha
                                        # tree( alpha ) ) ;
```

which we wish to represent by an array of triples, each comprising the data item of type alpha stored in the corresponding node of the abstract tree, and two numbers which define the connectivity of the tree by indexing the array. For a leaf node, both numbers are zero, otherwise the triples indexed in the array by the first and second numbers correspond to the root nodes of the left and right subtrees of the non-leaf node respectively. The concrete type therefore has the declaration

```
type row_num == num ;
data array( alpha ) == empty_array ++
                       assign(array # row_num # alpha #
                          num # num ) ;
```

The empty array does not represent any tree, and the second sub-type represents the array formed from the array which is the first argument of the constructor assign by setting the row numbered by the second argument to the triple having as components the third, fourth and fifth arguments. Thus, for example, the tree shown in Figure 17.1 is represented by the

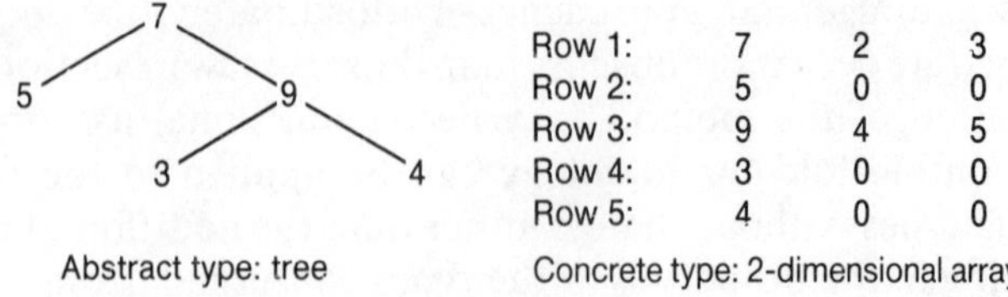

Figure 17.1 Representation of trees by arrays.

array beside it, and this array could be written (non-uniquely) as

```
assign( assign( assign( assign( assign( empty_array, 1, 7, 2, 3 ),
  2, 5, 0, 0 ), 3, 9, 4, 5 ), 5, 4, 0, 0 ), 4, 3, 0, 0 )
```

The concrete form of the abstract type has selector functions associated with it which determine how data items stored in objects may be accessed, i.e. which provide the indexing operations. These selectors are in general recursive and may be provided by the programmer in the form of recursion equations. Being recursive, they cannot be represented by normal pattern matching. In fact if the data type is regarded as axiomatic, the defining equations of the selector functions constitute its axioms. In our present example, we define the functions read_data, read_left and read_right, corresponding to the data item, left pointer and right pointer respectively in an array triple representing a node, as follows:

```
dec read_data : array( alpha ) # num → alpha ;
--- read_data( assign( ar, n, a, i, j ), m ) <= if m = n
    then a else read_data( ar, m ) ;

dec read_left : array( alpha ) # num → num ;
--- read_left( assign( ar, n, a, i, j ), m ) <= if m = n
    then i else read_left( ar, m ) ;

dec read_right : array( alpha ) # num → num ;
--- read_right( assign( ar, n, a, i, j ), m ) <= if m = n
    then j else read_right( ar, m ) ;
```

(We have omitted the equations with empty_array in their patterns, these resulting in errors since the functions read_data, read_left and read_right are undefined on empty arrays.)

The final responsibility of the programmer is to provide the mapping between the concrete type and the original abstract type. We call this abs, for 'abstraction' mapping, which is simply defined as follows:

```
dec abs : array( alpha ) → tree( alpha ) ;

dec abs1 : array( alpha # num ) → tree( alpha ) ;
--- abs( ar ) <= abs1( ar, 1 ) ;
--- abs1( ar, rn ) <= if read_left( ar, rn ) = 0
                      then leaf( read_data( ar, rn ) )
                      else node( abs1( ar, read_left( ar, rn ) ),
                                 read_data( ar, rn ),
                                 abs1( ar, read_right( ar, rn ) ) ) ;
```

Note that the expression abs1(ar, rn) evaluates to the subtree with root node represented by row number rn in the array ar.

Having given these definitions, the programmer should be free to write any function on the abstract type tree, and the transformation system should synthesize the corresponding function on the concrete arrays. Assuming that both the abstract and concrete type for numbers is the type num, let us consider the function sum which adds up the numbers in a tree, and see how we can apply the unfold/fold methodology to derive a concrete version of sum. The abstract function is defined as follows:

```
dec sum : tree( num ) → num ;
--- sum( leaf( n ) ) <= n ;
--- sum( node( t1, n, t2 ) ) <= sum( t1 ) + n + sum( t2 ) ;
```

The transformation of the abstract function, sum, into its concrete version, concsum, proceeds via the following primitive steps, which could be applied under the control of a meta system such as the one outlined in Section 17.2. We begin with the introduction of the new, concrete function's definition in terms of the abstract function:

```
dec concsum : array( num ) → num ;
--- concsum( ar ) <= sum( abs( ar ) ) ;
                  <= sum( abs1( ar, 1 ) ) ;        Unfolding
```

Corresponding to abs1, we introduce the function concsum1:

```
dec concsum1 : array( num ) # num → num ;
--- concsum1( ar, rn ) <= sum( abs1( ar, rn ) ) ;   Definition
```

so that,

```
--- concsum1( ar, 1) <= sum( abs1( ar, 1 ) ) ;      Instantiation
```

and therefore

```
--- concsum( ar ) <= concsum1( ar, 1 ) ;            Folding
```

Now, by unfolding the definition of abs1 in the equation for concsum1, we obtain

```
--- concsum1( ar, rn ) <= sum(
        if read_left( ar, rn ) = 0
        then leaf( read_data( ar, rn ) )
        else node( abs1( ar, read_left ( ar, rn) ),
                   read_data( ar, rn ),
                   abs1( ar, read_ right( ar, rn ) ) ) ;

        <= if read_left( ar, rn ) = 0
           then sum( leaf( read_data( ar, rn ) ) )
           else sum( node( abs1( ar, read_left ( ar, rn ) ),
                           read_data( ar, rn ),
                           abs1( ar, read_ right( ar, rn ) ) ) ) ;
```

using the distributive law satisfied by the **if_then_else** construct. This states that for function f and expressions A, B, C,

```
f( if A then B else C ) = if A then f( B ) else f( C )
```

Thus, unfolding sum gives

```
--- concsum1( ar, rn ) <=
        if read_left( ar, rn ) = 0
        then read_data( ar, rn )
        else sum( abs1( ar, read_left( ar, rn ) ) )
             + read_data( ar, rn )
             + sum( abs1( ar, read_right( ar, rn ) ) ) ;
```

and finally folding concsum1 yields the equation

```
--- concsum1( ar, rn ) <=
        if read_left( ar, rn ) = 0
        then read_data( ar, rn )
        else concsum1( ar, read_left( ar, rn ) )
             + read_data( ar, rn )
             + concsum1( ar, read_right( ar, rn ) ) ) ;
```

Thus, we can define the summation of the data items in an abstract tree purely in terms of the concrete representations of those trees, namely arrays of triples and functions defined on them – by the equation

```
--- concsum( ar ) <= concsum1( ar, 1 ) ;
```

where the right-hand side is defined by the equation for concsum1 derived by the transformation.

EXAMPLE 2: REVERSAL OF A LIST REPRESENTED BY A TREE

In the previous example, the ranges of the abstract function, sum, and of its concrete version, concsum, were the same, namely numbers, and alternatively we might have considered that the abstraction mapping between the range types were the identity function. In the next chapter we will see how this type of transformation may be regarded as 'triangular', the vertices of the triangle corresponding to the abstract domain type, the concrete domain type and the common range type. In this example, we consider a full 'square', although the domain and range types of the abstract function (and so also of the associated concrete function) are the same. However, a fully general example involving distinct domain and range abstract types which are also different from their concrete counterparts would introduce only much more tedium and no more insight.

Suppose that we wish to represent lists by binary trees, perhaps with a view to exploiting parallelism, so that several processors could manipulate different, independent segments of the list, represented by disjoint subtrees, at the same time. For example, the Hope list, [2, 8, 4, 6, 9], might be represented by the tree

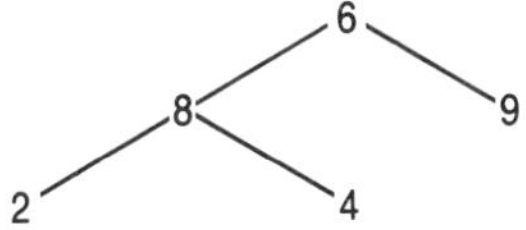

Formally, we define in Hope the concrete data type tree of objects of polymorphic type alpha by:

```
data tree( alpha ) == empty ++ node( tree( alpha ) # alpha #
                                     tree( alpha ) ) ;
```

Note that these trees are not quite the same as the trees of the previous example, in that the respective base types are different; here the empty tree and there a single-node tree, or 'leaf', containing one item of data. The abstraction function, abs, mapping concrete trees to abstract lists is therefore defined by the programmer as:

```
dec abs : tree( alpha ) → list( alpha ) ;
--- abs( empty ) <= nil ;
--- abs( node( t1, n, t2 ) ) <= abs( t1 ) <> [ n ] <> abs( t2 ) ;
```

where the infix operator <> denotes the append function defined on lists, and [n] denotes the singleton list comprising the element n.

Now suppose the abstract function, reverse, for which the concrete form, revtree, is to be synthesized, is defined by:

```
dec reverse : list( alpha ) → list( alpha ) ;
--- reverse( nil ) <= nil ;
--- reverse( x :: l ) <= reverse( l ) <> [ x ] ;
```

Then a specification for the function revtree is

```
dec revtree : tree( alpha ) → tree( alpha ) ;
--- revtree( t ) <= tr st abs tr = reverse( abs t ) ;
```

The connective **st** stands for 'such that'; this is not standard Hope syntax but is provided in the extended functional language UnifHope which was mentioned briefly in Chapter 5. So, although this will be a runnable specification in UnifHope, here we shall aim to remove **st** from our definition of revtree by the use of fold steps in our transformation sequence.

For the base case of revtree, the transformation proceeds as follows:

```
--- revtree( empty ) <= tr st abs( tr ) = reverse( abs( empty ) ) ;
                                              Instantiation
                     <= tr st abs( tr ) = reverse( nil ) ;
                                              Unfold abs
                     <= tr st abs( tr ) = nil ;  Unfold reverse
                     <= tr st abs( tr ) = abs( empty ) ;
                                              Fold abs
                     <= tr st tr = empty ;    Law*
                     <= empty ;
```

A sufficient condition for the law, marked*, to generate the step shown would be that abs is a one-to-one function, but for now we only need abs tr ≠ nil if tr ≠ empty, which clearly is the case. The transformation steps which produce the recursive case of revtree involve more intricate reasoning, and are:

```
--- revtree( node ( t1, n, t2 ) )
      <= tr st abs( tr ) = reverse( abs( node( t1, n, t2 ) ) ) ;
                                                  Instantiation
      <= tr st abs( tr ) = reverse( abs( t1 ) <> [ n ]
                           <> abs( t2 ) ) ;        Unfold abs
      <= tr st abs( tr ) = reverse( abs( t2 ) ) <> [ n ] <> reverse
                           ( abs( t1 ) ) ;         Law for reverse$
      <= tr st abs( tr ) = abs( revtree( t2 ) ) <> [ n ] <> abs
                           ( revtree( t1 ) ) ;     Fold revtree†
      <= tr st abs( tr ) = abs( node( revtree( t2 ), n,
                           revtree( t1 ) ) ) ;     Fold abs
      <= tr st tr = node( revtree( t2 ), n, revtree( t1 ) ) ;
                                                  Law#
      <= node( revtree( t2 ), n, revtree( t1 ) ) ;
```

Thus we have a complete definition of revtree, the concrete version of reverse, defined only in terms of the concrete type tree and functions which manipulate objects of this type. However, three of our steps, marked $, † and #, have not been explained fully, and do not even appear to be necessarily valid. Considering the last of these first, we clearly do not have a one-to-one function in abs, since, for example, there are two tree representations of the list [1, 2]. Thus it would seem that we cannot justify stripping off the functions, abs, on the right-hand side of the equation as we have done. However, the equation resulting from this step clearly is valid, and so the resulting recursion equation does provide one definition of a function revtree which represents reverse faithfully in the concrete domain. Of course typically there will be just one (canonical) tree which represents a given list – for example the most evenly balanced tree (with at least as many elements in each of its left subtrees as in its corresponding right subtrees if the number of elements is not a power of 2). If this is the case, abs is one-to-one, and there is no problem.

In the case of the step marked † we simply apply abs to both sides of the defining equation for revtree to obtain

```
--- abs( revtree( t ) ) <= abs( tr ) st abs( tr ) = reverse( abs( t ) ) ;
                        <= reverse( abs( t ) ) ;          by definition
```

and the step follows by folding.

The law concerned in the transformation step marked $ states that for all lists A and B

reverse(A ⟨⟩ B) = reverse B ⟨⟩ reverse A

In fact this law is equivalent to the recursive defining equation of reverse, and together with the law reverse(nil) = nil could be used as an alternative specification. However, we can prove the result rigorously from the recursion equations defining ⟨⟩ and reverse, using only the primitive transformation steps and structural induction on the list A as follows.

In the base case, A = nil. Thus,

```
reverse(A ⟨⟩ B) = reverse(nil ⟨⟩ B)
                = reverse( B )                     Unfold ⟨⟩
                = reverse( B ) ⟨⟩ nil              By induction on B
                = reverse( B ) ⟨⟩ reverse( A )     Fold reverse
```

For the inductive step, assume the result is true for the list A, and consider the expression

```
reverse( ( a :: A ) ⟨⟩ B) = reverse( a :: ( A ⟨⟩ B ) )
                                                   Unfold ⟨⟩
                          = reverse( A ⟨⟩ B ) ⟨⟩ [ a ]
                                                   Unfold reverse
                          = ( reverse( B ) ⟨⟩ reverse( A ) ) ⟨⟩ [ a ]
                                                   Inductive hypothesis
                          = reverse( B ) ⟨⟩ (reverse( A ) ⟨⟩ [ a ])
                                                   Associativity of ⟨⟩
                          = reverse( B ) ⟨⟩ reverse( a :: A )
                                                   Fold reverse
```

which completes the proof.

These two examples are far more complex than any of the transformations we saw earlier in this chapter, and their structures are obscured by the presence of object variables which might, for example, impede the identification of simplifying laws. It is the absence of object variables in the corresponding algebraic approach which is in part responsible for its greater degree of automation, and this style of transformation is the subject of the following chapter.

SUMMARY

- Program transformation provides a way of optimizing functional programs whilst guaranteeing their meaning stays the same.

- The unfold/fold transformation methodology is based upon a set of six basic rules.
- Application of sequences of these rules generates a very wide range of transformations which are correct up to non-termination (i.e. are partially correct).
- Rule sequences are supplied by the programmer as part of the program development process.
- A meta-language can be used to support this process by allowing the programmer to specify transformations through meta-programs.
- The unfold/fold methodology may be used to transform abstract data types and functions defined on them into alternative concrete forms.

EXERCISES

17.1 The following Hope program defines a function treeaverage that computes the average of a tree of numbers:

```
data tree( alpha ) == tip( alpha ) ++ node( tree( alpha ) #
                                  tree( alpha ) ) ;
dec treeaverage, sum, count : tree( num ) → num ;
--- sum( tip( n ) ) <= n ;
--- sum( node( t1, t2 ) ) <= sum( t1 ) + sum( t2 ) ;
--- count( tip( n ) ) <= 1 ;
--- count( node( t1, t2 ) ) <= count( t1 ) + count( t2 ) ;
--- treeaverage( t ) <= sum( t ) div count( t ) ;
```

where div is the primitive divide function. Use the unfold/fold methodology to transform the definition of treeaverage into a more efficient form that requires only one pass over a tree.

17.2 Given the Hope definitions:

```
dec addn : num # list( num ) → list( num ) ;
dec sum : list( num ) → num ;
--- addn( n, nil ) <= nil ;
--- addn( n, m :: z ) <= (n + m) :: addn( n, z ) ;
--- sum( nil ) <= 0 ;
--- sum( n :: z ) <= n + sum( z ) ;
dec g : num # list( num ) → list( num ) ;
--- g( n, z ) <= sum( addn( n, z ) ) ;
```

transform the definition of g into a form that calls neither addn nor sum.

17.3 The expression listo(n) evaluates to the list of integers from 1 to n inclusive, where listo is defined by:

```
dec listo : num → list( num ) ;
dec append : list( alpha ) # list( alpha ) → list( alpha ) ;
--- listo( 0 ) <= nil ;
--- listo( n + 1 ) <= append( listo( n ), ( n + 1 ) :: nil ) ;
--- append( nil, z ) <= z ;
--- append( x :: z1, z2 ) <= x :: append( z1, z2 ) ;
```

This program is inefficient since the repeated calls to append involve copying its first argument. Systematically derive a more efficient version of listo which does not use append. (*Hint*: Define an auxiliary function and use the associativity of append.)

17.4 Explain why unification removal is important in the transformation of abstract data types. Use the unfold/fold methodology to remove the **st** operator (and so unification) from the following definition of the function g, carefully explaining every transformation step:

```
dec g : num → list( num ) ;
dec forall : list( alpha ) # ( alpha → truval ) → truval ;
dec length : list( alpha ) → num ;
dec isone : num → truval ;
--- g( n ) <= z st ( length( z ) = n, forall( z, isone ) = true ) ;
--- forall( nil, p ) <= true ;
--- forall( x :: z, p ) <= p( x ) and forall( z, p ) ;
--- length( nil ) <= 0 ;
--- length( x :: z ) <= 1 + length( z ) ;
--- isone( x ) <= x = 1 ;
```

17.5 The function factlist computes a list of factorials and is defined in Hope by:

```
dec factlist : num → list( num ) ;
dec factorial : num → num ;
--- factlist( 0 ) <= [ 1 ] ;
--- factlist( n + 1 ) <= factorial( n + 1 ) :: factlist( n ) ;
--- factorial( 0 ) <= 1 ;
--- factorial( n + 1 ) <= ( n + 1 ) * factorial( n ) ;
```

Why is this definition of factlist inefficient? By defining a suitable auxiliary function, transform it into a form that contains no redundant computation.

Chapter 18
Algebraic program transformation

Despite its near-completeness, the unfold/fold transformation methodology has limited scope for the automation we require for a viable transformation system, as we saw in the previous chapter. The transformations we consider in this chapter are based on the application of axioms and theorems which equate expressions and function definitions having certain structures – hence the term **algebraic** transformation. Instances of the left- (or right-) hand sides of these equations as sub-expressions are identified during the normal parsing of expressions, and any instance may be replaced by the correspondingly instantiated right- (or left-) hand sides (because of referential transparency). Optimization is, therefore, a consequence of some underlying analysis which establishes theorems equating an 'original', user-defined function with a more efficient version. In the object-oriented style of the Hope language, a typical axiom might be the following:

f(**if** p(x) **then** q(x) **else** r(x)) =
  if p(x) **then** f(q(x)) **else** f(r(x))

for all functions f, p, q, r and all objects x. Similarly, a theorem might equate the basic Fibonacci function with its linear version fib(n) = **let** (u, v) == g(n) **in** v

where the functions fib and g are as defined in the previous chapter. Thus, transformation based on this object-oriented presentation requires an analysis of expressions which considers both the functions called and the particular arguments to which they are applied. However, consideration of the object domain need not be crucial to the analysis of functions, which are the real objective of our optimization, and may well obscure it. By reasoning at the function level, where variables have been abstracted, there is no need to be concerned with an auxiliary domain of objects, the functional expressions acquire a simpler structure and equalities between functions can be expressed more concisely and are more readily recognized. As a result, more generally applicable transformations can be derived relatively easily because of the simpler syntax of the functional expressions. In fact the difficulties with automating the unfold/fold methodology may be partly attributed to its presentation in terms of objects which hides the functional relationships to some extent.

There are several transformation schemes based on the FP algebraic approach, and to describe them all in any detail would require a book in itself. One addresses the transformation of functions into imperative language loops, or equivalently tail recursion, by considering initially a class of *linear* functions; loosely speaking, a linear function makes a number of function calls proportional to the size of its argument. There are also schemes that transform certain classes of non-linear functions into linear form and hence tail recursion, the Fibonacci function being an example. Using an extended algebra which includes axioms for many-valued functions, it is possible to synthesize mechanically inverses for a significant class of recursive functions. For example, the function split may be derived as the inverse of append, yielding the set of all pairs of lists that when appended produce the list to which it is applied. Inverse functions have important applications in the optimizing of functional languages augmented with unification, and in the synthesis of efficient, concrete versions of abstract data types, as we will see in Section 18.5.

In this chapter, however, we will be primarily interested in the question of transforming linear functions into loops/tail recursive form, and merely summarize the principles behind the other schemes, providing references to the relevant research papers. Before embarking on this, we first describe the variable abstraction process which enables Hope programs, with user-defined data types, to be converted into FP. We then introduce the axioms of the FP functional algebra, giving some examples of their application, and go on to consider functional forms, and in particular their linear subset. This in turn leads on to linear functions, which satisfy the Linear Expansion Theorem, upon which the main theory of this chapter is based. An overview of some of the more advanced techniques referred to above is then given, before we close the chapter with a description of an alternative approach to transformation which is also algebraic in nature, but presented at the object level. This is based on the idea of passing *continuations*, which are essentially functions representing the 'work remaining to be done' in a partially evaluated function application. In this way it is possible to find, with a few Eureka steps, tail-recursive versions of many functions. The problem that remains, however, is how to represent the continuation efficiently as a data structure since it may well be a complex function.

18.1 Variable abstraction

The algebraic approach to transformation establishes theorems which state generic identities between functions, so that a transformation becomes an instance of an application of a theorem, rather than a prescription for determining the next rule to try in a transformation algorithm. The first problem is therefore to express all functional expressions in variable-free form, i.e. to abstract out all the variables in the program. We have come across this problem before, and we must first remove any pattern matching that may be present, as per Chapter 8, and then use an abstraction function of some sort to derive expressions in combinator form. The abstraction function defined in Chapter 12 to produce applicative expressions containing only the primitive combinators S, K and I (together with others such as B and C in an optimized implementation) is one possibility. In this chapter, however, we will be concerned only with first-order functions, and so a subset of the functional language, FP, described in Chapter 5 is most suitable in view of its established axioms and functional algebra.

Variable abstraction from languages with no pattern matching and no user-defined data types is easy, and essentially follows the method given in our discussion of the CAM at the end of Chapter 13. The compilation of pattern matching into conditional trees was described in Chapter 8, and we consider how to represent user-defined types in FP below. To illustrate the abstraction mechanism suppose we have the following first-order expression syntax:

$$E ::= constant \mid identifier \mid E : E \mid \langle\rangle \mid \langle E \{ , E \}^* \rangle$$

where, as usual, M^* denotes zero or more occurrences of M. Function application is written in infix notation using a colon and we use angle brackets to denote sequences to conform with the FP convention. The abstraction function, *abs*, for this syntax satisfies the equation $abs(x, E) : x = E$, and a function f of arity m may be expressed in variable-free form as follows. Given the definition $f(x_1, \ldots, x_m) = E$, f has the function-level form $f = abs(z, [(1 : z) / x_1, \ldots, (m : z) / x_m] E)$ since we may express the object-level definition as $f(z) = E$, where $z = (x_1, \ldots, x_m)$, i.e. where $x_i = i : z$.

The abstraction function is defined by the equations

$abs(x, x) = id$

$abs(x, y) = \underline{y}$ — for object y (more generally, if we had higher-order functions, this would be Ky)

$abs(x, f : E) = f \circ abs(x, E)$ — for functions f, which cannot be an expression containing objects in first-order FP

$abs(x, \langle E_1, \ldots, E_n \rangle) = [\, abs(x, E_1), \ldots, abs(x, E_n)\,]$

(In general, $abs(x, E_1 : E_2) = apply \circ [abs(x, E_1), abs(x, E_2)]$ where *apply* is the primitive functional, not in first-order FP, defined by $apply : \langle f, x \rangle = f : x$ for function-expression f and object-expression x. Thus the function *apply* is equivalent to the S combinator in that $(apply \circ [f, g]) : x = (f : x) : (g : x)$. We will not require this for our first-order analysis, however.)

Given that we can compile pattern matching into conditional trees, it now only remains to provide in FP a representation of user-defined data types. We take the same approach as in Chapter 8 except that we use sequences to represent compound data instead of tuples. Each constructor of a Hope data type is given a unique tag, e.g. an integer, and a structure formed by the application of an n-ary constructor is represented by a sequence of length $n + 1$, the first element of which is the constructor tag. The constructor code can then be accessed by extracting the head of a compound object's sequence representation. Selection of a particular component of a structure is represented by applying the FP selector function which is one greater than the parameter position of that component in the definition of its constructor. For example, suppose we have the following definition for the type tree in Hope:

```
data tree( alpha ) == leaf( alpha )
                      ++ node( tree( alpha ), alpha , tree( alpha ) ) ;
```

leaf and node will be given the tags 0 and 1 respectively so that, for example, the expression leaf(39) will be represented by the FP sequence ⟨0, 39⟩. Similarly, the object node(leaf(8), 7, leaf(9)) will be represented by ⟨1, ⟨0, 8⟩, 7, ⟨0, 9⟩⟩. Now we can easily translate a function defined on trees in Hope into FP. For example, the function depth, defined by

```
--- depth( leaf( x ) ) <= 0 ;
--- depth ( node( l, x, r ) ) <= 1 + max( depth( l ), depth( r ) ) ;
```

has the equivalent FP definition

$$depth = eq \circ [\ 1, \underline{0}\ ] \rightarrow \underline{0};\ + \circ [\ \underline{1},\ max \circ [\ depth \circ 2,\ depth \circ 4\ ]\ ]$$

Thus, we can now obtain equivalent FP functions for arbitrary first-order Hope functions; higher-order functions require no new techniques for their translation if we augment the FP language with extra combinators, such as *apply* and *K*, as discussed at the end of Chapter 13.

18.2 Axioms of the FP algebra and function-level equations

The functional algebra of FP is based upon a set of axioms which derive from the primitive functions and functionals (combining forms). The reader unfamiliar with the FP language is referred to Chapter 5 for an introduction, where our variant of the FP notation is defined. Each primitive will induce a number of axioms corresponding to its semantics, giving the appearance of the axioms associated with an abstract data type. The axioms are presented as equations in variable-free form, giving the functional algebra complete independence from the object domain, and so any set which does not give rise to a contradiction would define an algebra. However, to be useful, when the two sides of an axiom equation are applied to the same arbitrary object, the resulting equation must be known to hold at the object-level. For example, an axiom corresponding to the head selector function for sequences might be $hd \circ cons \circ [\ f, g\ ] = f$, for functions f, g where the range of g is sequences. When applied to an object, x, this yields the equation $hd : cons : \langle f : x, g : x \rangle = f : x$, which we know to be true. The same argument applies to all of the axioms we list below. Any further primitive data types, such as trees, could also be assumed to exist, each contributing its own set of axioms, but we just give the sequence axioms. The addition of the axioms for a new type is a simple exercise in the specification of abstract data types. The set of axioms that we will use for our function-level reasoning in this chapter now follows. All variables range over the set of FP functions, except the underlined ones which represent *constant* functions, the variable then being the *object* returned as the result.

18.2.1 Axioms for the primitive functions

First, we have two, type-independent axioms:

$id \circ x = x \circ id = x$ where *id* is the identity function

$\underline{x} \circ y = \underline{x}$ for constant function $\underline{x}$, in the domain that y is defined†

For the sequence manipulation functions, there are symmetrical sets of 'left' axioms and 'right' axioms, corresponding to the symmetry of definition of FP sequences. The 'left' axioms are:

$cons \circ [\, x, [\, y_1, \ldots, y_n \,]\,] = [\, x, y_1, \ldots, y_n \,] \quad (n \geq 0)$

$hd \circ [\, x_1, \ldots, x_n \,] = x_1$ in the domain that $[\, x_2, \ldots, x_n \,]$ is defined†

$tl \circ [\, x_1, \ldots, x_n \,] = [\, x_2, \ldots, x_n \,] \quad (n \geq 1)$ in the domain that x_1 is defined†

$k \circ [\, x_1, \ldots, x_n \,] = x_k \quad (1 \leq k \leq n)$ in the domain that $[\, x_1, \ldots, x_{k-1}, x_{k+1}, \ldots x_n \,]$ is defined†

(Thus the selector function, $k \equiv hd \circ tl^{k-1}$ for $k \geq 1$)

The corresponding 'right' axioms are:

$consr \circ [\, [\, y_1, \ldots, y_n \,], x \,] = [\, y_1, \ldots, y_n, x \,] \quad (n \geq 0)$

$hr \circ [\, x_1, \ldots, x_n \,] = x_n$ in the domain that $[\, x_1, \ldots, x_{n-1} \,]$ is defined†

$tr \circ [\, x_1, \ldots, x_n \,] = [\, x_1, \ldots, x_{n-1} \,] \quad (n \geq 1)$ in the domain that x_n is defined†

$k^r \circ [\, x_1, \ldots, x_n \,] = x_{n-k+1} \quad (1 \leq k \leq n)$ in the domain that $[\, x_1, \ldots, x_{n-k}, x_{n-k+2}, \ldots, x_n \,]$ is defined†

(Thus the selector function, $k^r \equiv hr \circ tr^{k-1}$ for $k \geq 1$.)

† A function f is defined in the domain D, if for $x \in D, f : x \neq \bot$ for $x \neq \bot$.

The primitive function, *null*, tests for empty sequences, and so induces the axiom

$$null \circ [\,] = \underline{T}$$

Note that [ ] is the empty construction which when applied to an object x yields the empty sequence ⟨⟩. Finally we have

$$\text{null} \circ (\, cons \circ [\, x, y \,]\,) = \underline{F} \qquad \text{in the domain that } cons \circ [\, x, y\,] \text{ is defined}^{\dagger}$$

There is also a similar 'right' axiom.

18.2.2 Axioms for the combining forms

We will use the axioms involving the primitive functionals of FP quite extensively, these functionals determining the structure of the function definitions that we wish to transform. The set given is not complete in that there are equalities between functions which are not derivable solely by application of the axioms. The most important axioms concern the combining forms of composition, conditional and construction which are essential for defining useful first-order functions. Any expression which uses the other combining forms is equivalent to one defined in terms of explicitly recursive functions which use only these three; refer to Chapter 5 where the use of higher-order functions is discussed. We do not include any of the axioms associated with the 'apply-to-all' functional α, but those of the 'insert' functionals / and \ will be required:

$$
\begin{array}{lll}
f \circ (\, g \circ h \,) & = (\, f \circ g \,) \circ h & \text{(associativity of composition)} \\
f \circ (\, p \rightarrow q \,;\, r \,) & = p \rightarrow f \circ q \,;\, f \circ r & \\
(\, p \rightarrow q \,;\, r \,) \circ f & = p \circ f \rightarrow q \circ f ;\, r \circ f & \\
p \rightarrow q \,;\, p \rightarrow r \,;\, s & = p \rightarrow q \,;\, s & \\
[\, f_1 , \ldots , f_n \,] \circ g & = [\, f_1 \circ g, \ldots , f_n \circ g \,] & \\
[\, \ldots (\, p \rightarrow f ; g \,) \ldots \,] & = p \rightarrow [\, \ldots f \ldots \,] ; [\, \ldots g \ldots \,] & \\
/ f \circ [\, x \,] = \backslash f \circ [\, x \,] & = \ x & \\
/ f \circ [\, x_1 , \ldots , x_n \,] & = f \circ [\, x_1 , / f \circ [\, x_2 , \ldots , x_n \,]\,] & (\, n \geq 2 \,) \\
\backslash f \circ [\, x_1 , \ldots , x_n \,] & = f \circ [\, \backslash f \circ [\, x_1 , \ldots , x_{n-1} \,], x_n \,] & (\, n \geq 2 \,)
\end{array}
$$

Just as we may define a function by its result expression, given in terms of its formal parameters, in an object-level language, so too we define a **functional** in terms of the result it produces when applied to formal **function** parameters. We consider only functionals of one argument in this chapter, and write the application of the functional H to the function f as $H(\, f\,)$, which we will often abbreviate by Hf, i.e. using juxtaposition. The expression Hf in the variable f is often referred to as a **form**, to distinguish it from the term 'functional', of which H is an example. A functional G of n variables would then be defined by the form $G(f_1, \ldots, f_n)$.

In our study of algebraic transformation techniques, we will consider functions defined by equations of the form

$$f = p \rightarrow q\,;\, Hf$$

for some functional H, where the functions p, q are fixed. Properties of such functions are then determined by the structure of H, which is frequently expressed in terms of **functional compositions**. The composition of the functionals H_1 and H_2 is also written as a juxtaposition, and $H = H_1H_2$ is defined by $Hf = H_1(H_2f)$ for function variable f. We also denote the *identity* functional by ID, defined by $ID(f) = f$, so that $ID\,H = H\,ID = H$. The n-fold functional composition of H with itself is written as H^n, and is defined by $H^0 = ID$, $H^nf = H(H^{n-1}f)$ for $n \geq 1$.

An easy example of function-level reasoning, which we will make use of later, is to evaluate the expresssion H^n1 where H is defined by $Hf = f \circ [j \circ 1, k]$ for fixed functions j and k. For $n = 1$, the result is $1 \circ [j \circ 1, k] = j \circ 1$ by the sequence axioms. Thus for $n = 2$, the result is $(j \circ 1) \circ [j \circ 1, k] = j^2 \circ 1$ and we can prove by induction that $H^n1 = j^n \circ 1$. We already have the base case, and assume that $H^n1 = j^n \circ 1$ for $n \geq 0$. Then,

$$\begin{aligned} H^{n+1}1 &= H(H^n1) = (H^n1) \circ [j \circ 1, k] \\ &= j^n \circ 1 \circ [j \circ 1, k] && \text{by the inductive hypothesis} \\ &= j^n \circ j \circ 1 && \text{by the sequence axioms} \\ &= j^{n+1} \circ 1 && \text{as required} \end{aligned}$$

We can now proceed to consider the special case in which the functional H is linear, defined formally in the next section, giving a linear function f and leading to a loop representation for f.

18.3 Linear functions and the Linear Expansion Theorem

Intuitively, a linear function is one that generates a number of function calls to itself which grows linearly in the magnitude of the argument to which it is applied. Thus, certainly, tail-recursive functions are linear, and these are defined, in the terminology of the previous section, by equations of the form $f = p \rightarrow q; f \circ x$ for some fixed function x, corresponding to a functional H defined by $Hf = f \circ x$. However, the tail-

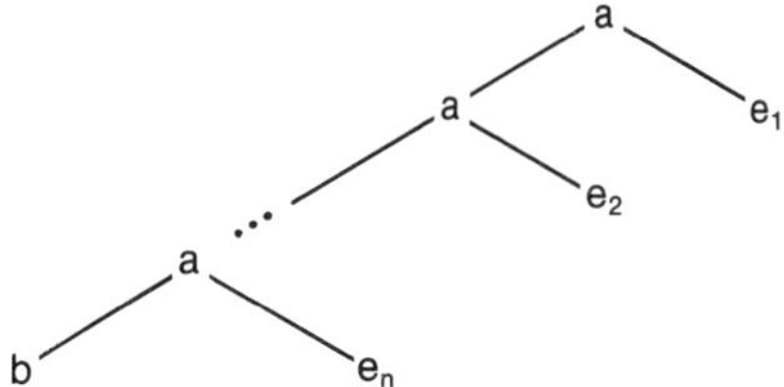

Figure 18.1 'Comb-shaped' reduction tree of a linear function.

recursive functions form but a small subset of the linear class, and any function with a 'comb-shaped' reduction tree, i.e. one that grows unidirectionally down its left spine as shown in Figure 18.1, must be linear; the factorial function is the archetypal example.

In the figure, the nodes labelled a represent calls to a fixed 2-argument function, a, which occurs in the defining expression of the linear function, f say, and the dependent subtrees of each represent its argument expressions. The nodes of the tree labelled e_i ($1 \leq i \leq n$) denote expressions which are unspecified as yet but do not involve calls to f; under applicative-order evaluation they would be leaves. The leaf b denotes a base-case application of f, i.e. of q, and the value of n is proportional to some measure of the size of the argument, which may be the magnitude of an integer (as with factorial) or the length of a list (as with reverse) for example. In the case of the application of the factorial function to the argument x, we would have $n = x$, $e_1 = n$, $e_2 = n - 1$, $\ldots, e_n = b = 1$ and $a = *$, the multiplication operator, giving the graph:

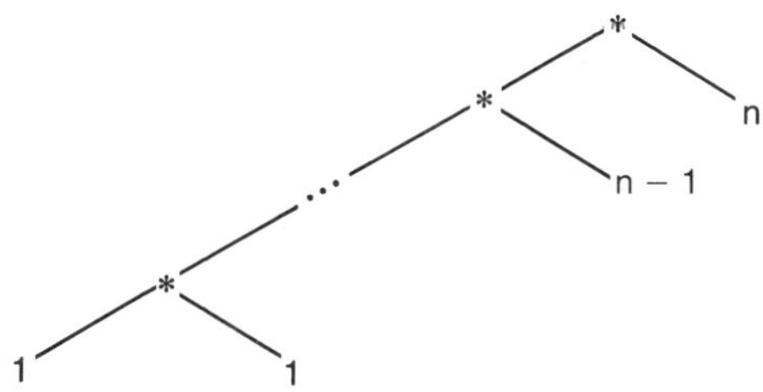

The question now is this: given the function f with defining equation $f = p \rightarrow q\ ;\ Hf$, what property of H can we determine that renders the function f linear in this sense? To answer this, we consider non-recursive expansions for f as follows.

Given the definition $f = p \rightarrow q\ ;\ Hf$, we can derive an expanded version by substituting the definition of f for the occurrence of f in the right-hand side. This gives the equation

$$f = p \rightarrow q\ ;\ H(\ p \rightarrow q\ ;\ Hf\ )$$

and repeating the operation gives

$$f = p \to q\,;\, H(\, p \to q\,;\, H(\, p \to q\,;\, Hf\,))$$

and so on. Now, this process can go on *ad infinitum* and the number of terms may grow in a highly non-linear manner, depending on the definition of H. For example the Fibonacci function is certainly non-linear intuitively, having a balanced reduction tree. Here each application of H in the expansion yields two more, so that the number of terms grows exponentially with the number of substitutions for f made in the right-hand side. In order to obtain a number of terms that grows linearly, we need the functional H to distribute through a conditional expression, and it is sufficient that we have the property that for all functions a, b, c,

$$H(\, a \to b\,;\, c\,) = H_t a \to Hb\,;\, Hc$$

for some functional H_t which is called the **predicate transformer** of H. This property defines H to be a **linear functional**, and equivalently Hf to be a **linear form.** (In fact, to ensure convergence of the expansion below, an additional condition must be satisfied by a linear functional H, namely that if for any object x, $H \underline{\perp} : x \neq \perp$, then, for all functions a, $H_t a : x = T$. Clearly this condition holds if the functional H is strict, i.e. $H \underline{\perp} = \underline{\perp}$.)

For a linear functional H, the above expansion then simplifies to

$$f = p \to q\,;\, H_t p \to Hq\,;\, \ldots\,;\, H_t{}^n p \to H^n q\,;\, H^{n+1} f$$

for all $n \geq 0$. Thus we have the **Linear Expansion Theorem** (LET):

If H is a continuous linear functional, then the function f defined by $f = p \to q\,;\, Hf$ for fixed functions p, q, is given by

$$f = p \to q\,;\, H_t p \to Hq\,;\, \ldots\,;\, H_t^n p \to H^n q\,;\, \ldots$$

The linearity condition, $H(\, a \to b\,;\, c\,) = H_t a \to Hb\,;\, Hc$, is clearly sufficient for f to have a non-recursive expansion, but it is *not* necessary, and the property that $H(\, a \to b\,;\, c\,) = H_t a \to H_1 b\,;\, Hc$ for some functional H_1 would also be sufficient. Indeed, this is still not necessary, and expansion theorems for certain classes of non-linear functions are considered by Williams (1982) and Harrison (1985).

Although quite correct, our statement of the LET is rather imprecise as it stands, and for the mathematically minded reader, we now formalize it a little more rigorously. If we define the sequence of functions, f_i, by

$$f_0 = \underline{\perp}$$
$$f_{n+1} = p \to q\,;\, H_t p \to Hq\,;\, \ldots\,;\, H_t^n p \to H^n q\,;\, \underline{\perp} \qquad \text{for } n \geq 0$$

then the LET states that for linear H, the least solution of the equation $f = p \rightarrow q\,;\, Hf$ is

$$lim_{(i \rightarrow \infty)}\, f_i$$

We can prove this result by first establishing the recurrence relation

$$f_{n+1} = p \rightarrow q\,;\, Hf_n$$

Certainly the recurrence relation holds if H is strict. If H is not strict, then for all objects x, either

$$H\,\underline{\perp} : x = \perp = \underline{\perp} : x$$

or

$$H\,\underline{\perp} : x \neq \perp \quad \text{and} \quad H_t p : x = T \quad \text{so that for } n > 0 \quad Hf_n : x = Hq : x$$

In either case, $f_{n+1} : x = (\, p \rightarrow q\,;\, Hf_n\,) : x$ as required.

Now, since the sequence $(\, f_0, f_1, \ldots)$ is increasing for continuous H (specifically, the ascending Kleene chain), it must have a limit in a function space which is a complete partial ordering (domain), and this limit is the least fixed point of the equation for f by the Fixed Point Theorem (see Appendix B).

The distribution axiom for conditionals extends to the infinite conditionals produced by the LET, that is, for continuous function g,

$$\begin{aligned}(\, p \rightarrow q\,;\ldots;\, H_t^n p \rightarrow H^n q\,;\ldots) \circ g = p \circ g \rightarrow q \circ g\,;\ldots;\\ (\, H_t^n p\,) \circ g \rightarrow (\, H^n q\,) \circ g\,;\ldots\end{aligned}$$

and

$$g \circ (\, p \rightarrow q\,;\ldots;\, H_t^n p \rightarrow H^n q\,;\ldots) = p \rightarrow g \circ q\,;\ldots;\, H_t^n p \rightarrow g \circ (\, H^n q\,)\,;\ldots$$

This follows if and only if $(\, lim\, f_i\,) \circ g = lim\,(\, f_i \circ g\,)$ and $g \circ lim\, f_i = lim\,(\, g \circ f_i\,)$, which follows by the continuity of the composition functional and of the function g.

Now, we can easily identify a basic set of elementary linear forms, by specifically testing for the linearity conditions, but more importantly, the set of linear forms is *closed:* if the functionals H and G are linear, then their composition, HG, is also linear and has predicate transformer $H_t G_t$, the composition of the predicate transformers of H and G respectively. This result is called the **Functional Composition Theorem** (Backus, 1981). If we write $L = HG$, we can easily show that for arbitrary functions a, b and c

$$L(\, a \rightarrow b\,;\, c\,) = L_t a \rightarrow Lb\,;\, Lc$$

Table 18.1 Simple linear forms

Linear form, Hf	*Predicate transformer form,* $H_t a$		
r	$\underline{T}$		
$f \circ r$	$a \circ r$	$(H_t = H)$	
$r \circ f$	a	$(H_t = ID)$	
$[\ldots, f, \ldots]$	a	$(H_t = ID)$	*f occurs only once in*
(for example $Hf = [f, r]$ and $Hf = [r, f]$ are common)			*the construction*
$p \rightarrow q ; f$	$p \rightarrow \underline{T} ; a$		
$p \rightarrow f ; r$	$p \rightarrow a ; \underline{T}$		
$f \rightarrow q ; r$	a	$(H_t = ID)$	

where $L_t = H_t G_t$:

$$\begin{aligned} L(a \rightarrow b ; c) &= H(G(a \rightarrow b ; c)) \\ &= H(G_t a \rightarrow Gb ; Gc) && \text{since } G \text{ is linear} \\ &= H_t(G_t a) \rightarrow H(Gb) ; H(Gc) && \text{since } H \text{ is linear} \\ &= L_t a \rightarrow Lb ; Lc \end{aligned}$$

The difficult part of the proof of the theorem lies in establishing the additional condition for L that we mentioned above when defining a linear functional, and we omit it.

The basic collection of linear functionals – called **simple linear functionals**, or SLFs for short – that we consider are defined together with their predicate transformers in Table 18.1. The letters f and a are used to denote function variables, all other letters denoting arbitrary fixed functions, and the sequence of three dots ... denotes a finite sequence of fixed functions, say $r_1, \ldots, r_n$ for $n \geq 0$.

Each of the forms listed in the table can be shown to be linear very easily. For example, in the case of the first, for arbitrary functions a, b, c,

$$H(a \rightarrow b ; c) = r = \underline{T} \rightarrow r ; r = H_t a \rightarrow Hb ; Hc$$

In fact, in place of $\underline{T} \rightarrow r ; r$ we could also write $\underline{F} \rightarrow r ; r$, or indeed $b \rightarrow r ; r$ for any Boolean-valued function b. Consequently the predicate transformer $\underline{T}$ given in Table 18.1 is not unique. In the second case we have

$$\begin{aligned} H(a \rightarrow b ; c) &= (a \rightarrow b ; c) \circ r \\ &= a \circ r \rightarrow b \circ r ; c \circ r && \text{by the conditional axioms} \\ &= Ha \rightarrow Hb ; Hc && \text{so that } H_t = H. \end{aligned}$$

The proofs for the other cases are equally straightforward, and are left as exercises. Although these proofs are sufficient for strict functionals H (H is always strict in the cases $Hf = f \circ r$, $r \circ f$ and $[\ \dots, f, \dots\ ]$), in general it is also necessary to show that the second condition for linearity is satisfied. This is also left as an exercise.

By applying the composition theorem to these SLFs we can identify a very rich class of linear forms and their predicate transformers. It is the corresponding linear functions that we will transform into iterative form – loops or tail recursive functions – in the next section. Notice that all forms Hf which are built from the three primitive functionals of function composition, construction and conditional and which contain only a single occurrence of the function variable f, must be linear.

Thus, for example, the form $Hf = h \circ [\ i, f \circ j\ ]$ is linear and has predicate transformer defined by $H_t a = a \circ j$. This follows since $H = H_1 H_2 H_3$ where $H_1 f = h \circ f$, $H_2 f = [\ i, f\ ]$, $H_3 f = f \circ j$. Thus $H_{1t} = ID$, $H_{2t} = ID$, $H_{3t}\, a = a \circ j$, and $H_t = ID.ID.H_{3t} = H_{3t}$. In fact such a form can immediately be identified as linear by applying the above heuristic rule, and its predicate transformer can be found by finding the 'composition of all functions composed with f on the right'. The significance of this example is that it encapsulates the factorial example given above. If $f = p \rightarrow q\ ; Hf$, then assigning the functions $eq0$ to p, $\underline{1}$ to q, $*$ to h, id to i and $sub1$ to j gives the definiton of factorial. It also covers other functions, however. For example, the assignments $null$ to p, $[\,]$ to q, $consr$ to h, hd to i and tl to j yield the function *reverse* that reverses a given sequence.

Despite the convenience of the above heuristics for hand calculations, clearly the systematic decomposition of a form into SLFs is most appropriate for mechanical compilation. In fact such a decomposition is precisely what must be performed by the parser of any implementation of such expressions, and minimal extra effort is needed to obtain the predicate transformers. We will extend this discussion in the next section where we will also build the loops corresponding to linear functions during parsing.

18.4 Iterative forms of linear functions

Using the LET of the previous section, we may form an iterative implementation corresponding to a linear function f with definition of the form $f = p \rightarrow q\ ; Hf$. Such an implementation may take the form of either a loop (or pair of loops) defined on objects, or an equivalent tail-recursive version of f. We consider the first alternative, which is slightly the simpler and requires no further transformation for an imperative implementation; the second may be found in Harrison and Khoshnevisan (1986).

Now, given an object x as argument, if $f : x$ is defined, then by the

LET, $f: x = (H^n q): x$, where n is the smallest integer such that $(H_t^n p): x = T$. Thus, for the application of f to x, f can in principle be 'computed' iteratively in a loop, starting with the known function q in an accumulator and applying H to the accumulator n times. The result of the application is then obtained by applying the final contents of the accumulator to x. Of course, in general, the increasing complexity of the functions in the sequence q, Hq, $H^2q, \ldots$ renders this approach impractical, and we have to work a little harder to find a loop at the object level. The idea behind the forthcoming analysis is that if a loop implementation does exist for the expression $f : x$, the loop should comprise the assignment to an accumulator of an expression which depends on two variables: the current accumulator and some loop input variable, x_i, given by the loop count i on the ith iteration.

To this end let $r_i = (H^i q): x_i$ for $0 \le i \le n$ and some set $\{x_i \mid 0 \le i \le n\}$ with $x_n = x$, where n is the integer defined above. Then $r_n = f: x$ by the LET, and if we can find an object level expression E_H corresponding to H with the property that $r_i = E_H(r_{i-1}, x_i)$ for $1 \le i \le n$, the set of objects $\{r_i \mid 1 \le i \le n\}$ can be computed iteratively in a loop using destructive assignment to an accumulator variable, $r := E_H(r, x_i)$, giving the result $r = r_n$ in the accumulator as required after the final iteration. E_H may therefore be regarded as the a that labels the nodes in the linear expression graph shown in Figure 18.1. If the functional H is built entirely from SLFs, we will see that n and $\{x_i\}$ can be computed for any object x from p and H_t, which can be obtained as described in the previous section. Since we also know that the initial value of the accumulator is $r = r_0 = q : x_0$, it remains only to determine the expressions $E_H(u, v)$ for object variables u, v.

Again, we first determine the expression E_H when H is an SLF, and then define it for the case in which H is a composition of SLFs. That is, if $H = H_1 \ldots H_n$ where each H_i is a SLF $(1 \le i \le n)$, E_H is defined in terms of $E_{H1}, \ldots, E_{Hn}$ (and also, in fact, the predicate transformers, $H_{1t}, \ldots, H_{nt}$). For the sake of simplicity, we shall consider only functionals C which are compositions of the following three SLFs introduced in the previous section: $Hf = f \circ r$, $Hf = r \circ f$ and $Hf = [\ldots, f, \ldots]$, where r is an arbitrary fixed function, and ... represents a finite sequence of fixed functions. We shall call functionals C of this type **composite** linear functionals, or CLFs.

The SLF case that $Hf = r$ for all functions f is trivial, the function defined by the equation $f = p \rightarrow q\,; r$ being non-recursive; the same also applies if H is a composition of SLFs that includes one of this type. The SLFs that involve conditionals may be handled analogously to the third type of SLF that we do consider, involving constructions. In fact, in Harrison and Khoshnevisan (1986), an extended set of simple linear functionals is considered, for example including the functional H defined by $Hf = [\ldots, Af, \ldots, Bf, \ldots]$, where A and B are both linear functionals with equal predicate transformers, $A_t = B_t$. In this way, the class of linear functions that can be transformed into iterative form is much more general than the class we address here. However, the examples we give here should be sufficiently general to explain the principles involved.

We first derive the following important lemma which will be used in the proof of the theorem given below.

Lemma 18.1 Given CLF H, $H_t f = f \circ H_t id$ for all functions f.

Proof We denote the function $H_t id$ by j, and in fact it is *equal* to j in the case of the factorial-like form $Hf = h \circ [\, i, f \circ j\,]$. The proof of the lemma is by induction on the number of SLFs in the composition H. (The predicate transformers for each of the SLFs considered are given in Table 18.1.)

Base case: If $Hf = f \circ r$, then $j = H_t id = id \circ r = r$. Thus, $H_t f = f \circ r = f \circ j$
If $Hf = r \circ f$, then $j = H_t id = id$. Thus, $H_t f = f = f \circ j$
If $Hf = [\ldots, f, \ldots]$, then $j = H_t id = id$. Thus, $H_t f = f = f \circ j$

Inductive step: Suppose that $H = H_1 \ldots H_m$ for $m \geq 2$, and let $L = H_1 \ldots H_{m-1}$. Then we may assume inductively that $L_t f = f \circ L_t id$ for all functions f. But

$H_t f = L_t(H_{mt} f)$	by the Functional Composition Theorem,
$= H_{mt} f \circ L_t id$	by the inductive hypothesis
$= f \circ H_{mt} id \circ L_t id$	by the base case
$= f \circ L_t(H_{mt} id)$	by the inductive hypothesis
$= f \circ H_t id$	by the Functional Composition Theorem

This completes the proof.

Consider, then, the function f defined by the equation $f = p \rightarrow q\,;\, Hf$, and the non-bottom valued application $f : x$. The first consequence of the above lemma is that the least integer n such that $H_t^n p : x = T$ is the least n such that $p : j^n : x = T$, which can be computed easily in a simple while loop, by successively applying j to x and then p to the result. In fact we make further use of this same while loop by defining the set $\{x_i \mid 0 \leq i \leq n\}$ by $x_n = x$ and $x_{i-1} = j : x_i = j^{n-i+1} : x$ for $1 \leq i \leq n$. We will see that this set is indeed the required one in the forthcoming theorem.

Now, we saw how to compute the predicate transformer, H_t, of a CLF, H, in the previous section, and we now need to determine the expression E_H in a similar fashion. The key property that we require of this expression is that $(Hf):x = E_H((H_t f):x, x)$ for all functions f and objects x. For then we have the following theorem:

Theorem 18.1 Given CLF H, integer $n \geq 0$ and object r_0, let the set $\{r_i | 1 \leq i \leq n\}$ be defined by $r_i = (H^i q):x_i$, where the set $\{x_i | 0 \leq i \leq n\}$ is defined as above. Then $r_i = E_H(r_{i-1}, x_i)$ for $1 \leq i \leq n$.

Proof: $r_i = (H^i q):x_i = (H(H^{i-1}q)):x_i$ for $1 \leq i \leq n$

$= E((H_t(H^{i-1}q):x_i, x_i)$ by hypothesis, substituting $H^{i-1}q$ for f, and abbreviating E_H by E

$= E((H^{i-1}q \circ H_t id):x_i, x_i)$ by Lemma 18.1, substituting $H^{i-1}q$ for f

$= E((H^{i-1}q):x_{i-1}, x_i)$ by definition of x_{i-1} for $i \geq 1$

$= E(r_{i-1}, x_i)$ by definition of r_{i-1} for $i \geq 1$

From this, the iterative implementation of the expression $f:x$ follows immediately as a pair of loops: the while loop referred to above which computes n and the set $\{x_i | 0 \leq i \leq n\}$, and the for loop which is entered n times to compute $f:x$ as r, by starting with $r := q:x_0$ and successively assigning (n times) $r := E(r, x_i)$.

We therefore only have to define appropriate expressions E_H for arbitrary CLFs H, which satisfy our hypothesis. The required definitions are given next, and their validity is established in the lemma that follows them.

If $Hf = f \circ r$, then $E_H(u, v) = u$ for object variables u, v

If $Hf = r \circ f$, then $E_H(u, v) = r:u$ for object variables u, v

If $Hf = [r_1, \ldots, r_i, f, r_{i+1}, \ldots, r_n]$, then

$E_H(u, v) = \langle r_1:v, \ldots, r_i:v, u, r_{i+1}:v, \ldots, r_n:v \rangle$

for object variables u, v

If $H = BC$ where B is one of the three SLFs considered in this analysis and C is a CLF, then $E_H(u, v) = E_B(E_C(u, B_t id:v), v)$

The theory is therefore completed with the following lemma:

Lemma 18.2 The above definition of the expression E_H associated with a CLF H satisfies the property that $(Hf):x = E_H((H_t f):x, x)$ for all functions f and objects x.

Proof We again use induction on the number of SLFs in the composition H.

Base case: If $Hf = f \circ r$, then $E_H(H_t f : x, x) = H_t f : x = (f \circ r) : x = Hf : x$
If $Hf = r \circ f$, then
$$E_H(H_t f : x, x) = r : (H_t f : x) = r : (f : x) = (r \circ f) : x = Hf : x$$
If $Hf = [r_1 , \ldots , r_i , f, r_{i+1} , \ldots , r_n]$, then
$$E_H (H_t f : x, x) = [r_1 : x, \ldots , r_i : x, H_t f : x, r_{i+1} : x, \ldots , r_n : x]$$
$$= [r_1 , \ldots , r_i , ID(f), r_{i+1} , \ldots , r_n] : x = Hf : x$$

Inductive step: Suppose that $H = AB$ where A is an SLF of the base case and B is a CLF. Then,

$$\begin{aligned} E_H(H_t f : x, x) &= E_A(E_B(H_t f : x, A_t id : x), x) && \text{by definition of } E_{AB} \\ &= E_A(E_B(B_t f : A_t id : x, A_t id : x), x) \end{aligned}$$

since

$$\begin{aligned} H_t f &= A_t(B_t f) && \text{by the Functional Composition Theorem} \\ &= B_t f \circ A_t id && \text{by Lemma 18.1} \end{aligned}$$

Thus,

$$\begin{aligned} E_H(H_t f : x, x) &= E_A(Bf : A_t id : x, x) && \text{by the inductive hypothesis} \\ &= E_A((Bf \circ A_t id) : x, x) \\ &= E_A(A_t(Bf) : x, x) && \text{by Lemma 18.1} \\ &= A(Bf) : x && \text{since } A \text{ is an SLF of the base case} \\ &= Hf : x \end{aligned}$$

completing the proof.

Thus, any linear recursive function defined by an equation of the form $f = p \rightarrow q \,;\, Hf$, where H is a CLF, may indeed be implemented by the pair of loops described above; a while loop and a for loop which are simple to write down in terms of p, q, $H_t id$ and E_H (which is left as an exercise).

We can see how the transformation works by considering the generalized factorial function as an example. This is given by the equation $f = p \rightarrow q \,;\, Hf$, where $Hf = h \circ [i, f \circ j]$. As in the previous section, we write $H = H_1 H_2 H_3$ where $H_1 f = h \circ f$, $H_2 f = [i, f]$, $H_3 f = f \circ j$, so that $H_{1t} = ID$, $H_{2t} = ID$, $H_{3t} = H_3$ and so $H_t id = j$. Now, for the SLFs H_1, H_2, H_3 we have the respective expressions $E_1(u, v) = h : u$, $E_2(u, v) = \langle i : v, u \rangle$, $E_3(u, v) = u$. Thus, by Theorem 18.1, the assignment statement in the for loop is

$$r := E_H(r, x_i) = E_1(E_2(E_3(r, H_{1t}H_{2t}id : x_i), H_{1t}id : x_i), x_i)$$
$$= E_1(E_2(E_3(r, x_i), x_i), x_i) \quad \text{substituting for the predicate transformers}$$
$$= E_1(E_2(r, x_i)x_i)$$
$$= E_1(\langle i : x_i, r \rangle, x_i)$$

i.e.

$$r := h : \langle i : x_i, r \rangle$$

In the case of the factorial function, therefore, where $p = eq0$, $q = \underline{1}$, $h = *$, $i = id$ and $j = sub1$, we obtain the loop assignment $r := * : \langle x_i, r \rangle$, and $H_t id = j = sub1$. For reverse, where $p = null$, $q = [\,]$, $h = consr$, $i = hd$ and $j = tl$, we get $r := consr : \langle hd : x_i, r \rangle$, and $H_t id = j = tl$.

In fact, the transformation given so far provides only a minimal improvement in performance, since it is only the calls to the recursive function that have been removed. However, this is not surprising in view of the generality of the scheme, which applies to all linear recursive functions defined by a CLF, some of which cannot be optimized any further, an example being the function given to reverse the elements of a given sequence. Such a function would first generate a sequence of recursive calls to itself until its argument reached the base case and would then complete the corresponding function applications using the arguments which must have been saved in the initial calling sequence. If it is impossible to reconstruct these arguments by starting with the argument of the base case and repeatedly applying some fixed function, there is no direct alternative to implementing the function's application in two phases: one to pre-compute and stack all of the arguments and reach the base case, the other to successively complete the evaluations of the function's defining expression instantiated with the stacked argument values. In the case of the reverse function, each argument stacked after the first (that of the top-level application) is the tail of the previous one, which cannot therefore be reconstructed because of the destructive nature of the *tl* function, which discards the head of its argument. However, in the case of factorial, the next argument stacked is the integer one less than the current one, and so in this case the previous argument can be reconstructed by adding one. Thus there is no need to stack the arguments in an implementation of the factorial function.

In general, the 'next' argument is obtained by applying the known function $j = H_t id$ to the 'current one'. Thus we can avoid building a stack if we know that j has an inverse, j^{-1}, and are able to determine it. In this way we avoid building the intermediate stack, but we cannot dispense with the while loop entirely since we need to find the number of iterations required in the for loop, n, and also the value of the argument, x_0, in the base case. For certain functions, however, these two values can be determined without recourse to executing a while loop. For example, if the predicate function $p = eq0$ and $j = sub1$, then $n = x$ (the top-level argument) and $x_0 = 0$. Similarly, if $p = null$ and $j = tl$, then $n = length(x)$ and $x_0 = \langle\rangle$, where application of the function *length* is a simple operation if the length of a list is maintained in its descriptor. However, in the latter case, recall that we do not know j^{-1}, and so we cannot dispense with the while loop, the only saving being a simplification of its body by omitting the updating of a count.

Thus we can eliminate the while loop only in the case that j has a known inverse and it is possible to generate at compile-time the code necessary for deducing x_0 and n at run-time. In practice the function j tends to have a very simple structure, for example it may be primitive, such as *sub*1 or *tl* in our examples. Moreover, the theory of inverse functions referred to in this chapter could be used to extend significantly the range of these functions for which inverses can be found. Thus, under the above conditions, the resulting loop corresponding to the application to the argument, a, of the function, f, defined by $f = p \rightarrow q\ ;\ Hf$ is as follows:

```
n := NumberOfIterations( j, p, a ) ;
x := BaseValue( j, p, a ) ;
r := q : x ;
for i := 1 to n
    x := j^-1 : x ;
    r := E_H( r, x )
end
```

The code for the functions NumberOfIterations and BaseValue is generated by the compiler, as it is for the function E_H. In the case of factorial, this becomes

```
n := a ;
x := 0 ;
r := 1 ;
for i := 1 to n
    x := add1 : x ;
    r := * : ⟨r, x⟩
end
```

This is the normal imperative implementation of factorial, working from the base case upwards toward a, and we now note that an equally common loop implementation of this function works 'downwards' from the top-level argument, i.e. in reverse. Such loop reversal depends here on the property that the primitive function multiply, i.e. $*$, is associative and commutative. In general, we may dispense with the for loop by reversing the while loop if a similar, less restrictive, associativity condition holds which fits very naturally into the above transformation scheme. This condition relates to the function E_H, and we do not need j ($= H_t id$) to possess an inverse since the while loop uses this function as it stands to drive its iteration. We state a result based upon Harrison and Khoshnevisan (1986), using the notation we have defined above:

Let $a_0 = y_0 = x$, and $a_i = E_H(y_i, a_{i-1})$, $y_i = j : y_{i-1}$ ($i \geq 1$)
Then $Hf : x = E_H(q : y_n, a_{n-1})$ where $n = min_i \{ p : j^i : x = T \}$
if $E_H(u, E_H(v, w)) = E_H(E_H(u, v), w)$ for all objects u, v, w

Under this condition, it can be shown similarly that the equivalent tail-recursive form of the function f is

$$f = p \rightarrow q ; E \circ [q \circ j \circ 1, 2] \circ g \circ [j, id]$$

where

$$g = p \circ 1 \rightarrow id ; g \circ [j \circ 1, E]$$

and the FP function E is defined by $E : \langle u, v \rangle = E_H(u, v)$.

A result of Kieburtz and Shultis (1981) which, under appropriate conditions, gives a tail-recursive form for the factorial class of functions defined above, is actually a special case of this transformation – or rather an immediate generalization of it. The result states that given functions f and f^*, defined by

$$f = p \rightarrow q ; h \circ [i, f \circ j] \text{ and } f^* = p \circ 1 \rightarrow h \circ [2, q \circ 1] ; f^* \circ [j \circ 1, h \circ [2, i \circ 1]]$$

where the fixed function h is associative with left unit object u, then $f = f^* \circ [id, \underline{u}]$. (The object u is a left unit of the function h if and only if $h \circ [\underline{u}, x] = x$ for all functions x.)

We now prove this result by using the LET and comparing the general terms in the expansions of each side of the claimed equality. If each corresponding pair of terms can be shown to be equal, then the (convergent) expansions, and hence their functions, must also be equal.

Considering first the left-hand side, we define the functional H by $Hx = h \circ [i, x \circ j]$ for function variable x, so that $H_t x = x \circ j$, as we saw in Section 18.3. Thus $H_t^n p = p \circ j^n$.

Now,

$$\begin{aligned} H^n q &= h \circ [\, i, (\, H^{n-1} q \,) \circ j \,] && \text{for } n \geq 1 \\ &= h \circ [\, i, h \circ [\, i, (\, H^{n-2} q \,) \circ j \,] \circ j \,] && \text{for } n \geq 2 \\ &= h \circ [\, i, h \circ [\, i \circ j, (\, H^{n-2} q \,) \circ j^2 \,] \,] && \text{by the FP construction/composition axiom} \\ &= h \circ [\, i, h \circ [\, i \circ j, h \circ [\, i \circ j^2, \ldots, h \circ [i \circ j^{n-1}, (\, H^0 q \,) \circ j^n \,] \ldots \,] \,] \,] \\ &= /h \circ [\, i, i \circ j, \ldots, i \circ j^{n-1}, q \circ j^n \,] && \text{for } n \geq 0 \end{aligned}$$

which may be proved rigorously by induction on n. Note that this result holds for $n = 0$ under the convention that the sequence $i, i \circ j, \ldots, i \circ j^{n-1}$ is then empty, giving $/h \circ [\, q \,]$ which is equal to q as required by definition of $/h$. Thus, the general term for the left-hand side is

$$p \circ j^n \rightarrow /h \circ [\, i, i \circ j, \ldots, i \circ j^{n-1}, q \circ j^n \,] \qquad \text{for } n \geq 0$$

Turning now to the right-hand side, we define the functional G by $Gx = x \circ k$, where the fixed function $k = [\, j \circ 1, h \circ [\, 2, i \circ 1 \,] \,]$, so that $G_t = G$. Then if $q^* = h \circ [\, 2, q \circ 1 \,]$, the function f^* has the defining equation $f^* = p \circ 1 \rightarrow q^*; Gf^*$, and the predicate of the general term in its expansion is $G_t^n (\, p \circ 1 \,) = p \circ 1 \circ k^n = p \circ j^n \circ 1$ by the result derived in Section 18.2.

Now,

$$\begin{aligned} G^n q^* &= q^* \circ k^n \\ &= h \circ [\, 2 \circ k^n, q \circ 1 \circ k^n \,] && \text{by the FP construction/composition axiom} \\ &= h \circ [\, 2 \circ k^n, q \circ j^n \circ 1 \,] && \text{by the same result from Section 18.2} \end{aligned}$$

But,

$$\begin{aligned} 2 \circ k^n &= h \circ [\, 2, i \circ 1 \,] \circ k^{n-1} && (\, n \geq 1 \,) \\ &= h \circ [\, 2 \circ k^{n-1}, i \circ j^{n-1} \circ 1 \,] && \text{using the same result} \\ &= h \circ [\, h \circ [\, 2 \circ k^{n-2}, i \circ j^{n-2} \circ 1 \,], i \circ j^{n-1} \circ 1 \,] \\ &= \backslash h \circ [\, 2, i \circ 1, i \circ j \circ 1, \ldots, i \circ j^{n-1} \circ 1 \,] && (\, n \geq 0 \,) \end{aligned}$$

by repeating the same argument. Again, it is easy to prove this result rigorously by induction on n, and the proof will be set as an exercise. Thus,

$$\begin{aligned} G^n q^* &= h \circ [\, \backslash h \circ [\, 2, i \circ 1, i \circ j \circ 1, \ldots, i \circ j^{n-1} \circ 1 \,], q \circ j^n \circ 1 \,] \ (\, n \geq 0 \,) \\ &= \backslash h \circ [\, 2, i \circ 1, i \circ j \circ 1, \ldots, i \circ j^{n-1} \circ 1, q \circ j^n \circ 1 \,] \end{aligned}$$

The general term of the right-hand side is therefore

$$p \circ j^n \circ 1 \circ [\, id, \underline{u} \,] \rightarrow \backslash h \circ [\, 2, i \circ 1, i \circ j \circ 1, \ldots, i \circ j^{n-1} \circ 1, q \circ j^n \circ 1 \,] \circ [\, id, \underline{u} \,]$$
$(n \geq 0)$

i.e. $p \circ j^n \rightarrow \backslash h \circ [\, \underline{u}, i, i \circ j, \ldots, i \circ j^{n-1}, q \circ j^n \,]$ by the FP selector/construction axiom

i.e. $p \circ j^n \rightarrow /h \circ [\, \underline{u}, i, i \circ j, \ldots, i \circ j^{n-1}, q \circ j^n \,]$ since h is associative

i.e. $p \circ j^n \rightarrow h \circ [\, \underline{u}, /h \circ [\, i, i \circ j, \ldots, i \circ j^{n-1}, q \circ j^n \,]\,]$

i.e. $p \circ j^n \rightarrow /h \circ [\, i, i \circ j, \ldots, i \circ j^{n-1}, q \circ j^n \,]$ since u is the left unit of h

This is the same as we obtained for the left-hand side for all $n \geq 0$, and so the equality is proved.

Intuitively, the second argument of the function f^* corresponds to the accumulator variable in an imperative while loop, set initially to the unit object of the function h according to the composition of f^* with the construction $[\, id, \underline{u} \,]$. The first argument corresponds to the loop's input variable which is set initially to the argument of f, according to the composition of f^* with $[\, id, \underline{u} \,]$ similarly, and is successively 'reduced' (on recursive calls to f^* corresponding to cycles of the loop) until it satisfies the exit condition of the loop.

For the factorial function, for example, we would have $p = eq0$, $h = *$, $j = sub1$, $i = id$, $u = 1$, so that f^* is defined by the equation

$$f^* = eq0 \circ 1 \rightarrow * \circ [\, 2, \underline{1} \,] ; f^* \circ [sub1 \circ 1, * \circ [\, 2, 1 \,]\,]$$

The expression $f^* \circ [\, id, \underline{1} \,]$ reflects the conventional loop that begins with 1 in its accumulator and its input variable set to the value of the argument of the top-level expression. The loop then repeatedly multiplies its accumulator by its input variable, which it decrements until it becomes zero (the exit condition).

18.5 Other applications

The appeal of the function-level algebraic approach to transformation is that it applies to substantial classes of functions – we have only considered part of the linear class for which the transformations are mechanizable. All of the information required for the translation of the linear class of functions considered in this chapter into iterative form, for example, can be obtained during the parsing of the functions' defining equations, which would still be necessary in any implementation. However, the approach is certainly not limited to linear functions, many non-linear functions having equivalent linear versions, from which iterative implementations follow from the above results. We call such a transformation **linearization**. The non-linear functions concerned are called **degenerate multilinear**, the defining equation of such a function, f, having the form $f = p \rightarrow q\,;\, Hf$ where $Hv = M(v, \ldots, v)$ for function variable v, and M is a **multilinear** functional of n parameters. An n-multilinear form $M(f_1, \ldots, f_n)$ is independently linear in each of its arguments considered separately, i.e. for $1 \leq i \leq n$,

$$M(f_1, \ldots, f_{i-1}, a \rightarrow b\,;c, f_{i+1}, \ldots, f_n) = M_i a \rightarrow M(f_1, \ldots, f_{i-1}, b, f_{i+1}, \ldots, f_n)\,; \\ M(f_1, \ldots, f_{i-1}, c, f_{i+1}, \ldots, f_n)$$

for some fixed functionals M_i. (In fact, as in the definition of a linear form, we also require that if there exists an object x such that $M(f_1, \ldots, f_{i-1}, \underline{\perp}, f_{i+1}, \ldots, f_n) : x = \perp$, then for all functions a, $M_i a : x = T$, which always follows if M is strict.)

We do not give the details here, these being rather lengthy and available in Harrison (1985), but simply illustrate the transformation by considering one example, the Fibonacci function which is degenerate **bilinear** (2-multilinear):

$$fib = le1 \rightarrow \underline{1}\,;\, + \circ [\, fib \circ sub1,\; fib \circ sub2\,]$$

where $le1$ is defined by $le1 : x = T$ if $x \leq 1$, and F if $x > 1$ for integer x. This can be written as

$$fib = le1 \rightarrow \underline{1}\,;\, G(f, f)$$

where

$$G(u, v) = + \circ [\, u \circ sub1,\; v \circ sub2\,]$$

It is easy to see that G is bilinear, with predicate transformers G_1, G_2 respectively given by $G_1 a = a \circ sub1$ and $G_2 a = a \circ sub2$ for function variable a. It is easily shown that G satisfies the conditions of the main linearizing theorem for multilinear functions in particular because G_2 is a power of G_1, i.e. $G_2 = G_1{}^n$ for some integer $n \geq 2$, here $n = 2$. (The enthusiastic reader should note that although this property is sufficient for one of the theorem's conditions, the corresponding necessary condition is rather more general. Also, in the case that $n = 1$, the function would already be linear, as may be shown easily. The linearization theorem has some further lesser conditions, but we will not worry about them here.)

Given that a degenerate bilinear function, f, satisfies the conditions of the theorem, we define the linear function g by

$$g = p \rightarrow [\, q, G_1 q\,]\,;\, [\, G'(1 \circ g, 2 \circ g), G_1(1 \circ g)\,]$$

where

$$G'(u, G_1 v) = G(u, v) \qquad \text{for function variables } u, v$$

(that such a functional G' exists is one of the 'lesser' conditions). Then $f = 1 \circ g$. Thus, in the case of *fib*, we have $G'(u, v) = + \circ [\, u \circ sub1, v \circ sub1\,]$, $p = le1$ and $q = \underline{1}$, so that its linear form is given by

$$fib = 1 \circ g$$

where

$$g = le1 \rightarrow [\,\underline{1}, \underline{1}\,]; [\, + \circ [\, 1 \circ g \circ sub1, 2 \circ g \circ sub1\,], 1 \circ g \circ sub1\,]$$

upon direct substitution. The generalized scheme for transforming linear functions into loops referred to in the previous section could indeed now generate the usual loop implementation of the Fibonacci series, but some very straightforward simplification yields

$$g = le1 \rightarrow [\,\underline{1}, \underline{1}\,]; [\, + \circ [\,1, 2\,], 1\,] \circ g \circ sub1$$

Thus we obtain $g = le1 \rightarrow [\,\underline{1}, \underline{1}\,]; [\,+, 1\,] \circ g \circ sub1$ using the fact that $[\,1, 2\,] = id$ for correctly typed expressions, i.e. when each side is applied to a sequence of two elements. Applying the Linear Expansion Theorem to this function, we get

$$\begin{aligned}
fib : x &= 1 : (g : x) \\
&= 1 : (H^n[\,\underline{1}, \underline{1}\,] : x) \qquad \text{where } n = min_i \{\, le1 : sub1^i : x = T\} \\
&= 1 : ([\,+, 1\,]^n : [\,\underline{1}, \underline{1}\,] : sub1^n : x) \\
&\qquad\qquad\qquad \text{where } n = min_i \{x - i \leq 1 = T\} \\
&= 1 : ([\,+, 1\,]^{x-1} : \langle 1, 1\rangle) \quad \text{since } n = x - 1 \\
&= 1 : ([\,+, 1\,]^{x-2} : \langle 2, 1\rangle) \\
&= 1 : ([\,+, 1\,]^{x-3} : \langle 3, 2\rangle) \\
&= 1 : ([\,+, 1\,]^{x-4} : \langle 5, 3\rangle) \\
&\ldots
\end{aligned}$$

This reflects precisely the iterative implementation of the Fibonacci function, which uses a pair of accumulators, repeatedly swapping and adding them.

A further important application of algebraic techniques is the synthesis of recursively defined *inverse functions*. This is a rather more complex subject, beyond the scope of this book, since inverse functions are not in general single valued, and the underlying theory introduces logical function variables and involves power domains. To synthesize the inverse of a given function may seem a strange thing to want to do. However, there are at least two important roles for this type of transformation. One of these is to enhance the performance of functional languages which have been augmented to enable functions to be used as relations in any of their modes, as in logic programming. For example, we may define the function *append* to concatenate two lists in the usual way, but also need a function that, when applied to a single list as its argument, returns all pairs of lists that produce that argument when appended together. This function, call it *split*, could be written independently but is already fully specified by *append* and so, in this sense, is redundant and involves unnecessary effort on the part of the programmer. The definition

$$split(x) = \{(y, z) \quad \text{such that} \quad append(y, z) = x\}$$

is sufficient from the program designer's point of view. Similarly, the difference between two lists may be required, defined to be the list which when appended to the right of the second list gives the first:

$$difference(x, y) = z \quad \text{such that} \quad append(y, z) = x$$

Again this function is fully specified by *append* and it should not be necessary for the programmer to define the same logical function – or rather relation – two or three times.

Unfortunately, implementations of extended functional languages must evaluate applications of implicitly defined functions such as *split* and *difference* using unification, as with implementations of the logic languages such as PROLOG, which is generally less efficient than the reduction-based evaluation of functional expressions. Moreover, it is frequently known that recursive, i.e. purely functional, implementations also exist, as in our example. If it were possible to compile a recursively defined inverse of the function defining one of the modes of the corresponding relation, then all of its modes could be implemented without recourse to run-time unification. For example, $split = append^{-1}$, and *difference* can then be synthesized from this. Current techniques can indeed synthesize a recursive definition for $append^{-1}$, and for a significant class of recursively defined functions (Harrison, 1988).

The second application of inverse functions arises in the transformation of abstract data types, introduced in the previous chapter. We may express this problem in terms of a commutative square of functions between the abstract and concrete types, and find that a natural solution can be given in terms of function composition and inverse functions, and hence by an algebraic approach.

Suppose we have a pair of user-defined, abstract data types α, β, and the corresponding concrete pair α', β' which provide realizations of α, β respectively. Then, given any function $f: \alpha \rightarrow \beta$, we wish to synthesize a corresponding function, say $f' : \alpha' \rightarrow \beta'$, which performs operations on objects of type α' which are isomorphic in some sense to the operations performed by f on corresponding objects of type α. The function f' is then the concrete, 'implementation version' of f that we seek and we have the commutative square shown in the following diagram:

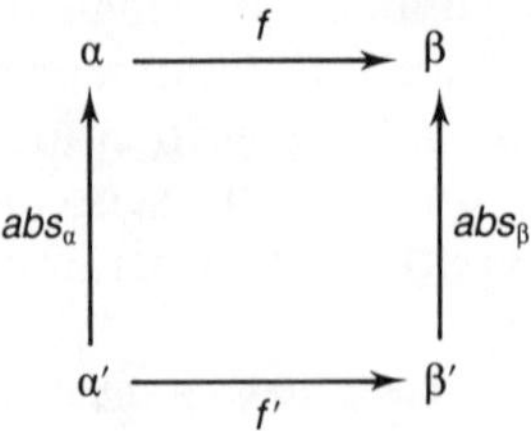

Here the abstraction function for an abstract type σ is denoted by $abs_\sigma : \sigma' \rightarrow \sigma$ where σ' is the concrete type corresponding to σ. Thus, in the notation of the FP functional algebra,

$$f \circ abs_\alpha = abs_\beta \circ f' \qquad \text{or} \qquad f' = abs_\beta^{-1} \circ f \circ abs_\alpha$$

assuming that the inverse function, abs_β^{-1}, exists. In the special case that $\beta = \beta'$, i.e. the concrete range type is the same as the abstract range type, we have a triangle:

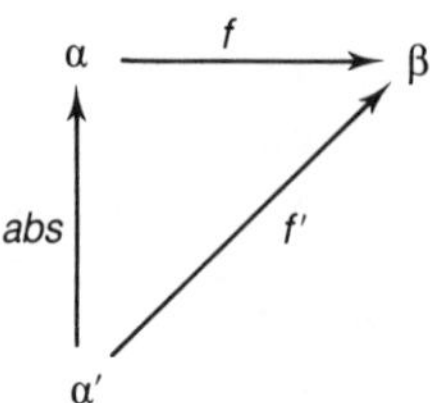

so that $f' = f \circ abs$. Such a situation would arise, for example, if the type β were a base type such as the integers – as we had in the first example of data type transformation that we considered in the previous chapter.

The simple idea of the commutative square forms the basis of a whole algebraic approach to data type transformation (Harrison and Khoshnevisan, 1988). This transformation system operates by repeatedly rewriting the expressions defining the functions abs^{-1} and f' using a set of axioms which includes the FP axioms and those relating to function inversion. In addition, the user-supplied definitions of the abstract data types are also used as the basis of further axioms for their own particular transformations; in the same way that they were in the unfold/fold approach to this problem described in Section 17.3. In this way, many functions $f' : \alpha' \rightarrow \beta'$ corresponding to $f: \alpha \rightarrow \beta$ supplied by the programmer may be synthesized mechanically, without recourse to Eureka steps other than in specifying the axioms appropriate for the particular user-defined types concerned. In particular, the algebraic approach is easily applied to the examples of Section 17.3.

We have seen that the algebraic approach to program transformation provides mechanizable optimization for a number of classes of functional programs, all of the information required being obtainable during parsing. By way of comparison, the unfold/fold methodology too could derive, as a result of an appropriate sequence of the elementary steps described in the previous chapter, any functional equivalence obtained by the algebraic approach. However, how to choose the right 'appropriate steps' without the benefit of hindsight is a substantial problem, and the choice would appear difficult, if not impossible, to automate with the generality required. For the present, the most effective answer appears to be a compromise in which a type of transformation meta-system discussed in Section 17.2 is extended to include new higher-level steps, or tactics, to apply each algebraic equivalence between functions (or between functions and loops). In this way, the increased automation of the algebraic approach could be acquired whilst still preserving the near completeness of the unfold/fold methodology. Indeed, such an approach might even provide a means by which new tactics, and possibly new functional equivalences, could be derived for use by the meta-system.

18.6 Transformation by continuation passing

A rather different approach to program transformation simplifies the calling mechanism of a recursive function at a cost of introducing higher-order functions which it then attempts to represent efficiently. Given a function of one argument, the idea is to find an equivalent tail-recursive function of two arguments, the first of which is a data object of the same type as the argument of the original function, and the second is a function called a **continuation**. In general, a continuation may be viewed as a mapping that, when applied to some partially evaluated object, will yield the fully evaluated object, that is, the final result. If we can find a sequence of object/continuation pairs, from each of which the final result may be obtained by applying the continuation to the object, the pairs may be regarded as defining the invariant of an iterative process and hence a tail-recursive function. Continuations were first introduced to provide a denotational semantics for goto statements in imperative languages essentially, the continuation computes the final semantic value of a program when applied to an intermediate program state.

It is usually not too hard to define the new, tail-recursive function independently of the original function and it is always possible to define it mutually recursively as we shall see. But the price to pay for so easily deriving an iterative implementation is the continuations themselves and the higher-order function applied to them. As we have seen, such objects are much less efficient to implement than data, and the continuations passed as parameters in an application of the transformed function become increasingly complex, rendering the transformation worthless. Typically what happens is that the tail-recursive version *f-tr* of a function f is initially applied to the argument of f and a simple continuation such as the identity function, *id*. Subsequently it is applied to object/continuation pairs in which the object becomes simpler, eventually reaching the base case that terminates the computation, and the complexity of the continuation increases. The benefits of the method are gained only when the continuations can be represented by simple data structures themselves, such as counters or lists. The continuation is then analogous to an accumulator.

Suppose then, that the function f is defined by $f(x) =$ **if** p **then** q **else** E, where the variable x may occur in any of the expressions p, q and E, and E has a single occurrence of f which is applied to the sub-expression $s(x)$ – i.e. $f(s(x))$ is a sub-expression of E. Then if f is applied to the non-base case argument a (i.e. $[a/x]$p evaluates to **false**) the computation proceeds by first applying f to $s(a)$, giving the result r say, and then evaluating the expression produced by substituting r into E in place of $f(s(x))$. This gives the result $f(a) = E_r$, where for variable w we define $E_w = [w/f(s(x))]E$. Another way of expressing this is to say that the function $\alpha = \lambda w.E_w$ is applied to the argument $r = f(s(a))$. It is the function α which is the continuation, representing the remaining evaluation to be performed in computing $f(a)$ after the evaluation of $f(s(a))$ is complete. The object/continuation sequence has general term $(\alpha^m, f(s^m(a)))$ and so, noting that $\gamma \circ \alpha = \lambda w.\gamma E_w$, an equivalent definition of f is

$$f(x) = \textit{f-tr}(x, id)$$

where

$$\begin{aligned}\textit{f-tr}(x, \gamma) &= \gamma(f(x)) \\ &= \textbf{if } p \textbf{ then } \gamma(q) \textbf{ else } \textit{f-tr}(s(x), \lambda w.\gamma E_w)\end{aligned}$$

The validity of this will be clear to the experienced functional programmer, and we can prove the equivalence informally by showing that $\textit{f-tr}(x, \gamma) = \gamma(f(x))$ by induction as follows. First, if x is such that p evaluates to **true**, then $\textit{f-tr}(x, \gamma) = \gamma(q) = \gamma(f(x))$. Otherwise,

$$\begin{aligned}\textit{f-tr}(x, \gamma) &= \textit{f-tr}(s(x), \lambda w.\gamma E_w) \\ &= (\lambda w.\gamma E_w) f(s(x)) && \text{by the inductive hypothesis} \\ &= \gamma(E) && \text{by definition of } E_w \\ &= \gamma(f(x)) && \text{in the non-base case as required.}\end{aligned}$$

We have not defined the induction mechanism that we have used, in particular the underlying ordering, but the method is essentially the subgoal induction used for the same purpose by Wand (1980).

A typical example of this style of transformation is the function rev that reverses a list, defined by

```
rev( x ) <= if null( x )
            then nil
            else rev( tl( x ) ) ⟨⟩ [ hd( x ) ] ;
```

Here, when applied to a non-nil list , rev first calls itself with argument tl(x) and then applies the continuation $\lambda w.w\langle\rangle[\, hd(x)\,]$. Thus, the tail-recursive version is

```
rev( x ) <= rev-tr( x, id ) ;
```

where

```
rev-tr( x, γ ) <= if null( x )
                  then γ( nil )
                  else rev-tr( tl( x ), λw.γ( w⟨⟩[ hd( x ) ] ) ) ;
```

Now, in this case we can represent the continuations by lists, since all of them are of the form $\lambda v.v\langle\rangle k$ for some list k. To prove this, we first note that id is of this form ($k = nil$), and assume inductively that $\gamma = \lambda v.v\langle\rangle k$. Then

$$
\begin{aligned}
\lambda w.\gamma(\, w\langle\rangle[\, hd\ x\,]\,) &= \lambda w.(\, w\langle\rangle[\, hd\ x\,]\,)\langle\rangle k && (\beta\text{-reduction}) \\
&= \lambda w.w\langle\rangle cons(\, hd(\,x\,), k\,) && (\text{associativity and definition of } append)
\end{aligned}
$$

as required, the next continuation passed being represented by the list $hd(\,x\,) :: k$. Hence, rather than pass a continuation $\gamma = \lambda v.v\langle\rangle k$, we may pass the list k that represents it. Thus, noting that in the base case $(\ \lambda v.v\langle\rangle k\ )(\ nil\ ) = k$, we get the normal tail-recursive function for reversing lists

```
rev( x )          <= rev-tr* ( x, nil ) ;
rev-tr* ( x, k )  <= if null( x )
                     then k
                     else rev-tr* ( tl( x ), hd( x ) :: k ) ;
```

In fact this result can easily be generalized in the same way to establish the loop-reversal result we derived in Section 18.4 using the LET.

The continuation passing method is not restricted to functions with only one occurrence of their name in the right-hand side of their defining equation, and we now derive the iterative form of the Fibonacci function using it. We start with the definition

```
fib( x ) <= if x ≤ 1
            then 1
            else fib( x − 1 ) + fib( x − 2 );
```

In the evaluation of fib(n) for argument n > 1, fib is first applied to (n − 1) and (n − 2) separately, giving the result-pair (fib(n − 1), fib(n − 2)). The evaluation is then completed by applying the continuation $\lambda uv.(u + v)$ where $\lambda uv.$ denotes the lambda abstraction of the *pair* (u, v). The next step is a little tricky. Since the first part of the computation produced a pair, we need a new function that produces a similar pair rather than just fib, because our continuations must be applied to pairs (they have arity 2). Thus we define

```
g( x ) <= ( fib( x ), fib( x − 1 ) );
       <= if x ≤ 1
          then ( 1, 1 )
          else ( fib( x − 1 ) + fib( x − 2 ), fib( x − 1) );
```

Applying the same continuation strategy as we used for fib(n) above, we obtain the same result pair, (fib(n − 1), fib(n − 2)), but now the continuation is $\lambda uv.(u + v, u)$. After this admitted Eureka-ish step, we can easily derive a tail-recursive form for g from which fib can be extracted as follows:

```
g( x )       <= g-tr( x, id );
g-tr( x, γ ) <= if x ≤ 1
                then γ( 1, 1 )
                else g-tr( x − 1, λuv.γ( u + v, u ) );
```

Now, $\lambda uv.\gamma(u + v, u) = \gamma \circ \lambda uv.(u + v, u)$ and we can see that all continuations are of the form $\{\lambda uv.(u + v, u)\}^n$, i.e. $[+, 1]^n$ in FP notation. (This can be proved rigorously by induction as before.) The continuation passed can therefore be replaced by n, which is a simple count, and we get

```
g( x )         <= g-tr* ( x, 0 );
g-tr* ( x, n ) <= if x ≤ 1
                  then [ +, 1 ]^n( 1, 1 )
                  else g-tr* ( x − 1, n + 1 );
```

Finally, therefore, we obtain the result $g(x) = [+, 1]^x(1,1)$, as we saw before using both the unfold/fold methodology and the algebraic approach.

In fact the continuation-passing style can also be applied to some more unusual functions with some success. We consider one example, the highly non-linear '91-function' of McCarthy, defined by

```
f( x ) <= if x > 100
          then x - 10
          else f( f( x + 11 ) ) ;
```

We can immediately express this in the tail-recursive continuation-passing form

```
f( x )       <= f-tr( x, id ) ;
f-tr( x, γ ) <= if x > 100
                then γ( x - 10 )
                else f-tr( x + 11, λw.γ( f( w ) ) )
```

Here, however, we have not got rid of the occurrence of f in its tail-recursive version, but we can obtain a simple expression for the continuation passed: it is of the form $\lambda w.f(\,f(\ldots f(\,w\,)\ldots))$ for some number of applications of f which we can again represent by a counter. The problem has not gone away entirely though, as we need to be able to simulate the multiple applications of f to evaluate $\gamma(\,x - 10\,)$. This can be done by introducing the auxiliary function sim-app, to give

```
f( x )          <= f-tr* ( x, 0 ) ;
f-tr* ( x, i )  <= if x > 100
                   then sim-app( x - 10, i )
                   else f-tr* ( x + 11, i + 1 ) ;
sim-app( v, i ) <= if i = 0
                   then v
                   else f-tr* ( v, i - 1 )
```

The correctness of the mutual recursion may be seen by noting that f-tr* (x, i) $= \gamma(\,f(\,x\,)\,) = f^i(\,f(\,x\,)\,)$.

The continuation-passing style of transformation is quite generally applicable, but relies on finding an efficient representation for the continuations generated, since otherwise any gain in efficiency would be prevented by the overheads incurred in the management of cumbersome higher-order functions. Often no such representation can be found, which is not really surprising in that some recursive functions are optimal, or near optimal, anyway by virtue of the nature of the problems they are solving, for example those involving tree manipulation. When a suitable representation can be found for the continuations, it may be a simple counter or a list, but in every example that we considered, which were not complex, Eureka steps were needed. Continuation passing provides a transformation system which is rather more mechanical than the unfold/fold methodology and more generally applicable than the algebraic methods which provide the best prospects for automation. In any event, it presents a novel approach of interest in its own right.

SUMMARY

- The algebraic style of program transformation is based upon finding equivalences for generic classes of functions.
- It is convenient to present the formal analysis in variable-free form.
- The axioms of FP simplify and help to mechanize the manipulation of programs.
- The linear functions constitute a large class which is closed under a functional composition operation.
- Linear functions may be transformed into loops or tail-recursive form using the Linear Expansion Theorem.
- Loop reversal may be performed when the linear function's defining expression possesses the appropriate associativity property.
- Degenerate multilinear functions are non-linear and may be transformed into linear functions under appropriate conditions.
- Many recursive inverse functions may be synthesized and used in the mechanization of data type transformations and removal of unification.
- A tail-recursive higher-order form of a function may be found which passes a function called a continuation in calls to itself.
- The continuation may sometimes be represented by a data structure, so producing a more efficient implementation of the function.

EXERCISES

18.1 Prove that each of the functionals given in Table 18.1 is linear and that the predicate transformers are as specified. If all FP functions are strict, which functionals must always be strict, and why?

18.2 In each of the following cases, prove that the functional H is linear, and find its predicate transformer. For function variable f:

(a) $Hf = Pf \rightarrow k\,;\,h$ where P is a linear functional and k, h are fixed functions

(b) $Hf = Pf \to Af; Bf$ where P, A, B are linear with $P_t = A_t = B_t$

(c) $Hf = Pf \to Af; k$ where P, A are linear with $P_t = A_t$ and k is a fixed function

(d) $Hf = p \to q; Af$ where A is linear and p, q are fixed functions

(e) $Hf = p \to Af; Bf$ where A and B are linear and p is a fixed function

18.3 If $Hf = p \to Af; Bf$ where p is a fixed function and A, B are linear with $A_t = B_t$, under what conditions is $H_t = A_t$?

18.4 Given the functional H defined by $Hf = h \circ [\, i, f \circ j \,]$ for fixed functions h, i, j, prove by induction on n that $H^n f = /h \circ [\, i, i \circ j, \ldots, i \circ j^{n-1}, f \circ j^n \,]$ for $n \geq 0$. What would the result be if we had $Hf = h \circ [\, f \circ j, i \,]$?

18.5 Prove by induction on n that $2 \circ k^n = \backslash h \circ [\, 2, i \circ 1, i \circ j \circ 1, \ldots, i \circ j^{n-1} \circ 1 \,]$ for $n \geq 0$, where $k = [\, j \circ 1, h \circ [\, 2, i \circ 1 \,]\,]$. Hence show that

$$h \circ [\, 2, q \circ 1 \,] \circ k^n = \backslash h \circ [\, 2, i \circ 1, i \circ j \circ 1, \ldots, i \circ j^{n-1} \circ 1, q \circ j^n \circ 1]$$

18.6 Given the bilinear form $G(u, v)$ with $G_1 = G_2$, show that the functional H defined by $Hf = G(f, f)$ is linear. Generalize the result to the n-multilinear case.

18.7 Show that the functional H defined by $Hf = Pf \to Af; Bf$ is linear if P, A, B are linear with equal predicate transformers. Theorem 18.1 can be generalized to apply to this functional H if P, A, B are CLFs and we define

$$E_H(u, v) = \textbf{if } E_P(u, v) \textbf{ then } E_A(u, v) \textbf{ else } E_B(u, v)$$

Using this result or otherwise, show that the square root approximation function sqrt is linear, where

```
sqrt( a, e ) = if a < e
               then 0
               else if square( x + e ) ≤ a
                    then x + e
                    else x
               where x = sqrt( a, 2 * e )
```

(*square* is the primitive arithmetic function defined by *square* $(x) = x * x$).

18.8 The Fibonacci function is defined in FP by

$$fib = le1 \rightarrow \underline{1}\ ;\ + \circ [\ fib, fib \circ sub1\ ] \circ sub1$$

If $g = [\ fib, fib \circ sub1\ ]$, show that $g = le1 \rightarrow [\ \underline{1}, \underline{1}\ ];\ Hg$ where the functional H is linear. Define H and outline a loop implementation for g and hence for *fib*.

18.9 The function *factlist* is defined in FP as follows:

$$factlist = eq0 \rightarrow [\ \underline{1}\ ]\ ;\ cons \circ [\ factorial, factlist \circ sub1\ ]$$
$$factorial = eq0 \rightarrow \underline{1};\ * \circ [\ id, factorial \circ sub1]$$

Give a recursive definition of the function $h = [\ factlist, factorial\ ]$ and show that h is degenerate multilinear but not linear. Now let $f = factlist \circ sub1$. Show that the function $h' = [\ f, factorial\ ]$ is linear and give its predicate transformer. (*Hint:* First observe that the predicate in the definition of *factorial* can be replaced by $eq1$.) Hence derive a loop implementation for *factlist*.

18.10 Express the following functions in continuation-passing form:

(a) *listo*, defined in Exercise 17.3;

(b) the *factorial* function.

In each case find an efficient representation for the continuation passed, stating any properties this requires of the primitive functions involved.

Chapter 19
Memoization

The technique called memoization was originally introduced by Michie (1968), and operates by replacing certain non-linear function definitions by corresponding **memo functions**. A memo function is like an ordinary function except that it 'remembers' some or all of the arguments it has been applied to, together with the corresponding results computed from them, by storing the appropriate pairs of values in a table – the **memo table**. If a memo function is ever re-applied to an argument, it does not recompute the result, but just reuses the same result computed previously. This is guaranteed to be correct because functional languages are referentially transparent so that there can be no side-effects. A very simple example is the function power defined by

```
--- power( 0 ) <= 1 ;
--- power( i ) <= power( i − 1 ) + power( i − 1 ) ;
```

which returns 2^n when applied to argument n. In a conventional implementation, this will involve a total of $1 + 2^n$ calls of power. However, if power is memoized, the second call in an invocation will be implemented by simply looking up its result in the memo table, and further calls will be avoided. Thus only $1 + n$ calls will be made by the memo function of power.

Therefore we can see that memoization can be used to replace a potentially expensive computation by a simple table look-up, enabling inefficient versions of functions which are close to their specifications to be used as an alternative to source-to-source program transformation. Indeed, memoization is obviously more generally applicable than transformation; any function may be memoized, although such memoization may not be beneficial – for example in the case of a linear function such as factorial, in which arguments are not used more than once in a single invocation. (Note, however, that in a function which makes several calls to factorial, such as a combinatorial, great performance improvements may be gained.) One could also claim that the destruction of the original function definition by transformation is a disadvantage avoided by memoization, but this is less clear since the optimized version of a function would rarely be accessed by (or accessible to) the programmer anyway. Conversely, purists might object that the implementation of a memo function normally involves non-functional operations, namely the dynamic updating of the memo table by destructive assignment. The alternative, purely functional implementation requires that a memo table be passed to a memo function, and a new one returned as a result. This is certainly more 'portable' than the destructive update approach, albeit less efficient. This will be considered further in Section 19.3.3, where we derive source-to-source transformations equivalent to memoization.

19.1 Principles of operation and the main problems

The Fibonacci function, fib, is the classic example of a function which becomes much more efficient when it is memoized. Each recursive call to fib generates two further calls, so the cost of computing fib(n) is exponential in n (actually of order fib(n)), but memoized fib will execute in linear time, since for each argument value n, fib(n) is evaluated only once. Logically, the memo function of fib might take the form:

```
memo_fib n <= if in_memo_table( n )
              then lookup( n )
              else insert( fib( n ) )
```

The auxiliary operations in_memo_table, lookup and insert maintain the memo table. Although the first two can be considered as functions, insert adds (non-functionally) to the memo table a new pair (n, fib(n)) and returns fib(n) as its result. Of course, these auxiliary operations are invisible to the programmer, and would not normally be implemented as proper functions at run-time. However, we will give a purely functional version of memo_fib when we consider source-to-source transformations in Section 19.3.3. In either case, given the usual definition of fib, a call to memo_fib will always give the same result as a call to fib with the same argument, i.e. memo_fib(n) = fib(n) for all objects n, so that memo_fib has the same semantics as fib, and clearly this applies similarly to all memo functions. This is a consequence of referential transparency, and is equally valid for call-by-value or call-by-need parameter passing (applicative-order or normal-order semantics). In the latter case, neither the argument values nor the results stored in the memo table will be fully evaluated in general, and the whole issue of lazy memoization will be discussed in the next section.

In fact, the Fibonacci example is a rather special case since its arguments are atomic, and memoization can also be used to great advantage to avoid 'walking over' the same part of a data structure more than once. It is particularly effective when used by *expression evaluators*, such as a normal-order eval-apply interpreter of the type considered in Chapter 9, where an argument expression is not evaluated until it is first required in the defining expression of an applied function, but is evaluated every time its value is needed. We consider this example in Section 19.2, where we also use pointers to provide efficient representations of the unevaluated arguments.

For all their attractive features, memo functions have serious problems with respect to their own implementation. First, the matching of an argument against the entries in a memo table is inefficient if the argument concerned is a compound data structure, for example a tree. The memo function must compare the argument with each entry for equality, using a recursive procedure to test each sub-structure of an object with a recursively defined data type. For example, if we have the data type declaration

```
data tree == leaf( num ) ++ node( tree # num # tree ) ;
```

then the function which compares two trees for equality might be

```
dec compare : ( tree # tree ) → truval ;
--- compare( leaf( n ), leaf( m ) )             <= (n = m) ;
--- compare( tree( s, n, t ), tree( u, m, v ) ) <= ( n = m ) and compare
                                                   (s, u) and compare(t, v) ;
--- compare( leaf( n ), tree( u, m, v ) )       <= false ;
--- compare( tree( u, m, v ), leaf( n ) )       <= false ;
```

Such tests are expensive, and must be performed every time the memo function is called, possibly several times as the memo table increases in size. The problem is worsened by the fact that, for compound structures, it is difficult to apply sophisticated techniques such as hashing to optimize the searching of the memo tables, or to organize the tables as ordered trees to the same end. In either case, to obtain the necessary unique characterization of a structure would again require a recursive function. A further disadvantage of this form of memoization is that the equality test forces the complete evaluation of arguments to their normal form, and we are therefore restricted to applicative order evaluation.

However, by far the most serious limitation of memoization is that memo tables forever grow as new entries continue to be added, and even if an entry's argument will never be passed to the memo function again, it will still remain in the table. It is difficult to know when it is safe to delete such entries, i.e. when one can be certain that an argument will never again be needed, but a continually growing memo table may ultimately bring expression evaluation to a halt by using up the entire storage available, and the cost of a memo table lookup will also be increasing with its size.

In the rest of this chapter, we consider how these drawbacks can be overcome to a great extent, so providing the basis for a viable implementation. The problem of compound arguments may be solved by the use of lazy memo functions (Hughes, 1985) which are described first; the control of the growth of the memo table is considered next. Finally, we discuss some of the problems that arise in the garbage collection of memo table entries.

19.2 Lazy memo functions

Lazy memo functions were introduced with the intention of being used in lazy implementations of functional languages, and simplify the representation, in memo table entries, of arguments which no longer need to be completely evaluated – only to WHNF. In this way the problems associated with recursive equality tests and hashing are greatly reduced, so that the technique is equally applicable to strict implementations. The basic idea is to weaken the requirement that a memo function must satisfy, but we will soon see that all memo functions can be defined in terms of lazy ones; in other words, the lazy technique does not lose any power. Ordinary memo functions, which we will call **full** memo functions, are required to reuse previously computed results if they are applied to arguments equal to previous ones. Lazy memo functions, however, need only do so if they are applied to arguments which are *identical* to previous ones, that is to arguments stored in the same place in memory. Two objects are therefore identical if

(1) they are stored at the same address, i.e. are accessed by the same pointer;

(2) they are *equal* atomic values, e.g. integers, characters, Booleans etc.

Thus it can be seen that in any implementation which provides memoization, pointer comparison must be a primitive operation. Note that atomic values are still tested for equality because they have no explicitly associated address; we could equally well interpret each atomic value as having a unique (implicit) address, whereupon equal atoms would be identical according to our definition above. There is now no need for the recursive equality test, this being replaced by a simple pointer comparison, and we can organize memo tables as hash tables or as ordered binary trees to facilitate ease of searching for an argument (pointer or atom). For example, the hash index to the table could be computed from the address or bit pattern of the pointer using standard techniques. A further advantage of this use of pointers to represent arguments in the memo table is that it aids garbage collection. We will see this in Section 19.4, but for now we note that when an argument stored in a memo table is reclaimed, its entry can also be deleted from the memo table, since it can never again be an argument to any function. In this way the growth of lazy memo tables can be restrained to some extent.

An important feature of this style of memoization is the way that it handles *cyclic* structures. These are used to represent, in bounded space, infinite objects which consist of a repeated finite pattern – i.e. cyclic objects. For example, the infinite list of 'ones', defined by the recursion equation:

```
--- ones <= 1 :: ones ;
```

can be represented by a single cons cell:

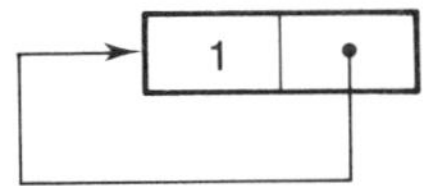

In other words, cyclic structures provide an optimization for a certain class of infinite objects. They can therefore be manipulated by ordinary lazy techniques and can represent unevaluated expressions with infinite values. For example, the expression hd(tl(tl(tl(ones)))), which evaluates to 1, would involve four calls to ones if the cyclic representation were not used, but no calls if it were, since then the expression would already have been compiled into the cyclic form. Thus, even if the result of applying a function to a cyclic structure can also be represented as a cyclic structure, ordinary lazy evaluation will still, in general, produce an infinite structure as its result, i.e. one including an unevaluated infinite expression. An example of this is the expression which evaluates to the infinite list of twos:

```
--- twos <= map double ones ;
--- double x <= 2 * x ;
```

A normal lazy implementation cannot distinguish a cyclic structure from any other, since it does not look at the contents of the cell representing the recursive part of an expression. Here twos would evaluate lazily to 2 :: map double ones, and the sub-expression, map double ones, would not be reduced further, and certainly not identified with the root cell of the whole expression, twos.

It is important to keep infinite structures cyclic wherever possible, since not only are they more compact, but they also take only a finite amount of work to build. Furthermore, once built they can be accessed cheaply, without additional function calls, in contrast to an infinite object, which consumes more and more computation time as more of it is created. In many cases, lazy memoization will keep cyclic structures cyclic automatically, by identifying an argument pointer with a pointer to an enclosing expression. For example, the lazy evaluation of the expression map double ones yields the structure:

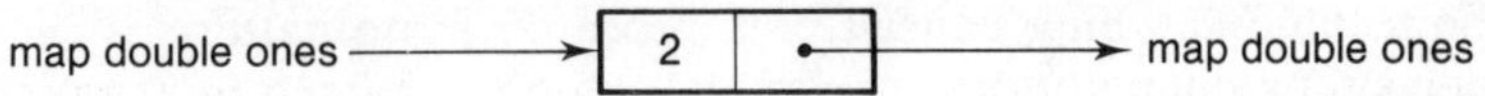

Now, the arguments of the recursive call to map are identical to those of the top-level call, so that if map is memoized, the original result will be re-used. This will generate the cyclic structure

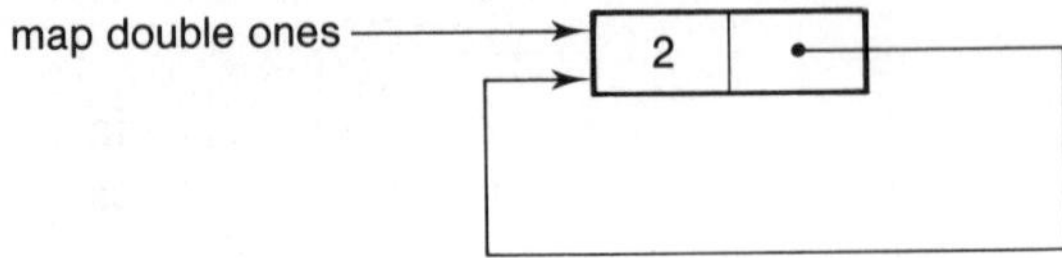

which is optimal. Thus we can see how memoization will automatically represent many infinite objects by cyclic structures which are as small as possible, and the reader is referred to the exercise involving the function zip at the end of the chapter for a more complicated example.

Memoization using lazy memo functions is particularly effective in the implementation of interpreters and compilers which manipulate abstract syntax trees, and may reuse many complex subtrees. For example, consider the following very simple interpreter for the (pure) lambda calculus which performs function application by explicit β-substitution:

```
data exp == id( char ) ++ app( exp, exp ) ++ lam( char, exp ) ;
dec eval : exp → exp ;

dec apply : (exp # exp) → exp ;

--- eval( app( f, x ) )       <= apply( eval( f ), x ) ;
--- eval( id( c ) )           <= id( c ) ;
--- eval( lam( c, e ) )       <= lam( c, e ) ;

--- apply( lam( c, e), a )    <= eval( subst( c, a, e ) ) ;
--- apply( id( c ), a )       <= app( id c, a ) ;
--- apply( app( f, x ), a )   <= app( app( f, x ), a ) ;
```

where subst(c, a, e) replaces all (free) occurrences of c in e by a. Normal-order semantics is ensured because arguments are not evaluated before they are substituted into the bodies of the functions applied to them, and the normal forms (WHNFs) are either lambda abstractions, with constructor lam, or applications of an identifier, with constructor id, to zero or more arguments. Although an argument expression is not evaluated until it is first required in the body of an applied lambda abstraction, if it occurs several times in the body it is re-evaluated every subsequent time it is needed. However, if eval is a lazy memo function, the address and value of an evaluated argument expression will be stored in its memo table, and the value will just be looked up if needed again. In this way memoization provides a call-by-need implementation from a functionally defined interpreter with call-by-name semantics. We saw in Chapter 9 that the crucial property of sharing necessary in a lazy interpreter was not easy to provide in a purely functional way, requiring a trick using the lazy constructors of Hope; also, in Chapter 10 we had to introduce destructive assignment to provide an implementation of the lazy SECD machine. Here, however, we find that lazy memoization provides this efficiency automatically by mimicking the conventional lazy evaluation mechanism; the sharing is indirect via the memo table, with efficiency that is slightly inferior to that which can be achieved by destructive assignment.

A similar example is provided by the incremental compiler, which maintains a representation of the user's program together with its compiled code. When the user edits a program, as little recompilation as possible is performed, by the compiler's keeping track of which code is affected by a change and so must be regenerated. Memo functions can maintain this information automatically. For example, if an ordinary compiler is modified by adding a structure editor to enable changes to be made to abstract syntax trees, and memoizing the code generation functions, then the result will be an incremental compiler. The code generator may be applied to the whole abstract syntax tree at any time, and new code will be created only for those parts that have been changed.

To end this discussion on lazy memo functions, we show how full memoization can be achieved by lazy memo functions. The key to this is to ensure that the test for identity becomes equivalent to the test for equality. This is already the case for atoms, and would also be the case if all data structures were stored uniquely. This means that if any pair of data structures are the same, whether or not the arguments of memo functions, they must share the same locations in storage, imposing a severe overhead on expression evaluation in general. However, we can define full memo functions in terms of lazy ones by this approach, using a 'hashing cons' (Spitzen and Levitt, 1978).

A hashing cons (hcons) is the same as the constructor function, cons, but does not allocate a new cell if one already exists with identical head and tail fields. Of course, a hashing version can be defined for any constructor function, but we will restrict our discussion to the list constructor cons for simplicity. We can easily define hcons as a lazy memo function; we shall use the Hope notation but will annotate the declaration with **memo** to indicate that the function is to be memoized:

```
dec memo hcons : ( alpha # list( alpha ) ) → list( alpha ) ;
--- hcons( a, b ) <= a :: b ;
```

Now, using hcons, we can define the function unique that makes a unique copy of an object

```
dec unique : alpha → alpha ;
--- unique( a :: b ) <= hcons( unique( a ), unique( b ) ) ;
--- unique( x )      <= x ;
```

(Notice the use of overlapping patterns in this definition.)

Thus, if a and b are two equal structures, unique(a) and unique(b) are identical, which follows easily by structural induction, the claim being true by definition for atomic a and b. To convert a function, f : $\alpha \rightarrow \beta$, into a full memo function, f′, we now just have to lazily memoize f and apply f′ to unique arguments, hence obtaining:

```
dec memo f : α → β ;
dec f′ : α → β
--- f′ x <= f( unique x ) ;
```

When f′ is applied to an argument which is equal to a previous argument, unique ensures that the lazily memoized function f will be applied to corresponding identical arguments, so that recomputation of the result will be avoided according to the scheme defined above. Of course, this scheme incurs the same penalties as any other that implements full memo functions, namely complete evaluation of arguments, inefficiency in the comparison of argument values (unique is a recursive function), and increased difficulty in managing the size of the memo table.

19.3 Control of the size of memo tables

If no action is taken to remove entries from a memo table, the table will grow inexorably, a new entry being added whenever the associated function is applied to a new argument for the first time. It is this excessive waste of storage that originally prevented memoization from becoming a widely used optimization, but more recently the problem has been tackled with some success. There are two ways in which the growth of a memo table can be checked. One is by extending the operation of the garbage collector, so that inaccessible entries may be reclaimed whenever the collector is run; we discuss this in Section 19.4.

The other is for a memo function to include information that indicates for which argument values memo table entries may be deleted and under what conditions the deletion is safe, i.e. the entries are guaranteed no longer to be required. Often the programmer will be able to provide such information, and it would not be a difficult task for the compiler to encode it suitably. Moreover, in contrast to other programmer-defined optimizations, any misguided deletion strategy cannot affect the correctness of the program, only its efficiency, since the result of an inadvertently deleted entry might have to be recomputed.

In particular, the programmer may well know when the memo table can be cleared, i.e. completely discarded. In our example of the previous section, which maps the function double over the cyclic list of ones, it is important that the memo table should remain intact whilst a particular cyclic list is being mapped with some function. Otherwise, an infinite list might be computed in the usual, non-memoized way. However, as soon as the mapping of that list is complete, all entries for it can reasonably be deleted – even if the programmer can predict that map will be applied again to an identical function and list, the main concern is that a cyclic structure be formed wherever possible on subsequent applications, the cost of doing this being minimal. In this case, therefore, it is sufficient to create a *local* memo table for each top-level application of map, which can be completely disposed of on return. Thus we may define a local memo function, m, for map, corresponding to the particular function being mapped, in a qualified expression as follows (omitting the Hope declarations):

```
--- map( f, z ) <= m( z )
                          where memo m == lambda nil => nil |
                                                 a :: x => f( a ) :: m( x ) ;
```

19.3.1 Dynamic memo table management

The type of local memoization described above does not allow for the possibility of dynamic management of a memo table where, as new entries are added, old ones which will never be needed again are deleted without complete disposal of the table. By doing this the size of many memo tables is kept to manageable levels, in many cases to a small fixed number of entries. We will be concerned mainly with local memoization, in which a memo table is created for each top-level application of a memoized function, and only the applications of this function occurring within its own defining equations, or in those of other functions called from them, are memoized. This is a little restricting in that, for example, two top-level applications of fib(20) would each execute in linear time if they were locally memoized, whereas the second could execute in constant time by simply looking up its result in the memo table of the first, had this not been discarded. In fact, with this restriction, we will see later that it is possible for the compiler to determine automatically in many cases the dynamic deletion strategy, by simply parsing the defining expression of the memo function.

First, however, we consider the additional primitives needed to implement such table management, and how the programmer can make use of them. Deletion of entries in a memo table is performed by a function called a **table manager**, which may be provided by the user or generated by the compiler for certain classes of functions. The table manager of the function f of type $\alpha \rightarrow \beta$ has type $\alpha \rightarrow$ list α, and is executed after computation of a result of f immediately prior to insertion of the new entry into the memo table of f. It identifies the values of the arguments whose entries can be safely deleted (or overwritten) from the memo table, in the sense that these arguments can never again be passed to f in the current top-level call. For example, one would expect the table manager function for fib to be **lambda** x => [x - 2] in Hope syntax, since the evaluation of any Fibonacci number requires only the values of the previous two. In this example we have specified a list which has just one element in it, but for a function that manipulates trees, the table manager might be

```
lambda leaf( x ) => nil | node( l, x, r ) => [ l, r ]
```

In the latter case, if the current argument is represented by a pointer ptr to a node cell, application of the table manager would indicate that the memo table entries with keys (argument components) equal to ptr.left or ptr.right (the pointers to the left and right subtrees of the cell respectively) are no longer required and so can be deleted. The insert operation does not need to scan the entire table to delete the entries identified by the table manager. It can simply do a look up operation on the table to locate each entry for deletion, hence making the most of hashing or a tree organization of the table.

The space gains obtained by dynamic memo table management are acheived by increasing the cost of insert a little, since it is now always necessary to execute the table manager. However, no extra apparatus is needed to execute the table managers since they are simply expressed in the functional language being compiled, and they are non-recursive functions. In the execution of a memo function, the base case conditions are tested for prior to doing a look up. Should a base case condition be true then the memo function returns the base case result and will not alter the memo table. Otherwise the memo function will proceed by doing a look up to see if the result is already known. Hence base case entries are never inserted in the memo table and so need not be tested for in the table manager. Thus for the above unspecified tree manipulation function, the table manager function would now become **lambda** node(l, x, r) ⇒ [l, r], since we know that the table manager will never be applied to a leaf.

19.3.2 Automatic generation of table managers

For a significant class of non-linear functions, not only can the table managers of the memoized functions be synthesized automatically by the compiler, but the size of the memo table is bounded, by a value that can also be determined at compile time (Khashnevisan, 1987). It can be shown that this is possible for any function defined by an FP equation of the form f = p → q ; M(f, . . . , f), where M is an m-multilinear functional, defined in Section 18.5, with predicate transformers $M_1, \ldots, M_m$ which are all positive powers of some functional, M_0, called their **highest common generator**. The maximum size that the memo table can reach is then the **lowest common sum**, lcs, of those powers, where the lowest common sum of a set of integers $\{ a_1, \ldots, a_n \}$ is the least integer L such that $L - a_i$ may be expressed in the form $k_1a_1 + \ldots + k_na_n$ for some non-negative integers $k_1, \ldots, k_n$ $(1 \leq i \leq n)$ – compare this with the definition of 'lowest common denominator'.

The table manager generated for f is then **lambda** x => [$LCC\,x$], where $LCC = M_0^{lcs}\,id$ (in other words, the LCC is a kind of 'lowest common *composition*' of the functionals $M_1, \ldots, M_m$). Thus, once the memo table has reached its maximum size, whenever a new entry is added, another is deleted, or alternatively an old entry is overwritten by the new one.

Of course, the Fibonacci function satisfies these conditions, $LCC = sub2$ as we noted above, the memo table never contains more than two entries and the function will run in linear time. We also saw how to achieve this by linearization in Section 18.5, and the memo function would actually run a little slower than the corresponding linear transformed function because of its greater run-time overheads. Indeed, the same applies to all functions satisfying the conditions of the linearization theorem – these conditions include all of those necessary for memoization and more. Thus any function that can be linearized in this way may also be memoized, and the necessary conditions will be easier to test. In this way memoization provides a more practical alternative than the transformation of non-linear functions. In fact the automatic generation of table managers, and of upper bounds for memo table sizes, can be extended to degenerate multilinear functions with predicate transformers which are *incompatible*, i.e. which have no highest common factor. The table manager identifies one entry to delete for each subset of predicate transformers which do have a highest common factor. For example, if no two predicate transformers have a highest common factor, each compatible subset will have exactly one member which will be both the subset's highest common factor and its LCC. Thus one memo table entry will be deleted for every predicate transformer, which might sound good as far as controlling the size of the table is concerned, but in fact is immaterial since in this case the memo function can *never* be reapplied to the same argument.

The only time a local memo function will be applied to the same argument value more than once is when that argument is passed to different instances of the function in its defining expression, corresponding to different predicate transformers. These must be in the same compatible subset, for otherwise it would not be possible for equal arguments to be generated during the evaluation of a single top-level function application. The problem for the compiler is how to find out which predicate transformers are compatible and which are not. Some are defined by quite complex expressions and it is not always possible to simplify them sufficiently to determine their compatibility. Thus, if there is a subset of 'don't knows', members of which may or may not be compatible, it is not safe to delete any memo table entries, although doing so would not, of course, cause the implementation to compute incorrect results, but would reintroduce unnecessary recomputation.

As an example of this type of memoization, consider first the following naive definition of the function depth, which computes the depth of a tree as the maximum of the distances of its leaves from its root node.

```
dec depth : tree → num ;
--- depth( leaf( n ) ) <= 0 ;
--- depth( node( l, n, r ) ) <= if depth( l ) > depth( r )
                               then 1 + depth( l )
                               else 1 + depth( r ) ;
```

To translate this definition into its FP form, we first assign the tags 0 and 1 to represent the constructors leaf and node respectively, as discussed in Section 18.1. We then obtain the FP definition

$$depth = eq0 \circ 1 \rightarrow \underline{0}\,;\, gt \circ [\, depth \circ 2,\, depth \circ 4\,] \rightarrow + \circ [\,\underline{1},\, depth \circ 2\,]\,;\\ + \circ [\,\underline{1},\, depth \circ 4\,]$$

which may be written as

$$depth = eq0 \circ 1 \rightarrow \underline{0}\ ;\ Hdepth$$

where the functional H is degenerate 4-multilinear, defined by $Hf = M(f, f, f, f)$, where $M(a, b, c, d) = gt \circ [\, a \circ 2, b \circ 4 \,] \rightarrow + \circ [\, \underline{1}, c \circ 2 \,]; + \circ [\, \underline{1}, d \circ 4 \,]$ for function variables f, a, b, c, d. Now, $M_1 f = M_3 f = f \circ 2$ and $M_2 f = M_4 f = f \circ 4$ (see the Chapter 18 exercises), so that we have two compatible subsets of predicate transformers, each having only one distinct member. Thus, the table manager for the memoized FP function depth is **lambda** x => [2 : x, 4 : x], and the corresponding function for the original Hope definition is **lambda** node(l, n, r) => [l, r].

A more complex example is provided by the function deepest which, when applied to a tree, returns the list of all of the values stored in the leaves at the greatest depth in the tree. The definition of this function is given below in terms of the function depth, which we now write in a more concise form.

```
dec depth : tree → num ;
--- depth( leaf ( x ) ) <= 0 ;
--- depth( node( l, n, r ) ) <= 1 + max( depth( l ), depth( r ) ) ;
dec deepest : tree → list( num ) ;
--- deepest( leaf ( x ) ) <= [ x ] ;
--- deepest( node( l, n, r ) ) <= if depth( l ) > depth( r )
                                  then deepest( l )
                                  else if depth( l ) < depth( r )
                                       then deepest( r )
                                       else deepest( l ) <> deepest( r ) ;
```

In this case, we cannot simply memoize depth locally as above because reuse of the same arguments does not occur within a single, top-level application of depth, but rather in separate applications, made within a single top-level application of deepest. We therefore wish to memoize depth more fully, but only for calls to it from deepest. The memo table of depth should then be deleted after the completion of the top-level application of deepest.

Alternatively, mutually defined functions can often be optimized by combining them into a single function definition, h say, where h is the construction of the two functions, to use the FP terminology. Very briefly, here h is defined by $h = [\, depth', deepest' \,]$ where $depth'$ and $deepest'$ are the FP expressions defining $depth$ and $deepest$ in which all occurrences of $depth$ and $deepest$ have been replaced by $1 \circ h$ and $2 \circ h$ respectively. In this way the new FP definitions for $depth$ and $deepest$ become $depth = 1 \circ h$ and $deepest = 2 \circ h$. It is now straightforward to show that h is degenerate multilinear (see the exercises). Thus local memoization can be used to implement the function h efficiently and generates the table manager **lambda** node(l, n, r) => [l, r], as we surmised above.

When the memoized version of the combined depth and deepest function is applied to a tree, the depth and deepest values of the subtrees are found successively, starting from the leaves. The corresponding values for the internal nodes, moving up the tree, are then computed using the look up operation to obtain the results for their immediate children. This achieves an efficient implementation which limits the size of the table to the depth of the tree, since on inserting the result for a given internal node into the memo table, two entries are deleted, leaving only one entry corresponding to the whole subtree with this internal node at its root.

19.3.3 Memoization as a source-to-source transformation

In the preceding presentation of memoization, we have assumed that the run-time machine provides the primitives necessary to access and maintain the memo table, namely the operations in_memo_table, lookup and insert. We may combine the first two of these operations into a proper function, which returns a pair consisting of a Boolean value, indicating whether the look up was successful or not, and the result if it was, or a 'don't care' otherwise. The operation insert, however, must apply the table manager function provided for the memo function (either by the programmer directly or by the compiler for a degenerate multilinear function) and then create a new table entry after possibly deleting old ones. The most efficient implementation of this operation is non-functional, using destructive assignment, but it may be simulated functionally by modifying the memo function to take a memo table as an extra argument, and to return its updated version as an extra (part of its) result. In this way we can express the memoized version of a function in the source language of its original definition, and the Hope version of the Fibonacci memo function is shown below. We require the Hope definitions listed below to be predefined, but omit the more obvious recursion equations.

```
type arg_type == alpha ;
type res_type == beta ;
type table == list( arg_type # res_type ) ;
type manager == arg_type → list( arg_type ) ;
dec lookup : table # arg_type → truval # res_type ;
  (returns true and the result if it finds an entry for the given argument;
   returns false otherwise)
dec delete_entry : table # list( arg_type ) → table ;
  (finds the entries of the arguments supplied, if they exist, and deletes
   them from the table)
```

```
dec insert : table # ( arg_type # res_type ) # manager → table ;
--- insert( tab, ( arg, res ), man ) = ( arg, res ) :: delete_entry( tab,
                                                  man ( arg ) ) ;
```

The reconstructed Hope definition for fib will now be as follows:

```
--- fib ( x ) = let ( FinalTab, Answer ) == Mfib( nil, x ) in Answer
```

where the memoized version of fib, Mfib is defined by

```
--- Mfib( tab, x ) <=
     if x =< 1
     then ( tab, 1 )
     else let ( KnowIt, res ) == lookup( tab, x ) in
          if KnowIt
          then ( tab, res )
          else let ( tab1, A1 ) == Mfib( tab, x - 1 ) in
               let ( tab2, A2 ) == Mfib( tab1, x - 2 ) in
               let TheAnswer == A1 + A2 in
                  ( insert( tab2, ( x, TheAnswer ), lambda y => [ y - 2 ] ),
                    TheAnswer ) ;
```

19.4 Garbage collection of memo tables

In full memoization, it is impossible to predict that a function will never again be applied to an argument equal to one with an entry in its memo table, and we have also seen that such prediction is possible in the case of local memoization only for particular classes of degenerate multilinear functions, together with functions for which the programmer can spot the appropriate table manager. However, with lazy memoization, if the garbage collector detects that an object which is identical to the argument of an entry in the memo table can be deleted, since there are no references to it, then the entry is no longer needed and the garbage collector can delete it too. However, all arguments with entries in accessible memo tables are accessible by definition, and so a standard garbage collector which preserves all accessible structures would not reclaim them. Thus, references from memo table entries to stored argument structures must be ignored by the garbage collector, but we still have a problem with references from memo table entries to stored results. If an argument is preserved, then its result should be preserved too so that it can be returned if and when the memo function is applied to that argument and, conversely, if an argument is deleted then the reference to its result should be too.

We now have a circular problem. If the garbage collector is

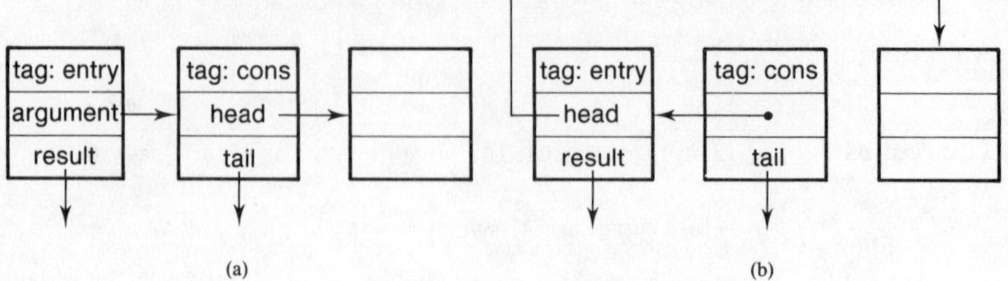

Figure 19.1 Pointer reversal on finding an unmarked argument: (a) memo table entry with unmarked argument and (b) after pointer reversal.

examining a memo table, but has not yet reached some of its stored argument structures, it cannot know which of the stored result structures to preserve, over and above any it has already marked as accessible before coming to this memo table. On the other hand, some data structures, including arguments with memo table entries, may only be accessible through the result structures of memo table entries. It is therefore not sufficient simply to delay the examination of memo tables until the end of garbage collection. This might involve some memo table entries being deleted when their arguments are still going to be passed to their memo functions via the result of a preserved entry further down the table. Although this is not catastrophic in that program correctness will not be lost, it may cause a significant loss of efficiency by diluting the effect of the memoization. In fact, as we shall see, it is not unduly difficult to modify the garbage collector so as to collect memo table entries and their results properly. In the example we consider we shall modify the mark–scan garbage collector for this purpose following the basic approach taken in Hughes (1985).

Let us consider a simple system in which all storage cells available for compound data contain fields for two pointers and a tag to indicate their type. We assume that a memo table is implemented as a list of entries and that its head cell has type memo table. Since cells have only two pointer fields and a tag, the memo table list is represented as a separate structure, with its first pointer field linking the list elements and its second pointing to a cell of type entry, representing the memo table entry. A binary tree would be a more suitable structure in practice, and would benefit from an additional cell-pointer field since otherwise two linked cells would be needed for each node. Efficiency would also be increased if the memo table entries could be incorporated into the cells forming the list or tree structure of the memo table, rather than be accessed indirectly, and a practical implementation would normally use variable sized cells; in this case with four pointers, or five with a tree-structured memo table.

During the mark phase, when the garbage collector finds a cell of type memo table (the head of a list or root of a tree), it marks it and then

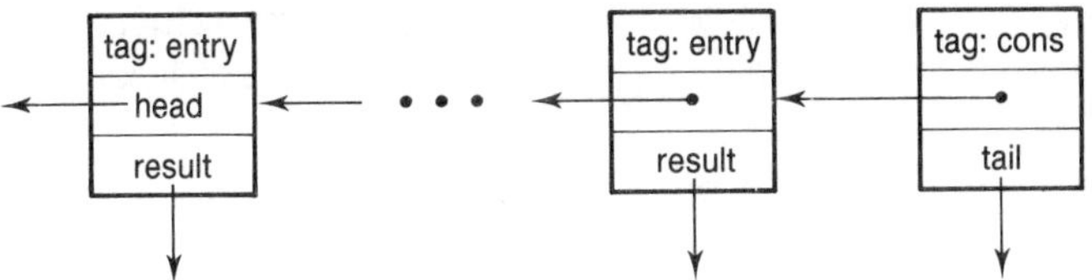

Figure 19.2 Chain of entries with a shared unmarked argument.

scans the memo table. For each cell in the memo table, it fetches the associated entry (represented by the cell of type entry pointed to by this cell) and inspects its argument. If the argument is already marked or is atomic, both the entry and its result are marked. Otherwise, we have the structure shown in Figure 19.1(a), and the garbage collector interchanges the pointer to the argument in the entry (in its first pointer field) with the first pointer in the argument, producing the structure shown in Figure 19.1(b).

If several entries, in different memo tables, point to the same unmarked argument, the above procedure will produce a list with the unmarked entries forming its tail and the argument at its head, as shown in Figure 19.2. A newly added memo table entry is inserted immediately after the argument cell, i.e. in second position in the list, and the first entry found is always last in the list. This entry cell holds the original contents of the first pointer field of the argument cell.

Now, when the garbage collector marks a cell whose first pointer refers to a cell of type entry, it marks all of the entries in the list and their results, and restores the first pointer in each cell of the list back to its original state. Thus the argument cell is restored using the pointer saved in the last entry cell of the list, and each of the entry cells is set to point to the argument cell. In fact the first pointer stored in every cell could be specially tagged (if a bit is available) so that the indirection involved in testing whether or not it points to a cell of type entry could be avoided. At the end of the mark phase all entries, arguments and results that are still accessible will have been marked, and the sweep phase can proceed as normal, but must also update the memo table lists (or trees) by deleting all cells pointing to unmarked (reclaimed) entries, and reclaiming these too. Any such memo table entries will be incorrect because of the pointer reversal, but of course cannot be required anyway.

SUMMARY

- Memoization works by remembering the results computed by a function for each argument it is applied to by storing argument–result pairs in a memo table.
- When a memo function is re-applied to an argument value the result is looked up in the memo table rather than recomputed.

- Lazy memo functions test arguments for identity rather than equality and give lazy semantics together with more efficient argument comparisons.
- Lazy memo functions are particularly effective for representing cyclic structures.
- Full memoization may be implemented by lazy memoization using 'hashing' constructors.
- Table manager functions control the growth of the memo table by deleting certain table entries upon insertion of new entries.
- For certain degenerate multilinear functions the size of the memo table is bounded by a constant number of entries determined at compile-time.
- Memo tables and their entries are treated as special cells by the garbage collector.

EXERCISES

19.1 The function zip, which forms a list of corresponding pairs from its two list arguments, is defined by

```
--- zip( [ ], [ ] ) <= [ ] ;
--- zip( a :: x, b :: y ) <= [ a, b ] :: zip( x, y ) ;
```

Given the cyclic lists ab = a :: b :: ab and abc = a :: b :: c :: abc, find the lazy form of the expression zip(ab, abc) after six applications of zip, and show how this would be represented as a cyclic structure by a system which supports lazy memo functions. What cyclic structure would represent the expression zip(ab, ab)?

19.2 When applied to the integer n, the function comb defined below returns all combinations of the numbers 2, 3 and 5 which add up to n:

```
data combination == c235( num # num # num ) ;
dec addon : num # list( combination ) → list( combination ) ;
dec g, comb : num → list( combination ) ;
--- addon( a, nil ) <= nil ;
--- addon( 2, c235( ( x, y, z) :: L ) ) <= c235( x + 1, y, z ) :: addon( 2, L ) ;
--- addon( 3, c235( ( x, y, z ) :: L ) ) <= c235( x, y + 1, z ) :: addon( 3, L ) ;
--- addon( 5, c235( ( x, y, z) :: L ) ) <= c235( x, y, z + 1 ) :: addon( 5, L ) ;
--- g 2 <= [c235( 1, 0, 0 ) ] ;
--- g 3 <= [c235( 0, 1, 0 ) ] ;
```

```
--- g 4 <= [c235( 2, 0, 0 ) ] ;
--- g 5 <= [c235( 0, 0, 1 ), c235( 1, 1, 0 ) ] ;
--- comb n <= if n ≤ 5 then g n else addon( 5, comb( n − 5 ) ) <*>
                                   addon( 3, comb( n − 3 ) ) <*>
                                   addon( 2, comb( n − 2 ) ) ;
```

where the infix function ⟨∗⟩ appends two lists together, omitting duplications. Give a variable-free definition of comb and determine its table manager function. What will be the maximum size of the memo table during the evaluation of an application of comb?

19.3 Give the FP definition of the function *deepest* defined in Section 19.3.2, and hence write down an FP defining equation for the function h = [*depth*, *deepest*]. Prove that h is degenerate 8-multilinear with two classes of predicate transformers, and give the definitions of the single predicate transformer in each class. Hence show that the table manager for h is, in Hope,

```
lambda node( l, n, r ) => [ l, r ]
```

19.4 The degenerate bilinear function f that computes binomial coefficients may be defined by:

$$f = (or \circ [\, =, eq0 \circ 2\,]) \rightarrow \underline{1};\ + \circ [\, f \circ [\, sub1 \circ 1, sub1 \circ 2\,], f \circ [\, sub1 \circ 1, 2\,]\,]$$

What are the definitions of the predicate transformers M_1 and M_2 associated with this definition? Show that $M_1M_2 = M_2M_1$. Now consider the function g defined by:

$$g = p \rightarrow q\,;\ a \circ [\, g \circ b, g \circ c\,]$$

where $b \circ c = c \circ b$ for fixed functions p, q, a, b, c. If the predicate transformers have no common generator, i.e. there are no integers n, m for which $b^n = c^m$, how many times may g be applied to any one argument value in a top-level application? Can you suggest a suitable memo table deletion strategy?

Chapter 20
Abstract interpretation

Rather than convert a program into another equivalent program which executes more efficiently than the first on some chosen machine, a second route to optimization is to annotate the program so as to make it execute in some preferred way which does not change the results it produces. In fact, the two approaches are not mutually exclusive, and one strategy to the optimization of functional programs is to first transform them according to the methods discussed in the earlier chapters and then to derive semantically correct annotations to guide their execution. The main problem which abstract interpretation addresses is to determine when the execution characteristics of a program can be safely modified, that is modified in such a way as to preserve the program's semantics. The classic example is strictness analysis, as we mentioned in the introduction to Part III, and we investigate this more deeply in Section 20.2. First, however, we give a more general introduction.

20.1 General principles

The semantics of any functional language is expressed in terms of a domain of objects, such as the integers, Booleans, characters etc. or union of any of these, and continuous functions defined on it. Therefore any formal analysis of a functional program's execution must also be conducted in terms of domains rather than sets. Abstract interpretation analyses certain properties of a functional expression's evaluation by first defining an 'abstract domain' which is much simpler than the standard semantic domain of that expression, having a structure which is the minimum required to encapsulate these properties. An abstract version of each function occurring in the expression is defined on the abstract domain, and is 'applied' to abstractions of its arguments to give results, also in the abstract domain, from which the required properties of the function's real application can be deduced. The point is that the 'applications' in the abstract domain are normally sufficiently simple that they can be performed at compile-time, so facilitating the annotations required to guide the real expression's execution. In this way an equivalent operational semantics of the expression in question can be specified which is more efficient than the standard semantics, and the correctness of the annotations can be established.

A simple arithmetic example, in which we can in fact use sets rather than domains of objects, provides a good illustration of the general idea. Consider the set of integers, Z, with the multiplication function, $*$, and suppose that we wish to find the sign of the product of the integers 762 and -957. One way of doing this is to work out that the answer is -729234 and observe that this is a negative number. Thus the answer is 'negative'. However, few people would perform this calculation, of course, but instead use the 'rule of signs' which states that the product of two numbers of opposite sign is negative. This rule is a form of abstract interpretation, using the abstract set $Z^{\#} = \{\, plus, minus, zero \,\}$ which corresponds to the signs of the integers. The abstraction function, $abs_Z : Z \rightarrow Z^{\#}$ is defined by

$$
\begin{aligned}
abs_Z(x) &= plus && \text{if } x > 0 \\
&= minus && \text{if } x < 0 \\
&= zero && \text{if } x = 0
\end{aligned}
$$

and the abstraction function defined on pairs of integers (the domain of $*$) is the extension of this, $abs_{Z\times Z} : Z \times Z \rightarrow Z^{\#} \times Z^{\#}$, defined by

$$abs_{Z\times Z}(x, y) = (abs_Z(x), abs_Z(y))$$

If the abstract version of $*$ is denoted by $*^{\#}$, the rule of signs may be expressed as

$$*^{\#}(\,plus, plus\,) = *^{\#}(\,minus, minus\,) = plus$$
$$*^{\#}(\,plus, minus\,) = *^{\#}(\,minus, plus\,) = minus$$
$$*^{\#}(\,zero, a\,) = *^{\#}(\,a, zero\,) = zero \quad (\,a \in Z^{\#}\,)$$

It is common to overload the symbol # by using it to denote the postfix forms of both the function mapping ordinary functions such as $*$ to their abstract versions such as$*^{\#}$ and also of abs_Z which maps objects. Thus in the former case # has type $(\,Z \times Z \rightarrow Z\,) \rightarrow (\,Z^{\#} \times Z^{\#} \rightarrow Z^{\#}\,)$, and in the latter $Z \rightarrow Z^{\#}$. We now have $x^{\#} = plus$ for $x > 0$, $x^{\#} = minus$ for $x < 0$ and $0^{\#} = zero$, and it is easily seen that for any $x, y \in Z$,

$$*^{\#}(\,x^{\#}, y^{\#}) = (\,*\,(\,x, y\,)\,)^{\#}$$

by considering each of the six possible cases $x, y > 0, < 0, = 0$. In other words, the square of functions below commutes; in FP terms,

$$abs_Z \circ * = *^{\#} \circ abs_{Z \times Z}$$

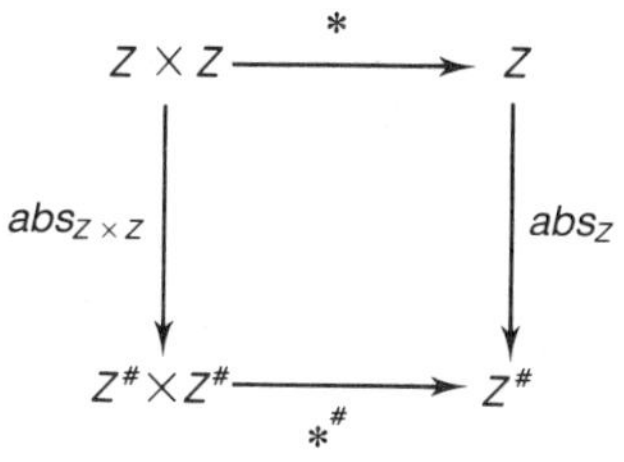

$$\begin{array}{ccc} Z \times Z & \xrightarrow{\;*\;} & Z \\ \downarrow{\scriptstyle abs_{Z \times Z}} & & \downarrow{\scriptstyle abs_Z} \\ Z^{\#} \times Z^{\#} & \xrightarrow[\;*^{\#}\;]{} & Z^{\#} \end{array}$$

This equation is the one that guarantees the correctness of our rule of signs, and we can see that it will always give us a definite answer, i.e. we will always be able to use the rule to get the sign of a product without having to compute that product.

However, suppose that we also have addition defined on Z, and wish to find a similar rule of signs for this. We will immediately define

$$+^{\#}(\,plus, plus\,) = +^{\#}(\,zero, plus\,) = +^{\#}(\,plus, zero\,) = plus$$
$$+^{\#}(\,minus, minus\,) = +^{\#}(\,zero, minus\,) = +^{\#}(\,minus, zero\,) = minus$$
$$+^{\#}(\,zero, zero\,) = zero$$

but we can't be sure when we come to $+^{\#}(\,plus, minus\,)$ and $+^{\#}(\,minus, plus\,)$. These cannot evaluate to any of *plus*, *minus* or *zero*, since whichever we pick we can find a counter example to the analogous correctness equation $+^{\#}(\,x^{\#}, y^{\#}) = (\,+\,(\,x, y\,)\,)^{\#}$. For example, if we decided that $+^{\#}(\,plus, minus\,) = plus$, then if $x = 1$ and $y = -2$ the left-hand side would be *plus* whereas the right-hand side would be $(\,-1\,)^{\#} = minus$. Thus we have to add (at least) a 'don't know' element to our abstract set.

To be precise, we must associate with each element of the abstract domain, here $Z^\#$, the subset of the standard domain, here Z, which that element represents. Here then we associate *plus* with the subset $\{ n \mid n > 0 \}$, minus with $\{ n \mid n < 0 \}$ and zero with $\{ 0 \}$. An abstract interpretation is 'correct', and said to be **safe**, if the real result of the application of a function is in the set represented by the result of the corresponding application of the abstracted function. Thus the correctness equation must be replaced by the *safeness criterion*

$$abs \circ * \subset *^\# \circ abs$$

where the set inclusion refers to the sets associated with the abstract values concerned. In our first example, we can see that this property holds because of the equality $abs \circ * = *^\# \circ abs$, but in the second example, to ensure safeness we must associate the elements $+^\#(\,plus, minus\,) = +^\#(\,minus, plus\,)$ with the whole set Z. We therefore have an additional element in $Z^\#$, say Φ associated with Z, and the extra rules for the abstract function $+^\#$

$$+^\#(\,plus, minus\,) = +^\#(\,minus, plus\,) = +^\#(\,a, \Phi\,) = +^\#(\,\Phi, a\,) = \Phi$$
$$\text{for } a \in \{\,plus, minus, zero, \Phi\,\}$$

(We should also now define corresponding new rules for $*^\#$, namely $*^\#(\,a, \Phi\,) = *^\#(\,\Phi, a\,) = \Phi$, so that the signs of arbitrary arithmetic expressions involving both addition and multiplication might be determined.)

By mapping certain expressions to Φ to ensure safeness, we are throwing away information with the result that we cannot determine the signs of certain expressions without performing the computation. If the abstract value of an expression is Φ all we can conclude about the value is that it may be positive, negative or zero, and we don't need abstract interpretation for this! For example, we would not deduce that the expression $39 - 24$ is positive. Sadly, this type of situation inevitably arises in almost all optimizations based on abstract interpretation – 'almost' because we have already seen that the rule of signs for multiplication provides complete information, but this is the exception. The reason is that we need to abstract properties which are undecidable, and to be certain of being correct, i.e. safe, we must consider every possible outcome of the computations represented by a given abstract value, only one of which will occur in any particular instance. Thus, in our case study of strictness analysis, we will find cases where an argument which could be passed by value will not be detected as strict, but we will be sure that any which must be passed by need will certainly not be detected as strict. Of course, by enriching the abstract domain sufficiently, we could represent any property completely, making precise prediction possible, but ultimately we could arrive back at the standard domain itself and have to do the whole computation anyway. This is the case with our example which considered the sign rule for addition.

20.2 Strictness analysis

The original idea of applying abstract interpretation to strictness analysis is due to Mycroft (1981), who also used the technique to investigate the complementary problem of detecting when an expression definitely will terminate. The main objective here is to improve the efficiency of a lazy implementation of a functional language by detecting when it is safe to pass arguments by-value rather than by-need without altering the termination characteristics of the program. As we have seen in the earlier chapters this obviates the need to construct a suspension for the argument in an SECD-based machine and at the same time reduces the number of run-time structures which have to be garbage collected. Furthermore, in the context of parallel graph reduction, knowing the strictness of each user-defined function enables the strict arguments of a function to be evaluated concurrently with the function thereby increasing the degree of parallelism available.

Mycroft initially worked with first-order functions and flat domains, and our discussion is based upon his approach. For higher-order functions, the work is generalized in the framework of the typed lambda calculus in Burn *et al.* (1986), and we sketch the ideas of this work in the next section when we consider the issues involved in proofs of safety.

Now, a function f of arity n is strict in its ith argument iff

$$f(x_1, \ldots, x_{i-1}, \bot, x_{i+1}, \ldots, x_n) = \bot$$
$$\text{for all objects } x_1, \ldots, x_{i-1}, x_{i+1}, \ldots, x_n \text{ in flat domain } A \ (1 \le i \le n)$$

Thus, for such a function, it is safe to evaluate its ith argument before applying it to a set of n arguments because if this computation does not terminate, i.e. has value $\bot$ in its semantic domain, then the same applies to the application of f to the complete set of arguments under any computation rule with the specified standard semantics. We can therefore pass the ith argument by value, and annotate the definition of f to reflect this information.

As may be seen in Appendix B, a flat domain A is a partially ordered set $(S_\bot, <)$, where S is any set of atomic data available in a typical programming language, such as the union of the Booleans, integers and characters, and $S_\bot = S \cup \{\bot\}$. The ordering, $<$, is defined by $\bot < a$ and $a < a$ for all $a \in S$; $<$ is not defined on distinct, non-$\bot$ elements. (As something of a technicality, note that this gives the 'coalesced' sum, denoted by $\oplus$, of the constituent domains, which has a single shared bottom element. The coalesced sum of the domains $D = (S_\perp, <_D)$ and $E = (T_\perp, <_E)$ is the domain $D \oplus E = ((S \cup T)_\perp, <)$ ordered by $x < y$ iff $x = \perp$ or $x <_D y$ or $x <_E y$, so that the coalesced sum of flat domains is also flat because for $x, y \in S$, $x <_D y$ iff $x = y$, and similarly for $x, y \in T$. In this way expressions are untyped, but this is not important here and we could have defined instead a separated sum, where the least element of each domain is retained and a new bottom element is introduced which is lower than both. The subtypes are then represented by complete domains rather than sets.)

For the purposes of strictness analysis, we define the abstract domain for A by $A^\# = \{0, 1\}$ where 0 is its bottom element which is associated with the set $\{\perp\}$, 1 is associated with A, and the ordering on $A^\#$ is $0 < 1$. We will represent *definitely non-terminating* expressions by 0 and expressions which *may* (but may not) terminate by 1, so that the abstraction function $abs_A : A \to A^\#$ is defined by:

$$
\begin{aligned}
abs_A(\perp) &= 0 \\
abs_A(a) &= 1 \qquad (a \neq \perp, a \in A)
\end{aligned}
$$

We wish to consider functions of any number of arguments, that is functions $f : A^n \to A$ of any arity $n \geq 2$, and so we extend our domain A to include tuples. We define the product domain A^n by $\{(a_1, \ldots, a_n) | a_i \in A, a_i \neq \perp, 1 \leq i \leq n\} \cup \{\perp\}$, that is we use the coalesced product with no bottom-valued tuple components. Thus, we consider the domain D which is the (coalesced) sum of the domains A^n for $n \geq 0$, denoted by $D = A \oplus A^2 \oplus \ldots$. The ordering $<$ is extended to tuples in D in the obvious way (see Appendix B for the discussion on Cartesian products) by defining $(d_1, \ldots, d_n) < (e_1, \ldots, e_m)$ iff $n = m$ and $d_i <_A e_i$ for $1 \leq i \leq n$, i.e. $d_i = e_i$ since A is flat and $d_i \neq \perp$. Thus the ordering on tuples is equality and so the domain D is also flat. We can now be slightly more general and admit functions of type $D \to D$, which can return tuples as results.

The abstract domain corresponding to D is now $D^\# = A^\# \oplus A^{\#2} \oplus \ldots$, and we extend the abstraction function to tuples by defining $abs_{A^n} : A^n \to A^{\#n}$ by

$$
abs_{A^n}(a_1, \ldots, a_n) = (abs(a_1), \ldots, abs(a_n)) \qquad (a_1, \ldots, a_n \in A)
$$

so that we can define the abstraction function $abs : D \to D^\#$ (dropping the subscript D) by

$$
\begin{aligned}
abs(d) &= abs_A(d) \qquad \text{if } d \in A \\
&= abs_{A^n}(d) \qquad \text{if } d \in A^n
\end{aligned}
$$

The 'superscripted postfix' function $\# : [\, D \rightarrow D\,] \rightarrow [\, D^{\#} \rightarrow D^{\#}\,]$ which maps a function f to $f^{\#}$ is then such that the square shown below has

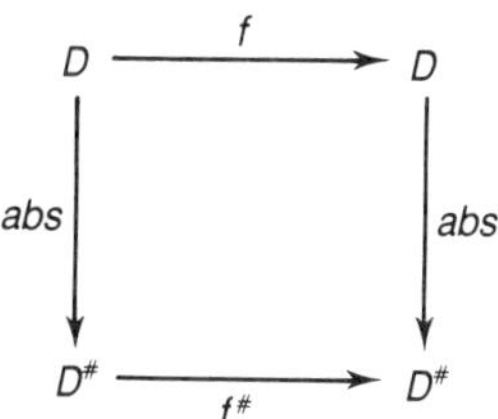

the property that $f^{\#}(\, abs(\, d\,)\,) \supset abs(\, f(\, d\,)\,)$ for a safe abstract interpretation. We will also use # to denote abs, i.e. $d^{\#} \equiv abs\ (\, d\,)$, and we write $\# \circ f \subset f^{\#} \circ \#$ with obvious overloading of $\subset$. We can use this relation to simplify our strictness tests as follows.

If $abs(\, f(\, x_1, \ldots, x_{i-1}, \perp, x_{i+1}, \ldots, x_n\,)\,) = 0$ for all objects $x_1, \ldots, x_{i-1}, x_{i+1}, \ldots, x_n \in A$, we know that $f(\, x_1, \ldots, x_{i-1}, \perp, x_{i+1}, \ldots, x_n\,) = \perp$ by definition of *abs*, since 0 is associated with the singleton set $\{\, \perp\,\}$. Then f would be strict in its ith argument. Assuming that we have a safe abstract interpretation, this condition is implied by $f^{\#}(\, x_1^{\#}, \ldots, x_{i-1}^{\#}, 0, x_{i+1}^{\#}, \ldots, x_n^{\#}\,) = 0$. Thus we can simplify the criterion for strictness to $f^{\#}(\, 1, \ldots, 1, 0, 1, \ldots, 1\,) = 0$, where the 0 appears in the ith argument position on the left-hand side. This follows if f and # are continuous since then $f^{\#}$ is continuous, and so

$$f^{\#}(\, x_1^{\#}, \ldots, x_{i-1}^{\#}, 0, x_{i+1}^{\#}, \ldots, x_n^{\#}\,) < f^{\#}(\, 1, \ldots, 1, 0, 1, \ldots, 1\,) = 0$$
$$\text{for all } x_1, \ldots, x_{i-1}, x_{i+1}, \ldots, x_n \in A$$

because $(\, x_1^{\#}, \ldots, x_{i-1}^{\#}, 0, x_{i+1}^{\#}, \ldots, x_n^{\#}\,) < (\, 1, \ldots, 1, 0, 1, \ldots, 1\,)$.

Of course, with this interpretation the abstract value 1 will sometimes be associated with an expression which will fail to terminate, with the result that certain strict arguments will not be detected as such, but this is the price of safety with a simple abstract domain. In general, we would expect to identify a high proportion of strict arguments, and as far as program execution is concerned, any is better than none.

We are now in a position to define our abstraction of *function definitions*, i.e. to complete our definition of #. As we will see next, all we do is define the abstract versions of the primitive functions and then a rule which abstracts first-order expressions formed using primitive functions, objects and recursion. We outline the steps necessary in a formal proof of the safeness of the abstract interpretation in Section 20.3, referring the reader to appropriate references for the details which involve some fairly heavy notation and algebra.

20.2.1 The abstraction of first-order expressions

Suppose we consider only the strict binary operators of our language such as $+$, $-$, $=$ etc. Because they are strict in both of their arguments their abstract versions are all the logical connective $\wedge$ given by the following table:

$$1 \wedge 1 = 1$$
$$1 \wedge 0 = 0$$
$$0 \wedge 1 = 0$$
$$0 \wedge 0 = 0$$

That is, $+^\# = \wedge$, $-^\# = \wedge$ and so on.

Now, for conditional expressions E of the form **if** x **then** y **else** z the situation is a little more complex. If x does not terminate, then E will not terminate either. However, if x does terminate, we can only be sure that E will not terminate if both of y and z do not, for we do not know which branch will be taken in the absence of more information about x. Thus, the abstract version of the conditional function is defined by **if**$^\#$ p **then**$^\#$ q **else**$^\#$ $r = p \wedge (q \vee r)$ for objects $p, q, r \in A^\#$ where the connective $\vee$ is given by

$$1 \vee 1 = 1$$
$$1 \vee 0 = 1$$
$$0 \vee 1 = 1$$
$$0 \vee 0 = 0$$

Since we are concerned with only first-order functions, we may assume that all are named and held in some function environment, so that we need only be concerned with applicative expressions. Thus, any expression E is either a constant, for which we have a definition of abs, or it is an application of the form E_1E_2, and we define $(E_1E_2)^\# = E_1{}^\# E_2{}^\#$. (In fact, for a syntax with only first-order functions, in the case of the application E_1E_2, E_1 would have to be a primitive function or a user-defined function name, but in fact the abstraction given for an application also holds with higher-order functions.)

Assuming that the definition of # which follows yields a safe abstract interpretation, we have defined all we need to convert an arbitrary first-order expression into its abstract form, from which we may be able to deduce termination and strictness properties. Let us consider the following example of a function f of three arguments, with the defining equation

```
--- f( x, y, z ) <= if x = 0 then y + z else x - y ;
```

To find its abstract form, we simply 'drive the # into the application' according to the rule given above, and apply the rule for abstracting conditionals to obtain

$$f^{\#}(X, Y, Z) = (x = 0)^{\#} \wedge ((y + z)^{\#} \vee (x - y)^{\#})$$

where X represents $x^{\#}$ and Y, Z similarly. Now, $(x = 0)^{\#} = X \wedge 1$ since $=$ is strict in both its arguments and $0^{\#} = 1$, 0 being a constant. By similar arguments for $(y + z)$ and $(x - y)$ we obtain

$$\begin{aligned} f^{\#}(X, Y, Z) &= (X \wedge 1) \wedge ((Y \wedge Z) \vee (X \wedge Y)) \\ &= X \wedge Y \qquad \text{after easy simplification} \end{aligned}$$

Of course, we can always choose parameters x, y, z to produce any value in $D^{\#}$ we want for X, Y, Z (e.g. $x = \bot$ gives $X = 0$, $y = 3$ gives $Y = 1$). Thus we can regard X, Y, Z as formal parameters of the function $f^{\#}$. Finally, therefore, we have $f^{\#}(0, 1, 1) = f^{\#}(1, 0, 1) = 0$ and $f^{\#}(1, 1, 0) = 1$, from which we conclude that f is strict in its first two arguments but not in its third.

There are a number of points brought up by this example. The first is that although this particular conclusion could have been drawn by inspection, the method we used is mechanizable and guarantees correctness since the safeness of the method has been proved (elsewhere). Secondly, we needed some intelligent steps in the simplification of the logical expressions, which in a more general case might not be easy to derive, let alone automate. However, in view of the smallness of the abstract domain, it is often practical to use truth tables to perform the necessary logical computations; this is certainly so in the non-recursive case. Here, for example, we have three arguments, each of which may take either of two values, giving only eight rows in the truth table. The third point is that it is easy to apply this method to derive strictness properties for any non-recursive first-order function, but this is the relatively trivial case which needs little or no optimization and recursion is the crux of the matter, which we consider next.

20.2.2 Expressions with recursion

We abstract recursive function defining expressions in exactly the same way as we did in the non-recursive case, and duly obtain a corresponding recursion equation for the abstract function. However, this function is defined on a very small domain, and we exploit this to compute its least fixed point using its recursion equation directly in the Fixed Point Theorem given in Appendix B. We again consider an example which will amply define the method. Suppose the function f is defined by the equation

```
--- f( x, y ) <= if x = 0 then y else f( x − 1, y ) ;
```

Then, by applying the method used in the previous section, we obtain for the abstract function the equation

$$f^{\#}(X, Y) = (x = 0)^{\#} \wedge (y^{\#} \vee f^{\#}((x - 1)^{\#}, y^{\#}) \\ = X \wedge (Y \vee f^{\#}(X, Y))$$

where again $x^{\#}$, $y^{\#}$ have been replaced by the formal parameters X, Y. Since $f^{\#}$ is continuous (because f is and it can be shown that # is) we can now solve for it as a least fixed point by direct iteration. The computation is guaranteed to terminate since the domain $D^{\#}$ has finite depth, in fact is flat, so that there are no infinite increasing sequences, and the method is not infeasible on small domains. Thus, in general, a function $f^{\#}$ defined by the equation

$$f^{\#}(X_1, \ldots, X_n) = E \text{ where } f^{\#} \text{ occurs in } E \text{ (as may } X_1, \ldots, X_n \text{)}$$

can be found at compile-time using the following iteration. Let

$$f^{\#}_0(X_1, \ldots, X_n) = 0$$

and

$$f^{\#}_n(X_1, \ldots, X_n) = [f^{\#}_{n-1} / f^{\#}]E \qquad (n \geq 1)$$

Then $f^{\#} = f^{\#}_n$ for n such that $f^{\#}_n (X_1, \ldots, X_n) = f^{\#}_{n+1}(X_1, \ldots, X_n)$ for all $X_1 , \ldots , X_n \in D^{\#}$.

In our example, then, we obtain

$$f^{\#}_0 (X, Y) = 0 \\ f^{\#}_1 (X, Y) = X \wedge (Y \vee 0) = X \wedge Y \\ f^{\#}_2 (X, Y) = X \wedge (Y \vee (X \wedge Y)) = X \wedge Y$$

so that we can deduce that $f^{\#} (X, Y) = X \wedge Y$.

In general, the functions $f^{\#}_n$ will be expressed in the form of a table which defines the mapping explicitly, and the iteration will terminate only when the whole table is the same after successive iterations. It is important to avoid generating a sequence such as $f^{\#}_n(0, 1, 1, \ldots ,1)$

for $n \geq 0$ when testing the strictness of the first parameter, and stopping when consecutive values are the same. This will not necessarily be the result obtained by applying the fixed point to the same arguments since this sequence does not compute $f^{\#}$. The only way to perform the strictness test is to find the complete definition of the fixed point, by computing the whole table if necessary, although more efficient methods have been found than repeatedly applying approximations of $f^{\#}$ to every argument value combination (Peyton-Jones, 1985).

20.3 Proofs of safety

To complete our discussion of abstract interpretation techniques and their application to strictness analysis, we briefly consider the main results that have to be established in order to prove formally that an abstract interpretation is safe. The roots of the theory of abstract interpretation are in domain theory and a full treatment is not only outside the scope of this book but would require a book in itself. In the preceding sections we considered essentially two semantics: a *standard* semantics defined on the standard domain D and an *abstract* semantics on the abstract domain $D^{\#}$. Thus we must be concerned with two semantic functions, mapping a given expression syntax to values in the respective standard and abstract domains, together with a suitable abstraction function, abs_D, for which the safeness condition holds. The following description is based entirely on the approach of Burn *et al.* (1986) and applies in general to a functional language with higher-order functions, although the reference does not consider non-flat domains.

Suppose an interpretation I of a given syntax for functional expressions has semantic domain D^I, that its semantic function is sem^I and that its environment function, mapping variable names to values in D^I, is ρ^I. In our case I will be either the standard or the abstract interpretation, D^I will be respectively D or $D^{\#}$, and sem^I, ρ^I will be the corresponding standard or abstract semantics, environment. Semantic functions map syntactic expressions and environments into values in the semantic domains and are normally curried, so that sem^I has type $expressions \rightarrow environments^I \rightarrow D^I$ where $environments^I = [\, variables \rightarrow D^I \,]$, expressions and variables being given by the syntax.

It is sufficient to use the lambda calculus for our expression syntax since we know that any functional language can be represented by it and how to define the translation into it. To represent functions of more than one parameter, we could incorporate tuples into the lambda calculus as we described in Chapter 6. However, the correctness proof based on the approach that follows allows functions to be higher-order in any case and assumes that all functions are represented in their curried form. We therefore define sem^I by:

$$sem^I\ x\ \rho = \rho\ x$$
$$sem^I\ c\ \rho = \mathbf{c}$$

where c is a constant expression and **c** is a corresponding value chosen in D^I

$$sem^I\ (\ MN\ )\ \rho = (\ sem^I\ M\ \rho\ )\ (\ sem^I\ N\ \rho\ )$$
$$sem^I\ (\ \lambda x.M\ )\ \rho = \lambda d.sem^I\ M\ \rho\ \{\ d\ /\ x\ \}$$

where $\{\ d\ /\ x\ \}$ extends ρ to associate x with d.

Thus an interpretation I is determined solely by its domain D^I and the values it assigns to constants. (Higher-order functions are incorporated by Burn *et al.* (1986) by considering the typed lambda calculus, with a separate domain for each type. Then D^I is the separated sum of all of these, and an interpretation is determined by just the domains it assigns to the base types, together with the values it assigns to constants.)

For example, in the previous section, in the standard interpretation we would have had the following definition for the semantics of conditional expressions:

$$sem^{St}(\ \textbf{if}\ p\ \textbf{then}\ x\ \textbf{else}\ y\ ) = COND(\ p, x, y\ )$$
where $COND : A^3 \rightarrow A$ is defined by
$$COND(\ p, x, y\ ) = \bot \qquad \text{if } p \notin \{\ true, false\ \}$$
$$COND(\ true, x, y\ ) = x$$
$$COND(\ false, x, y\ ) = y$$

In the abstract interpretation we would have

$$sem^{\#}(\ \textbf{if}\ p\ \textbf{then}\ x\ \textbf{else}\ y\ ) = COND^{\#}(\ p, x, y\ )$$
where $COND^{\#} : A^{\#3} \rightarrow A^{\#}$ is defined by
$$COND^{\#}(\ 0, x, y\ ) = 0$$
$$COND^{\#}(\ 1, x, y\ ) = x \vee y$$

where $\vee$ is the least upper bound operator, equivalent to the 'logical or' connective used in Section 20.2.1.

The abstraction function, #, must relate the standard semantics and the abstract semantics in such a way that we can *correctly* infer strictness information for a function f by computing in the abstract domain the expressions obtained by applying the abstract semantic function to the expressions $f(\ x_1, \ldots, \bot, \ldots, x_n\ )$, where f has arity n. This notion of correctness is rather stronger than the safety property that we discussed in Section 20.1, and is called **soundness**.

In fact, for expressions of the typed lambda calculus, the soundness of this abstract interpretation may be established by choosing a definition for each typed abstraction function $abs_\sigma : D_\sigma \to D^{\#}_\sigma$ which satisfies the following conditions:

(1) $abs_\sigma(d) = \bot^{\#}_\sigma$ if and only if $d = \bot_\sigma$. This ensures that the bottom element of the abstract domain is associated with the singleton set $\{\bot\}$.

(2) For all expressions E of type σ and environments ρ,

$$abs_\sigma(\, sem^{St}\, E\, \rho\,) < sem^{\#}(\, E\, abs_\sigma \circ \rho\,)$$

(3) $abs_\tau(\, fd\,) < abs_{\sigma\to\tau}(\, f\,)\, abs_\sigma(\, d\,)$.

Given these conditions, we obtain the following soundness theorem (Burn *et al.*, 1986). (For simplicity we consider closed expressions, i.e. expressions with no free variables, and omit the terms representing the empty environment.) The theorem states that, for closed term $\mathrm{M} : \sigma_1 \to \ldots \to \sigma_n \to A$,

$$(\, sem^{\#}\, M\,)\, T^{\#}_{\sigma 1} \ldots \bot^{\#}_{\sigma i} \ldots T^{\#}_{\sigma n} = 0 \Rightarrow (\, sem^{St}\, M\,)\, d_1 \ldots \bot_{\sigma i} \ldots d_n = \bot_A$$

for all $d_1 \in D_{\sigma 1}, \ldots, d_n \in D_{\sigma n}$.

The term $T^{\#}_{\sigma j}$ denotes the *top* element of the domain representing type $\sigma_j\, (1 \leq j \leq n)$, which is greater in its domain's ordering than any other element – these domains are *lattices*. The domain A is the coalesced sum of each domain representing a base type, and is therefore the same as the domain A used in the previous section. This result is precisely what we need to justify the method used for strictness analysis previously. It is straightforward to prove, given the conditions on the abstraction functions, but it is not easy to find these and prove that the conditions hold. For the base types our definition of the previous section for a first-order analysis suffices, namely $abs_A(\, d\,) = 0$ if $d = \bot_A$ and 1 otherwise. The extension to higher types is much harder and is the subject of Burn *et al.* (1986) and of Abramsky (1985), which puts the ideas into a wider context.

20.4 Other applications in program optimization

Abstract interpretation is a currently active research area (Abramsky and Hankin, 1987), and so far the only optimization for which it has been used in practice is strictness analysis, which we discussed at some length. However, there are a number of other opportunities for its application in the optimization of functional programs by means of semantically correct annotation. We have already seen one example that might be viewed as abstract interpretation in the type inference system discussed in Chapter 7, which forms the basis of type checking algorithms. Type checking is clearly a static, compile-time analysis, and it could in fact be formulated in terms of mappings between different semantic domains, which is what characterizes abstract interpretation. Then appropriate safety and soundness properties could be established.

A second additional application concerns the use of destructive assignment in the execution of a functional program, called 'in-place updating'. Because of referential transparency, opportunities for the reuse of storage locations are limited for functional languages in any direct implementation. In fact, apart from the sharing of a repeated argument in a call-by-need implementation, reuse of storage is possible only in stack manipulation and indirectly through the garbage collector. However, garbage collection imposes a significant overhead on expression evaluation and its onset should be postponed for as long as possible. It is therefore desirable to destroy a data object, by overwriting it or by adding it to the free list, as soon as possible after it becomes inaccessible. For example, the function squall that squares all the elements of a list of integers,

```
dec squall : list( num ) → list( num ) ;
--- squall( x ) <= map( square, x ) ;
```

where map and square are primitive, will create a new list in a direct implementation, whereas once an element has been squared it will become inaccessible unless it is shared by another part of the computation. Thus ideally, when walking over an unshared list which is the argument to squall, the list's elements should be overwritten and all of its cons cells should remain unchanged. The pointer to the result will then be the same as the pointer to the argument at the time the function was invoked. By considering the different possible sharing characteristics that a node might have in an expression graph of the sort considered in Chapter 11, such as 'singly referenced', 'not necessarily singly referenced', abstract interpretation may be able to identify at compile-time and so annotate appropriately, dereferencing operations which address a singly referenced cell. This would immediately make such a cell available for reuse, possibly in the same right-hand expression of a recursion equation. For example, in the equation map(f, a :: y) <= f(a) :: map(f, y) the cons cell referred to in the left-hand pattern would become inaccessible after the evaluation of the arguments of the cons on the right-hand side, unless it were shared elsewhere. Some progress has been made using this kind of approach, and Hudak gives a functional version of the Quicksort algorithm which runs in linear space in Abramsky and Hankin (1987).

Other applications which are more speculative at the time of writing include 'relevant clause analysis' and 'complexity analysis'. The former is concerned with identifying which of the recursion equations of a function's definition will be required on particular calls to that function. This is important in parallel architectures where remote access to shared code may be required. By identifying which parts of that code are required (the relevant clause(s)) the amount of communication required to transmit those clauses can be significantly reduced. Complexity analysis also has an important role in parallel machines, especially fine grain machines. When an expression contains sub-expressions which can be evaluated independently, for example the arguments of a function application or a function-valued expression which is applied to an argument expression, the independent computations are suitable for distributing, or 'spawning', to separate processors to be performed in parallel. However, this distribution imposes further communication overheads, and if the overhead associated with spawning a computation is not less than the time taken to perform that computation, there is no point in increasing the degree of parallelism in this way. The problem is then to know in advance, i.e. to detect at compile-time, how long the evaluation of a sub-expression will take. It is possible that this could be given by some complexity measure defined on expressions, and if this were expressed in terms of some non-standard semantics and domain, abstract interpretation techniques might provide the analysis with a formal basis.

SUMMARY

- Abstract interpretation determines characteristics about the execution of a program which enable the rules for its computation to be modified without changing its semantics.
- The arithmetic 'rule of signs' is an archetypal example.
- A major application is strictness analysis, which identifies arguments that are definitely needed and so can be passed by-value.
- In flat domains the abstract forms of first-order functions are derived by replacing the (standard) primitive operators in their defining expressions by abstract versions.
- Recursively defined abstract functions are computed at compile time by finding their least fixed points iteratively.
- Basic strictness analysis generalizes naturally to higher-order functions and non-flat domains.
- Proofs of safety of abstract interpretations are exercises in denotational semantics.
- Other applications of abstract interpretation include in-place updating of data structures, complexity analysis and relevant clause analysis.

EXERCISES

20.1 In ordinary arithmetic on the integers, we have 'rules of signs' which enable the sign of a calculation to be determined without working out the result. Similarly we can devise rules to determine the 'order of magnitude' of a result, i.e. the number of digits it contains; sometimes exactly, sometimes only within a certain range.

(a) What is the abstract set A which represents all possible 'orders of magnitude'?

(b) Given integers x, y with abstract interpretations $X, Y \in 2^A$ (the power set of A), define the abstract versions of the addition and multiplication operators, $+^\#$, $*^\#$ by defining the two subsets of A: $X +^\# Y$ and $X *^\# Y$.

(c) What does your abstract interpretation predict for the possible number of digits in the value of the expression $(-9 * 100) + 99$?

20.2 Explain what is meant by the *safety* of an abstract interpretation and give a formal description in terms of appropriate semantic domains. Prove that the 'order of magnitude' example of Exercise 20.1 is safe.

20.3 Determine the arguments in which the following functions are strict:

(a) $f(x, y, z) =$ **if** $x \leq y$ **then** 1 **else if** $y = f(x - 1, y, z)$ **then** y **else** $z * f(x, y + 1, z + 1)$

(b) $f(x, y, z) =$ **if** $x \leq y$ **then** z **else if** $y = f(x - 1, y, z)$ **then** y **else** $z * f(x, y + 1, z + 1)$

Appendix A
Hope language summary

A.1 The Hope BNF

The language described in this book is an extension of the Edinburgh Hope language and is officially known as Hope$^+$. The following BNF is complete and includes a number of features not covered in Part I of the book. These are numbered and briefly summarized in the notes below. In the BNF notation used { E }$^+$ means one or more occurrences of E; { E }* means zero or more occurrences of E, and [E] indicates that E is optional. Reserved words are written in boldface.†

⟨program⟩	::= { ⟨module⟩ ; }* { ⟨statement⟩ }$^+$	
⟨module⟩	::= **module** ⟨module name⟩ { ; ⟨dec⟩ }$^+$ **end**	(1a)
⟨statement⟩	::= { ⟨dec⟩ | ⟨free exp⟩ } ;	
⟨free exp⟩	::= ⟨exp⟩	
⟨module name⟩	::= ⟨identifier⟩	
⟨dec⟩	::= ⟨type dec⟩	
	| ⟨type variable dec⟩	
	| ⟨object dec⟩	
	| ⟨equation⟩	
	| ⟨operator dec⟩	
	| ⟨import dec⟩	
	| ⟨export dec⟩	
⟨operator dec⟩	::= **infix** ⟨op name⟩ : ⟨precedence⟩	
	| **infixrl** ⟨op name⟩ : ⟨precedence⟩	(2)
⟨op name⟩	::= ⟨object name⟩ | ⟨data constructor⟩	
⟨precedence⟩	::= 1 | . . . | 9 | 10	
⟨type dec⟩	::= ⟨data dec⟩	
	| ⟨synonym dec⟩	
	| ⟨constructor dec⟩	

† The material in this appendix is based on the Hope$^+$ language definition (Perry, 1987) and includes sections extracted directly from the text therein. This material is reproduced with kind permission of Nigel Perry and International Computers Ltd (ICL).

```
⟨data dec⟩              ::= data ⟨data type dec⟩
                            { with ⟨data type dec⟩ }*                              (3)
⟨synonym dec⟩           ::= type ⟨type name⟩ == ⟨type exp⟩
⟨constructor dec⟩       ::= type ⟨type constructor⟩ ⟨type parameters⟩
                            == ⟨type exp⟩
⟨data type dec⟩         ::= ⟨type name⟩ == ⟨data element⟩
                            { ++ ⟨data element⟩ }*
                            | ⟨type constructor⟩ ⟨type parameters⟩ ==
                            ⟨data element⟩ { ++ ⟨data element⟩ }*
⟨type variable dec⟩     ::= typevar ⟨type variable⟩ { , ⟨type variable⟩ }*
⟨type variable⟩         ::= ⟨identifier⟩
⟨type parameters⟩       ::= ⟨type parameter⟩
                            | ( ⟨type parameter⟩ { , ⟨type parameter⟩ }* )
⟨type name⟩             ::= ⟨identifier⟩
⟨type constructor⟩      ::= ⟨identifier⟩
⟨type parameter⟩        ::= ⟨identifier⟩
⟨data element⟩          ::= ⟨data constant⟩
                            | ⟨data constructor⟩ ⟨type exp⟩
                            | ⟨type exp⟩ ⟨data constructor⟩ ⟨type exp⟩
⟨type exp⟩              ::= ⟨type variable⟩
                            | ⟨type name⟩
                            | ⟨tuple type⟩
                            | ⟨function type⟩
                            | ( ⟨type exp⟩ )
                            | ⟨type constructor⟩ ⟨type exp⟩
⟨tuple type⟩            ::= ⟨type exp⟩ { ⟨hash symbol⟩ ⟨type exp⟩ }+
⟨hash symbol⟩           ::= # | X
⟨function type⟩         ::= ⟨type exp⟩ → ⟨type exp⟩
⟨data constant⟩         ::= ⟨identifier⟩
⟨data constructor⟩      ::= ⟨identifier⟩
⟨export dec⟩            ::= pubtype ⟨type name⟩ { , ⟨type name⟩ }*                 (1b)
                            | pubconst ⟨data identifier⟩ { , ⟨data identifier⟩ }*(1c)
                            | pubfun ⟨object name⟩ { , ⟨object name⟩ }*           (1d)
⟨import dec⟩            ::= use ⟨module name⟩ { , ⟨module name⟩ }*                (1e)
⟨data identifier⟩       ::= ⟨data constant⟩
                            | ⟨data constructor⟩
⟨object dec⟩            ::= dec ⟨object name⟩ : ⟨type exp⟩
⟨object name⟩           ::= ⟨identifier⟩
⟨exp⟩                   ::= ( ⟨exp⟩ )
                            | ⟨literal⟩
                            | ( ⟨exp⟩ { , ⟨exp⟩ }+ )
                            | ⟨data constant⟩
                            | ⟨data constructor⟩ ⟨exp⟩
                            | if ⟨exp⟩ then ⟨exp⟩ else < exp >
                            | let ⟨pattern⟩ == ⟨exp⟩ in ⟨exp⟩
                              otherwise ⟨exp⟩                                       (4)
                            | ⟨exp⟩ where ⟨pattern⟩ == ⟨exp⟩ end                    (5)
                            | lambda ⟨pattern⟩ => ⟨exp⟩
                              { | ⟨pattern⟩ => ⟨exp⟩ }* end                         (5)
```

```
                              | ⟨exp⟩ ⟨exp⟩
                              | ⟨exp⟩ ⟨op name⟩ ⟨exp⟩
                              | ⟨exp⟩ ( ⟨argument exp⟩ { , ⟨argument exp⟩ }⁺ )
                              | ⟨object name⟩
                              | ⟨pattern variable⟩
                              | error ⟨exp⟩
⟨application exp⟩          :=  ⟨exp⟩ | ?                                        (6)
⟨equation⟩                 ::= - - - ⟨object name⟩ [ ⟨pattern⟩] <= ⟨exp⟩
                              | - - - ⟨pattern⟩ ⟨object name⟩ ⟨pattern⟩ <= ⟨exp⟩
⟨pattern⟩                  ::= ( ⟨pattern⟩ { , ⟨pattern⟩ }* )
                              | ⟨data constructor⟩ ⟨pattern⟩
                              | ⟨pattern variable⟩
                              | ⟨literal⟩
                              | ⟨data constant⟩
                              | _
                              | error ⟨pattern⟩                                  (7)
                              | ⟨pattern variable⟩ & ⟨pattern⟩
⟨pattern variable⟩         ::= ⟨identifier⟩
⟨literal⟩                  ::= ⟨integer literal⟩
                              | ⟨real literal⟩
                              | ⟨character literal⟩
                              | ⟨truval literal⟩
                              | ⟨void literal⟩
⟨integer literal⟩          ::= [ - ] ⟨digit⟩ { ⟨digit⟩ }*
⟨real literal⟩             ::= [ - ] ⟨digit⟩ { ⟨digit⟩ }* . ⟨digit⟩ { ⟨digit⟩ }*
⟨digit⟩                    ::= 0 | . . . | 9
⟨character literal⟩        ::= ⟨single quote⟩ ⟨character representation⟩
                                 ⟨single quote⟩
⟨single quote⟩             ::= '
⟨character representation⟩ ::= ⟨graphic char⟩
                              | ⟨newline⟩
                              | ⟨tab⟩
                              | ⟨double quote⟩
                              | ⟨formfeed⟩
                              | ⟨backslash⟩
                              | ⟨hex representation⟩
⟨graphic char⟩             ::= any printable graphic character (including space),
                                 except backslash
⟨newline⟩                  ::= \n
⟨tab⟩                      ::= \t
⟨formfeed⟩                 ::= \f
⟨double quote⟩             ::= \"
⟨backslash⟩                ::= \\
⟨hex representation⟩       ::= \ ⟨hex digit⟩ ⟨hex digit⟩
⟨hex digit⟩                ::= 0 | . . . | 9 | A | . . . | F
⟨void literal⟩             ::= ( )                                              (8)
⟨truval literal⟩           ::= true | false
⟨identifier⟩               ::= ⟨letter⟩ { ⟨letter⟩ | ⟨digit⟩ }*
                              | { ⟨compoundable symbol⟩ }⁺
```

⟨letter⟩ ::= a | . . . | z | A | . . . | Z | ⟨other alphabetic characters in standard set⟩
⟨digit⟩ ::= 0 | . . . | 9
⟨compoundable symbol⟩ ::= @ | £ | $ | % | ^ | & | * | − | + | / | \
| : | < | > | = | ' | | | ? | ~
| ⟨other symbol characters in standard set⟩

Notes on the BNF

(1) Declarations may be collected together into modules which are the units of separate compilation. Modules may export some or all of the objects and types declared in them, and may import objects and types from other modules. Modules and statements are collected into a program, which is the basic unit of execution. A program module may be combined with other pre-compiled modules to form a program.

(1a) The module name serves to identify the module. If an object declaration occurs in a module then its defining equation(s) should also be in the same module. (*Note:* Modules cannot contain other modules.)

(1b) Types declared in a module may be exported from a module using a **pubtype** declaration.

(1c) If the exported type is a constructed type then its data constant(s) and constructor(s) are not exported with the type. Data constants and data constructors declared in a module may be exported using a **pubconst** declaration.

(1d) Functions declared in a module may be exported using a **pubfun** declaration.

(1e) All the items exported by a module may be imported, and hence referred to, by another module by means of **use** declarations.

(2) **infixrl** is the same as **infix** except that the declared operator associates from right to left. For example we could declare :: using **infixrl**, in which case we could write 1 :: 2 :: nil omitting the parentheses otherwise required around 2 :: nil.

(3) **with** is used to define mutually recursive data types. For example,

data D1 == . . . D2 . . . **with** D2 == . . . D1 . . . ;

(4) If the pattern in a qualified expression fails to match, then the **otherwise** expression is evaluated; the **otherwise** is optional. e.g. **let** x :: l == E **in** E1 **otherwise** E2 evaluates to E2 if E is nil.

(5) The **end**s in the BNF may be omitted in some implementations and this has been done in the text. These **end**s were not part of the original Hope language and the option to omit them is attributable to the desire to make Hope$^+$ upwards compatible with Hope.

(6) ? is used as a shorthand for generating **lambda** expressions. For example, f(a, ?, b, ?) is equivalent to **lambda** (x, y) => f(a, x, b, y).

(7) Hope has an error value which is a member of every possible type. error can be viewed as a constructor whose argument is a list of error number,

error message pairs (of type list(num # list(char))). An error produced by the application of a function f may be trapped by pattern matching the result against a pattern of the form error(m), where m is the current list of messages. Subsequent error messages may be added to the existing list arbitrarily by forming a new error expression, e.g. error((13,"Something is wrong") :: m).

(8) void is a special type and can be viewed as an empty tuple.

A.2 Predefined types and functions

Type variables

```
alpha, beta
```

Types

```
num, real, char, void, truval, list( alpha ), filename, file
( infix :: : 7 ; data list( alpha ) == nil ++ alpha :: list( alpha ) ; )
```

Character conversion functions

```
dec ord : char → num ;
dec chr : num → char ;
```

Real conversion functions

```
dec floor, ceil, trunc, round : real → num ;
dec float : num → real ;
```

Arithmetic functions (note the use of overloading)

```
infix + , − : 5 ;
infix * : 6 ;
infix ^ : 7 ;
dec + , − , * , ^ : num # num → num ;
dec + , − , * , ^ : num # real → real ;
dec + , − , * , ^ : real # num → real ;
dec + , − , * , ^ : real # real → real ;
infix div, mod, divmod : 6 ;
dec div : num # num → num ;
dec mod : num # num → num ;
dec divmod : num # num → num # num ;
infix / : 6 ;
dec / : num # num → real ;
dec / : num # real → real ;
```

```
dec / : real # num → real ;
dec / : real # real → real ;
dec – : num → num ;
dec – : real → real ;
```

Boolean functions

```
infix < , =<, >, >= : 4 ;
dec <, =<, >, >= : num # num → truval ;
dec <, =<, >, >= : real # real → truval ;
dec <, =<, >, >= : char # char → truval ;
dec <, =<, >, >= : list( char ) # list( char ) → truval ;
        nil ⟨op⟩ nil <= true ;
        nil ⟨op⟩ ( _ :: _ ) <= ( ⟨op⟩ = < ) or ( ⟨op⟩ = =< ) ;
        ( _ : _ ) ⟨op⟩ nil <= ( ⟨op⟩ == > ) or ( ⟨op⟩ == >= ) ;
        ( h :: t ) ⟨op⟩ ( g :: s ) <= if h ⟨op⟩ g then t ⟨op⟩ s else false ;
infix =, /= : 3 ; dec =, /= : alpha # alpha → truval ;
```

List processing functions

```
infix <> : 5 ;
dec <> : list( alpha ) # list( alpha ) → list( alpha ) ;
```

Input/output functions

dec fromfile : filename → list(char) ;

(returns contents of named file)

dec tofile : filename # list(char) → file ;

(creates a new external file and sets its value to the list of characters. Returns an internal value of type file)

dec fromfile : file → list(char) ;

(returns the list of characters associated with file)

Appendix B
Basic domain theory

B.1 Introduction

Our discussion of the lambda calculus in Chapter 6 was purely syntactic in nature. We defined only what structure a lambda expression must have to be valid and how certain expressions and sub-expressions may be replaced textually by others according to reduction rules. The same observation applies equally to all programming languages, and syntax alone is insufficient to explain fully the effect of executing a program. Domain theory and denotational semantics (considered in Appendix C) were introduced to give meaning to syntactic expressions, and so to the recursive programs of functional languages in particular. Formally, we consider the meaning of an expression to be a value taken from some set, or domain, with well understood mathematical properties. For example, expressions might be formed from five Roman numerals, I, II, III, IV, V and the operator *plus*. Although we determine what are the grammatically correct expressions, such as II *plus* II or V, we do not yet know how to interpret these symbols – what is IV for example? Typically, we might be talking about apples, and by IV we mean that we have four apples in our hands which we can confirm by counting them. Under the usual interpretation of *plus*, therefore, we would expect I *plus* III (one apple in one hand and three in the other) and II *plus* II (two apples in each hand) to mean the same thing – four apples altogether, also the meaning of IV.

In more abstract terms, the meaning of such expressions might be given by the integers 1, 2, 3, 4, 5, which represent the numerals I, II, III, IV, V respectively. As a matter of terminology, we also say that I *denotes* 1 etc, since the numeral expressions are concrete objects which can be written down whereas the integers are a mathematical abstraction, and not the only possible representation. With this set of values, the meaning of *plus* may be, not surprisingly, addition modulo 5, i.e. the meaning of the expression E *plus* F is the sum of the integer representations of E and F modulo 5. With this semantic definition the meanings of the expressions I *plus* III, II *plus* II, IV are all the same, namely the integer 4.

As a first attempt at finding a suitable domain of values for the meanings of syntactic expressions, we might try to base our theory on ordinary sets and functions defined on them, but we immediately run into inconsistencies. For example, we could have the syntactically correct Hope definition of the function 'silly':

```
dec silly : truval → truval ;
--- silly ( x ) <= not ( silly x ) ;
```

If we consider the type *truval* to be the set $Bool = \{ true, false \}$ and **not** to be the logical negation operator, *neg*, we cannot find any function f: $Bool \rightarrow Bool$ to satisfy the equation representing *silly*, that is the equation $f(x) = neg(f(x))$ for $x \in Bool$. For example, if $f\,true = true$, then $f\,true \neq neg(\,f\,true\,)$, contradicting the defining equation, and similarly if $f\,true = false$. In practice, if *silly* were applied to any object in *truval*, the computation would not terminate, but there is no representation of non-termination in *Bool*.

If we now add the single new element $\perp$, pronounced 'bottom', to the set *Bool* to give the set $Bool_\perp$ (where for any set S, $S_\perp$ denotes the set $S \cup \{ \perp \}$) we can obtain consistency by making f, and so *silly*, become a well-defined function. This requires that we extend the definition of *neg* appropriately, i.e. that we define $neg \perp = \perp$, and the definition of f that satisfies its defining equation is then $f x = \perp$ for all $x \in Bool_\perp$. Since the bottom element $\perp$ represents the undefined value, or non-termination, it contains less information than the elements of *Bool*, and by defining an 'information ordering' on *Bool* in this way, $Bool_\perp$ becomes a domain. In fact for functions defined only on sets which do not include compound data such as lists, this domain construction is sufficient for defining a consistent semantics as we shall soon see when we consider flat domains in the next section.

B.2 Complete partial orderings and continuous functions

As we have just seen, we can construct some domains so as to provide a consistent semantics by simply 'lifting' a set of values above an undefined element. However, for many reduction rules with various associated normal forms, the situation is not black or white in that the result of a reduction may be neither a fully evaluated expression nor non-existent, but *partially evaluated.* For example, the infinite list of ones defined by:

```
--- ones <= 1 :: ones ;
```

has an infinity of partially evaluated results, ones, 1 :: ones, 1 :: (1 :: ones), 1 :: (1 :: (1 :: ones) etc. Thus if our domain is to properly represent the results of all computations, it must include *partial elements* which represent approximations to completely evaluated, or *total,* elements which may be infinite, as in the case of ones for example. We therefore require an ordering, $<$, on the domain to reflect these approximations, i.e. to show which elements are approximations of which, and are approximated by which. The notation $a < b$ means that a is an approximation of b, also read as 'a approximates b'. We also require that domains include the limits of infinite chains of approximating partial elements, for example nil $< [\,1\,] < [\,1, 1\,] < [\,1, 1, 1\,] < \ldots$. These limits are total, and in the above example we would want the infinite list of ones to be a member of the domain representing *lists* – it is after all the true value of ones.

In the case of a flat domain $A_\perp$, the ordering $<$ is very simple, namely that $\perp < a$ for all $a \in A_\perp$ and for $a, b \in A$, $a < b$ if and only if $a = b$. The set A is said to have been 'lifted' to form the domain $A_\perp$, i.e. lifted above a new bottom element. The ordering is not defined on distinct members of the subset A of the domain, and it is this uniformity over all elements other than the bottom element that gives rise to the term 'flat'. Thus, the set $Bool_\perp$ introduced above is a flat domain, and the domain of integers $Z_\perp$ (where $Z = \{ 1, 2, \ldots \}$) is also flat: different integers are not comparable, i.e. cannot approximate each other, and we have only $1 < 1, 2 < 2, \ldots$ for the relation on Z.

In general, a domain must satisfy the following two axioms, the second being a consequence of the first for flat domains:

(1) A domain is a partially ordered set $(D, <)$ with least element $\perp_D$ such that $\perp_D < d$ for all $d \in D$, where the ordering $<$ is
   - (i) reflexive, i.e. $d < d$ for all $d \in D$,
   - (ii) transitive, i.e. if $d < e$ and $e < f$ for $d, e, f \in D$, then $d < f$,
   - (iii) antisymmetric, i.e. if $d < e$ for $d \neq e \in D$, then it is not the case that $e < d$.

(2) For each increasing sequence $x_1 < x_2 < \ldots < x_n < \ldots$ in D, the *least upper bound*, $\bigsqcup_{n \geq 1} x_n \in D$, exists. This states that a domain is a *complete* partial order (or cpo). The least upper bound of the above sequence is defined as follows:
   - (i) It is an *upper bound*, i.e. for all $n \geq 1$, $x_n < \bigsqcup_{n \geq 1} x_n$.
   - (ii) It is *least*, i.e. if $x_n < u$ for all $n \geq 1$ and some $u \in D$, then $\bigsqcup_{n \geq 1} x_n < u$.

It is not easy to give an intuitive explanation of the need for Axiom 2 in a few sentences, and the reader is referred to Stoy (1977) for a full account. However, we can give an analogy involving the rational numbers. Consider the set Q of rationals in the closed real interval $I = [0, 3]$, i.e. the rational numbers r such that $0 \leq r \leq 3$. Then if $\leq$ denotes the ordering 'less than or equal to' defined on the real numbers, it is easily checked that $(Q, \leq)$ is a partially ordered set. (However, note that this ordering is not an approximation ordering in the above sense; again a flat domain would be used for this purpose.) Now consider the sequence $1, 1 + 1, 1 + 1 + 1/(2!), 1 + 1 + 1/(2!) + 1/(3!), \ldots$. The nth term is $\Sigma_{1 \leq i \leq n} 1/(i - 1)!$, the sequence is clearly increasing and its elements are clearly all rational. However, its limit is e which is known to be irrational and not a member of Q. Thus $(Q, \leq)$ is not a cpo, but $(I, \leq)$ is a cpo since it contains all such limits.

Domains provide a suitable abstract representation of the data objects that we are concerned with, and we now turn our attention to functions defined on domains. Informally, all we require is that computable functions between domains preserve the structure of these domains, i.e. their ordering, so that the more information given to a function (the better the approximation of its argument) the more information it returns (the better the approximation of its result). Thus, in particular, computable functions must be **monotonic**, the definition of monotonicity being

$$f: D \rightarrow E \text{ is monotonic iff for all } d, e \in D, \text{ if } d < e \text{ then } f(d) < f(e)$$

However, in non-flat domains we require also that limits are preserved, and this is embodied in a third axiom:

(3) Computable functions are continuous, where $f: D \rightarrow E$ is continuous iff for every increasing sequence $x_1 < x_2 < \ldots < x_n < \ldots$ in D, $f(\bigsqcup_{n\geq1} x_n) = \bigsqcup_{n\geq1} f(x_n)$.

We can use our example of an interval on the real line as an analogy to motivate this axiom, computability arguments again being available in Stoy (1977). Suppose we have a rational sequence t_n ($n \geq 0$) where $t_0 = 3$ and $t_n = t_{n-1} + 2^{-n}$ for $n > 0$, so that the limit of the sequence is 4. Now let the function $f: Q \rightarrow Q$ be defined by $f(t_n) = t_n - 1$, and suppose that we wish to extend f to map $[3, 4] \rightarrow [2, 4]$ in a structure-preserving way. How do we define $f(4)$? We could choose *any* real number in the closed interval [3, 4] and still keep f monotonic, but if, say, we choose $f(4) = 4$, in the range of f we would have an increasing sequence $f(t_n)$ ($n \geq 0$) getting closer and closer to the value 3 as n increases and t_n approaches 4. However, *at* the point 4, there would be a 'jump' in the value of f, from 3 to 4. Continuity essentially says that there must be no jumps.

Note that continuity implies monotonicity since if $d < e$ for $d, e \in D$, we may consider the sequence $d < e < e < e < \ldots$ which has least upper bound e. Then if f is continuous we have $f(e) = \bigsqcup\{f(d), f(e)\}$, but $f(d) < \bigsqcup\{f(d), f(e)\}$, by definition and so $f(d) < f(e)$.

B.3 Constructions on domains: new domains from old

Given domains D and E we can construct new domains, and we just give four which are needed in various places in this book: the Cartesian product, $D \times E$, which corresponds to Hope tuples, the function space, $[D \rightarrow E]$, the separated sum, $D + E$, which represents a union of data types, and the coalesced sum, $D \oplus E$, which we use in our discussion of abstract interpretation in Chapter 20.

The product $D \times E$ is the set of pairs $\{(d, e) \mid d \in D, e \in E\}$ and has ordering defined by $(a, b) < (d, e)$ iff $a < d$ and $b < e$ in the domains D and E respectively. The least element, $\perp_{D \times E} = (\perp_D, \perp_E)$, and given the increasing sequence $\{(d_n, e_n) \mid n \geq 1\}$ in $D \times E$ we must have increasing sequences $\{d_n \mid n \geq 1\}$ and $\{e_n \mid n \geq 1\}$ in D and E respectively. We therefore define the least upper bound of the increasing sequence $(d_1, e_1) < (d_2, e_2) < \ldots$ in $D \times E$ by

$$\bigsqcup_{n\geq1}(d_n, e_n) = (\bigsqcup_{n\geq1} d_n, \bigsqcup_{n\geq1} e_n)$$

Similarly, the m-fold product $D_1 \times \ldots \times D_m = \{(d_1, \ldots, d_m) \mid d_i \in D_i, 1 \leq i \leq m\}$, with analogous component-wise ordering, least element and least upper bound.

The function space $[D \rightarrow E]$ is the set of all continuous functions between D and E, which are ordered by $f < g$ iff $f(d) < g(d)$ for all $d \in D$. The least element is $\lambda d.\perp_E$ and the least upper bound of the increasing sequence $\{f_n \mid n \geq 1\}$ in $[D \rightarrow E]$ is defined by $(\bigsqcup_{n\geq1} f_n)(d) = \bigsqcup_{n\geq1} f_n(d)$.

The separated sum of domains is defined in terms of the **disjoint union** operation, $\underline{\cup}$, on sets. The disjoint union of sets differs from ordinary union in that each of its elements remains associated with the component set of the union to which it belongs, i.e.

$$A_1 \underline{\cup} \ldots \underline{\cup} A_m = \{x(\alpha) \mid \alpha = A_i, x \in \alpha, (1 \leq i \leq m)\}$$

Thus if an element is a member of $n \geq 1$ component sets, it will appear n times in the disjoint union – if $x \in A$ and $x \in B$ then $x(A) \neq x(B)$ in $A \uplus B$. Where there is no ambiguity, we will abuse our notation slightly when indicating the component set associated with an element $z \in A_1 \uplus \ldots \uplus A_m$, by referring to $z \in A_i$ if $z = x(A_i)$ for some $x \in A_i$ ($1 \leq i \leq m$).

The separated sum $D_1 + \ldots + D_m = (D_1 \uplus \ldots \uplus D_m)_\perp$ where $\perp$ is a *new* least element, i.e. the summands $D_1, \ldots, D_m$ are lifted above $\perp$. The ordering on $D_1 + \ldots + D_m$ is $a < b$ iff $a = \perp$ or $a \in D_i$, $b \in D_i$ and $a < b$ in the summand D_i for some i, $1 \leq i \leq m$.

Given the increasing sequence $\{ d_n \mid n \geq 1 \}$ in $D_1 + \ldots + D_m$, then either $d_n = \perp$ for all $n \geq 1$, in which case we define the least upper bound of the sequence to be $\perp$, or else there exists $N \geq 1$ such that for all $n \geq N$, $d_n \in D_i$ for some i, $1 \leq i \leq m$, and we may define the least upper bound to be the least upper bound in D_i, $\bigsqcup_{n \geq N} d_n$. More precisely we have the definition

$$\bigsqcup_{n \geq 1} d_n = \bigsqcup(i)_{n \geq N} x_n$$

where for $n \geq N$, $d_n = x_n(D_i)$ for some i ($1 \leq i \leq M$), and $\bigsqcup(i)$ denotes the least upper bound operator on D_i.

Notice that in the separated sum construction, two of the summands D_i ($1 \leq i \leq m$) may be the same domain. In other words we may have $D_i = D_j$ for some $i \neq j$, each element of D_i appearing twice in the disjoint union – e.g. we might define $D + D$. In fact it is common to 'tag' each element of the sum explicitly, defining

$$D_1 + \ldots + D_m = \{ \perp \} \cup \{ \langle i, d_i \rangle \mid d_i \in D_i,\ 1 \leq i \leq m \}$$

in which the elements are clearly distinct.

Technically, if $d \in D_1 + \ldots + D_m$ we should not write $d \in D_i$ for any summand D_i, $1 \leq i \leq m$, but instead we should use *injection* and *projection* functions, **in** and $|$ respectively, which are usually written in infix form. If D is a sum, these functions are defined by

(1) If $d' \in D'$ and D' is a summand of D, then d' **in** D is the image of d' under the injection of D' into D, i.e. d' **in** $D = d'(D')$. For example, if D' is the first summand and we have tagged elements in D, then d' **in** $D = \langle 1, d' \rangle$.

(2) If $d \in D$, then $d \mid D' = d'$ if $d = d'$ **in** D, $\perp_{D'}$ otherwise.

Instead of $d \in D_i$, we should therefore really write $d = d_i$ **in** $D_1 + \ldots + D_m$ for some $d_i \in D_i$, $1 \leq i \leq m$, but this is not necessary when there is no ambiguity in the overloading of the operator $\in$.

There is also another type of sum, the **coalesced sum** $D_1 \oplus \ldots \oplus D_m$, in which a new least element is not introduced, but instead the least elements of all of the summands are identified with $\perp$, the unique least element of the coalesced sum. The definitions of the ordering and least upper bound then become simpler, and the difference between the two types of sum are illustrated in Figure B.1.

It is left as a straightforward exercise to show that the definitions of these four constructs do satisfy the axioms given for domains, after which the reader should be familiar with the notation.

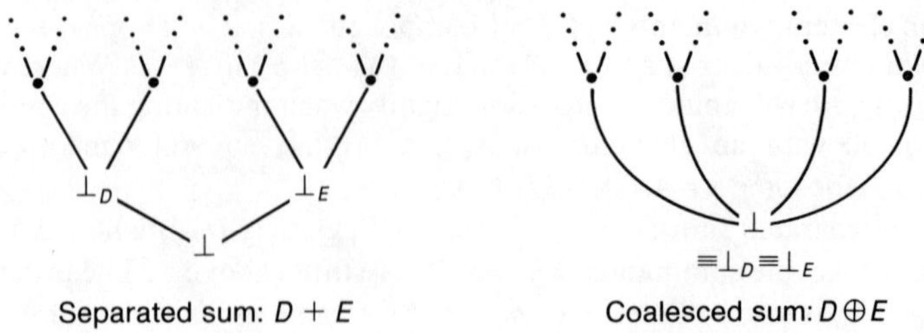

Figure B.1 Separated and coalesced sums of the domains D and E

B.4 Least fixed points

We conclude this brief introduction to domain theory with a result that gives meaning to the syntactic notion of a recursive function and to the fixed point combinator of the lambda calculus. This was specifically motivated by our discussion in Chapter 6, and the result is the following theorem:

Fixed Point Theorem If $f : D \rightarrow D$ is a continuous function on the domain D, then

(1) f has a least fixed point $d \in D$, i.e. d satisfies $f(d) = d$ and if $f(e) = e$ for some $e \in D$, then $d < e$.

(2) The least fixed point of f, $d \in D$, is defined by $d = \sqcup_{n \geq 0} f^n(\bot_D)$.

Proof The proof, which uses all of the axioms for domains and computable functions defined on them, considers the elements $f^k(\bot_D((k \geq 0)$ and uses induction on k as follows: First we show inductively that $\{f^k(\bot_D) \mid k \geq 0\}$ is an increasing sequence and that its least upper bound d is a fixed point.

In the base case, $f^0(\bot_D) = \bot_D < f(\bot_D)$ since $\bot_D$ is the least element.

For the inductive step, assuming that $f^k(\bot_D) < f^{k+1}(\bot_D)$ for $k \geq 0$, we have

$$f(f^k(\bot_D)) < f(f^{k+1}(\bot_D)) \qquad \text{since } f \text{ is monotonic}$$

i.e.

$$f^{k+1}(\bot_D) < f^{k+2}(\bot_D)$$

Thus the sequence $\{ f^k(\bot_D) \mid k \geq 0 \}$ is increasing with least upper bound d, say. But

$$\begin{aligned} f(d) = f(\sqcup_{n \geq 0} f^n(\bot_D)) &= \sqcup_{n \geq 0} f^{n+1}(\bot_D) && \text{since } f \text{ is continuous} \\ &= \sqcup_{n \geq 0} f^n(\bot_D) && \text{since } f^0(\bot_D) < \sqcup_{n \geq 0} f^n(\bot_D) \\ &= d \end{aligned}$$

Thus d is a fixed point.

Now suppose that x is also a fixed point of f. Then $f^k(\bot_D) < x$ for all $k \geq 0$, which may also be shown by induction. In the base case $\bot_D < x$ since $\bot_D$ is the least element.

For the inductive step, if $f^k(\bot_D) < x$ for $k \geq 0$, then $f^{k+1}(\bot_D) < f(x) = x$ since f is monotonic and x is a fixed point of f by hypothesis.

Thus x is an upper bound for the increasing sequence $\{ f^k(\bot_D) \mid k \geq 0 \}$, and so is above its least upper bound, i.e. $\bigsqcup_{n \geq 0} f^n(\bot_D) < x$. Therefore $\bigsqcup_{n \geq 0} f^n(\bot_D)$ is the least fixed point of f.

Because of the Fixed Point Theorem, we can now interpret recursively defined functions as least fixed points, and give meaning to fixed point operators, in particular the least fixed point combinator, Y.

Appendix C
Formal semantics

Many of the problems encountered with implementations of programming languages arise because certain semantic features are not fully specified in the languages' definitions. One simple example typical in imperative languages is that variables may or may not have preassigned values the first time they are used. A second example is that the effect of accessing an array item with an index which is out of range may not be detected at run-time, giving unpredictable effects possibly involving the corruption of the compiled program itself. Similarly, we were unable to achieve strict evaluation using an interpreter written in a lazy functional language because we were defining the semantics of our source language in terms of another functional language. Although an interpreter obviously provides a precise definition of the language's semantics, that definition also depends on the semantics of the second language used for the implementation. This semantics too must therefore be formally defined if we are to obtain a complete and unambiguous definition for the source language.

To resolve such issues rigorously, and others such as the meaning-preserving optimizations considered in Part III of this book, a mathematical semantics must be provided for any programming language; because of their sound theoretical foundations, functional languages are particularly well suited to such analysis. A number of alternative approaches to formal semantics have been followed. *Operational semantics* prescribes how expressions are evaluated in terms of transitions between states which are defined so as to represent partially evaluated expressions; the end of a transition sequence represents some fully reduced, or ground, value. Another approach which has been used to describe the semantics of imperative languages is *axiomatic*, where an axiom is associated with each type of syntactic statement. Given a set of assumptions representing the state of a program's execution at the point immediately before a statement is executed, the set of assumptions at the point immediately after it has been executed may be inferred from the axiom associated with that statement. However, since there is no natural notion of 'program point' in a declarative program (unless its computation sequence is represented explicitly), the axiomatic approach is difficult for functional languages.

For functional languages, then, we consider here **denotational semantics**, which defines a mapping to associate with each syntactically correct expression a value in some well-defined mathematical domain of the kind considered in the previous appendix. The expressions may therefore be said to *denote* their values –

hence the name of the approach – and the abstract domain of values will be isomorphic to the machine representation of the results of executed expressions. For example the domain of (a finite subset of the) integers with an undefined element is isomorphic to the set of bit patterns used to represent them together with the possibility of non-termination.

The denotational semantics of a language therefore specifies precisely *what* the value of any source expression is, in the true spirit of functional programming, whereas its operational semantics prescribes *how* expressions are executed and is most appropriate for designing an interpreter. Nevertheless, if an existing functional language implementation is available, the denotational semantics could also be used directly as an interpreter, and this is essentially what we have done in Chapter 9. One of the key issues in current programming language theory is to prove that the operational semantics of a language, based upon which we wish to build implementations, is equivalent to its denotational semantics, which should be part of the language definition. Such equivalences are established formally as correspondence theorems, which essentially prove the correctness of interpreters, assuming these programs really do conform with the operational semantics. However, the proofs involved are lengthy, and more research is required for the approach to become established as a practical technique for software production.

Instead, here we shall consider the semantics of certain salient features of typical functional languages such as Hope, showing for example how we can distinguish between applicative-order and normal-order reduction. Notice, however, that call-by-name and call-by-need parameter passing compute the same value for every expression since each implements normal-order reduction. The two computation rules are therefore semantically identical and cannot be distinguished by their denotational semantics, although they could be by an operational semantics. We begin by considering the lambda calculus since all functional languages are mathematically equivalent to it, and its semantics provide a relatively simple introduction to the subject.

C.1 Denotational semantics of the lambda calculus

There is actually a quite fundamental question which has to be answered before any meaningful semantics can be defined for the lambda calculus at all – and the same therefore applies to any functional language, in particular those in which there are no restrictions on the use of higher-order functions. The problem is that all of the conversion rules defined for the lambda calculus relate pairs of syntactic expressions, so that the reduction rules of any interpreter based solely upon them make only syntactic manipulations. This may be of academic interest in its own right, but for practical purposes we normally require the data objects in a program to have a concrete interpretation, e.g. integers, characters and in general (higher-order) functions too. From what we have studied so far, we cannot even be sure that there *is* a set, D say, of values which is isomorphic to the complete set of normal forms of the lambda calculus. In the case of the pure lambda calculus, all of these normal forms are functions and so D must be isomorphic to its own function space; but if all functions are admitted into the function space, the isomorphism is impossible unless D has only one element by countability and cardinality arguments. The only semantics of the lambda calculus we would then be able to find would have every expression denoting the same value!

This appeared to be a fatal flaw in the lambda calculus for many years until certain restrictions relating to computability were placed on the functions admissible in the function space. If we require that D be a cpo (defined in Appendix B) and that all functions be continuous, then we can find non-trivial solutions to the domain equation $D \cong [\, D \rightarrow D \,]$ and generalizations of it such as $D \cong A + [\, D \rightarrow D \,]$ where A is a domain of atomic data such as the integers (with an undefined element).

One semantic domain D for lambda expressions is a subset of $\mathscr{P}\omega$, the power set of the non-negative integers (i.e. the set of all sets of non-negative integers) with subset inclusion for its ordering. A theory of continuous functions on $\mathscr{P}\omega$ can be formulated in which each such function is identified with some element of $\mathscr{P}\omega$, and based upon this a model of the lambda calculus can be defined. In this model there is an abstraction operator and an application operator which obey the same conversion rules as the corresponding operators denoted by λ and juxtaposition in the lambda calculus.

We will not pursue this further here, referring the reader instead to Stoy (1977), but we again emphasize the importance of knowing that some non-trivial model does exist; for if there were none the semantic equations given below would be quite vacuous, reflecting merely the translation between one syntax in which we write λ for the abstraction operator into another syntax in which we write Λ! The theory of domains and denotational semantics is a very substantial subject which was initiated by Strachey, Scott, Plotkin and others in the early 1970s, and an excellent exposition with good intuitive supporting reasoning is provided by Stoy (1977); a more recent account is Schmidt (1986).

We are now in a position to define a semantics for the lambda calculus – both in its pure form and extended with primitive data types and functions. Here we use the following expression syntax for the pure lambda calculus:

$$E ::= x \mid \lambda x.E \mid E\ E'$$

where $x \in \mathit{Identifiers}$ is a variable name. Now, assuming that we have a non-trivial semantic domain D with suitable representations of function abstraction and application (the '$\mathscr{P}\omega$-model' being one example), three equations suffice to define the required semantic function, one for each syntactic type. We use the name d to denote a variable representing a value in D and $\rho : \mathit{Identifiers} \rightarrow D$ to denote an environment function (in the set *Environments*) which maps syntactic variable names to values.

The semantic function $S : \mathit{Expressions} \rightarrow \mathit{Environments} \rightarrow D$ is therefore defined by:

$$\begin{aligned} S[\![\, x \,]\!]\rho &= \rho[\![\, x \,]\!] \\ S[\![\, \lambda x.E \,]\!]\rho &= \Lambda d.S[\![\, E \,]\!](\rho\{d/x\}) \\ S[\![\, E\,E' \,]\!]\rho &= (S[\![\, E \,]\!]\rho)(S[\![\, E' \,]\!]\rho) \end{aligned}$$

where Λ is the semantic abstraction operator and $\rho\{d/x\}$ is the environment ρ extended to include the association of x with d, defined by

$$\rho\{d/x\}\,y = \textbf{if } x = y \textbf{ then } d \textbf{ else } \rho\, y.$$

Function application in D is denoted by juxtaposition, as in the syntax. We have also followed convention by enclosing syntactic constructs in double square brackets. Notice that these equations define normal-order semantics because of the definition of Λ and its associated rule for β-reduction. The corresponding applicative-order semantics may be obtained by modifying the equation for lambda abstraction, as we will see in the next example.

If we add constants into our syntax, obtaining $E ::= x \mid k \mid \lambda x.E \mid E\,E'$, our semantic domain becomes the least solution of an equation of the form $D \cong A + [\,D \rightarrow D\,]$ where A is a set of primitive values. Since this domain is a separated sum with more than one component, we will need to use projection and injection functions, denoted in infix form by $\mid$ and **in** respectively, to enable an element to be considered either in D or else in its own component, either A or $[\,D \rightarrow D\,]$. Our equations for the function S then become

$$\begin{aligned}
S[\![\,x\,]\!]\rho &= \rho[\![\,x\,]\!]\\
S[\![\,k\,]\!]\rho &= K[\![\,k\,]\!]\\
S[\![\,\lambda x.E\,]\!]\rho &= \Lambda d.S[\![\,E\,]\!](\,\rho\{d/x\}\,)\ \textbf{in}\ D\\
S[\![\,E\,E'\,]\!]\rho &= (\,S[\![\,E\,]\!]\rho \mid [\,D \rightarrow D\,]\,)(\,S[\![\,E'\,]\!]\rho\,)
\end{aligned}$$

where K: *Constants* $\rightarrow D$ is some mapping given for syntactic constants (in the set *Constants*). Note that the range of K need not be A since some primitive *functions* may also be associated with the constants; recall from Chapter 3 that the set of constants may include both base types, e.g. the integers, and their associated operators, e.g. $+$.

Again, the above equations define the semantics of normal-order reduction (by the definition of Λ), and to give the corresponding equations for applicative-order reduction we use the function $\mathit{strict} : (\,D \rightarrow D\,) \rightarrow D \rightarrow D$ defined by:

$$\begin{aligned}
\mathit{strict}\ f\,x &= f\,x \text{ if } x \neq \bot\\
\mathit{strict}\ f\,\bot &= \bot
\end{aligned}$$

We then change the equation defining the value of an abstraction to

$$S[\![\,\lambda x.E\,]\!]\rho = (\,\mathit{strict}\,(\,\Lambda d.S[\![\,E\,]\!]\rho\{d/x\}\,)\,)\ \textbf{in}\ D$$

However, this rather innocent looking modification leads to problems with β-conversion, and the fixed point combinator Y no longer computes fixed points, but always $\bot$, with obvious repercussions on properties of recursively defined functions (recall the SECD machine in Chapter 10). This is the source of a number of theoretical objections to applicative-order interpreters.

C.2 Extension to functional programming languages

The analysis introduced for the lambda calculus in the previous section also provides the basis for the denotational semantics of functional languages in practical use, for example Hope. However, we consider just the most significant additional features of such languages and show how to devise the appropriate semantic equations for them, since it would be too substantial an undertaking to provide a full semantics for a language as complex as Hope. Some of these features do not require new techniques since they can be represented directly in the lambda calculus – for example functions with arity greater than one can be defined in curried form with their formal parameters abstracted as the bound variables of lambdas, and recursion may be expressed in terms of the Y-combinator. On the other hand pattern matching does require special treatment, and we postpone its consideration to Section C.4.

Here we give the semantic function $\mathcal{E}$ for the syntax of a typical functional programming language which includes tuples, denoted by bracketed sequences of expressions but, for now, not full pattern matching. In this language, all functions take only a single argument, which may be a tuple; a function of arity $n \geq 2$ is then applied to a tuple with n components. This scheme is consistent with the functional language Hope, but we could equally well have restricted functions to one argument only by means of currying, whereupon a function of arity n would be applied successively to each of its arguments, one at a time.

Consider, therefore, the syntax:

$$\begin{aligned} \mathsf{E} ::= \mathsf{x} \mid \mathsf{E}\ \mathsf{E}' \mid \textbf{if}\ \mathsf{E}\ \textbf{then}\ \mathsf{E}'\ \textbf{else}\ \mathsf{E}'' \mid (\mathsf{E}_1, \ldots, \mathsf{E}_n) \mid \lambda \mathsf{x}.\mathsf{E} \mid \textbf{fix}\ \mathsf{x}.\mathsf{E} \mid \textbf{let}\ \mathsf{x} = \mathsf{E}\ \textbf{in}\ \mathsf{E}' \\ \mid \upsilon(\mathsf{x}_1, \ldots, \mathsf{x}_n).\mathsf{E} \mid \textbf{let}\ (\mathsf{x}_1, \ldots, \mathsf{x}_n) = \mathsf{E}\ \textbf{in}\ \mathsf{E}' \end{aligned}$$

where $\mathsf{x}, \mathsf{x}_1, \ldots, \mathsf{x}_n$ $(\mathsf{n} \geq 2)$ are variable names. As in Chapter 7, we use the 'nu-abstraction' operator, υ, which denotes an uncurried function of several arguments; if the function f of arity n is defined by $\mathsf{f}(\mathsf{x}_1, \ldots, \mathsf{x}_n) = \mathsf{E}$, then we write $\mathsf{f} = \upsilon(\mathsf{x}_1, \ldots, \mathsf{x}_n).\mathsf{E}$. Also, $\textbf{fix}\ \mathsf{x}.\mathsf{E}$ denotes the least fixed point of the equation $\mathsf{f} = [\mathsf{f}/\mathsf{x}]\mathsf{E}$ so that functions defined by expressions of the form $\mathsf{f}\ \mathsf{y} = \mathsf{E}_\mathsf{f}$, where f occurs in E_f, are written as $\mathsf{f} = \textbf{fix}\ \mathsf{f}.(\lambda \mathsf{y}.\mathsf{E}_\mathsf{f})$ in this syntax. Notice too that although we have included conditional expressions as a separate syntactic type, we could have defined a conditional function of three arguments as a primitive instead.

We take our semantic domain D to be the separated sum (defined in Appendix B) of the base domains $B_0, \ldots, B_m$, a single-point domain, W, which represents an error, the domains of tuples with two or more components, and the (continuous) function space $F = [D \rightarrow D]$. We prefer the separated sum over the coalesced sum so that each summand is a domain that represents a complete type of objects, with its own undefined element, and we now describe these summands individually.

(1) First, B_0 is the flat domain of truth values, $\{\perp_{B0}, \textbf{true}, \textbf{false}\}$, and for $1 \leq i \leq m$, B_i represents some base type such as numbers, characters etc.

(2) W is the single-point domain $\{\perp_W\}$, and we could omit it from our definition of D by representing errors as $\perp_D$. However, in this way we would not be able to distinguish a type error from a non-terminating computation.

(3) For the tuple domain, for $n \geq 2$, we define the domain U_n that represents n-tuples by $U_n = D \times \ldots \times D$, the Cartesian product domain with n Ds for its components.

(4) The definition of the space of continuous functions, $F = [\,D \to D\,]$, was given in Appendix B.

The domain D is therefore defined by the set of domain equations:

$$D \cong B_0 + \ldots + B_m + W + F + U_2 + U_3 + \ldots$$
$$\text{where } W = \{\bot_W\},\ U_n = D \times \ldots \times D\ (n \geq 2)$$
$$\text{and } \quad F = [\,D \to D\,]$$

Domain theory tells us that these equations do have a solution.

In our semantic domain, we will use a curried conditional function, $cond : B_0 \to D \to D \to D$, and we write $cond\ p\ d\ d'$ in the form $\underline{\text{if}}\ p\ \underline{\text{then}}\ d\ \underline{\text{else}}\ d'$, where

$$\underline{\text{if}}\ \mathbf{true}\ \underline{\text{then}}\ d\ \underline{\text{else}}\ d' = d$$
$$\underline{\text{if}}\ \mathbf{false}\ \underline{\text{then}}\ d\ \underline{\text{else}}\ d' = d'$$
$$\underline{\text{if}}\ \bot_{B0}\ \underline{\text{then}}\ d\ \underline{\text{else}}\ d' = \bot_D$$

We will also use the injection and projection functions, **in** and $|$ respectively, defined in Appendix B, and the indexing function $\downarrow : (\,D \times Z^+\,) \to D$ which selects components from tuples in D, defined by:

$$
\begin{array}{lll}
(\,e_1, \ldots, e_m\,) \downarrow i = e_i & & \text{if } 1 \leq i \leq m \\
& \bot_W \ \mathbf{in}\ D & \text{otherwise} \\
d \downarrow i & = \bot_W \ \mathbf{in}\ D & \text{if } d \notin U_m \text{ for any } m
\end{array}
$$

In order to define our semantic function, it is necessary to test if a member d of D belongs to a particular summand of D, S say. However, if d is $\bot$, the test will not terminate, so its result is $\bot$. Thus we will use the domain-membership function $\textsc{e}$, pronounced 'squarely in', defined by

$$
\begin{array}{ll}
d\ \textsc{e}\ S = \mathbf{true} & \text{if } d = s\ \mathbf{in}\ D \text{ for some } s \in S \\
\quad\ \ = \bot & \text{if } d = \bot \\
\quad\ \ = \mathbf{false} & \text{otherwise}
\end{array}
$$

(The astute reader will have noticed that we have essentially already used the function $\textsc{e}$ in our definition of the separated sum construction in Appendix B. However, there we chose not to introduce new notation and overloaded the ordinary set-membership symbol $\in$ instead.)

We are now in a position to define the semantics for our functional language syntax. Given the environment function $\rho : Identifiers \to D$, and omitting the last two syntactic types which involve tuples initially, the semantic function $\mathcal{E} : Expressions \to Environments \to D$ is defined by the following equations:

$$
\begin{array}{ll}
\mathcal{E}[\![\mathsf{x}]\!]\rho & = \rho[\![\mathsf{x}]\!] \\
\mathcal{E}[\![\mathsf{E\,E'}]\!]\rho & = \underline{\text{if}}\ d\ \mathrm{E}\ F \\
& \quad \underline{\text{then}}\ \underline{\text{if}}\ d'\ \mathrm{E}\ W\ \underline{\text{then}}\ \bot_W\ \underline{\text{else}}\ (\,d\,|\,F\,)\,d' \\
& \quad \underline{\text{else}}\ \bot_W \\
& \qquad\qquad \text{where } d = \mathcal{E}[\![\mathsf{E}]\!]\rho,\ d' = \mathcal{E}[\![\mathsf{E'}]\!]\rho \\
\mathcal{E}[\![\textbf{if}\ \mathsf{E}\ \textbf{then}\ \mathsf{E'}\ \textbf{else}\ \mathsf{E''}]\!]\rho & = \underline{\text{if}}\ d\ \mathrm{E}\ B_0 \\
& \quad \underline{\text{then}}\ \underline{\text{if}}\ d\,|\,B_0\ \underline{\text{then}}\ \mathcal{E}[\![\mathsf{E'}]\!]\rho\ \underline{\text{else}}\ \mathcal{E}[\![\mathsf{E''}]\!]\rho \\
& \quad \underline{\text{else}}\ \bot_W \\
& \qquad\qquad \text{where } d = \mathcal{E}[\![\mathsf{E}]\!]\rho \\
\mathcal{E}[\![(\,\mathsf{E}_1, \ldots, \mathsf{E}_n\,)]\!]\rho & = (\,\mathcal{E}[\![\mathsf{E}_1]\!]\rho, \ldots, \mathcal{E}[\![\mathsf{E}_n]\!]\rho\,)\ \textbf{in}\ D \\
\mathcal{E}[\![\lambda \mathsf{x.E}]\!]\rho & = (\,\Lambda d.\mathcal{E}[\![\mathsf{E}]\!]\rho\{\,d\,/\,\mathsf{x}\,\}\,)\ \textbf{in}\ D \\
\mathcal{E}[\![\textbf{fix}\ \mathsf{x.E}]\!]\rho & = Y(\,\Lambda d.\mathcal{E}[\![\mathsf{E}]\!]\rho\{\,d\,/\,\mathsf{x}\,\}\,) \\
\mathcal{E}[\![\textbf{let}\ \mathsf{x} = \mathsf{E}\ \textbf{in}\ \mathsf{E'}]\!]\rho & = \underline{\text{if}}\ d\ \mathrm{E}\ W\ \underline{\text{then}}\ \bot_W\ \underline{\text{else}}\ \mathcal{E}[\![\mathsf{E'}]\!]\rho\{\,d\,/\,\mathsf{x}\,\} \\
& \qquad\qquad \text{where } d = \mathcal{E}[\![\mathsf{E}]\!]\rho
\end{array}
$$

where Λ is the abstraction operator defined on D and $Y: F \rightarrow D$ is the least fixed point operator of D (which always exists). Notice that the semantics given for an application $E\ E'$ is *eager*, i.e. corresponds to applicative-order reduction, because the test $d'\ \mathrm{E}\ W$ ensures that the semantic value of $E\ E'$ is $\bot_D$ whenever this is true of E' – by our definition of the conditional function on D. We can obtain call-by-name/need semantics, corresponding to normal-order reduction, by omitting the test.

If we had considered all functions to be curried, the above equations would be sufficient to provide a complete semantics for a language with functions of more than one argument. However, our use of tuples for this purpose introduced two further syntactic types and hence the following additional semantic equations:

$$
\begin{array}{l}
\mathcal{E}[\![\upsilon(\mathsf{x}_1, \ldots, \mathsf{x}_n).\mathsf{E}]\!]\rho = (\,\Lambda d\ \mathrm{E}\ U_n.\mathcal{E}[\![\mathsf{E}]\!]\rho\{\,(\,d \downarrow i\,)\,/\,\mathsf{x}_i\,|\,1 \le i \le n\,\}\,)\ \textbf{in}\ D \\
\mathcal{E}[\![\textbf{let}\ (\,\mathsf{x}_1, \ldots, \mathsf{x}_n\,) \quad = \mathsf{E}\ \textbf{in}\ \mathsf{E'}]\!]\rho \\
\quad = \underline{\text{if}}\ d\ \mathrm{E}\ U_n\ \underline{\text{then}}\ \mathcal{E}[\![\mathsf{E'}]\!]\rho\{\,(\,d \downarrow i\,)\,/\,\mathsf{x}_i\,|\,1 \le i \le n\,\}\ \underline{\text{else}}\ \bot_W \\
\quad \text{where } d = \mathcal{E}[\![\mathsf{E}]\!]\rho
\end{array}
$$

where the typed version of the abstraction operator Λ is defined by

$$\Lambda d\ \mathrm{E}\ S.e = \Lambda d.(\,\underline{\text{if}}\ d\ \mathrm{E}\ S\ \underline{\text{then}}\ e\ \underline{\text{else}}\ \bot_W\,)$$

for summand domain S and $e \in D$.

Thus, for example, the value of the expression $(\upsilon(\,\mathsf{x}, \mathsf{y}\,).\mathsf{x} + \mathsf{y})\ (\,2, 3\,)$ is

$$
\begin{array}{l}
\quad (\,\Lambda d\ \mathrm{E}\ U_2.\mathcal{E}[\![\mathsf{x} + \mathsf{y}]\!]\rho\{\,(\,d \downarrow 1\,)\,/\,\mathsf{x}\,\}\{\,(\,d \downarrow 2\,)\,/\,\mathsf{y}\,\}\,)\,(\,2, 3\,) \\
= (\,\Lambda d\ \mathrm{E}\ U_2.(\,d \downarrow 1) + (d \downarrow 2)\,)\,(\,2, 3\,) \\
= (\,(\,2, 3\,) \downarrow 1) + (\,(\,2, 3\,) \downarrow 2\,) \\
= 2 + 3 \\
= 5
\end{array}
$$

In fact we could have represented functions of two or more arguments as curried functions in our semantic domain, by simply adding the equation

$$\mathcal{E}[\![\upsilon(\mathrm{x}_1, \ldots, \mathrm{x}_n).\mathrm{E}]\!]\rho = (\Lambda d_1. \ldots \Lambda d_n.\mathcal{E}[\![\mathrm{E}]\!]\rho\{ d_i / \mathrm{x}_i \mid 1 \le i \le n \}) \text{ in } D$$

However, this would allow the partial application of a function of arity $n \geq 2$ to less than n arguments, giving a higher-order function as the result. This would be perfectly valid in some languages, but is not allowed in Hope where a partial application must be expressed explicitly using the lambda operator – see Chapter 4.

Apart from the cases of a non-Boolean predicate and application of an expression which is not a function, a type error would only be revealed in the denotational semantics by an expression evaluating to the application of a primitive function to an object of the wrong type, the valid types being part of the primitive function's specifications. However, we saw in Chapter 7 that any expression which is well typed (according to $\mathcal{W}$ for example) cannot result in such a semantic type error, so the equations given above are actually sufficient. In fact the type checker would certainly also find any type error arising from the application of a non-function-valued expression, and if we were to represent conditionals by a primitive three-argument function, *cond* : *truval* $\rightarrow \alpha \rightarrow \alpha \rightarrow \alpha$, we would not have to mention types in the semantic equations at all; the type checker would find any type errors in conditional expressions too. However, this does not mean that the semantics of types are not important. On the contrary, the above arguments depend upon the *semantic soundness theorem* for well-typed expressions, the proof of which represents types as subdomains of the semantic domain D with certain properties – the interested reader is referred to Milner (1978).

C.3 Constructed data types

A constructed data term is expressed as the application of a constructor function to the appropriate number of arguments of the appropriate types. We represent the types of such elements by new domains defined by domain equations corresponding to the declarations of the compound types. More precisely, suppose we have the declaration:

$$\textbf{data}\ \mathrm{t} == \mathrm{c}_1(\tau_{11}\#\ldots\#\tau_{1,\mathrm{a}_1}) ++ \ldots ++ \mathrm{c}_\mathrm{n}(\tau_{\mathrm{n}1}\#\ldots\#\tau_{\mathrm{n},\mathrm{a}_\mathrm{n}});$$

where a_j is the arity of the constructor c_j and τ_{jk} are types ($1 \le \mathrm{j} \le \mathrm{n}$, $1 \le \mathrm{k} \le \mathrm{a}_\mathrm{j}$). These types may include t, yielding a recursive definition. Let C_{jk} be the domain representing the type τ_{jk}, then the domain, T, representing the type t is the (least) solution of the domain equation:

$$T \cong (C_{11} \times \ldots \times C_{1,a_1}) + \ldots + (C_{n1} \times \ldots \times C_{n,a_n})$$

The domain equation for D now becomes:

$$D \cong B_0 + \ldots + B_m + W + F + U_2 + U_3 + \ldots + T_1 + \ldots + T_u$$

where the summands T_i represent all user-defined compound types such as T above ($1 \le i \le u$).

For example, lists of truth values might be declared explicitly as:

data listbool == nilbool ++ consbool(truval, listbool) ;

so that the domain of such lists is the solution of $T \equiv N + (B_0 \times T)$ where N is a one-point domain (like W) representing the empty Boolean list.

Given type t with associated domain T, the meaning of the constructor c_i of t is now given as an element of $C_{i1} \times \ldots \times C_{ia_i} \rightarrow T$, namely:

$$\mathcal{E}[\![\mathrm{c_i}]\!]\rho = (\Lambda d \in C_{i1} \times \ldots \times C_{ia_i}.(d \downarrow 1, \ldots, d \downarrow a_i) \,|\, T) \textbf{ in } D$$

All this is fine for monomorphic types: for polymorphic types we obtain a family of domain equations, one for each instantiation of the type variables contained in the declaration. Thus, given the declaration:

data p($\alpha_1, \ldots, \alpha_m$) == $\mathrm{c_1}$($\tau_{11}\#\ldots\#\tau_{1,a_1}$) ++ ... ++ $\mathrm{c_n}$($\tau_{n1}\#\ldots\#\tau_{n,a_n}$) ;

where the type variables α_i $(1 \leq i \leq m)$ occur in the right-hand side, we obtain an infinite number of domain equations corresponding to the assignment of any monotype to each α_i. Of course, we could define a domain which contained every domain corresponding to the polymorphic type p, namely $P \equiv D^{a_1} + \ldots + D^{a_n}$, where D^i is the product $D \times \ldots \times D$ with i Ds, but it would then be possible to represent many expression types which are not defined in the syntax, for example lists with elements of different types. The semantics of polymorphic types is outside the scope of this book, however, and the interested reader is referred to Kahn *et al.* (1984).

C.4 Pattern matching

A function which is (partially) defined by a recursion equation with pattern matching may be expressed in terms of the nu-abstraction operator introduced in Chapter 7. Given the function f defined by the equation f P = E, we write f = υP.E for pattern P. Thus, if P is a single variable identifier, we have $\upsilon = \lambda$, and we have already given the semantics for f in the case that P is a tuple of variables (in Section C.2). In this section, we first give a denotational semantics for functions defined by only one equation using pattern matching and then generalize to the case of multiple equations. To do this we shall introduce the semantic operator **∇** which gives the result of matching the patterns of *all* of the defining equations of a function when it is applied to an argument (or arguments).

There are two syntactic types of pattern: a variable identifier and the application of a constructor function of arity $i \geq 0$ to i patterns. A *constant* is defined to be a constructor of arity 0 for the purposes of the present discussion. (This is convenient mathematically but not the definition used in the rest of the book.) First, we consider the function f defined by the single equation, f P = E, where the expression P is a pattern. Intuitively, the expression f A reduces to UE where, in the notation of Chapter 7, U = $\mathscr{U}$(P, A) is the substitution of the identifiers in E obtained by unifying P and A, provided this succeeds. For example, if P is the formal parameter x, then we might say that f A reduces to [A / x]E, which is just a syntactic form of β-substitution as expected. If the unification fails, then so does the pattern match, and if there is no other defining equation for f the result is an error; the type of the function must be inconsistent with that of the argument A. However, since this intuitive view relates only to syntax, it is not directly useful in our consideration of denotational semantics.

Instead, therefore, we provide a definition of the function corresponding to f in the semantic domain D with environment ρ, and so define the semantics of υ by:

$$\mathcal{E}[\![\upsilon \mathrm{P.E}]\!] \rho = U \Lambda a.(\mathcal{E}[\![\mathrm{E}]\!] \rho^*) \textbf{ in } D$$ provided the unification below succeeds,

where $U = \mathcal{V}((\mathcal{E}[\![\mathrm{P}]\!] \rho^*), a), \rho^* = \rho\{ d_1 / \mathrm{x}_1 \} \ldots \{ d_n / \mathrm{x}_n \}$, and $\mathrm{x}_1, \ldots, \mathrm{x}_n$ are the variables that occur in P.

If the unification fails, we need a special value, *wrong*, in D to represent a 'failed pattern match', and we choose our error value, $\bot_W \equiv$ *wrong*, the least (and only) element in the summand W of D.

Notice that the unification is now performed on terms in D, yielding the substitution U for the semantic variables d_i which represent values in D; i.e. we have simply renamed the variables x_i in the same way that we renamed x by d in the rule for lambda abstraction previously.

In the special case that P is the identifier x, we have $\rho^* = \rho\{ d / \mathrm{x} \}$ so that $U = \mathcal{V}((\mathcal{E}[\![\mathrm{x}]\!] \rho\{ d / \mathrm{x} \}), a) = [a / d]$, and

$$\begin{aligned} \mathcal{E}[\![\upsilon \mathrm{P.E}]\!] \rho &= \Lambda a.[a / d](\mathcal{E}[\![\mathrm{E}]\!] \rho^*) \textbf{ in } D \\ &=_\alpha \Lambda d.(\mathcal{E}[\![\mathrm{E}]\!] \rho^*) \textbf{ in } D && (\alpha\text{-conversion}) \\ &= \mathcal{E}[\![\lambda \mathrm{x.E}]\!] \rho && \text{by the equation for } \mathcal{E} \text{ given in the previous section} \end{aligned}$$

The unification which comprises pattern matching is a special case of general unification since all of the variables occur in only one of the terms – the pattern – and we can write the semantic equations for υ directly in the form of a set of recursion equations as follows:

$$\begin{aligned} \mathcal{E}[\![\upsilon \mathrm{x.E}]\!] \rho &= (\Lambda d.\mathcal{E}[\![\mathrm{E}]\!] \rho\{ d / \mathrm{x} \}) \textbf{ in } D \qquad \text{for identifier x} \\ \mathcal{E}[\![\upsilon(\mathrm{c} (\mathrm{P}_1, \ldots, \mathrm{P}_n)).\mathrm{E}]\!] \rho &= \Lambda d \,\mathbf{E}\, C.(\mathcal{E}[\![\upsilon \mathrm{P}_1 . \ldots . \upsilon \mathrm{P}_n.\mathrm{E}]\!] \rho) \\ &\qquad (d \downarrow 1) \ldots (d \downarrow n) \qquad \textbf{in } D \end{aligned}$$

where c is a constructor of arity n with associated semantic domain C, and $\mathrm{P}_1, \ldots, \mathrm{P}_n$ are patterns. If $n = 0$ (constant pattern) the second equation reduces to

$$\mathcal{E}[\![\upsilon \mathrm{c.E}]\!] \rho = \Lambda d \,\mathbf{E}\, C.\mathcal{E}[\![\mathrm{E}]\!] \rho$$

(henceforth we drop the injections into D for brevity) where C is the single point domain $\{ Kc \}$. Denoting this value by f we have, for $e \in D$,

$$fe = \textbf{if } e \,\mathbf{E}\, C \textbf{ then } [e / d] \; \mathcal{E}[\![\mathrm{E}]\!] \rho \textbf{ else } \bot_w$$

so that unless $e = Kc$ the match fails as required. (Note that we still do not allow partial applications because of the typed Λ-abstraction.)

For example, a function which flattens a list of lists might be defined by the equations

```
--- f nil              <= nil ;
--- f( nil :: z )      <= f( z ) ;
--- f( ( x :: y ) :: z ) <= x :: ( f( y :: z) ) ;
```

Taking the third equation, we obtain

$$\mathscr{E}[\![\upsilon((x :: y) :: z).(x :: (f\ y :: z))]\!] \rho$$
$$= \Lambda d \,\mathrm{E}\, Lists.(\mathscr{E}[\![\upsilon(x :: y).\upsilon z.(x :: (f\ y :: z))]\!] \rho) \, d \downarrow 1 \; d \downarrow 2$$
$$= \Lambda d \,\mathrm{E}\, Lists.(\Lambda e \,\mathrm{E}\, Lists.(\mathscr{E}[\![\upsilon x.\upsilon y.\upsilon z.(x :: (f\ y :: z))]\!] \rho) \, e \downarrow 1 \; e \downarrow 2) \, d \downarrow 1 \; d \downarrow 2$$

At this stage the υs can be replaced by λs and we are back to the case of no pattern matching. The concerned reader who has noted that the variable f occurs free on the right-hand side need not worry since it would actually be bound if we had given the full semantics of the recursive function f, as we consider below.

Finally, we extend the above results to give a complete semantics for a function defined by one or more pattern matching equations. To do this we define the function $\nabla : D \times D \rightarrow D$ to combine matches of patterns during function application as follows:

$$\begin{aligned} \nabla(d, e) &= d \quad \text{if } d \neq wrong \text{ and } d \neq \bot \\ \nabla(wrong, e) &= e \\ \nabla(\bot, e) &= \bot \end{aligned}$$

Application of ∇ represents the sequential matching of two patterns of a function's defining equations upon application of that function to an argument. If the first equation matches, it is used to compute the result; if it fails, the second equation is used; if the match fails to terminate, the result of the function's application must also be non-terminating. It is clear that ∇ is associative, and we will use it in infix form without brackets (or ambiguity) to give the semantic value of applying a function defined by any number of equations to an argument.

Given a function f defined by m recursion equations f P_i <= E_i where P_i is a pattern and E_i is an expression ($1 \leq i \leq m$) the semantic equation for f is:

$$\mathscr{E}[\![f]\!] \rho = /\nabla \circ ((\mathscr{E}[\![\upsilon P_1.E_1]\!] \rho), \ldots , (\mathscr{E}[\![\upsilon P_m.E_m]\!] \rho))$$

where / and $\circ$ denote the reduce (or insert) and composition operators respectively, so that

$$(/\nabla \circ (d_1, \ldots , d_n)) \, e = (d_1 \, e) \, \nabla \ldots \nabla \, (d_n \, e)$$

cf. the FP language introduced in Chapter 5.

This almost completes the discussion, but we have not yet considered the case in which f is recursively defined, i.e. where there are occurrences of f in the expressions E_i. This case is easily handled using the semantic fixed point operator, Y, as follows:

$$\mathscr{E}[\![f]\!] \rho = Y \, \Lambda d.(\mathscr{E}[\![\upsilon P_1.E_1]\!] \rho\{ d / f \}) \, \nabla \ldots \nabla \, (\mathscr{E}[\![\upsilon P_m.E_m]\!] \rho\{ d / f \})$$

Outline solutions to selected exercises

Chapter 2

2.1 (a)

```
--- convert( n ) <= if n = 0 then 0 else convert( n div 2 ) * 10 +
        if ( n mod 2 ) = 0 then 0 else 1 ;
```

(b)

```
--- sum( m, n ) <= sum2( m, n, 0 ) ;
--- sum2( m, n, c ) <=
        if n = 0 then c
                  sum2( m div 2, n div 2, c2 ) * 10 + s2
              where ( c2, s2 ) == ( total div 2, total mod 2 )
              where total == ( n mod 2 ) + ( m mod 2 ) + c ;
```

2.3

```
type bag( alpha ) == list( alpha # num ) ;
--- add( e, nil ) <= [ ( e, 1 ) ] ;
--- add( e, ( entry & ( x, n ) ) :: s ) <= if e = x then ( x, n + 1 ) :: s
      else entry :: add( e, s ) ;
--- remove( ( x, n ) :: s ) <= ( x, if n = 1 then s else (x, n - 1 ) :: s ) ;
```
will do assuming bag is non-empty
```
--- union( ( x1, n1 ) :: s1, s2 ) <= if n1 = 0 then union( s1, s2 )
      else union ( ( x1, n1 - 1 ), add( x1, s2 ) ) ;
--- union( nil, s ) <= s;
```
not the most efficient version, but an interesting one!

2.5

```
dec isort : list( num ) -> list( num ) ;
dec insert : num # list( num ) -> list( num ) ;
--- isort( nil ) <= nil ;
```
this version works 'backwards' from the one suggested in the question but is slightly simpler
```
--- isort( x :: s ) <= insert( x, isort( s ) ) ;
```

2.7

```
data truval == true ++ false ;
--- and( false, false ) <= false ;
--- and( true, true ) <= true ; . . .
```
(declaration should be obvious) and similarly for (true, false) and (false, true) which are both false

2.8 (a) This will do, but is only one of many possible solutions:

```
type name == list( char ) ; data sex == male ++ female ;
type date == ( num # num # num ) ;
type DateOfBirth == date ; type EnrolmentDate == date ;
type address == list( char ) ;
type StaffInfo == ( name # sex # DateOfBirth #
EnrolmentDate # address ) ;
type course == num ;
data Section == Systems ++ Software ++ Theory ;
data SupportClass == Secretarial ++ ComputerSupport
++ Maintenance ;
data StaffRecord == Teacher( StaffInfo # Section #
list( course ) ) ++ Support( StaffInfo # SupportClass ) ;
type Database == list( StaffRecord ) ;
```

(b) (i) **dec** CountTeachers : Database → num ; similarly for support staff

```
--- CountTeachers( nil ) <= 0 ;
--- CountTeachers( Teacher( _,_,_ ) :: Rest ) <=
      1 + CountTeachers( Rest ) ;
--- CountTeachers( Support( _,_ ) :: Rest ) <=
      CountTeachers( Rest ) ;
```

2.9 Associativity as for Join given in the text. For commutativity, we first show by induction on m that add(n, succ(m)) = add(succ(n), m) for all n, m of type nat. In the base case, m = zero and we have add(n, succ(zero)) = succ(add(n, zero)) = succ(n) = add(succ(n), zero) for all n of type nat.

Now assume that add(n, succ(u)) = add(succ(n), u) for all n, u of type nat. Then we have add(n, succ(succ(u))) = succ(add(n, succ(u)) = succ(add(succ(n), u)) by the inductive hypothesis = add(succ (n), succ(u)) as required.

Commutativity now follows by induction on n. For n = zero, add(zero, m) = add(m, zero) by a second induction on m and using the result just derived. Finally, assuming that add(u, m) = add(m, u) for all u, m : nat, add(succ(u), m) = add(u, succ(m)) by the above result = succ(add(u, m)) = succ(add(m, u)), by the inductive hypothesis, = add(m, succ(u)) as required.

Note that a simpler proof uses induction on the pairs (n, m) defined by the base value (zero, zero) and by the inductive case that if (n, m) is a pair then so are (succ(n), m) and (n, succ(m)). This still needs the hint though.

Chapter 3

3.1

```
--- map ( f, l ) <= reduce( lambda ( x, y ) => f(x) :: y, nil, l ) ;
--- l1 <> l2 <= reduce( :: , l2, l1 ) ;
```

3.3
```
--- gen( n ) <= map(lambda x => lambda y => y + x, from( 1, n ) ) ;
--- from( n, m ) <= if n > m then nil else n :: from( n + 1, m ) ;
```
(suitably declared)

3.4 (c)
```
--- C( F ) <= reduce (compose, lambda y => y, F) ;
```

3.5 (a) This is essentially the same as reduce except that the reducing function is of type $\alpha \rightarrow \beta \rightarrow \beta$ instead of type $\alpha \# \beta \rightarrow \beta$. / returns a function which when applied to the 'base case' yields the resulting reduced list.

(b)
```
--- sum( l ) <= ( ( lambda a => lambda b => a + b ) / l ) 0 ;
```

(c)
```
--- add( n ) <= lambda nil => nil |
         x :: s => if n < x then n :: ( x :: s ) else x :: ( add( n )( s ) ) ;
```

(d)
```
( add / [ 4, 2, 7, 3 ] ) 0
```

Chapter 4

4.1 We can define a function which generates an infinite list of random numbers, e.g.

```
dec Randoms : real → list( real ) ;
--- Randoms( seed ) <= let ( next, newseed ) ==
         Generate( seed )
         in next :: Randoms( newseed ) ;
```

This can be passed to all functions requiring a random number; the next random number is obtained by taking the head of the infinite list.

4.4 (a)
```
--- pipe( F ) <= lambda stream =>
                   reduce( compose, lambda y => y, StreamFuns)
                   where StreamFuns == map( lambda f =>
                   ( lambda s => map( f, s ) ), F ) ;
```

StreamFuns simply translates each function, f, in F (of type $\alpha \rightarrow \alpha$) into a *stream processing* function (of type list(α) $\rightarrow$ list(α)) by mapping f over the stream argument, s, to which it is ultimately applied by reduce. Using sequential lazy evaluation this obviously won't (can't) behave like a pipeline: each value on the input stream will be processed by every function in F before the next input value is ever processed. However, the list of stream processing functions can be viewed as a description of a physical pipeline of processes and each such function could be implemented on a separate processor. It is then possible to obtain the pipeline parallelism implied by the solution.

(b)
```
--- Intersection( S, T ) <= Filter( pipe( F )( map( lambda s =>
      ( s, false ), S ) ) )
    where F == map( lambda x => lambda ( v, f ) =>
      ( v, if v = x then true else f ), T ) ;
--- Filter( nil ) <= nil ;
--- Filter( ( v, b ) :: s ) <= ( if b then v :: r else r )
      where r == Filter( s ) ;
```

Chapter 5

5.3 This depends on how we define the lambda expression. Clearly, any function can be written in its curried form by writing it explicitly as a 'nest' of lambda expressions, e.g. f x y = E in Miranda becomes f = **lambda** x => **lambda** y => E in Hope. However, if in Miranda we have f x y z = E, and similarly --- f′(x, y, z) <= E in Hope, then G = f a is not always the same as H = **lambda** (x, y) => f′(a, x, y); it depends on how G is used. If G is always applied to two arguments then the two are equivalent: G a b ≡ H(a, b); however, if G is subsequently partially applied, as in G b, then the lambda notation requires this to be written **lambda** y => H(b, y). Currying is, in this sense, more general; whether it results in clearer programs is, however, a matter of personal judgement.

5.5 (b) Def app = /cons ∘ consr

Chapter 6

6.2 (c) Case (iii) We shall reduce the leftmost-outermost β/δ-redex at each step

$$(\,\lambda h.(\,\lambda x.h(\,x\,x\,)\,)\,(\,\lambda x.h(\,x\,x\,)\,)\,)\,(\,(\,\lambda a.\lambda b.a\,)\,(\,+\,1\,5\,)\,)$$
$$\rightarrow (\,\lambda x.(\,(\,(\,\lambda a.\lambda b.a\,)\,(\,+\,1\,5\,)\,)\,(\,x\,x\,)\,)\,)\,(\,\lambda x.(\,(\,\lambda a.\lambda b.a\,)\,(\,+\,1\,5\,)\,)\,(\,x\,x\,)\,)\,)$$
$$\rightarrow (\,(\,(\,\lambda a.\lambda b.a\,)\,(\,+\,1\,5\,)\,)\,(\,\lambda x.(\,(\,\lambda a.\lambda b.a\,)\,(\,+\,1\,5\,)\,)\,(\,x\,x\,)\,)\,)\,(\,(\,\lambda x.(\,(\,\lambda a.\lambda b.a\,)\,(\,+\,1\,5\,)\,)\,(\,x\,x\,)\,)\,)\,)\,)\,)$$
$$\rightarrow (\,(\,(\,\lambda b.(\,+\,1\,5\,)\,)\,)\,(\,\lambda x.(\,(\,\lambda a.\lambda b.a\,)\,(\,+\,1\,5\,)\,)\,(\,x\,x\,)\,)\,)\,(\,(\,\lambda x.(\,(\,\lambda a.\lambda b.a\,)\,(\,+\,1\,5\,)\,)\,(\,x\,x\,)\,)\,)\,)\,)\,)$$
$$\rightarrow (\,+\,1\,5\,)$$
$$\rightarrow 6$$

6.4 $(\,\lambda f.+\,(\,f\;1\,)\,(\,f\;2\,)\,)\,(\,\lambda x.(\,\lambda y.y\,)\,7\,)$

	$\rightarrow +\,(\,f\;1\,)\,(\,f\;2\,)$	**where** $f = (\,\lambda x.(\,\lambda y.y\,)\,7\,)$
	$\rightarrow +\,(\,(\,\lambda x.(\,\lambda y.y\,)\,7\,)\,1\,)\,(\,f\;2\,)$	**where** $f = (\,\lambda x.(\,\lambda y.y\,)\,7\,)$
	$\rightarrow +\,(\,(\,\lambda y.y\,)\,7\,)\,(\,f\;2\,)$	**where** $f = (\,\lambda x.(\,\lambda y.y\,)\,7\,)$
*	$\rightarrow +\,7\,(\,f\;2\,)$	**where** $f = (\,\lambda x.(\,\lambda y.y\,)\,7\,)$
	$\rightarrow +\,7\,(\,(\,\lambda x.(\,\lambda y.y\,)\,7\,)\,2\,)$	
*	$\rightarrow +\,7\,(\,(\,\lambda y.y\,)\,7\,)$	
	$\rightarrow +\,7\,7$	
	$\rightarrow 14$	

$(\lambda y.y)$ 7 is reduced twice, in the steps marked $*$. We can avoid this duplicated effort by reducing the function body before completing the application. This reduction order is called **innermost spine reduction**. This reduces redexes in the body once and for all. However, it requires us to reduce 'through lambdas' so we end up with the free variable and name clash problems again, making it impractical.

6.5 (a) (i) $\lambda x.x$ (ii) $\lambda x.6$ will do

(b) $\bot$ since $* \bot \bot = \bot$ and $\bot$ is least defined (see Appendix B). The other fixed points are 0 and 1.

(c) 6.2(c)(iii) computes the least fixed point of $(\lambda x.\lambda y.x)(+\ 1\ 5)$ i.e. of $\lambda x.6$ since the function being applied is the lambda calculus version of the Y-combinator. This explains why the answer is 6!

6.7 (a) (i) NOT $\equiv \lambda x.x\ FALSE\ TRUE$ (ii) XOR $\equiv \lambda a.\lambda b.a\,(\text{NOT}\ b)\ b$

6.8 (b) $\lambda.(\lambda.L0\ L0)(\lambda.L0(\lambda.L1))$

Chapter 7

7.1 (a) For predicate $a(b) : truval \Rightarrow b : \beta,\ a : \beta \rightarrow truval$
For consequent $[c] : list(\alpha),\ c : \alpha$
For alternative $[b :: c] : list(\gamma), b : \gamma, c : list(\gamma) \Rightarrow \gamma = \beta, \alpha = list(\gamma)$ $= list(\beta)$
Hence $f : ((\beta \rightarrow truval)\ \#\ \beta\ \#\ list(\beta)) \rightarrow list(list(\beta))$

(b) $(\alpha\ \#\ (\alpha \rightarrow truval)) \rightarrow (\alpha \rightarrow truval) \rightarrow \alpha \rightarrow truval$ (remember consequent and alternative always have the same type in a conditional expression)

(c) $(\alpha\ \#\ ((\alpha\ \#\ num) \rightarrow \beta)\ \#\ (\beta \rightarrow \alpha \rightarrow \gamma)) \rightarrow list(\alpha \rightarrow (\beta\ \#\ \gamma))$

7.2 Begin with rule (d):

$$\mathcal{W}(nil, \lambda f.\lambda g.\lambda a.\lambda b.pair\ (f\ a)\ (g\ b)) = (R_1, R_1\,\beta_1 \rightarrow \rho_1)$$

where β_1 is a new type variable and

$$(R_1, \rho_1) = \mathcal{W}(f : \beta, \lambda g.\lambda a.\lambda b.pair\ (f\ a)\ (g\ b))$$

Keep cranking the algorithm to get the result

$$funpair : (\alpha \rightarrow \beta) \rightarrow (\gamma \rightarrow \delta) \rightarrow \alpha \rightarrow \gamma \rightarrow (\beta \times \delta)$$

Similarly

$$tagpair : \alpha \rightarrow \beta \rightarrow \beta \rightarrow ((\alpha \times \beta) \times (\alpha \times \beta))$$

7.3 (a) *apply* : $((\alpha \rightarrow \beta) \times \alpha) \rightarrow \beta$

(b) --- *apply* (*tuple-2* f x) <= $f\,x$

(c) In general we have υ (*tuple-n* $x_1 \ldots x_n$) instead of $\upsilon(x_1, \ldots, x_n)$ and use the assumption for *tuple-n* rather than rule (g) to infer the type of the pattern.

7.4 ---curry3 f <= **lambda** x => **lambda** y => **lambda** z => f(x, y, z) ;
curry3 : $((\alpha \times \beta \times \gamma) \rightarrow \delta) \rightarrow \alpha \rightarrow \beta \rightarrow \gamma \rightarrow \delta$

7.5 For constructor c of arity $n > 0$, $\mathcal{W}(A, \upsilon(c\,p_1 \ldots p_n).e) = U\beta \rightarrow U\sigma$ where $U = \mathcal{V}(\gamma, \rho_1 \rightarrow \ldots \rightarrow \rho_n \rightarrow \beta)$, $\mathcal{W}(A, c) = (I, \gamma)$ and $\mathcal{W}(A, \upsilon p_1 \ldots \upsilon p_n.e) = (R, \rho_1 \rightarrow \ldots \rightarrow \rho_n \rightarrow \sigma)$.
Base cases: for constructor c of arity 0, $\mathcal{W}(A.c : \gamma, \upsilon c.e) = (s, s\gamma \rightarrow \sigma)$ where

$$(S, \sigma) = \mathcal{W}(A.c : \gamma, e)$$

for variable x, $\upsilon x.e \equiv \lambda x.e$ and rule (d) applies.
(Note that $f\,p_1 \ldots p_n = e$ is represented as $f = \upsilon p_1 \ldots \upsilon p_n.e$.)

7.6 (a) '*Occurs check*' on disagreement pair (*num*, *num* $\rightarrow \tau$)

(b) '*Occurs check*' on disagreement pair (*bool*, *bool* $\rightarrow \tau$)

Chapter 8

8.1 (b) Constructors can be passed as arguments and returned as results. For a curried language we rely on the fact that TUPLE-n is itself curried. For example, the list constructor cons might be translated as the partial application TUPLE-3 1, assuming that 1 is the internal code for cons. In Hope we could have used a two-tier representation for compound data so that cons x y would be represented TUPLE-2 1 (TUPLE-2 x y). If cons were passed as a parameter then it should be passed as TUPLE-2 1, so that applying it to the tuple containing x and y would give the required result. Using our representation we have to decompose the tuple to which it is ultimately applied. cons is then passed as λT.TUPLE-3 1 (INDEX 1 t) (INDEX 2 t).

8.3 **data** Tree == NoMatch ++ Leaf(list(EquationNumber)) ++ Node (Position # list(Tree)) ; with EquationNumber and Position suitably defined.

Extending this for literals requires an extra node type:

data Tree == ... ++ Literal(Expression # Tree # Tree) ;

8.4 (a) (ii) TUPLE-3 2 (TUPLE-2 1 (TUPLE-1 0)) (TUPLE-1 0)

As an aside, there is an intermediate language called FLIC, based on the lambda calculus, which looks very similar to the one defined in this chapter. One of the major differences is that FLIC supports tagged tuples where it is possible to inject a tag into a tuple using an explicit injection function. This can be used to tag the arguments of a constructor with the constructor code. In this way the constructor code is no longer a component of the corresponding tuple so that the constructor zero, for example, would be represented by a tag-injected tuple of arity 0.

(d) The binding lists are empty for the first two equations; the third has a bind list of [("a", [3, 2]), ("b", [3, 3])].

8.5 Yes! The value node v is represented by a four-tuple whose first element is the tag for the node constructor and whose remaining three elements are the elements of v. To bind T to v we therefore have to extract these three elements and reconstruct a new three-tuple. The easiest way to do this is to replace T in the pattern by a tuple of variables, e.g. (x_1, x_2, x_3) for the purposes of the translation. An alternative would be to represent all constructed data by *pairs*, the first element being the constructor tag and the second the constructor argument (which may, of course, be a tuple). Data constants can again be represented as singleton tuples.

8.7 Because if we ever merge two nodes, one of which is a leaf node, the equations associated with those nodes must overlap: if they didn't we wouldn't be merging them.

8.8 Test constructor for nil / cons → call to isempty; indexing to get head and tail elements → direct calls to head and tail. The advantage is efficiency; list processing functions are likely to be highly optimized in the implementation.

8.9 The modifications are trivial. Instead of generating a single λ for each function we instead introduce a separate λ for each function argument. For the purposes of the matching tree we can still view the arguments as though they were in a tuple, as at present. The only change that is then required is in the final translation of positions. The position [n] now refers to the nth argument/bound variable (a_i, say) instead of the nth element of the argument tuple. Curried constructors are no problem. By the time a function is called all compound data arguments are stored as tuples and the prescribed indexing method still works.

Chapter 9

9.1 (a) (ii) LET("x", INT(4), LAM("y", APP(APP(PRIM("+"), INT(7)), INT(5))))

9.2 (c) --- empty <= **lambda** i => i ; this cannot arise because all expressions are closed

```
--- E :+: ( v, e ) <= lambda i => if i = v then e else E( i ) ;
```
:++: then follows

9.5 (a) We could represent primitive function applications by a special node type called PRIMAPP, e.g. + x y → PRIMAPP("+", [x, y]). Partial applications of primitives must then be represented by closures to get currying, e.g. + 6 → CLOSURE(LAM("x", * PRIMAPP("+", [INT(6), VAR("x")])), empty).

(b) This is all OK but there is now no difference between the internal interpreter representation of + 6 and λx. + 6 x. If the program produces this expression as a result and tries to print it λx. + 6 x will always be echoed back to the user. This might surprise him if he had typed + 6 as the expression to be evaluated.

9.7 (a) **data** AllPrims == plus ++ minus ++ ... ++ tuple(num) ++ ... ;

Then "+" is represented by plus, − by minus, ..., tuple-n by tuple (n) etc. ArityOf must be modified accordingly: ArityOf(plus) = 2 ; ... ; ArityOf(tuple(n)) <= n. The basic application mechanism is the same as before except that we now require a representation for the resulting tuples themselves since we are now supporting them as a new base type. A list of expressions will suffice:

```
data exp == INT( num ) ++ VAR( id ) ++ ... ++
  TUPLE( list( exp ) ) ;
```

(b) FunOf(tuple(n)) <= **lambda** Args => TUPLE(Args) ;

(c) We need a combination of the two interpreters: if the applied function is lazytuple-n then we must form suspensions from the arguments; otherwise we must evaluate them as per the eager interpreter.

```
--- Eval( APP( F, A ), Env ) <= Check( Eval( F, Env ), A, Env ) ;
--- Check( F & OP( lazytuple( _ ),_,_ ), A, Env ) <=
    Apply(F, SUSP( A, Env ) ) ;
--- Check( F, A, Env ) <= Apply( F, Eval( A, Env ) ) ;
```
using overlapping patterns

Chapter 10

10.1 Analogous to examples in Chapter 10.

10.2 Eager use of $Y = \lambda h.(\lambda x.h(xx))(\lambda x.h(xx))$ results in the application xx being reduced as soon as x is bound.

(a) In the evaluation of $Y f 3$ with eager evaluation, 3 is already in WHNF and Yf next reduces to DD where $D = (\lambda x.(\lambda f.\lambda n.cond\ldots)(xx))$. This reduces to $(\lambda f.\lambda n.cond\ldots)(DD)$ and eager evaluation then evaluates the argument DD and so on *ad infinitum*.

Using Y' we reach similarly the expression $D'D'$ in the evaluation of $Y'f$ where $D' = (\lambda x.(\lambda f.\lambda n.cond\ldots)(\lambda z.xxz))$ and this reduces to $(\lambda f.\lambda n.cond\ldots)(\lambda z.D'D'z)$ which is in WHNF.

Thus we apply it to 3 and find the subexpression $(\lambda z.D'D'z)\ 2 \rightarrow D'D'\ 2$ in the **else** part of the conditional, driving the recursion. However, in the base case (which this now is) the sub-expression $(\lambda z.D'D'z)$ is discarded.

(b) $f' = \langle f, \lambda n.cond\ 2\ (*\ n\ (f(-\ n\ 1)))\ (=\ n\ 2)\rangle$. Initial state is

$$
\begin{aligned}
()\,()\,(f'3)\,() &\rightarrow ()\,()\,(3, f', @)\,() \\
&\rightarrow (3)\,()\,(f', @)\,() \\
&\rightarrow (3)\,(f = \lambda n.cond \ldots)\,(\lambda n.cond \ldots, @)\,() \\
&\rightarrow ([\,n, cond \ldots, (f = \lambda n.cond \ldots)\,], 3) \\
&\quad\ (f = \lambda n.cond \ldots)\,(@)\,() \\
&\rightarrow \ldots
\end{aligned}
$$

f' is never again accessed.

10.4 Put the closure corresponding to the lambda expression of the labelled expression into the environment immediately – the free variable bindings will not change under reduction to WHNF.

10.5 $L_f = \langle f, \lambda x.cond\ 1\ (g\ x)\ (=\ x\ 0)\rangle$
$g\ = \lambda f.h\ f$
$h\ = \lambda y.f(-\ y\ 1)$
In the evaluation of $L_f\ 132$, x is bound to 132, then f is bound to 132 in the application of g. Thus in the body of h, f is bound to 132 whereas it should be bound to $\lambda x.cond \ldots$. The problem can be avoided by using unique names.

10.7 The assumptions that need to be modified are the state transition rules (cf. the call-by-name implementation described in the text) and the semantic function *eval* defining the substitution rules for β- and δ-reduction. Then follow through an analogous proof.

Chapter 11

11.1 (i)

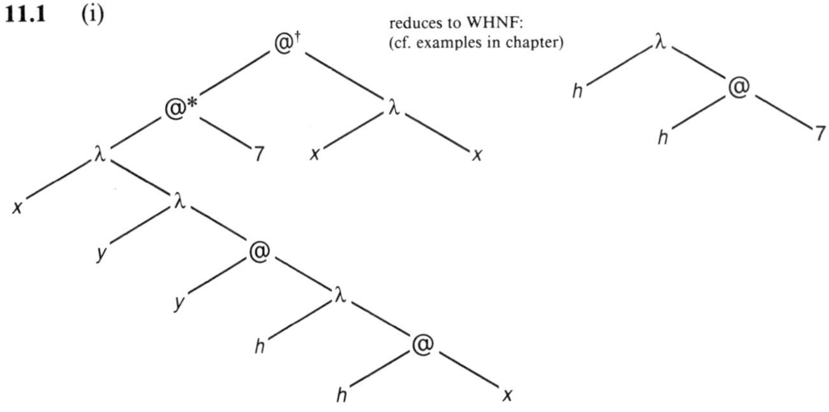

$*$ denotes first redex, † denotes second redex.

(ii) and (iii) similar.

11.2 Represent *cons* 4 as $(\lambda x.\lambda y.cons\ x\ y)\ 4$ or $\lambda y.cons\ 4\ y$ then follow the usual rules.

11.5 (a) Each node type contains a tag field and others as follows (there are various optimizations):

@ node	: two pointers	*λ node*	: *id* and a pointer
identifier	: *id*	*constant*	: value
cons	: two pointers	*tuple-n*	: a vector of *n* pointers

where *id* is some suitable numeric encoding of an identifier. The label to the left of the : in each case is the cell tag.

(b) The main advantage is that the tuple elements can be accessed in constant time. The disadvantage is that it requires variable-sized cells; for some implementations (particularly parallel implementations) this can significantly complicate the store manager and garbage collector.

11.6 In normal-order graph reduction the next redex is selected by scanning the graph in a depth-first left-to-right fashion. To evaluate arguments first, we move to the right at each @ node in the graph as far as possible; i.e. a depth-first right-to-left search.

Chapter 12

12.1 (a)
$$\begin{aligned} comb(\lambda x.+x\ 1) &= [x]comb(+x\ 1) = [x](+x\ 1) \\ &= S[x](+x)[x]1 = S(S[x]+[x]x)(K1) \\ &= S(S(K+)I)(K1) \end{aligned}$$

(b) $S(SI(KI))(K1)$

(c) $S(S(S(K\,cond)(S(S(K=)I)(K0)))(K1))(S(S(K-)I)(K1))$

12.3 (a) $X = Z\,Z$ where $Z = \lambda x.\lambda y.y\,(x\,x\,y)$.
Thus, for lambda expression E,

$$XE = (ZZ)E = (\lambda y.y(ZZy))E = E(ZZE) = E(XE)$$

(b) For all M, $SKKM = KM(KM) = M = IM$

(c) For all M, N, P,

$$\begin{aligned} S(KS)KMNP &= KSM(KM)NP = S(KM)NP \\ &= KMP(NP) = M(NP) = BMNP \end{aligned}$$

12.4 *Base cases*:

(i) $sub([x]x) = sub(I) = \lambda z.z =_{\alpha} \lambda x.sub(x)$

(ii) For constant m or variable $m \neq x$,

$$sub([x]m) = sub(Km) = (\lambda x.\lambda y.x)\,m =_{\beta} \lambda y.m =_{\alpha} \lambda x.sub(m)$$

Inductive step:

$sub([\,x\,]AB) = sub(S[\,x\,]A[\,x\,]B) = sub(S)\,sub([\,x\,]A)\,sub([\,x\,]B)$
$=_\alpha sub(S)\,(\lambda x.sub(A))\,(\lambda x.sub(B))$ (by the inductive hypothesis)
$= \lambda z.(\lambda x.sub(A))\,z\,(\lambda x.sub(B)\,z) =_\beta \lambda z.[\,z/x\,]\,sub(A)\,[\,z/x\,]\,sub(B)$
$= \lambda z.[\,z/x\,]\,(sub(A)\,sub(B)) = \lambda z.[\,z/x\,]\,sub(AB)$
$=_\alpha \lambda x.sub(AB)$

Rest as described in Chapter 12.

12.7 $comb(W) = S\,S\,(K\,I)$.

(a) Straightforward.

(b) 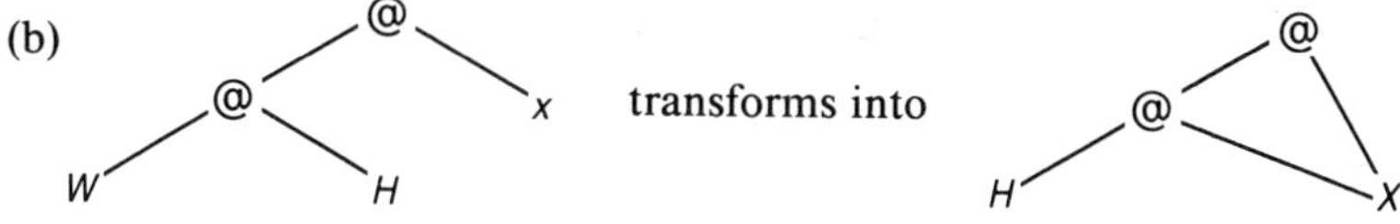

Graph reduction of $W + 2$ straightforward.

(c) E has the graph:

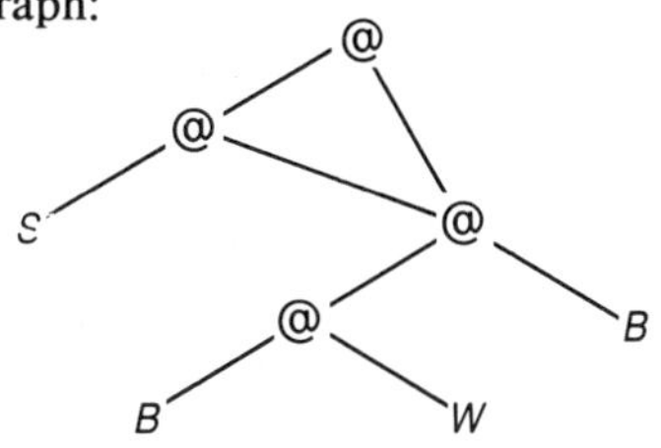

(d) More straightforward graph transformations.

12.8 The abstraction function *abs* can be defined as follows:

$abs(\lambda v.v) = I$	
$abs(\lambda v.w) = @\,K\,w$	(for identifier $w \neq v$)*
$abs(\lambda v.\lambda w.E) = abs(\lambda v.abs(\lambda w.E))$	
$abs(\lambda v.@\,\$\,E_1E_2) = @/\$\,abs(\lambda v.E_1)\,E_2$	if $v \in FV(E_1)$ and $v \notin FV(E_2)$
$= @\backslash\$\,E_1\,abs(\lambda v.E_2)$	if $v \notin FV(E_1)$ and $v \in FV(E_2)$
$= @\hat{}\$\,abs(\lambda v.E_1)\,abs(\lambda v.E_2)$	if $v \in FV(E_1)$ and $v \in FV(E_2)$
$= @-\$\,E_1E_2)$	if $v \notin FV(E_1)$ and $v \notin FV(E_2)$

12.9 (a) Use the K combinator: $\lambda x.\lambda y.7 =_\beta \lambda x.K\,7$.

(b) This is where variables are bound to arguments. If the bound variable does not occur in the body then we use a - at the root node. In the body graph the directors only send the argument where it is needed; thus if a variable did not occur below a given node it would not have been sent to that node in the first place, so no need for a -.

Chapter 13

13.1 (a) $mult = Y\ \lambda m.\lambda x.\underline{\lambda y.cond\ (\ =\ x\ 1\ )\ y\ (\ m\ (\ -\ x\ 1\ )\ y\ )}$

The innermost λ-abstraction (underlined) may be written $\alpha\ m\ x$ where α is defined by:

$$\alpha\ u\ v\ w = cond\ (\ =\ v\ 1\ )\ w\ (\ u\ (\ -\ v\ 1\ )\ w\ )$$

Then $mult = Y\ \lambda m.\lambda x.\alpha\ m\ x$ and we define β by $\beta\ u\ v = \alpha\ u\ v$ so $\beta = \alpha$, giving $mult = Y\ \lambda m.\alpha\ m = Y\alpha$ similarly (or by η-conversion). Note that you will need another combinator if you do not select the first two parameters of α in the order shown (see also Exercise 13.5).

(b) $Y\ \alpha\ 3 \rightarrow \alpha\ mult\ 3$ which is a partial application and cannot be further reduced. However,

$$\begin{aligned} mult\ 3 &= \lambda y.cond\ (\ =\ 3\ 1\ )\ y\ (\ mult\ (\ -\ 3\ 1\ )\ y\ ) \\ &= \lambda y.cond\ false\ y\ (\ mult\ 2\ y\ ) = \lambda y.mult\ 2\ y \end{aligned}$$

so that the values of the two constant sub-expressions $=\ 3\ 1$ and $-\ 3\ 1$ can be shared on a second application of *mult* 3. This possibility of sharing is lost in lambda lifting.

(c) Mfe's of the underlined expression are $cond\ (\ =\ x\ 1\ )$ and $m\ (\ -\ x\ 1\ )$ and we have

$$mult = Y\ \lambda m.\lambda x.\sigma\ (\ m(\ -\ x\ 1\ )\ )\ (\ cond\ (\ =\ x\ 1\ )\ )$$

where $\sigma\ u\ v\ w = v\ w\ (\ u\ w\ )$. The only mfe of the new innermost lambda body is m and we have

$$\begin{aligned} mult &= Y\ \lambda m.\tau\ m = Y\ \tau \\ &\text{where } \tau\ u\ v = \sigma\ (\ u\ (\ -\ v\ 1\ )\ )\ (\ cond\ (\ =\ v\ 1\ )\ ) \end{aligned}$$

Now the partial application of *mult* gives

$$\tau\ mult\ 3 = \sigma\ (\ mult\ (\ -\ 3\ 1\ )\ )\ (\ cond\ (\ =\ 3\ 1\ )\ )$$

so the constant sub-expressions' values can be shared.

(d) (τ rule only)

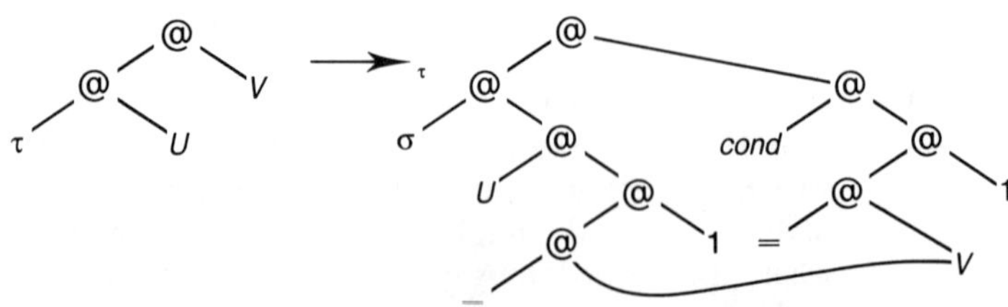

13.2 $f = Y\ \lambda f.\lambda x.\lambda y.cond\ (\ <\ x\ y\ )\ x\ (\ f(\ -\ x\ y\ )\ y\ )$ and the mfe's are $<x$, x, f, $-x$. There are no benefits over lambda lifting since the only non-variable

mfe's are partial applications of primitive functions which need all their arguments and so cannot be reduced. This is at a cost of 4 parameters as opposed to 2 with simple lambda lifting.

13.3 (a) $f = \lambda x_1.\lambda x_2 \ldots \lambda x_n.E = \alpha\ v_1 \ldots v_m$ where $\alpha\ v_1 \ldots v_m\ x_1 \ldots x_n = E$ (general lambda lifting).

(b) All function-valued objects become partial applications of combinators. This means that we can 'accumulate' the arguments of the combinator and only apply the combinator when all its arguments are available (cf. the normal mechanism for curried function application).

(c) Full laziness is preserved if no partial application of f ever becomes shared. If it does then it is possible that a sub-expression within the combinator body will be evaluated each time the shared partial application is applied. The compiler can determine whether f will ever be partially applied and, if so, whether the resulting function can ever become shared. Provided the sharing cannot occur the combinator can be left intact without losing full laziness. If it can become shared then mfe lifting must be applied in the manner described in Section 13.2 and at least one new combinator synthesized.

13.4 We need only consider expressions of the form $X = \lambda x_1 \ldots \lambda x_n.E$, where E is applicative, since otherwise we may assume inductively that the result holds for E (and similarly for expressions which are not lambda abstractions).

For general lambda lifting we get $glift(\ X\ ) = \alpha\ v_1 \ldots v_m$ where $\alpha\ v_1 \ldots v_m\ x_1 \ldots x_n = E$ and $v_1 \ldots v_m$ are the free variables in X.

For simple lambda lifting (with freest first parameter ordering) we get

$$slift(\ \lambda x_n.E\ ) = \alpha'\ w_1 \ldots w_m\ x_1 \ldots x_{n-1}$$

(provided each of $x_1, \ldots, x_{n-1}$ occur in E) where $\alpha'\ w_1 \ldots w_m\ x_1 \ldots x_n = E$ and $w_1, \ldots, w_m$ are the variables $v_1, \ldots v_m$ in freest first order. But

$$\lambda x_1 \ldots \lambda x_{n-1}.\alpha'\ w_1 \ldots w_m\ x_1 \ldots x_{n-1} = \alpha'\ w_1 \ldots w_m$$

by extensionality (η-conversion) and so sufficient conditions are that general lambda lifting must also select its free variable parameters in freest first order and that every variable with sub-expression E in its scope must occur in E. A counter example is $X = \lambda x.\lambda y.\lambda z.z\ x$ which gives under simple lambda lifting $X = \beta$ where $\beta\ x\ y = \alpha\ x$ and $\alpha\ x\ z = z\ x$, but general lambda lifting gives a single combinator.

13.6 (Expression (i) only)

(a) $(\ \lambda.\lambda.L1\ L0\ (\ +\ 1\ L0\ )\ )\ +\ 2$

(b) $S(S(\Lambda(\Lambda(\ S(\ S(\ 1!, 0!\ ), S(\ S('+, '1\ ), 0!\ )\ )\ )\ )\ ), '+\ ), '2\ )$ in WCCL

or
$App \circ \langle A,B \rangle$ where $A = App \circ \langle C,D \rangle$, $B = \Lambda(2 \circ Snd)$
where $C = \Lambda(\Lambda(App \circ \langle E,F \rangle))$, $D = \Lambda(+ \circ Snd)$
where $E = App \circ \langle Snd \circ Fst, Snd \rangle$, $F = App \circ \langle G,Snd \rangle$
where $G = App \circ \langle \Lambda(+ \circ Snd), \Lambda(1 \circ Snd) \rangle$

(c) Straightforward as per example in Chapter 13, giving WHNF of 5 using either the WCCL rules (applying expression to an empty environment) or CCL rules.

Chapter 14

14.1 (b) Using the format of Table 14.1 but omitting the number of inputs field:

(i)	1	copy	(4.2, 7.2)	(iii)	1	copy	(3.1, 5.2)
	2	copy	(5.2, 6.2)		2	value : 3	(3.2)
	3	value : 2	(4.1)		3	−	(7.2)
	4	*	(8.1)		4	value : +	(5.1)
	5	apply	(6.1)		5	apply	(8.2)
	6	apply	(7.1)		6	value : f	(7.1)
	7	apply	(8.2)		7	apply	(8.1)
	8	+	(output)		8	apply	(output)

14.2 This precludes the partial application of F. If we partially apply F we have no mechanism by which to refer to the resulting function and no mechanism by which to apply it. As an aside, this is the way many conventional dataflow machines implement function application; the fact that they cannot (or at least cannot easily) support higher-order functions makes them largely unsuitable for implementing functional languages.

14.3 (a) See the above example.

(b) A primitive function symbol can now appear on the function input of an apply node. The rules for apply must therefore be extended accordingly.

14.5 This is because the two arms are combined using a merge node which is non-strict in the T and F inputs. If the control input were true then a kill token on the F input would just be absorbed, and vice versa.

14.6 0.2 – this corresponds to the top of stack when it appears in the output list of the last instruction.

14.7 This simply says that we can use the input fields of an instruction to hold the source list entries.

Chapter 15

15.1 (d) (3 (if (af (fe (lv 3)) (lv 1) (cv 1)) (lv 2) (af (bi −) (lv 1) (cv 1))
(af (bi *) (lv 1) (lv 2))))

15.2 tv expressions can do unpacking of tuples; in this respect they can be viewed as implementing directly expressions of the form **let** (x_1, x_2, . . . , x_n) == T **in** . . .

15.4 (b) The important thing about the intermediate tuple is that it is not shared. It is in fact a shorthand for the expression (tv 1 E_1 (tv 1 E_2 (tv 1 E_3 E))).

(c) We could translate the expression into the equivalent 'longhand' above. However, by handling tuples directly in the code generator we end up with a more general solution. For example, if we were given (tv 3 (if (. . .) (lv 4) (mt E_1 E_2 E_3)) E) we could not apply the FC → FC translation so easily. The extension required is actually quite simple: we just need to add another parameter, n, to the compilation functions, which states a ground rule that if n > 1 then the result of evaluating the expression must be an n-tuple which must be left on the stack. This parameter is propagated through all arms of a conditional and through to the resultant in a (nested) tv expression. The 'base case' is in the rule for mt where the extra parameter determines where the resulting tuple must be left. The two most interesting rules are:

```
E [ (mt E1 E2 . . . En )] d l n = E [ En ] d l ; E [ En-1 ] d + 1 l ;
                                  . . . ; E [ E1 ] d + n − 1 l ;
                                  if n = 1 then COPY n
E [ ( tv k E1 E2 ) ] d l n = E [ E1 ] d l k ;
                             E [ E2 ] d + k   l ++ [ k, d ] ; DROP n, k
```

15.6 F ⟦ from n = cons n from(succ(n)) ⟧ = E ⟦ cons n from(succ(n)) ⟧ r_1 3 ; UPDATE 3 ; RET 2 by the F-scheme, where r_1 = r_0{ 2 / x } and r_0 is the empty environment. By applying the rules for the E- and C-schemes we obtain the code:

```
PUSH 1 ; PUSHFUN succ ; MKAP ; PUSHFUN from ;
         MKAP ; PUSH 2 ; CONS ; UPDATE 3 ; RET 2
```

Graph for from(succ(0)) is constructed by the code

```
C⟦ from( succ( 0 ) ) ⟧ r0 0 = PUSHINT 0 ; PUSHFUN SUCC ;
                              MKAP ; PUSHFUN from ; MKAP
```

Easy to derive stack and graph from this.

15.7
```
E⟦ hd ( tl ( from 1 ) ) ⟧ r0 0
  = E⟦ tl ( from 1 ) ⟧ r0 0 ; HD ; EVAL
  = E⟦ from 1 ⟧ r0 0 ; TL ; EVAL ; HD ; EVAL
  = C[ from 1 ] r0 0 ; EVAL ; TL ; EVAL ; HD ; EVAL
  = . . . = PUSHINT 1 ; PUSHFUN from ; MKAP ;
    EVAL ; TL ; EVAL ; HD ; EVAL
```

After the unwinding operation (in the first EVAL instruction) the expression to be evaluated is PUSH 1 ; PUSHFUN succ ; . . . ; RET 2 as in Exercise 15.6, and the stack/graph look like:

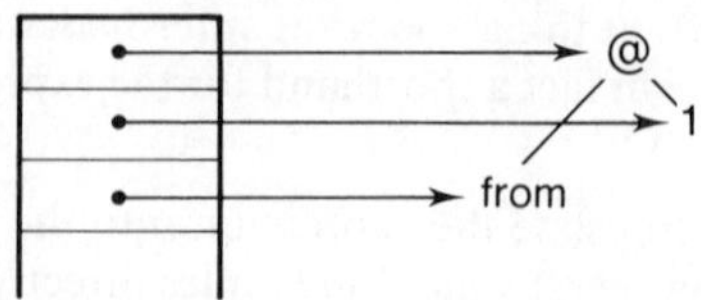

After the execution of RET 2 the expression TL ; EVAL ; HD ; EVAL is restored with stack/graph:

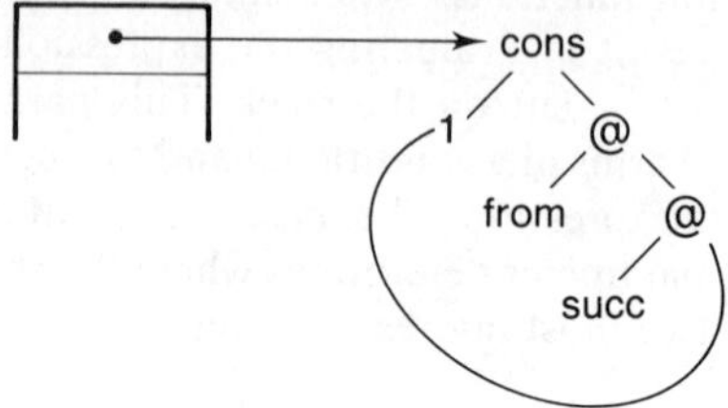

The evaluation of the tail (generated by TL) involves a second function call – from 2 – and the evaluation of the head of the result (the final EVAL) is null since the graph is then the single node 2, i.e. already in WHNF.

15.8 Y f = **let** D x_1 x_2 = x_1 (x_2 x_2) **in** D f (D f) and apply the compilation rules for c[Y f] r n as usual.

Chapter 16

16.1 The important feature of a copying garbage collector is that it visits only the active cells. The number of active cells required at any point in the evaluation of a program is independent of the total size of the heap. Consequently if we make each heap space N times larger then the garbage collector will be invoked approximately N times less often but will take the same time to execute. The propotion of time spent garbage collecting therefore approaches zero as N increases. This argument does not apply to a mark–scan collector because here every heap cell is visited so that the garbage collection time increases linearly with N (assuming no thrashing!)

16.2 (a) This is because the elements of tuples and the arguments of a constructor are all evaluated prior to the tuple/constructor cell being created. Using a multiple heap version of Baker's algorithm this means that no mapping table is required since all pointers point either to cells in the same region or to cells in older regions.

(b) This can happen in a lazy implementation when a suspension or graph redex node is overwritten by the result of evaluating the suspension/redex. This result may be another heap structure built some time after the construction of the suspension/redex node.

16.4 When we pop the TBD stack looking for a free cell we can pop the next address and then read the cell at that address. We can then modify the read cell in one of two ways: either we can decrement its reference count if its current count is greater than 1, or we can overwrite the cell by its new contents in the event that the reference count is zero (the pointer fields would also have to be pushed onto the TBD stack). Finally the modified cell can be written back, the whole process requiring a single read/modify/write cycle.

16.5 (a) Create an indirection cell (synonym cell) which contains a single pointer to the required cell with a weight of 1.

(b) If the initial reference count is 2^n for some n then the weights in each pointer need be only $\log_2 n$ bits in length. Duplicating a pointer then corresponds to decrementing the weight by one and allocating that weight to both pointers. The cell must have a reference count field of n bits; if a cell with a normalized weight of k is deleted then the cell reference count must be reduced by 2^k.

(c) Let w_p be the weight of pointer p and r_c be the reference count of cell c. At the end of the rewrite the counts/weights will be updated as follows:

```
WP := wp ; wp := wr − ( wr div 2 ) ; wr := wr div 2 ; DEC( B, WP )
```

where DEC(c, n) decrements the reference count of c by n and possibly garbage collects c. We can optimize this by inspecting the reference count of B explicitly:

```
rB := rB − wp ;
if rB =0 then        B is not shared and so will be returned to
                     the free list
  wp := wr ;
  DEC( C, wq )
else                 B is shared
  wp := wr − ( wr div 2 ) ;
  wr := wr div 2 ;
```

Chapter 17

```
17.1 --- g( t )             <= ( sum( t ), count( t ) ) ;                (definition)
     --- g( tip( n ) )      <= ( sum( tip( n ) ), count( tip( n ) ) ) ;(instantiation)
                            <= ( n, 1 )                                   (unfolds)
     --- g( node( t1, t2 ) )<= ( sum( node( t1, t2 ) ),
                               count( node( t1, t2 ) ) ) ;          (instantiation)
```

```
                          <= ( sum( t1 ) + sum( t2 ),
                                count( t1 ) + count( t2 ) ) ;            (unfolds)
                          <= ( u + x, v + y ) where ( u, v, x, y ) ==
                                ( sum( t1 ), count( t1 ), sum( t2 ), count( t2 ) )
                             ;                                 (where abstraction)
                          <= ( u + x, v + y ) where ( ( u, v ), ( x, y ) ) ==
                                ( g ( t1 ), g( t2 ) ) ;                    (folds)
    --- treeaverage( t )  <= u div v where ( u, v ) ==
                                ( sum( t ), count( t ) ) ;     (where abstraction)
                          <= u div v where ( u, v ) == g ( t ) ;           (fold)
```

17.3 (Transformation step names omitted henceforth)

```
    --- listo( n ) <= g( n, nil ) ;
    --- g( n, l )  <= append( listo( n ), l ) ;
    --- g( 0, l )  <= append( listo( 0 ), l ) <= append( nil, l ) <= l
    --- g( n + 1, l ) <= append( listo( n + 1 ), l )
                      <= append( append( listo( n ), ( n + 1 ) :: nil ), l )
                      <= append( listo( n ), append( ( n + 1 ) :: nil, l ) )
                                           (since append is associative)
                      <= append( listo( n ), ( n + 1 ) :: append( nil, l ) )
                      <= append( listo( n ), ( n + 1 ) :: l )
                      <= g( n, ( n + 1 ) :: l ) ;
```

17.4

```
    --- g( 0 ) <= z st ( length( z ) = 0, forall( z, isone ) )
               <= nil ;  (unify with first equations defining length and forall)
    --- g( n + 1 ) <= z st ( length( z ) = n + 1, forall( z, isone ) )
                   <= x :: z' st ( length( x :: z' ) = n + 1, forall( x :: z', isone ) )
                            (z cannot be nil so unify with the other equations)
                   <= x :: z' st ( 1 + length( z' ) = n + 1, isone( x ),
                                   forall( z', isone ) )                  (unfold)
                   <= 1 :: z' st ( length( z' ) = n, forall( z', isone ) )
                                   (isone( x ) iff x = 1)
                   <= 1 :: g( n )                                           (fold)
```

Chapter 18

18.1 First part straightforward, as in Chapter 18. $\underline{\bot} \circ a = \underline{\bot}$ by definition of $\underline{\bot}$, $a \circ \underline{\bot} = \underline{\bot}$ if a is strict, $[\ldots, \underline{\bot}, \ldots] = \underline{\bot}$ if sequences are strict. Hence the functionals defined by composition and construction must always be strict.

18.2 (b)

$$
\begin{aligned}
& H(a \to b\,;c) \\
&= P(a \to b\,;c) \to A(a \to b\,;c)\,;B(a \to b\,;c) \\
&= (P_t a \to Pb\,;Pc) \to (A_t a \to Ab\,;Ac)\,;(B_t a \to Bb\,;Bc) \\
&= P_t a \to (Pb \to Ab\,;Bb)\,;(Pc \to Ac\,;Bc) \\
&= P_t a \to Hb\,;Hc
\end{aligned}
$$

so $H_t = P_t$ provided the last condition holds:

$$H\underline{\bot} : x \neq \bot \Rightarrow P\underline{\bot} : x \neq \bot \Rightarrow P_t a : x = T\, \forall a \Rightarrow H_t a : x = T\, \forall a.$$

Other parts of the question similar.

18.3 $H_t a = p \rightarrow A_t a\, ; B_t a$. If $A_t = B_t$ then $H_t = A_t$ if $p : x \notin \{ T, F \} \Rightarrow A_t a : x = \bot$.

18.4 $n = 0 : H^0 f = /h \circ [\, f\,] = f$. $n = 1$: result true by definition of H.
Inductive step:

$$\begin{aligned} /h \circ [\, i, i \circ j, \ldots, i \circ j^n, f \circ j^{n+1}\,] &\\ = h \circ [\, i, /h \circ [\, i \circ j, \ldots, i \circ j^n, f \circ j^{n+1}\,]\,] &\\ = h \circ [\, i, /h \circ [\, i, \ldots, i \circ j^{n-1}, f \circ j^n\,] \circ j\,] &\\ = h \circ [\, i, H^n f \circ j\,] & \quad \text{(by inductive hypothesis)}\\ = H(H^n f\,) = H^{n+1} f & \end{aligned}$$

If $Hf = h \circ [\, f \circ j, i\,]$, $H^n f = \backslash h \circ [\, f \circ j^n, i \circ j^{n-1}, \ldots, i \circ j, i\,]$.

18.6
$$\begin{aligned} H(a \rightarrow b\, ; c\,) &= G(\, a \rightarrow b\, ; c, a \rightarrow b\, ; c\,)\\ &= G_1 a \rightarrow G(\, b, a \rightarrow b\, ; c\,)\, ; G(\, c, a \rightarrow b\, ; c\,)\\ &= G_1 a \rightarrow (\, G_2 a \rightarrow G(\, b, b\,)\, ; G(\, b, c\,)\,)\, ;\\ &\qquad\qquad (\, G_2 a \rightarrow G(\, c, b\,)\, ; G(\, c, c\,)\,)\\ &= G_1 a \rightarrow G(\, b, b\,)\, ; G(\, c, c\,) \text{ since } G_1 = G_2 \end{aligned}$$

If $H\underline{\bot} : x \neq \bot$, then $G(\, \underline{\bot}, \underline{\bot}\,) : x \neq \bot$ so $G_1 a : x = T\, \forall a$.
Thus H is linear with predicate transformer G_1.
Similarly if M is n-multilinear with $M_1 = \ldots = M_n$, $M(f, \ldots, f\,)$ is linear in f with predicate transformer M_1.

18.8 Since $fib \circ sub1 = le1 \rightarrow \underline{1}\, ; fib \circ sub1$,

$$\begin{aligned} g &= le1 \rightarrow [\, \underline{1}, \underline{1}\,]\, ; [\, + \circ [\, fib, fib \circ sub1\,] \circ sub1, fib \circ sub1\,]\\ &= le1 \rightarrow [\, \underline{1}, \underline{1}\,]\, ; [\, + \circ g \circ sub1, 1 \circ g \circ sub1\,] \end{aligned}$$

Thus $g = le1 \rightarrow [\, \underline{1}, \underline{1}\,]\, ; Hg$ where $Hg = [\, +, 1\,] \circ g \circ sub1$. Loop implementation as discussed in Chapter 18.

18.9 $h = eq0 \rightarrow [\, [\, \underline{1}\,], \underline{1}\,]\, ; [\, cons \circ [\, 2 \circ h, 1 \circ h \circ sub1\,], * \circ [\, id, 2 \circ h \circ sub1\,]\,]$
$h' = eq1 \rightarrow [\, [\, \underline{1}\,], \underline{1}\,]\, ; Hh'$

where

$$Hv = [\, cons \circ [\, 2 \circ v \circ sub1, 1 \circ v \circ sub1\,], * \circ [\, id, 2 \circ v \circ sub1\,]\,]$$

for function variable v. Thus H is linear (e.g. because it is degenerate multilinear with equal p.t.s, see Exercise 18.6) with $H_t a = a \circ sub1$.

18.10 (a) *listo*(x) = *listo-tr*(x, *id*), where
listo-tr(x, γ) = **if** $x = 0$
then γ(*nil*)
else *listo-tr*($x - 1, \lambda w.\gamma(w \langle\rangle (x :: nil\,)\,)$)

As with the reverse example in Chapter 18, we represent the continuations by lists to get:

$$
\begin{aligned}
listo(\, x\,) &= listo^*\,(\, x, nil\,)\\
listo^*\,(\, x, k\,) &= \textbf{if } x = 0\\
&\quad \textbf{then } k\\
&\quad \textbf{else } listo^*\,(\, x - 1, x :: k\,)
\end{aligned}
$$

(b)

$$
\begin{aligned}
fac(\, x\,) &= fac\text{-}tr(\, x, id\,) \text{ where}\\
fac\text{-}tr(\, x, \gamma) &= \textbf{if } x = 0\\
&\quad \textbf{then } \gamma(\,1\,)\\
&\quad \textbf{else } fac\text{-}tr(\, x - 1, \lambda w.\gamma(\, w{*}x\,)\,)
\end{aligned}
$$

This time we represent the continuations by a multiplicative accumulator, $a : \gamma = \lambda v.v{*}a$.

Thus since $\lambda w.\gamma(\, w{*}x\,) = \lambda w.(\, w{*}x\,){*}a = \lambda w.w{*}(\, x{*}a\,)$ by associativity of $*$, we obtain:

$$
\begin{aligned}
fac(\, x\,) &= fac^*\,(\, x, 1\,)\\
fac^*\,(\, x, a\,) &= \textbf{if } x = 0\\
&\quad \textbf{then } a\\
&\quad \textbf{else } fac^*\,(\, x - 1, x{*}a\,)
\end{aligned}
$$

Chapter 19

19.1 zip(ab, abc) = zip(a :: b :: ab, a :: b :: c :: abc) → [a, a] :: zip(b :: ab, b :: c :: abc) → . . .
→ [a, a] :: [b, b] :: [a, c] :: [b, a] :: [a, b] :: [b, c] :: zip(ab, abc)

after six reductions. The argumens of the call to zip are now identical to the original arguments and so a memo table look up is generated on the next reduction. This gives a circular structure of the form

z = [a, a] :: [b, b] :: [a, c] :: [b, a] :: [a, b] :: [b, c] :: z

For zip(ab, ab) we get similarly z = [a, a] :: [b, b] :: z

19.2 comb = le5 → g ; ⟨*⟩ ∘ [addon ∘ [$\underline{5}$, comb ∘ sub5],
⟨*⟩ ∘ [addon ∘ [$\underline{3}$, comb ∘ sub3],
addon ∘ [$\underline{2}$, comb ∘ sub2]]]

(Here we have used the prefix form of ⟨*⟩.)

This is degenerate 3-multilinear with compatible predicate transformers M_1, M_2, M_3 defined by M_1a = a ∘ sub5, M_2a = a ∘ sub3, M_3a = a ∘ sub2 so that the lowest common sum is 5 and LCC = sub5. Thus the table manager is **lambda** x => [x − 5] and the memo table never has more than 5 entries.

19.4 M_1a = a ∘ [s ∘ 1, s ∘ 2], M_2a = a ∘ [s ∘ 1, 2] where s = sub1. Thus

M_1M_2a = a ∘ [s ∘ s ∘ 1, s ∘ 2] = M_2M_1a ∀a

Thus $M_1M_2 = M_2M_1$. Given g as stated, if $b \circ c = c \circ b$ the predicate transformers commute similarly and if there is no common generator the argument calling graph looks like:

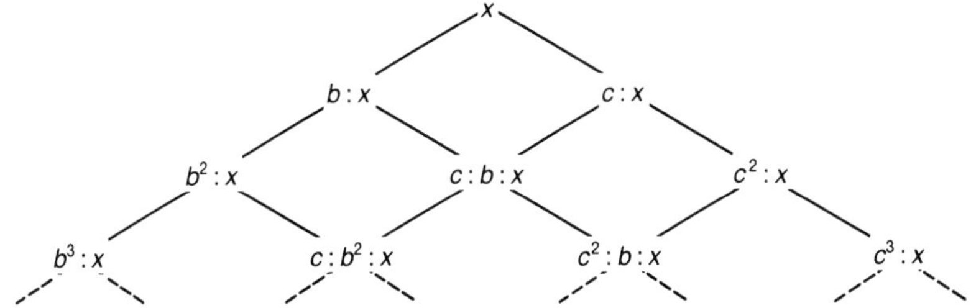

Hence interior nodes occur twice and spine nodes once. This suggests a deletion strategy in which a table entry is deleted after it is first looked up.

Chapter 20

20.1 (a) A is the set of non-negative integers, and if the integer x has d digits, its abstract value in A is $(d - 1)$. The abstract domain is 2^A and $x^\# = \{d - 1\}$.

(b)

$$X +^\# Y = \bigcup_{\substack{x \in X \\ y \in Y}} \{ m + 1, m, m - 1 \mid m = max(x, y) \}$$

$$X *^\# Y = \bigcup_{\substack{x \in X \\ y \in Y}} \{ x + y, x + y + 1 \}$$

(c)

$$\begin{aligned}(-9 * 100) + 99 &=> (\{0\} *^\# \{2\}) +^\# \{1\} = \{2, 3\} +^\# \{1\} \\ &= \{3, 2, 1, 4, 3, 2\} = \{1, 2, 3, 4\}\end{aligned}$$

20.3 (a)

$$\begin{aligned}f^\#(X, Y, Z) = (X \wedge Y) \wedge (true \vee ((Y \wedge f^\#(X, Y, Z)) \wedge \\ (Y \vee (Z \wedge f^\#(X, Y, Z)))))\end{aligned}$$

(omitting some steps). Thus $f^\#(X, Y, Z) = X \wedge Y$ so f is strict in its first two arguments.

(b)

$$\begin{aligned}f^\#(X, Y, Z) = (X \wedge Y) \wedge (Z \vee ((Y \wedge f^\#(X, Y, Z)) \wedge \\ (Y \vee (Z \wedge f^\#(X, Y, Z)))))\end{aligned}$$

Let $f^\#_0(X, Y, Z) = 0$ for all X, Y, Z (where 0 denotes the value *false*) and substitute into the right-hand side to give $f^\#_1 = (X \wedge Y) \wedge (Z \vee 0) = X \wedge Y \wedge Z$. Repeating this gives $f^\#_2 = X \wedge Y \wedge Z$ giving convergence so that $f^\# = X \wedge Y \wedge Z$ and f is strict in all its arguments.

Thus $M_1 M_2 = M_2 M_1$. Given g as stated, if there were no [illegible] the predicate transformers commute similarly, and if there is no common generator the argument calling graph looks like:

Hence interior nodes occur twice and some nodes once. This suggests a deletion strategy in which a table entry is deleted after it is first looked up.

Chapter 20

20.1 (a) [illegible] is the set of non-negative integers, and if the integer x has d digits, its abstract value in [illegible] is [illegible]. The abstract domain is [illegible] and [illegible]

(b) [illegible]

[illegible]

[illegible]

[illegible]

[illegible]

Bibliography

Abramsky, S., (1985). 'Strictness analysis and polymorphic invariance'. In *Programs as data objects. LNCS* **217**. Springer Verlag

Abramsky, S., Hankin, C.L. (eds.), (1987). *Abstract interpretation of declarative languages*. Ellis Horwood

Aho, A.V., Hopcroft, J.E., Ullman, J.D., (1983). *Data structures and algorithms*. Addison-Wesley

Arvind, Kathail, V., Pingali, K., (1980). 'A dataflow architecture with tagged tokens'. *Proc. International Conference on Circuits and Computers*

Augustsson, L., (1984). 'A compiler for lazy ML'. In *Proc. ACM Symposium on Lisp and Functional Programming*, Austin, 218–27

Augustsson, L., (1985). 'Compiling pattern matching'. In *Proc. Conference on Functional Programming Languages and Computer Architecture*, Nancy, 368–81. *LNCS* **201**. Springer Verlag

Backus, J.W., (1978). 'Can programming be liberated from the von Neumann style? A functional style and its algebra of programs', *Communications of the ACM*, **21**, 613–41

Backus, J.W., (1981). 'The algebra of functional programs: function-level reasoning, linear equations and extended definitions'. *LNCS* **107**, 1–43. Springer Verlag

Backus, J.W., Williams, J.H., Wimmers, E.L. (1987). *FL language manual (preliminary version)*. IBM research report number RJ 5339 (54809)

Bailey, R., (1985). *FP/M abstract syntax description*. Internal report, Department of Computing, Imperial College, University of London

Bailey, R., (1987). 'Functional programming using abstract data types'. In S. Eisenbach (ed.) *Functional programming: languages tools and architectures* 57–68. Ellis Horwood

Baker, H., (1978). 'List processing in real time on a serial computer'. *Communications of the ACM*, **21**(4), 280–94

Barendregt, H.P., (1984). *The lambda calculus – its syntax and semantics*. North Holland

Bellegarde, F., (1984). 'Rewriting systems on FP expressions that reduce the number of sequences they yield'. In *Proc. Conference on LISP and Functional Programming*, 63–73. (Also in *Science of Computer Programming*, **6**(1), 11–34, January 1986.)

Bevan, D.I., (1985). *Distributed garbage collection using reference counting.* Research report, GEC Research Ltd, Hirst Research Centre, and also in *PARLE* 1987

Burge, W.H., (1978). *Recursive programming techniques.* Addison-Wesley

Burn, G., Hankin, C.L., Abramsky, S., (1985). *The theory and practice of strictness analysis of higher-order functions.* Internal report no. DoC 85/6, Department of Computing, Imperial College, University of London

Burstall, R.M., Darlington, J., (1977). 'A transformation system for developing recursive programs'. *JACM*, **24**(1), 44–67

Burstall, R.M., MacQueen, D.B., Sanella, D.T., (1980). *Hope: an experimental applicative language.* CSR-62-80, Department of Computer Science, University of Edinburgh

Cardelli, L., (1984). 'Basic polymorphic type checking'. *Science of Computer Programming*, **8**(2), 147–72, April 1987

Church, A., (1941). *The calculi of lambda conversion.* Princeton University Press

Clack, C.D. and Peyton Jones, S.L., (1986). 'The four-stroke reduction engine'. *Proc. of the ACM Conference on LISP and Functional Programming*, Boston, 220–32

Colmerauer, A., Kanoui, H., Pasero, R., Roussel, P. (1973), *Un système de communication homme–machine en Français.* Rapport, groupe intelligence artificielle, Université d'Aix Merseille, Luminy

Cousineau, G., Curien, P-L., Mauny, M., (1985). 'The categorical abstract machine'. In *Proc. Conference on Functional Programming and Computer Architecture*, Nancy, 50–64, *LNCS* **201**. Springer Verlag. (Also in *Science of Computer Programming*, **8**(2) 173–202, April 1987.)

Curien, P-L., (1986). *Categorical combinators, sequential algorithms and functional programming.* Pitman/Wiley

Curry, H.B., Feys, R., (1958). *Combinatory logic*, Vol. 1. North Holland

Darlington, J., Cripps, M.D., Field, A.J., Harrison, P.G., Reeve, M.J., (1987). 'The design and implementation of ALICE: a parallel graph reduction machine'. To appear in IEEE Press edition on Dataflow and reduction architectures, ed. by S. Thakkar

Davies, I.L., *PhD Report 1* (for R. Bailey). Research proposal, April 1985. Department of Computing, Imperial College, University of London

De Bruijn, N.G., (1972). 'Lambda calculus notation with nameless dummies'. *Indagationes Mathematicae*. **34**, 381–92

Dennis, J.B., (1980). 'Data flow supercomputers'. *IEEE Computer*, **13**(11), 48–56

Dijkstra, E.J.W., (1976). *A discipline of programming*. Prentice-Hall

Fairbairn, J. (1982). *The design and implementation of a simple untyped language based on the lambda calculus*. PhD thesis, University of Cambridge

Field, A.J., Hunt, L.S., While, R.L., (1988). *Best-fit pattern matching for functional languages*, Internal report, Department of Computing, Imperial College

Glaser, H., Hayes, S., (1986). 'Another implementation technique for applicative languages'. *Proc. European Symposium on Programming*, Saarbrucken, 70–81. *LNCS* **213**. Springer Verlag

Glaser, H.W., Thompson, P., (1985). 'Lazy garbage collection'. *Software – Practice and Experience*, **17**(1), 1–4

Gordon M.J., Milner, A.J., Wadsworth, C.P., (1979). 'Edinburgh LCF'. *LCNS* **78**. Springer Verlag

Harrison, P.G., (1985). *Linearisation: An optimisation for non-linear functional programs*. Research report, Department of Computing, Imperial College. (Also to appear in *Science of Computer Programming*, 1988)

Harrison, P.G., (1988). 'Functional inversion.' *Proc. Workshop on Partial Evaluation and Mixed Computation*, Denmark, 1987, North–Holland

Harrison, P.G., Khoshnevisan, H., (1986). 'Efficient compilation of linear functions into object-level loops'. *SIGPLAN '86 Symposium on Compiler Construction*, Palo Alto

Harrison, P.G., Khoshnevisan, H., (1988). *On the synthesis of function inverses*. Research report, Department of Computing, Imperial College, University of London

Henderson, P., (1982). 'Purely functional operating systems'. In J. Darlington, P. Henderson & D. Turner (eds.), *Functional programming and its applications*, 177–92. Cambridge University Press

Henderson, P., Jones, G.A., Jones, S.B. (1983). *The LispKit manual*, Vol. 1. Technical monograph PRG-32(1), Oxford University Computer Laboratory, Programming Research Group

Hindley, J.R., Seldin, J.P., (1986). *Introduction to combinators and λ-calculus*. Cambridge University Press

Hudak, P., (1985). *Para-functional programming – a paradigm for programming multiprocessor systems*. Internal report no. YALEU/DCS/RR-390. Department of Computer Science, Yale University (Also in *IEEE Computer*, 60–70, August 1986)

Hudak, P., Goldberg, B., (1985). 'Serial combinators: optimal grains of parallelism'. *Proc. Conference on Functional Programming and Computer Architecture*, Nancy, 382–99, *LNCS* **201**. Springer Verlag

Hughes, R.J.M., (1984). *The design and implementation of programming languages*. PhD thesis, University of Oxford

Hughes, R.J.M., (1985a). 'A distributed garbage collection algorithm'. *Proc. Conference on Functional Programming and Computer Architecture*, Nancy, 256–72, *LNCS* **201**. Springer Verlag

Hughes, R.J.M., (1985b). 'Lazy memo functions'. In *Proc. Conference on Functional Programming and Computer Architecture*, Nancy, 129–46, *LNCS* **201**. Springer Verlag

Hunt, L.S., (1986). *A Hope to FLIC translator with strictness analysis*. MSc dissertation, Department of Computing, Imperial College, University of London

IEEE Computer, (1982). Special edition on Data Flow Systems, **15**(2), February 1982

Johnsson, T., (1984). 'Efficient compilation of lazy evaluation'. In *Proc. ACM Conference on Compiler Construction*, Montreal, 58–69

Johnsson, T., (1985). 'Lambda lifting: transforming programs to recursive equations'. In *Proc. Conference on Functional Programming Languages and Computer Architecture*, Nancy, 190–203

Kahn, G., (1974). The semantics of a simple language for parallel programming. In *Information Processing 74*. North Holland

Kahn, G., MacQueen, D.B., Plotkin, G. (eds.), (1984). 'Semantics of Data Types'. *Proc. International Symposium*, Sophia-Antipolis, *LNCS* **173**, Springer Verlag

Keller, R.M., (1985). *Rediflow architecture prospectus*. Internal report no. UUCS-85-105, Department of Computer Science, University of Utah

Kelly, P.H.J. (1987). *Functional languages for loosely-coupled multiprocessors*. PhD thesis, Imperial College, University of London

Kennaway, J.R., Sleep, M.R., (1982). *Director strings as combinators*. Internal report, Computing Studies Sector, University of East Anglia

Khashnevisan, H., (1987). Automatic transformation systems based on function-level reasoning. *PhD Thesis*, Imperial College, University of London

Kieburtz, R.B., Shultis, J., (1981). 'Transformations of FP program schemes'. In *Proc. ACM Conference on Functional Languages and Computer Architecture*, Portsmouth, New Hampshire

Kott, L., (1978). 'About a transformation system: a theoretical study'. In *Proc. 3rd Symposium on Programming*, Paris

Landin, P.J., (1964). 'The mechanical evaluation of expressions'. *Computer Journal*, **6**, 308–20

Lieberman, H., Hewitt, C., (1983). 'A real-time garbage collector based on the lifetime of objects'. *Communications of the ACM*, **26**(6), 419–29

Lins, R.D., (1986). 'A new formula for the execution of categorical combinators'. In *Proc. 8th International Conference on Automated Deduction, LNCS* **230**, 89–98. Springer Verlag

McCarthy, J., (1960). 'Recursive functions of symbolic expressions and their computation by machine'. *Communications of the ACM*, **3**(4), 184–95

McCarthy, J., Abrahams, P.W., Edwards, D.J., Hart, T.P., Levin, M.I. (1962). *LISP 1.5 programmers manual*, MIT Press, 1962

Mauny, M., Suarez, A., (1986). 'Implementing functional languages in the categorical abstract machine'. In *Proc. Conference on Lisp and Functional Programming*

Michie, D., (1968). '"Memo" functions and machine learning', *Nature*, **218**, 19–22

Milner, R., (1978). 'A theory of type polymorphism in programming'. *Journal of Computer and System Science*, **17**, 348–75

Minsky, M.L., (1967). *Computation: finite and infinite machines*. Prentice-Hall

Morris, F.L., (1978). 'A time- and space-efficient garbage compaction algorithm', *Communications of the ACM*, **21**(8), 662–5

Mycroft, A. (1981). *Abstract interpretation and optimizing transformations for applicative programs*. PhD thesis, Department of Computer Science, University of Edinburgh

Perry, N., (1987). *Hope*$^{+}$. Internal research report ref. IC/FPR/LANG/2.5.1/7, Functional Programming Section, Department of Computing, Imperial College, University of London

Peyton Jones, S.L., Clack, C.D., Salkild, J., (1985). *GRIP – a parallel graph reduction machine*. Internal report, Department of Computer Science, University College, London

Plotkin, G.D., (1975). 'Call-by-name, call-by-value and the lambda calculus'. *Theoretical Computer Science*, **1**, 125–59

Robinson, J.A., (1965). 'A machine-oriented logic based on the resolution principle'. *Journal of the ACM*, **12**(1), 23–41

Spitzen, J.M., Levitt, K.N., (1978). 'An example of hierarchical design and proof'. *Communications of the ACM*, **21**(12), 1064–75

Stoy, J.E., (1977). *Denotational semantics: the Scott–Strachey approach to programming language theory*. MIT Press

Stoye, W.R., (1985). *The implementation of functional languages using custom hardware*. PhD thesis, University of Cambridge

Stoye, W.R., Clarke, T.J.W., Norman, A.C., (1984). 'Some practical methods for rapid combinator reduction'. *Proc. ACM Symposium on Lisp and Functional Programming*, Austin, 159–66

Thomas, R.E., (1981). *A dataflow computer with improved asymptotic performance.* MIT Laboratory for Computer Science report MIT/LCS/TR-265

Turner, D.A., (1976). *The SASL language manual.* University of St Andrews

Turner, D.A., (1979). 'A new implementation technique for applicative languages'. *Software – Practice and Experience*, **9**, 31–49

Turner, D.A., (1981). *Aspects of the implementation of programming languages.* PhD thesis, University of Oxford

Turner, D.A., (1982). 'Recursion equations as a programming language'. In J. Darlington, P. Henderson & D. Turner (eds.), *Functional programming and its applications*, 1–28, Cambridge University Press

Turner, D.A., (1985). 'Miranda – a non-strict functional language with polymorphic types'. In *Proc. Conference on Functional Programming Languages and Computer Architecture*, Nancy, 1–16., *LCNS* **201**, Springer Verlag

Wadler, P., (1985). *An introduction to Orwell.* Programming Research Group, University of Oxford

Wadler, P., (1987). 'Efficient compilation of pattern matching'. In S. Peyton Jones (ed.) *The implementation of functional programming languages* (Chapter 5), 78–103. Prentice Hall

Wadsworth, C.P., (1981). *Semantics and pragmatics of the lambda calculus.* PhD thesis, University of Oxford (Chapter 4)

Wand, M., (1980). 'Continuation-based program transformation strategies', *JACM* **27**(1), 164–80

Watson, I., Gurd, J., (1979). 'A prototype data flow computer with token labelling', *AFIPS Conference Proceedings*, **48**. 1979 National Computer Conference

Watson, P., Watson, I., Woods, V., (1986). *A model of computation for the parallel evaluation of functional languages based on a canonical representation of variables.* Internal report No. PMP/MU/PW/000001, Department of Computer Science, University of Manchester

Williams, J.H., (1982). 'On the development of the algebra of functional programs'. *ACM Transactions on Programming Languages and Systems*, **4**, 4

Index